EFFECTIVE READING INSTRUCTION IN THE ELEMENTARY GRADES

Donald J. Leu, Jr.
SYRACUSE UNIVERSITY

Charles K. Kinzer
VANDERBILT UNIVERSITY

MERRILL PUBLISHING COMPANY
A BELL & HOWELL COMPANY
COLUMBUS   TORONTO   LONDON   MELBOURNE

To our families—Alexandra, Debbie, Katie, Rita, and Sarah. With gratitude for your support and understanding over the past three years.

Cover art: Copyright © Sonny Zoback

Published by Merrill Publishing Company
A Bell & Howell Company
Columbus, Ohio 43216

This book was set in Usherwood.

Administrative Editor: Bev Kolz
Production Coordinator: Pamela Hedrick Bennett
Cover Designer: Cathy Watterson
Text Designer: Cynthia Brunk

Library of Congress Catalog Card Number: 86–61445
International Standard Book Number: 0–675–20695–2
Printed in the United States of America.
1 2 3 4 5 6 7 8 9 — 91 90 89 88 87

Credits

Donald J. Leu is an associate professor of education at the Reading and Language Arts Center of Syracuse University. He has an extensive range of teaching experiences at the elementary level including positions as a self-contained classroom teacher and reading specialist in California, as well as supervisor of English Education in the Marshall Islands. He received an Ed.M. degree in Reading at Harvard University and a Ph.D. in Language and Literacy at the University of California, Berkeley. Professor Leu has published articles on reading in a variety of journals including *Reading Research Quarterly, The Journal of Educational Psychology, The Journal of Reading Behavior, Reading Psychology,* and *Curriculum Review.*

Charles K. Kinzer is assistant professor of education and research scientist at the Learning Technology Center, Peabody College of Vanderbilt University. He teaches graduate and undergraduate courses in reading education and language arts. He has previously taught reading and remedial reading in middle and junior high schools, and has served as Language Arts Consultant (K–12) at the school district level. He received his M.A. in Education from the University of British Columbia, Canada, and his Ph.D. in Language and Literacy at the University of California, Berkeley. Professor Kinzer's current research interests include reading comprehension and vocabulary acquisition, as well as problem solving and computer applications in educational settings. He has published in scholarly journals across the reading education and computer fields and serves on several editorial review boards. His publications include *Computer Strategies for Education: Foundations and Content-Area Applications* and *Planning the School of the Future,* a special issue of the *Peabody Journal of Education.*

Preface

Developed as the basic text for preservice teachers in an elementary reading methods course, this book focuses on the teaching of reading from reading readiness to the comprehension of extended text. It is an integrative text, based on the assumption that effective reading teachers must understand both *what* to do during instruction as well as *why* it should be done. We have attempted to address specifically the comment often heard by graduates of reading methods courses: "Our course told us what to do, but not why it should be done or when, why, and how to modify lessons and methods."

During the last decade, there has been an explosion in reading research. Research findings on effective reading instruction, on the reading process, on readers' cognitive and linguistic processes, on teacher behavior and cognition, on classroom environments, on interest and attitude, and on different text structures have resulted in a knowledge base that has clear instructional implications. This text translates the most consistent of these research findings into practice. It presents the major perspectives in reading education, describes a comprehensive range of instructional practices, and shows teachers how to select and modify practices that are consistent both with their perspective and the individual needs of their students. In short, this text helps teachers become effective instructional decision makers in their classrooms. It goes beyond simply describing the materials, methods, and approaches to reading instruction by showing students how to develop and teach from an instructional framework to foster understanding of both what to do and why it should be done.

The text has been carefully structured to meet the needs of students in preservice elementary reading education classes. Chapters are of a constant length, facilitating consistent reading assignments. Additionally, comments from over twenty distinguished reviewers have guided the inclusion of model lessons on major teaching procedures, as well as over 300 sample activities. Questions and activities have been chosen to provoke additional thought, to be clearly relevant to each chapter's focus, and to solidify important concepts.

Instructional aids include an extensive teachers' guide, containing a range of additional questions appropriate for group work, individual projects, and for prediscussion before a chapter is read; a computerized test bank; and a set of overhead transparencies.

Special attention has been devoted to the layout and design of this text. These elements will aid initial reading, later studying, and reference when needed as a tool in student teaching, practicum, or later teaching environments. Each chapter is introduced by a relevant quotation and a clear statement of what will be presented and learned as the chapter is read. Key concepts and definitions have been highlighted in the text and have been placed as margin notes to facilitate understanding while reading and to serve as later study aids. Major points are itemized at the end of each chapter to facilitate review. Additionally, model lessons and sample activities have been set off from the text through the use of unique boxes and a second color, facilitating retrieval of instructional activities during field experiences. Headings have been clearly differentiated through the use of different type fonts and color to promote previewing and studying.

Included to promote interest and understanding throughout each chapter are elements called *Before Reading On* and *Point to Ponder*. The former serves as an advance organizer for upcoming information; the latter as a way to apply immediately preceding information. Finally, the provision of current, annotated references for further reading at the end of each chapter allow interested readers to further pursue a specific topic. These references also provide an initial source for literature searches appropriate for class assignments.

The text is divided into four major sections. The first contains two chapters. These chapters move from an introduction to reading education to a discussion of different instructional frameworks. They help the reader specify an explicit personal framework for reading instruction. This framework will be enhanced and modified as readers proceed through the text and continue to develop their knowledge throughout a teaching career.

The second section includes seven chapters which develop the reader's knowledge base about reading and reading instruction. The chapters move from readiness, decoding, and vocabulary through the comprehension of extended text. Each chapter has a separate focus, delineated by its respective title, but each recognizes that fluent reading in real reading materials is the goal of reading instruction. This section also includes separate chapters about the special reading and instructional demands of expository texts, and about the many and varied materials used in reading instruction—from basal reading programs and trade books through programs with modified orthographies.

Section three consists of two chapters about instructional needs and their determination. Chapter 10 presents and discusses different methods of assessment, across both individual and group situations with both formal and informal measures. This chapter considers the assessment of readers as well as reading materials. Chapter 11 presents instructional needs from the perspective of the individual learner as well as from the needs of special populations including the learning disabled, the gifted, and children with unique linguistic and cultural backgrounds.

Section four concludes with three chapters that present different patterns of instruction in reading: chapter 12 discusses organizational patterns; chapter 13 presents knowledge about patterns of effective teaching behavior; and chapter 14 examines changing instructional patterns due to the impact of microcomputer technology on reading instruction.

Several chapters reflect the currency of this text. At present, no other book offers separate chapters on content area reading, computer applications, classroom organization, and effective teaching practices. As a result, students receive up-to-date knowledge that will make them more effective teachers.

The chapters in this text have been ordered in a logical instructional sequence. However, they have been written to stand alone if one desires to alter their order of presentation. We strongly suggest that chapters 1 and 2 be read first regardless of any reorganization that may occur in other parts of the text because they set the foundation on which each subsequent chapter is based. They explain the instructional consequences of various instructional frameworks and begin the process of helping readers develop their own personal frameworks.

Finally, even as this volume goes to press, new research is appearing that holds important instructional implications for improving reading education. Future revisions will continually attempt to incorporate the best, most current knowledge about effective reading instruction and to present this knowledge in a useful manner. To this end, we welcome comments and suggestions from both instructors and students who use this text. Any recommendations for improvements in both clarity and content will be appreciated and considered.

The writing of this text has been both challenging and rewarding, and working together on this project has been an especially worthwhile experience. The text would not have its depth of coverage were it not for the combined knowledge of each author. In no other project that we have been associated with has there been a similar equality of effort—the text is a joint effort in the fullest sense of a partnership. Both authors participated equally throughout the project from its inception. We would like it clearly known that this book is a coauthored text in the fullest sense. Author order was determined randomly.

ACKNOWLEDGMENTS

As in any major project, the quality of the finished product results from the efforts and encouragement, of many individuals. It is impossible to individually recognize or thank each of the large number of friends and colleagues who have contributed to this text's successful completion. We beg the indulgence of any we may have inadvertently failed to acknowledge.

This text has benefited from extensive review. The number of reviewers, their variety of perspectives, and their unselfish giving of time and ideas has made this text current, complete, and accurate. Over twenty distinguished reviewers across Canada and the United States, with different perspectives and experiences participated in this project. The following friends and colleagues have our continuing gratitude for their professionalism and consideration.

> Donna E. Alvermann, University of Georgia
> JoAnn Brewer, Oregon State University
> Benita Blachman, Syracuse University
> Mark Conley, Eastern Michigan State University
> Susan J. Daniels, University of Akron
> Fredrick A. Duffelmeyer, Iowa State University
> Elizabeth B. Galloway, Clemson University
> Nathaniel Glaser, University of Northern Colorado
> Lee Gunderson, University of British Columbia
> William Harp, Oregon State University
> Kathy Hinchman, University of Wyoming
> E. Bess Osburn, Sam Houston State University
> Glennellen Pace, University of Wisconsin—Eau Claire
> John Pikulski, University of Delaware
> Thomas C. Potter, California State University, Northridge
> John Savage, Boston College
> Leo M. Schell, Kansas State University
> Barbara Schmidt, California State University, Sacramento
> Gary L. Shaffer, James Madison University
> Dorothy E. Smith, Western Michigan University

We also wish to thank the following individuals: Dorothy Carrick for her help in preparing margin notes and her many comments throughout the various drafts; Linda-Jo DeGroff for assistance with literature selections and for her comments throughout the various drafts; Joann Sweetland for her work on the index and her suggestions regarding several model activities; Katherine Misulis for her comments as we worked through the final draft; Bev Kolz, Pam Bennett, and Lynda Ward for their editorial work and support—without their belief and commitment to the project the text would not include the many design elements and stylistic features that make this text instructionally sound; our undergraduate students at Peabody College, Vanderbilt University and Syracuse University who read and responded to several earlier drafts, and whose comments helped make the presentation of material interesting and relevant to those who will ultimately use the text; our colleagues at Syracuse and Vanderbilt Universities who gave us the benefit of their support and experience, both formally and informally, as we worked through the various stages of the text and supplementary material.

Contents

SECTION TWO: DEVELOPING A KNOWLEDGE BASE

3
READINESS AND COMPREHENSION   67

4
DECODING AND COMPREHENSION   111

7
LITERATURE: AFFECT AND NARRATIVE DISCOURSE
239

8
CONTENT-AREA READING AND STUDY SKILLS: EXPOSITORY DISCOURSE
287

11
TEACHING READING TO CHILDREN WITH SPECIAL NEEDS

SECTION FOUR: INSTRUCTIONAL PATTERNS IN THE READING CLASSROOM

12
CLASSROOM ORGANIZATION

13
EFFECTIVE TEACHING OF READING   519

14
MICROCOMPUTERS IN THE READING
CLASSROOM   551

SECTION ONE
ENTERING THE
WORLD OF READING
INSTRUCTION

1 The Problem, the Challenge, the Rewards

TEACHING READING—A FUTURE NECESSITY? ■ ARRIVING AT A DEFINITION OF READING ■ THE CHALLENGE OF TEACHING READING ■ INSTRUCTIONAL FRAMEWORKS AND DECISIONS ■ THE REWARDS

Carmen, Dexter and Fox were on their way to school.
"I'm going to be a pilot when I grow up," said Carmen.
"I think I'll be a cowboy," said Dexter.
"What about you, Fox?" said Carmen.
"I'm going to be a teacher," said Fox.

From E. Marshall, *Fox at School* (New York: E. P. Dutton, 1983), p. 36.

This chapter addresses the future of reading education, given the widespread use and sophistication of technology in our society. In chapter 1, you will be shown some of the goals of reading instruction. You will become aware of how instructional frameworks help make teaching decisions.

After reading this chapter, you will be able to

1. specify the importance of reading and its purposes,
2. discuss several views and definitions of reading,
3. explain why a clear personal framework of reading is important to you as a future teacher of reading,
4. generally discuss the future of reading and reading instruction, given the impact of technology on communication.

TEACHING READING—A FUTURE NECESSITY?

A POINT TO PONDER Assume that you will be teaching a first-grade class in two years. Take this year's date (19_____) and add 2. Then add 12. Remember the total. Add 4 more. Your first total is the year that your first-grade students will graduate from high school. The final total is the year that your students would graduate from college with an undergraduate degree if they choose to attend and they go straight through. Will your first-grade instruction provide the foundation they will need to function in society?

During the past several years a tremendous change has taken place in education. In part, this change has resulted from the extensive development and rapid spread of technology in our society, including our schools. The ever-increasing emphasis on technology has resulted in speculation that a number of school subjects may need to be taught differently if our students are to be educated most effectively. Some may feel that certain traditional school subjects, such as reading and mathematics, will become obsolete since sophisticated and easy-to-use technology may soon read and perform mathematical calculations for us. As evidence for such a trend, these people could point to the increasing acceptance and use of calculators in arithmetic classes and the potential of microcomputers with **synthetic speech** capabilities.

synthetic speech: Sounds generated electronically, usually controlled by a computer.

Yet reading ability concerns parents, legislators, and educators alike. A major concern of all teachers is that students learn to read. In fact, many teachers feel they have succeeded with their students if they achieve nothing else but teaching them to read. Why is there this seeming discrepancy between viewpoints that reading may be relatively unnecessary in the future, and that reading ability is the most important aspect of education?

Partly, the discrepancy lies in one's conception of reading. If reading is largely equated with pronunciation, then a talking computer might indeed make the intermediate step of looking at printed symbols unnecessary. But is listening to or pronouncing print all there is to reading? Consider the example of a paid reader for a blind law student. The reader's job is to read assigned class material to the student. Whom would you say is reading, the sighted person who is pronouncing the material but who does not understand it, or the blind student who is not pronouncing the printed symbols, but who understands the material?

Most people would agree that reading includes, but goes beyond, decoding symbols and involves understanding. Thus, if we assume that reading goes beyond pronunciation to deriving meaning, then we see that it is the *process* of reading that must be taught. This process is not a mechanical skill, but is active and internal. In fact, teaching reading may be thought of as teaching thinking. When reading, one must organize information, recognize cause and effect, be aware of the ramifications of what is being read, and fit the material being read into one's beliefs and **knowledge base.** The fact that technology is allowing ever-increasing access to information makes effective teaching of the **reading process** more, not less, important. The increase in available information means that individuals will have to perform more **higher-level reading comprehension tasks** such as organizing available information, differentiating relevant from irrelevant facts, and deciding how to use these facts.

Although listening and reading are closely related **language processes,** they are not identical. As shown in figure 1–1, listening requires the processing of oral stimuli rather than the visual ones required in reading. Listening to a text presented by a computer would not allow certain common reading behaviors to occur easily. For example, have you ever gone back to check a fact, rereading where necessary, when reading a book? This might have happened when you realized that an interesting point needed additional thought, or if you realized that an important word or phrase might have been skipped. Silent reading is faster and more efficient than listening when attempting to learn a large amount of information. In silent reading you can proceed at your own pace or quickly scan for a piece of information rather than reading an entire segment for a particular item. When you use a telephone book, for example, you quickly search for a particular item rather than reading all of the page at the same speed.

Thus, you will be part of an aspect of education for which there is and will continue to be a great need. Only those who view reading as the mechanical skill of pronunciation rather than the complex process of comprehension can foresee the future elimination of reading instruction. Perhaps equating reading with a set of external skills may lead one to wonder why reading is not always taught much like typing—using a given set of sequential drills and much repetitive practice. To answer,

knowledge base: The organized store of a person's formal and informal learning experiences; general information about the world.

reading process: Active and internal operations involved in reading.

higher-level reading comprehension tasks: Analysis and synthesis skills (organizing information, recognizing and using relevant facts).

language processes: Communication skills related to speaking, listening, reading, spelling, and writing.

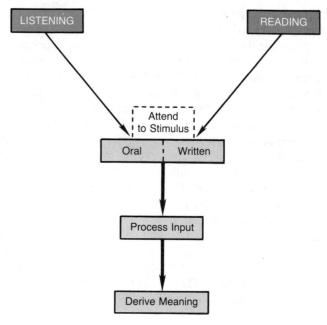

FIGURE 1–1
Reading-listening differences

one could say that when typing is taught, the learner's major objective is learning to type. When reading is taught, the learner's major objective is to develop, refine, and use high-level thought processes. The ultimate goal in reading instruction is to teach students to gain meaning—to comprehend. And although much is known about the comprehension process, much is still to be learned. This text takes the position that comprehension must be taught throughout the reading curriculum, and that if this is the intended outcome, then reading education will never become obsolete.

Reading: A Useful Tool

Good, adult readers often forget how difficult it might have been to learn to read, and also take for granted the many times that reading ability is used. Look around you now. How many things nearby need to be read? If you are at home, there might be a newspaper, TV guide, cereal box, or letter. If at school, perhaps a bulletin board, posters, books, or class notes. Now think of the things you have read so far today. If you define reading as translating printed symbols into meaning, then you might have "read" your watch, the morning paper, road signs, a map or other set of directions, or the numbers and letters on a dollar bill. Reading touches all aspects of life. For example, the inability to read directions on a prescription drug bottle or ingredients on a food label could be dangerous.

Reading ability, to a large extent, influences one's life style. How well one reads is a key factor in determining employment opportunities. This is recognized by legislators who are deeply concerned with literacy issues. Adult literacy classes, for example, try to make people more self-sufficient, thus easing both the political and human issues such as unemployment and welfare costs. Additionally, reading can help solve depression and boredom, as well as provide role models and inspiration.

Reading, then, can provide answers to questions, provide needed directions, or give relief from boredom. It can teach and transform, provide pleasure, and stimulate original thought. Reading ability is a social, political, and economic issue in our society. It touches our personal and professional lives.

In school, reading more than anything cuts across every subject area. Not being able to read textbooks, do research in the library, or read the teacher's notes on the blackboard directly affects the quality and amount of a student's learning. Small wonder, then, that teachers and parents, as well as students, are so concerned that reading be learned and taught properly. Yet there are many different perceptions about what reading is and how it is most effectively taught.

Reading for relaxation as well as for job-related purposes underscores the need for continued and effective teaching of reading.

ARRIVING AT A DEFINITION OF READING

The Importance of Establishing a Perspective

Your view of reading—the factors involved, their relative importance, and how reading takes place and develops—will have a direct and major impact on how you teach reading. Strang, McCullough & Traxler (1961), for example, state:

> If we think of reading primarily as a visual task, we will be concerned with the correction of visual defects and the provision of legible reading material. If we think of reading as word recognition, we will drill on the basic sight vocabulary and word recognition skills. If we think of reading as merely reproducing what the author says, we will direct the student's attention to the literal meaning of the passage and check his comprehension of it. If we think of reading as a thinking process, we shall be concerned with the reader's skill in making interpretations and generalizations, in drawing **inferences** and conclusions. If we think of reading as contributing to personal development and effecting desirable personality changes, we will provide our students with reading materials that meet their needs and have some application to their lives (pp. 1–2).

inference: A reasoned assumption using one's background knowledge to make decisions about meaning not explicitly stated in the text.

Teachers are often left to discover their view of the reading process on their own and are not told how various viewpoints will affect their instructional decisions. This text will provide guidance in specifying your view of reading into a framework on which you will ultimately make your instructional decisions. This will later allow you to consciously modify your viewpoint and instruction as appropriate. First, however, consider how others have defined reading and how reading is defined in this text.

Some Definitions of Reading

As our knowledge of the reading process has evolved, definitions of reading have become more complex. Although "getting meaning from print" is one way to define reading, such simplified definitions do not adequately present the complexity of the process, nor do they reflect the interaction of factors which enter into the reading act.

BEFORE READING ON

Try to specify as completely as possible your view of how we read. How do we get meaning from print? What factors do you think influence how effectively a reader translates abstract symbols into meaningful communication?

The following paragraphs present four different definitions of reading.

Rudolf Flesch relates reading to a set of mechanical skills: "Learning to read is like learning to drive a car. . . . The child learns the mechanics of reading, and when he's through, he can read (1981, p. 3). [Teach] the child [phonics] letter-by-letter and sound-by-sound until he knows it—and when he knows it he knows how to read" (1955, p. 121).

Dechant, however, feels that reading is more complex: "Reading cannot occur unless the pupil can identify and recognize the printed symbol, and generally the pupil must also give the visual configuration a name. Even so, it is only one aspect of the reading process. Meaning, too, is an absolute prerequisite in reading. Perhaps too much emphasis in reading instruction has been placed on word identification and not enough on comprehension" (1982, p. 166).

Relating reading to a type of guessing game based on one's knowledge of language, Goodman notes: "Reading is a **psycholinguistic** guessing game. It involves an interaction between thought and language. Efficient reading does not result from precise perception and identification of all elements, but from skill in selecting the fewest, most productive cues necessary to produce guesses [about meaning] which are right the first time" (1976, p. 498).

psycholinguistic: Psychological and linguistic processes involved in language.

Rumelhart, however, states: "Reading is the process of understanding written language. It begins with a flutter of patterns on the retina and ends (when successful) with a definite idea about the author's intended message . . . a skilled reader must be able to make use of sensory, **syntactic, semantic,** and **pragmatic** information to accomplish his task. These various sources of information interact in many complex ways during the process of reading" (1986, p. 722).

syntactic: The ordering of words to make meaningful phrases and sentences.
semantic: Word meanings.
pragmatic(s): Knowledge of the social appropriateness of speech acts in certain contexts.

The four definitions presented here are quite different, ranging from views of reading as strictly a mechanical sounding-out process to reading as an interaction between what is read and what is already known which allows meaning to occur. Different teaching emphases will result from these different definitions of reading. For example, a teacher who defines reading as strictly learning to sound out letters will spend more time at the early grade levels teaching letter-sound relationships and less time reading to students, presenting written forms of students' oral stories, and doing activities related to the overall meaning of stories or sentences.

All definitions of reading are personal, based on one's view of how one reads and how reading ability develops. The following definition of reading has guided the writing of this text. It views reading in a broad sense, recognizing that reading requires learned skills as well as a reader's existing knowledge. Arriving at meaning is considered the goal of reading. Remember, though, that any definition of reading is only a guide and must change as our knowledge of the reading process grows. Our definition has seven aspects, as shown in italic.

Reading is a *developmental, interactive,* and *global process* involving *learned skills.* The process specifically incorporates an individual's *linguistic* knowledge, and can be both positively and negatively influenced by nonlinguistic *internal* and *external* variables or factors.

The seven aspects of the definition are briefly explained in the following paragraphs. Each aspect will become clearer as you proceed through the remaining chapters in this text.

Developmental Process. This aspect recognizes that reading ability develops over time, and that readers read differently at different stages in their reading development. For example, the way that a beginning reader reads differs from the way in which a mature reader reads. The former, for example, attends more to individual letters than to words and general meaning.

Interactive Process. This aspect of the definition recognizes that reading is an interaction between the reader, the writer, and the text being read. Meaning is not only in the mind of the person doing the reading, nor is it only in the text being read. It is the interaction between the text being read and a reader's existing knowledge and expectations, which results in the amount and type of comprehension that takes place. Since readers' knowledge and expectations differ, this is one explanation for two readers' interpreting an identical text in different ways.

Global Process. This aspect recognizes that comprehension can occur at different levels of complexity, yet is a comprehensive and organized process. One can, for example, comprehend a letter, word, phrase, sentence, or an entire piece of discourse and, furthermore, can do so with varying degrees of proficiency. Yet all of these levels of comprehension must function in a coordinated manner and with some sophistication for reading to occur.

Learned Skills. This aspect recognizes that reading skill develops over time, and also incorporates our knowledge that instruction helps students learn to read. This also includes the fact that a reader must "learn how to learn," and needs not only to learn certain skills and strategies for reading, but must also learn when and how to use a strategy.

Linguistic Knowledge. This aspect acknowledges that one's (1) phonic (knowledge of sounds and their relationship to symbols); (2) semantic (knowledge of meanings); (3) syntactic (knowledge of word patterns); and (4) discourse (knowledge of how different written products are structured) backgrounds influence reading ability. All of these are linguistic abilities that affect reading and reading instruction. For example, a learner's knowledge of sounds in oral language helps the teacher teach the link between a certain letter and its sound(s), just as one's knowledge of word meanings helps one learn the written word that represents that meaning.

Internal Factors. Variables such as a reader's physical and mental well-being, general intelligence, specific developmental handicaps, and interest in or attitude toward reading and what is being read influence the reading process. This aspect also includes knowledge of pragmatics (the acceptability of speech acts in certain social contexts) and what has been called "world knowledge" and "general knowledge or experience." For example, knowing what might be said acceptably in certain situations helps a reader interpret what a character in a novel might be saying or might help distinguish sarcasm. Consider also how one's general knowledge about restaurants can help comprehension when reading a story that is set in a restaurant. A definition of reading that leaves out reader-based factors may not adequately explain individual differences in reading comprehension.

External Factors. This aspect recognizes that instructional and situational characteristics influence the reading act. These include the physical environment in which one reads, the instructional program (including the materials used in instruction), prereading home environment, teacher-student interactions in the classroom, and other factors that are not either controlled by or inherent to the reader.

The preceding paragraphs clearly define reading as being more than recognition or pronunciation of printed squiggles on a page. Although this is seen as necessary, reading is viewed as a process in which the reader and print interact. The material being read is a starting point from which the reader moves, incorporating existing knowledge to reason, learn, and ultimately go far beyond the assimilated printed symbols.

The view that reading is interactive and that the reader somehow processes the printed stimulus to gain meaning implies that all of the knowledge that a reader already has can be used in the attempt to comprehend symbols. Since reading is a language activity, the language and language-related skills already in a person's knowledge base are key factors in understanding and interpreting what is read. Remember that when children come to school they already have a wealth of language on which to build reading instruction. At very least, children come to school knowing how to speak—the miracle of language acquisition has already taken place. Children know that communication is possible and that the goal of communication is to transmit meaning. Further, all of the sounds of the English language are already known, even if the relationship of specific printed symbols to those sounds is not. Do not overlook the already highly-developed communication skills that are present in the children in your classroom, whatever grade level you teach.

As you read through the following chapters, try to look back periodically to our definition. Add to it or delete from it as your knowledge changes. Throughout this text, you will be asked to remember that your

As readers interact with print they both use and enhance their knowledge base.

view of reading will determine how you teach. Specifying a personal framework in order to develop and improve instructional strategies is an important part of being a reading teacher and will help you to meet the challenges outlined next. Guiding you in this task is a major goal of this text.

THE CHALLENGE OF TEACHING READING

As a future teacher of reading, you face one of the more challenging tasks in education. You have already seen how important reading is, and will continue to be, in our society. You will sense this importance as parents ask about their children's progress in reading, as administrators provide inservice workshops on teaching reading, as you see your school's reading test scores reported in the local newspaper, and especially as you look at the faces of your students who want very much to learn to read. Teaching reading is a challenge because many people consider reading an important part of the elementary curriculum and, therefore, pay close attention to what is done to teach it.

Teaching reading is also a challenge because reading is a complex developmental process. Learning how to teach reading requires some understanding of this complexity and, in addition, an understanding of effective instructional strategies. As you learn how to teach reading you will be developing answers to a number of important questions, such as:

■ What must readers know to comprehend complete stories, articles, and books? How can I help readers gain meaning from these and other kinds of writing?

■ What materials should be used to teach reading? How can I select and adapt appropriate materials for reading instruction?

■ What organizational patterns can be used to provide for the range of individuals in my classroom? How can I best organize my classroom?

■ What are the characteristics of effective teachers? What must I do to become an effective reading teacher?

Learning to teach reading would be complex even if there was clear agreement about how to define reading. As you have seen, however, there is wide variety in the definitions of reading proposed by different experts. Because there are so many different definitions of reading, there are different answers to each of these questions. No single, definitive answer exists to the question, How do I teach reading? because many different definitions of reading exist, and because learners do not all acquire knowledge equally well in the same way. This situation makes learning how to teach reading a wonderful challenge for a new teacher.

Another reason that reading presents a challenge is that the children you will teach are so diverse. Some of your students will be far beyond their classroom peers in reading ability; others will be somewhat below the class average. All will have individual needs and will exhibit individual difficulties in reading. Some may have difficulty with pronunciation in oral reading, while some will need help with understanding word meanings, and yet others may require assistance at interpreting or evaluating what is read. This diversity of needs and abilities makes teaching in general, and the teaching of reading in particular, so exciting and challenging.

Students' individual differences and needs require that you make informed instructional decisions in order to maximize students' learning. You will have to make informed decisions within the context of a busy classroom environment with many potential distractions. This is the final challenge you will face as a teacher of reading: learning how to make appropriate instructional decisions while you attend to the many events that take place during the course of a lesson.

Learning to manage classroom activities to provide the best possible learning environment is part of becoming a teacher. Do not be concerned that this is an impossible task. Remember how you felt when learning to drive a car? In that situation you were also confronted with important decisions that had to be made while many other things needed to be considered—the cars in front of and behind you, changing gears, actions of your passengers, the state of the road and of your car, among others. You now probably drive skillfully, and the uneasiness you may have experienced at first has disappeared. With a solid knowledge base, thought, and practice, you will master the decision-making process and management functions that will make your classroom a haven for learning.

As a future reading teacher, then, you face many challenges. To be successful, you must have a clear understanding of a complex subject, be able to make informed decisions, and accomplish all of this in a busy classroom environment. Yet teachers successfully meet these and other challenges. As one indication, remember that North America has one of the highest literacy rates in the world. When comparing the percentage of people who can read now to that of fifty years ago, it is clear that teachers are learning to teach reading and are doing so effectively. Through this text and through your own hard work and practice, you will develop into a teacher of reading who will be rewarded over and over as you see students become eager readers.

Reading teachers develop many tools for managing the complexities of reading instruction. One of the most useful tools is what we will call an instructional framework. We believe that teachers provide effective reading instruction in a busy environment by relying on different types of instructional frameworks. These frameworks are introduced briefly in the next section and are more fully presented in chapter 2.

Teaching reading provides many rewards as you see children's growth and know that you are helping them attain a skill that will be vital in later life.

INSTRUCTIONAL FRAMEWORKS AND DECISIONS

What is an instructional framework and how do teachers use frameworks to make decisions about reading instruction? An **instructional framework** consists of the materials, methods, and beliefs about reading that teachers use to guide their instructional decisions. Teachers use instructional frameworks to guide them in planning and teaching reading lessons in much the same way that drivers use road maps to guide them on trips, shoppers use lists to guide them during a trip to the grocery store, or readers use chapter outlines to guide them through understanding a complex subject.

> **instructional framework:** A set of beliefs about reading that guides instructional decisions.

Instructional frameworks provide structure and reduce the number of conscious decisions that teachers must make during interactions with students. Instructional frameworks are useful since they ease teachers' decision-making tasks in their complex and busy environments. Frameworks help teachers of reading decide both what to teach and how to teach.

Three Types of Frameworks

Teachers often use three types of frameworks to meet the challenges of reading instruction: frameworks based on a set of instructional materials; frameworks based on instructional methods; and frameworks based on an understanding of reading comprehension. Each may be used to guide the decisions teachers make regarding reading instruction.

A framework based on a set of instructional materials, or a **materials framework,** consists of the materials and lesson planning information available in a published set of materials, whether a kit of graded activity cards, computer software, or a complete reading program. A materials framework uses the detailed description of how a teacher is to teach reading using a particular set of instructional materials. As such, it reduces the number of instructional decisions that a teacher must make since the planning for lessons and activities are provided as part of the material. Notice how many instructional decisions have been made for the teacher in the sample lesson presented in figure 1–2.

> **materials framework:** A set of beliefs emphasizing materials and lesson plans provided by published reading programs.

Acquiring a materials framework typically means becoming familiar with the teacher's manual for a particular reading program. Teachers with materials frameworks generally follow the directions in the lesson plan of the teacher's manual quite closely. Many teachers begin their teaching experience with a materials framework because they are often busy trying to understand the many new things around them and have little time to modify or develop materials and specific plans for instruction. They are willing to accept decisions about what and how to teach that a teacher's manual presents them. This does not mean that careful evaluation of the material or a conscious choice has not been made, only that the guidelines provided by a set of materials provides the basis for specific instructional decisions.

3 Developing Reading Skills

VOCABULARY

Word Identification: Using new vocabulary words

MATERIALS
Word cards: *after, again, climb, cried, down, first, happened, happy, jumped, kittens, mouse, pond, saw, swim, they, thought, three, toad, turtle, walked, went, white, why, would*

Distribute the word cards among pupils, and have pupils take turns reading them. As each word is read, collect the card and display it. When all words have been read, shuffle the cards and distribute them again. Read each word aloud and have pupils raise their hands when they hear their word.

■ **Skillpack page 55**
This page is in the format used on the Unit Test and cannot be completed independently. Have pupils look at the first row. Say:

Read the three words. (*Pause.*) Now fill in the circle next to the word *first . . . first.*

Say the word twice. Follow this procedure with each row. Say the following words: (1) *first,* (2) *walked,* (3) *kittens,* (4) *climb,* (5) *turtle,* (6) *went,* (7) *down,* (8) *jumped,* (9) *they,* (10) *saw,* (11) *white,* (12) *happened.*

Additional practice: have pupils write sentences using two new words and illustrate the sentences.

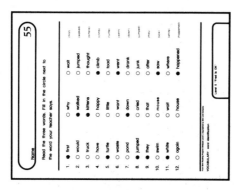

Name   55

Read the three words. Fill in the circle next to the word your teacher says.

1. ● first	○ why	○ wolf
2. ○ would	● walked	○ jumped
3. ○ truck	● kittens	○ thought
4. ○ have	○ happy	● climb
5. ○ turtle	○ little	○ toad
6. ○ waddle	○ went	● went
7. ○ pond	● down	○ drank
8. ● jumped	○ cried	○ junk
9. ○ they	○ that	○ otter
10. ● swim	○ mouse	○ low
11. ● white	○ wolf	○ where
12. ○ again	○ house	● happened

VOCABULARY: word classification

COMPREHENSION

Reality/Fantasy: Distinguishing between reality and fantasy (Review)

Write the following sentences on the chalkboard:

A duck can tell time.
A duck can swim.

Have volunteers read the sentences. Have a pupil identify the sentence that tells about something real. (*the second*) Now read the following sentence:

A dog would like a bone.

Ask:

Is this sentence real or make-believe? (*real*)

Ask volunteers to change this sentence so that it tells about something make-believe. (*For example: A dog would like a book.*)

■ **Skillpack page 56**
Additional practice: have pupils rewrite two sentences that tell about something make-believe, so that they tell about something real.

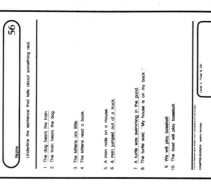

Name   56

Underline the sentence that tells about something real.

1. The dog hears the train.
2. The train hears the dog.
3. The kittens are little.
4. The kittens read a book.
5. A man rode on a mouse.
6. A man jumped out of a truck.
7. A turtle was swimming in the pond.
8. The turtle said, "My house is on my back."
9. We will play baseball.
10. The toad will play baseball.

COMPREHENSION: reality/fantasy

DECODING

Inflection: Decoding verbs with inflection -ed (Review)

Write *helped, looked,* and *liked* on the chalkboard. Have volunteers read each word and underline the ending *-ed* in each word. Remind pupils that the ending *-ed* shows that the action has already happened. Write the following incomplete sentence and answer choices on the chalkboard:

Yesterday she _____ the pail with water. (*rake, worked, filled*)

Ask volunteers to read the sentence and answer choices and to select the word that completes the sentence. Read the following sentences to pupils and write the answer choices on the chalkboard. Have pupils select the word that completes each sentence.

He hit the egg, and it _____. (*wanted, cracked, call*)
The toy in the window was the one she _____. (*wanted, walked, eat*)
Was that the flower he _____? (*played, going, picked*)

■ **Skillpack page 57**
Additional practice: have pupils select one of the words with the ending *-ed* and write two sentences. One sentence should include the word with the ending *-ed,* and the other sentence should include just the root.

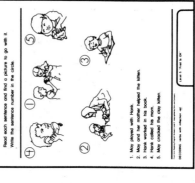

Name   57

Read each sentence and find a picture to go with it. Write the sentence number in the circle.

1. May played with Hank.
2. May and her mother helped the kitten.
3. Hank worked in his book.
4. Hank called his mom.
5. May cracked the day kitten.

DECODING: verbs with inflection -ed

FIGURE 1–2
A partial lesson plan from a published set of materials used to teach reading.

A framework based on an instructional method, or a **method framework,** consists of the knowledge of the procedural steps for one or more instructional methods and the options that may be selected at each step in a procedure. Here is an example of one type of method framework, a **directed reading-thinking activity.**

method framework: A set of beliefs based on a particular instructional method.

directed reading-thinking activity: An instructional method which includes three procedural steps repeated throughout a reading passage: predicting, reading, proving.

A Procedural Outline for a Directed Reading-Thinking Activity

1. *Predicting.* During this first step, ask students what they expect to find when they read. At the beginning ask questions like, What will a story with this title be about? Why? Later in a story, ask questions like, What do you think will happen next? Why? Each student should form a prediction and be able to support it.
2. *Reading.* During this second step, ask students to read up to a specified point in the story and check their predictions. They may read either orally or silently. For example, tell students to read up to the end of a certain page and see if their guesses were correct.
3. *Proving.* During this third step, ask students to evaluate their predictions within the context of a discussion. Ask questions like, Was your guess correct? Why or why not? At the end of the discussion, begin the procedural cycle again and have students predict what will take place in the next portion of the story. Continue in a similar fashion until you finish reading the story.

A method framework provides a general description of the steps to follow during instruction and a general indication of the activities that might be used at each step. A method framework, however, is not usually tied to a specific set of materials; method frameworks may be used with almost any set of materials, from selections found in published reading programs, to selections written by teachers or provided by students, or a piece of computer software. If instructional materials come with teaching suggestions that differ from a teacher's preferred method, then the suggestions would be substituted with activities appropriate to the chosen method framework.

Often teachers will employ several different method frameworks, using each for different instructional purposes. For example, a particular method or set of methods might be preferred for teaching decoding skills; others might be preferred for teaching study skills. The more frequently used method frameworks include **directed reading activities** (see chapter 9), **language experience activities** (see chapter 3), and directed reading-thinking activities (see chapter 6).

directed reading activity: A method framework for teaching reading, consisting of preparation, guided reading, skill development and practice, and follow-up enrichment activities.
language experience activity: A method emphasizing children's experiences and oral language.
comprehension framework: A set of beliefs based on understanding what we do when we read and how reading ability develops.

A framework based on understanding reading comprehension, or a **comprehension framework,** consists of answers to two questions: How does one read? and How does reading ability develop? A comprehension framework is more abstract than either a materials framework or a method framework since it is not based on any specific set of methods or materials. In many ways, it is similar to the definitions of reading that were described earlier. A comprehension framework is a perspective, based on understanding what we do when we read. It influences the many instructional decisions that are made in the classroom and necessitates an understanding of a wide range of materials and methods. Thus, a comprehension framework may be said to incorporate, but go beyond, the knowledge necessary to use the materials or method frameworks. This is why experienced teachers often arrive at a comprehension framework—they have been exposed to a wide variety of materials and methods, and have made clear decisions about how they feel that reading takes place and develops.

Thus, to teach from a comprehension framework, you must acquire a thorough understanding of instructional materials and methods as well as arrive at an answer to the questions, How does one read? and How does reading ability develop? Comprehension frameworks are used in two major ways, first, to select materials and methods, and second, to adapt methods and materials that are inconsistent with the answers to the two questions. Thus, teachers with comprehension frameworks may use the lesson plans and activities in a set of materials and one of several method frameworks as they teach a reading lesson. These choices would be deliberate, reasoned decisions. Each would be entirely consistent with the teacher's explanation for how one reads and how reading ability develops.

Given the relative difficulty of developing and using different types of frameworks, why should teachers be challenged to develop and use a comprehension framework? Why should they not learn how to teach reading with either a materials or method framework? We believe that acquiring and teaching from a comprehension framework is preferable for at least five important reasons.

1. A comprehension framework can be used in many more situations than can frameworks based on a set of materials or instructional methods. For example, materials and method frameworks are only helpful if the teacher-preferred methods or materials are those favored by the school district in which they are used. A comprehension framework can be used in any instructional situation.

2. A comprehension framework provides a clear sense of direction, especially as you decide when and how to modify instructional resources. All teachers adapt and supplement available instructional materials. A comprehension framework helps to quickly and efficiently make such decisions.

3. A comprehension framework provides more strategies for meeting individual needs. Within materials or method frameworks, individual needs are met by altering either the pace of instruction and/or the amount of practice. The materials or methods rarely change significantly. Within a comprehension framework, individual needs may be

met not only by altering pace and practice, but also by altering instructional materials, methods, and even skills that are taught.

4. A comprehension framework helps understanding of why certain decisions are made during reading instruction. Frameworks based on either materials or methods only tell teachers what to do. Knowing why something is being taught allows one to alter instruction for particular students more effectively and to better evaluate the success of an instructional activity.

5. A comprehension framework is frequently developed by teachers, on their own, after using a wide variety of methods and materials. Knowing in advance that you will probably develop a comprehension framework as you teach will facilitate your development; knowing where you are going always makes a journey shorter and easier. Learning about reading instruction from a comprehension framework, therefore, makes your learning process more effective and efficient.

Developing a comprehension framework is more difficult than developing either a materials or a method framework, partly because teaching from a comprehension framework means that you will have to have a comprehensive knowledge of a wide range of materials and methods. Yet there can be little doubt that such a wide-ranging knowledge will make you a more effective teacher. We believe that this knowledge can be gained by anyone who aspires to teach children to read. We are also convinced that the potential benefits to you and your future students are well worth the effort.

One of the major reasons that we feel it is important to acquire a comprehension framework is because it offers more flexibility in instructional decision making than do either materials or method frameworks. This is shown in the following illustration, where the arrows indicate that teachers making decisions based on comprehension frameworks choose from a range of methods and materials. Teachers with method frameworks choose from within a range of materials, as appropriate to their chosen method(s). No arrows move away from *materials,* however, teachers with materials frameworks are constrained by their set of instructional materials.

Decision Making and the Modification of Frameworks

Frameworks are modified as your knowledge about materials, methods, and the reading process develops and changes. Also, although you might use one framework predominately, the frameworks can interact with one another and are not used exclusively. To continue one of the examples used previously in this chapter, a driver might use predominately a road map to guide a trip, but rarely does a driver use *only* a map. A driver may also ask directions, rely on sense of direction, and use knowledge of major landmarks even though the map might be the main tool used for guiding the way.

Thus, instructional frameworks are not static devices used to guide decision making. Teachers continually modify their frameworks on the basis of what does and does not help children learn to read. Also, if they are knowledgeable about their instructional goals, their students, and about the reading process, teachers can shift from one framework to another while retaining the framework that is fundamental to their beliefs. This process is illustrated in figure 1–3 and described in the following list.

1. *Teachers use frameworks to help them make instructional decisions.* Teachers with a materials framework will generally follow the directions in a teacher's manual. Teachers with a method framework will choose one or several instructional activities for each step in a procedural outline. Teachers with a comprehension framework will select materials and methods consistent with their beliefs about how reading takes place and how reading develops.
2. *Teachers evaluate the appropriateness of their instructional decisions.* After an activity, teachers have a sense of whether or not the activity succeeded. Successful activities are apparent by the performance of your students. They will be able to perform the skill or skills that you taught and, as a result, they will have improved in their ability to read and comprehend. Both teachers and students sense a feeling of accomplishment.
3. *Teachers modify their frameworks based on the success or failure of instructional decisions.* Teachers with a materials framework who teach a successful activity will repeat that activity the next time they follow their manual. Unsuccessful activities are dropped or modified the next time a lesson is taught. Teachers with a method framework who teach a successful activity will tend to repeat it. Unsuccessful activities are dropped or modified. Teachers with a comprehension framework will find support for their beliefs when an activity meets with success. After a period of unsuccessful lessons, beliefs about how one reads and how reading ability develops tend to change.
4. These confirmed or modified frameworks are then used to make additional decisions and the process repeats itself.

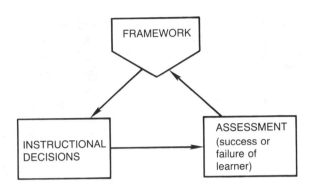

FIGURE 1–3
Illustration of the dynamics of frameworks and the decision-making process

Notice, however, that assessment leads to instructional decisions based on the framework. The arrows in figure 1–3 indicate that assessment does not lead directly to instructional decisions. Decisions are made by filtering assessment (that is, observations of the success or failure of certain instructional activities) through the framework. This can also modify the framework.

The decision-making process described here is similar to the process used by researchers or scientists. Just as researchers in any field use a theory to make predictions, so do teachers of reading use a framework to make instructional decisions. And just as researchers test their predictions in an experiment, so do teachers evaluate the appropriateness of their instructional decisions in classroom lessons. Finally, just as researchers modify their theories based on the results of experiments, so do teachers modify their frameworks based on the results of classroom lessons. Thus, although teachers are not true scientific researchers, they are involved in decision-making processes that share many similarities. Both use clear frameworks to help make decisions. Both use keen observational and assessment skills to evaluate these decisions. And both must be willing to modify their frameworks when results indicate a need to do so.

Frameworks are central to the decision you must make as a teacher of reading. They reduce complexity; allow you to make decisions quickly; and most importantly, allow you to meet the challenges faced by a teacher of reading. In chapter 2, you will begin defining your own framework to help in your future teaching decisions.

THE REWARDS

Assume you will teach an elementary classroom with twenty-five students. If you teach for ten years, you will have taught 250 students and, if you participate as a faculty sponsor in extracurricular activities such as clubs or sports, will have meaningfully touched the lives of perhaps that many more.

A POINT TO PONDER

Classroom teaching, particularly teaching reading, is not only a series of challenges. It is also immensely rewarding. Helping young children acquire one of society's most valued skills is, perhaps, one of the most satisfying feelings that teachers experience. You will play a central role in helping children gain access to the pleasure and power of reading. Each of the students you touch will be influenced by their interactions with you. As a teacher, you will have direct influence over their lives. Helping your students acquire needed skills and knowledge, and knowing that your work has helped them develop into productive adults, provides a feeling of reward and accomplishment that is rare in any profession.

It is difficult, though, to objectively describe the sense of accomplishment that comes from effective reading instruction. To put this feeling into more personal terms, consider the following case studies of how two students, with the assistance of a teacher, entered the world of readers.

CASE STUDY 1

Pat entered Mr. Nelson's first-grade class and looked forward to learning how to read. Her parents often read to her and she knew that books had lots of interesting things in them. She wanted to be able to read on her own so that she could find out what they had to say. Pat was a gentle child, a little shy around other students. Although she knew some of the children in her class, there were many who were strangers. Mr. Nelson knew that other children in his class were much like Pat, and he gave them lots of opportunities right away to get to know each other.

Mr. Nelson made a number of informal observations about Pat during her first week at school. Pat had very mature oral language skills, as well as an extensive oral vocabulary. She explained ideas clearly and asked interesting questions. She could identify most letters by name and enjoyed word games and rhyming activities. Mr. Nelson felt that Pat was average to above average in reading-related skills for her grade level, and he looked forward to helping her become a reader.

As the year went on, Mr. Nelson kept track of Pat's progress. Pat progressed normally through his reading program, and she looked forward to reading the short selections that were a part of Mr. Nelson's instruction. She particulary liked reading the short books that he allowed students to read on their own, and after doing so, the class would talk about them. As they became able to read, students were given short selections at their ability levels.

At parent conference time, Mr. Nelson found out that Pat's parents were pleased with her progress, and that Pat proudly read words out loud, such as signs when they were driving. They had continued to read stories to Pat after she entered school, and added books to her personal library. Pat's parents left the conference impressed with their daughter's new school and teacher.

By the end of the school year, Pat was eagerly reading independently books appropriate for a child of her age level. Mr. Nelson was happy with her progress and knew that it would continue throughout her school experience. He looked back at her reading ability when she entered his class, when she could only identify letters, and compared that with her reading ability now. He knew that he was instrumental in teaching her to read, and to enjoy it. As always, he would miss Pat and the other students in his class, but he looked forward to the students that he would teach next year. Thinking of the advantages that Pat's reading ability would provide her, Mr. Nelson was happy with his teaching decisions.

CASE STUDY 2

Jerry was a third grader in Ms. Dye's room. He was a precocious youngster, the son of a university professor in a midwestern college community. Jerry was a very verbal child who knew a great deal about the world and communicated this information effectively orally. Jerry was having a hard time, though, keeping up with his peers in reading. He scored at the bottom quarter of his class on a **standardized, norm-referenced test** in word recognition, sentence comprehension, and story comprehension. Jerry was having difficulty with almost all the skills that had been taught in his first two years of formal reading instruction. In addition, he was having extreme difficulty in spelling and writing. Jerry could spell only a small set of words correctly and never wrote more than a few sentences. Writing was a struggle for him.

standardized norm-referenced test: A published test including specific directions and procedures. Scoring is based on a comparison to a peer group.

Jerry considered both reading and writing to be unimportant to the life of a nine-year-old boy. Other things seemed far more promising—things like fishing, hiking, dirt bikes, and sports. During reading lessons, Jerry was not attentive. Ms. Dye had to regularly call on Jerry when his attention wandered in order to get him to focus on the learning task. This often resulted in Jerry not producing the correct answer, a fact that did not distress Jerry at all.

Ms. Dye was concerned about Jerry so she asked Jerry's parents to come for a conference to discuss the situation. Jerry's parents were equally concerned, but noted that Jerry had always seemed more interested in the outdoors than in books. The conference resulted in a sharing of information but produced no specific solutions.

Ms. Dye's greatest concern was that Jerry would get so far behind in reading achievement that he would never reach his potential, and that with each passing year, Jerry would fall further and further behind, eventually losing interest in reading and in school. Ms. Dye decided to try to use high-interest books as vehicles to build Jerry's awareness that books were things where joy and important information could be found.

Every day, Ms. Dye read aloud to the students in her room. This read-aloud session lasted about twenty minutes and took place immediately after lunch. Ms. Dye always selected what she considered to be quality literature for her students, stories that would catch their interest and carry an important meaning. She was just finishing the story *Charlotte's Web,* a story with a very sad, emotional ending for young children. She was amazed to see that Jerry, like several other students in her class, had tears in his eyes. He had obviously been touched by Charlotte's death.

Immediately after this session, Ms. Dye took Jerry aside and asked if he wanted to take the book home and share it with his parents. Jerry seemed very interested in this. Ms. Dye even suggested that Jerry's dad might reread the story aloud so he could enjoy it too. After school, Ms. Dye called home, explained what had happened, and suggested that Jerry's dad read a chapter aloud each night before Jerry went to bed. She also suggested that if this proved successful, Jerry and his parents could make regular trips to the city library for more books. Ms. Dye offered to provide a list of books that might be interesting to Jerry.

Meanwhile, at school, Ms. Dye put Jerry in touch with books about fishing and backpacking from the school's library. She made time for

Sometimes teachers need to find activities that are of special interest to students, and then bridge these activities into specific reading tasks.

Jerry to browse through these books every day. Although Jerry normally had difficulty attending to reading for more than a minute or two, he very much enjoyed these new tasks. Jerry's attention even improved in formal reading lessons. Within two weeks, Jerry's parents called Ms. Dye with the news that Jerry had brought books home from the library and was reading them with his dad. They reported that Jerry had a new interest in reading and asked for new titles they might check out from the library. Ms. Dye complied with this request and told them of Jerry's new interest at school. Both agreed to maintain regular communication about Jerry's reading interests and performance. By the end of the year, Jerry was "hooked on books" and was reading as well as Ms. Dye's average third graders. Ms. Dye's only concern was that Jerry's interests were very narrow, centered almost entirely on fishing and backpacking. She anticipated, though, that with sufficient guidance and encouragement, these narrow interests could easily be expanded now that Jerry was able to read and was interested in reading.

THE MAJOR POINTS

1. Reading ability is important. It is a key factor in one's job opportunities and quality of life.
2. Reading is not a mechanical skill, but is a thought and problem-solving process. Viewed in this way, the importance of reading and the teaching of reading will not become obsolete.
3. The teacher is an ongoing decision maker in the classroom, using observational skills to gather information on which to base instruction.
4. A teacher's view and definition of reading; that is, the framework of reading determines how reading will be taught.
5. Teaching reading to children in the elementary grades is one of the most rewarding tasks you will have an opportunity to perform. You will have the potential to help young children achieve one of their most important and exciting accomplishments: reading.

QUESTIONS AND ACTIVITIES

1. Interview as many of the following as you can: an elementary-grade student, a teacher, a parent, and a businessperson. Ask them (1) what they think reading is; (2) how important they think reading is now and will be in the future; and (3) to make a list of what they read in a normal day.
2. If you haven't already done so, state your definition of reading. Provide enough detail so that others can see how you arrived at your definition.
3. Why might different teachers, using the same information about their students (for example, test scores or observations), arrive at different instructional decisions?

FURTHER READING

Carroll, J. B. (1986). The nature of the reading process. In H. Singer & R. Ruddell (eds.), *Theoretical models and processes of reading*, 3rd Edition (pp. 25–34). Newark, DE: International Reading Association.

Discusses the nature of reading and points out that there is no real disagreement about what is involved in reading, but really only in the order of the steps that are involved.

Diehl, W. A., & Mikulecky, L. (1980). The nature of reading at work. *Journal of Reading, 24,* 221–27.

Discusses reading demands across different jobs and points out how these differ from what is expected in school.

Guthrie, J. T. (1983). Where reading is not reading. *Journal of Reading, 26,* 382–84.

Case studies of reading in fourteen occupational settings.

—. Worldwide sources for information about primary education. (1986). *The Reading Teacher, 39,* 572–75.

Lists worldwide sources that present issues in primary education. Acquiring literacy is a key element discussed on an intenational basis.

REFERENCES

Dechant, E. (1982). *Improving the teaching of reading* (3rd Edition). Englewood Cliffs, NJ: Prentice Hall.

Fingeret, A. (1983). A new perspective on independence and illiterate adults. *Adult Education Quarterly, 33,* 133–46.

Flesch, R. (1955). *Why Johnny can't read.* New York: Harper & Brothers.

Flesch, R. (1981). *Why Johnny still can't read.* New York: Harper & Row.

Goodman, K. S. (1976). Reading: a psycholinguistic guessing game. In H. Singer & R. Ruddell (eds.) *Theoretical models and processes of reading* (2nd Edition), pp. 497–508. Newark, DE: International Reading Association.

Heath, S. B. (1980). The functions and uses of literacy. *Journal of Communication, 30,* 123–33.

Miller, P. (1982). Reading demands in a high-technology industry. *Journal of Reading, 26,* 109–15.

Rumelhart, D. (1986). In H. Singer & R. Ruddell (eds.) Theoretical models and processes of reading (3rd Edition), pp. 722–50. Newark, DE: International Reading Association.

Samuels, S. J., & Kamil, M. L. (1984) Models of the reading process. In P. D. Pearson (ed.). *Handbook of reading research,* (pp. 185–224). New York: Longman.

Strang, R., McCullough, C., & Traxler, A. (1961). *The improvement of reading* (3rd Edition). New York: McGraw-Hill.

2 Specifying a Personal Framework

MAJOR COMPONENTS OF THE READING COMPREHENSION
PROCESS ■ HOW DOES ONE READ? ■ HOW DOES READING ABILITY
DEVELOP? ■ HOW A COMPREHENSION FRAMEWORK AFFECTS
INSTRUCTIONAL DECISIONS ■ DEVELOPING INDIVIDUAL FRAMEWORKS

"And so to completely analyze what we do when we read would almost be the
acme of a psychologist's achievements, for it would be to describe very many
of the most intricate workings of the human mind, as well as to unravel the
tangled story of the most remarkable specific performance that civilization has
learned in all its history."

E. B. Huey, *The Psychology and Pedagogy of Reading,* (Cambridge, MA: MIT Press, 1908), p. 6.

In chapter 2, you will first learn about the major components of the reading comprehension process. You will see how reading instruction attempts to develop these components in young readers so that comprehension may proceed smoothly. You will then learn how to define a comprehension framework. To accomplish this second task, you must consider answers to two questions, How does one read? and How does reading ability develop? As Edmund Burke Huey pointed out over seventy years ago, answering questions related to the reading process is not easy. Nevertheless, it is essential to begin to consider your responses to these two questions. Throughout your teaching career, the beliefs you have about reading comprehension will be central to the appropriateness of your instructional and assessment decisions, and to your development as a teacher of reading. This chapter will help you to begin that development.

After reading this chapter, you will be able to

1. identify the major components of the reading comprehension process,
2. explain how one reads,
3. explain how reading ability develops,
4. define alternative answers to questions regarding how one reads and how reading ability develops,
5. explain how instructional decisions are influenced by the nature of one's comprehension framework.

MAJOR COMPONENTS OF THE READING COMPREHENSION PROCESS

components of the reading comprehension process: Include readiness and affective aspects as well as decoding knowledge, vocabulary knowledge, syntactic knowledge, and discourse knowledge. See figure 2–1.

To understand issues related to how one reads and how reading ability develops, one must first become familiar with the major **components of the reading comprehension process:** decoding knowledge; vocabulary knowledge; syntactic knowledge; discourse knowledge; readiness aspects; and affective aspects. These components are thought to contribute in important ways to reading comprehension, as illustrated in figure 2–1.

While individuals may disagree about how these components are related, how they develop, or even how they should be labeled, most would agree that each exists and is an important part of the reading comprehension process. Indeed, much of reading instruction consists of activities designed to develop these six components. For example, teachers often spend a portion of each lesson discussing the meanings of unfamiliar words that will shortly appear in reading selections. These teachers are helping students develop vocabulary knowledge with the expectation that this will facilitate the comprehension process. Teachers also use similar instructional activities during reading lessons to develop each of the other components.

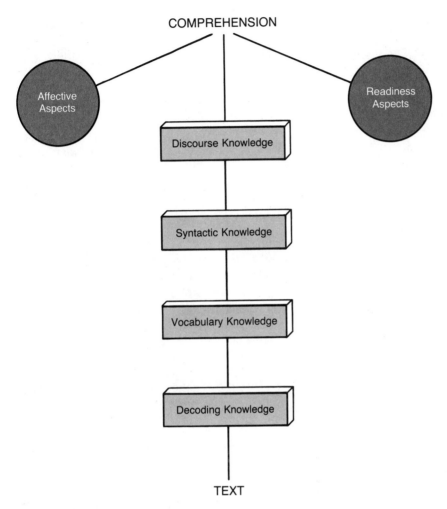

FIGURE 2–1
Major components of the reading comprehension process

Decoding Knowledge

Decoding knowledge refers to the knowledge readers use to determine the oral equivalent of a written word. As you work with instructional materials, you are likely to encounter a variety of other terms used to label what we shall refer to as decoding knowledge: recoding, word recognition; word identification; word attack; and others. All of these terms usually include the knowledge that readers use to determine the oral equivalent of written words. In addition, however, these other terms may sometimes be used to include knowledge that readers have about word meanings, or what we will call *vocabulary knowledge*.

Sometimes decoding knowledge is important for comprehension;

decoding knowledge: Knowledge used to determine the oral equivalent of a written word.

other times it is not. Decoding knowledge is important for comprehension when determining the oral equivalent of a word helps a reader identify meaning. This is frequently true for beginning readers who know the meanings of many words in spoken form but are relatively unfamiliar with printed words. Knowing how to determine the oral equivalent of a written word enables beginning readers to access the meanings of most words in their oral language.

Decoding knowledge is not important for comprehension when determining the oral equivalent of a word fails to help a reader identify its meaning. You can, for example, determine the oral equivalent of an unfamiliar word like *ethmoid,* but this does not help you understand its meaning.

Note, too, that decoding knowledge is not always necessary to determine a word's meaning. Frequently, readers determine the meaning of unfamiliar words like *ethmoid* not by using decoding knowledge to determine its oral equivalent, but rather by analyzing the surrounding context for clues about its likely meaning. You do this, for example, when you read a sentence like, "Joan broke her ethmoid bone at the point where her nose joins her skull." Thus, decoding knowledge is often, though not always, necessary for comprehension.

Developing decoding knowledge is almost always included in instructional programs. It is usually taught in the early grades, and is an important part of beginning reading instruction (Anderson, Hiebert, Scott, & Wilkinson, 1985; Chall, 1983). Teachers often use activities such as the following to teach various aspects of decoding knowledge.

SAMPLE ACTIVITIES

Rhyming Riddles. Give riddles to a group of children where the answers all rhyme with a key word and have the same spelling pattern at the end; for example, "I'm thinking of a word that rhymes with *make* and is something that you eat at a party" (cake), or "I'm thinking of a word that rhymes with *make* and is something that crawls in the grass" (snake). As students guess each riddle, write the answers on the board. When a number of words have been listed, help students identify the similar letter-sound relationship in all of the words (*ake* represents the sound /ache/). Then help students apply this generalization and read other similarly spelled words such as *take, lake,* or *rake.*

Letter Linking. To practice several letter-sound patterns that have been previously taught, prepare two sets of cards: one with initial consonant letters (*t, l, m, f,* and so on) and one with final letter patterns (*ake, ime, ame, ight,* and so on). Pass out the cards to a small group of students and have them find partners with whom to join cards and make a word. Have pairs of students read their word to the group.

BEFORE READING ON

Read the following passages and consider whether successful decoding is always important for comprehension.

> "Pupils who are below the average need the same program of instruction and practice and application of essential skills that average pupils do. But these pupils need to be more carefully paced through the program" (Scott Foresman, 1985, p. T13).

> "An analysis of variance of the syntactic appropriateness of the erroneous response compared the percentage of scores that fell into each of the three scoring categories, and then the interactions of syntactic appropriateness with experimental condition, passage difficulty, and mode of reading" (Haber, Haber, & Furlin, 1983, p. 181).

Can you determine the oral equivalent for all of the words in each passage? Can you understand the meaning of each passage? What does this suggest about the role of decoding during the comprehension process? What other type of knowledge is necessary for you to comprehend the second passage?

Vocabulary Knowledge

As the preceding example demonstrates, determining the oral equivalent of a word does not guarantee an understanding of its meaning. You may have been able to recognize the oral equivalent of "analysis of variance," but you probably could not understand its meaning. You lacked sufficient knowledge of the word meanings in this passage and you were probably unable to determine the necessary word meanings from context. Both of these aspects of the comprehension process are considered part of a reader's **vocabulary knowledge.**

vocabulary knowledge: The knowledge one has about word meanings used to determine the appropriate meaning for a word in a particular context.

Helping students develop vocabulary knowledge is important at all grade levels, but is a particularly important aspect of reading instruction as children develop and explore less familiar subject areas with somewhat specialized vocabularies. Before students read an article about the developmental stages of a butterfly, for example, you could explain the meanings of unfamiliar words that will appear such as *chrysalis, pupa,* and *metamorphosis.* You might also use activities such as the following to teach different aspects of vocabulary knowledge.

SAMPLE ACTIVITIES

Making a Pair Tree. On a bulletin board, put up the outline of a large tree made from construction paper. Cut out a number of blank word cards in the shape of a pear. Write difficult words that students will be encountering shortly on the word cards (one for each word card) and pin up on the tree. Have students attempt to discover synonyms for each word on the tree. When they have a correct synonym, write it on a blank word card, put the student's name at the bottom, and pin it with its synonym "pear" on the tree. Each day, place several new words up on the tree and, when the tree gets crowded, remove several old pairs for students to take home.

Context Clues. When teaching students how to determine an unfamiliar word's meaning from context, provide them with several sentences such as the following.

> Jim said, "This message can mean either that Tom is hurt or that he is well. It seems very *ambiguous* to me. What do you think?"
>
> Ambiguous is likely to mean _____
> Write another sentence with the word ambiguous. _____

Model your reasoning as you complete the first example for students so they might see the strategies you used. Have individual students model their reasoning for answers to the next couple of items. Then have students complete the remainder by themselves or with a partner. When all students have finished, have individuals explain their answers for each sentence as you check in responses.

Syntactic Knowledge

syntactic knowledge:
Knowledge of the word-order rules that determine grammatical function and sometimes the meaning and pronunciation of words.

Knowledge of sentence syntax, or word order, is also crucial for the comprehension process. **Syntactic knowledge** includes understanding word-order rules that exist within sentences and permit you to determine the grammatical function and often the meaning and pronunciation of words.

As an example, consider your ability to read and understand the following sentence:

Sarah will lead the miners to the lead.

In this sentence, syntactic knowledge enables you to determine that the third word is a verb meaning "to direct" and that it is pronounced /leed/ while the last word is a noun meaning "a heavy metal" and is pronounced /led/. Knowledge of word-order rules allows you to make these distinctions even though both words look the same in writing.

Most young children have already developed a substantial amount of syntactic knowledge by the time they begin school since children's oral language ability is fairly well developed at five or six years. Nevertheless, a number of more complex syntactic patterns appear in print, are often unfamiliar to young children, and, thus, need to be taught. For example, the structure and meaning of appositive phrases are often taught during reading instruction (e.g., Tom, *Bill's father,* came home late.). The way in which meaning can be derived from other complex syntactic patterns may be taught as well.

Familiarity with the more complex syntactic patterns in English becomes especially important as children develop reading ability, and as the structure of the sentences they encounter while reading becomes more complicated. Teachers often use activities such as the following to help students develop greater syntactic knowledge.

Paraphrase Pairs. After teaching the form and meaning of appositive phrases, have students practice by writing paraphrases of sentences like the following.

1. Robert picked out a car, the red one with a white roof, before he checked with his father.
2. Luis, Roberto's brother, bumped into Roxanne, George's sister.

Have students work individually, in pairs, or in small groups. Be certain to have students explain their reasoning when you check in responses.

Cause-and-Effect Patterns. Teach the meanings of various words and phrases designating cause-and-effect relationships (for example, *since, and therefore, as a result of, and thus,* and so on.) Show students how these words serve to communicate cause-and-effect relationships between two different ideas (Tom sat in the sun all day *and thus* he got very sunburned.) Then have students practice by completing the blanks in sentences like this:

Brian caught many fish ＿＿＿＿＿＿he was very happy when he returned.

because   and therefore   following

Ask students to explain their reasoning when you check in responses.

Discourse Knowledge

Discourse knowledge is the knowledge of language organization at units beyond the single sentence level. It includes knowledge of the structural organization of different types of writing. The structural organization of fairy tales, for example, leads readers to form certain expectations for a story beginning with, "Once upon a time . . . ." After reading this short phrase it is likely that you formulate very specific kinds of expectations including (1) this is a story, not a chapter in a social studies book; (2) the story is not true; (3) the story takes place in a kingdom "long ago and far away;" (4) there is likely to be a boy and a girl in the story and possibly a prince and princess; (5) there will be some conflict

discourse knowledge: Knowledge of language organization at units beyond the single sentence level. Includes knowledge of the structural organization of different types of writing.

Reading and discussing different types of literature is an enjoyable way to promote the development of discourse knowledge.

that the hero of the story will be forced to resolve; and (6) there will probably be a happy ending, perhaps conveying some sort of message to young children. Knowing the structural organization of different types of writing is useful during reading comprehension. Among other things, it permits you to know if you are reading information that is likely to be true or false.

Discourse knowledge often receives greater instructional emphasis at higher grade levels. Though discourse knowledge is often developed by simply having children read extensively in many different forms of writing, teachers may also use activities such as the following.

SAMPLE ACTIVITIES

Teaching Story Forms. Every day, read a selection characteristic of a particular type of writing (for example, a fable, folk tale, fairy tale, biography, autobiography). After completing several selections of a particular type, ask students to help you list the characteristics that were common to each. With fables, you may end up with a list that includes animals are the main characters; the animals talk and act like people; there is usually a lesson (moral) at the end of the story; and the story did not really happen. Then read, or have students read, another selection of this type in order to see if the same structural elements also appear in the new story.

Who, What, When, Where, How, Why. Explain to students that newspaper articles are written to inform readers of important events that have actually happened in the world. Explain that this form of writing usually contains answers to the questions who, what, when, where, how, and why. Then read several short articles together, identifying each of these elements in the articles. Provide students with several other short articles and have them work together to identify and underline each type of information. You may then wish to have students contribute articles about classroom and school events and put together a copy of a school newspaper.

Readiness Aspects

Readiness refers to two different concepts. Traditionally, **reading readiness** is the ability of a student to benefit from initial reading instruction. According to this view, a young child is either ready to begin reading instruction or else must continue to develop a number of readiness skills. Traditional readiness skills are important instructional considerations during kindergarten and the beginning of first grade. Some of the readiness skills which individuals (Aulls, 1982; Clay, 1980a, 1980b; Ollila, 1976) believe to be important during this readiness period include

reading readiness: Traditionally refers to the student's ability to benefit from initial reading instruction. Also refers to the student's ability to read and understand a particular selection.

1. knowledge of letter names,
2. knowledge of the left-to-right sequence of writing,
3. the ability to see similarities and differences in shapes,
4. oral language proficiency,
5. the ability to hear similarities and differences in sounds,
6. the ability to work cooperatively in small groups,
7. the ability to sustain independent work.

Recently, reading readiness has also included being ready to read and understand a particular selection. According to this perspective, reading readiness describes the abilities required for reading and comprehending any particular piece of printed material. Readiness instruction, in this sense, consists of activities that prepare students to read a specific story such as developing background knowledge about the topic of a selection, learning new vocabulary words, understanding the purpose for reading the selection, or learning a comprehension skill required to understand the selection.

Reading readiness, therefore, may describe instruction designed to assist both prereaders and children who already know how to read. Regardless of which definition is used, however, the level of reading readiness will influence how children comprehend written text. Thus, readiness needs to be considered in any discussion of reading comprehension.

SAMPLE ACTIVITIES

Developing Oral Language Proficiency. Regular show-and-tell or sharing sessions help young students to develop important speaking and listening skills in oral language.

Setting the Purpose for Reading. Before reading, tell students the purpose for reading a particular selection: to find out some specific piece of information; to evaluate a character's action; for enjoyment; or to learn about something new. Regularly discuss with students how knowing the reason for reading a selection influences how a person reads.

Affective Aspects

Much of the preceding discussion has focused on aspects of reading comprehension intimately related to language: decoding knowledge; vocabulary knowledge; syntactic knowledge; and discourse knowledge. Reading is a language process but it is also an affective process. **Affective aspects** of comprehension include a reader's attitude and interest in reading.

affective aspects: In reading comprehension, include both interest and attitude. These increase motivation and facilitate reading comprehension.

All readers comprehend better when they are interested in reading. The difference is especially noticeable among less proficient readers. Any teacher of reading knows students who had difficulty comprehending typical classroom assignments but had no difficulty when they were highly interested. Thus, to facilitate comprehension, always make reading and reading instruction as interesting and enjoyable as possible.

Affective aspects are important to consider at all age and grade levels. You can use activities such as the following to heighten students' attitude and interest.

SAMPLE ACTIVITIES

Regular Read-Aloud Sessions. Spend a short portion of each day reading books that you enjoy and that you think your students might enjoy. Get a collection of other books by the same author from your school library and make them available for students to read during their free moments in the school day, at lunch, or at home. For your most reluctant readers, stop reading a story at the most exciting part and suggest that they may wish to finish the book on their own.

Character Costumes. On Halloween, encourage your students to come dressed as a favorite storybook character. Have a contest to see who can identify the greatest number of impersonators.

HOW DOES ONE READ?

In the field of reading, there is substantial agreement that decoding knowledge, vocabulary knowledge, syntactic knowledge, discourse knowledge, readiness aspects, and affective aspects all exist in the mind of a reader and contribute to reading comprehension. There is far less agreement, however, about how these components contribute to reading comprehension (Rumelhart, 1976; Smith, 1979; Weaver & Shonhoff, 1984). Put more simply, there is substantial disagreement about exactly how one reads. Over time, several different explanations for how one reads have evolved. The most common types of explanations consist of

1. text-based explanations,
2. reader-based explanations,
3. interactive explanations.

While these three types of explanations will be discussed separately, you can view them as points on a continuum of explanations. Just as you can view different political philosophies on a continuum ranging from conservative to liberal with moderate perspectives situated somewhere in the middle, so you can view different types of explanations for how one reads on a continuum ranging from text-based explanations to reader-based explanations with interactive explanations situated somewhere in the middle (see figure 2–2).

We have chosen to discuss the major categories of explanations separately for instructional purposes; it is simply easier to describe a limited set of clear-cut categories of explanations than it is to discuss all of the possible points on a continuum of explanations. Recognize, however, that variations of the three major explanations for how one reads do exist at other points on the continuum illustrated in figure 2–2.

| Text-Based Explanations | Interactive Explanations | Reader-Based Explanations |

FIGURE 2–2
A continuum of explanations for how one reads

Text-Based Explanations

Some individuals (Gough, 1986) tend to adopt text-based explanations for how one reads, suggesting that reading consists largely of decoding or sounding out words on a page. This is because **text-based explanations** assume that (1) meaning exists more in the text than in the meaning a reader might bring to a text; (2) reading consists of translating

text-based explanation: An explanation for how one reads. Readers are thought to translate print into sounds to uncover meaning in a text.

printed words into sounds and sounds into meanings; and (3) readers begin by using the lowest knowledge source (decoding) and then sequentially apply higher knowledge sources (vocabulary, syntactic, and then discourse knowledge). According to text-based explanations, readers translate print into sounds so they might uncover the meaning in a story, article, book, or other form of writing.

One way to understand this type of explanation is to think about how you might read words like *Roskolnikov, Ekaterinburg,* or *Fedorachovna* in a Russian novel. Here you are likely to attempt to sound out these difficult Russian names hoping that hearing them will help you remember who they are or where they are located. You would, in effect, read these words in a text-based way.

Another way to understand this type of explanation is to consider how it might depict the activity going on in your mind as you read a story. Figure 2–3 illustrates how a text-based explanation for how one reads might describe this process. In this example, you have read and acquired an author's intended meaning for the first portion of the first sentence of a fairy tale that begins, "Once upon a time, a princess kissed a . . . ." You are now starting to process the symbols on the page representing the word *frog.* The process has been stopped in time at several points so that you might better understand how reading comprehension takes place according to a text-based explanation.

According to a text-based explanation, you would probably first perceive the word *frog* and attempt to sound out or determine the oral equivalent of this word using decoding knowledge. Once the oral equivalent of this word (/frog/) had been determined, you would use the sound of the word to search vocabulary knowledge and locate the word's meanings: (1) noun — a small green amphibian and (2) adjective — of or pertaining to a frog (e.g., frog legs). Both meanings would then be passed on to syntactic knowledge for a decision as to which is most appropriate in this sentence's context. Your syntactic knowledge would help you decide that the word *frog* is most likely being used as a noun, not an adjective, and so the first meaning of the word *frog* would be chosen. At this point, your discourse knowledge would begin to interpret the discourse aspects of the text. You would probably conclude that the selection is a fairy tale since the beginning of the story is consistent with what you know about the characteristics of this story type. You might also conclude that both the princess and the frog are the major characters in this story since major characters are often introduced early in a fairy tale. Thus, the complete meaning of the first sentence of the fairy tale would have been realized and you would begin to sound out the next word in the story. You would continue to read, translating the meaning on the page into your mind by sounding out words and sequentially applying each knowledge source from lowest (decoding) to highest (discourse knowledge).

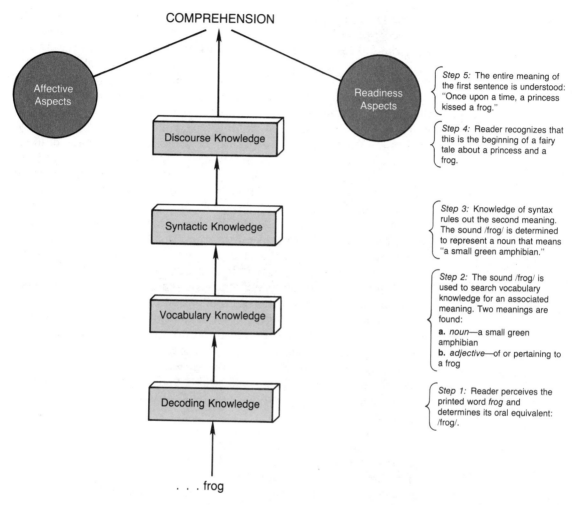

COMPREHENSION

Affective Aspects

Readiness Aspects

Discourse Knowledge

Syntactic Knowledge

Vocabulary Knowledge

Decoding Knowledge

. . . frog

Step 5: The entire meaning of the first sentence is understood: "Once upon a time, a princess kissed a frog."

Step 4: Reader recognizes that this is the beginning of a fairy tale about a princess and a frog.

Step 3: Knowledge of syntax rules out the second meaning. The sound /frog/ is determined to represent a noun that means "a small green amphibian."

Step 2: The sound /frog/ is used to search vocabulary knowledge for an associated meaning. Two meanings are found:
a. *noun*—a small green amphibian
b. *adjective*—of or pertaining to a frog

Step 1: Reader perceives the printed word *frog* and determines its oral equivalent: /frog/.

FIGURE 2–3
Reading comprehension according to a text-based explanation

Reader-Based Explanations

Other individuals (Goodman, 1976; Smith, 1979) adopt more of a reader-based explanation for how one reads, suggesting that readers use background knowledge and the evolving meaning of a text to help them make guesses and form expectations for upcoming words. Readers are thought not to sound out each and every word they encounter. Thus, **reader-based explanations** assume that (1) meaning exists more in what a reader brings to a text than in the text itself; (2) reading consists of expectations for upcoming words, not the translation of words into sounds and sounds into meanings; and (3) readers begin by using

reader-based explanation: An explanation for how one reads. The reader's prior knowledge is used to predict meaning. This prediction is then checked against the words in the text.

knowledge sources more associated with meaning (discourse, syntactic, and vocabulary knowledge) and only then apply decoding knowledge. According to reader-based explanations, readers continuously form hypotheses about upcoming words based on their understanding of a text, then look to the letters in words to see if their hypotheses were correct.

One way to understand this type of explanation is to think about how you might read one of today's popular "romance" novels. Before you even begin reading a story of this type, you probably have very clear expectations about how the story will be structured and what will likely take place. You do not need to pay careful attention to sounding out each and every word since your expectations for the plot are so strong and most of the words are familiar to you. Indeed, you are likely to finish the book in a single night since you read so quickly, skimming the incidental portions to get to the more interesting sections of the story. You certainly do not need to sound out each word the way you might sound out the names of characters and locations in a Russian novel. You would, in effect, read in a reader-based fashion.

A second way to understand a reader-based explanation is to consider how it might depict the comprehension process inside your mind as you were reading (see figure 2–4). Again, we have tried to show what it would look like if you had read the sentence beginning, "Once upon a time, a princess kissed a . . . ." You are now beginning to form an expectation for the final word in this sentence. The process has again been stopped at each of the steps so that you might better understand how reading comprehension takes place according to a reader-based explanation.

From the information at the beginning of this sentence, discourse knowledge would lead you to expect that you have started to read a fairy tale since this is exactly how fairy tales begin. A number of other expectations derived from discourse knowledge would also follow. One is that the beginning of most fairy tales contains information about the main characters in the story. You already have information about one of the characters (a princess). Since the princess is about to kiss someone, you would also expect that the second character in this story will be mentioned next.

Expectations from discourse level knowledge limit the possible expectations from syntactic level knowledge. Given previous context and the expectation that this is a fairy tale, you would expect to find a noun and the recipient of a kiss who is likely to be a main character in the story.

Your syntactic expectations limit, in turn, the possible expectations for word meaning generated from vocabulary level knowledge. There are a limited set of things that are nouns, recipients of actions, potential main characters in a fairy tale, and characters likely to be kissed by princesses. This set probably includes people like a king, a queen, and

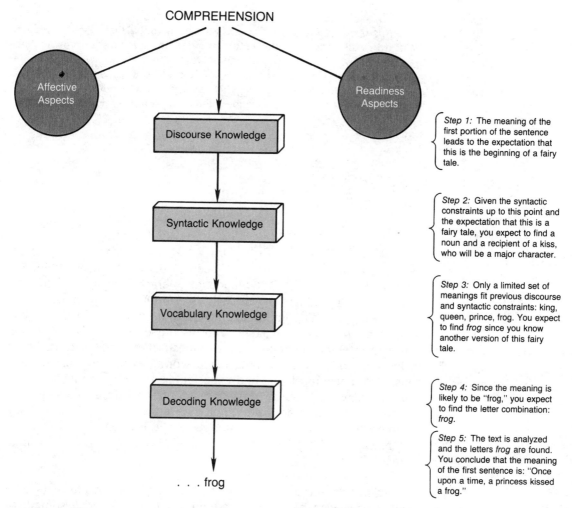

COMPREHENSION

Affective Aspects

Readiness Aspects

Discourse Knowledge

Step 1: The meaning of the first portion of the sentence leads to the expectation that this is the beginning of a fairy tale.

Syntactic Knowledge

Step 2: Given the syntactic constraints up to this point and the expectation that this is a fairy tale, you expect to find a noun and a recipient of a kiss, who will be a major character.

Vocabulary Knowledge

Step 3: Only a limited set of meanings fit previous discourse and syntactic constraints: king, queen, prince, frog. You expect to find *frog* since you know another version of this fairy tale.

Decoding Knowledge

Step 4: Since the meaning is likely to be "frog," you expect to find the letter combination: *frog.*

Step 5: The text is analyzed and the letters *frog* are found. You conclude that the meaning of the first sentence is: "Once upon a time, a princess kissed a frog."

. . . frog

FIGURE 2–4

Reading comprehension according to a reader-based explanation

a prince. The set would also include a frog, especially if you have read another version of the princess-kisses-frog-and-finds-a-prince story. Since you already know that some princesses do, indeed, kiss frogs, this might be the expectation generated by your vocabulary knowledge.

Finally, expectations from vocabulary knowledge constrain possible expectations from decoding knowledge; you expect to find the graphic representation for *frog* on the page. You then analyze the text for the expected graphic representation, find the letters for *frog* and begin to generate expectations for what might come next in the story, beginning with discourse knowledge and proceeding down to decoding knowledge.

> **A POINT TO PONDER**
>
> The terms *text-based* and *reader-based* are not the only labels used to describe these two explanations of the reading comprehension process. Others have been chosen by individuals (Rumelhart, 1976; Smith, 1979; Weaver & Shonhoff, 1984) to label their explanations for how one reads as well as the explanations of others. See if you can determine which explanation was referred to when the following terms were used to describe the reading comprehension process.
>
> 1. top-down
> 2. inside-out
> 3. bottom-up
> 4. outside-in

Interactive Explanations

interactive explanation: An explanation for how one reads. Reading is seen as an interaction between text and reader.

Yet other individuals (Anderson, Hiebert, Scott, & Wilkinson, 1985; Rumelhart, 1976; Stanovich, 1980) adopt an interactive explanation for how one reads, suggesting that you read by simultaneously sounding out words using decoding knowledge at the same time you form expectations from vocabulary, syntactic, and discourse knowledge. This is because an **interactive explanation** assumes (1) meaning is located both in the text and in the meaning readers bring to the text; (2) reading consists of both translation and expectation; and (3) reading proceeds as each knowledge source in one's mind interacts simultaneously with the print on the page and with other knowledge sources. Thus, reading comprehension is viewed as a product of the interaction between text and reader, taking place simultaneously at a number of knowledge sources.

It is somewhat difficult to understand the notion of reading as an interaction between text and reader. One way is to consider your own reading behavior when you are attempting to comprehend something like this text. At times, reading is very easy and it seems that you are able to anticipate what will come next. This is because the meaning you bring to the page matches closely the meaning that exists on the page. Your expectations help you read and comprehend. At other times, reading is somewhat difficult and you may sound out words like *syntactic* to see if hearing their oral equivalents helps you recall their meanings. Readers who shift quickly back and forth between expectation and translation are reading interactively. Comprehension is a result of the interaction between the meaning in a text and that which each reader brings to a text.

To understand the more specific ways in which a reader interacts with a text, it may be useful to consider how an interactive explanation might portray the reading process as depicted in figure 2–5. Again, we have stopped the comprehension process after you have read the first

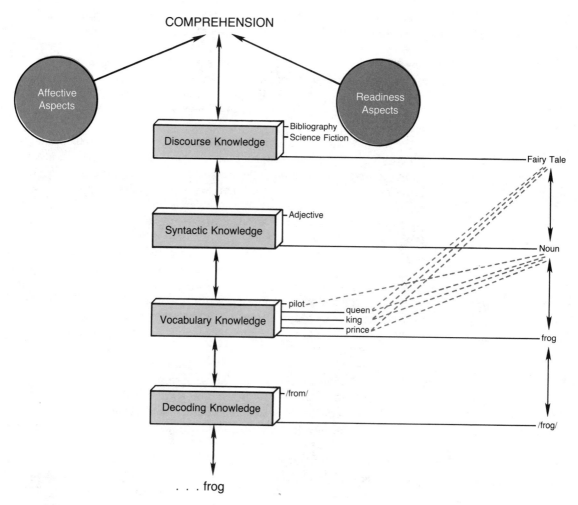

FIGURE 2–5

Reading comprehension according to an interactive explanation

Expectations at each knowledge level are simultaneously checked with expectations at all
other levels and with the text itself. Readers seek to find the one answer at each
knowledge level that is consistent with answers at all other levels. In this example, the
only answer consistent with expectations at each level is the word *frog*. It can exist in a
fairy tale, it is a noun, it carries the meaning "frog—a small green amphibian," and it has
the oral equivalent /frog/. Note that readers with large amounts of background
knowledge about fairy tales, princesses, and frogs would depend more on expectations
from higher knowledge levels. Conversely, readers with little background knowledge in
these areas would depend more on lower knowledge levels as they translated words into
sounds and sounds into meanings.

portion of the sample sentence and are beginning to read the symbols on the page that represent the word *frog.*

In an interactive explanation, the most difficult concept to understand is the way that the reader's knowledge sources simultaneously interact with the text and each other. Unlike text-based and reader-based explanations, there is not a fixed, sequential ordering in which knowledge sources are applied. Instead, each knowledge source simultaneously searches for an answer at its particular level by generating possible expectations and testing these against the expectations at all levels. The number of possible answers to a unit of text is ultimately narrowed as each level finds only a single answer consistent with previous information and with answers received from each of the other levels of processing.

We have attempted to illustrate this aspect of interactive explanations in figure 2–5 by using several conventions. First, you can see that multiple expectations have been simultaneously generated at each knowledge source by the solid lines extending to the right. Longer lines to the right represent a possible answer at one level that is consistent with one or more possible answers at other levels. Thus, at the vocabulary knowledge level, the meaning *pilot* has a short line because it is only consistent with the syntactic expectation for a noun. The meanings for *queen, king,* and *prince,* however, have longer lines because they are consistent with the discourse expectation for a fairy tale as well as the syntactic expectation for a noun. *Frog* has a longer line yet because it is consistent with expectations at all knowledge levels. In figure 2–5, a longer line to the right, therefore, represents a more likely answer at any level of the process.

Second, dotted lines have been drawn between expectations at several levels to indicate how an answer at one level is also consistent with an answer at another level. The meanings *queen, king,* and *prince,* for example, are consistent with *fairy tale* at the discourse level and *noun* at the syntactic level, but not consistent with the sound /frog/ at the decoding level.

Finally, the one answer at each level that is consistent with answers at all other levels is indicated by arrows extending simultaneously up and down. It is this answer *(frog)* that you are likely to achieve before moving on to the next word or phrase.

Now let us consider the process itself. From the information at the beginning of this sentence, the most likely answer at the discourse level is that the story is a fairy tale. When you read the first word in the sentence, it was possible for the story to also be science fiction or biography. When you read the phrase "upon a time," however, science fiction and biography became less likely candidates and the possibility that the story is a fairy tale increased (note the longer line to the right). The decision that this is a fairy tale was made as you found this answer to be consistent with answers at other knowledge sources, especially those at the syntactic and vocabulary levels.

At the syntactic level, you have decided that the symbols on the page represent a noun. They might also represent an adjective, but this is less likely since you know from previous sentence context that the word is probably going to be the recipient of a kiss. Also, knowing that the word is the final word in this sentence makes it unlikely that it will be an adjective. The decision that the word is a noun was made as you found this answer to be consistent with each of the other knowledge sources.

At the vocabulary level, you have decided that the meaning of this word is *frog*—a small green amphibian. At one point you also entertained the possibility that the word meant either *pilot, queen, king,* or *prince,* since each is a noun that a princess might kiss. The meaning *pilot* is less likely, though, because pilots seldom exist in fairy tales. The meanings *queen, king,* and *prince* are less likely since they are inconsistent with the most likely candidates from the decoding level: /from/ and /frog/. Only the meaning of *frog* is consistent with candidates in each of the knowledge sources.

At the decoding level, you have decided that the oral equivalent of the word on the page is /frog/. Before you had determined the oral equivalent for all four letters, the possibility existed that the symbols might represent the sound /from/. This possibility was reduced, however, because it was inconsistent with the most likely choice at each of the other knowledge sources.

At this point, you made a decision that everything points to the fact that the set of graphic marks on the page is, indeed, the word *frog* and that the meaning of this sentence is "Once upon a time, a princess kissed a frog." You would then continue reading, translating the oral equivalent from the text as you formed simultaneous and interactive expectations at each of the knowledge sources.

Affective Considerations

Notice that each of the previous explanations lack any specific mention of how the affective aspects (interest and attitude) influence motivation and the comprehension process. Affective aspects exert a powerful influence on comprehension, but we do not clearly understand how. We do not know, for example, if affective aspects influence each of the knowledge sources equally or if affective aspects influence some knowledge sources more than others. In figures 2–3, 2–4, and 2–5, affective aspects have been represented in a generalized fashion since we know that interest and attitude strongly influence the comprehension process and because we have no evidence that this influence is different at any of the processing levels. Do not conclude that affective aspects are relatively unimportant simply because we did not indicate how they influence comprehension. The opposite is actually true—we comprehend best what is perceived as meaningful, interesting, and important. We suspect, though, that affective aspects exert a general influence on each

Affective aspects such as interest and attitude contribute substantially to reading comprehension.

knowledge source involved in the comprehension process. Indeed, this is probably the reason why affective aspects are so important.

A POINT TO PONDER

Consider each of the following definitions of reading from experts in the field. Attempt to determine if each definition reflects more of a text-based, reader-based, or interactive explanation of how reading takes place.

1. "Reading typically is the bringing of meaning *to* rather than the gaining of meaning *from* the printed page" (Smith & Dechant, 1961, p. 22).

2. "Reading means getting meaning from certain combinations of letters. Teach the child what each letter stands for and he can read" (Flesch, 1955, pp. 2–3).

3. "Reading is a complex mental process that involves the doing of several things simultaneously. The reader must recognize the symbols that represent speech and must bring meaning to what he recognizes" (Strickland, 1969, p. 256).

4. "Reading is a process in which information from the text and the knowledge possessed by the reader act together to produce meaning. Good readers skillfully integrate information in the text with what they already know" (Anderson, Hiebert, Scott, & Wilkinson, 1985).

HOW DOES READING ABILITY DEVELOP?

Understanding how one reads is one-half of a comprehension framework. The other half is understanding how reading ability develops. Over time, at least three different types of explanations for how reading ability develops have evolved and been used by individuals (Goodman & Goodman, 1979; Shuy, 1979; Weaver & Shonhoff, 1984) to account for the developmental nature of reading comprehension:

1. mastery of specific skill explanations,
2. holistic language learning explanations,
3. differential acquisition explanations.

These explanations for the development of reading ability, like explanations for how one reads, are not discrete categories. Rather, they exist on a continuum as illustrated in figure 2–6. At one end of this continuum are explanations based on the idea that readers must learn to master specific skills. At the other end are explanations based on the idea that readers learn to read holistically. Somewhere in the middle are explanations based on the idea that development differs according to the nature of the student. Recognize that we have chosen to discuss these three categories of explanations separately for instructional purposes. Rather than attempting to describe all of the points on a continuum, we will describe a few reference points as clearly as possible.

Mastery of Specific	Differential	Holistic Language
Skills Explanations	Acquisition	Learning Explanations
	Explanations	

FIGURE 2–6
A continuum of explanations for how reading ability develops

Mastery of Specific Skills

A **mastery of specific skills** explanation for how reading ability develops is based on two assumptions: that reading ability develops to the extent that students master specific reading skills and that reading ability develops to the extent that these skills are taught by another person, usually a teacher, in an explicit and frequently **deductive** fashion.

According to mastery of specific skills explanations for development, a hierarchy of specific skills is often organized according to level of difficulty. Easier reading skills are taught first; harder reading skills are taught last. A reading program based on a mastery of specific skills explanation for development might include skills like the following.

mastery of specific skills: An explanation for how reading ability develops. Development is thought to be a result of direct instruction in specific skills.

deductive: In teaching, direct explicit instruction where a teacher states a rule to the student.

1. The student will be able to correctly pronounce words that begin with both hard *c* and soft *c* sounds.
2. The student will be able to correctly interpret cause-and-effect relationships within a sentence.
3. The student will be able to identify the main idea in a paragraph and also be able to identify the supporting details.

To ensure that children master each skill, a cycle of test, teach, retest (if necessary), and reteach (if necessary) is often recommended (Block & Burns, 1977; Bloom, 1976). Instruction usually teaches these skills separately from the reading of stories or articles.

In addition to believing that students must master specific reading skills, this type of explanation usually assumes that reading ability develops best when students are taught in a direct, and frequently deductive, way. Students are not usually assumed to induce major skills on their own. Thus, children are expected to learn best when teachers provide clear and explicit instruction on each separate skill.

In short, a mastery of specific skills explanation of development is skill specific and teacher generated. Specific skills are mastered by students who are taught directly by their teachers.

Holistic Language Learning

holistic language learning: An explanation for how reading ability develops. Development takes place as students engage in meaningful, functional, and holistic experiences with print.
inductive: In teaching, indirect instruction where the student infers or generalizes a rule from examples.

A **holistic language learning** explanation is based on the twin beliefs that reading ability develops as students engage in meaningful, functional, and holistic experiences with print and that much of their learning takes place in a largely **inductive** fashion. Reading comprehension is perceived as a unified entity which is difficult to break down into a fixed set of separate skills. In addition, students are believed to induce most of the important generalizations required for proficient reading based on their experiences with print and observations of others interacting with print.

Individuals who have developed different versions of a holistic language learning explanation for development (Clay, 1980b; Goodman & Goodman, 1979; Holdaway, 1979; Taylor, 1984) believe that reading comprehension is not easily separated into a hierarchy of distinct skills. They argue that comprehension is a holistic process and that separating reading into a number of separate skills removes the context in which each takes place. This, they explain, makes for an artificial explanation of the skills we teach children and, in many instances, communicates inappropriate information about comprehension.

Advocates of a holistic language learning explanation assume that written language skills (reading and writing) and oral language skills (speaking and listening) develop similarly (Weaver & Shonhoff, 1984). There is fairly clear evidence that oral language skills develop inductively as a result of meaningful language interactions (Anderson & Lapp, 1979; Slobin, 1979). Children induce the rules of their language as they listen, speak, and interact with other language users, not as a result of direct instruction. Individuals who believe in a holistic language explanation suggest that reading and oral language proficiency develop similarly since reading is also a language process. According to this explanation, children should be presented with a rich written language environment, examples of others engaged in literacy tasks, and a functional need for communicating in a written language form. If these conditions exist, children will induce all of the necessary generalizations. Reading, like oral language, should be encouraged to develop in a very natural manner.

In short, a holistic language learning explanation is skill general and student generated. Reading, as a holistic entity, is acquired by students who learn inductively.

Differential Acquisition

According to a **differential acquisition** explanation, the development of reading is thought to occur differently depending on the reading ability of the individual student. With less proficient readers development is thought to be enhanced more as a result of direct instruction in specific skills; deductive learning is emphasized. With more proficient readers, development is thought to be enhanced as students engage in functional reading experiences; inductive learning is emphasized.

differential acquisition: An explanation for how reading ability develops. Development occurs differently depending on the reading ability of the individual.

In short, a differential acquisition explanation views development as skill specific and teacher generated among less proficient readers, but skill general and student generated among more proficient readers.

The Development of Automaticity

In addition to these three types of explanations for how reading ability develops, there is another aspect of reading development often used in conjunction with each explanation—that reading comprehension develops as the reading process becomes automatic. It is usually called the development of automaticity (Samuels & Eisenberg, 1981).

Automaticity describes situations where a complex activity can be performed by an individual without requiring attention to any of the component parts of that activity. Consider the physical movements of a concert pianist during a performance. Playing any single note properly on a piano requires that the pianist perform a complex sequence of finger and foot movements. Playing an entire piece of music requires many complex sequences of movement. Proficient pianists have learned how to perform these movements automatically without attending to the location of their fingers. We say that concert pianists have developed automaticity with respect to their finger movements during a perfor-

automaticity: Situations where a complex activity is performed without attention to the component parts of that activity.

mance. Similar explanations can be given to almost any complicated physical activity such as throwing a football, catching a baseball, hitting a golf ball, or whistling a tune. Each of these actions can be performed automatically by a person who is proficient at the skill without attending to any of the components of the task.

When you first learned how to play a piano, throw a football, or perform a similar skill, however, you did have to attend to each of the component parts of the task. You learned where a finger should be placed to achieve a particular note, for example. Thus, when you begin to learn a complicated process, you often must attend to the indivdual aspects of that process. Gradually you learn how to automatically perform each aspect without thinking about it. That is, your development is best explained in terms of the development of automaticity.

Reading is also a complicated process like playing a piano or throwing a football. As such, it requires attention to the many small aspects of the process when one is first learning the skill. As one practices the many small aspects of the process, these components become increasingly automatic. As the processing at each of the knowledge sources (decoding knowledge, vocabulary knowledge, syntactic knowledge, and discourse knowledge) becomes automatic, one is able to completely attend to the developing meaning of the text. Occasionally, one must direct attention to one of the lower levels to correct an error made during reading, when the text information is inconsistent with expectations, or when encountering an unfamiliar word or idea that cannot be processed automatically. Most of a mature reader's attention, though, can focus on comprehension, not on the components of comprehension.

Considering the development of reading ability as the development of automaticity accounts for a number of phenomena. It explains, for example, the behavior of beginning readers struggling to determine the oral equivalents of unknown words by sounding out the individual letters. We see evidence that beginning readers consciously attend to the decoding level of the process. It also explains the difficulty young readers have with comprehension as well as the difficulty experienced by older readers who do not automatically process written text. In both cases, a student's attention is often directed at decoding levels at the expense of overall text meaning. Comprehension suffers at the expense of decoding. Automaticity, therefore, appears to be a powerful concept to include in your explanation of how reading develops.

A POINT TO PONDER	Mature readers seldom are aware of the sounds of words when they read. If you ask beginning readers what they do when they read, however, they are likely to say that they sound out the words. How can you explain this discrepancy?

HOW A COMPREHENSION FRAMEWORK
AFFECTS INSTRUCTIONAL DECISIONS

Understanding how one reads and how reading ability develops are extremely difficult for someone who has not previously considered these issues. A clear framework of reading comprehension is, by definition, an abstract and complex concept. It is, however, more practical than almost anything else you will learn about reading instruction because it facilitates many of the decisions you will make. A framework of the comprehension process will assist you with the instructional choices you must make as a teacher of reading.

As you become familiar with the content and methods of reading instruction in Section 2, you will quickly see how some instructional goals are consistent with one type of comprehension framework but inconsistent with others. It is possible now, however, to generally demonstrate how a framework of reading comprehension will help determine many instructional decisions.

A comprehension framework consists of answers to the two questions, How does one read? and How does reading ability develop? Answers to each question influence different aspects of instruction. Your answer to the first question, How does one read? influences what will be taught and emphasized in your instructional program (i.e., the knowl-

Developing a comprehension framework helps you make informed instructional decisions, anticipate problematic aspects of children's texts, understand why a reader has failed to comprehend a story, and know when to use particular instructional strategies.

edge sources that students will be expected to learn). Your answer to the second question, How does reading ability develop? influences how you will promote the development of those knowledge sources (i.e., the way in which you will structure learning opportunities for students).

Consider, for example, how each type of explanation for how one reads (text-based, reader-based, and interactive) influences what will be taught. The assumptions behind each of these explanations lead to different instructional recommendations about the knowledge sources that are most important to acquire and develop.

Recall that a text-based explanation assumes that:

1. Meaning exists more in the text than in the meaning a reader might bring to a text.
2. Reading consists of translating printed words into sounds and sounds into meanings.
3. Readers begin by using the lowest knowledge source (decoding) and then sequentially apply higher knowledge sources (vocabulary, syntactic, and then discourse knowledge).

A teacher with a text-based explanation for how one reads stresses the acquisition of decoding knowledge during instruction more than any other type of knowledge source. This teacher tends to believe that strong decoding skills lead to successful translation of text meaning. Instruction, especially for younger readers, emphasizes activities such as those described earlier as rhyming riddles and letter linking (see decoding knowledge, page 32). Learning how to sound out words is an important part of the instructional program. Far less time would be devoted to developing higher-level knowledge sources such as discourse knowledge, syntactic knowledge, and vocabulary knowledge, especially among younger readers.

A reader-based explanation, on the other hand, contains this different set of assumptions.

1. Meaning exists more in what a reader might bring to a text than in the text itself.
2. Reading consists of expectations for upcoming words, not the translation of words into sounds and sounds into meanings.
3. Readers begin by using knowledge sources more associated with meaning (discourse, syntactic, and vocabulary knowledge) and only then apply decoding knowledge.

A teacher with a reader-based explanation for how one reads stresses the acquisition of discourse, syntactic, and vocabulary knowledge during instruction more than decoding knowledge. This teacher tends to believe that adequate higher-level knowledge leads to accurate expectations for upcoming meaning. As a result, instruction emphasizes activities such as those described earlier as who, what, when, where, how and why (see discourse knowledge, page 37), paraphrase pairs (see syntactic knowledge, page 35), or making a pair tree (see vocabulary knowledge, page 33). Any activity designed to help students generate or practice expectations is especially valued, such as teaching story forms (see discourse knowledge, page 36), cause-and-effect patterns (see syntactic knowledge, page 35), and context clues (see vocabulary knowledge, page 34). Learning how to sound out words is not an important part of the instructional program. Far more time is devoted to developing higher-level knowledge sources.

The assumptions behind an interactive explanation for how one reads also influence what will be taught. Recall that the assumptions of this type of explanation include:

1. Meaning is located both in the text and in the meaning readers bring to the text.
2. Reading consists of both translation and expectation.
3. Reading proceeds as each knowledge source in one's mind interacts simultaneously with the print on the page and with other knowledge sources.

A teacher with an interactive explanation for how one reads devotes relatively equal attention to the acquistion of decoding-, vocabulary-, syntactic-, and discourse-level knowledge during instruction. This teacher tends to believe readers need to develop knowledge that will help them simultaneously engage in translation and expectation. All activities described earlier might be used by a teacher with an interactive explanation for how one reads. Learning how to sound out words would be just as important as learning how to form accurate expectations.

Now consider how different answers to the second part of your comprehension framework will also influence instructional decisions. Answers to the question How does reading ability develop? strongly influence the manner of instruction—that is, how you will structure learning opportunities for students. This again is a direct result of the assumptions behind each explanation.

A mastery of specific skills explanation for development assumes that:

1. Reading ability develops to the extent that students master specific reading skills.
2. Reading ability develops to the extent that these skills are taught by another person, usually a teacher, in an explicit and frequently deductive fashion.

A teacher with a mastery of specific skills explanation teaches hierarchically organized skills in a direct, explicit way. Students are then tested on these specific skills to determine whether they have been mastered. If students have mastered a particular skill, they would then receive instruction in the next skill of the hierarchy. If not, additional instruction in that skill would be provided. Deductive learning is emphasized.

A holistic language learning explanation for development assumes that:

1. Reading ability develops to the extent that students engage in meaningful, functional, and holistic experiences with print.
2. Reading ability develops to the extent that students learn about reading inductively.

A teacher with a holistic language learning explanation provides opportunites for students to see literacy skills in action, always in the context of actual use. Many opportunities are also provided for students to both read and write so they may induce the generalizations required for proficient reading. Isolated skills are not taught to mastery directly. Inductive learning is emphasized.

A differential acquisition explanation assumes that:

1. Among less proficient readers, development is enhanced more by direct instruction. Mastery assumptions are thought to apply more frequently.
2. Among more proficient readers, development is enhanced as students engage in functional reading experiences. Holistic assumptions are thought to apply more frequently.

A teacher with a differential acquisition explanation for development varies instruction according to the students' proficiency level. Less proficient readers receive more direct instruction following a set of hierarchically organized skills. More proficient readers receive more meaningful, functional, and holistic reading experiences.

Thus, you have seen how answers to the two different questions associated with a comprehension framework influence different aspects of your instructional program. Keep in mind that a comprehension framework consists of two different explanations to two different questions. Perhaps the best way to explain this is to consider three of the more common comprehension frameworks that teachers use, as illustrated in figure 2–7.

One common comprehension framework consists of a text-based explanation for how one reads and a mastery of specific skills explanation for how reading ability develops. A teacher with this type of comprehension framework likely devotes much time to developing decoding knowledge, especially with younger children. This type of person also teaches a set of hierarchically organized skills directly and explicitly,

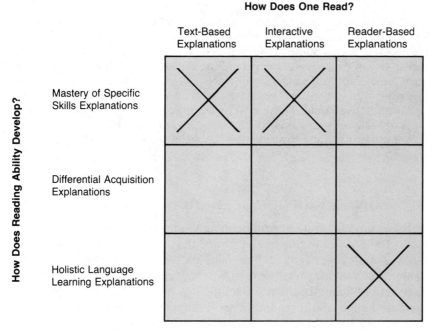

How Does One Read?

FIGURE 2–7

A matrix illustrating the various types of comprehension frameworks with the most common types of frameworks designated

being certain that students had mastered one skill before moving on to the next. Deductive learning is emphasized. A second comprehension framework that is frequently found consists of an interactive explanation for how one reads and a mastery of specific skills explanation for how reading develops. A teacher with this type of comprehension framework likely spends relatively equal amounts of time developing each of the knowledge sources and teaches a set of hierarchically organized skills directly and explicitly, being certain that students had mastered one skill before moving on to the next. Deductive learning is again emphasized. Finally, a third type of comprehension framework commonly found consists of a reader-based explanation for how one reads and a holistic language learning explanation for how reading ability develops. A teacher with this type of comprehension framework likely devotes more time to developing vocabulary, syntactic, and discourse levels of knowledge and very little time to developing decoding knowledge. Learning takes place as a result of functional reading experiences such as reading a self-selected story for pleasure. Inductive learning is emphasized.

Each of the chapters in section 2 will more precisely define the effect of different comprehension frameworks on instructional decisions. Be aware of the assistance a well-specified framework can provide.

<table>
<tr><td>

**A POINT
TO PONDER**

</td><td>

Some instructional programs teach discourse-level knowledge about the structural characteristics of a fable; that is, the characters in a fable are animals, these animals have human characteristics, a conflict is resolved to the advantage of one of the animals, a moral or lesson is explicitly stated at the end, and so on. How important would this knowledge be in the instructional program of a teacher with a text-based, reader-based, or interactive explanation for how one reads? How would this knowledge be developed in the instructional program of a teacher with a mastery of specific skills, holistic language learning, or differential acquisition explanation for how reading ability develops?

</td></tr>
</table>

DEVELOPING INDIVIDUAL FRAMEWORKS

It is now time for you to begin defining your own comprehension framework. To help you in this task, examine the statements about reading in tables 2–1 and 2–2. Table 2–1 contains statements about how one reads. Table 2–2 contains statements about how reading ability develops. In each set of fifteen questions, select the five that *best* represent your preliminary beliefs about reading. Choose only five statements in each list. *Do this now before you read any further.*

In table 2–1, there are five statements which are most consistent with each of the three explanations for how one reads: text-based, reader-based, and interactive. The text-based statements are numbers 1, 3, 5, 10, and 12. The reader-based statements are numbers 2, 4, 9, 11, and 15. The interactive statements are numbers 6, 7, 8, 13, and 14. If you selected a majority of text-based statements or a majority of reader-based statements, your preliminary framework shares one of these explanations for how comprehension takes place. If you selected a majority of interactive statements, if your statements were fairly evenly distributed between reader-based and text-based statements, or if your statements were fairly evenly distributed between all three categories of statements, your preliminary framework probably contains an interactive explanation for how reading comprehension takes place.

Similarly, in table 2–2 there are five statements which are most consistent with one of the three explanations for how reading ability develops: a mastery of specific skills explanation, a holistic language explanation, and a differential acquisition explanation. The mastery of specific skills statements are numbers 1, 5, 6, 11, and 12. The holistic language statements are numbers 2, 4, 8, 9, and 14. The differential acquisition statements are numbers 3, 7, 10, 13, and 15. If you selected a majority of either mastery of specific skills or holistic language statements, your preliminary framework shares one of these explanations for how reading develops. If you selected a majority of differential acquisition statements, if your statements were fairly evenly distributed between mastery of specific skills and holistic language statements, or if

TABLE 2–1

How does one read?

1. Before children can comprehend they usually must be able to recognize all of the words on a page.

2. Children's knowledge about the world plays a major role in their comprehension during reading.

3. Children who are weak at word recognition skills usually cannot overcome this weakness with strengths at other levels of the comprehension process.

4. Before young children read about something, it is often useful for them to share an experience similar to that depicted in the text.

5. There is usually only one acceptable answer to a question from a story.

6. Teachers should normally give equal emphasis to instruction aimed at developing each knowledge source.

7. If children are weak in one knowledge source important to the comprehension process it is still possible for them to read and comprehend.

8. The meaning of a text is usually a joint product of text and reader.

9. Teachers should normally expect and encourage children to have different interpretations to a story.

10. If a reader does not comprehend a text in the way an author intended, we can usually say that they have misunderstood the text.

11. Teachers should normally inquire what children know about the topic of each story before they begin reading.

12. When children retell a story they should usually attempt to use the author's words.

13. Expectations are often as important as accurate recognition of words during the reading process.

14. Readers use a variety of strategies as they read—from sounding out unfamiliar words to guessing familiar words in rich context.

15. The best readers are usually those who have learned to be accurate in their expectations for upcoming text.

your statements were fairly evenly distributed between all three categories of statements your preliminary framework probably contains a differential acquisition explanation for how proficiency at reading comprehension develops.

It is likely that your responses for each set of statements were not completely consistent. That is, few individuals ever select five statements reflecting a single explanation to either question. This brings us back to a point mentioned earlier. We have presented explanations to each of the questions associated with a comprehension framework as if they were distinct explanations. This was done for instructional pur-

TABLE 2–2
How does reading ability develop?

1. It is important for teachers to provide clear, precise presentations during reading instruction.

2. Children should receive many opportunities to read materials unrelated to specific school learning tasks.

3. In deciding how to teach reading, one should carefully consider the nature of the children.

4. Reading, writing, speaking, and listening are closely related learning tasks.

5. Children learn reading best when the task is broken down into specific skills to be taught by the teacher.

6. Children should be tested frequently to determine if they have learned what was taught. These tests should match very closely the nature of the instruction.

7. Some children learn best by reading widely and often; others learn best through direct instruction.

8. Children should be frequently read to while they are young so they acquire a "feel" for what reading is like.

9. Opportunities should be created in the classroom to provide children with a reason to read.

10. Less proficient readers often benefit from more direct and structured learning experiences.

11. Teachers should have a list of separate reading skills appropriate for their grade level and make certain that each student masters these skills, and only these skills.

12. Much of what children learn about reading can be attributed directly to what a teacher taught in the classroom.

13. It is important to individualize reading instruction as much as possible by taking into consideration the children's reading abilities.

14. Children learn a great deal about reading by watching their parents at home.

15. A teacher should generally spend greater time in the classroom with less proficient readers than with more proficient readers.

poses. We wanted you to understand the assumptions behind each explanation by considering each explanation separately. Understand from this exercise, however, that one seldom expresses a pure explanation for either of the questions associated with a comprehension framework. Instead, teachers' beliefs often fall somewhere between two different explanations on each of the continua illustrated earlier in figures 2–2 and 2–6.

Often, for example, teachers believe that one reads interactively but that slightly greater emphasis should be given to decoding knowledge compared to other knowledge sources. Thus, their explanation for how one reads would fall between an interactive and a text-based explanation on the continuum in figure 2–2. Similarly, teachers often believe that children learn to read holistically, but provide slightly more structured and deductive learning opportunities for their weakest readers. Thus, their explanation for development would fall between a holistic explanation and a differential acquisition explanation on the continuum in figure 2–6. Individuals seldom express pure explanations for each question associated with a comprehension framework. Consider where, exactly, you fall on each continuum.

You now have a beginning framework of the reading comprehension process. Expect to have a more refined framework at the end of this text, and a still more refined framework after your first year of teaching. If your framework did not change over time you are probably not sufficiently perceptive about children's behavior in the classroom. It is important to continually refine the nature of your framework as you observe the effects of your instructional decisions.

1. The reading comprehension process involves a number of important components: decoding knowledge; vocabulary knowledge; syntactic knowledge; discourse knowledge; readiness aspects; and affective aspects. Reading comprehension instruction seeks to promote the development of these components through carefully designed learning activities.
2. A comprehension framework consists of explanations to two different questions, How does one read? and How does reading ability develop?
3. There are three major types of explanations for how one reads: text-based explanations; reader-based explanations; and interactive explanations. Explanations for how one reads exist on a continuum ranging from text-based to reader-based explanations with interactive explanations existing somewhere near the middle.
4. There are three major explanations to how reading ability develops: explanations based on mastering specific skills, explanations based on holistic language learning, and explanations based on differential acquisition. Explanations for how reading ability develops exist on a continuum ranging from mastery of specific skills to holistic language learning explanations with differential acquisition explanations existing somewhere near the middle.
5. Instructional decisions are influenced by the nature of one's comprehension framework. Your explanation for how one reads will influence what you teach. Your explanation for how reading ability develops will influence how you teach.

THE MAJOR POINTS

QUESTIONS
AND
ACTIVITIES

1. Recall the six components of the comprehension process: decoding knowledge; vocabulary knowledge; syntactic knowledge; discourse knowledge; readiness aspects; and affective aspects. The following skills were taken from the list of skills taught in several instructional programs. Match each skill with the component in the reading comprehension process that it is most likely to promote.
   a. knows the sounds represented by the consonant digraphs *ch, sh, th,* and *wh*
   b. recognizes types of literature: autobiography, historical fiction, or informational articles
   c. relates word order to sentence meaning
   d. recognizes multiple meanings of words
   e. knows left-to-right and top-to-bottom progression of print
   f. enjoys reading

2. The three explanations for how reading comprehension takes place are not new ideas. Consider Edmund Burke Huey's description of the following methods for teaching reading and determine which explanation of the comprehension process is behind each method.

   "It is a spelling method, but the word is spelled by its elementary sounds and not by the letter names. The word is slowly pronounced until its constituent sounds come into consciousness. . . . Drill in this sound analysis trains the articulation, trains the ear and the ability to sound the letters of any new word, and gives the power to pronounce it by blending the sounds suggested. . . ." (Huey, 1908, p. 266).

   "In using the sentence method, the teacher has come to make much use of the blackboard. A sketch of some object or scene interesting to the child suggests to the child a thought which he expresses in a sentence. The teacher writes this sentence and it is read, naturally with expression since the child's own thought here leads the expression. . . . The important thing is to begin with meaning wholes and sentence wholes, make thought lead, and thus secure natural expression, letting analysis follow in its own time" (Huey, 1908, pp. 273–74).

3. In looking at writing instruction, Janet Emig (Emig, 1982) concludes that both "magical thinking" and "non-magical thinking" exist. She defines magical thinking as the belief that children learn how to write only from instruction. She defines non-magical thinking as the recognition that writing proficiency develops from exposure to print and opportunities to write. Emig argues strongly that non-magical thinking is required in school writing programs. Speculate about Emig's likely explanation for how reading proficiency develops. Why do you think her framework of reading would include this explanation?

4. You have defined a beginning framework of reading comprehension as a result of reading and thinking about the information in this

chapter. Will it change in the future? Why? How can you ensure that the changes you make in your framework are reasoned and not random changes? What type of evidence will you require before you consider revising your framework?

FURTHER READING

Blachowicz, C. L. Z. (1984). Showing teachers how to develop students' predictive reading. *The Reading Teacher, 36,* 680–84.

Describes a method framework that can be used to help readers generate and test their expectations for upcoming meaning. The approach is very consistent with reader-based or interactive explanations of how reading takes place.

Brazee, P. E. & Kristo, J. V. (1986). Creating a whole language classroom with future teachers. *The Reading Teacher, 39,* 422–28.

Describes a set of experiences for new teachers showing how a classroom would function if organized around holistic language learning assumptions.

Gemake, J. (1984). Interactive reading: How to make children active readers. *The Reading Teacher, 37,* 462–66.

Describes a method framework that encourages children to interact with the print on the page as they read. Outlines the procedural steps involved in this method and defines different activities for each step. The instructional approach is consistent with interactive explanations of how reading takes place.

Samuels, S. J. & Schachter, S. W. (1984). Controversial issues in beginning reading: Meaning versus subskill emphasis. In A. J. Harris & E. R. Sipay (eds.) *Readings on reading instruction* (3rd Edition). New York: Longman.

Specifies the two extreme explanations for how reading develops: holistic and subskills perspectives. Also discusses instruction consistent with each competing explanation.

Shannon, P. (1984). Mastery learning in reading and the control of teachers and students. *Language Arts, 61,* 484–93.

A critique of mastery learning of specific skills in reading instruction. The author points out a number of difficulties that resulted when mastery learning was implemented in two large school districts.

Smith, F. (1979). Conflicting approaches to reading research and instruction. In L. B. Resnick & P. A. Weaver (eds.). *Theory and practice of early reading* (vol. 2). Hillsdale, NJ: Erlbaum.

Outlines the three competing explanations for how reading takes place and describes the instructional practices consistent with each explanation.

REFERENCES

Anderson, P. S. & Lapp, D. (1979). *Language skills in elementary education* (3rd Edition). New York: Macmillan.

Anderson, R. C.; Hiebert, E. H.; Scott, J. A.; & Wilkinson, I. A. G. (1985). *Becoming a nation of readers: The report of the commission on reading.* Washington, DC: National Institute of Education.

Aulls, M. W. (1982). *Developing readers in today's elementary school.* New York: Allyn & Bacon.

Block, J. & Burns, R. (1977). Mastery learning. In L. S. Schulman (ed.) *Review of research in education* (Vol. 4). Itaska, IL: Peacock.

Bloom, B. (1976). *Human characteristics and school learning.* New York: McGraw-Hill.

Chall, J.S. (1983). *Stages of reading development.* New York: McGraw-Hill.

Clay, M. M. (1980a) *The early detection of reading difficulties: A diagnostic survey* (2nd Edition). New York: Heinemann.

Clay, M. M. (1980b). *Reading: The patterning of complex behavior* (2nd Edition). London: Heinemann.

Emig, J. (1981). Non-magical thinking: presenting writing developmentally in schools. In C. H. Frederiksen and J. F. Dominic (eds.) *Writing: Volume 2.* Hillsdale, NJ: Erlbaum.

Flesch, R. (1955). *Why Johnny can't read.* New York: Harper & Row.

Goodman, K. S. (1976). Reading: A psycholinguistic guessing game. In H. Singer & R. Ruddell (eds.), *Theoretical models and processes of reading* (2nd Edition). Newark, DE: International Reading Association.

Goodman, K. S. & Goodman, Y. M. (1979). Learning to read is natural. In L. B. Resnick and P. A. Weaver (eds.) *Theory and practice of early reading* (Vol. 1). Hillsdale, NJ: Erlbaum.

Gough, P. B. (1986). One second of reading. In H. Singer & R. Ruddell (eds.), *Theoretical models and processes of reading* (3rd Edition). Newark, DE: International Reading Association.

Haber, L. R.; Haber, R. N.; & Furlin, K. R. (1983). Word length and word shape as sources of information in reading. *Reading Research Quarterly, 18* (2), 165–89.

Harris, A. J. & Sipay, E. R. *How to increase reading ability* (8th Edition). New York: Longman, 1985.

Holdaway, D. (1979). *The foundations of literacy.* Exeter, NH: Heinemann.

Huey, E. B. (1968). *The psychology and pedagogy of reading.* Cambridge, MA: MIT Press. (Original Edition: The Macmillan Company, 1908.)

Ollila, L. O. (1976). Reading: preparing the child. In P. M. Lamb & R. O. Arnold (eds.) *Reading: Foundations and instructional strategies.* Belmont, CA: Wadsworth.

Rumelhart, D. (1976). *Toward an interactive model of reading.* Center for Human Information Processing, University of California, San Diego. LaJolla, CA. Report Number 56.

Samuels, S. J. & Eisenberg, P. (1981). A framework for understanding the reading process. In F. J. Pirozzolo, M. C. Wittrock (eds.) *Neuropsychological and cognitive processes in reading.* New York: Academic Press.

Scott Foresman. (1985). *Kick up your heels* (Teacher's Edition).

Shuy, R. W. (1979). The mismatch of child language and school language: Implications for beginning reading instruction. In L. B. Resnick and P. A. Weaver (eds.) *Theory and practice of early reading* (Vol. 1). Hillsdale, NJ: Erlbaum.

Slobin, D. (1979). *Psycholinguistics.* (2nd Edition). Glenview, IL: Scott Foresman.

Smith, F. (1979). *Understanding reading: A psycholinguistic analysis of reading and learning to read* (2nd Edition). New York: Holt, Rinehart & Winston.

Smith, H. & DeChant, E. V. (1961). *Psychology in Teaching Reading,* Englewood Cliffs, NJ: Prentice-Hall.

Stanovich, K. E. (1980). Toward an interactive-compensatory model of individual differences in the development of reading fluency. *Reading Research Quarterly, 16,* 32–71.

Strickland, R. (1969). *The language arts in the elementary school* (3rd Edition). Lexington, MA: D. C. Heath & Co..

Taylor, D. (1984). *Family Literacy.* Exeter, NH: Heinemann.

Weaver, P. & Shonhoff, F. (1984). Subskill and holistic approaches to reading instruction. In A. J. Harris and E. R. Sipay (eds.) *Readings on Reading Instruction* (3rd Edition). New York: Longman.

SECTION TWO
DEVELOPING A
KNOWLEDGE BASE

3 Readiness and Comprehension

THE CONCEPT OF READING READINESS ■ FACTORS AND STAGES IN
READING READINESS ■ EVALUATING THE PREREADER ■ READINESS
AND PROFICIENT READERS ■ DIFFERENT FRAMEWORKS AND
READINESS INSTRUCTION

"When will I read?" Jim asked.

"Soon," the teacher said.

"But when?" said Jim.

"You know what the signs in our room say," the teacher said.

"Yes," said Jim. . . .

"You can read your name," the teacher said.

"But that's not really reading," said Jim. . . .

"Don't worry," the teacher said. "There's no hurry. You will read when you are ready."

"But when will I be ready?" Jim asked.

"You are getting ready all the time," she said.

M. Cohen, *When Will I Read?* (New York: Wm. Morrow & Co., Inc., 1977).

After you complete this chapter, you will be asked to develop several lessons designed to promote reading readiness skills. As you work through the chapter, you will receive clear indications of the factors affecting readiness and the reading process. Try to keep your framework of reading in mind as you read.

After reading this chapter, you will be able to

1. discuss reading readiness and how it differs from prereading activities;
2. specify the skills and knowledge required before reading can take place;
3. point out the skills and knowledge that children have when they enter school and how a reading teacher might capitalize on these already acquired abilities.

THE CONCEPT OF READING READINESS

reading readiness: The time when a prereader has the skills and knowledge for reading instruction. For readers, having the knowledge required to comprehend a specific selection.

What does the term **reading readiness** mean to you? To reading teachers, it usually identifies the period of time in which students acquire the specific skills and abilities that allow reading to take place. The *Dictionary of Reading and Related Terms* (Harris & Hodges, 1981) defines readiness as "preparedness to cope with a learning task," and goes on to state that

> readiness for learning of any type at any level is determined by a complex pattern of intellectual, motivational, maturational, and experiential factors in the individual which may vary from time to time and from situation to situation (p. 263).

fluent reading: Reading unhindered by word identification or comprehension problems.
prereading activities: Activities that aid comprehension and take place before a selection is read.
prereading stage: The time before a child has learned to read.

A related term to reading readiness is *prereading,* sometimes used to describe activities designed to help teach skills which result in **fluent reading.** Yet **prereading activities** also describe activities which set the stage for reading a particular selection or story after the student has learned to read. For clarity, **prereading stage** will be used to describe the point in time before a child is able to read, and *prereading activities* will describe activities that take place before a selection is to be read.

BEFORE READING ON

Read each of the following and specify which appear to be easy to read, which are difficult, and why. What do you know, as a good reader, which helps make the passages readable? What would have to be taught so children could begin to master the skills necessary for fluent reading? *Hint:* For example 1, the code is:

a	=	*	f	=	-	m	=	>	s	=	$
b	=	/	g	=	™	n	=	]	t	=	!
c	=	†	h	=	@	o	=	%	u	=	¶
d	=	[	i	=	<	p	=	&	w	=	®
e	=	#	l	=	§	r	=	©	.	=	:

1. !@#$# $@%©! &*$$*™#$ ®<§§ <§§¶$!©*!# $%># %- !@# &©%/§#>$ †@<§[©#] -*†# ®@#] §#*©]<]™ !% ©#*[:

2. ?seldoop ekil uoy oD .reh rof ynapmoc doog si eldoop ehT .ti ot desu eb tsum ehS .eciton t'nseod ehs syas robhgien ym tub ,tol a skrab tI .eldoop a sah robhgien yM

3. dogsareinterestinganimalseventhoughtheycanbenuisancesattimestheyare usuallyfriendlyandarenicetohavearound doyouhaveadog

4. Somepeopledon'tlikedogs. Myfriend,forexample,isa "catperson." Hesaysthat dogsaredumbandthatcatsaremuchmoresophisticated. Whatdoyouthink?

Most people who try to read the first example agree that reading difficulty is caused by not knowing symbol-sound relationships. Using the key provided for example 1, it is certainly possible to puzzle out the meaning, and doing so provides some idea of what beginning readers face. Teaching symbol-sound relationships is teaching a **decoding** process. But in terms of readiness, there is a more basic step of understanding that there is a relationship between a symbol and a sound; that there is a relationship between oral and written language. You may have forgotten that this is something you had to learn.

decoding: The process of determining the pronunciation of a written word.

Example 2 violates a **convention** that proficient readers take for granted but that beginning readers must learn: the left-to-right, down, and left-to-right way that readers of English expect material to be written. Did you notice that there were no "nonsense" symbols in example 2, but that the text was written backwards? Try reading it again from the bottom right-hand corner. Notice that it is entirely possible to read this way—we simply don't do so in English. The left-to-right sequence is something that must be taught in the readiness program.

convention: The common way language is used by a particular group of people.

Example 3 may have caused some difficulty because of the lack of spaces between words. In fact, this written representation can be compared to speech, where there is no white space around individual words to signal where one word begins and another ends. Individuals asked to read this set of sentences often say that they are confused when they get to *animalseven,* reading the words initially as *animal seven* rather than as the intended *animals even.* Thus, the white space around words provides important clues to pronunciation and meaning. As good readers, we are aware of what the white space on a page can tell us, but the concept of *word* is something that beginning readers must learn.

In example 4 the upper-case letters and punctuation allowed you to use your knowledge about writing conventions to divide the passage into sentences. Don't forget, however, that many beginning readers have not yet learned upper- and lower-case letters; nor might they realize that punctuation can signal meaning, making text easier to read.

As you proceed through this chapter, remember how difficult it was for you to read the preceding examples. Although all the skills that readers must use were not demonstrated, consider the underlying knowledge that is necessary for reading to occur—that is, awareness that symbols stand for sounds; left-to-right progression and the concept of *word, sentence,* etc.; and discrimination between upper- and lower-case letters and words. These skills are incorporated into the following seven general goals of reading readiness programs (Durkin, 1980, pp. 96–97).

1. to motivate children to want to learn to read
2. to help children acquire some understanding of what reading and learning to read are all about
3. to teach the left-to-right, top-to-bottom orientation of written English
4. to teach the meaning of *word* and the function of space in establishing word boundaries
5. to teach children the meaning of terms that figure in reading instruction
6. to teach children to discriminate visually among both letters and words
7. to teach children the names of letters

A POINT TO PONDER

For a 15- to 20-year period beginning in the early 1920s, reading readiness was defined as maturity in terms of *mental* age, largely because of the work of Morphett & Washburn (1931). Mental age is determined by the formula

$$\text{Mental Age} = \frac{\text{Intelligence Quotient (IQ)} \times \text{Chronological Age}}{100}$$

It was thought that if a child did not have a mental age of 6.0 to 6.5, the child was not ready and instruction would be wasted. Gradually, readiness for reading was viewed as something that could be developed rather than something to be waited for. Now, readiness programs take into account students' individual differences and assume that readiness is something that can be taught (see Harris & Sipay, 1985).

FACTORS AND STAGES IN READING READINESS

There are many skills which a child must learn upon entering school. Yet much has already been learned before the child enters kindergarten or first grade.

BEFORE READING ON

Make a list of what you think a child entering first grade might already know that would help in learning to read. Try to state how the things you have identified relate to reading ability.

Before children enter school, they have already acquired spoken language. Children who enter kindergarten or first grade are good users of their native language and are able to understand almost all basic types of English sentences, including questions, statements, and exclamations. Children also have the perceptual abilities to discriminate between different objects. As good users of oral language, school-age children have highly-developed speaking vocabularies. Researchers differ in their estimations of the size of children's vocabularies in first grade. Early studies indicated that a first grader's vocabulary averaged about 2,500 words, while more recent studies have estimated as many as 8,000 words (Dale, 1965; Smith, 1972). Regardless of the specific number of words that first graders bring to school, their vocabularies are completely adequate for normal communication. The teacher can use all these language-related abilities to develop students' reading potentials.

Oral Language Factors

The language base of beginning readers is critically important to learning to read. A solid language foundation allows children to generalize from what they already do well. Children who do not have well-developed aural and oral language skills have more difficult times learning to read.

Children's acquisition of language progresses through three basic stages: babbling, **holophrastic speech,** and **telegraphic speech.** In the initial babbling stage, the infant generates random sounds. Although it is generally thought that the infant is not attempting to actively communicate the infant appears to be experimenting with the vocal system. The infant generates sounds which include, but go beyond, the sounds that will eventually become the native language. At this stage, it is thought that children can learn any language equally well. Only later, when children learn which sounds make up the language of the communicating group to which they belong, are unnecessary sounds dropped. Later, perhaps because of lack of need and practice, adult speakers have great difficulty in pronouncing and even hearing sounds which are not used in their native language.

Following the babbling stage, the infant appears to apply words to events, apparently labeling complete thoughts using single words logically and consistently. A single word such as *milk* or *doll* might be used to communicate thoughts like "I want more milk" or "Give me the doll."

holophrastic speech: A stage of early language acquisition when a child uses a single word to express meaning.

telegraphic speech: A stage of oral language development when all but essential words are omitted.

This stage, beginning in the mid- to late-first year of the infant's life, is called the holophrastic speech stage.

Early in this stage, parents might hear the child say *papa* or *mama,* even though the infant might not always recognize the adult as being the father or mother. We know that children, at a certain stage of cognitive development, overgeneralize and might call all adult males or females *papa* or *mama.* Furthermore, when we analyze the order in which children appear to consciously use the sounds of English, it appears that early sound combinations are the ones which are farthest apart relative to the **vocal tract.**

vocal tract: Speech organs used to make oral sounds.

BEFORE READING ON

Try to say the following sounds while consciously noting what is happening in your vocal tract.

/b/ as in *boy*	/ɔ/ as in *call*
/p/ as in *pen*	/l/ as in *late*
/m/ as in *mat*	/k/ as in *kite*
/g/ as in *got*	/s/ as in *send*

Did you notice that your vocal tract can be relatively wide open (as in the *call* example) or relatively closed (as in the *kite* example)? Were you aware that some sounds originated from the front of your mouth (note the part your lips played in the /p/ sound in *pen*), while other sounds seemed to originate from the rear of your vocal tract (note the /g/ in the *got* example)?

Since the /m/ *(mama)* and /p/ *(papa)* are sounds which are formed using the front of the vocal tract with the mouth closed, while the /ɔ/ sound is formed at the back with the tract open, it appears easy to rock back and forth between the two sounds of mama. The infant does not need fine motor adjustments to create the sounds and it is easy for the child to alternate between the opposite sounds.

Soon after the holophrastic stage, the child begins to string two or three words together in telegraphic speech. Examples of such utterances are *milk here, allgone milk,* or *baby milk.* The child's speech is not in the form of complete sentences, yet it appears that thoughts are grouped in sentence form. One problem with interpreting what the child means by *milk here* is, of course, that we really have no way of knowing whether the child means "Bring the milk here," "The milk has spilled over here," or "Here is the milk." In many instances, it may be that what we think the child means is not, in fact, the intended meaning. This applies equally well to the kindergarten or first-grade student as to the infant. Teachers must be careful not to impose their adult meanings on what young children say.

Ultimately the infant becomes a good and fluent user of oral language. The need for communication appears to be a key motivational force in language acquisition. Not only is language learned, but it is learned through meaningful communicative acts. Children must be participants rather than just observers in the language process.

It may not be children's speaking ability that fosters later reading acquisition, but the knowledge that language is communication—that one must seek to make meaning out of what is heard. In other words, the ability to understand spoken language may be closer to reading than is language production. **A POINT TO PONDER**

It is very important that parents and teachers provide many opportunities for oral expression. Storytelling by children is a beneficial activity, as is the recapping or retelling of what happened in a story which has been told to the child. In fact, at the readiness level, structured oral language activities should form an ongoing part of the instructional program. These teach good listening and speaking behavior, and can include activities ranging from dictating a story to the teacher, through explaining or describing an event, to planning a class play.

SAMPLE ACTIVITIES

- Show a picture or sequence of two or three pictures and have students tell a story relating to what was shown. Other students can build on the original story.

- Have students pretend they are certain animals or objects in a given situation and talk about their feelings.

- Have students think of a specific, sequential activity (such as getting ready for school in the morning, going home from school, or getting from the classroom to the library). Students are to tell a partner or group specific directions on how to perform the activity. If the activity is not first stated, then other students can try to guess the activity from the set of directions.

- Tell a story to students. Then tell it again, varying tone of voice and general expression. Discuss how the different readings made the story seem different (scarier, happier, and so on). Have students try to vary expression on sentences they repeat after you. Other students guess mood based on each student's expression.

- Students sit in a circle. The teacher begins a story with one sentence. Each student adds a sentence to the story until it gets back to the teacher. This can be tape recorded and the teacher can transcribe the whole story with students watching. Students can later illustrate their story and it may be posted on the classroom bulletin board.

■ Ask students to bring something special to them from home. They are to show the item and talk about it (show and tell).

Pay careful attention to each child's oral language and expression. Provide opportunities to build conversational skills such as turn-taking, listening, and **intonation.**

intonation: The voice's rise, fall, stress, and pauses in speaking.

The Language Experience Approach in Readiness Instruction. It is easy to overlook young children's experiences and language in beginning reading instruction. Many individuals, however, have attempted to demonstrate the power of both factors in helping young children learn to read (Allen & Allen, 1976; Ashton-Warner, 1963, 1972; Nessel & Jones, 1981; Stauffer, 1980). The generic term **language experience approach** has come to represent efforts to teach reading using children's language and experiences as a base.

language experience approach: A method framework for teaching reading based on children's language and experiences.

At beginning levels, the language experience approach uses transcriptions of children's oral language for learning about reading. The most typical language experience activity at this level is an experience story, beginning with a memorable experience. A rabbit might be brought to the class for petting; the class might go on a field trip to an apple orchard; the class might have just seen an interesting slide show

Here, a teacher provides an experience through show-and-tell. It will later form the basis for a language experience activity.

or traveling music ensemble, or heard an interesting presentation by a parent. Then the teacher elicits a description (story) of the experience from the children. The teacher transcribes each student's contribution just as it was spoken. This can be done on chart paper (if a group activity) or on lined paper while the student watches (if done individually).

When the story is completed, the teacher uses it to teach a variety of reading-related concepts. In the readiness program, the teacher might simply read the story back, moving a hand under the words as they are read. The teacher could comment about one of the more frequently occurring words, or point out the left-to-right progression of words. At a slightly more advanced level, a repeatedly occurring letter-sound pattern might be pointed out, possibly with comments about the phonic generalization that it illustrates. At any level, the teacher might read a portion of the story and then stop before a word that is highly predictable from the context and ask for someone to "read" the word.

Saving the stories over a period of time allows students and teacher to go back, "read," and enjoy together stories based on memorable past experiences. Further, experience stories can be generated by several small groups and individuals. If the original stories are transcribed on the chalkboard or chart paper, a teacher could copy them to lined paper, ask one child to illustrate each story, bind them with colored, appropriately illustrated posterboard covers, and put them in the reading corner for children and parents to enjoy. Covers can be attached by using a punch to make holes in the posterboard and story papers, and then binding with colored yarn.

A Language Experience Story. The first-grade students have just returned from a September field trip to an apple farm. The teacher wishes to use this experience and the children's language to show children how to use contextual information during reading and to give everyone a positive experience with reading.

MODEL LESSON

Teacher:	Boys and girls, let's write a story about our field trip today. We can use it to practice our reading and to put in the hall to tell the rest of the school where we went and what we did. What do you think we should call our story? What should be the title?
Jaime:	I know. Let's call it *Apples, Apples, Everywhere!*
Teacher:	(Writing) Good Jaime. I like that. Look at these capital letters. Titles always have capitals at the beginning of each word. Now how shall we start our story?
Maggie:	I want to start. How about We had a special day. We had an apple day.
Teacher:	(Writing) Good. Now what shall we say?
Tom:	We went to Beak and Skiff Apple Farm. (Teacher writes.)
Pam:	And we got to ride on the tractor. (Teacher writes.)

Katie: And we got to pick apples. (Teacher writes.)
Jason: And we got to eat apples. (Teacher writes.)
Sarah: And Tom got his shoes wet. (Teacher writes.)
Kerrie: We saw the bees. (Teacher writes.)
Del: When we got back we were tired and we still had to do our
           math. (Teacher writes.)

The teacher then explains to the students how sometimes they can use other words to help them when they read. Next, the teacher reads the first two sentences, stopping at the last word (We had a special day. We had an apple _____. The teacher lets the class read the last word together.

Teacher: See, sometimes you just know what a word in a sentence has to be from what came before.

Then the teacher gives children a chance to practice using context. In the readiness program, the teacher in this example would read all of the sentences except the last word and would then wait for the students to complete the sentence. Sometimes students might say the sentence along with the teacher, or might be able to "read" a sentence on their own, especially if they were the individuals that contributed the sentence to the story. The teacher then restates the generalization regarding context use.

After reading the story, the teacher has each student draw a picture of their trip. Walking around the room, the teacher helps some students copy words and possibly short sentences from the experience story to write a sentence as a caption or description for their picture. With others, the teacher transcribes a dictated sentence or word on the bottom of their picture. Afterward, the teacher places the experience story on the hall bulletin board surrounded by the students' pictures.

An experience story is not the only language experience activity that might be used at beginning levels. Other examples of language experience activities are listed here.

SAMPLE ACTIVITIES

■ Make name labels for each student in the class. Be certain to place these on students' desks before the first day of school.

■ Have students suggest names for items in the classroom and watch as you make labels for important objects.

■ Take a fall (winter, spring) walk and listen for sounds (look for colors, touch different textures, identify different smells). Write an experience story when you return.

- Take the students on a walk around the playground or around the block. Talk about what is around them. Later, make up word cards about some of the things seen. Use the word cards as "triggers" for oral language. Students can randomly pick a card, think of the walk, and talk about the specific thing on the card. The teacher will need to read the card for some students.

- When children come to school in the fall (or after winter vacation) have children draw a picture of an exciting summer (winter) experience. Circulate and ask students to dictate a sentence or two about their pictures. Write this down, ask students to read their sentences, and then bind the "stories" in a book for the reading center.

- Keep a regular class diary, making entries each day. Include, where you can, photos of class activities. Keep in the reading center for children to read and recall memorable class events.

- Construct "helper charts" with movable name tags. Alternate regularly.

- Write class-dictated letters to authors of books that you have read to your students.

The Language Experience Approach beyond the Readiness Level. With older students, experience and language may also be mobilized to develop reading comprehension through language experience activities. Two differences exist, however, when compared to typical language experience activities for young children. First, at higher levels the children should, if possible, do the writing themselves. Second, language experience activities at higher levels involve literacy experiences where students are asked to both write and then read their own work as well as the work of others. Any functional writing tasks can be used as language experience tasks with older students. Maintaining a diary; writing letters to pen pals in other states or countries; interviewing older members of the community and then reporting to the class on local history and traditions; writing get-well cards to any member of the class who is sick for more than two consecutive days; writing a regular class newspaper; writing candidates' ads for class elections; and a host of other functional literacy activities are all possible. Each requires writers to read and re-read their own writing. Each may also be used in conference situations where readers share their "work-in-progress" with other students to elicit comments, reactions, and suggestions from friendly but knowledgeable readers (Calkins, 1983; Graves, 1983).

The resulting dialogue between writers and readers can lead to significant insights for each about both reading and writing. The important aspect of these tasks is that they serve personally meaningful functions for students. They are not contrived and accomplished solely to develop a particular skill associated with reading comprehension. Rather, rich understandings about the nature of written language, the communicative needs of a reader, and the responsibilities of a writer are woven into comprehensive and real language experiences.

Cognitive Factors

cognition: Knowing.

All human beings have the capability to progress through four levels of **cognition:** sensorimotor; preoperational; concrete operations; and formal operations (Piaget, 1963; Inhelder & Piaget, 1964). Table 3–1 illustrates age ranges and certain behaviors associated with the four cognitive levels. Remember, though, that the ages are only approximate.

Cognitive science provides insight into the relationship between stages of cognitive development and behaviors or abilities necessary for mature reading. As a reading teacher, you must realize that this does not mean that educators can simply wait until students are ready to acquire a skill. Too often, the criterion for reading readiness has been mastery of specific tasks, with poor performance being excused as a lack of readiness. Good instructional practice can do much to facilitate reading readiness.

The benefit of cognitive science to reading lies in attempts to specify language tasks and their possible relationship to students' cognitive levels. Table 3–1 illustrates some of the reading-related behaviors and abilities at the various cognitive levels, and clarifies the statement that demands of specific reading tasks can be related to **cognitive development.**

cognitive development: One's growth in mental abilities and thought processes.

Several cognitive operations are related to reading (Almy, Chittenden & Miller, 1966; Bybee & Sund, 1982; Waller, 1977). These include:

seriation: The ability to order a set of objects logically.
temporal relations: Either the passage of time or a particular interval of time.
conservation: The thinking ability required to keep an unchanging property of something in mind when perceptual conditions are changed.

- **seriation**
- ordering
- **temporal relations**
- **conservation**
- one-to-one correspondence
- spatial relations
- classification
- number

Seriation and ordering, for example, play a part in realizing that letters and words go together in sequence and in learning left-to-right progression. One-to-one correspondence is a factor in learning letter-sound relationships, and classification relates to such tasks as learning upper- and lower-case letters. To demonstrate the importance of these operations for text comprehension, consider the following sentences.

The boy was hungry. He stole some food. He hid under a table that had a large pot of flowers on it.

TABLE 3–1

Cognitive levels and associated behaviors/abilities

Cognitive Level	Age (Years)	General Behaviors or Abilities
Sensorimotor	0–2	No concept of space, time, cause and effect, or self. No object permanence. Actions are reflexive.
Preoperational	3–7	Aware of past, present and future; has fairly broad concept of space; awareness of self is egocentric. Conceptualizes some cause-and-effect relationships. Egocentric language.
Concrete Operational	8–11	Conceptualizes and relates temporal order and duration. Conserves quantity, number, seriation. Recognizes multiple class membership. Exhibits logical, reversible thought related to concrete situations. Understands cause and effect in concrete problems. Egocentrism reduced; language reflects this reduction.
Formal Operations	12+	Comprehends relative space and time. Exhibits combinatorial logic. Controls and separates variables in complex problems. Can deal with abstractions and "ideal" situations. Understands others' viewpoints. Uses abstract language and concepts.

Attempting to answer the following questions also requires the cognitive operations noted by Bybee & Sund (1982).

- What happened first: the boy being hungry or stealing the food? (seriation, ordering, and temporal relations)
- What do you think the boy will do next? (ordering)
- Where was the food at the end of the story? (Choose one or more: under a table, on a table, under a large pot of flowers) (spatial relations)

Questions such as those on the "boy was hungry" passage are often asked by teachers and can be found in any reading workbook or teacher's guide. Yet, too often little attention is given to the cognitive demands of the questions being asked. Although questions that extend and appropriately challenge students are necessary for learning, questions that are too difficult can frustrate and result in the student giving up prematurely. For example, in their questions to students, teachers must be careful not to use concepts that are beyond the level of beginning readers. Some terms that adults take for granted may not be fully grasped by the young child. One aspect of readiness programs attempts to provide activities that can be used to build concepts such as *before, in front of,* or *under.*

Take opportunities to demonstrate such concepts in everyday teaching routines. Provide ample chances for students to "stand beside Jack but in front of Sue." Let students manipulate objects, placing them *on, under* and *around* other objects. Have students perform a sequence of activities and then allow others to describe the order of events.

Similarly, following directions can be a cognitively difficult task. Teachers at times ask students to do many things at once, forgetting that their pupils may have difficulty grasping multiple directions such as, "Put your pencil down and then get the coloring book before you get your crayons." Try to provide specific activities targeted toward building listening skills and following directions. A simple game such as "Simon Says" is one such activity, as is a classroom "treasure hunt," which depends on the precise following of instructions. Other activities related to concepts such as *over, under,* and *on,* left-to-right progression, and following directions are noted here.

SAMPLE ACTIVITIES

- Ask students to point to the place on the page where you should start and stop writing. Ask them to do this as they watch you write; for example, as they dictate a simple story or sentence to you. Draw their conscious attention to where you start and stop a line.

- Cut simple cartoon strips into individual frames. Have the children arrange the frames from left to right so that the story is told. After the frames are arranged, have the students tell the story in their own words, frame-by-frame, pointing to each frame as appropriate.

- Have children draw lines from left to right between two pictures that, when joined, make sense. For example, down the left side of a page there might be pictures of a squirrel, a car and a boat; on the right are a nut, a garage, and a lakeshore (water). Say to the children, "Help the squirrel (car, boat) get to the nut (garage, water) by drawing a line (from left to right) between the two."

- Have students repeat a string of directions.

- Supply students with pictures and ask them to listen for specific, sequential instructions (for example, "color the duck," "put an *X* below the house, then circle the dog").

- Provide motor activities such as drawing pictures to certain specifications ("Draw a man in one corner, two dogs in the middle, and a car between the man and the dogs"). Then help the students label their pictures.

- Have students give directions to the teacher or another student to perform a simple task.

- Use a simple board game and explain the directions. Have students repeat the directions to check for understanding. After playing the game, change the directions and discuss how this changes the game.

- Teach the concept of the importance of directions by bringing a simple recipe to class (popcorn or Jell-O, for example). Make the recipe item while reading and following the directions step-by-step. Discuss how the directions help complete the task.

The Home Environment

Before students come to school they have had vast learning experiences. In fact, what children have accomplished before entering school far exceeds what even a successful learner will grasp through normal school experiences. Before coming to school, children have already learned how to communicate, having **internalized** their set of language rules in addition to a sophisticated awareness of behaviors necessary for effective communication (for example, turntaking, intonation, gestures, and facial expressions).

internalize: To make external ideas or rules part of one's existing knowledge.

During the formative years at home, children develop speech patterns and usage conventions based on exposure to the language around them. Although all human beings, regardless of language and dialect, can communicate effectively within their own communicative group, several home environment factors have been identified as being highly **correlated** to reading achievement. Through interviews with parents of early readers, Durkin (1966, 1972, 1978) has discovered that

correlated: To show a relationship to something else.

1. parents of early readers spend much time in conversation with their children.
2. children who are early readers ask many questions, and parents of early readers take time to answer their children's questions.
3. a common question asked by early readers is "What's that word?"

The importance of home environment and parental involvement has also been noted by the Commission on Reading (Anderson, Hiebert, Scott & Wilkinson, 1985), which has stated that

parents play a role of inestimable importance in laying the foundations for learning to read. Parents should informally teach preschool children about reading and writing by reading aloud to them, discussing stories and events, encouraging them to learn letters and words and teaching them about the world around them. These practices help prepare children for success in reading (p. 57).

Parents who demonstrate a love of reading and who provide experiences with print from an early age foster a desire to read, and aid later reading success.

Other factors related to children's later reading success are:

- a stress on the value of literacy by adults in the home;
- the amount of reading done by adults in the home (modeling);
- the amount of reading material available in the home;
- the amount of language-based games and activities in the home;
- the availability of personal reading materials for the child.

Children who come from home environments where reading is perceived as a valued activity by adults who read on an on-going basis appear to become active readers. The number of reading materials available in the home (books, magazines, posters, comics, or newspapers) and the availability of a personal library for the child correlate highly to later reading achievement.

Reading to the child from an early age plays an important role in establishing later success in reading. There are literally thousands of books available for the preschool child, ranging from colorful picture books, with and without story lines, to fairly complex stories. One type of book that is popular with young children contains highly predictable patterns of language—perhaps rhyming patterns, repetition of words and phrases, or predictable concepts. These books allow children to begin quickly to read along with the parent or teacher. It is highly motivational for children to realize that they know what is coming next in the book. At one level, this use of prior knowledge to predict and thus aid in reading is what all readers do when using context and prior knowledge to help in understanding. An example of predictable text is given in *Ten Little Caterpillars,* which includes the following lines of text on four successive pages:

> The first little caterpillar crawled into a bower.
> The second little caterpillar wriggled up a flower.
> The third little caterpillar climbed a cabbage head.
> The fourth little caterpillar found a melon bed.
>
> B. Martin, Jr. (1967). New York: Holt Rinehart & Winston, pp. 3, 5, 7, 9.

Parents often ask their children's kindergarten or first-grade teacher to suggest appropriate reading materials. There are numerous reference sources which provide titles, critiques, and suggestions for parents about reading to their child at home. Here are three.

1. Arbuthnot, M. H.; Clark, M. M.; Long, H. G.; & Hadlow, R. M. (1979). *Children's books too good to miss* (7th Edition). New York: University Press Books.
2. Lamme, L. L.; Cox, V.; Matanzo, J.; & Olson, M. (1980). *Raising readers: a guide to sharing literature with young children.* New York: Walker and Co.
3. Trelease, J. (1985). *The read-aloud handbook.* New York: Penguin Books.

Additionally, the International Reading Association, 800 Barksdale Road, Newark, Delaware, 19711, publishes numerous small, inexpensive books aimed at informing parents about appropriate activities. The amount and frequency of language-based interaction between adults and children is equally important both in the home and in school. Good reading habits are built when children are read to with appropriate intonation and evident pleasure and when their attention is drawn to the reading material. Reading a wide variety of materials to children helps to build discourse knowledge, use of syntax, and use of context. As parents read to their child and use specialized reading vocabulary ("Let's turn the page," or "Isn't that a funny title?") the child learns terms which will serve well in the school reading situation. When playing guessing games such as "I Spy" ("I spy something with a color that rhymes with bed. What is it?"), the manipulation of language and auditory discrimination skills are enhanced.

MODEL LESSON

Fostering Discourse Knowledge and Predicting Outcomes. Choose an interesting story to read to the children and divide it into two parts. Have chartpaper or a blackboard available.

Read the first part of the story. At the end of the first section, and following discussion of what was read, ask students to make suggestions about what might come next; what might happen in the rest of the story. Record students' responses on the chartpaper. Ask why they made the predictions they did (you may have to clarify or make explicit the information in the text that was used as a basis for the prediction).

Read the next section of the story.

Go back to the predictions. Discuss and confirm the predictions. Discuss why some predictions may not have appeared in the story.

The preceding section pointed out that cognition and language are interrelated. Games and activities which, at a young age, allow children to classify ("Let's put all the blocks with the big letters together"); to match items ("Let's see if this puzzle piece will fit in this slot"); to discriminate ("Let's see if we can find what's wrong in this picture"); or to build concepts of *same* and *different* ("Let's see if we can find a word that looks the same") can all be done in the home and all aid in the future successful completion of reading tasks.

Perceptual Factors

Perception deals with the senses and is divided into visual (seeing), auditory (hearing), tactile (touching), olfactory (smelling), and tasting categories. In reading readiness, however, most emphasis is placed on **visual and auditory perception** because the normal reader depends on vision to read print and hearing is instrumental in matching sounds to symbols.

When speaking of perceptual factors, there are four important terms to remember.

visual perception: In reading, the ability to see characteristics of things such as letters, words, or lines of print.
auditory perception: Being aware of the presence of sound.

Acuity	The "strength" of the signal. Questions relating to acuity include How well does the child hear? and How good are the child's eyes?
Discrimination	The ability to notice similarities and differences.
Recognition	Awareness that something being experienced is the same as something previously experienced. If you visually *recognize* a word, you are aware that you have seen the word before.
Identification	Deals specifically with identifying meaning. If you *identify* a word, you have grasped its meaning.

These definitions are consistent with the *Dictionary of Reading and Related Terms* (Harris & Hodges, 1981).

Visual Perception. At its basic level, visual perception is the ability to notice that there are lines and squiggles on a page. Reading in total darkness is impossible because visual perception is not possible, yet light intensity can vary widely without affecting reading. Think of the variety of places where you have read today and try to remember the variance in lighting. Indeed, reading does not depend on vision. There are many people who read Braille text and depend on tactile rather than visual perception. The more important aspect of visual perception is *discrimination*. Visual discrimination allows recognition that letters (*D* or *F*) and words (*dog* or *dug*) differ.

Appropriate activities to build the concept of same and different through visual discrimination include matching words, letters, or combinations of these in different sizes, shapes, and colors. Normal classroom surroundings can provide such practice. Even simple questions, such as asking if anyone can see a chair that is the same as the teacher's can provide practice in understanding *same* and *different* given that discussion centers around this concept.

Remember that the goal of readiness activities is to facilitate later fluent reading. It is best to provide activities that use reader-related items. Practice in discriminating words and letters is more valuable than practice in discriminating flowers or colors and should be the focus of the readiness program. Yet all discrimination activities in some sense teach the underlying concept of *same* and *different,* and this concept can be taught using objects in addition to words and letters. Once the concept has been established, discrimination activities should move more and more into discriminating reading-related items.

Print-Based Visual Discrimination Activity (Small Group)

Purpose: To teach visual discrimination in a context using children's language and background.

Materials: 1) experience story (for example, the story developed after a visit to an apple farm, as in the model lesson on language experience; 2) words printed on 3" × 5" cards, selected from the experience story. For example:

| had | day | wet | ride | pick | apple | tractor |

Procedure: After the experience story has been developed and printed on chartpaper, read the story to the children.

Give one 3" × 5" word card to each child. Tell them to look carefully at the words on their cards.

Point to a word in the story, and focus especially on its beginning and ending. Ask if any child has a card with the same word you are pointing to. Ask them to hold up their cards if the words are the same. Read the word to the children.

Ask the child who has identified the word to place it under the word in the story. Ask the child to verify the match and (with your help if needed) say the word.

Ask if there are any more words in the story that look exactly like the one on the card. If the word appears more than once in the story, repeat the preceding step.

If a child raises a card with a word that does not match the target word in the story, ask the child to identify what is similar and different about the two words (for example, beginning letter, ending letter, or shape), and ask again if the word is the same.

Continue until every child has had a chance to match a word. After this has been done, write the child's name on the card and attach it to the chartpaper story under its matched word.

To build the concepts of *same* and *different,* teachers must move beyond children's answers to a discussion and examination of how items are the same or different (that is, why a particular response has been made). Understanding the reasoning behind responses helps both the children who provide a correct answer (by forcing an examination of their mental process), as well as those who may not have answered appropriately (by showing where their logic had broken down).

Careful questioning can point out the similarities and differences between letters or other print-based items. For example, ask the children to do the following with *m, n,* and *mother.*

Trace the two letters. Are they the same?

Do both have straight lines? Where?

Do both have curved lines? Where? How many?

Are the curved lines the same? How are they different?

Trace the word *mother.* Is there a letter in *mother* that is the same as one of the two letters? Where is it? Underline it.

Such questioning helps students to differentiate between particular features of letters and trains them to examine details that make up overall configurations.

One way to help children internalize the similarities and differences between letters and words is to have them copy or, at beginning stages, trace print-based material: letters, letter combinations, and words. Such activities focus their attention, are print-based, and make them attend to all parts of the item. Since the goal is to develop visual discrimination, not writing skills, the activity must include a discussion of the similarities of and differences between what is being traced or copied.

- Divide a piece of poster paper into large rectangles. Print a word in each rectangle. Make a matching set of rectangular word cards. Have students cover the words on the paper with the appropriate word cards.

- You can turn this activity into a bingo game. Students, perhaps in pairs, can cover the words which you point to on your "bingo card".

- Make labels for objects around the classroom (desk, chair, stool, book, table, shelf, window, or door). Attach an envelope below the label on each item. Give children a set of cards containing the labeled items. They are to place their word cards in the envelopes under the appropriate labels. Placing each child's name on a set of cards provides a quick check of who has difficulty matching cards to the labels.

- Using plastic or paper letters, arrange groups of letters which are the same, except for one that is obviously different (for example, C C X C C and F S F F F). Ask children to find and correct the one that is different. Gradually, increase the similarity of the letters.

- Help children perceive the differences between letters by discussing and pointing out the features of letters (curved lines, straight lines, or height). Provide two letters with color on the parts that make them different.

- Ask children to discriminate between similar words, drawing a circle around the part(s) that are different (for example, *near/rear; rat/rut; or window/widow*).

- Discuss similarities of and differences between words of clearly different shapes and lengths. For example, write *mow* and *motorcycle* on the board or on chartpaper. Discuss how they are the same and different (one is longer, two of the letters in mow are in motorcycle, one has a letter with a "tail", and so on).

Auditory Perception. Auditory perception is the ability to notice the presence of sound. More important for reading, however, is the ability to discriminate the similarities of and differences between the sounds of various letters, syllables, and words.

There is a controversy about what should be taught in the **auditory discrimination** component of reading readiness programs. For example, Gibson & Levin (1980) state that

auditory discrimination: The ability to hear likenesses and differences between sounds.

> auditory perceptual analysis of words is an important skill for learning to read and training in it helps and does show transfer, at least in the initial stages of learning to read . . . . Clapping for each unit, marking (with

dashes), deleting sounds, producing omitted sounds, and substituting sounds are successive stages of training, with apparently successful results in kindergarten and first grade. (p. 260)

Burns, Roe & Ross (1984) agree, noting that teachers must progress from talking about things in the classroom that sound the same and different (the scraping of a desk across the floor, the closing or opening of a window), to activities that deal with rhyming words; hearing similarities and differences in word endings, beginnings, and middles; and finally to blending individual sounds into a whole word (p. 58). Yet Durkin (1983) disagrees with the value of some of these activities "because they do not contribute to success with reading . . . distinguishing among musical and environmental sounds, for instance" (p. 73).

Aulls (1982) is even more definite, citing a number of studies supporting his conclusion that

emphasizing reading tasks such as sounding out words or emphasizing phonics may be a waste of time for many kindergartners. . . . Teaching auditory discrimination and blending appears to be clearly a waste of time according to a number of research studies . . . although there seems to be little justification for attempting to teach kindergartners auditory discrimination, blending or rhyming, there does appear to be justification for teaching auditory segmentation *to those children who have naturally begun to sound out words and who have already begun to read* (p. 99, emphasis added).

Partly, auditory discrimination activities provide a common terminology for both the teacher and the student. This has been clearly demonstrated in teacher's guides for some time.

The purpose of giving practice in listening for beginning sounds is not to teach children to "hear" sounds or to distinguish sounds from one another. Children who understand and reproduce their language do this automatically. However, many pupils in kindergarten or first grade have trouble with the concept that a word has a beginning because they think of a word as one undifferentiated sound. Since the children will be taught in a later lesson that one sound to use in decoding is the sound "at the beginning of a word", they need to know exactly what this expression means (Teachers' guide, Houghton-Mifflin's *Getting Ready to Read,* p. 21, 1979).

This goal of teaching common terminology is also a factor in using environmental sounds to build the concepts of *same* and *different* (Burns, Roe & Ross, 1984). As in visual discrimination, later transfer to print is better when auditory discrimination tasks center around reading-related materials.

- Provide magazines and blunt scissors. Have students find and cut out pictures that have sounds beginning with the same sound as their names. Later, have them say the names of the things they have cut out and let the other students agree or disagree that the beginning sounds are the same.

- Take the cut-out pictures and place them in a box. Provide containers and label each with a word. Students take pictures out of the boxes and place them in the containers that have labels beginning with the same sounds as the pictures they chose.

- Find or make up simple tongue twisters (for example, "Six silly sheep saw a slippery snake."). Have them repeat after you, first going slowly, then slightly faster. Put several of these into a box. Have students choose ones for you to say. Have them suggest other words that have sounds which might make the tongue twister longer (for example, slippery snake *sliding*).

- Draw a spaceship beginning on Earth, aiming toward the Moon, on a large piece of posterboard. Children provide words or pictures that have words with sounds relative to a target word provided by the teacher. For every three words the ship moves closer to the Moon. Dividing students into teams makes this into a motivational game.

- Use key words that begin or end with a specified sound. Provide other words so that students can decide whether the sounds are the same.

Auditory/Visual Integration. The beginning reader must learn that oral language can be represented in symbolic form, that symbols and sounds are linked, and that the purpose of reading is for meaning. Activities that attempt to build these concepts relate to **auditory/visual integration.**

In these activities, the child is presented with both the visual material and the sound(s) which it represents. The child must see and hear the symbol(s) and sound(s) at the same time, perhaps saying the item together with the teacher while looking at it, perhaps simply attempting to follow along with the teacher while being read to and being asked what word might come next.

Thus, activities to promote auditory/visual integration differ somewhat from those noted in preceding sections. To promote integration, students need to hear and see the stimulus at the same time. For example, where a purely auditory activity might ask the student to repeat the beginning sound in *baby,* a corresponding auditory/visual integration activity would present the visual image

<u>b</u>aby

auditory/visual integration: The linking or association of sound and sight.

In readiness programs many activities are available that use motivational auditory activities in ways that relate print-based and auditory modes.

while the teacher said the word. Students might be asked to repeat the beginning sound, or to point to the part of the word that has the /b/ sound as the teacher says the word. Such activities build the concept that specific sounds are associated with specific parts of a word, and can be used with sounds in beginning, medial, and ending positions, as well as with units larger than single letters. One of the best ways to build awareness that print has meaning is to read to children. This has the added benefit of creating positive attitudes toward reading and promoting a desire to read.

Affective Factors

We have all experienced tasks that seemed to be completed in record time, while others seemed to drag on and on. There are some things that we never tire of doing, while others need a great deal of mental strength to complete. If you think back to tasks of both types, you will probably find that those which flew by were those you found pleasant, while the others were ones that you did not enjoy. Further, you probably looked forward to performing the same or similar tasks if they were in the enjoyable category. Stated another way, your affective set—the way you feel about something—influences your motivation and performance. This applies equally well to beginning (indeed, to all) readers.

Any readiness program must foster a desire to read. Many children come to school with a desire to learn to read and view reading as potentially exciting (Downing *et al.,* 1979). Much of this feeling results from having had interesting and exciting stories read to them at home. This leads to the realization that the pleasurable experiences of being read to have originated from a book, and learning to read is viewed as achieving independence. Reading to students is a vital part of a readiness program.

BEFORE READING ON

Try to differentiate between *attitude* and *interest.* How do you think the terms are related? How do they differ? How might aspects of both affect your readiness instruction?

Affective factors address issues of motivation that are closely tied to how one feels about something. Is a specific activity liked or disliked? This is called **attitude.** A closely related term is **interest,** which indicates not how someone feels about something, but rather relates to the importance placed on pursuing a given topic or activity. To illustrate, it is possible to dislike something, yet be interested in finding out more about it. Perhaps one might have an intensely negative attitude toward snakes, but have a strong interest in finding out where they are most likely to be found. Conversely, one may feel very positively about something, but have no interest in studying it further. You may find Gothic architecture visually pleasing, but have no interest in studying its history or specific characteristics.

attitude: The way one feels about something.
interest: Intentional focusing of attention to something because one is motivated.

In reading readiness, as in all instruction, teachers need to be aware of both the interests and attitudes of their students. Though students' attitudes toward learning to read may be positive, their interest in performing specific readiness tasks may be quite low. To generate interest in required assignments, teachers must (1) be aware of students' attitudes toward and interest in the specific task, and (2) make each task inherently motivational, thereby creating a positive attitude toward the task being performed. Young children have great difficulty using long-term goals as motivating factors. Telling students they need to do a task so they will eventually become good readers is not conceptually relevant. The immediate task must, in itself, be motivational.

The administration of a short attitude survey will help you to choose instructional tasks and materials which will motivate your students. A sample is provided in figure 3–1.

FIGURE 3–1

Sample from Heathing-
ton Scales

Heathington Primary Scale

SAMPLE OF PARTIAL ANSWER SHEET

1.

The following directions should be followed in administering the primary scale:

> Your answer booklet is made up of two pages. Page one goes from
> number 1 to number 10, and page two goes from number 11 to number
> 20. Beside each number are five faces; a very unhappy face, an un-
> happy face, a face that's neither happy nor unhappy, a happy face, and
> a very happy face. I will ask you how you feel about certain things
> and you will put an X on the face that shows how you feel. Suppose
> I said, "How do you feel when you eat chocolate candy? Which face
> shows how you feel?" Someone may have chosen an unhappy face
> because he doesn't like chocolate candy; someone else may have
> chosen a happy face because he likes chocolate candy. Now, I'll read
> some questions to you and you mark the face that shows how you feel
> about what I read. Remember to mark how *you* feel because everyone
> does not feel the same about certain things. I'll read each question
> two times. Mark only one face for each number. Are there any
> questions? Now listen carefully. "Number 1 . . . ."

Certain groupings of questions can be considered diagnostic. That is,
they indicate specific areas of a child's reading environment toward which
he may feel positively or negatively. The following groupings are
suggested:

1. Free reading in the classroom (items 3, 17)
2. Organized reading in the classroom (items 4, 7, 8, 13)
3. Reading at the library (items 1, 18)
4. Reading at home (items 6, 12, 15, 19)
5. Other recreational reading (items 2, 5, 9, 16)
6. General reading (items 10, 11, 14, 20).

Primary Scale

How do you feel . . .

1. when you go to the library?
2. when you read instead of playing outside?
3. when you read a book in free time?
4. when you are in reading group?
5. when you read instead of watching TV?
6. when you read to someone at home?
7. about the stories in your reading book?
8. when you read out loud in class?
9. when you read with a friend after school?
10. when you read stories in books?
11. when you read in a quiet place?
12. when you read a story at bedtime?
13. when it's time for reading circle (group)?
14. when you read on a trip?
15. when you have lots of books at home?
16. when you read outside when it's warm?
17. when you read at your desk at school?
18. when you find a book at the library?
19. when you read in your room at home?
20. when you read instead of coloring?

Heathington (1976) has developed attitude scales for use in primary and intermediate grades. The answer sheets for the Heathington primary scale asks students to show how they feel about questions starting with "How do you feel . . ." by marking one of a set of faces that range from smiling to frowning. These scales provide a range of pertinent questions for teachers who wish to assess students in this area, but teachers sometimes supplement with questions like: What do you like to do most?; What are your favorite TV shows?; Do you have (want) any pets? They can also ask open-ended questions like: Your favorite story is . . . ?; The best day of the week is . . . ?; When you grow up you'd like to be . . . ? Chapter 11 also provides a discussion and more examples of attitude and interest assessment.

Building positive attitudes toward reading requires a rich oral reading environment. Read to beginning readers often—sometimes individually, sometimes in small groups or in whole-class situations. The interest/attitude survey will help you choose interesting reading material. You may wish to pick stories likely to be of high interest to students who have somewhat poor attitudes toward reading. You will need to make a special effort to identify materials of motivational value for such students, and spend some extra time reading to them and discussing their interest in the stories.

Although an attitude/interest inventory can be a valuable tool, teachers in readiness programs need to recognize that young children have short attention spans and that their interests are not as stable as those of older students and can change fairly quickly. Provide time to talk to young students often to keep abreast of their current interests.

Allowing time for discussion of what was read, pointing out pictures and interesting drawings, and leaving time for discussion after reading are all important to fostering positive attitudes and story comprehension. Encouraging students to talk about personal experiences relating to the reading selection is also of high motivational value, especially because beginning readers are often **egocentric.**

egocentric: When used to describe young children, it means self-centered because the child is unable to take another's point of view.

EVALUATING THE PREREADER

Teachers are decision makers, continually making instructional decisions based on the information around them. The three ways in which you will gather information influencing your instructional decisions in teaching beginning readers relate to

1. formal and informal readiness tests
2. observations of students' behavior and abilities
3. information from parents and students

Formal Readiness Tests

Four areas appear to predict success in reading: knowledge of letter names; general oral vocabulary knowledge; recognition of whole words; and visual discrimination ability (Silvaroli, 1965; Bond & Dykstra, 1967; Loban, 1963; Richek, 1977–78; Barrett, 1965). Although some studies have failed to replicate results showing that these four areas are predictive of later reading ability (Calfee, Chapman & Venezky, 1972; Olson & Johnson, 1970; Samuels, 1972). They are generally included in formal readiness tests. Formal readiness tests usually measure the following abilities:

auditory perception	auditory discrimination
visual perception	visual discrimination
auditory/visual integration	motor skills
concepts of *same, different, over,* and *under*	awareness of left-right sequence
letter identification and recognition	oral sentence or short passage comprehension
	word identification and recognition

Tests range from paper-and-pencil tests given to groups of students to tests administered individually. Figure 3–2 presents examples of different kinds of test activities.

Generally, readiness tests require that students match pictures, words, letters, or shapes to either visual or auditory stimuli. Children may be asked to listen to or look at an item then find the item in a series of choices, or to complete an incomplete item to match a stimulus. Although seemingly a simple task, teachers must be careful that their students clearly understand the test directions, for beginning readers easily confuse the test item under discussion (thus marking the wrong question), and are sometimes unable to grasp instructions such as:

> From the pictures on the *right, mark* the one that is *the same as* the one on the *left.*

You will need to make sure the test clearly relates to the skill being measured, and does not evaluate the student's ability to follow directions unless that is the specific objective of the test.

Another caution when testing young children relates to their attention spans. Teachers must ensure that the testing tasks are within the attention span of the child. The kindergarten or first-grade student is often a bundle of energy, frequently unused to the necessity of sitting still and focusing attention for long periods. Most readiness tests contain time lines beyond which rest periods or other activities are suggested. Do not ignore these instructions.

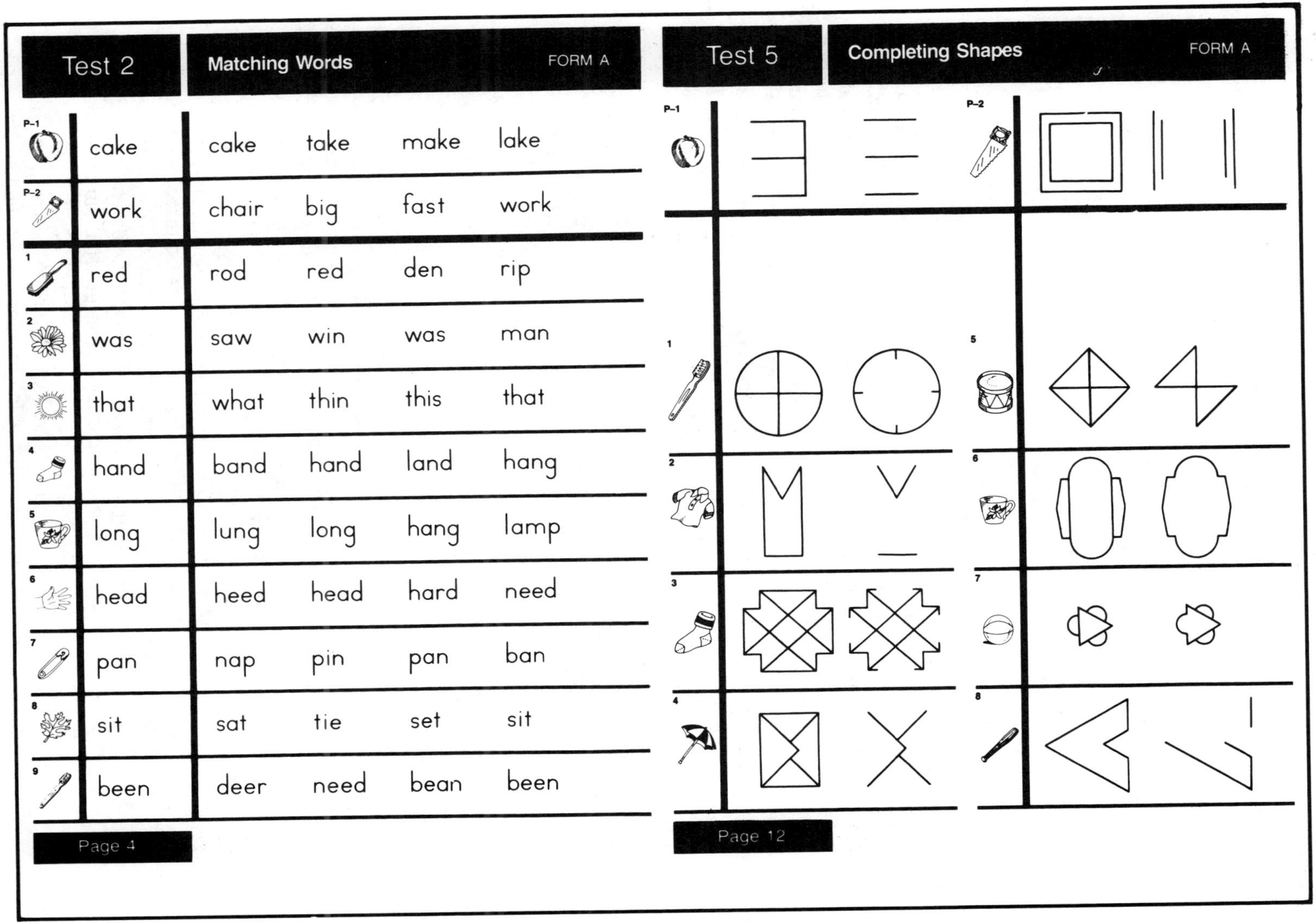

FIGURE 3–2
Sample readiness test pages: Clymer-Barrett Readiness Test

It will be your responsibility to find answers to the following questions.

1. What, exactly, do I want to measure, and why?
2. What, exactly, does the test measure, and how?
3. Does the test, in fact, measure what it says it is measuring?
4. Is there a close relationship between what I want to measure and what the test measures?

To answer these questions, you must be familiar with the test being given and take the time to preview it, thinking about each item. In addition to examining the test, however, read the test's manual carefully. (Chapter 11 discusses this and other measurement issues in more depth.) A test's manual contains valuable information on administration procedures and the intent of the test. Decide whether it is useful to spend time which would otherwise be used for instruction on testing. Once you have selected a test and administered it to your students, keep careful records and update them. Most readiness programs and formal, published tests provide a convenient format to record student data. Figure 3–3 shows an example of a student record sheet from a popular reading series. This record sheet corresponds to one level in the series.

Formal readiness tests were developed mainly in the 1920s to 1950s, but have been less popular in recent times. This is partly due to studies that have shown that the predictive power of readiness tests is fairly low. That is, a good score on a readiness test does not always predict with a high degree of certainty how well a student will learn to read. This is why many now advocate using more informal measures in reading readiness programs (Durkin, 1980; Lapp & Flood, 1981).

Observational Data

The school environment provides a wealth of opportunity for the observant teacher to informally assess students' abilities, interests, attitudes, and social skills. Assignments, oral responses to questions, student-initiated questions, attention span, speed of task completion, and patterns of correct/incorrect responses all provide data on which to base instructional decisions.

The checklist presented in figure 3–4 can help draw attention to specific behaviors and abilities. Some items can be discovered by observation. Others require input from parents or students' answers to questions. As with any informal evaluative instrument, you are free to modify items as appropriate to the respective instructional situation in which the test will be used.

Group activities and observation of a child's behavior on the playground can also provide valuable information. Is the child an active par-

GINN READING PROGRAM   **LEVEL 1 LEVEL TEST**

CLASS RECORD SHEET

SCHOOL _____ TOWN_____

TEACHER_____ YEAR/GRADE _____ DATE_____

PUPILS' NAMES	Suggested Passing Score	VOCABULARY Word Identification 16	DECODING Beginning Consonants 12	Test Total 28
1.				
2.				
3.				
4.				
5.				
6.				
7.				
8.				
9.				
10.				
11.				
12.				
13.				
14.				
15.				
16.				
17.				
18.				
19.				
20.				

FIGURE 3–3
Student record sheet from a popular reading series

INFORMAL READINESS CHECKLIST

Student's Name: _____   Date: _____

Age: Years _____   Months _____

Use the following scale in the "decision" column: 1 = YES, 2 = SOMEWHAT, 3 = NO. Comments should be added whenever possible, especially if "somewhat" is the decision.

	Decision	Comments
1. Knows alphabet (can say it with little or no help).	_____	
2. Can write alphabet.	_____	
3. Can distinguish between upper & lower case letters.	_____	
4. Recognizes written letters by name.	_____	
5. Can rhyme words.	_____	
6. Can count to 20.	_____	
7. Can state numbers from written form.	_____	
8. Can write numbers.	_____	
9. Recognizes and matches items that are the "same."	_____	
10. Knows relational words (before, after, back, front, under, above, until).	_____	
11. Can describe (tell) a picture-based story.	_____	
12. Can appropriately order a simple picture-story (i.e., a cartoon strip).	_____	
13. Can read common words (stop, dog, run).	_____	
14. Can read own name when written by teacher.	_____	
15. Can write own name.	_____	
16. Knows own age.	_____	
17. Can repeat sequence of events in a simple story.	_____	
18. Speaks in sentences rather than words or phrases.	_____	
19. Knows simple reading terms (page, word, story).	_____	

General comments (e.g., attentiveness, concentration, ability to follow directions, shy, pronunciation of words/sounds, general verbal fluency):

_____

_____

_____

FIGURE 3–4
Informal readiness checklist

Games that allow peer interaction and require players to follow directions can provide observational data for teachers as well as valuable learning experiences for children.

ticipant in games? Does the child take leadership or passive roles? In what kinds of activities? Is the child shy or somewhat of a bully? How do other students react to the child? Answers to these questions provide valuable insights. Record your informal observations along with your formal test data. Together, these pieces of information can make you a more effective teacher by allowing you to plan instructional activities according to student needs. For example, the checklist is an informal indication of which students might be grouped for activities such as visual discrimination of letters, numbers, or learning to write their names. The checklist can provide indications of activities or items that might be motivational, or show which students might need a little special consideration due to shyness or other personality traits.

Parental Input

Informal discussions with parents can prove very productive, helping provide information about your students. Through parent conferences, parent-teacher association (PTA) meetings, and notes or questionnaires sent to parents you can capture valuable information about siblings, motivating factors, attitudes about school, and home reading environment. Parents can also be a tremendous help in more direct instructional aspects of your readiness program. Young children are often proud when their parents come to their class (this sometimes changes as students get older), and try hard to do their best. Parents usually are aware of the value and importance of developing good reading and are willing to help in whatever way they can. Parental involvement often helps foster positive student attitude and motivation. Using parents as storytellers, to provide demonstrations, or to help in class activities can be valuable, especially when these are later used as a base for other oral, written, or art experiences.

Working parents who are unable to come to class during school hours might be willing and able to arrange an interesting field trip to their business or place of work, or may have a hobby that can be brought to school after class for discussion by the teacher and students on the next day. These types of parental involvement can form the basis for highly motivating lessons that build experiential background, oral language, and vocabulary.

READINESS AND PROFICIENT READERS

So far we have discussed the importance of oral language, cognitive factors, home environment, perceptual, and affective factors as they relate to the beginning reader. Yet, readiness can apply beyond the beginning stages of reading acquisition.

BEFORE READING ON

Read the following text and answer the questions which follow it.

Comprehensive allocation is more consistent with the accounting for liabilities than roll over, such as accounts payable. New accounts payable continually replace accounts being paid, much the same as originating timing differences replace timing differences that reverse. Each creditor's account is accounted for separately, even though aggregate accounts payable continue to roll over. Consistency requires that timing differences related to a particular asset or liability likewise be accounted for separately (Davidson, Stickney, & Weil, 1980, p. 20–26).

1. Why is comprehensive allocation more consistent with liabilities than roll over?
2. Explain the concept of timing differences and their importance to accounts payable.
3. In your own words, explain what the paragraph is about.

An accountant would not have difficulty answering the questions following the passage. There are several reasons, however, which you might have for not understanding the above passage—perhaps having to guess at some pronunciations or not knowing terms which the author assumed were in your background. Yet you are a good, fluent reader.

In a sense, you are not ready to read the accounting text example. Thus, you need some prereading activities, possibly including building background knowledge, defining new vocabulary, and discussing the overall meaning of the passage.

This example demonstrates that readiness does not stop once decoding activities have been acquired. Although *readiness* is commonly used to describe the stage relating to the time when children have not yet mastered basic decoding skills, a broader view acknowledges that we all encounter text which we are unprepared to read, given our current levels of knowledge.

DIFFERENT FRAMEWORKS
AND READINESS INSTRUCTION

Of necessity, the various components of the readiness program were presented separately in preceding sections. But the activities provided in each component are not intended to be used independently. Remember that the ultimate goal of reading readiness is fluent reading. Since comprehension necessitates the interrelation of all the components of the readiness program, do not view them as separate entities. The readiness program, as all aspects of reading instruction, must focus on comprehension within the components. When teaching the features of a letter, you are teaching comprehension of that letter; when teaching the concept *same,* you are teaching comprehension of that concept. Make questions that extend the student and that target conceptual understanding a major part of the readiness program.

Although this chapter presents various factors prerequisite to the acquisition of reading and provides sample activities to be used in a readiness program, the way that you implement readiness instruction will depend on your instructional framework. If your comprehension framework is based on explanations that feel reading takes place through exact pronunciation of what is written, you may lean toward perceptual, discrimination activities in your readiness program. Such an approach has as its goal the eventual direct teaching of sound-symbol relationships, and you would provide many activities that are aimed at students' conceptualizing that letters and sounds are related.

Although few would argue that readiness programs should exclusively teach either sound-symbol relations or getting meaning from print, there is an argument about the balance or degree of emphasis of one over the other. There are those who advocate a focus on sound-symbol relationships (Chall, 1979; Liberman & Shankwiler, 1980). Others (Goodman & Goodman, 1979; Smith, 1980) feel that decoding is not central to reading and imply that readiness programs should focus on meaning. Still others argue that reading is an interactive process between text and reader and that whether meaning or decoding is a reader's initial focus depends on factors such as overall reading ability, the reader's purpose for reading, and the difficulty of what is being read (Danks & Fears, 1979; Frederiksen, 1979). Those who hold this interactive view suggest that both perceptual- and meaning-based instructional activities should receive equal attention.

The discussion of the three classrooms in the following sections represents potential differences resulting from different instructional frameworks, that is, materials, method, and comprehension frameworks. Recall that comprehension frameworks are based on two questions: How does one read? and How does reading ability develop? We encourage you to refer to pages 15–19 and 53–56 if you are unsure about the difference between frameworks and their assumptions.

Three Different Classrooms

Ms. Smith, Mr. Jennings, and Ms. Jones each teach kindergarten classes with approximately the same student makeup. Some students in their classes are bussed from other neighborhoods. There is a mixture of races—Hispanic, Black, White, and a Korean student whose parents speak little English at home. Although the majority of students in each class has a keen interest in learning to read, two appear to have poor attitudes toward school in general, while one already reads simple storybooks independently.

Ms. Smith's Class. Ms. Smith spent much of the first week of school using reading readiness tests to determine which students need practice on specific skills. She feels that this is valuable, since she views reading acquisition as mastering a set of skills. She carefully completes student record cards and selects materials and activities that reflect the skills that she feels are needed by her students. Students are generally grouped according to needs in Ms. Smith's class. She makes sure that each of the important readiness skills is specifically taught, although there is special emphasis placed on auditory discrimination activities.

Ms. Smith's classroom contains many different kinds of readiness workbooks. Although Ms. Smith provides time for students to talk to each other about their activities, and they have adequate opportunity to work individually with her, Ms. Smith feels that it is vital for her students to gain early awareness that reading involves getting the meaning from what is written—that the author's message is contained in the text. Her students spend much of their time performing readiness activities in workbooks or on sheets of paper, thus out of the context of their oral language. After she reads stories to her students, much discussion focuses on what was stated in the story and what the author was trying to say.

Ms. Smith has carefully chosen workbooks that are colorful and, she hopes, motivational. Furthermore, she has spent a great deal of effort in trying to match specific workbook activities to the specific skills examined in her readiness testing program. Since Ms. Smith recognizes that the students in her class have diverse abilities, she provides exercises of differing levels for her students. She feels that the materials she uses are well designed and should be followed. She carefully examines the teacher's manual and prepares supplementary activities and lessons as suggested therein. Ms. Smith believes that it is very important to closely follow the teacher's manual, and she does so very conscientiously.

Ms. Smith's day, and that of her students, is full. She carefully segments her class time so that important activities are not inadvertently left out. Part of her day is devoted to record keeping: attendance, testing, recording lunch money, and so on. Other parts of her day are taken up by activities in music, artwork, physical education, reading readiness, recess, lunch, and rest periods. Ms. Smith tries to separate activities from each other to preserve their unique aspects, since she thinks it is important for children to realize that there are different skills and subject areas to be mastered in school.

Her specific activities are generally presented out of context, and she does not encourage guessing. For example, she teaches visual discrimination by using isolated words, rather than words appearing in the context of an experience story.

Mr. Jennings' Class. Mr. Jennings also spends time on testing, but his individual student records additionally contain tabulations of informal observations that he has made during class and play time, as well as data from parent interviews. He uses informal techniques to update his records. He feels this is vital, since he attempts to draw on the children's backgrounds and existing knowledge. Students are used as often as possible to help with administrative functions such as attendance checks or charts of their progress. Progress charts appear on the classroom walls, and the students update their charts with Mr. Jennings' supervision.

Mr. Jennings' classroom contains a wide variety of posters, pictures, labels for items, and a great deal of students' work—from simple drawings and colorings to stories which the students have dictated to him. Mr. Jennings' lessons are usually structured around a particular method. In fact, one of Mr. Jennings' favorite methods is the language experience approach that culminates in an experience story. These stories are posted and are frequently changed, with the children helping both to decide which things go on the wall and to take old items down and put new ones up. When teaching readiness skills, he uses activities that are in context. For example, when teaching visual discrimination, he has students match word cards to words appearing in students' experience stories.

Most of the readiness activities that Mr. Jennings provides are based in his students' oral language and experiences. He often starts the schoolday with a story, then asks students to tell each other or the whole class a story of their own. Sometimes he uses a tape recorder to capture the students' stories; sometimes he will write someone's story on the chalkboard or on a piece of paper as it is being told. These form the basis of discussion, and are frequently used as bases for illustrations and drawings in the art instructional component. In fact, conscious use of the students' oral language and background is the base for almost all other activities: in music, simple poems, rhythms, or rhymes are sung or chanted; in physical education, movement is used to illustrate concepts such as *under, on, over,* or left-to-right progression. Everything is related to language—specifically, the students' oral language.

Mr. Jennings believes that all language skills are related and thus attempts to link oral and written language. He feels it important to discuss individual interpretations of experience stories and things that he reads to his students, since he believes that comprehension is an interaction between what readers know and what is stated in the text.

Ms. Jones' Class. Ms. Jones does little formal assessment, preferring to use informal measures and close observation of each student's motor, cognitive, and oral language skills. Ms. Jones does not use any one, formally prepared readiness program in her classroom, but rather chooses and adapts activities from a range of materials and techniques. She feels that readers vary in the skills they need to know and use. At times she teaches lessons targeted at mastering specific skills such as visual discrimination; at other times she targets conceptual knowledge while relating student's background and experience to the activity. Ms. Jones has a clear understanding of how reading takes place and develops, and incorporates this knowledge into her reading lessons.

Her instructional program consists of a wide variety of activities. When one enters her classroom, it is not unusual to see children in different parts of the room pursuing different activities. Those students with poor motor skills might be tracing felt letters with their fingers, while those with better-developed fine motor skills might be tracing letters on paper. Ms. Jones tries very hard to change instructional tasks as students' abilities grow.

With an eye to future skilled reading demands, Ms. Jones uses story time to ask high-level questions aimed not only at comprehension of the story, but also at identifying story structure and to play with sentences and language. Even though her students are not readers, Ms. Jones knows that their listening and conversational skills are well developed, and she thus asks questions which, though currently applicable to oral language, will be paralleled in later reading activities. These include questions on opinions, cause and effect, sequence, main idea, and relationships of stories to personal experiences.

As does Mr. Jennings, Ms. Jones uses language experience activities, teaches readiness skills in context and attempts to provide awareness of story structure while building discourse knowledge. Additionally,

Ms. Jones teaches specific skills when she feels such skills are necessary for comprehension. For example, visual discrimination may be first taught in isolation, and then in the context of an experience story. When teaching a particular skill or concept, Ms. Jones asks comprehension questions in all types of activities. Ms. Jones tries to use students' strengths to improve their weaknesses.

THE MAJOR POINTS

1. Reading readiness is not a fixed point in time. It refers equally well to proficient readers who are not ready, due to experiential background or other factors, to read selections (for example, an insurance policy or legal document) and to children who are at the prereading stage. In effect, building required background takes place with both fluent and prereaders.
2. Readiness programs for prereaders generally stress auditory and visual perception; stress that sounds and symbols are related; and build understanding of reading-related concepts.
3. Readiness activities for prereaders are most effective when they deal specifically with print-related items (letters, letter groups, and words).
4. Prereaders in readiness programs must be given opportunities to trace and copy letters, letter groups, and words; should be read to often; and should be allowed to use their oral language skills.
5. Observational data, in addition to more formal readiness tests, form an integral part in the assessment of prereaders.

QUESTIONS AND ACTIVITIES

The first two activities relate to the three typical classrooms described in this chapter.

1. Which of the three classroom scenarios do you think most closely approximates a materials framework? A method framework? A comprehension framework? Defend your opinion. (A discussion of the various frameworks was presented in chapters 1 and 2.)
2. Reread the section on the three typical classrooms. Outline (1) which classroom situation most closely approximates your framework of reading at this point; (2) which aspects of *each* class profile you feel to be good instructional practice; (3) which aspects of *each* class profile you disagree with; (4) what you would add to and/or take away from any given profile in order to create your "ideal" situation (remember that each class consists of a diverse group of children); and (5) specify why the practices with which you agree and disagree cause the reaction they do.

3. If possible, visit a kindergarten classroom to observe what is taking place. Try to spend some time with the teacher and discuss how activities are planned, which seem to be most appropriate for the students, and why.

4. Go to your curriculum library and examine a basal reader intended for kindergarten level. Look at the activities suggested for auditory discrimination, visual discrimination, and oral language development. Look closely at the stated goals of each activity. Do you think the goals and activities are appropriate?

5. Design a readiness lesson in each of the following areas: auditory discrimination; visual discrimination; following directions; and auditory/visual integration.

FURTHER READING

Ellis, D. W. & Preston, F. W. (1984). Enhancing beginning reading using wordless picture books in a cross-age tutoring program. *Reading Teacher, 37,* 692–98.

Discusses the value of wordless picture books and describes how they were used in a tutoring program between fifth and first graders. Provides a list of 162 wordless picture books published in the United States.

Lass, B. (1982). Portrait of my son as an early reader. *Reading Teacher, 36,* 20–28.

Provides a brief overview of research on characteristics of early readers and provides a timeline of emerging reading behaviors.

McCormick, S. & Collins, B. M. (1981). A potpourri of game-making ideas for the reading teacher. *Reading Teacher, 34,* 692–96.

Points out general guidelines for use of games (for example, they should provide academic learning, not busywork; they should teach, not test) and provides list of supplies generally needed to construct instructional materials, where to get them, and what to do with them.

Ollila, L., (1977). *The kindergarten child and reading.* Newark, Delaware: International Reading Association.

Collection of brief articles on various aspects of reading in the kindergarten.

Read, D. & Smith, H. M. (1982). Teaching visual literacy through wordless picture books. *Reading Teacher, 35,* 928–33.

Provides a brief overview of the potential of wordless picture books and discusses appropriate skills that can be taught using these materials.

Tovey, R. T. & Kerber, J. E. (eds.) (1986). *Roles in literacy learning: A new perspective.* Newark, DE: International Reading Association.

A selection of short articles discussing the roles and responsibilities of parents, teachers, children, administrators, and researchers in literacy acquisition.

Vukelich, C. (1984). Parents' role in the reading process: a review of practical suggestions, and ways to communicate with parents. *Reading Teacher, 37,* 472–77.

Points out the most frequent suggestions made to parents and provides suggestions, methods, and activities to involve parents.

REFERENCES

Allen, K. K. (1982). The development of young children's understanding of the word. *Journal of Educational Research, 76,* 89–92.

Allen, R. V. & Allen, C. (1976). *Language experience activities.* Boston: Houghton Mifflin.

Almy, M.; Chittenden, E.; & Miller, P. (1966). *Young children's thinking: studies of some aspects of Piaget's theory.* New York: Teachers College Press.

Anderson, R. C.; Hiebert, E. H.; Scott, J. A.; & Wilkinson, I. A. G. (1985). Becoming a nation of readers: The report of the commission on reading. National Institute of Education: Washington, DC.

Ashton-Warner, S. (1963). *Teacher.* New York: Simon & Schuster.

Ashton-Warner, S. (1972). *Spearpoint.* New York: Knopf.

Aukerman, R. C. (1984). *Approaches to beginning reading instruction* (2nd Edition). New York: John Wiley & Sons.

Aulls, M. W. (1982). *Developing readers in today's elementary schools.* Boston: Allyn & Bacon.

Barrett, T. C. (1965). Visual discrimination tasks as predicators of first grade reading achievement. *Reading Teacher, 18,* 276–82.

Bond, G. L. & Dykstra, R. (1967). The cooperative research program in first grade reading instruction. *Reading Research Quarterly, 2,* 5–142.

Burns, P. C.; Roe, B. D.; & Ross, E. P. (1984). *Teaching reading in today's elementary schools* (3rd Edition). Boston: Houghton Mifflin.

Bybee, R. W. & Sund, R. B. (1982). *Piaget for educators.* Columbus, Ohio: C. E. Merrill.

Calfee, R.; Chapman, R.; & Venezky, R. (1972). How a child needs to think to learn to read. In L. Gregg (ed.), *Cognition in learning and memory* (pp. 139–82). New York: John Wiley & Sons.

Caulkins, L. (1983). *Lesson from a child.* Exeter, NH: Heinemann.

Cazden, C. (1983). Adult assistance to language development: scaffolds, models, and direct instruction. In R. P. Parker & F. A. Davis (eds.), *Developing literacy: young children's use of language* (pp. 3–18). Newark, DE: International Reading Association.

Chall, J. S. (1979). The great debate: ten years later, with a modest proposal for reading stages. In L. B. Resnick & P. A. Weaver (eds.), *Theory and practice of early reading* (vol. 1, pp. 29–55). Hillsdale, NJ: Lawrence Erlbaum Associates.

Clay, M. M. (1980a). *The early detection of reading difficulties: a diagnostic survey* (2nd Edition). New York: Heinemann Educational Books.

Clay, M. M. (1980b). *Reading: the patterning of complex behavior* (2nd Edition). New York: Heinemann Educational Books.

Dale, E. (1965). Vocabulary measurement: techniques and major findings. *Elementary English, 42,* 895–901, 948.

Danks, J. & Fears, R. (1979). In L. B. Resnick & P. A. Weaver (eds.), *Theory and practice of early reading* (Vol. 3). Hillsdale, NJ: Lawrence Erlbaum Associates.

Davidson, S.; Stickney, C. P.; & Weil, R. (1980). *Intermediate accounting concepts, methods and uses.* Hinsdale, IL: Dryden Press.

Downing, J.; Dwyer, C. A.; Feitelson, D.; Jansen, M.; Kemppainen, R.; Matihaldi, H.; Reggi, D. R.; Sakamoto, T.; Taylor, H.; Thakary, D. V.; & Thomson, D. (1979). A cross-national survey of cultural expectations and sex-role standards in reading. *Journal of Research in Reading, 2,* 8–23.

Durkin, D. (1966). *Children who read early: two longitudinal studies.* New York: Teachers College Press, Columbia University.

Durkin, D. (1974–75). A six-year study of children who learned to read in school at the age of four. *Reading Research Quarterly, 10,* 9–61.

Durkin, D. (1980). *Teaching young children to read* (3rd Edition). Boston: Allyn & Bacon.

Durkin, D. (1983). *Teaching them to read* (4th Edition). Boston: Allyn & Bacon.

Evans, M.; Taylor, N; & Blum, I. (1979). Children's written language awareness and its relation to reading acquisition. *Journal of Reading Behavior, 11,* 7–9.

Gibson, E. J. & Levin, H. (1980). *The psychology of reading* (3rd Edition). Cambridge, MA: MIT Press.

Ginsburg, H. & Opper, S. (1969). *Piaget's theory of intellectual development: an introduction.* Englewood Cliffs, NJ: Prentice Hall.

Goodman, K. S. & Goodman, Y. M. (1979). Learning to read is natural. In L. B. Resnick &

P. A. Weaver (eds.), *Theory and practice of early reading* (Vol. 1, pp. 137–54). Hillsdale, NJ: Lawrence Erlbaum Associates.

Groff, P. (1979a). Reading ability and auditory discrimination: a further consideration. *Academic Theory, 14,* 313–19.

Groff, P. (1979b). A critique of teaching reading as a whole-task venture. *Reading Teacher, 32,* 647–52.

Hammill, D. D. & McNutt, G. (1981). *The correlates of reading: the consensus of thirty years of correlational research.* Austin, TX: Pro-Ed Books.

Hare, V. C. (1984). What's in a word? A review of young children's difficulty with the construct "word". *Reading Teacher, 37,* 360–64.

Harris, A. J. & Sipay, E. R. *How to increase reading ability* (8th Edition). New York: Longman.

Harris, T. L. & Hodges, R. E. (eds.). (1981). *A dictionary of reading and related terms.* Newark, DE: International Reading Association.

Heathington, B. S. (1976). Scales for measuring attitudes. In J. E. Alexander & R. C. Filler (eds.), *Attitudes and reading* (pp. 27–32), Newark, DE: International Reading Association.

Hiebert, E. H. (1983). Knowing about reading before reading: preschool children's concepts of reading. *Reading Psychology, 4,* 253–260.

Inhelder, B. & Piaget, J. (1964). *The early growth of logic in the child.* New York: Norton.

Liberman, I. Y. & Shankwiler, D. (1980). In L. B. Resnick & P. A. Weaver (eds.), *Theory and practice of early reading* (vol. 2). Hillsdale, NJ: Lawrence Erlbaum Associates.

Loban, W. D. (1963). *The language of elementary school children.* Urbana, IL: NCTE.

Mason, J. M. (1980). When do children learn to read: an exploration of four year old children's letter and word reading competencies. *Reading Research Quarterly, 15,* 203–23.

Morphett, M. V. & Washburn, C. (1931). When should children begin to read? *Elementary School Journal, 31,* 496–503.

Nessel, D. & Jones, M. (1981). *The language experience approach to reading.* New York: Teachers College Press.

Ollila, L. O. (ed.). (1980). *Handbook for administrators and teachers: reading in the kindergarten.* Newark, DE: International Reading Association.

Ollila, L. O. (ed.). (1981). *Beginning reading instruction in different countries.* Newark, DE: International Reading Association.

Olson, A. V. & Johnson, C. (1970). Structure and predictive validity of the Frostig Development Test of Visual Perception in grades one and three. *Journal of Special Education, 4,* 49–52.

Piaget, J. (1963). *The origins of intelligence in children.* International Universities Press, 1952. Reprinted by Norton, New York.

Richek, M. A. (1977–78). Readiness skills that predict initial word learning using two different methods of instruction. *Reading Research Quarterly, 13,* 209–21.

Samuels, S. J. (1972). The effect of letter-name knowledge on learning to read. *American Educational Research Journal, 9,* 65–74.

Silvaroli, N. J. (1965). Factors in predicting children's success in first grade reading. In J. A. Figure (ed.), *Reading inquiry international* (vol. 10, pp. 296–98). Newark, DE: International Reading Association.

Smith, F. (1980). In L. B. Resnick & P. A. Weaver (eds.). *Theory and practice of early reading* (Vol. 2). Hillsdale, NJ: Lawrence Erlbaum Associates.

Stauffer, R. (1980). *The language experience approach to the teaching of reading* (2nd Edition). New York: Harper & Row.

Waller, G. T. (1977). *Think first, read later! Piagetian prerequisites for reading.* Newark, DE: International Reading Association.

4 Decoding and Comprehension

DECODING DEFINED ■ DEVELOPING CONTEXT KNOWLEDGE ■ DEVELOPING PHONIC KNOWLEDGE ■ DEVELOPING WORD STRUCTURE KNOWLEDGE ■ DEVELOPING DICTIONARY KNOWLEDGE ■ DEVELOPING SIGHT WORD KNOWLEDGE ■ HOW A COMPREHENSION FRAMEWORK AFFECTS INSTRUCTIONAL DECISIONS

. . . Miss Binney . . . was standing in front of the class holding up a brown paper sack with a big *T* printed on it . . . "Now who can guess what I have in this bag with the letter *T* printed on it? Remember it is something that begins with *T*. Who can tell me how *T* sounds?"

"T-t-t-t," ticked the kindergarten.

"Good," said Miss Binney. "Davey, what do you think is in the *b*ag?" Miss Binney was inclined to bear down on the first letters of words now that the class was working on the sounds letters make.

"Taterpillars?" said Davey hopefully.

Beverly Cleary, *Ramona the Pest* (New York: William Morrow & Co., 1968), p. 115.

I n chapter 4, you will learn about a second component of the reading comprehension process: decoding. This chapter will describe five different sources of information readers use to decode the pronunciations of words. In addition, this chapter will describe a wide range of instructional activities for developing each type of decoding knowledge. Finally, you will see how your developing framework of reading comprehension influences the nature of decoding instruction.

After reading this chapter, you will be able to

1. define decoding;
2. explain when decoding is and is not important for comprehension;
3. describe five different types of decoding knowledge;
4. identify at least two instructional activities for developing each of the five types of decoding knowledge;
5. indicate how your framework of reading comprehension influences instructional decisions about decoding.

DECODING DEFINED

decoding: The process of determining the oral equivalent (pronunciation) of a written word.

Decoding is the process used to determine the oral equivalent (pronunciation) of a written word. Decoding contributes to the comprehension process when determining the oral equivalent of a word helps a reader determine its meaning. Decoding knowledge is especially important for beginning readers. Being able to determine the oral equivalent of a word provides young readers with a reasonable opportunity to determine its meaning since many of the printed words they encounter are known in oral language. Within the elementary reading program, instruction in decoding skills receives the greatest attention during the primary grades (K–3). It receives relatively less emphasis during the intermediate grades (4–6).

Decoding does not contribute to the comprehension process when determining the oral equivalent of a word does not help a reader determine its meaning. Sometimes, for example, readers will encounter words with unfamiliar meanings as they explore new concepts and knowledge areas. Sounding out an unfamiliar word like *esophagus,* for example, does not help a young reader to comprehend unless the meaning of that word is already known or can be determined from context.

Readers use five different types of decoding knowledge to determine the oral equivalent of written words:

1. context knowledge
2. phonic knowledge
3. word structure knowledge
4. dictionary knowledge
5. sight word knowledge

Decoding instruction seeks to develop each type of knowledge and teaches students how to flexibly apply all aspects of decoding knowledge during reading comprehension. It is important to provide children with flexible and alternative methods for recognizing the oral equivalents of words so that when one strategy fails, alternative strategies can be employed quickly.

DEVELOPING CONTEXT KNOWLEDGE

The Content

Contextual information includes the meaning of the text surrounding a particular word and any related illustrations. Contextual information is useful to readers who often depend on **context knowledge** to determine the oral equivalent and the meaning of a word. Context knowledge consists of one's ability to use contextual information from the text in conjunction with background knowledge in order to determine the pronunciation and the meaning of a word. Readers sometimes use context knowledge when they are unable to recognize the pronunciation of a word from its spelling.

contextual information: The meaning of the text surrounding a particular word and any related illustrations.

context knowledge: The ability to use the contextual information and background knowledge to determine the pronunciation and meaning of a word.

Sarah went swimming in Nita's swimming _____.

In this example, you relied on the contextual information in the sentence along with your own background knowledge to determine that the missing word was *pool.* That is, you used your context knowledge. From the contextual information in the sentence you knew that the word was something in which one could go swimming and that it was a noun. Your background knowledge let you know that the word *pool* fit both conditions and, therefore, was a likely candidate. Readers can use context knowledge to recognize the pronunciation and meaning of a word without even perceiving the letters when there is sufficient contextual information to limit the possible choices and when they have appropriate background knowledge.

It is easy to demonstrate that readers use context knowledge during decoding, even when words are not left blank. Consider, for example, the following sentence.

A POINT TO PONDER

He will read your book after you have read it.

Notice that even though the same word, *read,* appears twice, you pronounced it differently each time. How does the contextual information differ at each location?

Instruction

Before children learn how to read, they have already developed some context knowledge from oral language experiences; children know how to use contextual information in conjunction with background knowledge to help them recognize spoken words. Helping children to use contextual knowledge during reading, then, does not mean teaching a new skill as much as it means teaching children not to abandon an existing skill when they interact with print. Many activities can help students see the utility of using contextual information to recognize words in print.

cloze tasks: Used to develop context knowledge. Presented as a piece of writing with at least one word deleted. Readers fill in the missing word.

Cloze Tasks. Cloze tasks are often used to develop context knowledge. A cloze task presents a reader with a piece of writing where at least one word has been deleted and replaced with a blank. The reader's task is to complete the blank with the missing word.

My mother comes home late at _____.

Cloze tasks provide opportunities for students to experience situations where they might be unable to recognize the pronunciation of a word from its spelling and must rely, instead, upon contextual knowledge.

When using cloze tasks to provide instruction in context use, teachers use commercial materials or sometimes create their own materials. In either case, you may provide instruction and practice on different aspects of context knowledge by varying one of several elements associated with the task: passage length, target word information, target word location, or the nature of the available contextual information.

One variable to consider manipulating for specific instructional purposes is the length of the cloze passage. It is possible to use a single sentence to create a cloze task. Another alternative is to use a longer piece of writing such as a paragraph, a story, or an article. Single sentences are especially useful for providing students with instruction and practice at using syntactic (word order) and vocabulary (word meaning) context. Longer selections can be used in addition to provide students with instruction and practice at using discourse context (meaningful relationships between sentences). Usually, longer selections will be easier than single sentences, although this depends greatly on which words are actually omitted. Notice how greater available contextual information at the discourse level makes the second passage substantially easier to complete.

1. "He knew how to ride a _____, but he had never had one of his own" (Rey, 1952, p. 6).
2. "He took George out to the yard, where a big box was standing. George was very curious. Out of the box came a bicycle. George was delighted; that's what he had always wanted. He knew how to ride a _____, but he had never had one of his own" (Rey, 1952, pp. 5–6).

Within longer selections, it is also possible to delete more than a single word, providing more opportunities to practice the use of contextual knowledge, especially at the discourse level.

"He took George out to the yard, where a big box was standing. George was very curious. Out of the _____ came a bicycle. George was delighted; that's what he had always wanted. He knew how to ride a _____, but he had never had one of his own" (Rey, 1952, pp. 5–6).

A second variable that may be manipulated for instructional purposes is the nature of the information available at target word locations. Traditionally, only a blank space is presented. The task can be made slightly easier, however, by providing the first letter or two of the target word. It can be made easier yet by placing two or more words underneath the blank and having students choose the correct word.

1. We went to the _____.
2. We went to the <u>st</u>_____.
3. We went to the _____.

                       run   store

If only a blank space is provided, students receive practice at using contextual information alone to recognize words. If the first letter or two of the target word is provided, students receive practice at simultaneously using contextual information and letter-sound information. The same is true, of course, if several words are available and students must pick the one that best fits the context.

When planning an instructional activity, you may also wish to consider the location of the target word. Putting the target word at the end of a sentence or passage provides practice at using preceding context to recognize a word. Usually, it also makes the task somewhat easier than when the target word appears at the beginning. Sometimes, however, you may wish to show children how to use the contextual information following an unknown word. In this case, locate the target word early in the sentence. Notice how different strategies are required in the following sentences:

1. A _____ is a person who delivers mail.
2. A person who delivers mail is a _____.

Finally, you may wish to manipulate the nature of the contextual information for specific purposes. Certain types of sentence patterns provide useful clues to readers attempting to recognize a word: definition patterns, comparison patterns, contrast patterns, and example patterns. It is important to show children how to take advantage of these types of sentence patterns by giving them guided practice with each type.

Definition patterns define the meaning of a word within the sentence, often with a clause following the word *is* or with an appositive phrase set off by commas or parentheses. Children need to be shown how to read around the troublesome word in order to acquire this information. Once students read the definition, they can usually recognize the word if it is in their oral vocabularies.

1. _____ is a force that keeps you from floating out into space.
2. The plane was _____, or made late, by the weather.
3. The _____ (a person who flies airplanes) enjoyed his job.

Comparison patterns compare one word or phrase with another. If a word at either location is hard to recognize, readers can acquire useful contextual information by reading words at the other location.

1. My ancient car is as _____ as this earth.
2. I don't _____ going to bed early. In fact, I hate it.

Contrast patterns contrast one word or phrase with another. If a word at either location is hard to recognize, readers can acquire useful information by reading words at the other location.

1. My sister is _____, unlike her noisy brother.
2. It is _____ during our winters, unlike the warm weather that you have.

Example patterns provide a reader with examples of the troublesome word. When the example follows the difficult word, readers need to learn how to read past the word in order to acquire this contextual information.

1. We saw several _____, but the Empire State Building was the tallest.
2. There are seven _____: Europe, Asia, North America, South America, Africa, Australia, and Antarctica.

deductive method: A method where the teacher first states an explicit rule and then uses examples to show how the rule operates.

inductive method: A method where the teacher first provides students with examples and guides students to discover and state the rule themselves.

Deductive and Inductive Methods. Two different instructional methods, or method frameworks, are possible when teaching context knowledge through cloze tasks: a deductive method or an inductive method. A **deductive method** is one where the teacher states a rule (When you cannot recognize a word, keep reading past the word and see if this information helps you.) and then shows students how the rule operates with several examples. An **inductive method** is one that provides students with several examples (A _____ is a person who teaches. A _____ is a person who works.) and then guides students to discover and state the rule themselves. Both instructional methods conclude with students practicing the particular aspect of context knowledge that was taught. Procedural outlines for both methods are listed here.

Deductive Instruction

1. *State the skill you want students to learn.*   Explicitly state the aspect of context knowledge that you want children to learn; for example, reading past a troublesome word.
2. *Provide several examples.*   Read each one aloud so students can see how this particular aspect of context knowledge is used.
3. *Provide guided practice.*   Have students do several similar cloze tasks orally. Check to make certain they have grasped what you have taught.
4. *Have students practice the skill independently.*   Give students written cloze tasks of a similar nature to be completed at their seats.

Inductive Instruction

1. *Provide an experience with the target skill.*   Allow students to read aloud previously prepared cloze sentences that all require the same type of context knowledge; for example, sentences that require readers to read past the missing word.

When using a deductive strategy, the teacher first states a rule and then shows students how it operates using several examples.

2. *Discover the target skill.* Have individuals explain how they were able to complete each sentence. List effective strategies.

3. *Provide guided practice.* Have students do several similar cloze tasks orally. Check to make certain they have grasped what you have taught.

4. *Have students practice the skill independently.* Give students similar written cloze tasks to be completed at their seats.

Additional Instructional Activities. In addition to using written cloze tasks to develop knowledge of contextual analysis, there are many other instructional activities that may be incorporated into your reading program. A few are listed here.

SAMPLE ACTIVITIES

Using Oral Cloze Tasks. When reading children's literature aloud to your class, periodically leave off the last word in a sentence and look for students to complete the sentence for you.

Presenting New Words in Context. As often as possible, introduce new vocabulary words to children within sentence contexts.

When they fight, pirates use sharp *swords.*

Before the ship could leave, the pirates had to pull up the *anchor.*

This encourages students to make context use a habit.

Generating Expectations for Words. When introducing a new reading selection, identify the topic (This is a story about pirates.) Then ask students to guess words that they might find in the story (*cutlass, galleon, sword, pirate, treasure,* or *shipwreck*). Write these words on the board. After reading the story, see how many of the words actually appeared.

Guiding Oral Reading. When children have difficulty recognizing a word during oral reading, suggest that they read the sentence over from the beginning and make a guess about what might make sense at that location. Then have them check to see if their guess is consistent with the initial letter. If useful contextual information follows an unknown word, encourage students to read past the word in order to take advantage of this information.

DEVELOPING PHONIC KNOWLEDGE

phonic knowledge: The knowledge of letter-sound relationships and the ability to blend sounds represented by letters.

Phonic knowledge consists of a reader's understanding of letter-sound relationships and the ability to put together, or blend, sounds represented by letters. Although English is a language without a perfect match between letters and sounds, knowledge of letter-sound relationships often is useful in recognizing many of the words we encounter, especially at beginning levels.

To understand the following section on phonic knowledge, familiarize yourself, first, with these terms.

- *grapheme* A grapheme is the smallest distinctive unit of graphic information in a written language. In English, it includes letters *(a, f, or g)*, numbers *(1, 2, or 3)*, punctuation marks (", ;, or .), and other symbols that are sometimes used (*, %, or $). Phonics instruction is only concerned with graphemes that are letters.
- *phoneme* A phoneme is the smallest distinctive unit of speech sound in a language. In English, it includes all of the distinctive sounds which we use in our language (for example, /k/, /f/, or /r/).
- *grapheme-phoneme relationships* While this term may refer to relationships between all types of graphemes and phonemes, in phonics instruction it refers only to relationships between letters and sounds. The term *grapho-phonic relationship* may also be used to capture the more limited nature of this relationship.

The Content

No other topic in reading inspires more controversy and less agreement than what the content of phonics instruction should be (Chall, 1983). The diversity of opinions stems largely from the fact that English does not have a perfect one-to-one relationship between its letters and sounds; many letters may represent several different sounds and many sounds may be represented by several different letters. In addition, no simple set of rules accounts for all of the letter-sound relationships existing in English; almost every phonic generalization has at least one exception. Note, for example, a common phonic generalization that many readers learn in school: "When two vowels are together, the first is long and the second is silent." Many exceptions exist for this generalization, especially words containing the vowels *au, ou, oi,* and *ie* such as *taught, drought, boil,* and *thief.*

That English does not have a perfect one-to-one relationship between letters and sounds has been used by some (Smith, 1978; Hittleman, 1983) to argue against the utility of extensive phonics instruction. On the other hand, there is a certain amount of consistency in the grapheme-phoneme relationships of English. Enough, at least, for others (Durkin, 1983; Harris & Sipay, 1985; Resnick & Beck, 1984) to argue in support of phonics instruction. Experts who advocate phonics instruction, however, all seem to have their own unique ideas about which specific grapheme-phoneme relationships need to be taught and how to state them. This text will present consonant and vowel generalizations that have the most use for readers (Clymer, 1963; Lesiak, 1984) and are most frequently included in instructional programs. If you wish other, more extensive treatments of the topic, Durkin (1983) and Burmeister (1983) may be consulted.

Consonants. The grapheme-phoneme relationship(s) for each of the following single consonants are often taught to young readers. The words next to each consonant illustrate the phoneme(s) children learn to associate with the appropriate grapheme. For example, the consonant grapheme *s* may represent the phoneme /s/ as in *sat*, /z/ as in *has*, /sh/ as in *sure*, or /zh/ as in *measure*. Also, note that each grapheme-phoneme relationship illustrated may often occur in either initial *(sat)*, medial *(ransom)*, or final position *(hits)*. Often, published instructional materials devote a separate lesson to teaching the same grapheme-phoneme relationship in each of these three positions.

b as in *boy*	*c* as in *cent* *cat*	*d* as in *did*	*f* as in *feet*
g as in *gem* *go*	*h* as in *home*	*j* as in *job*	*k* as in *king*
l as in *like*	*m* as in *make*	*n* as in *no*	*p* as in *pan*
q(u) as in *queen* *bouquet*	*r* as in *rat*	*s* as in *sat* *has* *sure* *measure*	*t* as in *time*
v as in *very*	*w* as in *we*	*x* as in *six* *exam* *xylophone*	*y* as in *yes*
z as in *zoo*			

The graphemes *c* and *g* are special cases of the single consonants since they can each represent two different phonemes depending on the following vowel. The generalizations for *c* and *g* likely to be taught include:

1. *c* often represents the beginning sound of *city* (/s/) before the letters *e, i,* and *y*. In other situations (after *a, o,* and *u*) it represents the beginning sound of *cat* (/k/).

/s/ or soft *c*	/k/ or hard *c*
c as in *cent*	*c* as in *cat*
as in *city*	as in *coat*
as in *cymbal*	as in *cut*

2. *g* often represents the beginning sound of *gem* (/j/) before the letters *e, i,* and *y*. In other situations (after *a, o,* and *u*) it represents the beginning sound of *gun* (/g/).

/j/ or soft *g*	/g/ or hard *g*
g as in *gem*	*g* as in *game*
as in *ginger*	as in *go*
as in *gym*	as in *gun*

Note: Some exceptions exist such as *finger, forget, forgive, get, girl,* and *give.*

Consonant clusters consist of two or three consonant graphemes that often appear together; for example, *st, th,* or *scr.* One type of consonant cluster, the **consonant digraph,** contains two different consonant graphemes representing a single phoneme (such as *sh, ck,* or *kn*). Some consonant digraphs represent phonemes not usually associated with either separate grapheme; for example:

ch as in *child*	*ng* as in *sing*	*ph* as in *phone*
as in *chorus*		
as in *chef*		
sh as in *should*	*th* as in *thin*	
	as in *the*	

Other consonant digraphs represent phonemes associated with one of the graphemes (for example, *kn, wr, ck, gn, mb,* or *gh*). Because the remaining grapheme is silent, these digraphs are called **silent letter combinations.** Common silent letter combinations include:

gn as in *sign*	*wr* as in *write*
kn as in *knit*	*mb* as in *comb*
ck as in *check*	*gh* as in *ghost*

A second type of consonant cluster is the **consonant blend.** This combination of graphemes represents a sound that combines, or blends, the phonemic qualities of each of the separate graphemes. Consonant blends include:

bl as in *blue*	*br* as in *brick*	*sc* as in *scare*
cl as in *close*	*cr* as in *cream*	*scr* as in *screen*
fl as in *fly*	*dr* as in *drop*	*sk* as in *skip*
gl as in *glass*	*fr* as in *free*	*sm* as in *small*
pl as in *play*	*gr* as in *green*	*sn* as in *snow*
sl as in *sleep*	*pr* as in *present*	*sp* as in *spot*
spl as in *splash*	*tr* as in *tree*	*sq* as in *squirrel*
	str as in *street*	*st* as in *still*
	thr as in *three*	*sw* as in *swim*
	spr as in *spring*	

consonant clusters: Two or three consonant graphemes that often appear together; for example, *st, th,* or *scr.*

consonant digraph: Two different consonant graphemes representing a single phoneme; for example, *sh, ck,* or *kn.*

silent letter combinations: Two or more different consonants where the phoneme normally associated with one grapheme is not heard; for example, *mb* or *kn.*

consonant blend: A consonant cluster representing a sound that combines the phonemic qualities of each of the separate graphemes; for example, *bl, br,* or *tr.*

consonant twin: Two identical graphemes that represent a single phoneme; for example, *dd, tt,* or *mm.*

A third type of consonant cluster is a **consonant twin.** Consonant twins (or consonant doubles) contain two identical graphemes. Consonant twins represent only a single phoneme, the phonemic quality normally associated with the particular grapheme. The exceptions usually are *cc* and *gg,* depending upon dialect. The set of consonant twins includes:

bb as in *robber*	*mm* as in *summer*
cc as in *raccoon*	*nn* as in *inn*
as in *succeed*	*pp* as in *happen*
dd as in *daddy*	*rr* as in *hurry*
ff as in *off*	*ss* as in *hiss*
gg as in *egg*	*tt* as in *mitt*
as in *suggest*	*zz* as in *buzz*
ll as in *fall*	

Vowels. There are four categories of single vowels often included in any program of phonics instruction: long vowels, short vowels, *r*-controlled vowels, and *y,* when it functions as a vowel. A **long vowel sound** is identical to the name of each of the five traditional vowel letters: *a, e, i, o,* and *u.* Long vowel sounds are sometimes indicated by a macron (a short horizontal line) over the vowel letter: *ā, ē, ī, ō, ū.* Long vowel sounds occur most frequently in two types of environments.

long vowel sound: A sound identical to the name of one of the five traditional vowel letters: *a, e, i, o,* and *u.*

1. A vowel letter usually has a long sound when it occurs at the end of a syllable. This is especially true for the vowel letters *e, o,* and *u (me, no,* and *tuber).*
2. A vowel letter may have a long vowel sound when it is followed by a consonant plus the letter *e (mane, theme, time, rope,* and *cute).* The final *e* in this pattern is usually silent.

short vowel sound: One of five vowel sounds at the beginning of *apple, egg, ink, octopus,* and *umbrella.*

The set of **short vowel sounds** is usually learned with a set of key words, each of which contains a short vowel sound at the beginning (see figure 4–1).

Short *a* as in *apple*
Short *e* as in *elephant*
Short *i* as in *ink*
Short *o* as in *octopus*
Short *u* as in *umbrella*

In many first grade classrooms, you will find a set of key word pictures above the chalkboard. The pictures help children to remember the appropriate short vowel sound for each letter. Short vowel sounds are sometimes indicated by a breve (a curved horizontal line) over the vowel letter: *ă, ĕ, ĭ, ŏ,* and *ŭ.* Short vowel sounds occur most frequently in syllables that end in a consonant or consonant cluster *(man-tle, let, win, ot-ter, bunt).*

FIGURE 4–1
Key words used to help students remember short vowel sounds

When a vowel is followed by *r* within a syllable, the vowel sound is neither long nor short. The sound of the vowel is strongly influenced by the following *r* sound. In this environment there may be as many as six different **r-controlled vowel sounds:** /ir/ as in *fur, bird,* or *her;* /ar/ as in *car, arm,* or *tar;* /or/ as in *corn,* or *sore;* /ear/ as in *gear;* /air/ as in *hair;* and /ure/ as in *sure.*

The final type of vowel sound occurs when **y functions as a vowel.** The letter *y* may function as a consonant in words like *yes.* In some environments, however, it may function as a vowel.

1. When *y* appears at the end of a word with more than one syllable, it usually stands for the long *e* sound *(sandy, baby,* or *sixty).*
2. When *y* appears at the end of a word with only one syllable, it usually stands for the long *i* sound *(try, my,* or *cry).*

Vowels, like consonants, often appear in clusters. **Vowel clusters** consist of two or three vowel graphemes that frequently appear together; for example, *ou, ee, ai, ew, oy.* Notice that both *w* and *y* may function as vowels when they appear in a vowel cluster. One type of vowel cluster is a **vowel digraph.** Like consonant digraphs, vowel digraphs contain two different graphemes that represent a single phoneme *(oo, au, ea,* or *oa).* Some vowel digraphs represent phonemes not usually associated with either separate grapheme.

r-controlled vowel sounds: Sounds that are strongly influenced by a following *r* sound.

y functions as a vowel: *Y* often functions as a vowel when it appears at the end of a word.

vowel clusters: Two or three vowel graphemes that frequently appear together; for example, *ou, ee, ai, ew,* or *oy.*

vowel digraph: A vowel cluster containing two different graphemes representing a single phoneme; for example, *oo, au, ea,* or *oa.*

oo as in *shoot*   ew as in *new*   aw as in *saw*   au as in *auto*
     (long)
as in *took*
     (short)

Other vowel digraphs represent a phoneme usually associated with one of the graphemes *(ay, ea, ee, oa, ai, ey, ei, ie,* or *ue)*.

A second type of vowel cluster results in a blending of two vowel sounds. Technically, these are called **diphthongs.** Sometimes they are called vowel blends to be consistent with similarly designated consonant patterns. Diphthongs include:

diphthongs: A vowel cluster representing a blending of two vowel sounds; for example, *oi* or *oy*.

oi as in *soil*   ou as in *mouse*
oy as in *toy*   ow as in *cow*

Instruction

Phonics instruction usually takes place in conjunction with a wide variety of commercially available materials. Sometimes instructional materials for developing phonics knowledge will be a part of a comprehensive published reading program. At other times a separate set of phonics materials will be used to either replace or supplement the materials in a school reading program.

synthetic approach: A phonics approach that first teaches separate grapheme-phoneme relationships and then teaches how to blend sounds to recognize a word.

Two major approaches to phonics instruction are incorporated into commercially available materials: synthetic and analytic. A **synthetic approach** to phonics instruction first teaches a number of separate grapheme-phoneme relationships (c = /k/, u = /u/, t = /t/, d = /d/, g = /g/, or o = /o/) and then teaches children how to combine or blend individual sounds in order to recognize a word (/k/ + /u/ + /t/ = *cut*, /d/ + /o/ + /g/ = *dog*). Synthetic approaches proceed from small parts to entire words.

According to Resnick & Beck (1984), instruction in combining or blending sounds within a synthetic approach should follow a five step procedure.

1. Model the blending procedure. Point to each letter separately, indicating the equivalent phoneme for each (c = /k/, u = /u/, t = /t/). Then slide your finger under the first portion of the word *(cu)* and say this blended sound (/ku/). Slide your finger under the final portion of the word *(t)* and say this sound (/t/). Slide your finger under the entire word and say the blended sound (/kut/). Circle the word with your finger and say, "The word is *cut.*"

2. Have children imitate the model with you. Maintain your use of verbal cues and finger cues to assist them.

3. Repeat step 2, but do not say either the sounds or the blends. Have students say these as you continue the verbal cues and finger cues.

4. Repeat step 3. This time, also remove the verbal cues, giving only finger cues.

5. Independent blending practice. Children independently perform the pointing, sounding, and blending steps.

Analytic approaches to phonics proceed in a direction opposite to that of synthetic approaches: from entire words to small parts. In an analytic approach, students are first taught to recognize a basic set of words as wholes (*cat, dog, on,* and so on). Then, these words are used to demonstrate grapheme-phoneme relationships such as "The letter *c* often represents the sound appearing at the beginning of the word *cat.* The letter *o* often represents the sound appearing at the beginning of the word *on.* The letter *t* represents the sound appearing at the end of the word *cat.* The letter *d* represents the sound appearing at the beginning of *dog.*" Finally, knowledge of the separate letter sound relationships is used to recognize new words such as *cot, dog,* or *cod.* Seldom are sounds isolated or is blending ability taught as a specific skill in an analytic approach.

analytic approach: A phonics approach that first teaches whole words and then uses these words to demonstrate separate grapheme-phoneme relationships.

Deductive and Inductive Methods. Two instructional methods, or methods frameworks, may be used to teach phonics knowledge: a deductive method and an inductive method. Each may be used within either a synthetic or an analytic approach to phonics. When teaching

A wide variety of methods exist to promote the development of phonic knowledge.

phonic knowledge in a deductive method, the teacher states a general rule ("Vowels in closed syllables usually represent the short sound") and then shows students examples of that rule *(cat, pet, sit, on,* or *funny).* When teaching phonic knowledge in an inductive method, children are provided with examples of words reflecting a common pattern *(my, try, sky,* and *fly)* and are then guided to discover the general rule ("*Y* at the end of one-syllable words usually represents the long *i* sound."). Both instructional methods conclude with students practicing the particular aspect of phonic knowledge that was taught. The following model activities demonstrate how deductive and inductive instructional methods would be used to teach an identical phonic generalization: hard *c.*

MODEL
LESSON

A Deductive Lesson in Phonics: Hard *C*

1. *State the Skill.* First, the teacher states the phonic generalization: "Sometimes you will find words with the letter *c* followed by *a, u,* or *o. C* followed by *a, u,* or *o* usually represents the sound of /k/. Look at these examples."
2. The teacher then reads or has students attempt to read the following words, pointing out that in each word the letter *c* is followed by either *a, u,* or *o* and that in each case the letter *c* represents the /k/ sound.

cat	cut	cot
can	cup	corn
cap	cub	come

3. *Guided Practice.* To determine if students have internalized the phonic generalization, the teacher might ask students to read a new set of words.

cab	cud	cob
car	cub	cod
camp	curl	coal

4. *Independent Practice.* The teacher explains how to do the following activity and lets children complete the task independently.

Draw a circle around every word where the letter *c* makes the same sound as the beginning sound in kite.

1. Can you come to the party?
2. Certainly. What should I bring?
3. Bring a batch of cinnamon cookies.
4. Bring a knife, too, so I can cut my cake.

Which letters follow *c* when it sounds like *k?* Write them here:

_____ .

An Inductive Lesson in Phonics: Hard *C*

1. *Provide an Experience with the Target Skill.* Write the following words on the chalkboard and ask or help the students to read them.

cat	*cut*	*cot*
can	*cup*	*corn*
cap	*cub*	*come*

2. *Discover the Target Skills.* Then ask questions to help children notice both the consistent sound represented by the letter *c* and the environment where this sound occurs: "What is the same in all of these words? Yes, they all begin with the letter *c.* Is the sound for *c* the same in all of these words? What sound does *c* make in these words? Do you notice anything else about these words? What letters follow the letter *c*? I wonder if the letter *c* always makes the sound of *k* when the next letter is an *a, u,* or *o*? Let's see. Does anyone else know a word that has a *c* in it?" Write other words on the board which have *c* followed by *a, o,* or *u* and represent /k/. Words which have *c* and are not followed by *a, o,* or *u* can also be used to show how the /k/ sound only occurs in certain environments. Ask if someone can make up a rule for the sound of *c* that accounts for all of the words they have seen with *c* in them; that is "*C* followed by *a, u,* or *o* usually represents the sound of /k/."

3. *Guided Practice.* Write a new list of words where *c* is followed by *a, u,* or *o* and test the utility of the new rule with students.

car	cube	coat
cab	cute	comb
cast	cure	coke

4. *Independent Practice.* To practice the use of this generalization, ask the students to complete an activity like the following.

> Draw a circle around every word where the letter *c* makes the same sound as the beginning sound in *kite.*
>
> **1.** Can you come to the party?
> **2.** Certainly. What should I bring?
> **3.** Bring a batch of cinnamon cookies.
> **4.** Bring a knife, too, so I can cut my cake.
>
> Which letters follow *c* when it sounds like *k*? Write them here:
>
> _____.

Additional Instructional Activities. Learning letter-sound relationships can be difficult for beginning readers. Thus, the development of phonic knowledge usually requires substantial amounts of repetition, review, and practice. It is thought that repetition, review, and practice lead students to develop the automatic use of letter-sound relationships during reading, freeing them to consider meaningful relationships between words and sentences.

Most instruction in phonics consists of either a synthetic or analytic approach using deductive and/or inductive methods. In addition to these general considerations, there are many different instructional activities you may use to help children develop phonic knowledge. Several are listed here.

SAMPLE ACTIVITIES

Sound Boxes. Place one letter (or letter cluster) representing a particular sound on the front of a small box. After introducing the target sound, have children cut pictures out of old magazines for words that contain the sound. Have students place their pictures in the box. Periodically, take out the pictures and check them in with the class. Ask students in the class if the particular sound occurs at the beginning, middle, or end of the word.

Sound Bags. Create a series of sound bags, each with a letter on the outside and one object inside beginning with the sound represented by that letter *(b = book, c = cup,* or *d = doll).* Each day introduce a new bag and have children guess what might be inside. Write down all of the students' guesses on the chalkboard. At the end of the day, just before students go home, take out the object and see who has correctly guessed the object.

Vowel Volumes. Make ditto masters for each vowel letter. Each page should contain one vowel letter and several words that begin with either the long or short sound for that letter. Have children cut out pictures from old magazines containing the sound represented by the target letter. Paste these pictures on the correct page. You, or the students, may wish to label each picture on each page. When pages for all of the vowels are completed, make a book cover and staple all the pages together. Give the books a title like *X's Short Vowel Volume* or *X's Long Vowel Volume.*

Make or Purchase a Phonics Concentration Game. Card pairs may consist of letters, letter combinations *(sh, oa,* or *e),* or words. To match a pair, require children to read the word or produce the correct sound. After introducing the game to the class, set up a round-robin team tournament putting one weaker reader with one stronger reader on each team.

Final Letter Patterns. To review consonant generalizations that have been previously taught, present a common final letter pattern such as *oot* on the chalkboard. Then write different initial consonant letters at the beginning (*sh, t, h, sc, r,* and so on) and have children read each new word *(shoot, toot, hoot, scoot,* and *root).*

General Principles for Phonics Instruction. Certain principles in phonics instruction apply regardless of your particular comprehension framework. If phonics is to be taught, students will benefit from your attention to several concerns.

1. Be consistent. It will help your students if you are consistent in the terms you use for instruction and in the way you state phonic generalizations.
2. Encourage students to be flexible in their application of phonic strategies. Students need to know that there are exceptions to every rule. They should also understand that alternative letter sound relationships are possible when one particular generalization fails to yield a familiar word.
3. Give more attention to consonants than vowels during instruction. Consonants tend to have more consistent grapheme-phoneme relationships than vowels.
4. Be certain that your students actually internalize phonic generalizations. Do not assume that students have internalized a generalization like the hard *C* rule when they are finally able to verbalize it. The point of learning any phonic generalization is to provide a strategy for determining the pronunciation of a difficult word, not to be able to parrot back a verbal rule.
5. Provide many opportunities for students to apply phonic generalizations in functional settings. Make certain your students have a chance to read widely and often outside of the regular instructional materials.

One reason that consonants must receive more attention than vowels is because consonants have more regular letter-sound relationships. A second reason is that consonants contribute more information to the decoding process. You can test this second reason yourself by attempting to read the following sentence with only the vowels and then with only the consonants available:

A POINT TO PONDER

——o——o——a————— ——e——e——a————y ——u———— ——e——ei——e
——o——e a——————e————io—— ————a— ——o——e———— ——u——i————
i——u————io——.

c——ns——n——nts g——n——r——ll—— m——st r——c————v—— m——r——
——tt——nt————n th——n v——w——ls d——r——ng ——nstr——ct————n.

Do vowels or consonants provide more information during the decoding process?

DEVELOPING WORD STRUCTURE KNOWLEDGE

The Content

word structure knowledge: A type of decoding knowledge that includes common structural patterns of letters and sound equivalents.

Word structure knowledge consists of knowledge of common structural patterns of letters and their sound equivalents. You often use word structure knowledge to recognize the oral equivalent of words, especially words with more than a single syllable such as *anthropomorphic, hopeful,* or *bidialectal.* You can tell that you are using word structure knowledge when you attempt to sound out the separate portions of each word *(an-thro-po-mor-phic, hope-ful, bi-di-a-lec-tal).* There are at least two types of word structure knowledge that may help a reader to recognize the oral equivalent of words: morphemic knowledge and syllabication knowledge.

morphemic knowledge: Knowledge of the smallest meaningful units of a language, or morphemes. One aspect of word structure knowledge.

Morphemic knowledge consists of a reader's knowledge of the smallest meaningful units of a language, or morphemes. Morphemes include prefixes such as *re-, bi-, anti-;* suffixes such as *-ful, -some, -ly;* and root or base words such as *hope, plane,* and *skill.* Knowledge of the oral equivalents for common morphemes is often useful during the decoding process. It allows readers to segment long and unfamiliar words into more manageable units. Typically, however, both the oral equivalents and the meanings for common morphemes are taught simultaneously. Thus, instructional practices designed to develop morphemic knowledge is usually considered within discussions of vocabulary knowledge. We will also follow this convention by considering instructional practices related to the development of morphemic knowledge in the next chapter. Recognize, however, that morphemic knowledge contributes to both decoding and vocabulary knowledge.

syllabication knowledge: Consists of the ability to determine syllable boundaries and use this information to assist decoding.

Syllabication knowledge consists of the ability to determine syllable boundaries and use this information to assist decoding. It is often necessary for applying phonic generalizations to words with more than a single syllable, particularly in relation to vowel sounds. This is true since many phonic generalizations, such as the following, are based on syllabic units.

> When there is a single vowel in a syllable that ends in a consonant, the vowel usually has the short sound (for example, *candle, pencil,* or *bottle).*

syllable: A unit of pronunciation containing only one vowel or diphthongized vowel sound.
open syllables: Syllables that end in a vowel sound (*sea, be-*tween, *o-*pen). Usually have long vowel sounds.
closed syllables: Syllables that end in a consonant sound (*set, run, af-*ter). Usually have short vowel sounds.

A **syllable** is a unit of pronunciation that contains only one vowel or diphthongized vowel sound. In writing, syllables may contain one vowel letter *(run)* or more than one vowel letter *(boat).* There are two types of syllables: open syllables and closed syllables. **Open syllables** end in a vowel sound *(sea, be-tween, o-pen).* They usually have a long vowel sound. **Closed syllables** end in a consonant sound *(set, run, af-ter).* Closed syllables usually have a short vowel sound.

Four syllabication generalizations are most frequently taught.

1. **The definition of a syllable.** A syllable is a continuous unit of sound that must contain a vowel and may also contain one or more consonants *(shoot* or *hap-py)*
2. **The VCCV rule.** When two consonants are surrounded by two vowels, the word is usually divided into syllables between the two consonants *(af-ter, com-pute,* or *im-por-tant)* and the first vowel is usually short.
3. **The VCV rule.** When a single consonant is surrounded by two vowels, the word is usually divided into syllables after the first vowel and the first vowel is usually long *(be-fore, pi-lot,* or *ho-tel)*. Note: Exceptions to this rule frequently occur when the consonant letter is *b (hab-it), r (chor-us), x (ex-it),* or *v (riv-er)*.
4. **The C + *le* rule.** When a word ends in a consonant plus *le*, the word is usually divided into syllables before the consonant *(ta-ble, tur-tle,* or *ap-ple)*.

Instruction

Initially, the concept of a syllable is almost always taught by having children listen to the continuous nature of syllabic units and having them clap out the separate syllables which they hear. This is usually taught early in the instructional program and may be accomplished with or without the students seeing the visual representation of the word. Eventually, however, the written words are presented so that children come to understand the notion that each syllable must have at least one vowel letter.

As with previous aspects of decoding knowledge, these four syllabication generalizations may be taught in either a deductive or an inductive fashion. The most frequent approach is to explicitly state the rules and teach the generalizations in a deductive fashion. Practice is often provided by having children divide a set of words into the appropriate syllables. A typical syllabication activity is presented in figure 4–2. There are two important problems with respect to instruction in syllabication. Each must be clearly understood by a teacher who intends to develop this knowledge source. First, recognize and communicate to students that the basic syllabication rules apply to vowels and consonants *and* to common consonant combinations that function together (digraphs and blends). With this understanding, students can correctly divide words like *im-press, fur-thest,* and *con-struct* according to rule 2 since *pr* and *str* are blends and *th* is a digraph. Words like *de-scribe, e-ther,* and *de-gree* can be correctly divided according to rule 3 since *scr,* and *gr* are blends, while *th* is a digraph. Amending the rules in this fashion requires that students are already familiar with the set of consonant digraphs and clusters.

FIGURE 4–2
A typical syllabication
activity

Directions: Read the following rules for dividing words into syllables.
Draw a line between the syllables in each word below.
Write the number of the rule you followed next
to each word.
The first has been done for you.

Rule 1: When two consonants are surrounded by two vow-
els, divide the word between the two consonants.
Examples: af/ter, com/fort, lad/der.
Rule 2: When one consonant is surrounded by two vowels,
divide the word after the first vowel.
Examples: me/ter, la/ter

fe/ver	_2_	butter	_____	yellow	_____
orbit	_____	fifty	_____	before	_____
happen	_____	over	_____	older	_____

A second problem is more difficult to solve: children typically attempt to solve syllabication tasks like figure 4–2 by first pronouncing
the word and then listening for the syllable break. Thus, they practice
recognizing the pronunciation of a word *before* dividing the word into
syllables. This is exactly the opposite of what the task intends to accomplish: dividing a word into syllables in order to assist decoding. As a
result, students seldom practice the use of syllabication generalizations
in a manner consistent with the way in which they are supposed to be
used. This problem has caused several authorities (Johnson & Pearson,
1984; Hittleman, 1983) to question the use of extensive instruction in
syllabication.

DEVELOPING DICTIONARY KNOWLEDGE

The Content

dictionary knowledge:
An aspect of decoding
knowledge that permits
use of a dictionary to determine word pronuncia-
tion and meaning.

Dictionary knowledge includes those skills necessary for using a dictionary to determine the pronunciation and meaning of a word. There are
a number of dictionary skills important for young children to acquire,
including but not limited to:

1. knowing how to determine word meanings, including secondary meanings;
2. knowing how to use phonetic respellings to recognize the pronunciation of a word;
3. knowing how to interpret accent marks in order to determine stress.

The last two skills are most directly related to decoding. Knowing how to use phonetic respellings and interpret accent marks provides students with yet another method for recognizing the pronunciations of words. Each will be discussed in this section.

When teaching dictionary skills related to decoding, keep in mind that a dictionary should only be used after other decoding strategies (context use, phonic analysis, and structural analysis) have failed. Comprehension is severely impeded whenever readers must stop and look up the oral equivalent of words they have failed to recognize. Indeed, in most situations, it is preferable to have readers ask someone how to pronounce a troublesome word, not look it up in a dictionary.

Using Phonetic Respellings. A **phonetic respelling** is used by a dictionary to represent the correct pronunciation of a word. There are two components to a phonetic respelling: the pronunciation key and the respelling itself (usually contained within parentheses). Children need to learn how to use the pronunciation key to be able to sound out the phonetic respelling in parentheses.

> **phonetic respelling:** A dictionary spelling system to represent the correct pronunciation of a word.

If dictionaries all used the same pronunciation key, a teacher's task would be straightforward—teach the key to students and have them practice using the key to determine pronunciations. Unfortunately, almost every dictionary uses a different key. Thus, what is important to teach students is not how to use any single system of phonetic respelling. Instead, it is important for children to learn how to use all systems of phonetic respelling by teaching them the general principles for using any pronunciation key.

Interpreting Accent Marks. An **accent mark (´)** is used to represent stress patterns in dictionaries. Sometimes both a primary (´) and a secondary (´) mark will be used to represent two levels of stress in a word (for example, *mul' ti pli ca' tion*). Knowing how to interpret accent marks is important in determining the pronunciation of an unknown word from a dictionary. It is especially important in cases where changes in accent produce a change in meaning, such as in *con'tent* and *con tent'*.

> **accent mark (´):** A symbol used in dictionaries to represent stress patterns.

Instruction

Using Phonetic Respellings. In learning how to use phonetic respellings, the basic learning task consists of understanding how pronunciation keys represent letter-sound relationships. Generally vowels present greater difficulties than consonants since they use unfamiliar diacritical marks as in ö, ô, or ō. Activities such as the following may be used to develop knowledge of phonetic respellings.

SAMPLE ACTIVITIES

■ Circle the word, or words, containing the same vowel sound as the word on the left. Check the answers in your dictionary. Write the entire respelling from your dictionary under the word(s).

ô as in *paw*	*dad, taught, bought, hope*
ōi as in *boy*	*oil, take, bowl, royal*
ûr as in *fur*	*bird, door, air, dirt*

■ Use the key below to determine the pronunciations for the following words. Match the pronunciations with the words on the right.

(fûr)	*four*
(kärv)	*curve*
(skâr)	*scar*
(măt)	*mate*
(māt)	*carve*
	scare
	fur
	mat

KEY

ûr as in *hurt*	är as in *bar*
âr as in *care*	ā as in *ate*
ă as in *at*	

■ Before students arrive at school, write a secret message on the chalkboard using the phonetic respelling system from the class's dictionary. Recognize those students who can decode the message by putting their names up on a "Dictionary Detectives" bulletin board. You may use messages like the following.

hwĕn yo͞o kăn rēd thĭs, rīt yōr năm ŏn ā pēs ŭv pāpûr ănd gĭv ĭt to͞o mē.

■ Show students how to write their names in a phonetic respelling. For younger students, use the key in the classroom's dictionary and, for one week, require that all names must be written in phonetic respelling. For older students make the same requirement during the week, but each day put a different key on the board for them to use.

Interpreting Accent Marks. Teach the concept that some syllables receive greater stress in pronunciation orally before you introduce written accent marks. This can be accomplished in tasks like the following.

Name Tapping. Say the names of students in your class. Show them how to tap their tables for each syllable: *Re-ne, Rob-ert, Da-vid, Fer-nan-do, Mar-y.* Then show students how to tap harder for the syllable that receives greatest stress: *Re-ne', Rob'-ert, Da'-vid, Fer-nan'-do, Mar'-y.*

Word Clapping. Have students clap out the syllables for words, clapping louder on the syllable that receives the greatest stress: *run'-ning, be-hind', af'-ter, af-ter-noon'.*

After students have developed the concept of stress and can identify stressed syllables in an oral mode, activities like the following may be introduced.

■ Show students how to mark the one syllable in a word that receives greatest stress. Then have them practice marking words that have already been divided into syllables: *in-deed, be-tween, li-brary,* or *car-riage.*

■ Have students decide which word should be used in each sentence.
   1. I am very _____ to stay here.
        con'-tent con-tent'
   2. I like the _____ in your paper.
        con'-tent con-tent'
   3. We can go in a _____.
        min'-ute min-ute'
   4. Another word for small is _____.
        min'-ute min-ute'

DEVELOPING SIGHT WORD KNOWLEDGE

The Content

Sight word knowledge consists of the ability to immediately recognize the pronunciation of words automatically, without conscious application of other strategies. You, as a mature reader, recognize most words by relying upon your extensive sight word knowledge. Beginning readers

sight word knowledge: An aspect of decoding knowledge that consists of the ability to recognize word pronunciation automatically.

have sight word knowledge that is far less developed. Often, they can only recognize the pronunciation of a word by consciously using other aspects of decoding knowledge: context knowledge, phonic knowledge, word structure knowledge, or dictionary knowledge.

If beginning readers understood that they must learn to recognize so many different words by sight they might give up the task in frustration. Memorizing the pronunciations of thousands of separate, yet highly confusing items, would be a tremendous feat for a young child. Fortunately, two factors make the task of developing sight word knowledge somewhat less demanding. First, a small set of words appear in writing with a high degree of frequency. By knowing the appropriate 200 to 400 words, young readers can immediately recognize fifty to sixty-five percent of the running words they encounter in almost any selection (Harris & Sipay, 1985). Learning to recognize these words by sight is a much less formidable challenge for beginning readers than setting out to memorize each and every word in our language. And it yields clear rewards. Being able to immediately recognize over half of the words one encounters substantially eases the comprehension task for a young student. Second, most of the other words incorporated into one's sight word knowledge base are acquired over a period of time as a reader repeatedly encounters them in print. Sight words are acquired more from use than by deliberate instruction, though many will be taught to students.

What appears to take place is that, initially, readers consciously attempt to recognize each new word using one of the other decoding strategies (phonic analysis, structural analysis, context use, and dictionary use). After a number of these experiences with a word, however, a reader seems to be able to recognize the word automatically, without using an overt strategy to determine its pronunciation. That is, the word becomes a part of that reader's sight word knowledge.

Among beginning readers, then, our object in developing sight word knowledge is a bit more limited than being able to recognize all the words in our language by sight. The sight word knowledge that needs to be developed at beginning stages consists of a limited set of words which share several characteristics. The first two characteristics are mandatory, the last two often, but not always, apply.

1. Frequency. Initial sight words should appear very frequently in print. Words like *is, a, to,* and *she* are much more likely candidates to be taught as initial sight words than words like *ray.*
2. Familiarity. The primary meaning of initial sight words should be familiar to beginning readers from their knowledge of oral language. It would serve no purpose to teach young children to recognize the pronunciations of words whose meanings are unfamiliar to them.
3. Low phonic regularity. Words taught as initial sight words often can not be recognized by resorting to phonic analysis. Words like *one, some, where,* and *said* appear frequently and have pronunciations

that are inconsistent with the vowel generalizations taught in phonic analysis. They are, therefore, more likely to be included in an initial sight word list than words that appear with equal frequency but can be recognized by applying a set of phonic generalizations.

4. No visual meaning. Many initial sight words contain no visual meaning *(a, of, could, may,* or *because).* This is true since some of the most frequent words in our language are **function words;** words whose meanings depend on the function they serve in specifying relationships among other words. Function words include forms of the *to be* verb, conjunctions, articles, auxiliary verbs, pronouns, and prepositions. They are often called the "glue words" of our language since they carry little meaning by themselves but cement the important relationships between the more meaningful words of our language.

> **function words:** Words that facilitate comprehension by connecting other words and phrases.

Which specific words, though, need to be taught? Here you have at least two different options. Comprehensive reading programs usually have their own list of words that students are expected to master as sight words. If you find yourself in a school that has adopted a particular reading series you may wish to strictly follow this list. Or, you may wish to rely on a sight word list based on a wider range of reading material, not solely on the stories found in a particular reading program. There are a number of different lists that may be used. Some sample selections in several basal programs to determine the most frequent words. Others sample a wider range of written material. Figure 4–3 presents one of the lists that sampled a wider range of reading selections. This list includes words appearing frequently in the oral language of kindergarten and first grade students and in printed English. Others by Fry (1980), Dolch (1960), and Harris & Sipay (1985) may also be consulted.

Instruction

Teaching in Context. Whenever possible, present sight words within sentence contexts. There are several reasons for this. First, children are less likely to be confused about a word's meaning when it appears in a sentence or phrase. The potential vocabulary confusion when words are presented in isolation is greatest among words that look or sound alike yet have different meanings such as:

1. The book was *red.* The book was *read.*
2. The play was *close.* The play will not *close.*

A second reason for initially presenting sight words in context is to more closely approximate the actual reading task. As much as possible, it is important to establish the habit of using context, even when the purpose of instruction is immediate word recognition. Always presenting

Johnson's First-Grade Words

a	day	had	make	really	under
above	days	hand	making	red	up
across	did	hard	man	right	very
after	didn't	has	may	room	want
again	do	have	me	run	wanted
air	don't	he	men	said	was
all	door	help	miss	saw	way
am	down	her	money	school	we
American	end	here	more	see	well
and	feet	high	most	seen	went
are	find	him	mother	she	what
art	first	his	Mr.	short	when
as	five	home	must	six	where
ask	for	house	my	so	which
at	four	how	name	some	who
back	gave	I	never	something	why
be	get	if	new	soon	will
before	girl	I'm	night	still	with
behind	give	in	no	table	work
big	go	into	not	than	year
black	God	is	now	that	years
book	going	it	off	the	yet
boy	gone	its	old	then	you
but	good	it's	one	there	your
came	got	just	open	these	
can		keep	or	they	
car		kind	out	think	
children		let	over	this	
come		like	past	those	
could		little	play	three	
		look	point	time	
		love	put	to	
				today	
				too	
				took	
				top	
				two	

Johnson's Second-Grade Words

able	called	great	need	same	until
about	change	group	next	say	us
almost	church	hands	nothing	says	use
alone	city	having	number	set	used
already	close	head	of	should	water
always	company	heard	office	show	were
America	cut	idea	on	small	west
an	different	knew	only	sometimes	while
another	does	know	other	sound	whole
any	done	last	our	started	whose
around	each	leave	outside	street	wife
away	early	left	own	sure	women
because	enough	light	part	take	world
been	even	long	party	tell	would
believe	ever	made	people	their	
best	every	many	place	them	
better	eyes	mean	plan	thing	
between	face	might	present	things	
board	far	morning	real	thought	
both	feel	Mrs.	road	through	
bought	found	much		together	
by	from	music		told	
	front			town	
	full			turn	

FIGURE 4–3
Johnson's first- and second-grade word lists

words in isolation sometimes provides children with the mistaken idea that reading is simply recognizing the pronunciations of separate words. Slow, inefficient, word-by-word reading without concern for comprehension is sometimes the result.

A Traditional Whole-Word Method. Walk into most first- or second-grade classrooms and you are likely to see initial sight word instruction follow a **traditional whole-word method.** This is a method framework devised to teach words as whole units to beginning readers. According to Durkin (1983), whole-word methods often follow several steps.

1. Write, or present, the new word for children to see (in context).
2. Read, or have children read, the entire sentence. Have children read the new word.
3. Point to the new word. Have students read, spell, and reread it.
4. Check to make certain the meaning is understood.
5. List similar appearing words. Discuss similarities and differences in appearance.
6. Erase all but the new word. Have students read, spell, and reread it.

It is crucial during sight word instruction to make certain that students actually look at each word as you present it. Often this is overlooked. Calling students' attention to the spelling is often used to direct their attention to the word on the board. Usually, no more than three or four words are presented in a single session (Jolly, 1981).

After teaching the sight words for any particular lesson, some type of practice activity follows. A number of different types of activities may be used.

> **traditional whole-word method:** A methods framework devised to teach words as whole units to beginning readers.

SAMPLE ACTIVITIES

Sight Word Cards. Give each student a set of small cards with one sight word written on each card. Have students follow your oral directions such as:

1. Put your finger above/below the word *some*.
2. Draw a line/circle with your finger under/around the word *one*.
3. Turn over the card with *where* on it. Turn it back.
4. Spell the word *some*. Write it with your finger on the table.
5. Give me the card with the word *where* on it.

Sight Word Practice Pages. Make and duplicate sets of sight word practice pages (see figure 4–4). Give students directions like the following:

1. In line 1 draw a straight line under the word *here*.
2. In line 1 draw a circle around the word *a*.
3. In line 1 draw an *X* under the word *there*.

4. In line 1 draw a box around the word *here.*

5. In line 2 draw a straight line under the word *book.*

FIGURE 4–4
A sight word practice
page

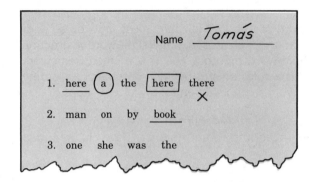

Word Banks. Sight word knowledge may also be developed through the use of word banks. Word banks consist of small, index card boxes (shoe boxes make an inexpensive substitute) with index cards or computer cards inside. Words that children have not yet learned are written on the cards by the teacher and practiced individually or with a partner. On one side of the card, words may be written in isolation. On the other side of the card, words may be written in context (see figure 4–5).

When a sufficient number of words are accumulated, they are organized either on an alphabetical basis or by categories. Often word banks are used in student-centered programs where the students themselves decide which words they need to learn. Sometimes word banks are used in conjunction with writing instruction. In this case, the teacher will write a new word on a card whenever a child asks for its spelling.

FIGURE 4–5
A word bank for sight
words

Sight Word Envelopes. Another method to develop initial sight word knowledge consists of using sight word envelopes, illustrated in figure 4–6. Sight word lists are prepared in a block on ditto masters, duplicated for the entire class, and then cut out and placed in separate envelopes for each student. On one side, a sight word is written in context. On the other side, the same sight word is written in isolation. Students practice, alone or with a friend, reading the sentences or the individual words. The teacher, on a regular basis or when a child requests, "checks in" students' ability to quickly recognize the words in their envelopes. When a student correctly recognizes one of the words, the teacher places a small dot in the corner of the slip of paper with the sight word on it. When a student has correctly recognized a word twice in context and twice out of context (that is, when two dots appear on each side) they can remove the slip from their envelope. When all of the slips from a set of sight words are removed, the date and the description of the sight word set (for example, SET III) are recorded on the front of a student's envelope. This allows you, at a glance, to monitor the progress of individual students and provide additional instructional time for those who require it.

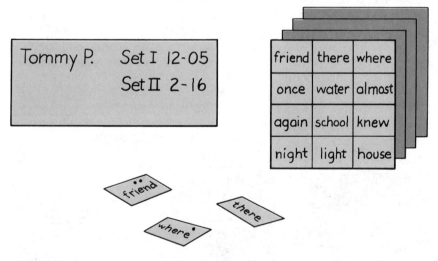

FIGURE 4–6
A sight word envelope

Sight Word Games. If you use a bit of imagination, the number and types of sight word games are almost limitless. Almost any type of game which the students enjoy (football, basketball, baseball, and others) can be translated into a board game with successful sight word recognition used to advance or score points. Almost any card game that is popular with children (Old Maid, Crazy Eights, or Fish) can also be translated into a sight word recognition activity by making cards with sight words rather than numbers or characters. Sight Word Lotto, Sight Word Bingo,

Sight Word Dominoes, or Sight Word Candy Land are also possible. Finally, many TV game shows can be translated into a sight word context. An especially popular format replicates the game show Concentration. Ask the students in your class for their favorite game show, athletic activity, card game, or board game and then translate these into sight word equivalents. Many of these games are also available commercially.

Daily Development of Sight Word Knowledge. An aphorism known to most reading teachers is "The best way to learn how to read is to read." There is a great deal of sound advice in this statement. The more opportunities to read real texts, the more students will encounter the frequently appearing words of our language. Sight word knowledge promotes the development of reading, but reading also promotes the development of sight word knowledge.

There are many opportunities to develop sight word knowledge within any classroom. Labeling objects, pictures of objects, and art work; and prominently displaying weather charts, calendars, and job charts present excellent opportunities to give children exposure to the sight words you want them to know. Creating a literacy environment will do much to accomplish your objectives in developing sight word knowledge. Writing activities, in particular, create excellent opportunities. Reading your own words and the words of others enhances any program of sight word instruction.

A classroom environment provides many meaningful opportunities to develop sight word knowledge.

**A POINT
TO PONDER**

You use all five types of decoding knowledge described here. You are not likely, however, to be explicitly aware of the nature of your decoding knowledge. To help make your tacit knowledge about decoding explicit you should read the following passages *after* you have finished reading this paragraph. Consciously attend to the decoding behavior you exhibit at each of the italicized target word locations. (Try not to look at these words before you read each paragraph). Each target word will require that you use at least one type of decoding knowledge. Which types of decoding knowledge did you use at each target word location? Did you use more than a single type of decoding knowledge in order to recognize a word? What are the characteristics of words you recognized by sight? By contextual analysis? By phonic analysis? By structural analysis?

1. "*When* Mr. Bilbo Baggins of Bag End announced that he would shortly be celebrating his eleventy-first birthday with a party of special magnificence, there was much talk and excitement in Hobbiton" (J. R. R. Tolkien, *The Fellowship of the Ring*. New York: Ballantine, 1965, p. 43).
2. "The charge is confirmed by three people only—the two brothers of the prisoner and Madame *Svyetlov*" (F. Dostoevski *The Brothers Karamazov*. New York: The New American Library, 1957, p. 639).
3. "You too have seen our city's affliction, caught
   In a tide of death from which there is no escaping—
   Death in the fruitful flowering of her soil;
   Death in the pastures; death in the womb of woman;
   And pestilence, a fiery demon gripping the city,
   Stripping the house of *Cadmus*, to fatten hell
   With profusion of lamentation" (Sophocles, *The Theban Plays,* Baltimore: Penguin Books, 1965, p. 26).
4. "She raised such a din
   That finally her uncle, the doctor, gave in
   And he told her just where she could find such a pill
   On a pill-berry vine on the top of a *hill*"
   (T. S. Geisel, *Yertle the Turtle and Other Stories*. New York: Random House, 1958, p. 35).

HOW A COMPREHENSION FRAMEWORK
AFFECTS INSTRUCTIONAL DECISIONS

You now have a clear understanding of decoding and the major sources of knowledge that contribute to the decoding process: contextual knowledge, phonic knowledge, word structure knowledge, dictionary knowledge, and sight word knowledge. Recall that instructional decisions in reading are often influenced by the type of comprehension framework you possess. With respect to instruction in decoding, decisions in three areas depend greatly upon the type of comprehension framework you currently possess: the amount of time to spend developing decoding knowledge, the content of decoding instruction, and how decoding should actually be taught. Now that you have acquired an understanding of the range of instructional possibilities for developing decoding knowledge, it is possible to see how your comprehension framework affects decisions in these three areas.

How Much Time Should I Spend Teaching Decoding?

One important decision regarding decoding instruction is how much time to spend teaching it. Should more time, for example, be spent developing decoding knowledge, vocabulary knowledge, syntactic knowledge, or discourse knowledge? Deciding about the relative importance of decoding instruction within the total reading program is determined largely by your answer to the first question in a comprehension framework: How does one read? The constraints on this instructional decision are due to the different assumptions inherent in each type of explanation for how one reads. Table 4–1 summarizes the assumptions behind each explanation for how one reads. It also indicates the effects of each set of assumptions on how much time should be spent helping children to develop decoding knowledge.

To the extent that you possess a text-based explanation for how one reads, you are likely to place greater emphasis on decoding instruction than any other aspect of reading instruction. Because you assume that meaning exists more in the text than in the meaning a reader might bring to a text, you believe that strong decoding skills lead to successful translation of text meaning. You do not believe that readers' expectations for upcoming words contribute greatly to the decoding process.

To the extent that you possess more of a reader-based explanation for how one reads, you are likely to feel that decoding is the least important portion of your instructional program. Since you believe that meaning exists more in what a reader might bring to a text than in the text itself, you believe that comprehensive discourse, syntactic, and vocabulary knowledge lead to accurate expectations for upcoming words. Thus, the development of decoding knowledge only receives minimal attention. Greater instructional time is spent on tasks promoting the development of discourse, syntactic, and vocabulary knowledge.

To the extent that you possess an interactive explanation for how one reads, decoding becomes an integral portion of your instructional program, receiving as much attention as all other aspects. Because you believe that meaning exists both in the text and in the meaning a reader might bring to the text, you devote relatively equal amounts of time developing decoding, vocabulary, syntactic, and discourse knowledge.

Which Aspects of Decoding Knowledge Should I Teach?

A second decison you must make as a teacher concerns the particular aspects of decoding knowledge that you will emphasize in your instruc-

TABLE 4–1

Two instructional decisions influenced by your explanation for how one reads: How much time should I spend teaching decoding knowledge? and Which aspects of decoding knowledge should I teach?

With this explanation for how one reads	You believe these assumptions about how one reads	You will probably spend this much time on decoding instruction	And you will probably emphasize these aspects of decoding
Text-based	1. Meaning exists more in the text. 2. Reading is translation. 3. Reading begins with lower level knowledge sources (e.g., decoding knowledge).	Much	1. Phonic knowledge 2. Word structure knowledge 3. Dictionary knowledge 4. Sight word knowledge
Reader-based	1. Meaning exists more in what the reader brings to the text. 2. Reading is expectation. 3. Reading begins with higher level knowledge sources (e.g., discourse, syntactic and vocabulary knowledge).	Little	1. Context knowledge
Interactive	1. Meaning exists in both the text and in the reader. 2. Reading is both translation and expectation. 3. Reading results from the interaction between text and reader which takes place simultaneously at each knowledge source.	Roughly the same amount of time as you devote to developing vocabulary, syntactic, and discourse knowledge	1. Context knowledge 2. Phonic knowledge 3. Word structure knowledge 4. Dictionary knowledge 5. Sight word knowledge

tional program: context knowledge; phonic knowledge; word structure knowledge; dictionary knowledge; or sight word knowledge. Here, again, the answer to this question is strongly influenced by your explanation for how one reads. This is also demonstrated in table 4–1.

Because a text-based explanation assumes that the direction of processing proceeds from lower to higher levels and that reading is largely a translation process, context knowledge and the use of contextual analysis is not strongly emphasized. Contextual analysis, you will recall, involves using higher-level vocabulary, syntactic, and discourse knowledge to facilitate decoding through the generation of expectations. This is inconsistent with the assumptions of a text-based explanation; that is, that the reading process proceeds from lower to higher levels as the reader translates the print on the page into meaning. Teachers with more of a text-based explanation tend to emphasize instruction in phonic knowledge, word structure knowledge, dictionary knowledge, and sight word knowledge. They tend not to emphasize the development of context knowledge, nor do they often encourage children to use contextual analysis strategies in order to recognize words.

A reader-based explanation assumes that the direction of processing proceeds from higher to lower levels as a result of progressively refined expectations. Teachers with a mostly reader-based explanation emphasize the development of contextual knowledge and encourage children to use contextual analysis strategies in order to recognize words. They tend not to emphasize the development of the knowledge sources important for translation: phonic knowledge, word structure knowledge, dictionary knowledge, or sight word knowledge. It is not unusual to find some phonic knowledge taught, but this usually consists of a limited set of letter sound relationships such as initial consonants and consonant clusters. Initial consonants and consonant clusters are taught in the belief that they are sufficient for readers to confirm well-constrained expectations.

An interactive explanation assumes that processing takes place simultaneously at all levels. Thus, all five aspects of decoding knowledge receive approximately equal attention. The decoding portion of the reading program will include instruction in contextual analysis, phonic knowledge, word structure knowledge, dictionary knowledge, and sight word knowledge. In addition to developing all five aspects of decoding knowledge, teachers with more of an interactive explanation for how one reads encourage students to flexibly apply all aspects of decoding knowledge during reading comprehension. Children are shown how to attempt alternative strategies during decoding when either one strategy or another fails.

How Should I Teach Decoding Knowledge?

How much relative time to spend teaching decoding knowledge and which aspects of decoding knowledge to teach are relatively global decisions. They do not tell you exactly which of the instructional activities or approaches described in this chapter should be used. They are, nevertheless, important preliminary decisions.

The answer to the more specific question of how to teach decoding knowledge is determined largely by your answer to the second question associated with a comprehension framework: How does reading ability develop? Mastery of specific skills, holistic language learning, and differential acquisition explanations for development all have different instructional consequences because each explanation is based on a different set of assumptions. Table 4–2 summarizes the assumptions behind each explanation of how reading ability develops. It also indicates how these assumptions influence decisions about how to teach decoding.

Mastery of Specific Skills. Teachers with more of a mastery of specific skills explanation for development favor learning experiences for children that are largely deductive in nature and focus on specific skills. Deductive methods would be used to teach context knowledge, phonic knowledge, word structure knowledge, or dictionary knowledge. The traditional whole-word method described in this chapter would be favored for developing initial sight word knowledge.

TABLE 4–2
How should I teach decoding knowledge?

With this explanation for how one reads	You believe these assumptions about reading	And you will probably favor these types of instructional activities
Mastery of Specific Skills	1. Reading ability develops as students master specific reading skills. 2. Reading ability develops as students are taught deductively.	Whenever possible, deductive instruction.
Holistic Language Learning	1. Reading ability develops as students engage in meaningful, functional and holistic experiences with print. 2. Students learn about reading in a largely inductive fashion.	Whenever possible, inductive instruction. In addition, many functional, meaningful, and holistic experiences with print are provided to develop a large sight word base.
Differential Acquisition	1. The assumptions of a mastery of specific skills explanation apply more to lower ability students; the assumptions of a holistic language learning explanation apply more to higher ability students.	Lower ability students receive more deductive learning opportunities. Higher ability students receive more inductive learning opportunities.

Holistic Language Learning. Teachers with more of a holistic language learning explanation for development favor learning experiences that are largely inductive in nature. Context knowledge, phonic knowledge, or word structure knowledge would be taught with inductive methods. Dictionary knowledge would be either taught inductively or taught individually as each child found a functional reason for acquiring these skills.

Teachers with a mostly holistic language learning explanation for development would probably find three sight word activities most consistent with their beliefs: word banks; sight word games; and the development of sight word knowledge through daily classroom life. When using word banks, each child, rather than the teacher, would determine which words would be entered. Sight word games would not be seen as only providing practice and reinforcement opportunities; they would be viewed as important learning experiences in their own right. More than either of these two activities, though, a teacher with a holistic language learning framework would probably rely upon developing sight word knowledge through daily classroom life. Reading widely and interacting with print throughout the classroom would be viewed as integral to developing a large sight word base.

Differential Acquisition. Teachers with a mostly differential acquisition explanation for development tend to vary instruction according to the proficiency level of their students. Less proficient readers tend to receive deductive instruction consistent with a mastery of specific skills explanation. More proficient readers tend to receive inductive learning opportunities consistent with a holistic language learning explanation.

THE MAJOR POINTS

1. Decoding is the process that readers use to determine the oral equivalent of a written word. It contributes to the comprehension process when determining a word's pronunciation helps a reader to determine its meaning. Decoding is especially important for beginning readers.
2. Readers use at least five different types of decoding knowledge to determine the oral equivalent of written words: context, phonic, word structure, dictionary, and sight word knowledge.
3. A variety of instructional activities may be used to develop each type of decoding knowledge. Deductive and inductive methods may often be used to teach decoding knowledge.
4. Teachers with more of a text-based explanation for how one reads emphasize decoding instruction and spend time teaching phonic, word structure, dictionary, and sight-word knowledge. Teachers with more of a reader-based explanation do not spend much time on decoding. They tend to only teach context knowledge. Teachers with more of an interactive explanation spend equal time on decoding

and other skill areas. All five aspects of decoding knowledge are often taught.

5. Generally, teachers with a mastery of specific skills explanation favor deductive methods. Teachers with a holistic language learning explanation favor inductive methods and view functional classroom interactions with print as integral to developing decoding knowledge. Teachers with a differential acquisition explanation tend to favor deductive methods for less proficient readers and inductive methods for more proficient readers.

**QUESTIONS
AND
ACTIVITIES**

1. The following teaching suggestion appears in the teacher's manual of a popular reading series. Notice how it combines both inductive and deductive instructional strategies. Which portion of the lesson is taught inductively? Which portion is taught deductively?

"Before class time write the following riddle on the chalkboard:

I'm in step but not in stop.
I'm in get but not in got.
I'm in men but not in man.
What letter am I?

Call on volunteers to read the riddle and to supply the answer if they can. If the answer isn't forthcoming, underline the letter *e* in *step, get,* and *men,* reading each word as you do so. Tell the children that the sound heard in the middle of these words is a short vowel sound. Confirm the similarity of sound by having all three words read together." (Laidlaw, 1980, p. T163)

How could the entire lesson be taught inductively?

2. Test the claim made in this chapter that fifty to sixty-five percent of the running words in writing consist of the same 200 to 300 high-frequency sight words. Select two 100-word passages from children's literature or stories from a basal reader. What is the average percentage of words from the passages appearing in the list in figure 4–3? Do the same type of analysis with material that you frequently read such as newspapers or textbooks. Is the claim supported? What differences did you find between the two sets of material? Speculate on the implications of your results for instructional decision making.

3. When teaching contextual analysis with cloze tasks, it is important to match children's learning tasks with their learning needs. In the following cloze passages, determine which information sources are required to successfully complete each task: discourse, syntactic, and/or vocabulary information.

   a. In the summer, I like to _____ swimming, hiking, and fishing.

    b. The owl flew so quietly that he didn't make a _____.

    c. A boy got on the sled. Then the sled went fast.
A girl got on the sled. Then the sled went fast.
A bird got on the _____. Then the sled went fast.
A snake _____ on the sled. Then the sled went _____.
Then they all fell off.

How could each task be made easier?

4. Which syllabication generalizations apply to the following words?

> *buggy*   *enter*   *trouble*
> *evil*   *uncle*   *after*

Did you make this determination by analyzing the letter patterns in each word or did you first say each word to yourself? What does this suggest for how students perform during word structure learning tasks? How would you attempt to overcome the problem?

5. Consider the following list of decoding skills which are taught in one reading series. Match up the name of the skill with the decoding knowledge source it develops: context knowledge, sight word knowledge, phonic knowledge, or word structure knowledge.

    a. Recognizes mastery words in isolation and in context.

    b. Decodes the appropriate sound for *f*.

    c. Uses picture context.

    d. Uses meaning and syntax to recognize words.

    e. Uses syllables to recognize a word.

    f. Knows that one sound is represented by different letters.

    g. Knows the *r*-controlled vowel sounds.

    h. Recognizes the common words: *the, a, one, he, she, here, we, run,* and *goes.*

6. Describe the comprehension framework of a second-grade teacher who made the following instructional decisions about decoding:

    a. Decoding will receive far greater attention than the development of vocabulary, syntactic, or discourse knowledge.

    b. Within decoding instruction, the following will be developed: sight word knowledge, phonic knowledge, dictionary knowledge, and word structure knowledge. Context knowledge will not receive much attention.

    c. The traditional whole-word method will be used to develop sight word knowledge.

    d. A deductive method will be used to teach phonic knowledge, word structure knowledge, and dictionary knowledge.

7. Are teachers who make the following instructional decisions being consistent with their framework of reading comprehension? Why or why not?

a. Decoding will receive equal instructional emphasis compared to developing other knowledge sources important to the comprehension process.

b. Within decoding instruction, developing context knowledge will be a priority. Developing sight word knowledge, dictionary knowledge, phonic knowledge, and word structure knowledge is not viewed as important.

c. A traditional whole word methodology will be used to teach initial sight word knowledge.

d. Inductive strategies will be used to develop context knowledge.

FURTHER READING

Durkin, D. (1983). *Teaching them to read.* (4th Edition). Boston: Allyn-Bacon.

A reading methods text that tends to emphasize the importance of decoding instruction, especially to young readers. Contains several useful chapters on decoding instruction.

Fry, E. & Sakiey, E. (1986). Common words not taught in basal reading series. *The Reading Teacher, 39,* 395–98.

Identifies several hundred very common words not taught in basal reading programs that teachers may wish to include in their reading programs.

Johnson, D. D. & Pearson, P. D. (1984). *Teaching reading vocabulary* (2nd Edition). New York: Holt, Rinehart and Winston.

Describes a wide range of instructional activities for promoting the development of decoding and vocabulary knowledge.

Jolly, H. B., Jr. (1984). Teaching basic function words. In A. J. Harris & E. R. Sipay (eds.) *Readings on reading instruction.* (3rd Edition) New York: Longman.

Presents several principles and strategies to follow when teaching initial sight words to children.

Lesiak, J. (1984). There is a need for word attack generalizations. In A. J. Harris & E. R. Sipay (eds.) *Readings on reading instruction* (3rd Edition). New York: Longman.

Defines thirty-two high-utility phonic, syllabication, and accent generalizations.

REFERENCES

Burmeister, L. E. (1983). *Foundations and strategies for teaching children to read.* Reading, Mass.: Addison-Wesley.

Chall, J. S. (1983). *Stages of reading development.* New York: McGraw-Hill.

Cleary, B. (1968). *Ramona the pest.* New York: Scholastic Book Services.

Clymer, T. (1963). The utility of phonic generalizations in the primary grades. *The Reading Teacher, 16,* 252–58.

Dolch, E. W. (1960). *Teaching primary reading.* Champaign, IL: Garrard Press.

Durkin, D. (1983). *Teaching them to read.* (4th Edition). Boston: Allyn-Bacon.

Fry, E. (1980). The new instant word list. *The Reading Teacher, 34,* 284–89.

Harris, A. J. & Sipay, E. R. (1985). *How to increase reading ability* (7th Edition). New York: Longman.

Hittleman, D. R. (1983). *Developmental reading.* (2nd edition). Boston: Houghton Mifflin.

Johnson, D. D. & Pearson, P. D. (1978). *Teaching reading vocabulary.* New York: Holt, Rinehart and Winston.

Jolly, H. B., Jr. (1984). Teaching basic function words. In A. J. Harris & E. R. Sipay (eds.) *Readings on reading instruction.* (3rd Edition). New York: Longman.

Lesiak, J. (1984). There is a need for word attack generalizations. In A. J. Harris & E. R. Sipay (eds.) *Readings on reading instruction.* (3rd Edition). New York: Longman.

Resnick, L. B. & Beck, I. L. (1984). Designing instruction in reading: Initial reading. In A. J. Harris & E. R. Sipay (eds.) *Readings on reading instruction.* (3rd Edition). New York: Longman.

Rey, H. A. (1952). *Curious George rides a bike.* Boston: Houghton Mifflin.

Smith, F. (1978). *Reading without nonsense.* New York: Teachers College Press.

5 Vocabulary and Comprehension

THE MANY MEANINGS OF WORDS ■ MEANING ACQUISITION: A BRIEF
LOOK ■ CLASSROOM ISSUES ■ SPECIAL CASES: HOMONYMS AND
REFERENTIAL TERMS ■ TEACHING VOCABULARY FROM YOUR PERSONAL
FRAMEWORK

"Dictionopolis will always be grateful, my boy," interrupted the king, throwing
one arm around Milo and patting Tock with the other. "You will face many
dangers on your journey, but fear not, for I have brought you this for your
protection."

He drew from inside his cape a small heavy box about the size of a
schoolbook and handed it ceremoniously to Milo.

"In this box are all the words I know," he said.

Norton Juster, *The Phantom Tollbooth.* (New York: Random House, Inc., 1961), p. 98.

Vocabulary knowledge is one of the most important factors in comprehending text. Not knowing the concept represented by a word makes understanding the author's intended meaning difficult, if not impossible. Of course, readers can and do use a number of techniques and strategies to infer what is meant, but these are not always accurate and can slow reading considerably, although they are important skills to learn. Teaching the concepts represented by words as well as teaching the strategies and techniques that can be used to infer an unknown word's meaning, is part of a reading teacher's role. This chapter examines the importance of vocabulary knowledge for reading comprehension. As you progress through the chapter, think carefully about how you use words in different situations and how you choose the words you use.

After reading this chapter, you will be able to

1. discuss the role of concept development in teaching and learning new vocabulary;
2. specify how pronunciation and meaning for words like *read* and *conduct* are decided on when reading;
3. state how vocabulary teaching differs across primary and intermediate grades;
4. discuss different ways to teach and learn new meanings for words.

THE MANY MEANINGS OF WORDS

As good readers and speakers of English, you almost unconsciously use and understand appropriate meanings of words from a large selection of possibilities. Yet even the simplest words often have more than one meaning, as well as a large number of shades or gradations in meanings. Here are some examples.

1. Copper is a good *conductor* of electricity.
2. Give your ticket to the *conductor*.
3. The orchestra *conductor* was quite young.

1. The *staple* went into his finger.
2. Corn was a *staple* in some Native Americans' diet.

1. The *frog* jumped into the pool.
2. He started coughing because he had a *frog* in his throat.

1. Write it down on *paper*.
2. We are going to *paper* the bedroom wall this weekend.

1. The fire glowed *red*.
2. The sunset was fiery *red*.
3. She has *red* hair.
4. The fire engine was bright *red*.

You probably changed the meaning of *conductor, staple, frog, paper,* and *red* each time the words were used.

While the *conductor, staple,* and *frog* examples show that words can have more than one meaning, the *paper* and *red* examples demonstrate that words often have shades of meaning. Did you "see" the same color for red in both 1 and 4? Almost all words in our language have such minute differences in meaning, yet we use them appropriately from a very young age. We sometimes forget that even the most common words have different meanings in different situations. Consider the word *up.*

1. Look *up* at the sky.
2. Look *up* the word in the dictionary.
3. Lock *up* the car!
4. The pipe is stopped *up.*
5. He can't come to the phone because he's tied *up.*

In oral communication, school-age children easily and unconsciously use needed words in their appropriate gradations of meaning. Thus, the fact that words have a range of meanings is really only of passing interest. It is the fact that we can remember, access, and use the meanings correctly in any given situation that is worthy of note. The important question for the reading teacher is not Can children learn a variety of word meanings fairly rapidly? (they do), but rather How are varieties of word meanings learned and appropriately accessed?

Categories of Words

We ask students to acquire and use many different types of vocabulary. Point out the differences between the various types of words.

BEFORE READING ON

The following words may be categorized into three lists. Two words in each list have already been provided. Place each word into one of the three lists. State how the lists differ.

is	that	microchip
shelf	table	at
beaker	cat	molecule
car	cumulus	and

LIST A	LIST B	LIST C
door	on	ledger
shelf	is	beaker
_____	_____	_____
_____	_____	_____
_____	_____	_____

function vocabulary:
Words that facilitate comprehension by connecting other words and phrases.
content vocabulary:
Words with clear-cut, concrete definitions.
content-specific vocabulary: Words representing concepts specific to a content area and that are not used in everyday language.

Vocabulary can be divided into two general types: **function** and **content.** A subcategory called **content-specific** words is a part of content vocabulary. In the preceding example, list *A* consists of the content vocabulary words *door, shelf, car, cat,* and *table.* List *B* contains the function words *on, is, that, at,* and *and.* The content-specific words *ledger, beaker, microchip, cumulus,* and *molecule* make up list *C.* Figure 5–1 illustrates these categories and provides examples of each.

Function words are often called the "glue" that holds a sentence together. Frequently occurring words such as articles, conjunctions, prepositions, pronouns, and adverbs are function words. They serve to make a sentence cohesive, providing links between words and phrases so that understanding can occur. Function words are frequently irregular in spelling and/or pronunciation and, if taught out of context, can be difficult for young children to conceptualize. This is because words like *but, and,* and *some* cannot easily be made concrete. This is especially true if you attempt to teach meanings of words like *but* in isolation. Such an approach is not only difficult for the teacher, but can be quite confusing for the student. Although there are times when it is appropriate to present words in isolation (perhaps when discussing word parts

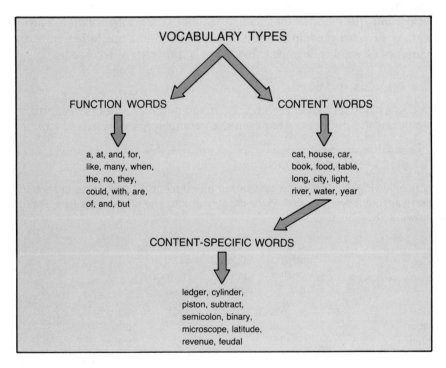

FIGURE 5–1
Examples of different vocabulary types

such as prefixes) we advocate teaching vocabulary in context. Context generally serves to clarify meanings.

Content words such as nouns, verbs, adjectives, and adverbs have concrete meanings and are not usually difficult for students to conceptualize. Content words considered to be everyday vocabulary such as *dog* or *car* are sometimes called general vocabulary words. Notice, however, that a word can have both general-use and specific meanings, depending on the context in which it is used.

> The *race* was run yesterday.
> The Oriental *race* has a long and fascinating history.

You cannot assume that students know both meanings unless the word is appropriately used in both contexts. Thus, teaching vocabulary requires the use of context to clarify intended meaning.

Although some content words have meanings only in the domain of general vocabulary, and others (such as *race*) have meanings ranging across both general and specialized domains, some vocabulary is content or subject specific. Such words have specialized meanings within a particular subject area and must be learned within the context of that area. For example, the word *race* has both general and specialized meanings. Words like *beaker* or *isotherm,* however, do not have general-meaning counterparts. These words have meanings specific to their subject areas. Content-specific vocabulary is usually taught in meaningful context to aid reading comprehension.

Teachers throughout the middle grades should spend time teaching their students the meanings of words that will be encountered in their reading material. This is especially true in content-area subjects such as science, social studies, and mathematics, where words often have content-specific meanings. Not knowing a word's content-specific meaning can quickly detract from comprehension. Be especially conscientious in teaching such vocabulary. Chapter 8 deals with this issue in more depth.

MEANING ACQUISITION: A BRIEF LOOK

To understand the value of different vocabulary teaching techniques you should have a basic knowledge about how concepts are acquired and stored in memory. This section briefly discusses meaning acquisition to provide a background for teaching techniques in vocabulary acquisition. First, however, think back to chapter 1 where it was noted that words themselves have no meanings. Words are simply labels for concepts. When we read, we attempt to match the printed label with a concept in memory. It is the concept that has meaning. The word-label can be thought of as a trigger for accessing the concept.

The preceding paragraph implies that a concept must be present before the word for a concept can be taught. To clarify this point, think about the following questions.

- Can or do we know something without "labeling" it through language? For example, do we know the concept *chair,* and can we access it, without using the language label to do so?
- Is it possible to have an internalized concept in memory without thinking of it in language-related terms?

Such questions are important, for if we only knew concepts as a result of language, then it would be necessary to teach word-labels and concepts as single units. However, if we can internalize a concept without attaching a label to it, then it may be better to first learn the concept and later attach a label to it. Perhaps a simple example will help resolve this issue.

Have you ever had the experience of trying to say something, and not being able to do so, even though you know for certain that you know what you are trying to say? Often we say that something is on "the tip of our tongues," but that we simply can't say it at that particular time. Usually, the desired term or concept makes itself available soon after we stop trying so hard to say it. This **tip of-the-tongue phenomenon** has been studied (Brown & McNeill, 1966) and supports the belief that we do have internalized representations for concepts accessed or triggered by language processing. Further, this phenomenon implies that we can and do know things without a labeling term being accessible at all times. Although some theorists (e.g., Vygotsky, 1962) argue that thought and language interact, others feel that the relationship between thought and language is such that thought precedes language (Ginsburg & Opper, 1969; DeHaven, 1983), and that concepts are well established before they are labeled.

The teacher's role when attempting to teach new vocabulary is to ensure that the concept for the new term is clearly known when attempting to forge a link between word and concept. In primary grades, it is often recommended that students have a word in their speaking vocabulary before they are taught the word in its printed form. This is one way to ensure that the concept exists in memory before the link between written word and concept is established. But there is a difference between what a teacher does when teaching vocabulary in the beginning grades as opposed to intermediate grades and beyond.

In the beginning grades, children are learning how to decode. They are still attempting to understand what the "squiggles" on the page represent. Thus, oral vocabulary is a bridge for linking written word and concept. Further, since vocabulary in beginning reading materials is controlled, generally using words in the speaking vocabulary of children for whom they are intended, primary-grade vocabulary lessons are often

"tip-of-the-tongue" phenomenon: Having a concept and word in memory, but being unable to access the knowledge at that time.

Discussing shared knowledge and pre-teaching new vocabulary is a common and useful activity before reading a selection.

presented to teach the written form of an already known concept. The teacher, although needing to ensure that a word is indeed in a student's speaking vocabulary before introducing it in print, does not have to spend much effort in actually teaching the concepts underlying most primary-level words. In later grades, however, when children are relatively competent decoders, they will be confronted with both new concepts and new word-labels for those concepts. This is especially true in the content-area subjects such as social studies, mathematics, and science. In the intermediate grades and beyond, a teacher must not only forge the link between word and concept, but must teach and build the concept as well.

The Role of Shared Experience in Meaning Acquisition

Theorists have noted that it is the commonality of shared experiences within a culture or social group that allows communication to take place (Carroll, 1967a, b). Because individuals within a society confront essentially similar experiences, they can refer to the experiences, and communication results. A word-label which has been accepted as referring to an experience or concept allows accessing of the concept among many individuals. If the word-label has not been agreed upon for use within a culture or societal group, then communication does not occur, or occurs with great difficulty.

It is for such reasons that individuals from different societies or cultures do not readily understand each other. If people from France and the United States were attempting to communicate about a furry animal that barks and has fleas, there are three possible reasons why communication may not occur. First, the possibility exists that there is no shared background experience. That is, both communicating parties need to have the concept in their memory of experiences. The second possibility is that there is a commonality of experiences, but that the two societies or cultures have evolved a different convention for labeling the furry-barking-has-fleas concept. The third possibility is that the label is the same but represents different concepts.

The second possibility is, in fact, the most likely. Since we know that people in France also keep dogs as pets, it is probable that a difference in word-labels is causing communicative difficulties. In France, such a creature is called *le chien* rather than *dog*. Since shared background between the two individuals does not extend to the knowledge of each other's word-labels, communication does not take place. In classrooms, you will find students who may have difficulty with vocabulary for any of these three reasons: they may not have the relevant concept as part of their knowledge base; they may have a different label for a to-be-learned concept; or they may, due to different background experiences, have evolved a somewhat different or unique meaning for a label. Effective teachers are aware of the diversity in their students' backgrounds, and ensure that vocabulary lessons are related to students' prior knowledge and shared experiences to mitigate possible communicative difficulties in their classrooms.

The Importance of Examples

As infants interact with the world, they encounter many new things. They in some way catalog each new experience and place it into memory. If you have a child or younger brother or sister, you might have noticed that, for a little while, all furry, four-legged animals may have been called *doggie*. Overgeneralizing certain perceived features of an item or entity may cause this. For example, the child may have noticed that furry, four-legged animals with ears are called *doggie,* and this set of features was generalized to include any four-legged, furry animal with ears. Later, as the child has more experience with different kinds of animals and is able to focus on finer discriminations, features such as barking, having fleas, having a cold nose, and chewing bones are added. The set of things to call *dogs* is thus narrowed to include only the appropriate animals. The following example shows how features may be used to discriminate among similar items.

BEFORE READING ON

In the blank to the right of each clue, write all possible choices from the following word list.

dog   cat   horse   poodle   stuffed animal (dog)

1. Has four legs: _____
2. Is alive: _____
3. Eats meat: _____
4. Barks: _____
5. Has a long nose and is often trimmed to have a ball of hair at the end of its tail:

_____

The example is by no means a completely accurate representation of how we identify perceived items. But it does demonstrate that internalized features provide the basis for judgments regarding the concept classification. We do not actually have to hear or read the word *dog* to know what is being discussed in the phrase "a furry animal that barks and has fleas." Both *dog* and "a furry animal that barks and has fleas" elicit the same concept. Thus, as more features of an item are recognized, classes of objects become defined. The barking feature, for example, distinguishes *dog* from *animal* because it narrows our possible choices. Animals that meow, hiss, or quack are excluded. As more features are recognized by infants, they make fewer overgeneralization errors. They move from calling all adult males *daddy* to calling only their father *daddy* when they become aware that their father has some distinctive features when compared to other adult males.

What you did while working through the preceding example is a type of **feature analysis.** When linguists analyze words to determine differences in meaning, they often use a feature analysis with plus and minus signs to indicate the presence or absence of a given feature (Katz, 1972, 1974; Leech, 1974; Lyons, 1977). For example:

feature analysis: A linguistic method that specifies differences in the meanings of words. Can be adapted for classroom use to aid understanding of new vocabulary concepts.

boy		*man*		*girl*	
+	animate	+	animate	+	animate
+	male	+	male	−	male (or + female)
−	adult	+	adult	−	adult

Often, developing a clear chart of this type through purposeful discussion aids students' understanding of a new concept and relates it to already known terms.

This discussion clearly applies to teaching vocabulary. First, concepts are continually refined as one identifies and clarifies features. This means that concepts are not learned on a one-shot basis. Further, concepts and vocabulary taught by one teacher in one grade can be refined and clarified by teachers at higher grades. Second, concepts are acquired through experiences leading to recognition of specific features. Teachers must, therefore, provide clear examples focusing on the salient features of the concept to be acquired. Third, activities must include both positive and negative examples of a concept. This helps delineate the boundaries of a concept, showing how it is similar to and different from other already known items. For example, if the concept *cup* is to be learned, present and discuss several kinds of cups. Also show things similar to, but different from cups—perhaps drinking glasses and coffee mugs. A discussion focused on how the various items are both similar and different will result in a clearer understanding of what a cup is. It is vital to provide and discuss examples of concepts to be learned, including the features of those concepts, in any vocabulary lesson.

Examples can take many forms. Use concrete examples where possible and appropriate. Providing the opportunity to see, touch, smell, and otherwise experience something which will form a new concept and result in a new vocabulary term is very important. A picture or facsimile of the item to be learned is also concrete, but not as much as is the item itself. Discussing the new term or concept and relating it clearly to already known concepts is also a valuable, but less concrete, way of teaching new concepts.

MODEL LESSON

Discussion of Features

Word to be learned: *canoe*

In this lesson, the teacher tries to relate the students' prior knowledge about different kinds of boats to the new word *canoe*. The word to be learned was chosen because it appears in a story to be read following the vocabulary lesson. The teacher shows the class a picture of a rowboat. Pointing to the rowboat, she asks, "Who can tell me what this is?" She writes the students' response *(boat)* on the chalkboard.

Pointing to the picture of the canoe, she says, "Raise your hands if you know what this is called."

Three of the eight students in the instructional group raise their hands. The teacher asks one of the students to name the item in the picture and receives the response *canoe*. She writes *canoe* on the blackboard beside the word *boat*.

She shows the students a picture of a sailboat and asks the class if this is also a boat. With her guidance, the class decides that the word *boat* is not specific enough and that one should be called a rowboat; the other a sailboat. The teacher erases the word *boat* from the blackboard and replaces it with *rowboat*.

The teacher says, "Let's list how a rowboat and a canoe are the same and how they are different. Tell me how they are the same."

The blackboard now looks like this:

                    ROWBOAT   CANOE

        Same

        Different

As the students provide responses, the teacher writes them on the blackboard in the appropriate columns. Near the end of the discussion, the teacher may write the word *sailboat* to the right of the other two words and ask which of the items beside *same* and *different* apply to the sailboat. She ends her lesson by asking the students to make up sentences using the word *canoe*. The sentences should reflect the word's meaning and be specific enough so that a reader will not be able to confuse it with another kind of boat.

Building Concepts: Some Teaching Implications

Experience. Experience is the most concrete way of teaching a new concept. Often, teachers will take their classes on field trips and point out and discuss things which will form the basis for a vocabulary lesson when the class returns. Remember that a field trip does not necessarily mean an expensive outing. It can be as short as walking around the block. Other concrete experiences can be established by bringing an object to the classroom, or having someone else do so. It is important, however, to focus the student's attention on the object. They must actively perceive the object, not simply look at it. Provide opportunities, as appropriate, for the students to touch, see, smell, and otherwise experience the object. As in all teaching of concepts, point out and discuss important features to develop and elicit associations between the new concept and related, known concepts, and to clarify and establish relationships between items that are known and to be learned.

Facsimile. Often, it is not possible to provide hands-on experience when teaching a new concept. Providing a facsimile can be nearly as relevant. Common facsimiles are drawings, photographs, filmstrips, videotapes, and recordings of sounds related to the object or concept under discussion. Use the facsimile to actively build the concept, not simply to allow passive observation.

Discussion. Although less concrete than experience or providing a facsimile, a meaningful discussion of the concept to be learned can lead to understanding and acquisition of new vocabulary. Discussion must relate to things already a part of students' knowledge, while focusing on the unique features of the new concept. For example, if it were necessary to teach *gorilla,* you might begin by asking if anyone knows of any animals that lived in trees in the jungle. If students respond with *monkey,* then use the students' knowledge of *monkey* to elicit responses to questions such as What is a monkey like? and What makes a monkey a monkey and not an elephant? Then discuss the similarities between monkeys and gorillas. Conclude the discussion by establishing similarities and differences between gorillas and other animals.

Context. While reading, we often encounter new words in context and use context clues to acquire new terminology and concepts. Context is a powerful tool that helps readers derive meanings for unfamiliar words. Relying only on context, however, is more appropriate for good readers and older students. We must be careful not to assume that everyone will understand new concepts simply because they have been used in written context. **Contextual** presentations require both good language facility and appropriate background knowledge. Context clues are only valuable when background knowledge and adequate decoding skills allow us to relate new, unknown terms to what is already known. Thus, discussion providing appropriate background knowledge is needed before full use can be made of context clues embedded in a sentence or story.

contextual presentation: A teaching technique that introduces new words in sentences. Allows students to infer definitions from known concepts.

Structured, group vocabulary games can be used to increase students' word knowledge. When carefully planned, they can use both context and dictionary knowledge.

Students without appropriate background knowledge will not learn new word meanings through just seeing a new word in context. Consider the following examples.

1. A common practice, especially when the salvage value is assumed to be zero, is to apply an appropriate percentage, known as the depreciation rate, to the acquisition cost in order to calculate the annual charge. (Davidson, S.; Stickney, C. P. & Weil, R. L. [1980]. *Intermediate accounting concepts, methods and uses.* Hinsdale, IL: Dryden Press, 13–17.)
2. The giraffe, a tall animal with a long neck, lives in Africa.

Unless the concepts for *salvage value, depreciation rate,* and *annual charge* are already a part of your background knowledge, it is unlikely that the context clues embedded in the first example will aid in your acquiring the concept of *annual charge.* If, in the second example, you had never before seen *giraffe* in print, but knew what a giraffe was and had the word in your speaking vocabulary, then the context would facilitate acquisition of the written word *giraffe.* However, unless more background is provided, perhaps in the form of a picture, it is unlikely that a student who knew nothing about giraffes would acquire the concept from passage context.

SAMPLE ACTIVITIES

Experience Activity. Have students see, touch, smell, taste, and use an item (as appropriate) and then discuss the name and features of the thing that is being experienced.

Experience Activity. Have the students walk around the schoolyard. Take a pad of paper and a marking pen. Stop periodically to write vocabulary items on the pad, taking time to discuss the word before moving on. On returning to the classroom use these words in other language activities. This can be done on any field trip (to the airport, zoo, newspaper printing plant, and so on).

Activity Using Facsimiles. Using a picture, videotape, movie, audio tape, or other secondary source, have students focus closely on the features of the item as seen in the facsimile. Discuss the item's possible uses, looks, size, and so on.

Context Activity. When discussing a new vocabulary item, have students close their eyes and present a detailed, verbal picture of the concept. Later, use sentence examples that have strong context clues and have students choose the appropriate word out of several possible choices to complete the picture or context.

If you keep in mind the goal of reading instruction—comprehension of text—then teaching words as isolated units is inappropriate. Children need to see that the vocabulary being taught is useful which is best done by using the new words in meaningful text. Further, using new vocabulary in context teaches something in addition to a word's meaning: its appropriate use in sentences. Knowing a word's meaning is sometimes not enough. One must also know if the word is used as a verb, noun, adjective, and so on. Thus, when teaching a new vocabulary item, present both the meaning and its use in text in the lesson. Figure 5–2 presents some suggestions for practicing the appropriate use of words in context.

Note that the instructions in figure 5–2 do not actually state that *clock* is a noun. Memorizing the part of speech does relatively little to facilitate proper use of a word in text. Only actual practice with appropriate usage will result in students' internalizing a word's use in a sentence. Further, teaching by definition is often confusing and faulty. For example, saying that a noun is a person, place, or thing is relatively meaningless in out-of-context situations. Defining *chair* and *fly* as nouns results in confusion when students encounter sentences such as:

> She will *chair* the meeting.
> The pilot will *fly* to Denver tomorrow.

This is not to say that discussions regarding parts of speech are not important or need not be part of a vocabulary lesson. But if the goal of instruction is students' proper use of new vocabulary in good sentences, then practice in context will be of more value than memorizing part-of-speech definitions.

Dictionaries. Dictionaries can be used to create vocabulary learning experiences and can help in meaning acquisition. They are also reference sources for students during independent reading activities. Dictionaries can be used in even the early grades, beginning with picture dictionaries. Perhaps you think of the dictionary as a large volume sometimes used in the library, but there are many attractive and useful dictionaries aimed at elementary-age students. These typically use large print and a page layout attractive to primary-grade readers. Such dictionaries also make effective use of color, drawings, photos, and other visual aids to explain and define concepts. Popular primary dictionaries include

1. Halsey, W. D. (Editorial Director). (1981). *First dictionary*. New York: MacMillan.
2. Jenkins, W. A. & Schiller, A. (1982). *My first picture dictionary*. Glenview, IL: Scott, Foresman & Company.

As noted in chapter 4, however, dictionaries are a last resort for finding meanings. One reason is that it takes a number of skills to use

---

Item to be learned: *Clock*

1. Modified Cloze (fill in the blank) Procedure:

   Instructions to students: A clock is something used to tell time. It is used in sentences in the same way that the word *boy* is used. From the words provided, place the word *clock* in the proper blanks.

   (a) Don't touch the _____
                           eat
                           clock
                           big

   (b) My house is _____
                   big
                   eat
                   clock

2. Categorization Exercises:

   Instructions to students: Make two lists of words. Circle all the words that can be used in sentence (a). Underline all the words that can be used in sentence (b).

   sit   eat   clock   jump   dog   table   go   spoon

   (a) She is looking at the _____.

   (b) He will _____ soon.

3. Correcting Exercises:

   Instructions to students: Put a check mark in front of the sentence(s) where *clock* is used properly. If *clock* is not used properly, cross it out, choose a word from the following list, and write it above the word *clock*.

   sit   jump   eat   go

   _____ (a) He will <u>clock</u> on the chair.

   _____ (b) The <u>clock</u> was on the table.

FIGURE 5–2
Techniques for practicing word use

---

a dictionary to look up an unknown word's meaning. For example, a child must (1) be able to alphabetize by (at least) the first letter of a word; and (2) be able to locate a word without turning every page; (3) be able to associate word and meaning; (4) be aware a word often has more than one meaning; and (5) use context to select one meaning from alternatives. Of course, assuming the needed skills are present, the dictionary can be a useful tool, especially as students encounter unfamiliar words in their content-area subjects. It is not enough, however, to simply have students copy dictionary definitions. The meanings need to be discussed, used in meaningful examples, and related to students' prior knowledge.

To teach students the value of using a dictionary, model its use, drawing students' attention to the reason the dictionary is being consulted. This is also true for sources such as a thesaurus and a glossary. Incidental instruction can result in students' using such tools independently when unknown words are found in reading assignments. For this to be effective always have a class dictionary and a thesaurus, at the appropriate level for the students, readily available for student use.

SAMPLE ACTIVITIES

Incidental Instruction. Pick an interesting, unknown word and use it incidentally during the day, showing how the dictionary can help find the word's meaning. For example, say, "Yesterday I heard someone say that he really doesn't like *canines*. I'd like to use the dictionary to find out what *canine* means and would like you to help me." Go on to use the dictionary to find the word, read the meaning, and relate it to previous knowledge.

Finding Correct Meanings. Use sentences like "He put the fish on the *scale* to find out how heavy it was. Her wedding dress had a long *train*." Use the dictionary to find the word and decide which of the listed meanings make sense in the sentence context.

CLASSROOM ISSUES

Deciding What to Teach

In general, teachers determine the vocabulary they will teach in one of three ways:

1. predetermined, graded word lists
2. words to be encountered in current reading materials
3. words used by students in their natural, oral language

Although a teacher uses all three methods for determining vocabulary to be taught, most lean toward one approach over the others. There are many published word lists available that indicate the frequency of words encountered by students in specific grade levels. These lists are usually developed from analyzing reading materials, including textbooks, which children are expected to read in each grade. Some teachers feel that, if their students encounter the words noted on a word list, it aids students' reading comprehension if the words on the list have been systematically taught. Teachers with this viewpoint sometimes construct pretests, using the word list, and teach only necessary, unknown words to specific students.

Word lists can provide much useful information for teaching vocabulary. Some common lists include:

1. Dale, E. & O'Rourke, J. (1976). *Living word vocabulary: The words we know.* Elgin, IL: Dome, Inc.
2. Fry, E. B.; Polk, J. K.; & Fountoukidis, D. (1985). *The reading teacher's book of lists* (2nd Edition). Englewood Cliffs, NJ: Prentice Hall.
3. Harris, A. J. & Jacobson, M. D. (1982). *Basic reading vocabularies.* New York: MacMillan.

Word lists can provide information such as the number of students in a given grade level who may not know a specific word; a frequency-ordered list of words encountered by students in elementary reading materials, or lists of roots, prefixes, suffixes, synonyms, antonyms, homophones, commonly misspelled words, and so on. Systematic teaching from a list, however, can mean that the words taught may not be seen by students in their presently used reading materials.

Another method of deciding which vocabulary items to teach is based on the philosophy that vocabulary is best learned and retained when the items to be learned occur in real, meaningful situations. Many teachers feel that this results in students' becoming more aware of the importance and relevance of learning the vocabulary. In this approach, vocabulary identified as critical to students' understanding of a passage or story that is about to be read is pretaught. Time must be taken to determine which words in the text are important for overall passage understanding. Sometimes this is done for the teacher; for example teacher's guides often present lists of words introduced in each unit and each story. It is intended that teachers focus on the list of important and new words in the selection to be read.

All reading materials do not, however, introduce the same vocabulary at identical grade levels. For example, *biscuit* and *regret* first appear in basal readers at substantially different grade levels, depending on the reading series being used.

Reading Program	Biscuit	Regret
American	Sixth Grade	Sixth Grade
Economy	Fourth Grade	Seventh Grade
Ginn & Company	Second Grade	Third Grade
Holt Rinehart & Winston	Second Grade	Fifth Grade
Houghton Mifflin	Fourth Grade	Sixth Grade
MacMillan	Third Grade	Seventh Grade
Scott, Foresman	Third Grade	Fifth Grade

From A. J. Harris & M. D. Jacobson, *Basic reading vocabularies.* (New York: MacMillan, 1982), p. 48, 122.

Notice that the word *biscuit* is introduced in a range from the second- to the sixth-grade level, while *regret* is first found in third-grade material in some readers, and in seventh grade in others. In our highly mobile society, where a significant number of children might change school districts from one year to the next (thus also often changing the reading materials used for instruction), differences in vocabulary can easily occur. If you are aware that vocabulary is different between reading series, you can mitigate the sometimes adverse effects that a change in instructional materials can cause. Do not assume that second-grade students who are learning to read from different materials encounter or master the same vocabulary.

Teachers use one other major approach to decide which vocabulary to teach. This method centers around the children's use of oral language and is closely related to the language experience approach discussed in chapter 2. A teacher may have a student dictate a story, which the teacher writes. This story forms the basis for vocabulary instruction, often through pointing out synonyms which might be appropriate substitutions for some of the student's words. Having the child attempt to read the story after the teacher has written it down may also show that some words are in a student's speaking vocabulary, but not in the reading vocabulary. This is a highly motivational approach and relates to forging the link between an already known concept and print, rather than strictly to concept development.

Using the child's oral language as a base for vocabulary lessons sometimes leads to criticisms that vocabulary is not being expanded because only known vocabulary is being used. Here are some activities intended to expand a child's vocabulary while using oral language as a foundation.

SAMPLE ACTIVITIES

logical cloze: A vocabulary-building activity based on the procedure of omitting words from sentences. Uses children's oral language to help select newly introduced words to complete the sentences.

Logical Cloze. After writing a story that has been provided by a student or students, delete words and present logical replacements for the original words. Teach and discuss each new word before asking children to place them in the appropriate blanks. For example, assume that the words to be taught are *morning, cape, previous,* and *annoyed.*

> The girl was on her way to school. It was a rainy _____(day) and she had her _____(raincoat) and her umbrella with her. She hoped that she wouldn't forget her umbrella at school like she did the _____(last) time. Her mother was _____(upset) with her when she didn't bring her umbrella home.

Thesaurus Detective. Cut pages out of a newspaper. Have students work in pairs. Each student circles five words that the other students are to replace with words found in the thesaurus. Students trade newspapers after circling the words. After synonyms have been found, students read the words to each other one at a time, with the listener attempting to provide the meaning of the synonym and the original word. Attempt this activity only after the skills necessary to use a thesaurus have been mastered.

Once a teacher has decided what to teach, a decision must be made about how to proceed. The choice depends on whether students know the concept to be taught, and consists of two general directions. Figure 5–3 illustrates the two options. For clarity, the figure represents concepts as being either known or unknown. In reality, we may have a rough or partial idea about what something is or means. It is really the degree to which something is known that determines whether the concept must be further taught. Vocabulary knowledge changes throughout our lives, with new concepts being learned and others being increasingly refined. Notice that the difference shown in figure 5–3 lies in whether the concept and oral vocabulary term is already known. In one instance, the concept must be taught. In the other, only the bond between written word-label and concept must be made. This choice applies to all vocabulary lessons, although the latter is more common in primary grades; the former, in higher grades.

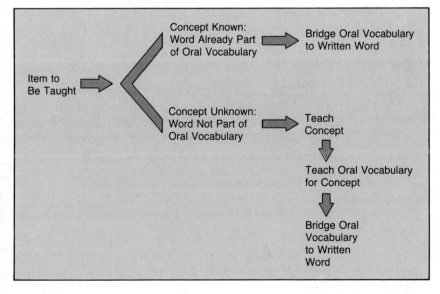

FIGURE 5–3
Decisions in teaching vocabulary

Use of Word Parts

Although knowledge of word parts can help in word recognition, it also helps readers discover the meanings of words and thus expands their vocabularies. When readers use word parts as clues to meaning, they use knowledge about affixes (prefixes and suffixes), as well as knowledge of root words to aid in determining meaning. Recall that **morphemes,** the smallest meaningful parts of language include prefixes, suffixes, and root words. For example, the following words contain one morpheme each:

> morphemes: Prefixes, suffixes, and roots.

play   run   cow

These contain two morphemes each:

playful   rerun   cows

Knowing common prefixes and suffixes helps to determine meaning. For example, knowing that the prefix *non-* means *not* helps a reader discover the meaning of words such as *nonprofit, nonsense,* or *nonstop,* providing the word's root is known. Similarly, knowing prefixes and roots can help in vocabulary acquisition. Thus, prefixes and suffixes are often taught as vocabulary items in reading instruction. Although it is impossible for you to teach all prefixes, suffixes, and roots, teaching the most common ones is worthwhile. There are many published lists that contain the most useful morphemes (for example, Fry, Polk, & Fountoukidis, [1985]. *The reading teacher's book of lists.* Englewood Cliffs, NJ: Prentice Hall). You can use activities such as the following to teach the meaning of affixes and roots.

SAMPLE ACTIVITIES

- Write several sentences containing words with the same prefix (or suffix) that have the same meaning. Have students state the meaning of each underlined word. Cross out the affix. Lead a discussion about how the meaning of the word has changed, moving toward a discussion about the meaning of the affix. For example:

    He had to <u>reheat</u> the food because it had cooled down.
    After she used the towel, Mary had to <u>refold</u> it.
    Since the color came out of his shirt after it was washed, Sam had to <u>redye</u> it.

- You can change this activity to use sentences that provide the long form of the meaning, with students required to use the appropriate affix. For example:

    Re- is a prefix that means *again. Un-* is a prefix that means *not.* Use one of these prefixes to revise the underlined words in the sentences.

Because the food had cooled down, he has to heat it <u>again</u>.
After she used the towel, Mary had to fold it <u>again</u>.
Since the color came out of his shirt after it was washed, Sam had to
<u>dye</u> it <u>again</u>.

- Affixes can be written on the blackboard, and students should supply
root words to which they can be added. For example:

-<u>less</u> (without)	-<u>en</u> (like)
care(less)	wool(en)
thought(less)	gold(en)
hope(less)	wood(en)

- Present students with a sentence and have them provide a suffix or
prefix that changes the word's meaning. Discuss how the affix has
not only changed the meaning of the word, but also of the sentence.
For example:

The prefix *un-* means *not.*
They were welcome at the picnic.
They were _____ at the picnic.

- Have students look through a reading selection and circle certain
prefixes, suffixes, and/or roots. Students then present their findings,
including how the meaning of the word would be different had the
prefix or suffix not been used.

Pretesting: A Helpful Step

BEFORE READING ON

Can you think of ways to quickly test students' vocabulary knowledge? Here
are some examples. With a little thought, you should be able to add to these.

Oral Question. Who knows what _____ means? (This is perhaps
the most common, yet most ineffective way of finding out. Can you state why?)

Oral or Written Question. Say (or write) _____ in a sentence.

Matching Activity. Match the word with the meaning.

     (a) house _____   1. grows in the garden
     (b) flower _____   2. a place to live

Fill in the Blank. From choices provided, place the appropriate words in the sentences.

house   flower

(a) The_____ grows in the garden.
(b) The_____ has three bedrooms.

Short Multiple Choice Test.

house

(a) a place to live
(b) something to eat
(c) a large animal

Although it is both appropriate and desirable to reinforce previously taught vocabulary, it is not a good use of time or resources to teach already known words. Thus, it is sometimes a good idea to quickly and informally pretest terms thought to be new or necessary for comprehension to occur. You may recall the analogy of the teacher as an instructional decision maker which has been used in earlier chapters. Pretesting to identify students who will benefit from instruction and those who may not need instruction is a part of making reasoned instructional decisions. Your students will not have identical needs when it comes to vocabulary instruction. Deciding which students to target for instruction will make your teaching more effective, interesting, and relevant to your students. It will also resolve potential problems resulting from boredom or frustration.

If you determine that the child already knows the item to be learned, then the link between the oral and written word-label needs to be established. The child needs to be shown the word in written form, and the techniques discussed in chapter 4 can be used to make the child aware that the written item represents the already known, oral term. When presenting a word, make sure that the student is actively attending to what is being presented. Questions such as What are the first two letters? What is the suffix? How many letters are in the word? and Which letters (if any) are silent? help focus the student's attention on the word-label.

If the concept is unknown, then it must be taught before the link between word-label and concept is established. Some techniques that build conceptual awareness are

- to use a range of examples;
- to provide practice in categorizing and classifying the new item;
- to relate the new concept to past experience;
- to use the concept in meaningful context.

Logistically, it is impossible to teach individual vocabulary lessons to each student in the class. That is, if one student does not know any of the words to be taught, another knows all but three, and yet another knows all but a different three, then difficulties result in deciding how to group them for instruction. Yet general groups can be formed where the ratio of known to unknown words is minimized. For example, consider that five words are to be taught (1, 2, 3, 4, 5) to a group of five students (perhaps those in the highest reading group). The teacher has identified the words and provided a brief pretest the day before the words are to be taught. The following list shows which words are unknown by which students.

Student	Unknown Word	Group Placement
A	1, 2	1
B	3, 4, 5	2
C	1, 2, 3	1
D	1, 3, 5	2
E	4	1

By using such a grouping, students are exposed to fewer already known words. Notice that students in group 1 are exposed to a maximum of two already known words; those in group 2, only one. Teaching the five students as one group would result in exposure of as many as four already known words (for student E). This example is simplified to make the point that pretesting does not result in perfect matches, but that it can help in targeting vocabulary instruction. Also, the example may seem somewhat trite because of the relatively low number of already known words taught due to the grouping arrangements. In reality, where more words are used with a greater number of students, the number of already known words taught is greatly reduced.

Conceptual Links: Instructional Implications

Research indicates that certain concepts are closely linked or interwoven with each other (Adams & Collins, 1979; Anderson, Reynolds, Schallert & Goetz, 1977). If people are asked to say the first word that comes to mind when presented with list A, most will respond with those in list B.

List A	List B
mother	father
boy	girl
man	woman

In fact, research in **schema theory** implies that there are sets or networks of concepts which appear to help trigger each other. If one is asked to respond to the stimulus word *restaurant,* for example, *menu,*

schema theory: A plan for organizing knowledge in memory in which objects and their relationships form a network.

food, or *waiter* is a more likely response than is *car* or *television.* Such results support instructional practices that attempt to link words into meaningful networks rather than teaching each word separately.

The fact that concepts seem to cluster; that is, that one concept seems to facilitate accessing related concepts (as in the restaurant-food example), implies that vocabulary may be effectively presented in **thematic units.** Figure 5–4 presents practice activities often found in commercially available materials.

thematic units: Lessons designed around a single topic.

In figure 5–4, note that pictures as cues and words are presented. The activities shown are intended for children in kindergarten or beginning first grade. The child's task is to match the picture to its appropriate word, and then write the word. Such activities are worthwhile since they allow the matching of word-label and pictured clue, yet additionally present the opportunity to write the word (although not in context—such an activity will need to be added).

MODEL LESSON

Linking Vocabulary

One popular and effective way of teaching vocabulary links meanings into a web of coherent context. Children seem better able to learn and retain vocabulary presented cohesively. If teaching the words

barn   *difficult*   *handle*   *horse*   *cheerful*

for example, after classification and discussion activities have taken place, appropriate instruction includes using the words in a related manner. One way to do this easily and effectively is to write a brief story, as a class or individually, using the words. The following is a story suggested by a group of four first-grade students. They each presented the teacher with a sentence orally and the teacher wrote the sentences on the blackboard while the students copied them into their notebooks. The last sentence was provided by the teacher. The vocabulary words were then underlined and discussed.

> There was a cheerful horse who lived in a barn. The horse was cheerful because he got to live in a big barn and had lots to eat. There was a big handle on the door of the barn. It was difficult to turn. The horse was cheerful because his barn was beautiful.

Webs of related concepts can also be prepared and added to, to present vocabulary in thematic units. For example, restaurant terms might be presented and diagrammed into a web, with the central component being the most general or generic concept and outlying concepts being added in terms of their importance to the central theme or con-

FIGURE 5–4
An example of a practice activity

cept. The amount of detail in these semantic webs will vary depending on the level of student. The following is a reasonably complex semantic web.

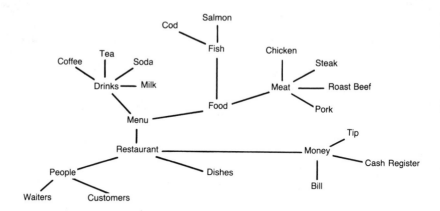

We know that after reading individuals use their interpretive abilities and remember things which were not actually specifically stated in what was read. For example, readers who are presented with sentences such as:

The woman was outstanding in the theater.

often believe that *actress* was stated in the sentence. This indicates that readers attempt to remember what appears to be most appropriate or the essence of what was read. The process of remembering the key item appears to be based on context and has been called **instantiation** (Anderson, Pichert, Goetz, Schallert, Stevens & Trollip, 1976). Research on instantiation has provided one rationale for using synonyms as well as appropriate, logically related examples when teaching vocabulary. Additionally, such research provides a reason for using examples that make sense. When teaching the word *hammer,* for example, you might say:

instantiation: Remembering what is perceived as the most important information in the material read.

He hit the nail with a _____.
What word fits in the blank? What other words could be used? Which is most appropriate? Why? What do all the words have in common?

as well as:

He hit the nail with the <u>*hammer.*</u>
What other words can be used instead of *hammer*? (for example, *rock, wrench,* and so on) Why can we use the other words? (All of the items can be used to hammer.) Why might *hammer* be the best choice? (It is used most often; it is the tool specifically made for hammering.) Where might a hammer be found? (Workbench, toolbox, or with other tools).

Such discussion methods use children's prior knowledge and help to place the new concept into a network of similar items (tools; items used to hammer), thus facilitating learning. These activities are similar to those using analogies and continuums or gradations of meanings to teach new concepts. This is because these activities, as well as the two following activities, use already known concepts to build new ones, implying that knowledge is organized as a series of related, linked concepts.

Using analogies to teach students new words and their uses may be done at all grade levels. Students are presented items such as:

>   Pipe is to *water*   as   *conductor* is to *electricity.*
>   Dog is to *puppy*   as   *horse* is to *foal.*

Analogies, used with discussion, foster concept development because they show the relationships between items that are known, comparing them to one item that is unknown in ways that allow the student to infer the meaning of the item to be learned. In these examples, *conductor* and *foal* are the words to be learned. Be sure that all other words in the analogy are known. Provide discussion that targets the relationship among the already known half of the analogy, moving on to questions about what the relationship might be between the words on the other side of the analogy.

Continuums, using meanings that are known as well as one or more to be taught, also facilitate vocabulary development in ways that use prior knowledge. For example, students might be shown the following:

>   *freezing*   *cold*   *tepid*   *hot*   *boiling*

Discussions of the changes in gradation of meaning from left to right with, in this case, *tepid* being the vocabulary item to be learned, present a scheme in which to fit the new term.

Learning Centers and Response Cards

Learning centers lend themselves well to teaching vocabulary, whether in thematic or unrelated word units. A learning center is an area in a classroom that contains a variety of instructional materials dealing with a specific goal or objective. They often are used independently by students, and provisions for self-evaluation are usually made.

A learning center, sometimes called an activity center or learning station, contains a set of activities designed to build specific skills. Since students work independently at a learning center, they must be aware of acceptable behavior while at the center and must also be aware of the purposes and goals of the activities. Good planning is required to

learning center: A classroom location where self-correcting instructional materials for a specific skill are used independently by students.

create an effective learning center. Huff (1983) and Sherfey & Huff (1976) suggest that the following steps be considered when planning a learning center.

1. Clearly define the center's purposes.
2. Consider the characteristics and needs of students who will be using the center.
3. Define the concepts and skills to be developed in the center.
4. Outline expected learning outcomes.
5. Select appropriate activities and materials.
6. Evaluate the center.
7. Implement needed changes.

Children can use learning centers individually or in groups of two or three. Make the center sturdy enough to withstand classroom use and include a variety of activities targeted toward the skill to be developed. Students should expect to spend no more than fifteen minutes at the center at a time.

In a teacher's busy day, effective activities and methods that lead to reduced time spent correcting students' work are always welcome. Learning centers where students work individually and where self-evaluation is used provide one such activity. Another that is especially useful in vocabulary teaching and evaluation uses *A-B-C* and true-false **response cards** to replace papers and pencils. For these activities, construct cards with the vocabulary words to be learned clearly printed on them. The cards consist of a maximum of three words, or can be single-word flashcards. The single-word cards are used for true-false; multiple-word cards for *A-B-C* activities. Figure 5–5 shows both types of cards.

response cards: Provide the teacher with immediate information about a child's response.

FIGURE 5–5
These vocabulary cards can be used with true/false or A-B-C response cards.

Response Cards. Students are asked to tear a piece of paper into either two (for true-false activities) or three (for *A-B-C* activities) parts and write either *true* and *false* or *A, B,* and *C* on their papers. The teacher then holds up a vocabulary card and provides context clues for students to choose the appropriate word from the cards. Children should not say the word, but simply hold up the letter which is under the word they think is appropriate, based on the teacher's clue. For the true-false activity, the teacher holds up the word card and provides a statement which is either true or false. Students hold up either *true* or *false* in response.

MODEL LESSON

These simple activities can be modified easily. They are valuable, however, for four reasons.

First, children are not self-conscious about responding. Since the response is not oral and all students face the teacher, others cannot see an incorrect response. Second, teachers do not have to spend a great deal of time grading papers or worksheets, yet have an overview of which students responded incorrectly. If the teacher has a class list of names handy, students who show problems with certain words can quickly be noted for later, individual help. Third, the cards are inexpensive, easy to make, and can be copied by students for inclusion in their word banks. Fourth, the activity provides a quick way to review and repeat previously presented vocabulary.

One hint for making the cards: make sure you place the clues or statements you want to use, as well as the words themselves, on the backs of the cards. It is very distracting to students and detrimental to the activity to either constantly flip the card back and forth so that you can look at the front or to have students waiting between clues while you think of what to say. Be prepared.

SPECIAL CASES: HOMONYMS AND REFERENTIAL TERMS

A Note on Homonyms

BEFORE READING ON

Using these examples, state the differences between **homographs, homophones,** and **homonyms.**

Homograph
(a) He *read* the book yesterday.
    He will *read* the book tomorrow.
(b) The metal looked like *lead.*
    Lead me to the table!

homographs: Words with the same spellings, but different pronunciation and meanings.
homophones: Words with the same pronunciation, but different spellings and meanings.
homonyms: Words with the same pronunciation and spellings, but different meanings.

Homophone

(c)　He *led* his horse to water.
　　His arms were so tired they felt like *lead.*

(d)　His *heir* will inherit the estate.
　　The *air* was clean and fresh.

Homonym

(e)　The fish *scale* looked like a speck of silver.
　　He weighed himself on the bathroom *scale.*

(f)　He sat in the *chair.*
　　He was *Chair* of the English Department.

There is often confusion in terminology when deciding what to call words that sound the same. Try to learn the following precise terms because there is a difference between words that sound the same and are spelled the same and words that sound the same and are spelled differently. One difference lies in the greater difficulty children have in learning the former when compared to the latter. Calling them all *homonyms* is inaccurate and can lead to confusion in the instructional situation. Learning the precise terms will also help when you encounter them in teacher's guides.

Homophones:　Words that sound alike, are spelled differently, and mean different things.

Homographs:　Words that do not sound alike, are spelled alike, and mean different things.

Homonyms:　Words that sound alike, are spelled alike, and mean different things.

Homonyms present an interesting methodological challenge to the teacher. Since neither the written (graphemic) nor the oral (phonological) form of a homonym changes with the meanings, young children sometimes become confused when the two meanings are presented together. Confusion and interference can result when a teacher focuses attention on the already known meaning of a homonym and then tells the students to learn the new meaning (Kinzer, 1982). Placing a heavy emphasis on the already known meaning and then, in effect, asking the child to forget that meaning because another must be learned is a poor practice. In fact, research has shown that young children who are taught new meanings for homonyms do better when not asked to say or focus on the meaning they already know (Kinzer, 1981). The following paragraphs relate learning multiple meanings to cognitive tasks and support this argument.

One indicator of cognitive level is the ability to classify and cross-classify. One way such ability is commonly tested is with items such as cardboard circles painted different colors. Students are asked to group the circles in any way they wish. Ability to do so indicates that the child can classify on a single dimension. A higher-level classification task, the ability to cross-classify or see multiple class membership, can be tested by presenting a child with squares and circles—some red and some yellow. Young children, when first asked to classify the items, generally do so on the basis of either color or shape. When the items are again mixed together, and the children are asked to group them in another way, they are generally unable to do so. Although cognitive levels are only loosely related to grade and age levels, the ability to perceive multiple class membership does not generally develop until approximately age eight or nine, or about third or fourth grade (Kofsky, 1966; Sigel, 1966, 1977; Ahr & Youniss, 1970; Klar & Wallace, 1976; Lowery, 1981).

When attempting to relate multiple class membership ability to learning multiple meanings for homonyms, one must think of what is being demanded in both tasks. When performing a multiple class membership task, one is being asked to perceive that an item can be classified as either a square or red. Similarly, a homonym may be classified by one of several meanings. In both cases, the actual item being perceived (the object or the word) does not change. Yet the item can be classified or viewed in different ways. As students develop and grow, it may be appropriate to teach new meanings for homonyms by relating a new meaning closely to a common word-label and an already known meaning. But for children in the primary grades, you must tread carefully. If the goal is to teach a new meaning for a homonym, then learning the meaning is of primary importance, not the fact that the word-label may have more than one meaning. Thus, teachers in the lower grades must consider teaching new meanings of homonyms in the same

As students read independently in materials of interest, they increase their vocabulary knowledge.

manner as teaching normal, single-meaning words. If the goal is to teach students that words might have more than one meaning, then focusing on homonyms as double-meaning words is appropriate.

We do not mean to suggest that young students do not use words in more than one way or for more than one meaning. Children know at an early age that an airplane can fly and that a fly is a sometimes bothersome insect. The confusion results when young children are asked to become consciously aware that the label for two separate concepts is the same. Young students seem to feel that the two words are separate items even though they sound the same. It is the ability to see similarity and difference across several dimensions at the same time which appears to be unavailable before the multiple class membership stage has been reached. An anecdote illustrates this point. Before attaining multiple class membership ability, youngsters who live in San Francisco answer yes to the questions

Do you live in San Francisco?

Do you live in California?

These same youngsters answer no when asked

Do you live in both San Francisco and California?

Do you live in San Francisco and California at the same time?

In the same manner, those youngsters who use multiple meanings before being able to multiply classify are not conscious of the similarity of the word-label. Attempting to teach a new meaning by drawing attention to the similarity of the label can cause confusion which may be detrimental to the goal of teaching the unknown meaning. In time, the ability to perceive the similarity of a label across meanings will develop naturally.

A Note on Referential Terms

BEFORE READING ON

In the following examples, decide where Steve is physically located.

(a) Steve, on the telephone, says, "Come to my house tonight."

(b) Steve, on the telephone, says, "Go to my house tonight."

In the following examples, decide where the food is physically located.

(c) Sally, Bill, and Tom are sitting at a table. Sally says to Tom, "He has the food."

(d) Sally, Bill, and Tom are sitting at a table. Sally says to Tom, "The food is over here."

(e) Sally, Bill, and Tom are sitting at a table. Sally says to Tom, "The food is over there."

These examples illustrate that certain vocabulary terms have **referential properties.** Such terms can be fully understood only through experiential knowledge which clarifies meaningful references that are not specifically stated in the text. You probably correctly stated that Steve was at home while on the telephone in example (a) and not at home in example (b). In example (c), Bill would have had the food, while in examples (d) and (e), respectively, the food would have been near Sally and with either Bill or Tom. Your ability to specify the locations in the examples indicates your facility with one kind of reference—place reference. Other forms of reference and their effects on comprehension of text are discussed in the next chapter.

In the context of this chapter's focus on the teaching and learning of vocabulary, however, note that referential terms can cause great difficulty for young children. Be aware that vocabulary items often have referential meanings that go beyond the word's literal use in the text being read. When teaching such terms, it is not enough to only explain the word's meaning. A discussion aimed at developing the students' understanding of the referential nature of the term to be learned, with several examples of its use, is necessary.

referential properties: Word characteristics requiring readers or listeners to use background knowledge to determine the object or person being mentioned.

SAMPLE ACTIVITIES

- In lower grades, use examples to teach pronoun reference in a number of sentence structures. For example, use sentences like

  The teacher gave *both* Sue and Joyce *erasers,* even though the girls didn't need *them.*
  Even though the girls didn't need *them,* the teacher gave *both* Sue and Joyce *erasers.*

  Chris wanted a drink of water because *she* was thirsty.
  Because *she* was thirsty, *Chris* wanted a drink of water.

  Bill said *the bike was new,* but Tipp did not believe *it.*
  Tipp did not believe *it,* but Bill said *the bike was new.*

  Discuss that some referential terms can refer to items in front of them or behind them. Also, draw attention to the fact that referential terms can refer to one thing, more than one thing, a phrase, clause, or sentence.

- For young children, use a gradual build-up of sentences, ultimately leading to replacement of a part or parts of the sentence with a referential term.

  Susie eats.
  Susie eats (lunch).
  Willy eats (lunch).
  Susie and Willy eat (lunch).
  (They) eat lunch.
  Susie and Willy eat (it).
  (They) eat (it).

Part of the difficulty children have in understanding referential terms can be related to both their cognitive level and to the differences between oral and written language. We know that children's understanding of time and place does not develop fully until about the third grade (Lowery, 1981; Bybee & Sund, 1982). Coupled with oral and written language differences, this results in confusion when children are asked to comprehend referential vocabulary terms in text. In oral communication, the sentence "The food is over there" or "He has the food" is usually accompanied by some form of gesture, such as pointing, which clarifies meaning and makes it more concrete. In text, quotation marks are an aid to meaning, but can easily cause confusion. Attempting to decide where the food is in written text such as

Sally said, "Tom said, the food is here."

is a high-level cognitive task. Does Sally or Tom have the food? Remember that saying that print is speech written down is often an inaccurate simplification.

TEACHING VOCABULARY FROM YOUR PERSONAL FRAMEWORK

As in other aspects of reading instruction, your view of reading will influence how you teach vocabulary lessons to your students. You are now familiar with the three possible explanations for how one reads (text based, reader based, and interactive) as well as the three explanations for how reading ability develops (mastery of specific skills, holistic language, and differential acquisition). Remember that a teacher's comprehension framework is formed by answers to questions about how one reads and how reading ability develops, and that teachers with comprehension frameworks modify their frameworks based on the success of their lessons. These teachers use their observations about their teaching and their students' success to modify their answers to these two questions, thus modifying their comprehension frameworks.

Your comprehension framework will influence the instructional decisions you will make in teaching vocabulary in much the same manner that was noted in the chapters examining readiness and decoding. The following paragraphs point out potential instructional differences in teaching vocabulary when comprehension frameworks result from different explanations to the questions about how one reads and how reading ability develops.

The Influence of Explanations for How One Reads

If you were to observe a teacher whose instruction evolves from a comprehension framework with a text-based explanation for how one reads, you would probably see vocabulary instruction being closely tied to a set of materials, possibly basal readers, used in class. The words to be taught would be those identified as important for the comprehension of the particular selection to be read. Vocabulary words outside those appearing in the reading material would not be keys in vocabulary teaching because, since this explanation states that meaning resides in the text, it would be important to know the words that were in the reading selection. The focus of instruction would most likely be based around the meaning of the vocabulary as found in the reading selection. There would be examples of each word's meaning in situations similar to those found in the reading selection, with little discussion about related terms or concepts that students might already know.

Teachers with reader-based explanations within their comprehension frameworks may choose to use activities to teach vocabulary that begin with the student's knowledge of related concepts. Areas of overlap regarding already known concepts and the one to be taught would be expanded until the new concept was learned. For example, if *conclusive* was the item to be learned, attention would be drawn to similarities to the structure of *conclude,* and a discussion of the relationship between the two words might follow. Synonyms would be a part of vocabulary instruction, with students encouraged to use the new vocabulary in situations that are already known to them. There would be effort taken to clearly relate the vocabulary to the student's current knowledge. Semantic webs, for example, would be a preferred method of instruction, as would use of analogies.

Comprehension frameworks built around interactive explanations for how one reads would emphasize vocabulary found in the student's reading selections, and also use the student's background knowledge to teach vocabulary items. Teachers with comprehension frameworks would try to teach the vocabulary within reading selections, and the specific meaning of the item(s) as used in the reading, but would go on to include alternate meanings and meanings that students already knew for the word.

The Influence of Explanations for How Reading Ability Develops

While the answers to questions about how one reads effect what vocabulary is taught, explanations for how reading ability develops have a greater impact on how vocabulary is taught. Teachers with different explanations for how reading develops will tend to choose different instructional methods to teach vocabulary lessons.

Mastery of specific skills explanations imply that there are a set of skills that can help in learning and that learning each skill results in overall mastery. A teacher with this explanation as part of the comprehension framework would teach vocabulary by focusing on word parts. Lessons could relate to the word's configuration and spelling, along with its prefix, suffix, and root. Indeed, since knowing prefixes and suffixes helps with vocabulary development, (1) teaching affixes separately from root words as a skill to be mastered; (2) teaching common Latin and Greek root words and their histories; (3) teaching dictionary skills; and (4) teaching other skills that would help in vocabulary acquisition would be important. Teachers with mastery of specific skills explanations may teach vocabulary in isolation since vocabulary knowledge may be viewed as one of the specific skills to be learned.

A teacher with a holistic language explanation would teach vocabulary in real-language settings, using more inductive methods. The teacher would present vocabulary in context, using experiential techniques, demonstrations, and oral discussion as much as possible. Vocabulary might be taught within a language experience approach, for example, where an experiential activity might provide the student with a number of concepts to which vocabulary would be provided. For example, a vivid picture might be provided and then vocabulary pertaining to the picture taught. If the picture contained a very large building, for example, the word *enormous* might be taught in the context of the picture. Then children would be encouraged to use the word in telling a language experience story based on the picture. A teacher with a comprehension framework that includes holistic language explanations for how reading ability develops would not spend much time teaching or focusing on specific word parts or teaching affixes as meaningful items in themselves, but would attempt to increase students' vocabularies through independent reading activities.

Teachers can also answer the question about how reading ability develops through a differential acquisition explanation. Such an explanation views reading as a process that is different at different stages of maturity. Consequently, a teacher whose comprehension framework includes such explanations would teach vocabulary differently depending on the reader's level. Beginning readers might be taught specific word meanings as they appear in reading materials. They might also be taught subskills such as the meaning of affixes and the use of surrounding context to find word meaning. As students become more proficient readers, the emphasis might shift to techniques using analogies, synonyms, and other techniques as appropriate to the students' reading abilities and cognitive skills.

THE MAJOR POINTS

1. In primary grades, teachers generally teach the word for an already known concept. In intermediate grades and beyond, teachers generally teach both a concept and its word-label.
2. Before presenting an unknown word, first teach the concept represented by the word.
3. Vocabulary lessons can be based on word lists, on reading materials, on children's oral language, or on a combination of these three.

4. When teaching vocabulary, give concrete examples as much as possible. A discussion of the features of the items to be learned compared to similar, known items is a valuable activity.
5. Homonyms and referential terms can be difficult to learn for children in lower elementary grades.
6. Be sure that vocabulary activities include many and varied examples of the item to be learned in context.
7. Vocabulary growth continues throughout one's life. Terms that are already known become increasingly refined while new terms are added to those we know.

1. Write a brief statement relating vocabulary development to concept development. How would this relationship influence your teaching of vocabulary in elementary grades?
2. You need to teach the following new terms for the words listed to second-grade students.

Word	Already Known	To Be Learned
scale	weigh scale	fish scale
race	run a race	human race
pen	writing instrument	a type of cage (pig pen)

Describe your lesson.

3. Provide three activities which you would use in teaching a set of vocabulary words (remember, you must provide a range of activities).
4. What is the role of pretesting in a vocabulary lesson?
5. What does it mean to use both positive and negative examples when teaching vocabulary?
6. How might vocabulary teaching differ in primary and intermediate grades? Why? You may wish to think of the words in question 2 as one source of difference. There are others.
7. Look at two different levels of a reading program. Examine the introductory material to see how vocabulary to be taught is identified and introduced. How are teaching strategies presented in the teacher's guide section?

Beck, I. & McKeown, M. G. (1983). Learning words well—A program to enhance vocabulary and comprehension. *Reading Teacher, 36,* 622–25.
    Describes a program to teach vocabulary using a varied method (involving cognitive, physical, and affective elements) to fourth-grade students.

Fry, E. & Sakiey, E. (1986). Common words not taught in basal reading series. *The Reading Teacher, 39,* 395–98.

Points out that basal series generally teach about 50% of the 3,000 most common English words. Also suggests that teachers may want to supplement basal lists with lists provided in the article.

Johnson, D. D. & Pearson, P. D. (1984). *Teaching reading vocabulary* (2nd Edition). New York: Holt, Rinehart & Winston.

A readable paperback including many ideas and suggestions for teaching vocabulary, as well as providing a good conceptual background.

Marzano, R. J. (1984). A cluster approach to vocabulary instruction: A new direction from the research literature. *Reading Teacher, 38,* 168–73.

Discusses teaching vocabulary in clusters of concepts and presents a list of clusters of words chosen from elementary textbooks.

REFERENCES

Ahr, P. & Youniss, J. (1970). Reasons for failure on the class inclusion problem. *Child Development, 41,* 131–43.

Anderson, R. C. & Ortony, A. (1975). On putting apples into bottles—a problem of polysemy. *Cognitive Psychology, 7,* 176–80.

Anderson, R. C. & Freebody, P. (1981). Vocabulary knowledge. In J. T. Guthrie (ed.), *Comprehension and teaching: Research Reviews,* (pp. 77–117). Newark, DE: International Reading Association.

Anderson, R. C.; Pichert, J. W.; Goetz, E. T.; Schallert, D. L.; Stevens, K. V.; Trollip, S. R. (1976). Instantiation of general terms. *Journal of Verbal Learning and Verbal Behavior, 15,* 667–79.

Anderson, R. C; Reynolds, R. E.; Schallert, D. L.; & Goetz, E. T. (1977). Frameworks for comprehending discourse. *American Education Research Journal, 14,* 367–81.

Anderson, R. C.; Spiro, R. J.; & Anderson, M. C. (1978). Schemata as scaffolding for the representation of information in discourse. *American Educational Research Journal, 15,* 433–40.

Bolinger, D. L (1961). Verbal evocation. *Lingua, 10,* 113–27.

Brown, R. & McNeill, D. (1966). The tip-of-the-tongue phenomenon. *Journal of Verbal Learning and Verbal Behavior, 5,* 325–37.

Bybee, R. W. & Sund, R. B. (1982). *Piaget for educators.* Columbus, OH: C. E. Merrill.

Carroll, J. B. (1964a). Words, meanings and concepts: Part I. Their nature. *Harvard Educational Review, 34,* 178–90.

Carroll, J. B. (1964b). Words, meanings and concepts: Part II. Concept teaching and learning. *Harvard Educational Review, 34,* 191–202.

Criscuolo, N. (1980). Creative vocabulary building. *Journal of Reading, 24,* 260–61.

Dale, E.; O'Rourke, J.; & Bamman, H. A. (1971). *Techniques of teaching vocabulary.* Palo Alto, CA: Field Enterprises.

DeHaven, E. P. (1983). *Teaching and learning the language arts* (2nd Edition). Boston: Little, Brown & Co.

Eeds, M. (1985). Bookwords: Using a beginning word list of high frequency words from children's literature K–3. *Reading Teacher, 38,* 418–23.

Fry, E. & Sakiey, E. (1986). Common words not taught in basal reading series. *The Reading Teacher, 39,* 395–98.

Ginsberg, H. & Opper, S. (1969). *Piaget's theory of intellectual development.* Englewood Cliffs, NJ: Prentice-Hall.

Gipe, J. (1978–79). Investigating techniques for teaching word meanings. *Reading Research Quarterly, 14,* 624–44.

Gold, Y. (1981). Helping students discover the origins of words. *Reading Teacher, 35,* 350–51.

Haggard, M. R. (1979). *Vocabulary acquisition during elementary and postelementary years: A preliminary report.* Unpublished manuscript, Northern Illinois University.

Halff, H. M.; Ortony, A.; & Anderson, R. C. (1976). A context-sensitive representation of word meaning. *Memory and Cognition, 4,* 378–83.

Huff, P. (1983). Classroom organization. In E. Alexander (ed.), *Teaching reading,* 2nd Edition (pp. 450–68). Boston: Little, Brown & Co.

Johnson, D. D. & Pearson, P. D. (1984). *Teaching reading vocabulary* (2nd Edition). New York: Holt, Rinehart & Winston.

Katz, J. J. (1972). *Semantic Theory.* New York: Harper & Row.

Kinzer, C. K. (1981). *Regular vs. mixed meanings effects on second and sixth graders' learning of multiple meaning words.* Unpublished doctoral dissertation, University of California, Berkeley.

Kinzer, C. K. (1982). *Interference effects of known meanings on vocabulary learning: Encountering the unexpected during the reading process.* Paper presented at the annual meeting of the International Reading Association, Chicago, IL.

Klar, D. & Wallace, J. (1976). *Cognitive development: A constructivist view.* New York: Erlbaum.

Kofsky, E. (1966). A scalogram study of classificatory development. *Child Development, 37,* 190–204.

Kurth, R. (1980). Building a conceptual base for vocabulary development. *Reading Psychology, 1,* 115–20.

Labov, W. (1973). The boundaries of words and their meanings. In Bailey, *et al.* (eds.). *New ways of analyzing variations in English.* Washington, D.C.: Georgetown University Press.

Leech, G. (1974). *Semantics.* New York: Penguin.

Lenneberg, E. H. (1967). *Biological foundations of language.* New York: John Wiley & Sons.

Lowery, L. (1981). *Learning about learning: Classification abilities.* Berkeley, CA: University of California, Berkeley, PDARC Department of Education Publication.

Lyons, J. (1977). *Semantics* (2 vols.). Cambridge, MA: Cambridge University Press.

Mason, J.; Kniseley, E.; & Kendall, J. (1979). Effects of polysemous words on sentence comprehension. *Reading Research Quarterly, 15,* 49–65.

Petty, W. T.; Petty, D. C.; & Becking, M. E. (1985). *Experiences in language: Tools and techniques for language arts methods* (4th Edition). Boston: Allyn & Bacon.

Rosch, E. H. (1978). Principles of categorization. In E. H. Rosch & B. B. Lloyd (eds.), *Cognition and categorization* (pp. 27–48). New York: Erlbaum.

Sherfey, G. & Huff, P. (1976). Designing the science learning center. *Science and Children, 14,* 11–12.

Sigel, I. (1966). Child development and social science education: Part IV. *Social Science Consortium,* mimeo.

Vygotsky, L. S. (1962). *Thought and language.* (E. Haufman & G. Vokow, trans.) Cambridge, Mass.: MIT Press.

Woodson, M. I. C. E. (1974). Seven aspects of teaching concepts. *Journal of Educational Psychology, 66,* 184–88.

6 The Comprehension of Extended Text

COMPREHENDING EXTENDED TEXT ■ DEVELOPING SYNTACTIC
KNOWLEDGE SKILLS ■ DEVELOPING DISCOURSE KNOWLEDGE
SKILLS ■ QUESTIONING STRATEGIES ■ HOW SPECIFIC FRAMEWORKS
AFFECT INSTRUCTIONAL DECISIONS

Mrs. Rogers came into the kitchen. "Good morning, Amelia Bedelia," she said.

"Good morning," said Amelia Bedelia.

"I will have some cereal with my coffee this morning," said Mrs. Rogers.

"All right," said Amelia Bedelia.

Mrs. Rogers went into the dining room. Amelia Bedelia got the cereal. She put
some in a cup. And she fixed Mrs. Rogers some cereal with her coffee. She
took it into the dining room.

"Amelia Bedelia!" said Mrs. Rogers. "What is that mess?"

"It's your cereal with coffee," said Amelia Bedelia.

From P. Parish, *Come Back, Amelia Bedelia,* (New York: Harper & Row, 1971), pp. 6–9.

This chapter is a bridge between the word-level aspects of reading comprehension discussed in chapters 4 and 5 and the longer and more complex aspects of reading comprehension that will be discussed in chapters 7 and 8. It describes two knowledge sources important to the comprehension of extended text: syntactic knowledge and discourse knowledge. In addition, it presents instructional activities designed to develop these two knowledge sources. Finally, the chapter demonstrates how the nature of a teacher's comprehension framework influences instructional decisions related to the development of syntactic and discourse knowledge. By the end of this chapter, you will be able to identify instructional activities consistent with your evolving framework of reading comprehension.

After reading this chapter, you will be able to

1. define inferencing and explain why inferential reasoning is important for reading comprehension;
2. identify several differences between oral and written language and explain how these create difficulties for young children learning to read;
3. identify at least two instructional activities that develop the use of syntactic knowledge during reading comprehension;
4. identify at least two instructional activities that develop the use of discourse knowledge during reading comprehension;
5. create discussion questions at literal, inferential, and evaluative levels of comprehension and indicate when to use each type of question;
6. explain how your comprehension framework influences instructional decisions regarding the development of syntactic and discourse knowledge.

COMPREHENDING EXTENDED TEXT

So far, we have been largely concerned with developing the components of reading comprehension that help children read and understand the meanings of individual words. You have learned, for example, about instruction in decoding knowledge (chapter 4) and vocabulary knowledge (chapter 5).

In the next three chapters, we will focus on the components of reading comprehension that help children read and understand sentences, paragraphs, and other more extensive units of writing such as stories, articles, letters, poetry, text books, manuals, or essays.

Units of writing that are at least a sentence in length are called **extended text.** When readers encounter extended text, they continue to use their decoding and vocabulary knowledge to assist comprehension. In addition, however, readers must also use at least two other knowledge sources: syntactic knowledge and discourse knowledge.

Syntactic knowledge includes one's understanding of the word-order rules that exist in a language at the sentence level and how they function to communicate meaning. Your syntactic knowledge, for example, helps you to distinguish the difference in meaning between *Tom saw Mary* and *Mary saw Tom,* two sentences containing identical words but ordered differently. Syntactic knowledge contributes to comprehending extended text.

Discourse knowledge also contributes to comprehending extended text (Fredricksen, 1975; Meyer, 1975; Beck, McKeown, Omanson, & Pople, 1984). **Discourse knowledge** consists of one's knowledge of language organization at units beyond the single sentence level. Just as syntactic knowledge allows you to understand the meaningful relationships among words when they appear in a particular order, discourse knowledge allows you to understand the meaningful relationships among sentences appearing in a particular order. Consider this paragraph.

> You can see that each animal is unique. Finally, a barracuda will bite. It releases a very strong odor. It also has a very thick skin. When a skunk gets excited it can ruin another animal's lunch. It has long sharp teeth. An armadillo likes to roll into a ball.

In this order, the preceding paragraph is meaningless except for the separate ideas expressed in the individual sentences. Meaningful relationships among sentences do not exist. As a result, it is difficult to comprehend. Note what happens, though, when the sentences are reordered and a single new sentence is added to the beginning.

> Animals protect themselves in different ways. An armadillo likes to roll into a ball. It also has a very thick skin. When a skunk gets excited it can ruin another animal's lunch. It releases a very strong odor. Finally, a barracuda will bite. It has long sharp teeth. You can see that each animal is unique.

In this order, you are able to understand more than the individual sentence meanings. You are also able to understand the meaningful relationships that exist among sentences. As a result, you have a clear sense of what the paragraph is about as a whole and your recall of the information in the paragraph is enhanced. It is your discourse knowledge that allows you to comprehend the relationships among individual sentences in this paragraph.

extended text: Units of writing at least a sentence in length, including sentences, paragraphs, stories, articles, and books.

syntactic knowledge: Knowledge of the word-order rules that determine grammatical function and sometimes meaning and pronunciation.

discourse knowledge: Knowledge of language organization at units beyond the single-sentence level.

This chapter describes instruction designed to help children develop and use syntactic knowledge. It also describes instruction designed to help children develop and use discourse knowledge, a discussion continued in chapters 7 and 8. First, however, it is important to consider two concepts intrinsic to any discussion of how syntactic and discourse knowledge function during the comprehension of extended text: the nature of inferential reasoning and the consequences of linguistic differences between oral and written language.

Inferences

inference: A reasoned assumption about information not explicitly stated in the text.

An **inference** is a reasoned assumption about information not explicitly stated in the text. Readers make inferences whenever they add meaning to the explicit meaning of the text. Some people refer to inferential reasoning as reading between the lines (Pearson & Johnson, 1978). Using syntactic and discourse knowledge to make correct inferences is often difficult for young readers as they read extended text. Perhaps this is why children get so much pleasure out of Amelia Bedelia's troublesome tendency to make inappropriate inferences, as demonstrated in the quotation at the beginning of this chapter.

One type of inference occurs when a reader connects two different pieces of information in a text. Consider the following sentences.

> The Marshall Islands consist of low coral atolls.
> Majuro is the capital of the Marshall Islands.

Notice these sentences do not explicitly specify that Majuro lies on a low coral atoll. Nevertheless, a proficient reader is likely to reason, or infer, that since the Marshall Islands are low coral atolls and since Majuro is the capital of the Marshall Islands, then Majuro must also lie on a low coral atoll. This first type of inference is called a **text-connecting inference** (Warren, Nicholas, & Trabasso, 1979) since it requires a reader to connect pieces of information existing in a text.

text-connecting inference: An inference requiring readers to connect two different pieces of information in a text to make a reasoned assumption about meaning.

A second type of inference takes place when readers fill in information from background knowledge not available in the text. If you have the appropriate background knowledge, for example, you can infer the correct activity in the following sentence.

> Dr. Christiansen made the cast quickly with his
> Orvis graphite containing a double-tapered line.

slot-filling inference: An inference requiring readers to fill in information from background knowledge not available in the text.

If you have adequate background knowledge, you are likely to infer that Dr. Christiansen was engaged in fly fishing and not the repair of a broken bone. This type of inference is called a **slot-filling inference** since you must fill in empty slots of meaning from your background knowledge (Warren, Nicholas, & Trabasso, 1979).

"Mary had a little lamb. Its fleece was white as snow." You are probably not aware of the many inferences you made as you comprehended these two sentences. Trabasso (1981) uses this short couplet to demonstrate the crucial, but often unnoticed, role played by inferences in even the simplest comprehension tasks. Consider a few of the inferences you made (and did not make) in each sentence.

A POINT TO PONDER

1. In "Mary had a little lamb", you made a number of slot-filling inferences. First, you inferred that Mary was a little girl. You could have inferred that *Mary* referred to a ewe. Second, you inferred that *had* meant *owned*. You could have inferred that *had* meant *ate* (that is, Mary had a little bit of lamb for her entree). You could have also inferred that *had* meant *gave birth to* (that is, Mary, the ewe, gave birth to a little lamb). Finally, you inferred that *lamb* referred to a live baby sheep. You could have inferred that *lamb* referred to a stuffed animal. You could also have inferred that *lamb* referred to a type of meat.

2. In the sentence "Its fleece was white as snow", you made at least one text-connecting inference. You probably inferred that *its* referred to the lamb. You could have inferred that *its* referred to Mary, the ewe giving birth to a baby lamb. You could also have inferred that *its* referred to the lamb which was eaten by Mary. In this case the inferred meaning of *was* changes to something like "had once been" (that is, Mary had a little bit of lamb for her entree. Its fleece had once been as white as snow).

3. You probably inferred that this was the beginning of a nursery rhyme. You could also have inferred that this was a descriptive account of an event such as a dinner or a ewe giving birth.

Readers frequently depend on background knowledge to make inferences (Anderson & Shifrin, 1980). Your inferences with respect to Mary and her little lamb in the preceding example are based on background knowledge about this particular poem. If you had never seen or heard this poem, you would have been more likely to make a different set of inferences.

Readers use their background knowledge to help connect implicit relationships in texts and to fill in missing information during the comprehension process. Comprehension of extended text thus appears to depend on what the reader knows about the world as much as it does on the information in the text itself. This is one reason that people often consider reading an interactive process (Anderson, Hiebert, Scott, & Wilkinson, 1985; Mason, 1984; Rumelhart, 1981). Much instruction in syntactic and discourse knowledge helps readers make appropriate inferences.

Differences between Oral and Written Language

A teacher of reading comprehension interested in developing students' syntactic and discourse knowledge must also understand a second concept: the consequences of linguistic differences between oral and written language. Consider, for a moment, children who arrive at school ready to begin formal instruction in reading. To a large extent, these children have already acquired a sophisticated understanding of oral language. What beginning readers need to acquire, then, consists primarily of those aspects of language that are somehow different in written language (Leu, 1982; Olson, 1977). Differences between oral and written language exist at each of the major knowledge sources associated with the comprehension process.

Differences Associated with Decoding Knowledge. With respect to decoding, there is one obvious difference between oral and written lan-

Virginia

Sleepy Dream.

One day sleepy had a dream, it was about. He was flying a kite in the park sleepy had a good time at the park when sleepy was flying his kite he. Bumped into a tree his kite flew in the air he. wood not fly a kite again. Then sleepy woke up he saw that he was at home.

The oral language that children bring to school is different from written language in predictable ways. Often this is most noticeable in their writing. Beginning readers (and writers) need to become familiar with the conventions of written language.

guage: separate symbol systems are used to represent meaning. In oral language, sounds are used to represent meaning; in written language, letters are used. Beginning readers are already familiar with how sounds are used to represent meaning; they are relatively unfamiliar, however, with how letters are used. To a certain extent, then, young readers must become familiar with relationships between letters and sounds in order to access meaning in written language. This aspect of reading comprehension was covered in chapter 4.

Differences Associated with Vocabulary Knowledge. With respect to vocabulary knowledge, young readers need to become familiar with the meanings of words they have not yet acquired from their oral language experiences. Often these new word meanings are peculiar or more frequently found in writing on specialized topics. The development of vocabulary knowledge was discussed in chapter 5.

Differences Associated with Syntactic Knowledge. With respect to syntactic knowledge, there are at least two important learning tasks as children move from oral to written language. First, children must become familiar with how punctuation is used to represent the stress and intonation patterns of oral language and, thus, communicate meaning. For example:

1. Now! I need your help! (Not Now I need your help.)
2. Bob talked to the teacher with Bill and Becky. Lou wanted to talk to them too. (Not Bob talked to the teacher with Bill and Becky Lou wanted to talk to them too.)
3. One day, Jim forgot to give his horse, Silver, food and water. (Not One day, Jim forgot to give his horse silver, food, and water.)

A second syntactic difference between oral and written language concerns the more complex word-order patterns typically used to communicate meaning in written language (Loban, 1976). In particular, writing tends to use more complex syntactic patterns to express sequence relationships (for example, After Tom read his book, he had dinner) and cause-and-effect relationships (for example, Because I had gone swimming, I was very tired). Often in writing, words like *because, consequently, before,* and *after* are used to explicitly mark sequence or cause-and-effect relationships within sentences. In oral language, less complex syntactic patterns are typically found. One tends to find both cause-and-effect and sequence relationships implicitly stated with coordinating conjunctions such as *and* in a chaining style.

Written Language

Before we went fishing last week, my dad fell in the water. *Because* he fell in the water, he caught a cold and *therefore* had to return home. Fishing alone, I caught a fish.

Oral Language

We went fishing last week . . . *and* . . . my dad caught a cold. He fell in the water . . . *and* . . . he had to go home . . . *and* . . . I caught a fish.

Thus, in addition to developing an understanding of punctuation conventions, young readers must become familiar with the syntactic markers of causation and sequence that appear more frequently in written language (Leu, 1982). They must also make the correct text connecting inferences when these markers are missing.

Differences Associated with Discourse Knowledge. With respect to discourse knowledge, two important differences between oral and written language exist. Each presents additional learning considerations for young readers who are unfamiliar with the characteristics of written language. First, written language requires that readers infer the meanings of implicit pronoun and adverbial referents (for example; *he, she, this, here, there,* or *now*) without a visible context (Rubin, 1980). Young children, who have experienced mainly oral language tasks, are accustomed to *seeing* the explicit references for these terms in the situation where a language event takes place. They are not as familiar with *imagining* the implicit meanings for pronoun and adverbial referents in written contexts. Although story illustrations provide some of the visual information for inferring the meaning of pronoun and adverbial referents, they can never capture all of the aspects in a continuously shifting situation. Making the text-connecting and slot-filling inferences demanded by pronoun and adverbial referents, therefore, presents an important learning task for beginning readers in written contexts.

A second difference also exists between oral and written language with respect to discourse knowledge, and presents difficulties for young children when learning to read. In their oral language experiences, children develop a clear knowledge of how oral conversations are organized and take place. The large majority of their oral language experiences require this discourse form. Children use their knowledge of conversational structure to make inferences during oral language experiences. Children who are learning to read, however, often lack an understanding of the structural characteristics of discourse forms commonly found in written language such as letters, fables, mysteries, newspaper articles, memos, or subject-area textbooks. They are, therefore, less likely to make inferences that require an understanding of written language forms. You must hear or read a number of fairy tales, for example, before you infer the significance of a sentence that begins "Once upon a time . . . ." Compared to oral conversations, children have fewer opportunities to develop an understanding of how stories (narratives) are organized (Sulzby, 1982). They have even fewer opportunities to develop an understanding of how informational writing (exposition) is organized. Beginning readers need to develop an understanding of the structural characteristics of those forms found much more frequently in written language such as narratives and exposition.

Helping Students to Comprehend Extended Text

BEFORE READING ON

If you analyze the comprehension skills taught by different reading programs, you will quickly notice that each program teaches a unique set of skills to help students comprehend extended text. Many skills are taught in one program but not in others. Other skills are listed in several programs but are uniquely labeled in each. Consider a sample of skills listed in two programs that promote the comprehension of extended text.

The Houghton Mifflin Reading Program (Durr, W. K. *et al.,* 1985)

1. Getting meanings from comparison and contrast.
2. Getting meanings from appositional constructions.
3. No similar skill.
4. Using punctuation marks and typographical variations as meaning aids.
5. Recognizing cause-and-effect relationships.
6. Noting correct sequence.
7. Understanding referents for pronouns and adverbs.
8. To infer: drawing conclusions.
9. To infer: predicting outcomes.

Scott Foresman Reading Series (Aaron, I. *et al.,* 1985)

1. No similar skill.
2. No similar skill.
3. Develops new levels of thinking.
4. Uses conventions of written English: punctuation.
5. Recognizes relationships: cause and effect.
6. Recognizes relationships: sequence.
7. Uses context to identify word referents: pronouns and adverbs.
8. Makes judgments about what is read: draws conclusions.
9. Makes judgments about what is read: predicts outcomes.

From looking at these data, what can you conclude about instruction in comprehending extended text? Which aspects are common to the two programs? If you have access to other reading programs, see if they also teach the skills that are common to these two programs. Do any programs teach the common skills identically? In an identical sequence?

Experts in reading do not agree about what children need to know to comprehend extended text. You can see this from the skills that are taught in different reading programs. Nevertheless, we do know something about the comprehension of extended text, and instructional activities exist that develop syntactic and discourse knowledge. This chapter covers aspects of text comprehension considered important by most experts, even though different experts will use different labels to describe them. Many of these skills require inferential reasoning. Most are related to the differences between oral and written language discussed earlier. The instructional aspects of text comprehension covered in this chapter include

skills often associated with syntactic knowledge

1. understanding punctuation
2. understanding sequencing
3. understanding cause-and-effect relationships

skills often associated with discourse knowledge

1. understanding pronoun and adverb referents
2. drawing conclusions
3. predicting outcomes

Recognize that each of these skills is not limited strictly to either syntactic or discourse knowledge. That is, understanding punctuation, sequence, and cause-and-effect relationships may, at times, be considered discourse level phenomena. Two paragraphs, not two sentences, for example, might be temporally sequenced or causally related. Conversely, the ability to understand pronoun and adverb referents, to draw conclusions, or to predict outcomes may be considered syntactic-level phenomenon when each takes place within a single-sentence context. Nevertheless, we will use this categorization system since it is similar to that used in many instructional programs.

DEVELOPING SYNTACTIC KNOWLEDGE SKILLS

Punctuation

A reader's ability to determine stress and intonation while reading contributes to the comprehension process (Cook-Gumperz & Gumperz, 1981). Knowledge of punctuation assists a reader in determining the correct stress and intonation in a sentence. Knowledge of punctuation usually includes familiarity with the following:

Period	.	Indicates a long pause and the end of a sentence.
Comma	,	Indicates a short pause and the end or beginning of an idea within a sentence. Also separates items in a list.
Exclamation Point	!	Indicates a long pause and a particularly strong feeling.

Quotation Marks	" "	Indicates what someone said (with appropriate intonation) or wrote. Also used to show some unique use of a word or phrase.
Internal Quotes	' '	Indicates what someone said or wrote that someone else said or wrote.
Question Mark	?	Indicates a long pause with prior "rounding", up or down, of intonation.
Semicolon	;	Indicates a short pause between two related propositions.
Colon	:	Indicates a long pause before a list.
Italic or Boldface	*italic* **bold**	Indicates greater stress, for contrastive emphasis.
Parenthesis	( )	Indicates an extra thought or aside.
Ellipsis	. . .	Indicates a long pause within a sentence or a break in a quotation.

Teaching Punctuation

Instruction in recognizing stress and intonation patterns through punctuation takes place early in the reading program, usually by the end of the third grade. Monitoring of this ability will continue, however, throughout the elementary years. Instruction in punctuation frequently takes place by the teacher linking children's oral speech to a written representation of that speech. You may wish to follow a method framework similar to the following as you teach punctuation.

1. *Elicit oral language.* Ask a student to orally produce a sentence containing the stress and intonation pattern you wish to teach.
2. *Write.* Write the sentence with the targeted punctuation pattern.
3. *Model.* Read and model the correct stress and intonation. Point out the punctuation marks you wish to teach. Define them.
4. *Practice.* Provide practice with similar sentences containing the same punctuation marks. Allow the students to read them.

Punctuation: The Comma in a Sequence

Teacher: Daria, tell us three things that you do before you come to school in the morning.

Daria: Let's see. I wake up, I eat breakfast, and I brush my teeth.

(Teacher writes on the blackboard: *Daria wakes up, eats breakfast, and brushes her teeth in the morning.*)

Teacher: Listen while I read this sentence. (Reads) Do you see how I wrote this little mark between each of the things which Daria does in the morning? This mark is called a comma. Can you say that word? Comma. What happens when I'm reading and come to a comma? Listen again. (Reads).

Sam: You kind of stop for a bit but not like at the end.

Teacher: Right. With a comma you should just stop reading for a little bit, but not as long as at the end of a sentence. Let's read some more sentences like this. Harry, what do you do when you get home after school? Tell us three or four things so we can write them and put commas between them.

Harry: I go home. I change my clothes and I have a snack, and I ride my dirt bike, and I have dinner.

(Teacher writes and has children orally read: *Harry goes home, changes his clothes, has a snack, and rides his dirt bike until dinner.*)

(Repeat with other children.)

Here are some additional instructional activities for teaching punctuation.

SAMPLE ACTIVITIES

Question Pairs. When teaching question intonation, make two sets of cards: one containing sentence beginnings like *Can Sandra* and the other containing a verb and a question mark like *swim?* (see figure 6–1). Pick one card from each pile, put them in the correct order, and read them to students. Have students answer questions about themselves. After explaining the role of the question mark, allow students to draw a pair and read the resulting sentence with correct intonation. Have the appropriate student answer the question.

FIGURE 6–1
Question pair cards

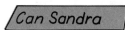

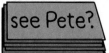

Dramatic Reading. Encourage groups of two or three students to choose a short selection (one or two paragraphs) for dramatic reading to the class. Be certain the selection contains a variety of punctuation marks. Allow each group a short period to practice and agree upon the exact intonation that will be used. This task may be used to introduce new books in either the class or the school library to your students. Have children read the most exciting parts in the story without giving away the ending.

Same Sentence; Different Meaning. Provide students with sentence pairs that are identical except for punctuation. Have students work in pairs to read each with the correct intonation and identify the correct meanings. You may wish to use sentence pairs like

> "Linda!" said Peter, "I need that paper done now."
> Linda said, "Peter, I need that paper done now."

Sequence Relationships

A **sequence relationship** is the time relationship that exists between two or more events. Often these events are expressed in the same or adjacent sentences. Sometimes they will be expressed in separate paragraphs. Sequence relationships are usually indicated in one of three ways:

sequence relationship: An implicitly or explicitly stated time relationship that exists between two or more events.

1. Sequentially ordered events that appear in separate sentences or paragraphs (for example, Tom finished his work. He went home.).
2. Sequentially ordered events that are linked with a coordinating conjunction (for example, Tom finished his work and he went home.).
3. Sequentially ordered events where the sequential relationship is indicated by a signal word.
   a. Where events appear in the order in which they happened (for example, Tom finished his work *before* he went home.)
   b. Where events appear in the opposite order in which they happened (for example, Tom went home *after* he finished his work.).

Sequence relationships may be stated implicitly or explicitly. Implicit sequence relationships may be indicated by sequentially ordered events within separate sentences or paragraphs (example 1) or by using the coordinating conjunction *and* within a single sentence (example 2). Implicit sequence relationships require inferential reasoning on the part of a reader. This type of inference is not unfamiliar to young readers, however. Sequence relationships in oral language are expressed identically.

Explicit sequence relationships are marked by signal words such as *before, after, then, later, following, first, initially, earlier, afterwards, next, finally* (example 3a and 3b). Young children are often unfamiliar with the meanings of some of these words. As a result, they need to learn their meanings. Most importantly, however, anticipate children having the greatest difficulty with the type of explicitly stated sequence relationship in example 3b (Pearson & Camperell, 1981; Pearson & Johnson, 1978). Here, events are listed in the opposite order from which they actually happened. In oral language, children are accustomed to events being stated in the order in which they occurred. Thus, they assume that a similar situation exists in written language and often interpret sentences like example 3b as Tom went home *and then* he finished his work. Pay particular attention to helping children comprehend sequence relationships like example 3b.

Teaching Sequence Relationships

With younger readers, sequence relationships can be taught using an adapted version of a language experience activity (LEA), a method often used during beginning reading instruction. Language experience activities often follow a procedural outline like the following.

1. Provide a vivid experience.
2. Elicit oral language that describes the experience.
3. Transcribe the children's oral language.
4. Help children to read the oral language that you have transcribed.

Throughout the LEA, discussion should help students identify the various events. Direct special attention to helping students understand the meanings of signal words and seeing how they are used to specify sequential relationships between events.

Language experience activities can take many forms and be used to teach many aspects of reading, especially to young children.

Teaching Sequential Relationships in a Language Experience Activity.

1. Provide children with an experience where sequentially ordered events take place. This might be an autumn leaf walk, a field trip, a story that you read to them, or even a short set of pictures that tell a story.
2. Elicit several sentences from the children, one for each event in the sequence they have just experienced. Transcribe these on the chalkboard as children produce them.

> We went to the library.
> Mrs. Koch showed us the bookshelves.
> We sat in a circle.
> Mrs. Koch read us a story.
> We came back to our room.

3. Have students read the entire sequence of sentences. Then initiate a discussion by asking questions such as What happened before we sat in a circle? What happened before Mrs. Koch read us a story? or What happened before we came back to our room? Write these responses next to the first set of sentences.

> Mrs. Koch showed us the bookshelves *before*
> we sat in a circle.
> We sat in a circle *before* Mrs. Koch read us a story.

4. After writing each sentence, discuss the meaning of the signal word and have children read. You may wish to elicit, write, read, and discuss other sentences off of the pattern you have chosen. Use events from the day's activities, events from a recent story they have read, and other sources.
5. Have students practice with similar types of sentences. Very young children may draw pictures, illustrating one of the sentences and then copying the sentence underneath it. More advanced readers may create their own set of sentences from personal events during the day.

Among older readers, instruction in understanding sequence relationships often takes place during the discussion of a story that has just been read. Questions that can direct students' attention to sequence relationships include:

- When did *X* take place?
- What happened before *X*?
- What happened before *Y*?
- Did *X* happen before or after *Y*?

An important distinction must be made here, though, between testing and teaching reading comprehension (Durkin, 1981; 1986). If you ask children only sequence questions and then either accept correct responses or reject incorrect responses (no matter how politely) you are testing children's comprehension rather than teaching comprehension. If, however, you follow sequence questions with requests to explain *how* students determined their answers, you are providing important learning opportunities for all children. This is especially true for those who may have missed the answer in the first place because they failed to either notice the signal word or make the appropriate inference.

Consider carefully the following points when teaching sequence relationships during the discussion of a story. Otherwise, the use of questions results in testing a student's understanding of sequence relationships, not teaching that student how to comprehend sequence relationships.

1. Ask a sequence question to focus children's attention on the part of the text you wish to use for instruction and to initiate a discussion about the sequence relationships that exist there. Do not ask a question merely to obtain a correct response.
2. A discussion must follow a question about a sequence relationship. You must ask children why they understood the story in a particular way if you hope to help those who failed to understand the sequence relationship. Demonstrate your reasoning process and have others demonstrate theirs.
3. Pay particular attention to sequence relationships when events are listed in the opposite order from which they actually happened. These, as mentioned, are likely to be particularly difficult for younger children to understand.
4. Before reading stories where you expect confusion about the sequence of events to impede comprehension, direct children to attend to the confusing portion of the text; that is, "Read and see if you can find out if *X* or *Y* happened first." Follow this with a discussion and have students explain their answers.

In addition to modifying language experience activities and using discussions to teach sequence relationships, a number of other instructional activities may be used. Here are several.

SAMPLE ACTIVITIES

Time Lines. Time lines can help children understand the sequence relationships in a text, particularly texts with a complicated or lengthy event sequence. Time lines may be used after the story is read, in a discussion. They may also be partially presented before reading a story to set up expectations and provide guidance during comprehension. See figure 6–2 for an example.

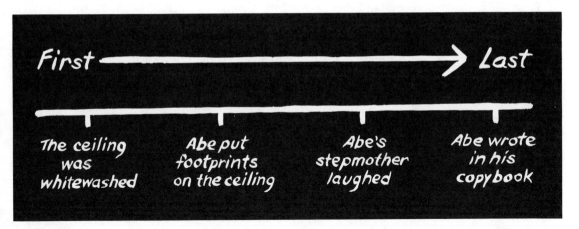

FIGURE 6–2
An example of a time line

Cloze Tasks. Cloze tasks can help children develop skill with sequence relationships. Discussions based on sentences like the following should not only focus on the words which were selected, but also on whether the sentences express the same meanings.

_____ putting on his shoe, Jim tied the laces.
   Before   After

Jim put on his shoe _____ he tied the laces.
               before   after

Out-of-Order Orders. Give children opportunities with sentences where events appear in the opposite order in which they happened. These can be taught by providing tasks like the following and discussing the reasons for children's choices.

Directions: Read the top sentence in each pair. Fill in the blank in the bottom sentence so that both mean the same thing.

1. **a.** Before eating dinner, Liz read a book.
   b. _____ reading a book, Liz ate dinner.
      Before   After
2. **a.** Jim saw his friend after he called home.
   b. _____ he called home, Jim saw his friend.
      Before   After

Cause-and-Effect Relationships

A **cause-and-effect relationship** is a meaningful relationship between two ideas where one idea is the consequence of the other. Sometimes the ideas will be expressed in separate paragraphs. More typically,

cause-and-effect relationship: An implicitly or explicitly stated causal relationship between two ideas, one the consequence of the other.

cause-and-effect relationships are expressed between two ideas within a single sentence or adjacent sentences. For example:

Candy is loaded with sugar. Thus, I never eat it for a snack.
(cause)   *(effect)*

Snow White fell asleep because she ate the poisoned apple.
(effect)   *(cause)*

Cause-and-effect relationships may be either explicit or implicit. Explicit relationships are indicated by signal words that signal the nature of the cause-and-effect relationship to the reader.

The hatch had just started *and therefore* the fish began to feed.
(cause)   *(signal words)*   *(effect)*

The most explicit and common signal word of causality is *because.* Other frequently used signal words are listed in table 6–1. Young children are often unfamiliar with these words and, thus, you may need to teach their meanings by following the procedures identified in chapter 5.

Implicit cause-and-effect relationships require that readers infer the appropriate relationship between two ideas since signal words are missing. Frequently, the coordinating conjunction *and* is used in place of a signal word or the two ideas are stated in separate sentences.

The hatch had just started and the fish began to feed.

The hatch had just started. The fish began to feed.

Implicit cause-and-effect relationships require readers to have the appropriate background knowledge in order to infer the correct meaning.

TABLE 6–1

Signal words for cause-and-effect relationships

Signal Words	Examples
because	He went home *because* he was ill.
(and) so	He was ill *and so* he went home.
(and) therefore	He was ill *and therefore* went home.
(and) hence	He was ill. *Hence* he went home.
(and) thus	He was ill *and thus* went home.
since	*Since* he was ill, he went home.
(and) as a result	He was ill *and as a result* went home.
(and) consequently	He was ill *and consequently* went home.
(and) for this reason	He was ill. *For this reason,* he went home.
that being the case	He looked ill. *That being the case,* he went home.
on account of	*On account of* his illness, he went home.
(and) accordingly	He looked ill *and accordingly* went home.

Without appropriate background knowledge, readers typically interpret the two ideas as temporally, but not causally, ordered. For example, "first, something hatched. Next the trout began to feed." The two events are not thought to be causally related.

Teaching Cause-and-Effect Relationships

Instruction designed to assist children's understanding of cause-and-effect relationships often takes place during a discussion, after students have either listened to or read a short passage. At beginning stages of formal reading instruction (in kindergarten or first grade), instruction usually takes place orally, after the teacher has read a selection to the students. Discussions focus on helping children understand causes, effects, signal words, and the way each serves to communicate meaning.

Cause-and-Effect Relationships in an Oral Context: Focus on Signal Words

MODEL LESSON

Teacher: I'm going to read you a short story about three children and I want you to see if you can find out why these children became lost.

> Once upon a time, three children went for a walk on a trail through the forest. They became lost because they left the trail. Two of the children started to cry since they were afraid. One child found the path again and showed everyone the way home.

Teacher: Does anyone know why the children became lost in this story?

Kurt: Yes, because they left the trail.

Teacher: Good. What word in the story helped you to know why they became lost?

Tama: *Because?*

Teacher: Right. We call words like *because* signal words since they act like a signal to tell us why things happened. Does anyone know why two of the children cried?

Erica: Because they were afraid.

Teacher: Yes. Listen to the sentence and see if you can hear a signal word that tells us why they cried. Two of the children started to cry since they were afraid.

Tim: I know. *Since.*

The teacher then reads a number of sentences with explicit cause-and-effect relationships indicated by signal words and asks students to identify the signal words that tell why something happened (for example, Joe went home *so* he could eat lunch.). Signal words are written on the board.

As with sequence relationships, instruction in cause-and-effect relationships among older readers often takes place during the discussion of a story. Questions that can direct students' attention to cause-and-effect relationships include

- Why did *Y* take place?
- What happened as a result of *X*?
- What caused *Y* to take place?
- What word tells us that *Y* happened because of *X*?

Be certain, again, that you use questions to initiate discussions that actually teach comprehension. It is important in these discussions to direct children's attention to the text so that concrete examples of the components of causal relationships (the cause, the signal word, and the effect) may be seen. The following model lesson shows how this might be done.

MODEL LESSON

Cause-and-Effect Relationships in a Written Context

Prior to reading, the concepts *cause, effect,* and *signal words* have been presented using familiar cause-and-effect sequences. The students have just finished reading silently a page with the following paragraph.

> The trouble was getting worse. In many villages, people were getting ready for war. Groups of men and young boys began training to be soldiers. They were called minutemen because they were ready to fight at a minute's notice (McGovern, 1975, p. 19).

Teacher: Look up at the first paragraph. Why were these soldiers called minutemen?

Tim: Because they could fight at a minute's notice.

Teacher: Tell us how you know that, Tim.

Tim: It says *because.*

Teacher: Right! *Because* is a signal word since it signals a special meaning between two ideas. It tells us why something happened. Can you see the two ideas in this sentence?

Linda: "They were called minutemen" and "they were ready to fight at a minute's notice."

Teacher: Good! Can anyone find the cause and the effect statements in this sentence?

Bonnie: I can. Let's see, "They were ready to fight at a minute's notice" is the cause and "They were called minutemen" must be the effect. Right! They were ready to fight at a minute's notice causes them to be called minutemen.

Teacher: Good! Now look at the first two sentences in this paragraph and read them again to yourself. Sometimes signal words are missing and yet we still have a special meaning between two ideas. One sentence can be a cause and another sentence can be an effect. Is there a cause sentence in the first two sentences? Which sentence causes the other sentence?

Joan: I think people were getting ready for war so the trouble was getting worse. "People were getting ready for war" is the cause.

Tim: But the people didn't cause the trouble, the British did. I think "The trouble was getting worse" is the cause.

Teacher: One way to test your answer is to put these two sentences together with a signal word like *because* at the beginning. That usually tells you which one is the cause and which one is the effect.

Joan: Because the trouble was getting worse, the people were getting ready for war. Yeah, that's what I mean. "The trouble was getting worse" must be the cause.

In addition to teaching cause-and-effect relationships through discussions in either an oral or written context, there are a number of other instructional activities that might be used.

SAMPLE ACTIVITIES

Marking Cause-and-Effect Relationships. Present cause-and-effect statements with and without signal words and show students how to identify each component in the relationship by marking them as follows.

The school bell rang for recess (so) the children went outside.
                   (c)   (e)

Cause-and-Effect Cloze Tasks. Teach the meaning of new signal words such as *and therefore* using the methods described in chapter 5. Then have students complete sentences like the following together or independently.

The wind was too strong for our sailboat and therefore —————————————.

————————————— and therefore we were late for dinner.

To reduce the difficulty level of the task you may wish to provide the answers at the bottom of the page:

we forgot the time   it tipped over

Signal Word Cloze Tasks. Teach the meanings of new signal words following methods outlined in chapter 5. Then have students practice using them in cloze sentences where the signal words have been deleted.

Debbie was ill _____ she went home.

and thus   previously   earlier   between

_____ the test, Bill was nervous.

On the other hand   On account of   On my own time

Discussing Selections in Science. Science lessons present excellent opportunities to apply skills related to cause-and-effect relationships. Be certain to capitalize on this during discussions of reading selections, film strips, and other experiences in the area of science.

DEVELOPING DISCOURSE KNOWLEDGE SKILLS

Pronoun and Adverbial Referents

pronoun referents:
Words that substitute for nouns or noun phrases in a text.
adverbial referents:
Words that substitute for specific location or time designations in a text.

Pronoun referents are words that substitute for nouns or noun phrases in a text. Pronoun referents include words like *I, you, he, she, we, they, us, them, him, her, me, this, that, these,* and *those.* **Adverbial referents** are words that substitute for specific location or time designations in a text. Adverbial referents include words like *here, there, over there, today, now, last week,* and *last month.* Readers must infer the meanings of pronoun and adverbial referents, usually without the visual information available in oral language contexts. This is especially difficult for young readers who are accustomed to seeing, not imagining, the meanings of these words.

Pronoun and adverbial referents are very common in writing. Consider the following example.

Heather and *her* friend were determined to see the unique solar event. *They* struggled with the box to get *it* right. First the hole was not big enough. Then *it* was too big. Finally, by putting tape across the biggest hole and poking a tiny hole in *it* with a toothpick, Heather was able to get the light to shine. "*We* can see *it here now*," *she* said.

anaphoric referents:
Referents that have explicit references in the text such as *he* in the sentence, "Bob went fishing but *he* did not catch any fish." Anaphoric referents require text-connecting inferences.
nonanaphoric referents: Do not have explicit references in the text. Non-anaphoric referents require slot-filling inferences.

Pronoun and adverbial referents may be either anaphoric or nonanaphoric. **Anaphoric referents** have explicit references in the text. The word *they* in the preceding paragraph is an example of an anaphoric referent since it refers back to the words *Heather and her friend.* Anaphoric referents require text-connecting inferences (see page 198) since the reader must connect the referent with the correct reference in the text. **Nonanaphoric referents** do not have explicit references in the text. The word *here* in the preceding paragraph is an example of a nonanaphoric reference since it refers to an unstated inside wall of the box. Nonanaphoric referents require slot-filling inferences (see page 198). They require that readers have appropriate background knowledge to fill in the correct meaning slots. Young readers need to develop proficiency in inferring the correct references for pronoun and adverbial referents to comprehend what they read (Anderson & Shifrin, 1980; Rubin, 1980).

Teaching Pronoun and Adverbial Referents

Instruction in comprehending pronoun and adverbial referents occurs early in the reading program. This happens because (1) pronoun and adverbial referents appear with great frequency in early readers' textbooks and (2) learning how to imagine references in written contexts is a new task for young children.

Instruction in comprehending anaphoric referents (referents with explicit references in the text) usually precedes instruction in comprehending nonanaphoric referents (referents without explicit references in the text). Both are often taught deductively.

1. *State the skill you want students to learn.* ("Some words refer to other words in a selection. Both words will mean the same thing." or "Some words in a selection are used to refer to other words. Sometimes only one of the words will be used and you have to imagine what it refers to.")
2. *Provide several examples.* Show children the relationships between anaphoric referents and their references. This can be accomplished by circling both referent and reference and then connecting the two with a line. Discuss with children how you determined the meaning of nonanaphoric references. Be certain not to use the technical terms for these words when working with young children.
3. *Provide guided practice.*
4. *Have students practice the skill independently.*

Pronoun and Adverbial Referents: Anaphora

MODEL LESSON

On the chalkboard:

I don't know if Hal was at work today. Was he there?
Mark isn't here. Where is he?

Teacher: Sometimes when you read, one word will take the place of another word or phrase. Both will mean the same thing. Look at these sentences. Can you read the first pair for us, Joan?

Joan: (Reads the first sentence pair.)

Teacher: What does *there* mean? Can you find any words in the first sentence that tell us where *there* is?

Kathy: At work. *There* means at work.

Teacher: Good. Let's circle the word *there* and draw a line back to *at work* to show how these two items are connected.

(Repeats for the words *Hal* and *he*. Then repeats with other sentences.) Independent practice might be provided with activities like those illustrated in figure 6–3.

You may want to consider also using the following activities.

Rewriting Repeated Words. Provide students with sentences like the following and ask them to rewrite the sentences using appropriate referents for any repeated words. To make the task easier, simply have them cross out the second instance of any word and write the correct referent above it. You may also wish to provide a list of possible words to use.

> Tom got on Tom's bike.
>
> Cindy went to school at noon. Did you see Cindy?
>
> Hello, Helene and Pat. I am by the table. Do Helene and Pat want to come by the table?
>
> his   you   here

Cloze Tasks. Follow standard cloze task procedures but only delete pronoun and adverbial referents. Have students complete the blanks. For a variation on this task, provide students with copies of a story with all of the referents crossed out. Have students work together in pairs and attempt to read the entire story aloud, filling in the correct referents. Get back together with all of the students and have groups read their solutions.

Predicting Outcomes and Drawing Conclusions

script knowledge:
Knowledge of common event sequences.

The abilities related to predicting outcomes and drawing conclusions have been grouped together since both rely on the same knowledge source: one's knowledge of common event sequences or scripts. **Script knowledge** is what you know about common event sequences in which you and others participate regularly. You have, for example, undoubtedly developed a script for the first day of class in a university course. You use this knowledge about the event sequences in a normal first class session to make inferences, either on the first day of class itself or when you read about someone experiencing their first day of class. Your script probably includes your arrival (the first event sequence). Within this event sequence, you probably have a preferred seating location based on previous experiences (in the front row, by the door, in the back, or on the aisle). You also know that certain meanings are normally associated with sitting in certain locations (in the front to make an impression; in the back to avoid making an impression). Your overall script probably also includes the arrival of your professor (the second

Ted can not see the turtle.

<u>He</u> can not see the turtle.

Fay ran to the pond.

<u>She</u> went to see the ducks.

Jack ran to the pond.

<u>He</u> went to see the ducks.

The ducks swam away.

<u>They</u> swam away.

Duck and Rabbit went
to Mr. Fig's house.

<u>They</u> went to the house.

Finding antecedents of pronouns.
Read each pair of sentences; then draw a line under the
word or words in the first sentence that mean the same as
the underlined word in the second sentence. (See T.E.
for complete directions.)

FIGURE 6–3

An example of a practice activity: pronoun and adverbial referents

event sequence). This may include the fact that professors are likely to be carrying a stack of syllabi which they set down at the table or lectern in the front of the class. Your script for the first day of class is also likely to include a number of other event sequences that define your expectations for the remainder of the class, such as passing out the syllabus, going over the syllabus, and making certain that students understand their assignments; finding out where the textbook can be purchased; and listening to the first lecture.

Your background knowledge includes literally thousands of scripts like this one. You have, no doubt, a script for eating at a restaurant, driving home, flying on an airplane, eating dinner at home, and many others. You use this background knowledge as you make inferences throughout the day and while you are reading. Consider, for example, the following paragraph.

> The two boys were across the street from Tom's house when they saw the ominous line of clouds approach and heard the thunder. They were playing under a large elm tree. Lightning was flashing all along the front as it came closer. "Hurry," said Tom.
>
> What do you think the two boys will do?

Most people would answer this question by making an inference from the available information in the text and from their "what to do in a lightning storm" script. If you know this script, you are familiar with the common event sequences that are followed in case of a lightning storm (for example, get away from trees, head for cover, look around to make certain you are not near metal objects, and so on). Based on your script knowledge and the information in the text, you probably inferred that the two boys would seek shelter across the street at Tom's house.

The question and the inference which you made nicely illustrate how script knowledge functions as one aspect of discourse knowledge during the comprehension process. Tasks similar to this are often called **predicting outcomes.** Predicting outcomes requires that a reader predict a future effect from a stated cause. Appropriate script knowledge is necessary to make the correct forward inference and predict what would be likely to happen next. Figure 6–4 illustrates several predicting outcome tasks from one reading series.

A related task, **drawing conclusions,** requires that a reader infer an unstated cause from a stated effect. It also requires script knowledge. But the inference, in this case, is backward to the unstated cause. Consider the following passage to see how this takes place.

predicting outcomes: A comprehension task requiring a reader to predict a future effect from a stated cause. Appropriate script knowledge is necessary.

drawing conclusions: A comprehension task requiring a reader to infer an unstated cause from a stated effect. Requires script knowledge.

> The team raced down to the far end of the court to cut the net down. The captain jumped up to the hoop, cut the net, put it around his neck, and let out a yell. The crowd was going crazy with excitement!
>
> Why was everyone so excited?

Stan sees the friends on the hill.

"I will run up to the friends," he says.

So Stan will _____.
    run slowly to the house
    run by the pond
    <u>run uphill</u>

Pam runs up to the house.

The house is very dark.

So Pam will _____.
    wash the dog
    <u>put on a light</u>
    play in the moonlight

Pam said, "I cannot find the dog."

Stan said, "I will help you."

So Pam and Stan will _____.
    clean the car
    ride in the wagon
    <u>look for the dog</u>

Inferring: predicting outcomes.
Read each story and underline the phrase that makes the
best ending. (See T.E. for complete directions.)

19

FIGURE 6–4
A practice activity in predicting outcomes

You are able to infer backward from the stated effects in this paragraph to determine that a basketball team had just won an important game, perhaps a championship. How could you do this when the cause was unstated? You relied upon your script knowledge of the events commonly associated with winning an important basketball game. When you draw a conclusion, then, you infer backward from an effect (or several effects) to an unstated cause. Figure 6–5 provides an example of a typical activity used to practice drawing conclusions.

Teaching Predicting Outcomes and Drawing Conclusions

directed reading-thinking activity (DRTA): Instructional method particularly appropriate for teaching children to predict outcomes and draw conclusions. Includes three steps: predicting, reading, and proving.

One of the most common methods used to help children predict outcomes and draw conclusions is the first phase of an instructional procedure developed by Stauffer (1976) known as a **Directed Reading-Thinking Activity (DRTA).** The first phase of a DRTA consists of three procedural steps, repeated as students read and discuss a selection.

1. *Predicting.* During this first step, students are asked to predict outcomes and model their inferential reasoning for others. At the beginning of a story, questions like the following might be used.

   What will a story with this title be about? Why?
   Who do you think will be in a story with this title? Why?
   Where do you think this story will take place? Why?

   Each student is expected to form a prediction and support it with a reasonable explanation. Teachers should encourage different predictions as long as a student can justify them logically.

2. *Reading.* Students are asked to read silently up to a predetermined point in the story and check their predictions. Directions like the following might be given.

   Now that you have all told me what you think this story is going to be about, who will be in it, and where it will take place, I want you to read and see if you were correct. Read up to the end of page 2, please.

3. *Proving.* During this third step, students are asked to draw conclusions and to model their reasoning process for others. In a discussion, students evaluate the available evidence in relation to their predictions. Questions like the following can be used to begin the discussion at this step.

   Was your guess correct? Why or why not?
   What do you think now? Why?
   Why do you think that X happened?
   Why did A (a character) do X (an event)?
   What do you think will happen next?

Drawing Conclusions

Read each paragraph and the numbered questions below it. In the blank before the number of each question, write the letter of the best answer.

This summer, Lori is earning some extra money by helping her father. She takes money from people who have had their gas tanks filled. She also cleans windshields and helps people put air into their tires. She is saving her money for the special shoes that she needs for the lessons she is taking.

_____ 1. **Where do you think Lori is working?**
    a. at a gasoline service station   b. at a bicycle repair shop
    c. at a supermarket

_____ 2. **What kind of lessons do you think Lori is taking?**
    a. weaving lessons   b. dancing lessons
    c. piano lessons

Dave was hammering a nail into a board. He thought to himself, "When I get this finished, it will make a nice home for my small feathered friends. I'll hang it in the tree beside my window." He was holding the nail to keep it steady while he hammered. All of a sudden he cried, "Ouch!" Then he dropped the nail.

_____ 3. **What do you think Dave was making?**
    a. a clubhouse   b. a doghouse
    c. a birdhouse

_____ 4. **When Dave said, "Ouch!" what do you think happened?**
    a. He hit his finger with the hammer.
    b. A bird pecked him on the nose.
    c. He put his finger between two boards.

Hank knew that the swimming test would be held today. He had a funny feeling in his stomach. He took his time getting dressed and eating breakfast. Slowly he walked to the pool where the test was being given. Two hours later when his mother saw him, Hank had a big smile on his face.

_____ 5. **How do you think Hank felt about taking the swimming test?**
    a. Hank was sure that he would pass the test.
    b. Hank was nervous.
    c. Hank wanted to take the test as soon as possible

_____ 6. **Why do you think Hank had a big smile on his face?**
    a. He did not take the test.   b. He failed the test.
    c. He passed the test.

FIGURE 6–5

A practice activity in drawing conclusions

At the end of this discussion, begin the three-step procedure again. Use questions like the following to help students make predictions for the next story portion.

Now what do you think will happen? Why?
How do you think *A* will solve the problem? Why?

This type of method framework can be used whenever you have a group of children read a story together. Its greatest advantage is that it encourages children to continually think about what they have read and what is likely to happen next. Other instructional activities may also be used, however, to develop students' ability to predict outcomes and draw conclusions. Here are several.

SAMPLE ACTIVITIES

Riddle Reading and Riddle Writing. Reading riddles provides opportunities for children to practice drawing conclusions in an enjoyable fashion. (Why did the man throw a clock out of the window? He wanted to see time fly.) You may want to write a riddle on the board each day and, at the end of the day, see who has figured out the answer. Older students may enjoy writing and sharing their own riddles. A class riddle book might even be developed and shared with other classes in your school.

Developing Scripts. Many school experiences that you build into your classroom program develop children's script knowledge, especially new experiences for children. Experiences provide children with a rich set of scripts they can use during comprehension. As you teach science, go on field trips, read literature selections to your students, show students how to make block prints during an art project, and as students themselves read, they acquire new script knowledge about the world they live in. You may want to consider planning experiences in other subjects to relate closely to the reading demands your students will encounter during the year. Thematic units that reach across all subjects for a given period of time are effective for this purpose.

Reading Mysteries. Mysteries are especially valuable for providing practice in predicting outcomes and drawing conclusions. Be certain to select mysteries for read aloud sessions (see chapter 7) and have students make predictions, draw conclusions, and explain their reasoning at various points in the story.

QUESTIONING STRATEGIES

Asking questions about what one is reading is important for both readers and teachers to consider, especially when attempting to comprehend units larger than a single word. For readers, questions serve to focus attention on puzzling aspects of a text and guide the search for answers. They are an integral part of the comprehension process. For teachers, questions serve a variety of functions, including:

1. *Assessment.* Questions can be used to monitor students' abilities to understand specific types of information after they have read a passage.
2. *Initiating a discussion.* Questions can be used to begin a discussion designed to increase the background knowledge of students before they read a passage. They can also be used to begin a discussion about what has happened in a text or about what will take place next.
3. *Focusing attention.* Questions can be used to focus attention on a specific portion of a text for subsequent instructional purposes.
4. *Modeling the reasoning process.* Questions, answers, and explanations of how answers were derived can be used to model reasoning for students. They can be used to demonstrate how proficient readers think while reading.
5. *Guiding students' reasoning processes.* Questions can be used to guide students' thinking. With questions you can have students replicate the reasoning process that you or other mature readers use.
6. *Practicing specific comprehension tasks.* Questions can be used to provide practice on specific types of comprehension tasks such as inferring cause-and-effect relationships, inferring sequence relation-

Questions, used carefully, can be an important component of reading instruction.

ships, inferring pronoun and adverbial references, predicting outcomes, or drawing conclusions.

It is important, therefore, that you understand the different types of questions often used during classroom reading lessons. It is also important that you consider several suggestions about the use of questions as you interact with students.

Levels of Comprehension Questions

While there are a variety of ways to organize the questions teachers use during reading instruction (Barrett, 1974; Bloom, 1956), the most common is usually called a levels approach to comprehension questions. This approach specifies several different levels of questions depending on the amount and type of information a reader must contribute to the answer. Three levels of questions are usually specified: literal, inferential, and evaluative. Each type of question is defined in relation to the following passage and the questions that follow. Read this paragraph and speculate about what, exactly, a reader must contribute to the text to answer each level of question.

> Bob and Diane wanted to go out to eat.
> Bob called in order to make a reservation and they went to the restaurant. When they arrived, no one was there. The door was locked and a sign said "Closed on Mondays." "How can this be?" asked Bob. "I just reserved a table over the phone." Diane asked, "You did call The Steak House, didn't you?" "Oh," apologized Bob. "I thought we were going to The Lake House."

Literal

1. Who wanted to go out to eat? *Bob and Diane.*
2. Why did Bob call? *To make a reservation.*

Inferential

3. When did Bob call and make a reservation? *Before they went to the restaurant.*
4. When did this story take place? *On Monday.*
5. Where did Bob make the reservation? *At the Lake House Restaurant.*
6. Where were Bob and Diane? *At the Steak House Restaurant.*

Evaluative

7. What would you have done next in this situation? *(Accept all logical answers.)*
8. What do you think Bob and Diane should have done differently? *(Accept all logical answers.)*

literal-level questions: Ask for information explicitly stated in the text.

Literal-level questions ask for information directly in the text. Readers can answer literal-level questions by relying on the literal, word-for-word, meaning that exists in a passage. Readers need to contribute little, if any, information to answer literal-level questions appropriately. Questions 1 and 2 are literal-level questions. Answers to each can be directly found in the text. Notice that question 2 is a literal question about an explicitly stated cause-and-effect relationship.

Inferential-level questions ask for information that is not explicitly stated in the text but, rather, must be supplied by reading between the lines. Inferential-level questions usually require that readers contribute background knowledge in conjunction with the literal meaning in a text to respond appropriately. Questions 3 through 6 are inferential-level questions. Question 3 is an inferential-level question about an implicitly stated sequential relationship. Questions 4 through 6 require readers to draw a conclusion based on information in the text in conjunction with script knowledge.

Evaluative-level questions ask readers to make a critical judgement about information in the text and, often, to relate the information in the text to their own past or future experiences. Evaluative-level questions often ask: Was X correct? What should X have done instead? What would you have done? Questions 7 and 8 are evaluative-level questions. Question 7 asks you to predict an outcome after evaluating the information in the text. Question 8 asks you to draw a conclusion after evaluating the information in the text.

> **inferential-level questions:** Ask for information not explicitly stated in the text but, rather, that must be supplied by reading between the lines. Require readers to contribute background knowledge in conjunction with literal meaning.

> **evaluative-level questions:** Ask readers to make critical judgments about information in the text and, often, to relate that information to past or future experiences.

Guidelines for Using Questions

Questioning is a teacher behavior that occurs with great frequency during classroom reading lessons. It is therefore important to give some thought to how you will employ questions during instruction. The following list of suggestions is intended to help you consider exactly how to use questions during your instructional program.

1. *Use questions for purposes other than assessment.* Durkin (1979, 1981) has found that teachers use questions largely to test, not to teach reading comprehension. Asking questions solely to obtain a correct response is testing, not teaching, reading comprehension. It results in playing "Guess the answer that I have in my head" with your students. To use questions for instructional purposes, consider following up questions with Can you tell us exactly how you got that answer? Asking students to explain their reasoning processes can provide effective models for less proficient students. This technique is especially appropriate when you want to focus students' attention on a specific aspect of comprehension (such as a particular cause-and-effect or sequence relationship) they have recently studied.

2. *Ask higher-level questions.* Generally, asking higher level questions (inferential and evaluative) is more appropriate than asking lower-level questions (literal). Higher-level questions provide more reasoning opportunities for readers. In answering an evaluative level question, for example, a reader must often consider information at both

literal and inferential levels of comprehension. In answering an inferential level question, a reader must also consider information at the literal level of comprehension. In answering a literal-level question, however, a reader needs only consider information at the literal level of comprehension. Higher-level questions also provide more useful discussion opportunities for students to model how, exactly, they determined the meaning of a passage.

3. *If students are unable to comprehend the answers to higher-level questions, a useful strategy is to ask a lower-level question that will help them answer the higher level question.* This is especially true with inferential-level questions where helping a student see the answers to two literal-level questions will sometimes allow them to make the required inference.

4. *Allow greater variation in responses as you ask higher-level questions.* Answers to literal-level questions are usually either correct or incorrect because the information is explicitly stated in the text. Answers to inferential- and evaluative-level questions rely more on background knowledge, information that is likely to be slightly different between individuals. As a result, higher-level questions often have more than one acceptable answer. Evaluative questions, in particular, have a wide range of acceptable answers that vary according to the individual's values and viewpoint.

5. *If students are unable to answer inferential or evaluative questions related to one of the specific skills discussed in this chapter (cause-and-effect relationships, sequence relationships, predicting outcomes, and so on), do not assume they cannot perform this skill.* The problem may be due to insufficient background knowledge or the failure to apply the appropriate background knowledge to the comprehension task. Test each possibility by probing for what the student knows about the topic.

6. *Ask questions before students read a story.* This helps students to focus attention on appropriate types of background knowledge. You can, for example, begin a story by asking students if they have ever experienced the particular problem they will read about. Have a short discussion on how they solved this problem. Then tell them they will read about someone else with a similar difficulty and to see how this person resolved the problem. Hansen & Pearson (1980) have found this to be a particularly effective questioning strategy.

7. *Plan your questions before beginning a discussion with students.* If you wait for the discussion to begin before considering the questions you want to ask, you will almost always end up asking many literal-level questions. It is nearly impossible to generate more complex questions on the spur of the moment.

8. *Help students ask their own questions as they read.* Herber & Nelson (1975) have proposed a method framework to facilitate this process. First, give students answers to questions (that is, statements) and the

general location of the supporting evidence. Have students identify the evidence that supports each answer. Second, give students answers to questions without the general location of the supporting evidence. Have students locate and identify the evidence supporting each answer. Third, give students questions with general locations where supporting evidence is given. Have them answer each question. Fourth, give students questions without locations where supporting evidence is given. Have them answer each question. Finally, have students form and answer their own questions.

HOW SPECIFIC FRAMEWORKS AFFECT INSTRUCTIONAL DECISIONS

This chapter serves as a bridge between the word-level aspects of reading comprehension discussed in chapters 4 and 5 and the longer and more complex aspects of reading comprehension discussed in chapters 7 and 8. Descriptions of instructional practices related to developing both syntactic and discourse knowledge will continue to be specified in later chapters. Nevertheless, it is now possible to begin considering how a comprehension framework influences the instructional decisions you must make with extended text. Three instructional decisions related to the comprehension of extended text are particularly important to consider: the relative importance of instruction with extended text; the content of instruction with extended text; and the nature of instruction with extended text.

The Relative Importance of Instruction with Extended Text

Deciding about the relative importance of instruction with extended text in the total reading program is determined largely by your answer to the question How does one read? Recall the three types of explanations often used to answer this question: a text-based explanation, a reader-based explanation, and an interactive explanation. Each explanation reflects unique assumptions about the reading process.

If you have more of a text-based explanation for how one reads, you are not likely to devote the major portion of your instructional time to developing syntactic and discourse knowledge. More instructional time will be spent developing decoding and vocabulary knowledge. You tend to emphasize the development of decoding and vocabulary knowledge because you believe that meaning is in the text and thus the reading process consists largely of translating printed words into sounds and sounds into meanings.

If you have more of a reader-based explanation for how one reads, you probably spend the majority of your instructional time developing syntactic and discourse knowledge. You emphasize the development of syntactic and discourse knowledge since you believe reading is largely a process of expectations that begins with these two sources of knowledge and proceeds down to the use of decoding knowledge. Strong discourse and syntactic knowledge greatly lessens the need for extensive decoding knowledge and somewhat lessens the need for extensive vocabulary knowledge. Note, also, that if you have a reader-based explanation you assume that meaning is largely in the reader's mind. This assumption is also consistent with the decision to spend a substantial amount of time teaching aspects of discourse and syntactic knowledge since much of that knowledge is associated with a reader's ability to apply background knowledge (or meaning) to make inferences.

If you have an interactive explanation for how one reads, you value instruction aimed at developing syntactic and discourse knowledge. You do not emphasize the development of syntactic and discourse knowledge, however, any more than you emphasize the development of decoding and vocabulary knowledge. All receive equal attention in your instructional program.

The Content of Instruction with Extended Text

Text-based, reader-based, and interactive explanations for how one reads also determine the aspects of syntactic and discourse knowledge that will receive the most attention in an instructional program. The greatest distinction between the different explanations for how one reads can be seen with respect to decisions about teaching punctuation and with respect to the amount of emphasis given to either predicting outcomes (forward inferencing) or drawing conclusions (backward inferencing).

Teachers with more of a text-based explanation for how one reads assume that meaning is in the text and that reading is a translation process. Therefore, these teachers tend to emphasize teaching punctuation. Generally, these individuals believe that children must first "hear" the words before they interpret them. Stress and intonation, of course, are critical to correctly "hearing" words and sentences during reading. Teachers with more of a reader-based explanation, on the other hand, assume that meaning is largely in the reader and, thus, a reader's expectations for upcoming text largely determine the correct stress and intonation. Stress and intonation are usually seen to follow, not precede, the meaning that a reader assigns to the words on a page. As a result, instruction in punctuation is not usually emphasized, although some of the more important graphic symbols of meaning may be taught, such as periods and question marks. A teacher with an interactive explanation would probably teach punctuation but not devote the time to this area that a teacher with a text-based explanation might.

Explanations for how one reads also influence the relative emphasis placed on tasks associated with predicting outcomes and drawing conclusions. A teacher with a reader-based explanation would spend far more time teaching children how to predict outcomes than a teacher with a text-based explanation. This is due to the greater importance assigned to the role of expectations for upcoming text in a reader-based explanation. A teacher with a text-based explanation would probably spend greater time on drawing conclusions. Greater emphasis is usually assigned to words that have already been read than to words that have yet to be read. A teacher with an interactive explanation would be likely to spend relatively equal amounts of time teaching the two types of tasks.

The Nature of Instruction with Extended Text

We now want to consider only two aspects of instruction related to the comprehension of extended text: the nature and the purpose of questioning activities. The answers to these two issues again depend on your explanation for how one reads. Text-based, reader-based, and interactive explanations for how one reads have different instructional consequences with respect to questioning strategies.

A major assumption of a text-based explanation is that meaning is largely in the text. A clear implication of this assumption is that readers' background knowledge is only minimally associated with comprehension. Questions, therefore, are frequently used to determine if a student has correctly translated the meaning in the text. Usually, little discussion ensues regarding how a reader inferred meaning; correct responses are simply accepted, incorrect responses are rejected. Students seldom have an opportunity to experience another student's reasoning process in a discussion. Also, most of the questions typically focus on relationships explicitly signaled in the text rather than those that are only implicitly signaled. Literal level questions occur more frequently than inferential or evaluative level questions.

A reader-based explanation assumes that a reader's background knowledge is crucially involved in determining meaning. A teacher with this type of explanation for how one reads is concerned with developing background knowledge and showing students how to use background knowledge during the reading process. Discussion questions focus more on how students derived answers than on the answers themselves. In addition, more time would be spent discussing implicitly signaled relationships rather than relationships which are explicitly signaled. Inferential and evaluative level questions occur more frequently than literal level questions.

An interactive explanation acknowledges both the explicitly signaled meaning in the text and the inferred meaning from background knowledge that a reader brings to the text. As a result, questions are probably equally divided between those with implicitly signaled answers and those with explicitly signaled answers. When questions are directed at explicitly signaled relationships, little discussion follows about how a student reasoned out the answer. When questions are directed at implicitly signaled relationships, students are encouraged to model their reasoning processes for others.

THE MAJOR POINTS

1. Extended text refers to units of writing that are at least a sentence in length. Comprehension of extended text requires the use of syntactic and discourse knowledge in addition to decoding and vocabulary knowledge.

2. An inference is a reasoned assumption about information that has not been explicitly stated. Readers make inferences whenever they add meaning that goes beyond the explicit meaning of the words on a page. Inferential reasoning is an important aspect of comprehending extended text and an important aspect of instruction in the use of syntactic and discourse knowledge.

3. Differences exist between oral and written language with respect to each of the major knowledge sources associated with comprehension: decoding; vocabulary; syntactic; and discourse knowledge. Learning to read requires that children become familiar with exactly those aspects of written language that differ from an already established knowledge of oral language.

4. Instruction in the use of syntactic knowledge often includes helping students understand cause-and-effect relationships, sequence relationships, and punctuation.

5. Instruction in the use of discourse knowledge often includes helping students understand pronoun and adverbial referents, draw conclusions, and predict outcomes.

6. Questions are frequently used during reading lessons for a variety of reasons. Three levels of questions are frequently used: literal, inferential, and evaluative. Increasing amounts of background knowledge are required to answer higher-level questions.

7. Your comprehension framework influences instructional decisions related to the development of syntactic and discourse knowledge. The answer to the question How does one read? is especially important to consider since it affects decisions about the relative importance of instruction with extended text, the content of instruction with extended text, and the nature of instruction with extended text.

QUESTIONS AND ACTIVITIES

1. Identify at least four inferences a reader must make to comprehend the following passage.

It was raining and they went inside the old barn. They unloaded their rifles and climbed the ladder to the loft. The hay was warm and dry. Craig and Bill sat swapping tales of their adventures with grouse and waiting for a chance to get back outside. They both enjoyed the chance to stretch the truth a bit. Finally the rain stopped and Bill said, "Let's get going. We have to bring something home for dinner." Craig noticed, though, that it was already dark outside.

2. Create two literal-level, two inferential-level, and two evaluative-level questions that might be used with the paragraph in question 1.

3. Using the paragraph in question 1, create at least one question that would help you initiate a discussion related to the following: cause-and-effect relationships; sequence relationships; pronoun or adverbial referents; predicting outcomes; and drawing conclusions.

4. Often you can informally determine young children's familiarity with the syntactic conventions of written language by listening to their speech. Consider the following transcriptions of two second-grade students. Determine which student is most familiar with the conventions of written language. Which child is likely to have greater difficulty in making the transition from oral language tasks like conversation to written language tasks like reading and writing? Why? How might the child who is less familiar with the conventions of written language acquire this familiarity?

Student 1

You see . . . there's a little frog, and he . . . *and* a little boy had him for a pet. *And* he had a little dog, *and* the frog was in the little bucket. *And* then they were walking, to do something, *and* the frog jumped out of . . . out of the bucket . . . *and* the frog just started looking at the flowers. *And* then they saw someone at a picnic, *and* they were having a picnic. *And* he got into their picnic basket, *and then* . . . the lady was gonna get . . . something out of her picnic basket . . . *and* the frog jumped on her hand . . . *and* . . . *and* then the lady got really mad.

Student 2

Um . . . *once upon a time,* there was a little boy . . . who had a little frog for a pet. *After* they were walking for a while. . . . the little frog jumped . . . out of the bucket *and* hopped away. The frog . . . saw two people who were having a picnic . . . *Because* he was a naughty frog . . . he hopped into their picnic basket. *After* the lady put her hand . . . into the picnic basket, the frog jumped out . . . *because* he thought . . . that she was gonna get him. The lady was scared . . . *since* she didn't like frogs.

5. The following skill objectives come from several different reading programs. Determine which objectives are related to the problems created for young readers by differences between oral and written language. Then determine which objectives develop skills often associated with syntactic knowledge and which develop skills often associated with discourse knowledge:

a. to recognize contractions
b. to recognize questions

    c. to use the table of contents

    d. develops vocabulary: antonyms

    e. can use punctuation to determine sentence meaning

    f. uses word structure: compound words

    g. recognizes implicit cause-and-effect relationships at the sentence level

    h. locates/interprets information in reference sources: encyclopedia

    i. recognizes implicit temporal relationships at the sentence level

6. Read the following paragraph from a popular children's literature selection. Would this paragraph lend itself more to teaching cause-and-effect relationships, sequence relationships, or both? Notice that most of the relationships are implicitly, not explicitly, stated. What questions might you ask to initiate a discussion of these relationships? What would you do if students gave you a correct response? An incorrect response?

I had now lived in this happy place three years, but sad changes were about to come over us. We heard from time to time that our mistress was ill. The doctor was often at the house, and the master looked grave and anxious. Then we heard that she must leave her home at once, and go to a warm country for two or three years. The news fell upon the household like the tolling of a death-bell. Everybody was sorry; but the master began to directly make arrangements for breaking up his establishment and leaving England. We used to hear it talked about in our stable; indeed, nothing else was talked about (Sewell, 1954, p. 89).

7. Create a lesson using the outline for a Directed Reading-Thinking Activity. Use a story from a reading program or a short children's literature selection. Indicate in your lesson where you would have the children pause in their reading. Also specify the questions you would ask at each location.

FURTHER READING

Bauman, J. F. & Schmitt, M. C. (1986). The what, why, how, and when of comprehension instruction. *The Reading Teacher, 39* (7), 640–45.

Describes a four-step method framework for direct comprehension instruction. This method framework is more consistent with mastery explanations of development.

Herber, H. L. & Nelson, J. B. (1975). Questioning is not the answer. *Journal of Reading, 18,* 512–17.

Defines an instructional method for helping students become independent questioners. Shows teachers of content-area subjects how to move from teacher-directed to student-directed questioning activities. These ideas apply as well to elementary classroom reading teachers.

Pearson, P. D. (1984). Asking questions about stories. In A. J. Harris & A. R. Sipay (eds.) *Readings on reading instruction* (3rd Edition). New York: Longman, Inc.

Describes a set of instructional guidelines to follow when using questions during comprehension instruction. Presents very practical suggestions based on four general principles.

Wilson, C. W. (1983). Teaching reading comprehension by connecting the known to the new. *Reading Teacher, 36* (4), 382–89.

> Provides practical suggestions for helping children apply their background knowledge and infer meaning. Specifies instructional activities that may be used before, during, and after reading.

Wixson, K. K. (1984). Questions about a text: What you ask about is what children learn. *The Reading Teacher, 37*(3), 287–93.

> Discusses the role that questions can play in helping children comprehend text and how questions may sometimes interfere with comprehension. Provides guidelines for using questions effectively in classroom reading lessons.

REFERENCES

Aaron, I., *et al.* (1983). *Scott, Foresman Reading Series.* Glenview, IL: Scott, Foresman.

Anderson, R. C.; Hiebert, E. H.; Scott, J. A.; & Wilkinson, I. A. G. (1985). *Becoming a nation of readers: The report of the commission on reading.* Washington, DC: National Institute of Education.

Anderson, R. C. & Shifrin, Z. (1980). The meaning of words in context. In R. J. Spiro, B. C. Bruce, and W. F. Brewer (eds.) *Theoretical issues in reading comprehension.* Hillsdale, NJ: Erlbaum.

Barrett, T. C. (1974). Taxonomy of reading comprehension. In R. C. Smith & T. C. Barrett (eds.) *Teaching reading in the middle grades.* Reading, MA: Addison-Wesley.

Beck, I. L.; McKeown, M. G.; Omanson, R. C.; & Pople, M. T. (1984). Improving the comprehensibility of stories: The effects of revisions that improve coherence. *Reading Research Quarterly, 19* (3), 263–77.

Bloom, B. S. (1956). *Taxonomy of educational objectives.* New York: Longmans.

Cook-Gumperz, J. & Gumperz, J. (1981). From oral to written culture: The transition to literacy. In M. F. Whiteman (ed.). *Writing: The nature, development, and teaching of written communication.* Hillsdale, NJ: Erlbaum.

Durkin, D. (1979). What classroom observations reveal about reading comprehension instruction. *Reading Research Quarterly, 14,* 481–553.

Durkin, D. (1981). Reading comprehension instruction in five basal reading series. *Reading Research Quarterly, 14,* 481–533.

Durkin, D. (1986). Reading methodology textbooks: Are they helping teachers teach comprehension? *The Reading Teacher, 39*(5), 410–17.

Durr, W. K., *et al.* (1983). *The Houghton Mifflin Reading Program.* Boston: Houghton Mifflin.

Fredericksen, C. H. (1975). Representing logical and semantic structure of knowledge acquired from discourse. *Cognitive Psychology, 7,* 371–458.

Hansen, J. & Pearson, P. D. (1980). *The effects of inference training and practice on young children's comprehension* (Tech. Rep. No. 166). Urbana, IL: University of Illinois, Center for the Study of Reading, April, 1980.

Herber, H. H. & Nelson, J. (1975). Questioning is not the answer. *Journal of Reading, 18,* 512–17.

Leu, D. J., Jr. (1982). Differences between oral and written discourse and the acquisition of reading proficiency. *Journal of Reading Behavior, 14* (2), 111–25.

Loban, W. (1976). *Language development: Kindergarten through grade twelve.* Urbana, IL: NCTE.

Mason, J. (1984). A schema-theoretic view of the reading process as a basis for comprehension instruction. In G. G. Duffy, L. R. Roehler & J. Mason (eds.) *Comprehension instruction.* New York: Longman.

McGovern, A. (1975). *The secret soldier.* New York: Scholastic Books.

Meyer, B. J. F. (1975). *The organization of prose and its effect on memory.* Amsterdam: North-Holland Publishing.

Olson, D. R. (1977). The languages of instruction: The literate bias of schooling. In Anderson, R. C., Spiro, R. J., & Montague, W. E. (eds.) *Schooling and the acquisition of knowledge.* Hillsdale, NJ: Erlbaum.

Parish, P. (1971). *Come back, Amelia Bedelia.* New York: Harper & Row.

Pearson, P. D. (1974–75). The effects of grammatical complexity on children's comprehension, recall, and conception of certain semantic relations. *Reading Research Quarterly, 10,* 155–92.

Pearson, P. D. & Johnson, D. D. (1978) *Teaching reading comprehension.* New York: Holt, Rinehart and Winston.

Pearson, P. D. & Camperell, K. (1981). Comprehension of text structures. In J. T. Guthrie (ed.) *Comprehension and teaching,* Newark, DE: International Reading Association.

Rubin, A. (1980). A theoretical taxonomy of the differences between oral and written language. In R. J. Spiro, B. C. Bruce, and W. F. Brewer (eds.) *Theoretical issues in reading comprehension.* Hillsdale, NJ: Erlbaum.

Rumelhart, D. E. (1981). Schemata: The building blocks of cognition. In J. Guthrie (ed.) *Comprehension and teaching.* Newark, DE: International Reading Association.

Sewell, A. (1954). *Black beauty.* Garden City, NY: Doubleday.

Stauffer, R. G. (1976). *Teaching reading as a thinking process.* New York: Harper & Row.

Sulzby, E. (1982). Oral and written mode adaptations in stories by kindergarten children. *Journal of Reading Behavior, 14*(2), 51–60.

Trabasso, T. (1981). On the making of inferences during reading and their assessment. In J. Guthrie (ed.) *Comprehension and teaching.* Newark, DE: International Reading Association.

Warren, W. H.; Nicholas, D. W.; & Trabasso, T. (1979). Event chains and inferences in understanding narratives. In R. O. Freedle (ed.), *New directions in discourse processing (Vol. 2).* Hillsdale, NJ: Erlbaum.

7 Literature: Affect and Narrative Discourse

LITERATURE FOR ALL REASONS: USING LITERATURE IN A CLASSROOM READING PROGRAM ■ LITERATURE FOR ALL SEASONS: DEVELOPING INDEPENDENT READERS ■ LITERATURE AND NARRATIVE DISCOURSE STRUCTURE ■ PROMOTING KNOWLEDGE OF NARRATIVE DISCOURSE STRUCTURE ■ HOW SPECIFIC FRAMEWORKS AFFECT INSTRUCTIONAL DECISIONS

November 13

Dear Mr. Henshaw,

   I am in the fourth grade now. I made a diorama of *Ways to Amuse a Dog,* the book I wrote to you about two times before. Now our teacher is making us write to authors for Book Week. I got your answer to my letter last year, but it was only printed. Please would you write to me in your own handwriting? I am a great enjoyer of your books.

   My favorite character in the book was Joe's Dad because he didn't get mad when Joe amused his dog by playing a tape of a lady singing, and his dog sat and howled like he was singing, too. Bandit does the same thing when he hears singing.

Your best reader,
Leigh Botts

Dear Mr. Henshaw, Beverly Cleary, (New York: William Morrow & Co., 1983), p. 3.

This chapter introduces you to the many reasons and methods for integrating children's literature into classroom reading instruction. You will see how literature can be used to promote the development of each aspect of comprehension: affective considerations; readiness considerations; decoding knowledge; vocabulary knowledge; syntactic knowledge; and discourse knowledge. Much of this chapter, however, focuses on the use of literature to accomplish two purposes. First, you will see how literature can be used to develop independent readers: readers who both know *how* to read and, actually *do* read for pleasure, information, and personal growth. Then, we will continue the discussion of discourse knowledge begun in chapter 6 and show how children's literature can be used to develop a very specific type of discourse knowledge: knowledge of narrative discourse structure. You will also see that regardless of one's comprehension framework, literature should always be incorporated into classroom reading activities. Thus, it is essential that you quickly develop a comprehensive understanding of children's literature as you become an effective teacher of reading.

After reading this chapter, you will be able to

1. explain why literature is a unique and powerful instructional tool;
2. describe several ways to develop independent readers;
3. define the structural organization of narratives and identify the unique characteristics of several specific narrative forms;
4. describe several different methods for promoting knowledge of narrative discourse structure;
5. explain how decisions related to the use of literature in a classroom are influenced by your comprehension framework.

LITERATURE FOR ALL REASONS: USING LITERATURE IN A CLASSROOM READING PROGRAM

BEFORE READING ON

If you are like many adults, you can recall some of your favorite books from childhood. Titles like *Babar, Where the Wild Things Are, Madeline, The Snowy Day, Little House in the Big Woods, Charlotte's Web, Ramona the Pest, Encyclopedia Brown,* or others may bring back very pleasant memories about reading. Your ability to retain this information when you have forgotten many other experiences from your childhood reflects the profound effect literature exerts on young children. As you read this chapter, consider what you might do to ensure that your students also have positive experiences with literature.

literature: Describes a variety of text types including fiction, nonfictional narratives, and poetry.

Literature describes a wide variety of text types including fiction, nonfictional narratives (for example, biographies and autobiographies), and poetry. Providing children with engaging literature experiences is central to effective reading instruction. When children interact with interesting literature selections, they are developing each aspect of the comprehension process discussed in chapters 2 through 6: affective considerations; readiness considerations; decoding knowledge; vocabulary knowledge; syntactic knowledge; and discourse knowledge. Literature, therefore, is a unique and powerful instructional tool; it may be used to promote all aspects of the comprehension process.

Literature for Promoting Affective Considerations

Literature probably has the greatest impact on affective considerations such as motivation and emotional response. Good literature captures the attention of readers; it increases students' attitude toward and interest in reading and learning to read. This has several important consequences. First, interested readers are motivated to work a little harder at uncovering the meaning of selections they read within your classroom. They spend additional energy attempting to recognize difficult words, recalling the meaning of new vocabulary items, or inferring implicitly stated relationships between several ideas. Thus, interested readers continuously learn and develop their ability to read within your instructional program.

Interested readers also carry their reading activities outside of your classroom. They are more likely to engage in independent reading activities after they leave school each day: reading an exciting book on the bus ride home, in the living room before dinner, or even under the covers after the lights have been turned off at night. When students choose to read independently, they have additional opportunities to practice and develop their ability to comprehend. Thus, getting students interested in reading can extend learning and practice opportunities beyond the limited amount of instructional time available at school.

Literature is also useful for children who are struggling to understand the realities of life. Children often seek and find emotional support in a story about an issue they are currently trying to understand. Death, love, fear, personal relationships, and developing a sense of self respect often are of great concern to young children as they struggle with the hopes, fears, and anxieties of childhood. Literature shows children that they are not alone in their emotions and provides them with possible solutions to personal concerns.

Literature for Promoting Readiness

Literature is also important for promoting reading readiness, both at home and at school. Parents who regularly read to their children are preparing them for later school reading experiences (Heath, 1982; Teale, 1982). Very young children can learn much about the nature of reading from informal reading experiences on a parent's lap: the left-to-right progression of print; how to turn pages; how words are related to sounds;

how different types of stories begin and end; what a word is; what a letter is; and many more important insights (Clay, 1972; Mason, 1984; Cochran-Smith, 1984; Taylor, 1983). Similar experiences with stories in preschool and elementary school classrooms continue this development (Mason, 1984). Schools can assist the transition to literacy among very young children by encouraging parents to read frequently to their young children and by incorporating informal literature experiences into readiness instruction.

A POINT TO PONDER	When student teachers are informally surveyed, we find that about ten percent remember learning how to read at home by listening to a favorite book that their parents repeatedly read to them. These students report learning how to read by first memorizing the oral version of a story and then matching the oral version with the words in their book. Test this observation by asking your colleagues if they recall similar experiences. Do approximately one out of ten respondents report important learning experiences from being read to at an early age? What does this suggest about literature, readiness considerations, and learning to read? As a classroom teacher of reading, what might you do to take advantage of this insight?

Literature for Developing Decoding Knowledge

A major goal of instruction at the decoding level is to develop automatic decoding skills, or the ability to rapidly recognize words without resorting to conscious "sounding out" strategies. Automatic decoding permits readers to focus their attention on the text's meaning. Comprehension usually increases with the development of automatic decoding (Biemiller, 1977; Stanovich, 1980).

Literature provides opportunities for children to develop automaticity. Good literature engages readers, drawing them into a book in order to discover how the story will turn out. Getting "hooked on books" (Fader, 1968, 1976) is a common experience for a child who discovers the rich and exciting possibilities that exist between the covers of a book; one book by an author is just not enough to satisfy the needs of a student who has had a memorable experience with literature. Children who become hooked simply have greater practice opportunities at recognizing words and, as a result, more rapidly develop automatic decoding skills.

Literature for Developing Vocabulary Knowledge

Literature allows a person to travel to the top of Mount Everest or to the bottom of the sea; to the edge of the galaxy or the center of the Earth; to the time of King Arthur or to the time of space traders all without ever leaving a comfortable chair. Literature can provide a range of vivid experiences that are impossible to physically replicate in a classroom. Participating in these experiences, if only vicariously, enriches a child's vocabulary and conceptual knowledge. What better way to develop an understanding of the meanings for words such as *Nazi, Jew, Europe, terror,* and *diary,* than to read *The Diary of Anne Frank?* What better way to develop an understanding of the meanings for words such as *prairie, headcheese, journey, pioneer, hearth, covered wagon, fiddle, threshing,* or *harvest* than to read the *Little House* series by Laura Ingalls Wilder? Literature increases vocabulary knowledge as it captures, entertains, and enriches the lives of readers.

Literature for Promoting Syntactic Knowledge

Chapter 6 discussed several important aspects of syntactic knowledge associated with reading comprehension:

1. developing familiarity with the more complex syntactic patterns found in written language
2. developing familiarity with ways in which punctuation represents stress and intonation in written language
3. developing the ability to infer several types of implicitly stated relationships

Each aspect of syntactic knowledge can be promoted through experiences with literature.

Reading to young children frequently and regularly can do much to promote familiarity with the more complicated syntactic patterns of written language. Listening to the more complex patterns by which meaning is expressed in written language benefits young children who have largely experienced the less complex syntactic patterns of oral language.

Literature also promotes familiarity with the way in which punctuation marks represent stress and intonation. Literature often portrays strong feelings. Thus, it is an excellent vehicle for helping children develop familiarity with punctuation because important stress and intonation patterns frequently appear.

Finally, the vivid contexts of literature are very useful in helping children develop the ability to infer implicitly stated meanings. Implicit cause-and-effect or sequence relationships, for example, are often easier to infer in the middle of an exciting adventure story than in a workbook activity. Literature makes situations come alive in the reader's mind and thus increases successful practice opportunities in inferential reasoning.

Literature for Promoting Discourse Knowledge

Literature facilitates greatly the development of discourse knowledge. So far, three aspects of discourse knowledge have been discussed: understanding pronoun and adverb referents; drawing conclusions; and predicting outcomes. Literature promotes the development of each of these abilities. The vivid and highly imagable contexts in literature provide rich opportunities for young children to learn how to visualize the meanings of pronoun and adverb referents. Mysteries, among other literature forms, encourage young readers to independently draw conclusions about who has done what to whom. Further, because literature engages the readers' attention so completely, children have continuous opportunities to anticipate upcoming events and predict outcomes.

In addition to facilitating the development of these three aspects of discourse knowledge, literature greatly promotes knowledge of narrative discourse structure. This aspect of discourse knowledge will be considered in greater detail later in this chapter. For now, it is enough to recognize that narratives are structured in regular and predictable ways and that developing an awareness of these patterns through literature experiences facilitates comprehension.

LITERATURE FOR ALL SEASONS: DEVELOPING INDEPENDENT READERS

The preceding discussion has focused on how literature promotes the development of specific components associated with the comprehension process. However, do not assume literature is used only to develop specific reading competencies (such as readiness considerations, decoding knowledge, vocabulary knowledge, syntactic knowledge, or discourse knowledge) and then put away when instruction is completed. Instead, classroom reading instruction must aggressively attempt to integrate literature into all aspects of the learning environment. It must also continuously attempt to put both children and books together in pleasurable settings. Literature must be a part of all of the seasons in your classroom.

Why should you integrate literature into your classroom? Why is it important to continuously put children and books together? The answer to these questions is related to the larger goal of reading instruction. The ultimate goal of any reading program is not to develop readers who only know how to read. Rather, the goal of any reading program should be to develop **independent readers,** readers who both know *how* to read and, in addition, actually *do* read for pleasure, information, and personal growth. Teachers of reading can use literature to develop independent readers by integrating literature into the learning environment and by putting children and books together in pleasurable settings.

independent readers: Readers who both know *how* to read and *do* read for pleasure, information, and personal growth.

Integrating Literature into the Learning Environment

Read-Aloud Sessions. There are many ways to integrate literature into the learning environment. One of the best ways is relatively simple: be

Perhaps the most important reason for integrating literature into your classroom reading program is to develop independent readers, readers who not only can read but also choose to read for pleasure, information, and personal growth.

an effective advocate and role model for literature. Enthusiasm is contagious. If children see your enthusiasm and interest in reading literature, they will be more interested in reading themselves. You can demonstrate the pleasures of a good book to your students by reading literature each day in a **read-aloud session.**

Read-aloud sessions with young children not only generate enthusiasm and interest in reading, but also allow the development of important readiness skills. They also can be used with older students to generate enthusiasm and interest in reading as you develop vocabulary knowledge and expose children to more complex written language forms. An ideal time for this activity is after lunch when it can serve as a transition from the relatively unstructured lunchtime activities to more formally structured classroom activities. For younger students, you may choose to read a single short book each day. For older students, you may read a chapter or two from a longer selection. In either case, consider the following suggestions from Coody (1983) for conducting successful read-aloud sessions.

read-aloud sessions:
Time regularly set aside for reading to students. Often used to generate enthusiasm and interest for reading.

1. *Choose a book with your students in mind.* Select books you think will be interesting to your students.
2. *Select a book with yourself in mind.* Be certain that you will enjoy the book. If you are not interested in the book, your students cannot be expected to enjoy it.

3. *Practice reading the book.* Prepare for the intonation patterns in unusual or vivid scenes. Be certain that you know what the book is about before you begin to read.

4. *Create an atmosphere for reading aloud.* If possible, gather the students in front of you in a cozy part of the room where they can get comfortable. Be certain that younger children can see the story's pictures.

5. *Eliminate undue distractions.*

6. *Read with feeling and expression.*

7. *Discuss unfamiliar words.*

8. *Teach the parts of a book.* This might include items like jacket covers, end pages, author and artist information, table of contents, or dedication pages.

9. *Give opportunity for responses to reading aloud.* When you finish, be certain to discuss and share reactions. If students liked the book, mention other titles by the same author and indicate where these books may be found.

SAMPLE ACTIVITIES

Counting Books. Use counting books such as *1 is One,* by Tasha Tudor; *My First Counting Book,* by Lilian Moore; or *The Very Hungry Caterpillar,* by Eric Carle to develop number concepts with preschool and kindergarten students. After reading one of these aloud, encourage children to create their own counting books. Provide blank pages to individual students and help them draw numbered sets of objects on each page (one book, two bikes, and so on); dictate a sentence for each page to you (write their words at the bottom of each page); and then staple the pages together. Be certain to have children number the pages, if they can.

Diaries. While reading *The Diary of Anne Frank* to fourth-, fifth-, or sixth-grade students, have students make and keep their own diaries. Encourage students to make an entry each day. You may want to make these completely private. Alternatively, collect them once a week and write a "private" response to each individual.

Recipe Reading. After reading books like *Cranberry Thanksgiving,* by Wendy and Harry Devlin; *The Gingerbread Man,* by Ed Arno; *Stone Soup,* by Marcia Brown; or *Rain Makes Applesauce,* by Julian Scheer, provide children with an experience in recipe reading. You may want to do this in the classroom or in the school kitchen with parent helpers. You could duplicate the recipe and send it home with children to share with their parents.

Reading Corners. Another way to integrate literature into your classroom is to devote a part of your room solely to reading. A **reading corner** with book shelves, a magazine rack, a newspaper rack, carpet, comfortable chairs or pillows, and a display table can be created without too much difficulty. Small classroom libraries initially can be established with the cooperation of your school library or media center. You may want to work with your librarian or media specialist to develop a rotating series of displays highlighting particular categories of books. Over time, you should develop your own classroom library.

reading corner: Portion of a classroom devoted solely to reading.

Classroom libraries can be started inexpensively with paperback versions of children's literature. Several publishers make these available at reasonable prices.

1. Scholastic Book Services, 904 Sylvan Avenue, Englewood Cliffs, NJ 07632.
2. Troll Associates, 320 Route 17, Mahwah, NJ 07430.
3. Xerox Educational Publishers, 245 Long Hill Road, Middletown, CT 06457.

Publishers of children's paperback books often manage book clubs for classrooms. Once a month, classrooms receive a listing of available titles and students can place orders through the teacher. Teachers and students are under no obligation to purchase books at any time. Teachers, however, usually receive free books for their classroom libraries if a purchase is made.

You might also decide to have your class subscribe to one or several magazines devoted to children. Be certain to announce and prominently display each issue in your magazine rack as it arrives. Popular children's magazines include the following:

1. *Cricket.* Open Court Publishing Company, Box 599, La Salle, IL 61301. Stories, poetry, and informative articles.
2. *Ebony, Jr.* Johnson Publishing Company, 820 South Michigan Avenue, Chicago, IL 60605. Articles, poetry, and stories about famous black Americans.
3. *Kids.* Kids Publishing, Incorporated, 777 Third Avenue, New York, NY 10017. A magazine written by children for children.
4. *Ranger Rick.* Ranger Rick, Membership Services, 1412 Sixteenth Street NW, Washington, DC 20036. Articles and stories on wildlife and conservation with color photographs.
5. *Sesame Street Magazine.* Sesame Street Magazine, P.O. Box 2896, Boulder, CO 80322. Thematic issues with games, activities, and at least one narrative.
6. *World Traveler.* Open Court Publishing Company, Box 599, La Salle, IL 61301. Material from *National Geographic* written at the primary-grade level.

SAMPLE ACTIVITIES

Book Swapping. Set up a swap table in your reading corner. A student who brings a book is entitled to take one. Or, require students to bring two books for every one they take. Use the extra book in your classroom library.

Book Talk Introductions. Regularly introduce new books into your classroom library during a book talk. Say a few words about the author and the book, and read a short paragraph that will catch children's attention. When you are finished, place the books on the display table in your reading corner and make them available to children.

Author of the Week. Create an "Author of the Week" bulletin board for your reading corner. Have different individuals research and put together a display for each author. The display might contain a short biography, titles of important books, and perhaps a picture. Give students their authors, or let them select a favorite author, several months in advance. Students may write to authors, in care of the publisher, informing them of the honor they have received. Some authors will respond to these letters. Responses can then be displayed.

reading center:
Learning center devoted specifically to reading activities.

Reading Centers. In addition to a reading corner, you may also want to establish a **reading center,** a learning center devoted specifically to reading activities. It consists of a single location in a classroom where children participate in a rotating series of independent, self-guided, reading activities. Reading-center activities are usually structured tasks as compared to the unstructured opportunities available in a reading corner. The content of reading-center activities varies widely. All, however, usually share four characteristics.

1. *Clear directions.* Reading center tasks have clearly written directions for students. In addition, teachers often go over the directions orally when new center activities are introduced.
2. *Necessary materials.* Usually all the materials required for any activity are placed in the center.
3. *A record-keeping device.* Often the students or teacher check their names off a list when an activity has been successfully completed.
4. *A place to turn in or display completed work.* Students can turn their work into a box at the center or display their work on an adjacent bulletin board.

It is important to remember to change reading-center tasks regularly so that fresh activities are always available. Also remember to formally introduce each new activity to arouse interest in the task and answer any questions about how to complete it.

Reading Center Activities for Primary-Grade Students. For primary-grade students, reading-center tasks might include listening and following along to a recorded reading of a book; reading a new book and drawing a more attractive cover; or reading a favorite story to a friend.

Reading Center Activities for Upper Elementary-Grade Students. For older students, reading-center tasks can include reading a book to a student in the primary grades; writing a letter to a favorite author; making a crossword puzzle for a favorite book; making an advertisement for a favorite book; or writing a review of a children's magazine.

Taking Advantage of Your School Library or Media Center. When considering how to integrate literature into your students' learning environment, do not be limited by the four walls of your classroom. Include the school library (or media center) in your plans. At least once a week, reserve time for a visit. School librarians often provide structured-learning experiences for children as well as time to browse and select books. Coordinating the literature experiences which you and the school library provide is an important aspect of a classroom reading program.

Lunchtime Library. If your library is unavailable to students during lunchtime, seek ways to make it available to supervised youngsters. Supervisors might be older students working as library assistants, parent volunteers, or yourself. You could eat lunch once or twice a week in the library and help check out books.

Related Readings. When students enjoy a particular story, make up a list of related titles by the same author or about the same topic. The librarian may be able to help you in this task. Pass the lists out just before a trip to the school library. Encourage students to find these books and check them out.

Working Together with Parents. Actively seek the assistance of parents in extending an environment of literature beyond school boundaries. Parents are usually more than willing to assist you in your efforts, but sometimes do not know what to do. Be certain to communicate the importance of establishing a supportive environment for reading at home. Provide clear examples of what parents can do to help their children. It is often useful to send a short note home at the beginning of each school year, listing ways in which parents can help. It might include ideas like the following.

Enlist parents in your attempts to surround children with literature. Provide clear examples of what they might do to help their children.

1. Set aside a regular time every day to read to your child. Sharing a good story at bedtime can be an enjoyable way to end the day together.
2. If you have not already done so, help your child establish a personal library. This may require some new furniture and a beginning set of books. Both can be acquired inexpensively. Shelving can be something as simple as a freshly painted set of boards and bricks. Books make excellent birthday and holiday presents.
3. Try to create a quiet place in the home where your child can read without being interrupted. This should be away from family traffic and the television.
4. If you have not already done so, help your child acquire a library card at the public library. Make a visit to the library a regular weekly event.
5. As a parent, your reading habits are an important model for your child. Your newspaper, magazine, and pleasure reading habits do not go unnoticed. When you come across something of interest to your child, be certain to share it. When you are looking for information in a reference book (a phone book, TV guide, dictionary, bird book, or repair manual) be certain to involve your child in the search if it seems appropriate. Explain what you are doing and how you are going about the task.
6. You may want to have your child join an inexpensive paperback book club. Several offer quality children's literature at inexpensive prices. Write to the Children's Book Council at 67 Irving Place, New York, NY 10003, for the names and addresses of reputable firms.

Additional Activities. There are many, many ways of integrating literature into children's learning environments. As you work in schools, you will probably encounter many new and useful instructional activities, bulletin board ideas, reading-center tasks, and other means to develop a classroom environment rich in literature. Begin now to collect and organize ideas that you think are useful. Keep a literature notebook and jot down descriptions of interesting ideas that you encounter in someone else's classroom, in a reading journal, or during your own professional education. Or, keep your ideas on separate 3- by 5-inch cards and organize them in a file box. Or, you can organize this information on a microcomputer using database management software. You might want to begin with some of the following:

1. *Book parties.* Have a short book party. Students can dress up in the afternoon as their favorite characters from a book read during the previous month. Have students wear name tags containing their character's name and the title of the book.
2. *Book cover doors.* Turn your classroom door into a book cover. In the higher grades, create a book cover on the door for the book you are currently reading aloud to students. Have your students help design and construct the cover. For lower grades, you could have your children vote on their favorite read-aloud book during the past month.
3. *Order literature motivators.* Write to the Children's Book Council at 67 Irving Place, New York, NY 10003, for a catalog of bookmarks, posters, and other promotional material.
4. *RIF.* Write to RIF (Reading is FUNdamental) at Department P, 600 Maryland Avenue SW, Smithsonian Institution, Washington, DC 20560. RIF has coordinated a nationwide program to provide each child with three free books. RIF will provide seventy-five percent of the costs including postage if local groups provide twenty-five percent. Inquire about the current procedures for including your students in this program.
5. *Book fairs.* Encourage your school's parent-teacher organization to sponsor a book fair. Invite book dealers to display and sell their new books each year in the school auditorium or cafeteria.
6. *Literature logs.* Encourage students to keep and maintain literature logs by writing short reactions after reading each new book. Periodically collect, read, and react to students in their logs. Have children design covers in the shape of a log.

Putting Children in Touch with Books

Many children will take advantage of an environment rich in literature to engage in independent reading. Your classroom environment has started these children on the road to becoming readers who both can and do read. Others, however, will still be reluctant to select and complete a book on their own, indicating that they find books boring and uninteresting. Despite your best intentions and a concerted effort to integrate literature into your classroom, some students may remain reluctant readers who will only read a book if it is required for an assignment. When you find yourself in this position, carefully consider the books you have selected for your classroom library, the interests of the students in your class, and the types of opportunities you provide for students to engage in literature experiences. Ask yourself several questions.

1. Are the books in my classroom library sufficiently interesting to capture students' attention?
2. Have I been able to match children's interests with suitable literature selections?
3. Do I provide appropriate and varied opportunities for students to interact enjoyably with literature?

Becoming Familiar with Popular Children's Literature. To answer the first question, you will need to become familiar with popular children's literature. You can begin by looking at books that have won The Newbery or Caldecott Medals. **The Newbery Medal** is awarded annually by the American Library Association and the Association for Library Service to Children to the author of the "most distinguished contribution to American literature for children published during the preceding year." **The Caldecott Medal** is awarded annually by the same organizations to the artist of the "most distinguished American picture book for children published in the United States during the preceding year." Lists of The Newbery and Caldecott Medal winners are provided for your use in table 7–1 and table 7–2, respectively. Understand, however, that The Newbery and Caldecott Medal winners are selected by adults. Excellence is thus defined by adult criteria and not necessarily the criteria of children. Although medal-winning books meet the highest standards of the two organizations which participate in their selection, they do not always meet the unique needs of individual children.

Another way to become familiar with popular children's literature is to look at books that have been selected as Children's Choices through the sponsorship of the International Reading Association and the Children's Book Council. Each year, a joint committee from these two organizations coordinates the choices of thousands of children who read new books and vote for their favorites. The results have appeared in the October issues of *The Reading Teacher* each year since 1974. You can obtain an annotated copy of the most recent choices by sending a self-addressed 6½- by 9½-inch envelope, stamped with first-class postage for two ounces to Children's Choices, International Reading Association, P.O. Box 8139, Newark, DE 19714. You can also purchase copies in bulk for parents.

Another method to become familiar with children's literature is to read issues of *Horn Book Magazine,* the major journal in the field. *Horn*

The Newbery Medal: Awarded annually by the American Library Association and the Association for Library Service to Children to the author of the "most distinguished contribution to American literature for children published during the preceding year."

The Caldecott Medal: Awarded annually by the American Library Association and the Association for Library Service to Children to the artist of the "most distinguished American picture book for children published in the United States during the preceding year."

Book Magazine reviews new children's books and contains articles on children's literature. It publishes six issues a year and can usually be found in your school or local library.

In addition, you may wish to talk to different individuals at your school about children's literature. Talk to the school librarian about books that are frequently checked out by students at your grade level. Inquire about topics, themes, authors, and narrative forms that are especially popular with your students. Talk with colleagues who also teach at your grade level to help you become familiar with popular children's literature. Ask about how they integrate literature into the reading program. Ask students in your school who are a grade or two above your class what they enjoyed reading when they were at your students' grade level. If you are working on graphs in your classroom, you could have your students collect this information by interviewing older students and then drawing a graph of the results.

Finally, you can consult one of several annotated bibliographies of popular children's literature. Frequently used annotated bibliographies include:

1. Association for Library Service to Children. (Annual). *Notable children's books.* Chicago, IL: American Library Association.
2. Tway, E. (ed.) (1981). *Reading ladders for human relations,* 6th Edition. Urbana, IL: National Council of Teachers of English.
3. White, M. L. (ed.) (1981). *A booklist for pre-k-grade 8.* Urbana, IL: National Council of Teachers of English.

All methods just described are useful for developing a greater understanding of children's literature. None, however, compensate for actually reading children's literature regularly. This will help you make appropriate choices as you build a classroom library and as you make suggestions for individual students. As you begin to rediscover the world of children's literature, you might take a few minutes after reading each book to jot down bibliographic information, a synopsis of the story, and questions you might use to begin a discussion. Write this information in a consistent format on index cards or on disc using database management software and develop an easy-to-access filing system. You will find your growing collection a useful aid for selecting books and discussing them with students after they have read a book. A sample literature card is illustrated in figure 7–1.

A POINT TO PONDER

Becoming Familiar with Your Students' Interests. As you develop confidence that your classroom library contains a wide range of interesting and engaging literature, you must also ascertain the unique interests of your students. There are many methods for evaluating students' interests. The most common is an interest inventory (see chapter 3). These assessment measures often provide useful information as you attempt

TABLE 7–1

Award-winning children's literature—The Newbery Medal winners

Year	Title	Author
1922	The Story of Mankind	Hendrik Willem van Loon
1923	The Voyages of Doctor Dolittle	Hugh Lofting
1924	The Dark Frigate	Charles Hawes
1925	Tales from Silver Lands	Charles Finger
1926	Shen of the Sea	Arthur Bowie Chrisman
1927	Smoky, the Cowhorse	Will James
1928	Gayneck, The Story of a Pigeon	Dhan Gopal Mukerji
1929	The Trumpeter of Krakow	Eric P. Kelly
1930	Hitty, Her First Hundred Years	Rachel Field
1931	The Cat Who Went to Heaven	Elizabeth Coatsworth
1932	Waterless Mountain	Laura Adams Armer
1933	Young Fu of the Upper Yangtze	Elizabeth Foreman Lewis
1934	Invincible Louisa	Cornelia Meigs
1935	Dobry	Monica Shannon
1936	Caddie Woodlawn	Carol Brink
1937	Roller Skates	Ruth Sawyer
1938	The White Stag	Kate Seredy
1939	Thimble Summer	Elizabeth Enright
1940	Daniel Boone	James Daugherty
1941	Call it Courage	Armstrong Sperry
1942	The Matchlock Gun	Walter D. Edmonds
1943	Adam of the Road	Elizabeth Janet Gray
1944	Johnny Tremain	Esther Forbes
1945	Rabbit Hill	Robert Lawson
1946	Strawberry Girl	Lois Lenski
1947	Miss Hickory	Carolyn Sherwin Bailey
1948	The Twenty-One Balloons	William Pène du Bois
1949	King of the Wind	Marguerite Henry
1950	The Door in the Wall	Marguerite de Angeli
1951	Amos Fortune, Free Man	Elizabeth Yates
1952	Ginger Pye	Eleanor Estes
1953	Secret of the Andes	Ann Nolan Clark
1954	. . . and now Miguel	Joseph Krumgold

to put reluctant readers and potentially interesting books together. Do not overlook, however, the information on students' interests that may be collected informally as you interact with children throughout the day. Often information about favorite activities, hobbies, games, or sports reveal themselves during sharing time or classroom discussions. Or, simply ask children during the first few weeks of school to tell you two or three things that they like the most. Parent conferences, which occur regularly throughout the year, are also useful for determining student

TABLE 7-1

continued

Year	Title	Author
1955	The Wheel on the School	Meindert DeJong
1956	Carry On, Mr. Bowditch	Jean Lee Latham
1957	Miracles on Maple Hill	Virginia Sorensen
1958	Rifles for Watie	Harold Keith
1959	The Witch of Blackbird Pond	Elizabeth George Speare
1960	Onion John	Joseph Krumgold
1961	Island of the Blue Dolphins	Scott O'Dell
1962	The Bronze Bow	Elizabeth George Speare
1963	A Wrinkle in Time	Madeleine L'Engle
1964	It's Like This, Cat	Emily Neville
1965	Shadow of a Bull	Maia Wojciechowska
1966	I, Juan de Pareja	Elizabeth Borten de Trevino
1967	Up a Road Slowly	Irene Hunt
1968	From the Mixed-up Files of Mrs. Basil E. Frankweiler	E. L. Konigsburg
1969	The High King	Lloyd Alexander
1970	Sounder	William H. Armstrong
1971	Summer of the Swans	Betsy Byars
1972	Mrs. Frisby and the Rats of NIMH	Robert C. O'Brien
1973	Julie of the Wolves	Jean George
1974	The Slave Dancer	Paula Fox
1975	M. C. Higgins, the Great	Virginia Hamilton
1976	The Grey King	Susan Cooper
1977	Roll of Thunder, Hear My Cry	Mildred D. Taylor
1978	Bridge to Terabithia	Katherine Paterson
1979	The Westing Game	Ellen Raskin
1980	A Gathering of Days: A New England Girl's Journal, 1830–32	Joan Blos
1981	Jacob Have I Loved	Katherine Paterson
1982	A Visit to William Blake's Inn: Poems for Innocent and Experienced Travelers	Nancy Willard
1983	Dicey's Song	Cynthia Voigt
1984	Dear Mr. Henshaw	Beverly Cleary
1985	The Hero and the Crown	Robin McKinley

interests. Record the information you collect in a log or individual file and update it as the need arises. Refer to your notes when you recommend books to reluctant readers.

Providing Independent Literature Opportunities for Students

Once you have put students and literature together, you must also provide sufficient opportunities for children to independently engage in lit-

TABLE 7–2
The Caldecott Medal Winners

Year	Title	Illustrator	Author
1938	Animals of the Bible	Dorothy P. Lathrop	Helen Dean Fish
1939	Mei Li	Thomas Handforth	Thomas Handforth
1940	Abraham Lincoln	Ingri and Edgar D'Aulaire	Ingri and Edgar D'Aulaire
1941	They Were Strong and Good	Robert Lawson	Robert Lawson
1942	Make Way for Ducklings	Robert McCloskey	Robert McCloskey
1943	The Little House	Virginia Lee Burton	Virginia Lee Burton
1944	Many Moons	Louis Slobodkin	James Thurber
1945	Prayer for a Child	Elizabeth Orton Jones	Rachel Field
1946	The Rooster Crows	Maud and Miska Petersham	Maud and Miska Petersham
1947	The Little Island	Leonard Weisgard	Golden MacDonald
1948	White Snow, Bright Snow	Roger Duvoisin	Alvin Tresselt
1949	The Big Snow	Berta and Elmer Hader	Berta and Elmer Hader
1950	Song of the Swallows	Leo Politi	Leo Politi
1951	The Egg Tree	Katherine Milhous	Katherine Milhous
1952	Finders Keepers	Nicholas Mordvinoff	William Lipkind
1953	The Biggest Bear	Lynd Ward	Lynd Ward
1954	Madeline's Rescue	Ludwig Bemelmans	Ludwig Bemelmans
1955	Cinderella, or the Little Glass Slipper	Marcia Brown	Charles Perrault
1956	Frog Went A-Courtin'	Feodor Rojankovsky	Retold by John Langstaff
1957	A Tree is Nice	Marc Simont	Janice May Udry
1958	Time of Wonder	Robert McCloskey	Robert McCloskey
1959	Chanticleer and the Fox	Barbara Cooney	translated by Barbara Cooney
1960	Nine Days to Christmas	Marie Hall Ets	Marie Hall Ets & Aurora Labastida

Year	Title		
1961	Babouska and the Three Kings	Nicolas Sidjakov	Ruth Robbins
1962	Once a Mouse	Marcia Brown	Marcia Brown
1963	The Snowy Day	Ezra Jack Keats	Ezra Jack Keats
1964	Where the Wild Things Are	Maurice Sendak	Maurice Sendak
1965	May I Bring a Friend?	Beni Montresor	Beatrice Schenk De Regniers
1966	Always Room for One More	Nonny Hogrogian	Sorche Nic Leodhas
1967	Sam, Bangs & Moonshine	Evaline Ness	Evaline Ness
1968	Drummer Hoff	Ed Emberley	Barbara Emberley
1969	The Fool of the World and the Flying Ship	Uri Shulevitz	Arthur Ransome
1970	Sylvester and the Magic Pebble	William Steig	William Steig
1971	A Story-A Story	Gail E. Haley	Gail E. Haley
1972	One Fine Day	Nonny Hogrogian	Nonny Hogrogian
1973	The Funny Little Woman	Blair Lent	Arlene Mosel
1974	Duffy and the Devil	Margot Zemach	Harve Zemach
1975	Arrow to the Sun	Gerald McDermott	Gerald McDermott
1976	Why Mosquitoes Buzz in People's Ears	Leo and Diane Dillon	Verna Aardema
1977	Ashanti to Zulu: African Traditions	Leo and Diane Dillon	Margaret Musgrove
1978	Noah's Ark	Peter Spier	Peter Spier
1979	The Girl Who Loved Wild Horses	Paul Goble	Paul Goble
1980	Ox-Cart Man	Barbara Cooney	Donald Hall
1981	Fables	Arnold Lobel	Arnold Lobel
1982	Jumanji	Chris Van Allsburg	Chris Van Allsburg
1983	Shadow	Marcia Brown	Blaise Cendrars
1984	The Glorious Flight: Across the Channel with Louis Bleriot	Alice and Martin Provensen	Alice and Martin Provensen
1985	St. George and the Dragon	Trina Shart Hyman	Margaret Hodges

> Dahl, Roald   Charlie and the Chocolate Factory   162 pp.
>   New York: Alfred A. Knopf, 1964
>
> Synopsis: Five children win a coveted prize: a tour of a mysterious
>   chocolate factory. During the tour, strange events befall
>   each of the children (and their parents). Marvelous
>   lyrical poetry in several locations!
>
> Discussion Questions
>
> 1. How would you describe the inner workings of the magical
>   chocolate factory? (Students may wish to make a map or a
>   board game based on the factory layout.)
>
> 2. Describe the main characters in this story.
>
> 3. Do you think the five children won their prizes by
>   chance? Why or why not?
>
> 4. Describe the life of an Oompa-Loompa. Would you enjoy
>   working in this chocolate factory? Why?

FIGURE 7–1
An example of a literature card

erature experiences. There are several ways to provide this type of experience in your classroom.

The most common, least structured, and perhaps least effective way for providing self-selected literature experiences takes place after students have completed their regular reading assignments. Often, teachers will encourage children to go to the reading corner or the reading center when regular reading assignments are completed early. During this free-choice time, students are allowed to select magazines, newspapers, or books for pleasure reading. Only a portion of the students in a classroom, however, usually have an opportunity to participate in this type of independent reading activity. Usually, those students who have the most to gain from this type of activity end up participating the least.

One method ensuring all students equal opportunities for independent reading is referred to by McCracken (1971) as **Sustained Silent Reading (SSR)** and by Hunt (1971) as **Uninterrupted Sustained Silent Reading (USSR).** SSR (or USSR) provides uninterrupted time for both students and teacher to read self-selected materials, without interruption, at a fixed time each day. Tierney, Readence, & Dishner (1980) give

Sustained Silent Reading (SSR) or Uninterrupted Sustained Silent Reading (USSR): Provides uninterrupted time for both students and teacher to read self-selected materials, without interruption, at a fixed time each day.

the following "cardinal rules" for USSR that capture the essential qualities of the methods advocated by both McCracken and Hunt.

1. Everybody reads. Both students and teacher will read something of their own choosing. Completing homework assignments, grading papers, and similar activities are discouraged. The reading should be for the pleasure of the reader.
2. There are to be no interruptions during USSR. The word "uninterrupted" is an essential part of the technique. Interruptions result in loss of comprehension and loss of interest by many students; therefore, questions and comments should be held until the silent reading period has concluded.
3. No one will be asked to report what they have read. It is essential that students feel that this is a period of free reading with the emphasis on reading for enjoyment. (p. 121).

Initially and for younger students, begin SSR for short periods (five minutes) on a regular basis. Gradually, the time allocated to this activity can be increased. Note that although SSR is usually implemented within individual classrooms, an entire school will sometimes participate in the activity. All children, teachers, and even staff members may read materials of choice for a specified time each session.

A third way to put readers and engaging texts together is to use a method framework called **Readers Theatre.** Typically, a Readers Theatre activity follows these procedural steps.

readers theatre: A group of students read a literature selection together, prepare a short script, practice reading the different parts, and then present a dramatic reading to the class without costumes or props.

1. A small group of students selects and reads a short literary selection together.
2. This group writes a short script (no more than a page or two) for presenting the selection to the class.
3. The students practice reading the various parts for intonation, expression, and eye or hand movements.
4. The students present the reading to the class.

Readers Theatre differs from the presentation of a play in that the message is usually communicated through the voices of readers rather than the appearance and movements of actors. Readers sit on chairs in the front of the room and props are not usually used. Readers carefully alter the rhythm, intonation, and pace of their reading to create an intended effect. More elaborate versions of Readers Theatre are also possible, however, in which props and movement by the actors are used.

Initially, Readers Theatre requires a certain amount of teacher direction and guidance. You should probably introduce the activity with teacher-selected scripts. If you wish to develop your own scripts, you might begin by looking at Dr. Seuss stories, fables, tall tales, short passages from longer books, and poems. Be certain to duplicate multiple

Readers theatre is one way to provide literature opportunities for students.

copies of each script for students. Commercially produced scripts are available from Readers Theatre Script Service, P.O. Box 178333, San Diego, CA 92117.

After all children have had several opportunities to participate in a Readers Theatre, they will be eager to select their own pieces, write their own scripts, and decide independently how a script is to be presented. A short five- to ten-minute period just before lunch might be regularly reserved for Readers Theatre presentations. Be certain to have the readers show the class the source of their script. Other students may be interested in reading the entire selection during SSR or free reading time.

A final method for putting readers and interesting, self-selected books together is somewhat more structured—**independent book projects.** As a regular part of your reading program, you might require that students independently read and discuss with you a minimum number of self-selected books. In conjunction with this task, students are sometimes asked to maintain reading logs, jotting down thoughts and reactions while they are reading a book. Frequently, they are asked to also write down a summary evaluation of the book. When students have completed a book, it is important for you to take a few minutes to discuss it with them. You may find your literature file useful for this purpose. Be certain that you use the discussion time to evaluate the student's response to the book. Use this information to make suggestions about additional books which might also be enjoyed.

Sometimes, children enjoy presenting their book to the class. Do not limit the form of this presentation to the traditional book report.

independent book projects: Students select a minimum number of books to read during a fixed time period. Often some form of presenting these books to others is also done.

When this format becomes the only method for sharing an independent book project, children quickly lose the excitement of reading and completing independent book projects. Here are some other ways of sharing an independent book project, besides the traditional book report.

1. Make a shoe box diorama of a vivid scene in your book.
2. Draw an illustrated map of the location of your story.
3. Create a board game based on the adventures in your story. Laminate with clear Con-Tact paper and place in your reading corner.
4. Make a mobile with the characters and several objects from your story. This is an especially effective way to present science fiction selections.
5. Create a crossword puzzle from your story. Duplicate the puzzle and let other readers of your book attempt to complete it.
6. Write a letter to the author of your book sharing your reactions. Post the letter and the response when it arrives.
7. Read a vivid scene from your book to the class.

It is important that children leave your room at the end of the year as better readers. It is equally important, however, that they leave your room as independent readers. Having good children's literature in the classroom, acquiring and using your knowledge of children's interests to help reluctant readers make choices, and providing sufficient varied opportunities for children to encounter literature are the three components of an effective independent reading program.

Do not give up, however, if your first few suggestions do not make a dramatic change in the independent reading habits of a reluctant reader. Developing interest and enthusiasm for literature is not a simple task when you confront a history of disinterest. A continuous program of recommending potentially interesting books and creating opportunities for children to interact with these books will ultimately yield gains in independent reading behavior.

LITERATURE AND NARRATIVE DISCOURSE STRUCTURE

Traditionally, literature is used in classroom reading programs to promote comprehension and to help students develop into independent readers. Increasingly, however, literature experiences are being viewed as especially important for developing one particular type of discourse knowledge: knowledge about **narrative discourse structure** or story structure (Applebee, 1978; Golden, 1984; Mandler & Johnson, 1977; Nessel, 1985).

Recall that readers use discourse knowledge to assist comprehension of units greater than a single sentence. In chapter 6, you learned about three types of discourse knowledge important for reading compre-

narrative discourse structure (story structure): The organizational structure common to all stories or narratives. Used by readers during the comprehension process.

hension: understanding pronoun and adverbial referents; drawing conclusions; and predicting outcomes. This chapter and the next will address a fourth form of discourse knowledge important for reading comprehension: knowledge of the structural organization of different text types.

Each category of text (narratives, exposition, poetry, fairy tales, mysteries, and so on) usually follows certain structural conventions. As a mature reader, you are familiar with these structural conventions. You know, for example, that fairy tales often begin with "Once upon a time . . . ." You also know that factual articles often use structural patterns such as "There are three reasons why . . . . First,. . . . Second,. . . . Finally,. . . ." Readers use their knowledge of these structural conventions during the comprehension process. Knowledge of structural organization at the discourse level assists comprehension in three ways: by helping readers to interpret appropriately what they have read; by forming expectations for upcoming meaning; and by filling in, or inferring, missing structural elements.

The organization of a text often provides clues to readers about how to interpret what they are reading. Consider, for example, what might happen if one reads an editorial as a newspaper article and not as a piece of persuasive writing: the reader would be likely to mistake opinion for fact. Knowing the structural organization of different text types permits a reader to interpret different forms of writing appropriately.

A POINT TO PONDER	First- and second-grade students often ask their teacher, after reading a particularly interesting story, "Is that true?" They want to know if what they read was fiction or nonfiction. Why do you think young readers are often unable to determine this for themselves? Why do older students seldom ask this question?

Knowing the structural organization of different text types is also important for a second reason: it enables a reader to anticipate upcoming meaning. Recall what happened in chapter 2 when you read the first sentence of a story beginning "Once upon a time . . ."; you immediately had specific expectations about this story—for example, it was not true, it took place in a kingdom long ago and far away, a prince and princess would appear as characters, a problem would require resolution, and there would be a happy ending. Knowing the likely structural characteristics for any text sets up expectations for what will come next and thus facilitates comprehension.

Finally, knowing the structural organization of different text types is important because it allows a reader to infer structural information omitted by an author. Just as authors omit signal words between ideas at the syntactic level, they similarly omit structural features character-istic of a particular type of text at the discourse level. An episode in a narrative, for example, will often be left out by an author who assumes that the reader will correctly infer what took place. Knowing that narra-tives contain episodic structure will make it more likely that a reader will infer the missing information.

What are the most important structural patterns at the discourse level with which young readers must become familiar? Generally, stu-dents encounter and must become familiar with two major discourse forms: narrative and exposition. **Narratives** tell a story. They appear most frequently during reading instruction in the elementary grades. Narratives include mysteries, fables, fairy tales, folk tales, historical fic-tion, and so on. **Exposition** is text that informs. Exposition appears most frequently during content-area instruction in the upper-elementary grades. Examples of expository forms include articles and textbooks in the various content areas: social studies, science, mathematics, and lan-guage arts. Narrative and expository selections are not the only forms of discourse that children encounter in the elementary grades. Neverthe-less, the emphasis of this chapter and the next will be on the develop-ment of narrative and expository discourse knowledge since these two categories of text types are the most frequently encountered by young readers.

narratives: Tell a story. Include mysteries, fables, fairy tales, and so on.

exposition: Informs by presenting factual infor-mation about the world we live in.

Knowledge of Narrative Discourse Structure Defined

The exact nature of readers' knowledge of narrative discourse structure is not yet completely clear. Researchers who are investigating this aspect of comprehension do not all agree on what it is that readers know about narrative structure and how they use this information during reading comprehension (Mandler & Johnson, 1977; Rumelhart, 1980; Thorndyke, 1977). Generally, however, researchers agree that readers take advan-tage of two types of knowledge: knowledge of the general structure of narratives and knowledge of the particular characteristics of specific nar-rative forms such as fairy tales, folk tales, mysteries, or historical fiction.

Knowledge of the General Structure of Narratives. Most researchers believe that narratives contain setting information, an initiating episode establishing a problem to be resolved in the story, and a sequence of episodes that explain how the problem gets resolved. Narratives often follow a structure similar to the following.

    I. Setting
        A. Character information
        B. Location information
        C. Time information

II. Initiating Episode (Story Problem)
   A. Initiating event
   B. Goal formation

III. Episode 1, 2, 3, 4, and so on. (Including the final, resolution episode)
   A. Attempt
   B. Outcome
   C. Reaction

setting information:
Found at the beginning of narratives. Includes information about the character(s), location, and time in the story.

Setting information usually occurs at the beginning of a narrative and includes information about the character(s) in the story, the location where the story takes place, and the time when the story takes place. For example:

Once upon a time, there was *a little girl with a red hood* who
     Time   **Character**
lived by *the edge of a forest.*
         Location

Not all stories contain character, location, or time information at the beginning; one or several may be missing. Nevertheless, knowing that character, location, and time *should* be at the beginning of a narrative leads proficient readers to infer this information when it is not explicitly stated.

initiating episode:
Usually the first organized sequence of actions in a story. Often specify a problem that is resolved in the story.

An **initiating episode** is usually the first episode in a narrative. Initiating episodes often specify a problem that will be resolved in the course of the story. They contain an initiating event ("One day, Little Red Riding Hood's mother gave her a basket of bread and jam.") and the formation of a goal by one or several of the characters ("She told Little Red Riding Hood to take the food to her grandmother's house in the woods."). Initiating episodes sometimes are not explicitly stated. Again, however, proficient readers usually infer this information when it is missing in a narrative.

succeeding episodes:
Sequences of actions in a story explaining how a character attempts to solve a problem or achieve a goal.

Succeeding episodes, including the concluding episode, are usually accounts of how the character attempts to solve the problem or achieve the goal established in the initiating episode. Succeeding episodes typically contain an attempt to accomplish the goal, an outcome of that attempt, and a reaction to the outcome. Succeeding episodes may also result in characters establishing new goals to be achieved in the course of the story.

BEFORE READING ON

The following story reflects the typical structural organization of a narrative. See if you can identify the following structural features in this piece:

1. A statement at the beginning establishing a setting for the story. (Note that

only character information is explicitly stated. The time and location for this story are unspecified and must be inferred.)

2. Three episodes expressed in a temporal order that describe unsuccessful attempts to achieve an unstated and implicit goal.

3. A fourth and concluding episode where the unstated and implicit goal is achieved.

"Mr. Randall had a hard time getting to the airport. First he took the wrong exit off the highway and had to drive eight miles to get back on. Then his car had a flat tire, and he had to fix it. When he was on his way again, he got stuck in a traffic jam. That took more time. Now he was an hour late! When angry Mr. Randall finally reached the airport, he discovered that the plane he was supposed to meet was an hour late too!" (Scott, Foresman, Golden Secrets, p. 41)

Readers often use their knowledge of narrative discourse structure to infer missing information in any text. When a structural component is not explicitly stated, readers will often infer its existence. Table 7–3 shows how this takes place with the short narrative selection you just read. Note how missing structural information such as the location, the time, the goal in an initiating episode, and the various reactions to outcomes are often inferred by readers.

Knowledge of narrative discourse structure is useful for readers. In addition, this knowledge is often very useful for teachers; it allows teachers to understand why some children fail to comprehend a story or a portion of a story. Some Children who read the following story without guidance, for example, fail to understand why the rabbit did a "spin dance." Given your knowledge of the structural organization of narrative discourse, what do you think might be the source of the problem? What inference do these readers fail to make?

A POINT TO PONDER

THE RABBIT AND THE BEAR

A rabbit was walking up a hill in the moonlight. She met a big bear on the hill. The bear jumped at the rabbit. "I have you!" called the bear. "Yes, you do," said the rabbit. The bear looked at the rabbit. "I am very hungry," he said. (Picture of the bear holding the rabbit)
The rabbit sat very still. Then she said, "Wait! I was going to dance my spin dance. You will not see my fast, fast spin dance. The bear did like to see a good dance. So he sat down. "I am not hungry," he said. "I'll wait. Dance your spin dance." The rabbit did the spin dance. Around and around she went. "Can you dance as fast as that?" said the rabbit. "Yes, I can," said the bear. The rabbit said, "No bear can spin around as fast as I can." "I can," said the bear. The bear went around and around. He was going very fast. He did not see the rabbit. The rabbit ran away. She hid in the grass. The she looked out at the bear. "Spin away, Bear," said the rabbit. And the bear went around and around and around in the moonlight (HBJ, Sun and Shadow, p. 66–70).

To help you identify the source of the problem, consider which of the following structural characteristics from narrative discourse are not explicitly stated in the story and, therefore, must be inferred by a reader:

1. setting information
2. an initiating event
3. the formation of a goal by the rabbit after the initiating event
4. an emotional reaction by the rabbit in the concluding episode

How might you help a reader who failed to understand why the rabbit did a "spin dance"?

TABLE 7–3

Using knowledge of narrative discourse structure to make inferences

Structural Feature	Narrative Text *(or Likely Inference)
I. *Setting*	
A. Character information	Mr. Randall had a hard time getting to the airport.
B. Location information	*(This story probably took place in the United States and in a metropolitan area where airports exist.)
C. Time information	*(This story probably took place in the recent past. It is unlikely it took place before the early 1900s.)
II. *Initiating Episode*	
A. Initiating event	*(Mr. Randall's boss directed him to go on a business trip. Other inferences are also possible at this point; that is, that someone called and informed Mr. Randall that she was arriving at the airport or that Mr. Randall worked for an airline.)
B. Goal formation	*(Mr. Randall wants to get to the airport.)
III. *Episode 1*	
A. Attempt	First he took the wrong exit off the highway
B. Outcome	and had to drive eight miles to get back on.
C. Reaction	*(Mr. Randall was concerned.)
IV. *Episode 2*	
A. Attempt	*(Mr. Randall got back on the highway.)
B. Outcome	Then his car had a flat tire, and he had to fix it.
C. Reaction	*(Mr. Randall was upset.)
V. *Episode 3*	
A. Attempt	When he was on his way again,
B. Outcome	he got stuck in a traffic jam. That took more time. Now he was an hour late.
C. Reaction	*(Mr. Randall was angry.)
VI. *Concluding Episode*	
A. Attempt	*(Mr. Randall continued on his way to the airport.)
B. Outcome	When angry Mr. Randall reached the airport he discovered that the plane he was supposed to meet was an hour late, too!
C. Reaction	*(Mr. Randall was angry no longer.)

Knowledge of Different Narrative Forms. In addition to knowing the structural characteristics of narratives in general, narrative discourse knowledge includes knowing the unique characteristics of a variety of narrative forms. This information is often crucial for effective comprehension of a particular narrative. Without knowing that you are reading a fable, for example, you are much less likely to infer an unstated moral or message. Similarly, your understanding of a story will be very different if you believe you are reading contemporary realistic fiction rather than science fiction; you may misinterpret many of the author's futuristic guesses about the nature of society for an accurate representation of contemporary reality. Table 7–4 lists the major narrative forms in both fiction and nonfiction. The defining characteristics of these forms are often taught to students in the elementary grades.

PROMOTING KNOWLEDGE OF NARRATIVE DISCOURSE STRUCTURE

You are now familiar with the structural characteristics of narrative discourse and the unique attributes of a variety of narrative forms. You have also seen how this information contributes to comprehension. The question now becomes How should we promote knowledge of narrative discourse structure? The answer is still being investigated. At least one study (Dreher & Singer, 1980) has concluded that instruction in the structural characteristics of narrative discourse does not lead to gains in comprehension. A number of other studies (Beck, Omanson & McKeown, 1982; Reutzel, 1985; Morrow, 1984), however, have demonstrated that several types of instructional strategies significantly improve students' abilities to comprehend narratives. Four will be described: questioning; writing activities; story mapping; and direct instruction.

Questioning

After Reading a Story or a Portion of a Story. It is possible to develop narrative discourse knowledge with discussion questions after reading a story or a portion of a story (Morrow, 1984). Discussion questions used to promote the development of narrative discourse knowledge must focus on the structural organization of narratives (or specific narrative forms) and be consistent with the questioning guidelines described in chapter 6. You may want to review these guidelines at this time.

The following types of questions can be adapted to the particular story students have read. Recall that questions requiring inferences are usually more useful for instruction than questions requiring literal recall of the facts.

TABLE 7–4 Major narrative forms and their defining characteristics

Form	Setting Information	Episodes	Examples
FICTION			
Historical Fiction	Time: In the past Characters: Fictional and historical	Fictional characters introduced into historically accurate episodes.	*Spies on the Devils Belt* *Searching for Shona* *Island of the Blue Dolphin*
Modern Realistic Fiction	Time: Contemporary	Realistic episodes. Contemporary issues.	*Stevie* *I Have a Sister - My Sister is Deaf* *From the Mixed up Files of Mr. Basil E. Frankweiler*
Folk Tales	Time: Long ago Characters: Average citizens or animals Location: Countryside	Magical or fantastic: animals often talk, a witch may cast a spell, and so on.	*The Three Billy Goats Gruff* *Hansel and Gretel*
Fairy Tales	Time: Long ago Characters: Royalty Location: Castle or kingdom	Magical or fantastic: animals often talk, a witch may cast a a spell, and so on	*Cinderella* *Sleeping Beauty* *Puss in Boots*
Fables	Time: Long ago Characters: Usually animals Location: Countryside	Magical or fantastic: animals take human characteristics. Moral often stated at end.	*Aesops' Fables* *Old Man Whickutt's Donkey*
Myths	Time: Long ago Characters: Cultural hero(ine)	Hero(ine) demonstrates extreme courage, bravery, and skill in resolving a serious challenge.	*Atalanta* *Odysseus* *Joan of Arc*
Modern Fantasies	Time: Contemporary Characters: Realistic	Magical or fantastic.	*James and the Giant Peach* *Charlotte's Web* *Where the Wild Things Are* *The Narnia Chronicles*
Science Fiction	Time: Future Characters: Usually realistic Location: Often outer space	Fantastic but logically predicted from time when the story was written.	*A Wrinkle in Time* *The Space Ship Under the Apple*
NONFICTION			
Biography	Character: An historically important individual	Factual account of an individual's life.	*What's the Big Idea, Ben Franklin?* *Can't You Make them Behave, King George?*
Autobiography	Character: An historically important individual	Factual account of the author's life.	*The Diary of Anne Frank* *Helen Keller*

Settings

1. Who can tell us something about the setting of this story? What do we mean by the setting for a story? Where do we usually find this information?
2. Who are the important characters in this story? Why are they important? How can you tell who the important characters are before you even finish the story?
3. When did this story take place? How do you know? Could this story have taken place today? How can you tell? What time words can you find in this story? Where do they appear? If there are no time words how can you figure out when a story took place?
4. Where did this story take place? How can you tell? Can anyone find the words in the story which tell us where the story took place? If there are no words which tell us where the setting is located how can we tell? Could this story have taken place in a different location? Why?

Initiating Episodes

1. Do stories usually have a problem in them? Where do you find this information? Are problems sometimes not mentioned in a story? What do you do when this happens? What problem (goal) did the main character have in this story? What in the story told you this was a problem? Why was this a problem for him?
2. What was the source of the problem? What caused the problem? How do you know?

Succeeding Episodes

1. How did the main character attempt to solve his problem? Do you think this was a good solution? Would you have done the same?
2. What happened? What was the outcome? Did this solve the difficulty?
3. How did the character react to the outcome? Is this how you would have reacted? Why?
4. How did the problem finally get solved? Was this an appropriate solution? How did the character feel then? Would you have felt the same? Why?

Before Reading a Story or a Portion of a Story. It is also possible to develop narrative discourse knowledge with discussion questions before reading a story or a portion of a story. This often is done by adapting a method framework initially described in chapter 1: the **Directed Reading-Thinking Activity (DRTA).** A DRTA includes three procedural steps repeated at several points as students read and discuss a selection: predicting; reading; and proving. When you want to develop knowledge of narrative discourse structure using a DRTA, guide students to make predictions related to structural elements such as setting information, the

Directed Reading-Thinking Activity (DRTA): An instructional method which includes three procedural steps repeated throughout reading a passage: predicting, reading, proving.

story problem in the initiating episode, and the solution to this problem in succeeding episodes. Then have students read a portion of the story to check their predictions. Finally, have students discuss why their predictions were correct or incorrect before making predictions about the next structural element. In the following model lesson, notice how the teacher follows the predicting, reading, proving format of DRTA.

A POINT TO PONDER It is important to reiterate that questioning often becomes an assessment activity, used only to test children's comprehension, not an instructional activity. Be certain that your questioning activities end up teaching, not simply testing, children's understanding of narrative structures. Discussion questions that focus on narrative structures might be used to begin a discussion of a story; for example, What information do we usually find at the beginning of stories? Did you find this information in this story? What do you think the problem was in this story? Discussion questions might also be used to guide students and help them make appropriate inferences; for example, You're right Bill, it doesn't tell us why the rabbit did a spin dance. Let's reread the first few paragraphs and see if there are any clues . . . . Now that you have read this again, can you figure out why the rabbit did a spin dance? Finally, discussion questions might be used to get students to model reasoning strategies, especially at locations where students must infer a missing structural element; for example, Tell us, Susan, how you figured out that the rabbit wanted to get away from the bear? The difference between testing and teaching with questions needs to be clear if you hope to promote the development of discourse knowledge and not simply to test it.

MODEL LESSON

Using a DRTA to Develop Knowledge of Narrative Discourse Structure. The teacher has followed the standard predicting-reading-proving format of a DRTA and guided students' reading of the first two paragraphs in "The Rabbit and the Bear."

> A rabbit was walking up a hill in the moonlight. She met a big bear on the hill.
>
> The bear jumped at the rabbit. "I have you!" called the bear. "Yes, you do," said the rabbit. The bear looked at the rabbit. "I am very hungry," he said.

The teacher is now directing students' attention to the problem in this story, the unstated goal of the rabbit, and the way in which the rabbit might achieve its goal.

Predicting

Teacher: Let's think a little bit now about the problem in this story. You remember that every story has some kind of problem. I wonder what it is in this story. Any guesses?

Bill: I think the bear's problem is how he's gonna cook this rabbit. He's got him now and he has to figure out how to cook him.

Teacher: Ok. Anyone else?

Tanya: I think the bear's problem is that he's hungry and he wants to find something to eat.

June: No. He's already got the rabbit to eat. I think the rabbit has a problem, not the bear. The rabbit is caught.

Teacher: Ok. What do you think the rabbit wants to do?

Bill: He wants to get away.

Tanya: Yeah. He wants to get home and be safe.

June: Yeah. The rabbit wants to run away.

Teacher: Ok. Now, how do you think the rabbit will try to get away? What would you do if a bear caught you and you wanted to get away?

Bill: I'd run away.

Tanya: You can't. The bear already has you. I know. I'd tell the bear I'd be his friend and help him if he let me go. You know, like that story about the lion and the mouse we read.

June: I'd give the bear a pot of honey if he let me go. Bears like honey more than anything else.

Teacher: Ok. Now let's read the next paragraph together and see what the problem is in this story and how it is solved.

Reading

Teacher: Why don't you start reading for us, Tanya.

(Tanya, Bill, and June each read several sentences and finish the story.)

Proving

Teacher: Ok. Now let's see who guessed the problem in this story.

Bill: I didn't. I thought the bear was gonna try and cook the rabbit. It didn't say that.

June: I did. I thought the rabbit had a problem. He needed to get away and he did. It says "The rabbit ran away."

Teacher: Good, June. Now let's see who guessed how the rabbit got away.

June: I didn't. I thought he would give the bear a pot of honey. It didn't say that.

Bill: I did. It says that the rabbit ran away. I thought he would run away and he did. Rabbits are fast.

Tanya: Yeah, but you didn't guess that the rabbit would trick the bear. He had to trick the bear first to get away.

Teacher: How did the rabbit trick the bear?

Tanya: He said he could dance faster than the bear and the bear wanted to beat him so they had a dancing contest and the bear put the rabbit down and the rabbit ran away.

Teacher: Can anyone read the part that tells us how the rabbit got away?

Bill: I can. It says "'Can you dance as fast as that?' said the rabbit.

Teacher: 'Yes, I can,' said the bear. The rabbit said, 'No bear can spin around as fast as I can.' 'I can,' said the bear. The bear went around and around. He was going very fast. He did not see the rabbit. The rabbit ran away."

Teacher: Good. It doesn't say that the bear put the rabbit down, though. How do you know that?

Tanya: Because the bear was dancing. He couldn't dance with the rabbit. No wait. It says the bear was dancing and couldn't see the rabbit. If he still had the rabbit in his hand he could see him. So he must have put the rabbit down.·

Writing Activities

Writing activities can be used to develop discourse knowledge. As students think about what to write, they often reflect on the structural characteristics of a particular discourse form. Thus, writing tasks designed to focus students' attention on the discourse structure of a particular form can provide useful learning experiences for children. Macro cloze tasks, story frames, and patterned writing tasks are several writing activities designed to enhance familiarity with narrative discourse structure.

A POINT TO PONDER   Haiku is a Japanese poetic form with a specific discourse structure. Haiku contain three lines: five syllables in the first line; seven, in the second; and five, in the third. The poem must be written in the present tense, must contain a reference to nature, and must not contain rhyme. Attempt to write a haiku. Notice how you continuously check your thoughts about what to write, what you are writing, and what you have written against the structural characteristics of that form. A similar process takes place with young writers when they attempt to write in a more frequently used but equally unfamiliar form such as a fable or other form of narrative.

---

macro cloze task: A writing activity in which students are asked to write and fill in a missing structural element.

Macro Cloze Tasks. A **macro cloze task** can be used to focus students' attention on the structural characteristics of a particular discourse form. Previously, you have considered cloze tasks at the micro level; that is, tasks where readers only filled in a missing word or phrase. Macro cloze tasks ask readers to fill in a missing unit at the discourse level; for example, setting information, a story problem in an initiating episode, or a resolution in a succeeding episode. This requires readers to write at least one, and usually several, sentences. Macro cloze tasks can promote knowledge of the structural organization of narratives.

One way to construct a macro cloze task is listed here.

1. Select a particular structural characteristic in a discourse form some-what unfamiliar to students. At beginning levels, this might be the setting information in a fable. At higher levels, this might be the initiating event in science fiction.
2. Find a selection containing this structural characteristic and delete it from the text. You may write your own short selection, leaving out the appropriate information. You may also locate a story that can be reproduced from your reading program, delete the appropriate portion of the text, and duplicate enough copies for your students.
3. Direct students to write, on a separate piece of paper, their best guess about what you have removed from the story. Encourage them to read both before and after the deleted section in order to pick up clues about what is missing.
4. After students complete the task, be certain to have students share their guesses with each other. Reading each other's solutions is one way to accomplish this. Be certain, also, to have students explain how they figured out what was missing and why they chose to write their particular story portion.
5. Share the deleted information with students so they can see what type of information the author included in the original story.

Macro cloze tasks can also be used with stories where authors have deliberately left out a structural feature. Simply have students attempt to write the missing portion of a story so that it might be clearer to a reader. An example of this type of macro cloze task is illustrated in figure 7–2. With this second type of macro cloze task, it is again important to "brainstorm" possible ways to fill in the missing information before writing. After writing, it is also important to jointly evaluate the extent to which students have made the missing information more explicit.

Rewriting Stories. Have students rewrite specific story elements. You may, for example, ask students to rewrite the ending to a story they have just read or rewrite the story with a different setting. If a story is told from the perspective of one character, you could have students rewrite the story from the perspective of a different character, retaining all of the structural elements of that particular story.

Oral Macro Cloze Tasks. For very young readers, you can present macro cloze tasks orally during a read-aloud session. Read a story with a missing structural element or omit this element when you read the story. Have students attempt to create the missing element orally. You may want, also, to turn this into a language experience activity, writing

SAMPLE ACTIVITIES

their solution on the blackboard. When finished, read the passage you omitted from the story and compare.

Students have just completed reading a story about a coyote that stole a sheep dog's pup and then returned it two weeks later. The story is told from the perspective of the sheepherder and his grandson, so the reader does not know what the coyote did with the pup before returning it. In addition, it is unclear what goal the coyote had in taking the pup away from the sheep camp, though several possibilities are mentioned in the story.

Creating an episode Have pupils speculate about what happened during the two weeks that the coyote had Blanca's pup. If pupils have some information about coyote habits, suggest that they consider these facts during their speculation. Pupils might like to write an additional episode for the story, describing events that could have taken place during that period of time (Scott, Foresman, 1983, Sky Climbers Teachers Manual, p. 276).

FIGURE 7–2
An example of a macro cloze activity

Story Frames. A second type of writing activity that may be used to develop familiarity with the structure of narratives is a **story frame** (Fowler, 1982). A story frame consists of a guided opportunity for students to reflect on the structural elements of narratives as they summarize the story or a portion of the story. Story frames are used after students have read a story. Fowler suggests that they are particularly useful for students in the primary grades (one through three). Examples of story frames focusing on setting information, the initiating episode (problem episode), and the structure of a fable can be seen in figures 7–3, 7–4, and 7–5.

story frame: A guided writing activity that promotes understanding of the structural characteristics of narratives.

Story Mapping. A **story map** is a graphic outline containing the major structural features of narratives (setting, initiating or problem episode, succeeding episodes, and resolution) as well as the specific information for a particular story at each structural location. A story map organizes and structures the information in a story for both students and teacher; it provides a "map" of a story's plot. A story map can guide the discus-

story maps: Graphic outlines containing the major structural features of narratives and the specific information for a particular story.

SETTING INFORMATION

An important character in this story is _____

_____ . This story takes place _____ .
                                        (location)
I can tell because the author uses the words "_____

_____ ."

The story takes place _____ .
                        (time)
I can tell because the author uses the words "_____

_____ ."

FIGURE 7–3
A story frame that focuses on setting information

sion of a story (Beck & McKeown, 1981; Pearson, 1982) and help students learn the structural characteristics of narratives (Reutzel, 1985). It may also be used to introduce a story. Most frequently, perhaps, a story map is used after students have read a story to organize the discussion and to develop greater understanding of narrative discourse structure.

To complete a story map, write down the major structural headings (story title, setting, story problem, episode 1, episode 2, and solution) and use this structure to ask questions such as Where did this story take place? When do you think it took place? or What was the problem in this story? As children answer the questions, fill in the story map with

STORY PROBLEM

The problem starts in this story when _____

_____ .

The main character, _____ ,
wants to _____ .

FIGURE 7–4
A story frame that focuses on the initiating episode (problem episode)

FABLE

The animals in this story are _____

_____.

The problem starts when_____

_____.

One of the animals, _____, wants to

_____.

First, _____

_____.

Then, _____

_____.

After that, _____

_____.

The problem is solved when _____

_____.

The moral of this story is _____

_____.

FIGURE 7–5
A story frame that focuses on the structure of a fable

the children's words. As you ask questions and guide the discussion, you may want to have students read aloud portions from the story to support their answers. In addition, encourage students to indicate how they inferred information missing from the text whenever an inference is required for an answer. Figure 7–6 provides an example of a story map completed after a group of first-grade students had read the story "The Rabbit and the Bear."

Note that for more advanced students, greater structural information about attempts, outcomes, and reactions might have been included in the story map outline. Also, as children help you fill in the structural information from a story, you can encourage them to consider which type of narrative they are discussing. Ask them, too, to list the evidence supporting their choice.

Direct Instruction. Often, the unique nature of each literary form's structure is taught using direct instruction. In direct instruction, a teacher explicitly defines the structural characteristics of a particular form to students and then provides opportunities for them to read examples of this form. In teaching the structural characteristics of a fable,

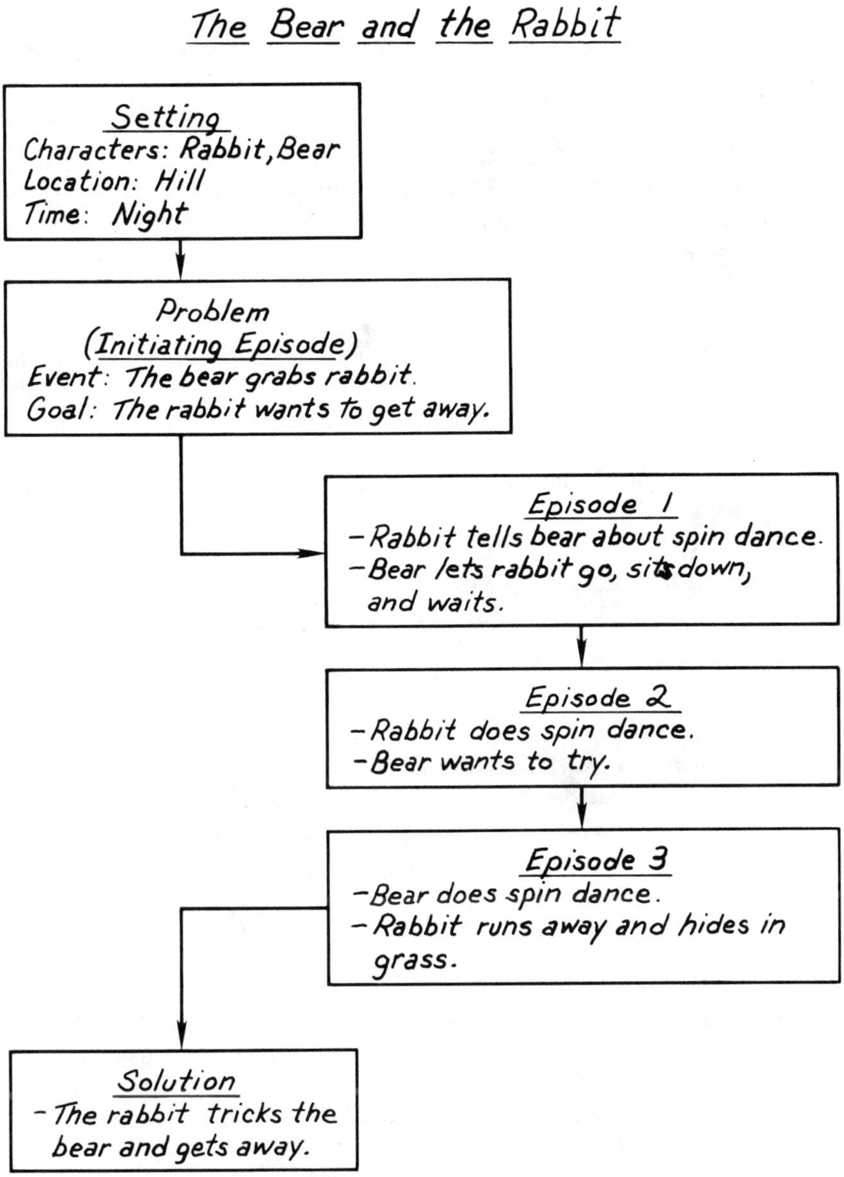

The Bear and the Rabbit

FIGURE 7-6
An example of a story map

Setting
Characters: Rabbit, Bear
Location: Hill
Time: Night

Problem
(Initiating Episode)
Event: The bear grabs rabbit.
Goal: The rabbit wants to get away.

Episode 1
- Rabbit tells bear about spin dance.
- Bear lets rabbit go, sits down, and waits.

Episode 2
- Rabbit does spin dance.
- Bear wants to try.

Episode 3
- Bear does spin dance.
- Rabbit runs away and hides in grass.

Solution
- The rabbit tricks the bear and gets away.

for example, the teacher would first define this form as a story (1) that is not true; (2) where animals are main characters; (3) where animals take on human characteristics; and (4) that often contains an explicitly stated lesson, or moral, at the end. Then a number of opportunities to read and discuss fables would be provided. The following model lesson shows how you could directly teach the structural characteristics of a fable to second-grade students.

MODEL	Using Direct Instruction to Teach the Structural Characteristics of a
LESSON	Fable

I. Before students read a fable for the first time and in addition to other instructional activities used to prepare students for reading the fable; that is vocabulary, word recognition, and so on:

    A. Have a discussion about a "special type of story" called a fable. Write *fable* on the blackboard. Ask if anyone has ever read or heard a fable before. Mention that a long time ago a man called Aesop often told fables to teach people how they should and should not act. Be certain to draw out or tell the students the four features which most fables share. Write these on the board: a story that is not true; a story where animals are often the main characters; the animals often take on human characteristics; and the story contains a lesson which is often stated at the end.

    B. Tell the students to read to see if this story is a fable and if it contains all four features mentioned.

II. After reading the fable and in addition to other postreading activities:

    A. Discuss with the students if they thought this was a fable. Be certain to ask for evidence in the story which supports their answers. See if they can find evidence for all four defining characteristics.

    B. Be certain to discuss the lesson of the fable. Ask the students if they think that all people should follow this advice. Why? Why not?

III. In the following weeks:

    A. Bring in other fables from your school library. Read them aloud to your students at appropriate times. Discuss whether or not these stories are fables. How do they meet the defining characteristics which were mentioned earlier? Make them available to the students in your reading corner.

    B. Whenever students encounter a fable in their regular instructional program, be certain to have children read to see if the story is a fable or another discourse form. Ask them to be able to support their answers after they read the story. What evidence can they find for each of the defining characteristics?

HOW SPECIFIC FRAMEWORKS AFFECT INSTRUCTIONAL DECISIONS

Literature can be used in a classroom reading program to serve a wide range of functions: to develop readiness skills among prereaders; to develop automaticity at decoding; to broaden vocabulary knowledge; to familiarize children with the syntactic patterns found more frequently in written language; to develop knowledge of narrative discourse structure; and to ensure that students develop into independent readers who not only can read but also choose to read outside of school settings. Since literature can serve multiple purposes, it is not possible to say that using literature is more consistent with some types of comprehension frameworks and less consistent with others. A reason for literature can always be found, regardless of the type of comprehension framework you have. Thus, literature should always be incorporated into classroom reading instruction. Three aspects of instruction with literature, however, are influenced by the type of comprehension framework you have:

1. the rationale for the use of literature in a classroom
2. the relative importance of instruction in narrative discourse structure
3. the nature of instruction in narrative discourse structure

Different Rationales for Instructional Decisions

The reasons that teachers use literature are not all the same. In fact, teachers' rationales for the use of literature in an elementary classroom are largely determined by their answer to the first question associated with a comprehension framework: How does one read? Text-based, reader-based, and interactive explanations are usually associated with different sets of rationales for the use of literature. This is due to the different assumptions about reading behind each explanation.

Teachers with more of a text-based explanation for how one reads emphasize the importance of developing decoding knowledge. Thus, these teachers value literature because it helps to develop automaticity at decoding. In addition, however, literature may be valued by these teachers for three other reasons: to develop important readiness aspects; to promote affective aspects of reading; and to develop independent readers. Teachers with more of a text-based explanation for how one reads tend not to value the use of literature for developing narrative discourse knowledge, developing syntactic knowledge, or developing vocabulary knowledge.

Teachers with more of a reader-based explanation for how one reads emphasize the prior knowledge that readers bring to a text. Thus, these teachers value literature because it helps develop discourse knowledge, syntactic knowledge, and vocabulary knowledge. In addition, teachers with more of a reader-based explanation, like teachers with more of a text-based explanation, value the use of literature to develop important readiness aspects, to promote affective aspects of reading, and to develop independent readers. Teachers with more of a reader-based explanation for how one reads, however, do not value the use of literature to develop automaticity at decoding.

Teachers with interactive explanations value literature for all of the reasons just listed. Literature is used in classroom activities because it (1) helps to develop automaticity at decoding; (2) broadens vocabulary knowledge; (3) familiarizes children with the syntactic patterns found more frequently in written language; (4) develops knowledge of narrative discourse structure; (5) develops important readiness aspects; (6) promotes affective aspects of reading; and (7) develops independent readers.

The Importance of Instruction in Narrative Discourse Structure

Within the entire scope of your reading program, how important is the development of knowledge about narrative discourse structure? The answer to this question is also dependent upon your answer to the question How does one read?

Teachers with more of a text-based explanation for how one reads believe that knowledge of narrative discourse structure is relatively unimportant. These teachers devote much more time to developing decoding knowledge than developing discourse knowledge. Literature is not excluded from classroom learning tasks. It is, however, used for purposes other than developing knowledge of narrative discourse structure.

Teachers with more of a reader-based explanation for how one reads believe that knowledge of narrative discourse structure is a very important part of the instructional program. A thorough understanding of narrative discourse structure is thought to be important since these teachers believe that discourse-related expectations profoundly constrain the comprehension process at syntactic, vocabulary, and decoding levels.

Teachers with more of an interactive explanation for how one reads also believe that knowledge of narrative discourse structure is relatively important. However, it receives no more and no less attention than instruction intended to develop the other knowledge sources associated with the comprehension process: decoding knowledge; vocabulary knowledge; or syntactic knowledge.

The Nature of Instruction in Narrative Discourse Structure

The nature of instruction in narrative discourse structure also appears to be influenced by the type of comprehension framework you have. The nature of instruction, though, is influenced more by your answer to the second queston: How does reading ability develop? If you have more of a mastery of specific skills explanation for development, you believe that children learn best when they are taught separate skills directly and explicitly. Thus, you would be likely to use the methods and activities described in this chapter that lend themselves to deductive methods. Direct instruction of narrative forms would be used frequently. Reading centers devoted to mastering a specific element of narrative structure also would be used. You also would use discussion questions to assess students' mastery of specific structural elements.

If, however, you have more of a holistic language learning explanation for development, it is unlikely that you would use many activities relying on direct instruction. Direct instruction is simply inconsistent with the belief that reading is learned inductively as students engage in functional, meaningful, and holistic experiences with print. Instead, activities that rely on students' discovery of narrative structures would be used. Read-aloud sessions would occur frequently. A well-stocked and attractive reading corner would be a central part of the classroom. In addition, activities like SSR, independent book projects, Readers Theatre, and macro cloze tasks might all be included in the instructional program since each more typically is associated with inductive methods.

If you have more of a differential acquisition explanation for development you believe that less proficient readers require deductive learning experiences while more proficient readers require inductive experiences. Thus, less proficient readers would tend to receive direct instruction in narrative discourse structure. More proficient readers, on the other hand, would tend to receive guidance in inductive discovery of narrative forms as they read a variety of literature.

THE MAJOR POINTS

1. Literature is a unique and powerful instructional tool; it can be used to promote all aspects of the comprehension process: affective aspects; readiness aspects; decoding knowledge; vocabulary knowledge; syntactic knowledge; and discourse knowledge. Providing children with engaging literature experiences is central to effective reading instruction.

2. Literature can also be used to develop independent readers; readers who both know *how* to read and, in addition, actually *do* read for pleasure, information, and personal growth. To accomplish this, reading teachers need to integrate literature into the learning environment and put children and books together in pleasurable settings.

3. Several different types of activities can be used to integrate literature into the learning environment: read-aloud sessions; reading corner activities; reading center activities; library activities; and working together with parents.

4. Several different types of activities can put children and books together in pleasurable settings: free-choice activities; sustained silent reading; Readers Theatre; and independent book projects.

5. Literature can help children develop understanding of the narrative structure, including setting information, an initiating episode that sets up the problem, succeeding episodes which are attempts to solve the problem, and a solution. Literature also can teach the unique characteristics of a variety of narrative forms.

6. Questioning activities, writing activities, the use of story maps, and direct instruction are four categories of instructional methods that develop knowledge of narrative discourse structure.

7. Several aspects of instruction with literature are influenced by the nature of one's comprehension framework: the rationale for the use of literature in a classroom; the relative importance of instruction in narrative discourse structure; and the nature of instruction in narrative discourse structure.

QUESTIONS AND ACTIVITIES

1. Develop a letter to the parents in your first classroom to briefly explain the importance of home environments for supporting your reading program. List several specific ways for parents to help their children. You might want to incorporate some of the suggestions listed on page 250 in your letter.

2. Begin a literature notebook containing ideas for integrating literature into classroom activities. This may contain specific instructional practices, descriptions of reading center activities, items to include in a reading corner, or other useful suggestions. Begin by including some of the suggestions on page 251. Then visit several classrooms known for their literature programs and gather additional ideas.

3. Read at least fifteen selections from children's literature and write up a literature card like the one on page 258 for each. You might visit your local library to help you complete this task. Look for books you think children will be interested in.

4. Interview five students and five teachers at a single grade level. Ask each to list five books they think are especially popular among students at the grade level you have chosen. Compare the results between teachers and students. Do teachers and students have similar answers? Which books appear to be the most popular at this level? Compare your answers with others who have also completed this task. What are the three or four most popular books? If you have not read these books you might want to look for them at a local library and read them.

5. Find a short narrative selection in a commercial reading program or from children's literature. Analyze its structural organization for set-

ting information, an initiating episode (problem episode), and succeeding episodes (including a resolution episode). Attempt to determine where children might be required to infer a missing structural element and, thus, have difficulty with comprehension. Explain how you would attempt to overcome this problem.

6. Create a macro cloze task using a short narrative selection. You can delete a portion of the story or have students rewrite an episode that is missing. Identify the type of structural knowledge your activity would promote.

7. Select an interesting piece of children's literature for a read-aloud session. Practice reading this aloud until you have a clear sense of how you want to read it to children. Then read your selection to a class or to your peers. Follow the suggestions by Coody listed on pages 245–46.

FURTHER READING

Ellis, D. W. & Preston, F. W. (1984). Enhancing beginning reading using wordless picture books in a cross-age tutoring program. *The Reading Teacher, 37*(8), 692–98.

Describes a wide range of uses for wordless picture books. Then explains how wordless picture books were used to promote readiness skills in first-grade classrooms by having fifth-grade students work as tutors. Lists 162 wordless picture books published in the United States that can be used for similar activities.

Nessel, D. D. (1985). Storytelling in the reading program. *The Reading Teacher, 38*(4), 378–81.

Describes how to tell stories to children in classrooms in a fashion similar to read-aloud sessions. Explains why storytelling is important for promoting knowledge of narrative structures and how to integrate it into classroom environments.

Rand, M. K. (1984). Story schema: Theory, research and practice. *The Reading Teacher, 37*(4), 377–82.

Reviews ten years of research on readers' knowledge of narrative discourse structure. Concludes that this knowledge is crucial for comprehension. Discusses instructional activities that might be used to promote knowledge of story structure.

Sloyer, Shirlee (1982). *Readers Theatre: Story Dramatization in the Classroom.* Urbana, IL: National Council of Teachers of English.

A monograph devoted to explaining Readers Theatre and showing teachers how to begin incorporating Readers Theatre into the classroom. Provides several examples of scripts for children to use.

Spiegel, D. L. & Fitzgerald, J. (1986). Improving reading comprehension through instruction about story parts. *The Reading Teacher, 39*(7), 676–83.

Describes how a set of specific teaching activities helped fourth-grade students gain a better understanding of story structure and how this assisted comprehension.

Vukelich, C. (1984). Parents' role in the reading process: A review of practical suggestions and ways to communicate with parents. *The Reading Teacher, 37*(7), 578–84.

Reviews articles on parental involvement in children's reading. Lists the most frequent suggestions and describes ways to communicate this information to parents.

REFERENCES

Applebee, A. N. (1978). *The child's concept of story.* Chicago, IL: University of Chicago Press.

Association for Library Service to Children. (Annual). *Notable children's books.* Chicago, IL: American Library Association.

Beck, I. L. & McKeown, M. G. (1981). Developing questions that promote comprehension: The story map. *Language Arts, 58,* 913–18.

Beck, I. L.; Omanson, R. C.; & McKeown, M. G. (1982). An instructional redesign of reading lessons: Effects on comprehension. *Reading Research Quarterly, 17,* 462–81.

Biemiller, A. (1977). Relationships between oral reading rates for letters, words, and simple text in the development of reading achievement. *Reading Research Quarterly, 13,* 223–53.

Clay, M. M. (1972). *Reading: The patterning of complex behavior.* New York: International Publications.

Cochran-Smith, M. (1984). *The making of a reader.* Norwood, NJ: Ablex.

Coody, B. (1983). Using literature with young children, (3rd edition). Dubuque, Iowa: Wm. C. Brown Co.

Fader, D. N. (1968). *Hooked on books.* New York: Putnam.

Fader, D. N. (1976). *The new hooked on books.* New York: Putnam.

Fowler, G. F. (1982). Developing comprehension skills in primary students through the use of story frames. *The Reading Teacher, 36,* 176–79.

Golden, J. M. (1984). Children's concept of story in reading and writing. *The Reading Teacher, 37*(7), 578–84.

Heath, S. B. (1982). What no bedtime story means: Narrative skills at home and school. *Language in Society, 11,* 49–76.

Hunt, L. C. (1971). Six steps to the individualized reading program. *Elementary English, 48*(1), 27–32.

Mandler, J. M. & Johnson, N. S. (1977). Remembrance of things parsed: Story structure and recall. *Cognitive Psychology, 9,* 111–51.

Mason, J. (1984). Early reading from a developmental perspective. In P. D. Pearson (ed.) *Handbook of reading research.* New York: Longman.

McCracken, R. A. (1971). Initiating sustained silent reading. *Journal of Reading, 14,* 521–24; 582–83.

Morrow, L. M. (1984). Reading stories to young children: Affects of story structure and traditional questioning strategies on comprehension. *Journal of Reading Behavior, 16,* 273–88.

Nessel, D. D. (1985). Storytelling in the reading program. *The Reading Teacher, 38*(4), 378–81.

Pearson, P. D. (1982). Asking questions about stories. *Ginn Occasional Papers,* No. 15. Columbus, OH: Ginn and Co.

Reutzel, D. R. (1985). Story maps improve comprehension. *The Reading Teacher, 38*(4), 400–404.

Rumelhart, D. (1980). Schemata: The building blocks of cognition. In R. Spiro; B. Bruce; & W. Brewer (eds.), *Theoretical issues in reading comprehension.* Hillsdale, NJ: Erlbaum.

Stanovich, K. (1980). Toward an interactive-compensatory model of individual differences in the development of reading fluency. *Reading Research Quarterly, 16,* 32–71.

Taylor, D. (1983). *Family literacy: Young children learning to read and write.* Exeter, NH: Heinemann.

Teale, W. (1982). Toward a theory of how children learn to read and write naturally. *Language Arts, 59,* 555–70.

Thorndyke, P. (1977). Cognitive structures in comprehension and memory of narrative discourse. *Cognitive Psychology, 9,* 77–110.

White, M. L. (ed.) (1981). *A booklist for pre-k-grade 8.* Urbana, IL: National Council of Teachers of English.

8 Content-Area Reading and Study Skills: Expository Discourse

TEACHING BOOK PARTS ▪ GENERAL RESEARCH SKILLS ▪ READING THROUGHOUT THE GRADES ▪ DIFFERENCES IN TEXT ORGANIZATION ▪ READING RATE: FLEXIBILITY IN CONTENT-AREA READING ▪ TEACHING APPROACHES FOR CONTENT AREAS ▪ READING IN FOUR CONTENT AREAS ▪ PERSONAL FRAMEWORKS AND TEACHING EXPOSITORY MATERIALS

"Miss Amburgy," asked Charley, "how can snakes run so fast when they don't have legs?"

"There are books in the library that tell all about snakes," Miss Amburgy said . . . . "I suspect they even tell how a snake can run fast when it hasn't any legs."

"Is that what books really do?" asked Charley. "Tell you about things?"

"Books tell you almost anything you will ever want to know," said Miss Amburgy. "Some things, of course, you'll have to find out for yourself."

"When do I go to the library again?" asked Charley.

R. Caudill, *Did you carry the flag today, Charley?* (New York: Holt, Rinehart & Winston, 1966), p. 60–61.

Previous chapters have stressed that not all reading is alike. Examples have been given to illustrate that even good readers have difficulty reading specialized text, such as law books, insurance policies, or tax forms. This chapter shows that materials that students are expected to read in different school subjects are also specialized, having varying structures that make different demands on a reader. Teaching content-area reading skills must not be ignored by the reading teacher since textbooks are still the predominant tool used in educating children. Students who are not able to read well are at a great disadvantage when required to read when learning mathematics, social studies, art, music, science, literature, and other subjects.

After reading this chapter, you will be able to

1. identify the structural characteristics of textbooks, the information each contains, and how each characteristic affects comprehension;
2. state the major differences between the kinds of reading material children encounter while learning to read and those they encounter in the various academic subject areas;
3. discuss the different reading demands required in different subject areas;
4. discuss how textbooks are structured differently in social studies, mathematics, and science;
5. use techniques designed to help students better read and study required reading material in content-area subjects.

TEACHING BOOK PARTS

Books are often composed of similar sections, usually including a title, copyright page, preface, table of contents, reference list, index, and glossary. Similarly, a chapter within a book usually contains a title, introduction, headings, subheadings, conclusion, questions, and references. Although not all books and chapters have each of these parts, most books that are not considered narratives (novels, plays, and so on) do.

Knowing about the information that is presented in each of a book's parts helps in comprehending what is presented. Think about the information found in each part and how it can help one's comprehension. For example, the copyright page can tell whether the information contained in the book is potentially out of date or whether the book was published by a special-interest group and might be potentially biased. The preface can point out the purposes for which the book was written. The table of contents presents an outline of what the book covers and helps to set up expectations regarding what will be found when reading. Each book part contains important information that can help the reader.

Lessons that teach the parts of books and how they can help the reader are a part of reading instruction. Students need to be aware of the various parts of a book, the information each contains, and their uses. The following sample activities include suggestions for teaching this aspect of reading.

■ Using the table of contents, have students predict what specific information might be found in various chapters, as well as in various sections and subsections. Write the predictions on the blackboard. Have students go to the appropriate pages to check their predictions.

■ Provide a list of specific items found in various chapters, sections, and subsections. Allow students to match the items on the list with the titles in the table of contents. Discuss reasons for the matches that were made, and check the appropriate sections to see if the matchups are correct.

■ Examine several copyright pages and tables of contents from books in the same subject area that span thirty years (science books, for example). Using the tables of contents, have students compare differences in topics. Then, using the copyright pages, have students attempt to match copyright pages to tables of contents. The teacher will have to provide guidance here, pointing out which topics are relatively "young" and thus would not have been included in earlier books.

■ Discuss the difference between a glossary and a dictionary. (A glossary only contains definitions for words that appear in the book, while a dictionary includes others, as well as more general words.) Find sentences in the book that contain content-specific vocabulary and have students look up their meanings in the glossary, then read the paragraph that contains the term to see if the definition is appropriate.

■ Compare pages in an index and glossary of a book. Have students brainstorm the differences, which are written on the blackboard (glossary contains definitions, index contains page numbers, and so on). Discuss the purposes of each and how the differences help to meet these purposes.

GENERAL RESEARCH SKILLS

Using Research Materials

As students move into higher grade levels and are required to study informational material, they are often expected to use the library to find background or supplementary material. This often requires students to use card catalogs, encyclopedias, almanacs, newspapers, books on related topics, atlases, and abstracts. Research abilities are important to achieving success in content-area subjects and require skills such as organizing, alphabetizing, and summarizing, in addition to knowing about reference tools and sources, what they contain, and how they are used.

The use of reference materials such as encyclopedias and tools such as the card catalog is usually part of the language arts program before specific content areas are encountered. In fact, trips to the library and a discussion of what the library contains should begin early in the primary grades. Similarly, encyclopedias specifically designed for young children, such as picture encyclopedias, should be used early to teach young readers that there are sources available that can teach them more about a topic of interest or that can provide background information. The following sample activities show some ways that children might be taught needed reference skills.

SAMPLE ACTIVITIES

Library Hunts. Each week, post a problem that requires students to use reference skills in the school library. You could ask older students questions like What is one book written by Judy Blume after 1979? Who illustrated *Where the Sidewalk Ends*? For younger students, you could ask questions like Where would you find a book by Ezra Jack Keats? or What are the titles of one fiction book and one nonfiction book? Put the question up just before library period and see who can return with the answer. Place a box below the question in which children can submit their answers. Read all answers at the end of the day.

Reference Match. After a discussion and demonstration of various types of reference materials, provide a list such as the following. Provide a list of reference materials and a separate list of information found in those materials. Have students match the information to the source. For example:

Atlas	_____	(a)	Maps
Encyclopedia	_____	(b)	Information about famous people
Thesaurus	_____	(c)	Use to find out which rivers flow through California
		(d)	Use to find out how the telephone was invented and how it works
		(e)	Use to find synonyms

Topic Sort. Place a number of topics in a box. On the blackboard, have a drawing of the spines of an encyclopedia. Students choose a topic and state which volume they would use to find information on the topic. For example:

1	2	3	4	5	6	7	8	9	10	11	12	13	14	15	16	17	18	19	20	21
A	B	C–Ch	Ci–Cz	D	E	F	G	H	I	J–K	L	M	N–O	P	Q–R	S–Sn	So–Sz	T	U–V	WX YZ

Newspaper Fact Hunt. After a discussion of the general purpose of an index, provide newspapers for a discussion of newspaper parts and the newspaper index. Have students use the index to find answers to such questions as Where would you look for information about football scores? Where would you find out about which movies are in town and their show times? What page are the comics on? On what page would you find the weather forecast and yesterday's highest and lowest temperature in the United States?

Dictionary Keys. Present and discuss the concept of key words in dictionaries (for example, How do you know which words are on any given page of a dictionary?). Provide key words for a dictionary page on the chalkboard, as well as words that would and would not appear on that page. Have students place the words in the proper order, stating whether or not they would be found on the page simulated by the key words.

Atlas Information. Have students use an atlas to find information such as which states border another; which is the longest river in a particular area; which two cities are farther apart than another two; which of two European countries is farther north, and so on.

Card Catalog Search. Visit the library and discuss the card catalog, what it does, and the three types of cards it contains (author cards, subject cards, and title cards). Then, present a two-column list with information desired in one column and type of card in the other. Have students match the columns. Have students use the card catalog to find out how many books by a particular author are contained in the library, how many books written on a given subject over the past two years are in the library, and so on.

Author Card	_____	(a) You want to find the book *The Black Stallion*.
Subject Card	_____	(b) You want to find another book by Walter Farley.
Title Card	_____	(c) You want to find a book that tells about different breeds of horses.

Organizing, Summarizing, and Notetaking

Many of the strategies and techniques discussed in this chapter require that information be organized or summarized, often in written form. These skills can be developed from the earliest stages of schooling. When children are asked to categorize similar items, they are developing categorizing skills that help in organizing information. When asked to restate or paraphrase a story, summarizing is enhanced, as are notetaking skills when summary statements or main points are compiled in written form. The following activities can be used to enhance these important skills.

SAMPLE ACTIVITIES

- Model and allow students to practice taking notes in point form, paragraph summary form, and outline form. Use a short reading selection, film, or audio tape to provide the basis for the note-taking activity. Be sure to discuss students' work, aiming the discussion toward reasons for including and not including certain information.

- Provide headings and subheadings in outline form. Leave the outline incomplete. Read a selection that pertains to the outline. Have students complete the outline. This is an activity that enhances both note-taking and summarizing skills.

- For use with young students, compile a set of pictures consisting of items in two categories. Mix the pictures and have students state which belong together. Alternately, state a category and have students state which pictures do not belong.

- Have students listen to a story or an expository reading. Allow them to restate, paraphrase, or provide the main idea of the selection. Conversely, students can provide a one- or two-sentence written statement.

READING THROUGHOUT THE GRADES

Think about the increase in what children learn relative to reading through the primary grades (one through three) the intermediate grades (four through seven), and the secondary grades (eight through twelve). Also, consider the demands on students in terms of the kinds of materials to be read and the amount of material to be read. When you think back to your own elementary school days, how would you describe the difference(s) between primary and intermediate grades? How much, in terms of reading instruction, is done as grade level increases?

The largest increase in reading ability takes place in the earliest stages of schooling. If one looks at how much new knowledge, relative to reading ability, is learned as one progresses through the grades, a graph something like that pictured in the margin note might be the result. This may be intuitively obvious. Think of the difference between an average reader in the middle of first grade and an average reader in third grade at the same point during the school year. Now try to specify the difference between an average tenth-grade reader and an average twelfth-grade reader. A one- or two-year grade difference results in much more obvious reading skill discrepancies in lower as opposed to higher grades.

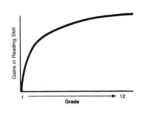

Although most reading instruction and most of what is learned about reading takes place in the early school years, this really refers to the "general" reading skills; that is, the skills that allow us to decode words and to string them together into meaningful units. Following this learning, specific reading instruction tapers off. Beginning about the third grade, emphasis is placed on learning specific content. In fact, school is often restructured as the child moves from primary to intermediate grades. Where the child had only one classroom and teacher, now there are different teachers and classrooms for different subjects. Where there was a great deal of stability, there is now a continually changing instructional environment. This continues throughout the in-

As readers mature, they will increasingly need to apply their study, note-taking, research, and reference skills.

termediate grades and becomes even more pronounced in secondary grades.

Within each of the diverse subject areas, in addition to the differences in content taught, there are different reading demands. In science, students are required to understand and manipulate various formulas and to learn many new terms. In mathematics, they must read many self-contained units, such as word problems, and are presented with many numerical examples as well as with capsulated rules in the form of theorems and laws.

Different types of texts demand different reading styles and skills. This is true both in terms of how reading material is approached and interpreted as well as in required background knowledge and recognition of text structure. If a reader is not aware that a text is designed to persuade, then the text might be interpreted as fact and be used incorrectly.

It seems fairly easy for people to accept that different text styles exist within narrative writing. After all, poetry is clearly different from dramatic scripts and both differ from stories in overtly visible ways. It also seems easy to accept that readers do not read texts in different narrative **genres** in the same way. That readers read poems differently from plays causes no great controversy. Yet the concept that texts in different subject areas make different demands on a reader and that, in general, **expository** texts are different from narratives seems somewhat more difficult to accept. Just as there are different narrative forms so are there different types of expository forms. An awareness of these differences and an understanding of what a reader does in trying to comprehend the different text types will make you a more effective teacher—one who better prepares students to read the range of materials commonly found in school settings and beyond.

genres: Categories of literary compositions, each having a special style, form, or content.
expository: Designed to explain or present.

> **A POINT TO PONDER**
>
> Normally, when reading content-area texts, one is reading for information while narratives are read for pleasure. Content-area textbooks and expository texts in general are read to discover, learn, and remember new information, or perhaps to reinforce and extend already known concepts. Narratives are read to entertain.

DIFFERENCES IN TEXT ORGANIZATION

Text structure is an important factor in the reading process. As pointed out earlier, the narrative texts used in reading instruction are not organized as are most texts found in content areas. Although different organizational patterns can and do appear both in texts used in reading lessons and in texts used in content areas, there are general differences in the organizational patterns of various written material.

The major difference between narrative and expository text is that narratives are usually written along a time sequence, while exposition is organized along **superordinate** and **subordinate** concepts. This difference is easy to see, not only in text itself, but even in tables of contents in different types of material. Look at the structure of two books, as reflected in the following partial tables of contents.

superordinate concept:
Part of the organizational pattern in expository text. A major unit supported by subunits.

subordinate concept:
Part of the organizational pattern of expository text. A subunit which supports a larger unit.

Table of Contents, Mathematics Textbook

Addition and Subtraction—Whole Numbers
> Rounding numbers through hundred thousands
> Finding sums and differences through 6-digits
> Estimating sums and differences by rounding
> Checking addition and subtraction
> Solving verbal and problems

Multiplication and Division—Whole Numbers
> Multiplying by 1- and 2-digit factors
> Estimating products by rounding
> Solving multiple-step problems

From O. C. Bassler; J. R. Kolb; M. S. Craighead; & W. L. Gray. *Succeeding in mathematics* (Revised). (Austin, TX: Steck-Vaughn Co., 1981), p. ii.

Notice how this following partial table of contents from a narrative book differs.

Table of Contents, Narrative Book

I Go to Sea

On the Island

We Plan to Leave the Island

The English Ship

Home!

From Daniel Defoe, *Robinson Crusoe,* Abridged and adapted by Ron King. (Pacemaker Classic Edition, 1967). Belmont, CA: Fearon.

The organizational differences in these examples become clear when attempting to answer the question What happened *first?* This question is meaningless in the mathematics example, while it is easily answered from the narrative table of contents.

Several different organizational patterns are found in all content areas, although some are found more often in some subjects than in others. For example, the next passage demonstrates the time-order sequence usually found in language arts materials. Try to specify the cues that tell the reader that time sequence is the overriding organizational factor in the following passage.

Tommy woke up, rubbed his eyes, and looked slowly around the room. Suddenly he jumped out of bed. He dressed quickly and ran down to breakfast. His father, already in his mechanic's uniform, was about to leave for work.

"What's your hurry?" his father said.

"I'm going fishing," Tommy announced.

"Bring home some big ones," Mr. Jackson said. "That little catfish you caught last time was hardly enough for one person."

From "Tommy and the Old Man" by Forrest L. Ingram, as printed in the Headway Reading Program (Level E). In M. Carrus; T. G. Anderson; & H. R. Webber; (eds.). *From sea to sea.* (La Salle, IL: Open Court, 1982), p. 167.

Did you pick out the background knowledge aspects that indicate a time sequence? Children know that waking up and rubbing one's eyes precedes looking around the room, just as getting dressed happens after getting out of bed. Conjunctions such as *and* can indicate sequential order, as can specific references such as *last time.* Since time-sequenced text patterns depend fairly heavily on common happenings that are part of background knowledge, students have less difficulty with this type of text than with some of the organizational patterns outlined below.

The following passage about Islam, from a social studies textbook, demonstrates how number order is often used as an organizational pattern. Notice how the structure of the passage outlines its content. The cues to passage organization reside in the enumeration of points *("first . . . second")* and in the two-part activity parallelling the two factual statements presented at the beginning of the paragraph.

Look at the map above. It shows you two things. First, it tells you the periods in which early Islam spread. Second, it shows the areas into which Islam spread. Islam began in the cities of Mecca and Medima. Use the map key to find the name of the area in which these two cities are found. Use the map key to find the territory that Muslims had conquered by Muhammed's death in 632.

From the Follett Social Studies Series. C. B. Meyers & G. Wilk. *People, time and change.* (Chicago, IL: Follett, 1983), p. 272.

Can you pick out the cues indicating that the next passage, taken from a science textbook, is organized in a comparison/contrast pattern? Notice the comparisons between radio and television, and the implicit assumption that the readers' background knowledge of each will help build new knowledge.

Television is the most popular form of communication in the world today. Television is very similar to radio. In radio, sound energy is changed to radio wave energy. Radio wave energy is sent through space. In television, both sound and light are changed to invisible waves. Television sets change the invisible waves back to light and sound.

From R. B. Sund; D. K. Adams; & J. K. Hackett. *Accent on science* (Level 6). (Columbus, OH: C. E. Merrill, 1980), p. 275.

The last organizational pattern discussed here is one of cause and effect. Often, facts or events happen because of other facts or events. This is especially true in history textbooks, for example, where an understanding of the causal relationship(s) between historical events, such as the causes of war, is a major goal. Yet there are more subtle cause-and-effect relationships found in texts, such as that demonstrated in the following example from an elementary mathematics textbook. Notice how the passage implies that a plane boundary is dependent on a plane region.

A closed plane figure together with its inside is called a plane region. The figure around the plane region is called its boundary. Plane regions are named for their boundaries.

From O. C. Bassler; J. R. Kolb; M. S. Craighead; & W. L. Gray. *Succeeding in mathematics* (Revised). (Austin, TX: Steck-Vaughn, 1981), p. 266.

Do not assume that students who can read one kind of text structure can read another with similar ease. Students need to be aware of the different structures both within narrative and expository material. To build this awareness, teachers might discuss the way that authors use language to signal the type of organization that is being used. Vacca (1981, p. 143) provides a list of signal words for the four organizational patterns discussed. Obviously, not all of the words will be found at all elementary grade levels. Teachers will have to choose those signal words appearing in the materials being used with their students.

TIME ORDER	ENUMERATION	COMPARISON/CONTRAST	CAUSE-EFFECT
on (date)	to begin with	however	because
not long after	first	but	since
now	second	as well as	therefore
as	next	on the other hand	consequently
before	then	not only/but also	as a result
after	finally	either . . . or	this led to
when	most important	while	so that
	also	although	nevertheless
	in fact	unless	accordingly
	for instance	similarly	if . . . then
	for example	yet	thus

SAMPLE ACTIVITIES

- Preread a future reading assignment. Choose a paragraph or page that demonstrates the overall structure of the selection. Tell students about the structure being used, including the signal words appropriate to that structure. On a copy of the paragraph or page chosen, have students mark any of the signal words that they find. Lead a discussion aimed at pointing out how each of the marked words specifically signals the pattern in the passage.

- If a selection has a time-sequenced or numbered, step-by-step organization, create an ordered list of the steps. Leave out some of the steps in the sequence. (For example, in a five-item sequence, steps 2 and 4 might be left out). Provide the list to students before they read the selection and discuss the concept of a sequenced organizational pattern. Have students check the steps on the list as they occur during their reading and add those that are missing.

- In a similar activity, create an out-of-order list of the sequence. In a prereading discussion, discuss the concept of ordered sequence and, before reading, have the students decide how to reorder the list so that it makes logical, sequential sense. Have students read to see if their reordered sequence holds true. A postreading discussion can reinforce the concept of sequence.

- For a superordinate/subordinate structure, preread a selection and note the major categories. In a prereading activity, discuss this pattern and list the major categories on the blackboard. Have students state what might be found under each category. Have students read to see if their predictions are accurate. In a postreading discussion, examine which of the predictions were and were not found. Discuss reasons why this might have happened.

READING RATE: FLEXIBILITY IN CONTENT-AREA READING

It is sometimes difficult for younger readers to realize that not all reading is done at the same speed. Reading rate depends on a number of factors, among them one's purpose for reading. Students need to be aware, for example, that reading a mathematics word problem and attending to every word differs in rate from reading a story for entertainment. Within some content-area texts, it is often vital not to miss even one word while reading. Consider how important it is to be sure to read every word carefully when reading the directions for a science experiment.

It is often suggested that one's reading rate be consciously changed to meet the demands of each reading task (Farr & Roser, 1979; Shepherd, 1982). **Skimming** refers to quickly moving through a text to discover key concepts and main idea. Awareness of headings and sub-headings is useful when skimming a text. Many content-area reading techniques discussed in this chapter require that a student first **preview** the reading material. Usually this entails a rapid movement through the text (skimming), so that the reader has some idea of what will be encountered on more detailed reading.

skimming: Reading quickly to find key concepts and main ideas.

preview: Reading rapidly to get a general idea of material which will be re-read in detail

There are many reasons for skimming and mature readers often use this skill. We may skim a newspaper to decide what to read in depth. We might skim an encyclopedia to decide whether all or only a part of the entry needs to be carefully attended to, or we might skim a journal article to determine whether it is appropriate and contains information relevant to a particular assignment. Well-developed skimming ability can result in valuable time savings. Provide activities that allow students to skim a selection followed by discussion of what was included in the selection.

SAMPLE ACTIVITIES

- Provide students with the front page of a newspaper and allow only enough time for students to skim the page. From a list of topics, have students identify those that were on the page. Follow up with a discussion of which are of most interest to them.

- Provide a passage that has a sequenced organizational pattern. Set the purpose for reading as determining the sequence of events in the passage. Have students skim to determine the sequence. As a pre-reading activity, discuss which words signal sequence; that is, discuss what to look for while skimming.

- Provide a paragraph or passage and set finding the main idea as the purpose for reading. Set a time limit for doing so that allows only for rapid skimming, not careful reading. After skimming, have students write down the main idea, then go back and carefully read the selection, writing down supporting details.

Closely related to skimming, **scanning** is rapid movement through a reading selection to find specific information. Again, this is a skill that mature readers use daily. Looking through a telephone directory to find a specific telephone number is one example. To foster this skill, give students the opportunity to practice it in their reading materials.

scanning: Reading quickly to find specific information.

Ask students to

- scan to find a particular date in a history selection;
- scan to find the murderer's name in a short mystery story;
- scan a chapter to find a specific heading in a science text;
- scan to find a specific ingredient in a recipe;
- scan a list of titles to answer questions like Who wrote _____?

Activities designed to enhance skimming and scanning abilities can be used to both build the concept that content-area reading materials need not always be read from beginning to end, and that reading speed does vary depending on one's reading needs and purposes. Note, however, that skimming and scanning might, in one sense, be considered alternatives to reading, since *reading* implies comprehending all or a large part of what was written, while skimming and scanning activities selectively look at parts of a piece of text.

Skimming and scanning are useful skills, Here, a student quickly searches a dictionary page for a particular item.

TEACHING APPROACHES FOR CONTENT AREAS

Although the general teaching strategies discussed throughout this text apply to reading both narrative and expository materials, some techniques are traditionally thought of as being specifically appropriate to content-area reading instruction. The following sections discuss several commonly used techniques to enhance content-area reading and study skills. When reading about the various instructional techniques, think about how they fit into the three instructional frameworks and explanations for how reading ability develops.

Keep in mind that this chapter does not include an exhaustive list of the content areas found in schools. In this chapter, we focus only on the four content areas commonly described as the "academic" subjects (mathematics, social studies, science, and language arts), not because they are in any way superior to the others, but because these subjects use reading material as a major instructional component. We recommend that you take a course in content-area reading as part of your teacher preparation. Some representative, readable texts in this area are listed at the end of this chapter.

Vocabulary and Concept Development

One of the major barriers to comprehension in content-area reading involves the high number of new concepts that are presented. When reading in science, mathematics, or social studies, students encounter words that they are familiar with in everyday use, but that have unfamiliar meanings within the subject. The example *race* (to run a race versus the Oriental race) illustrates this phenomenon. Also, students are confronted with new words and concepts that are subject specific—*beaker,* in science, is one example. Content-area teachers must identify and teach the vocabulary and concepts that are part of their subject areas. Students learn vocabulary best when it occurs in meaningful situations. This includes presenting content-specific vocabulary as part of the subject-area's reading assignment so that students realize that the concept is useful and will help them understand what they will be reading.

Directed Reading Activity in Content-Area Reading

The **directed reading activity** (DRA) is part of the lesson format commonly associated with a formal reading program. Yet the DRA is also applicable to content-area reading. The traditional DRA consists of four basic steps:

directed reading activity: A method framework for teaching reading, consisting of preparation, guided reading, skill development and practice, and follow-up enrichment activities.

1. *Preparation.* This involves providing needed background, preteaching necessary vocabulary (this is especially important in content-area reading), and providing motivation for reading.

2. *Guided reading.* Through purpose setting questions or outlines, readers' attention is directed while they proceed through the material. This step aids retention and comprehension of what is read.
3. *Skill development and practice.* Direct instruction in comprehension or other skills. Readers are provided with opportunities to practice the skills taught.
4. *Enrichment.* Activities based on the reading selection and skills learned. These are based on but go beyond the reading, often allowing children to pursue topics more specifically related to their interests.

In the content-area setting, steps 1, 2, and 4 are emphasized to a slightly greater extent when compared to instructional settings using narrative texts. Since the goal of reading content-area material is understanding concepts and facts, and is less that of increasing reading ability, step 3 is deemphasized, though not ignored.

We have discussed how one's background knowledge influences the comprehension process and the interpretation and potential understanding of what one reads. This is especially true when reading content-area material. The preparation stage, therefore, is critical in ensuring that students have the background to understand the selection to be read. Additionally, this step provides opportunities to discover and deal with potential problems arising from unknown vocabulary or lack of motivation. Before assigning reading material, teachers must make sure they have carefully and recently read the selection with their students in mind. Prereading discussion can then center around the concepts that are covered in the reading, with background knowledge provided as needed. Then, as another aspect of the prereading preparation activity, provide students with a clear and definite purpose for reading the assigned text.

The second step in content-area material requires an awareness that textbooks are usually not intended to be read at the **independent reading level.** They are to be used as instructional tools, and teacher guidance is expected. A study guide, outline, periodic help with vocabulary and concept load, and other support all must be available to students as they read their textbooks. Since readability and other analyses have consistently shown most content-area textbooks to be relatively more difficult for students than narrative materials intended for comparable grade levels, few students should be expected to read their textbooks on their own.

The skill-development and practice step of a DRA can, in content-area reading, provide practice with those vocabulary terms and concepts that are difficult for students. As in any vocabulary teaching and learning, remember that not all students will exhibit difficulty with identical vocabulary. Having students keep their own informal lists of difficult or unknown items that are encountered while reading can form the basis

independent reading level: Level at which students can read by themselves with few word recognition problems and excellent comprehension.

of a class discussion comparing students' listings and can also be the basis for specific vocabulary practice activities. This step also provides discussion about what was read. Discuss main ideas and their supporting details, check students' understanding of the selection, and point out relationships to previous work and knowledge. This discussion sets up the enrichment step of the DRA. As in a regular reading lesson, the enrichment stage in a content-area DRA must provide activities designed to allow application of new knowledge, thus allowing the student to go beyond the text.

Several authors have pointed out how the DRA can be applied to content areas (Rubin, 1983; Thomas & Alexander, 1982). They note that, as in all teaching, the activity must take into account the special demands of the appropriate subject area and individual differences among students. A model for a content-area DRA follows.

MODEL LESSON

Directed Reading Activity. Students will read a selection on Columbus discovering America.

Preparation. The teacher states what the reading selection is about and introduces vocabulary and concepts that might be difficult. The teacher notes that the popular belief at that time was that the world was flat and asks students why this might have been logical. The teacher asks students what ships were like at that time. After discussion, the teacher shows pictures of sailing ships and discusses hardships and reasons for those hardships while sailing for long periods of time. The teacher notes that Columbus set out with three ships and brainstorms the reasons why. The teacher sets purposes for reading: to find out why Columbus wanted to set sail; to find out some of the difficulties along the way; to find out the results of his discovery.

Guided Reading. The teacher provides a study guide (see the following section) to be used by students while reading. The teacher walks around and provides help to students who need it, asking individual questions periodically. When the reading and study guide activity has been completed, a class discussion about the selection takes place. It involves students' understanding of the reading, and includes main ideas and relationships between what was read and students' general knowledge.

Skill Development and Practice. The teacher has decided to focus in more detail on the vocabulary and concepts introduced in the preparation stage. This is done in combination with a scanning lesson. Students scan certain pages to find vocabulary items. Then a discussion takes place about how each word is used and its specific meaning in social studies as used in the selection. Discussion is also provided on potential purposes and benefits of scanning.

Students practice using the vocabulary items and concepts. They are also asked in what other materials scanning might be useful. Guided discussion results in agreement that telephone books and newspapers are places where scanning ability is important. The teacher provides such materials for further practice.

Enrichment. The teacher provides a list of three items and asks students which they are most interested in: other early explorers of America; Columbus' other journeys; and what happened to Columbus after his discovery. The class divides into groups and goes to the library to research their interests. A brief report is prepared by each group and is later presented to the others.

Study Guides

study guides: Teacher-designed aids that assist students in reading text.

literal level question: Asks for information directly stated in the text.
inferential level question: Requires readers to contribute background knowledge in conjunction with literal meaning.
evaluative level question: Asks readers to make critical judgments about information in the text and, often, relate that information to past or future experiences.

Study guides are constructed by a teacher to help students comprehend and remember what they read. Some guides are to be referred to during reading; others are used after the selection has been read to make students conscious of their reading processes. As noted by Herber (1978) and Tierney, Readence, & Dishner (1980), study guides should be written in three levels, with each level corresponding to one of the three general levels of comprehension questions: **literal; inferential;** and **evaluative.** The teacher must decide on the important content in the reading selection and on the organizational structure (for example, cause-and-effect, simple list, and so on) of the material. Also, the study guide must be constructed so that it is easy to read. The guide may include specific page and paragraph references or other aids, depending on the students' abilities and on the teacher's decision regarding how much help to provide. Finally, study guides are not intended to stand alone. They are to be used as part of an overall lesson, for example, within a directed reading activity.

MODEL LESSON

Study Guides. Students will be reading "Food for the Future" (Buggey, J. [1983]. *Our Communities* [Follett Social Studies, grade 3]. Chicago: Follett, pp. 231–34). This passage discusses how food might be grown to feed the world's increasing population. The teacher's objectives for assigning this reading are that students learn about different ways of growing food. The following three-level guide was constructed. The parenthetical information was included because the teacher felt students needed this additional help.

LEVEL I. Literal Level

Why will we need more food in the future?
Why will we not be able to use more land? (p. 213; par. 1)

What three methods of growing food, other than on farmland, are discussed? (look at subheadings)

Why are conditions inside greenhouses "perfect for growing crops"? (p. 232; par. 2)

What does *hydrophonics* mean? (p. 233, par. 2)

Will plants grow closer together in water or in soil? (p. 233; par. 2)

LEVEL II. Interpretive Level

Why does the author say that greenhouses can be used in many places where crops usually cannot grow? (p. 232; par. 2)

How does irrigation in deserts allow crops to grow? (p. 232; par. 1)

How are insects and weeds kept from getting inside a greenhouse?

What is the major difference between greenhousing and hydrophonics?

LEVEL III. Evaluative Level

Why do you think plants grown in water don't need as many roots as plants grown in soil?

How might greenhouses control growing conditions?

Do you think it would be better to irrigate in deserts instead of using greenhouses? Explain. (p. 232; par. 1 and 2)

Marginal Glosses

Another technique that is applicable to reading in all content areas is called glossing. This technique provides a system of marginal notes for a reader. The notes are designed to explain concepts, point out relationships, and otherwise clarify the text as the student reads. **Marginal glosses** are constructed by the teacher and are provided for the student when reading is assigned. In effect, the marginal glosses provide guidance while reading, in a way, reflecting the presence of the teacher. The glosses provide both a guide for the student-reader while teaching the kinds of questions and information to ask one's self while reading. Just as questioning strategies provide a model for students to follow when reading independently, so too are the glosses expected to model what should take place when students read on their own.

> **marginal glosses:**
> Teacher-constructed margin notes that aid students' comprehension by emphasizing and clarifying concepts, noting relationships, and modeling questions.

For teachers to prepare a relevant and useful gloss, Singer and Donlan (1985) suggest the following steps. An adaptation of the glossing technique is to have more able students prepare glosses for, or together with, less able readers.

Procedure for Preparing and Using a Marginal Gloss

MODEL
LESSON

1. Read through the text, identifying vocabulary or other material to emphasize or clarify.

2. Write marginal glosses on copies of the original passage (see figure 8–1). Glosses may be used for all or part of a selection.
3. Give copies of the passage, including glosses, to students to insert in the appropriate places in their texts and refer to them as they read.

An example of a text including marginal glosses is shown in figure 8–1. Note how the glosses attempt to clarify vocabulary, point out relationships, and pose questions that direct attention and generally emphasize the important points.

Herders and Nomads of the Steppe

Wanderers having no fixed home.

As You Read

You may need to look these up.

1. Think about these words.
   steppe clan khan yurt
2. Look for answers to these key questions.
   a. What were the three main areas of the Eurasian steppe?
   b. Why was the horse important to the nomads?
   c. What was the life of the steppe nomads like?
3. Use this reading skill.
   Recognizing generalizations, or statements about what certain groups may have in common, is an important reading skill. Few generalizations are true of all people, in all places, or at all times. Generalizations need to be limited by such words as many, few, some, usually, and nearly. Look carefully for generalizations as you read about nomads in this chapter.

Be sure to read this first.

Thousands of years ago nomads traveled the grasslands of Europe and Asia. Skilled at riding horses, they became warriors feared for their raids on settled communities. During the time of the Romans, some rode out of the north and east to attack cities of the empire.

The reason follows.

The Romans called the nomads "two-footed beasts." The nomads were small people, and to the Romans they seemed to be a part of their horses. They ate and even slept on their horses.

Rude and savage people.

The Romans thought the nomads were barbarians. The nomads had no great cities. They had no written language. They wore strange clothes. Yet these nomads conquered many lands, learned from other people, and built great empires of their own.

What was Roman dress like?

The nomads' accomplishments.

The Eurasian Steppe

The **steppe** region of Europe and Asia was home to the nomads. Because it covered parts of Europe and Asia, it has often been called the Eurasian steppe.

FIGURE 8–1
Text with marginal glosses

Advance Organizers

Although **advance organizers** are, technically, any prereading guide or aid that clarifies concepts, sets up expectations, or builds background, they are usually thought of as specific, brief selections or outlines that are read before attempting the main reading assignment. Advance organizers require that teachers present a brief outline, related to the assigned reading, that is written at students' independent reading level. After all, the organizer is to foster comprehension—it must not itself present difficult reading. An advance organizer, appropriate to a section in a science textbook dealing with the measurement of electricity, is shown in figure 8–2.

Advance organizers do not always appear in written form, although that is usual. If teachers provide **structured concept outlines,** as discussed in the following section, to students before a reading selection, then they serve the advance organizer function. Structured concept outlines that are used as advance organizers can be created by teachers or by advanced students. Further, if required texts do not change, the outlines can be reused with new students who are at the independent reading level relative to the organizer.

advance organizers: Enhance comprehension by explaining concepts, encouraging prediction, or establishing background knowledge.

structured concept outlines: Demonstrate the superordinate, coordinate, and subordinate relationships of the concepts in the text to be read.

You will be reading about measuring electricity. The unit you will read has three parts. The first part will tell you about one way of measuring electricity, using a unit of measurement called VOLTS. The other two parts in the reading will tell you about measuring electricity with units called AMPERES and WATTS.

When you read, try to find out why there are three different units to measure electricity. What is the purpose of each unit of measurement? Do you think we need three ways or units to measure electricity?

Before you start reading, write down a sentence or two about what you think you might find out about by reading the unit on measuring electricity:

_____

_____

_____

FIGURE 8–2
Sample advance organizer

Mapping and Other Schematic Overviews

There have been a number of techniques suggested that are intended to visually display and relate important concepts in what is being read. All attempt to enhance retention and provide a study guide. What these techniques have in common is a requirement, indeed an expectation, that the reader identify main idea(s) and important concept(s), together with their supporting details in the material being read. The following techniques all attempt to improve recall of content-area reading material, but poorer readers have difficulty identifying the main ideas needed to use the strategies successfully. Thus it is not enough to simply teach the technique. It is necessary to also discuss why certain concepts are identified as important—what it is in the text that suggests an item is related to another, perhaps in a subordinate role. Thus students need to practice not only the technique per se but, concurrently, skills related to identifying main ideas and supporting details.

semantic mapping: A note-taking and recall/study technique for identifying and recording main ideas and supporting details using graphic forms.

Semantic Mapping. Hanf (1971) has suggested **semantic mapping** as a method for organizing ideas to enhance note taking and as a recall and study technique. The technique consists of identifying and recording main ideas and related supporting details in visual, graphic form. Semantic mapping requires the following two steps.

1. Record the title or main idea anywhere on a page of note paper. Leave enough room so that additional information (the supporting details) can be added around the central idea.
2. Place the secondary, related ideas around the main idea in an organized pattern. Plan the placement of the secondary ideas so that proximity and linking lines reflect the "distance" or strength of relationship(s).

The semantic map can be created as a small group, whole class, or individual activity using either the chalkboard or chartpaper. Students should copy the map into their notebooks so that it can be used as a recall aid. As a prereading activity, teachers can provide a list containing main ideas and supporting details. Through a guided discussion, students decide which item is the main or superordinate idea, and rank order the supporting details by importance. The map is created based on the discussion. Reading then takes place. As a postreading activity, the map is reworked as necessary. Students can also generate the map during reading, noting ideas as they arise, or can create the map as a postreading activity. Figure 8–3 presents a sample semantic map that can be used as a recall and study aid either with or without reference to the original text.

Structured Concept Outlines. A structured outline is a schematic representation of the relationship between concepts presented in the ma-

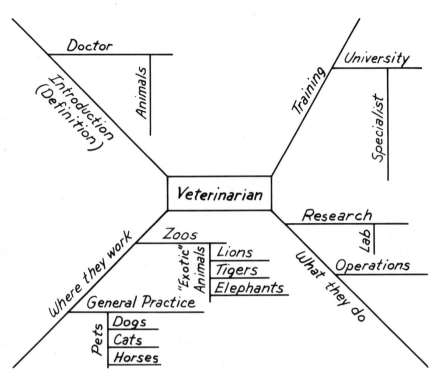

FIGURE 8–3
Based on a basal reader story on a veterinarian. This semantic map was developed, after reading the story, through discussion.

terial to be read. It may be used as an advance organizer or as an aid for postreading activities, as a study guide or to aid recall. This technique requires that concepts be ordered into superordinate, coordinate, and subordinate categories. For example, if a selection with the main idea *growing tomatoes* is to be read, the following outline might apply.

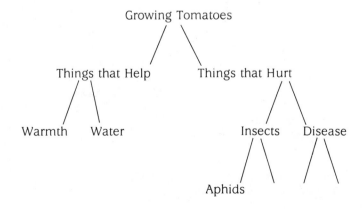

herringbone technique: Enhances retention by requiring readers to identify the main idea.

The outline is similar to the **Herringbone technique** (Tierney, Readence & Dishner, 1985), which uses answers to the questions who, what, where, when, why, and how, presented in a schematic format, to provide structure for recall and study. The following activities suggest how structured concept outlines might be used.

SAMPLE ACTIVITIES

- The teacher prepares the structured concept outline on ditto, hands it out, and uses it as a basis for discussion prior to students reading the selection.
- Certain parts of the outline can be left out (as in the preceding example under *insects* and *disease*), and students are told to complete the outline while they read. This has the advantage of providing a purpose for reading as well as allowing students to make active choices while reading.
- Combine the structured concept outline with marginal glosses and leave space around the individual entries. Students are expected to make notes or otherwise complete the outline, as requested by the gloss (see figure 8–4).

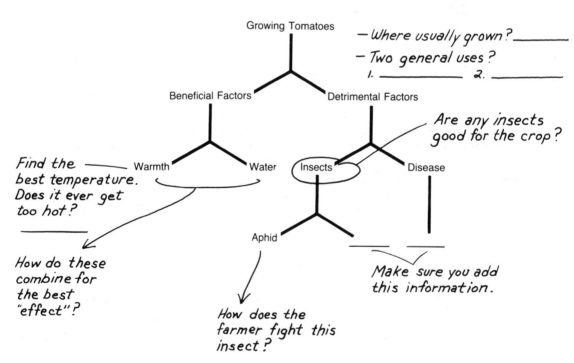

FIGURE 8–4
Example of marginal glosses used with structured concept outline

The structured concept outline provides a vehicle for teaching relationships: superordinate; subordinate; and coordinate concepts. Teachers who use this technique need to spend time building active awareness of the concepts and the structure employed in the outline. Students must understand that concepts are related to one another and that the outline provides a visual representation of such relationships. But it is important to explain and discuss how and why the concepts are related, not simply to point out that a relationship exists.

SQ3R

Originally developed by Robinson (1961) as a study strategy for college students, secondary- and upper elementary-grade teachers also teach SQ3R as a study tool. **SQ3R** stands for:

SQ3R: A study strategy using surveying, questioning, reading, reciting, and reviewing.

Survey	Quickly skim through the material. Focus on headings, titles, and generally "abstract" the material. After this stage, one should have a general feel for what the material covers.
Question	Ask questions, based on the survey just completed, to which answers are expected in the material to be read.
Read	Read the material to be able to answer the questions posed in the previous stage.
Recite	Specifically attempt to answer the questions posed during the question stage. This can be done orally or in writing.
Review	Reread portions of the material in order to check or verify the answers given during the recite stage.

SQ3R. The teacher has decided to use SQ3R with a science passage about inventing the telephone. The passage has a title "The Telephone: A Useful Invention" and three subheadings: "Before the Telephone"; "The Invention"; "After the Invention".

MODEL LESSON

The teacher begins with a discussion of SQ3R, reminding students of the steps. Students are asked to SURVEY, quickly skimming for headings and overall content. A short period of time is allowed. Students are asked to provide title and headings. Teacher lists these on the board and asks what QUESTIONS might be answered in each subsection. Students generate questions that are written under the headings on the board; for example:

The Telephone: A Useful Invention

    Q: Why is the telephone useful?
    Q: What makes the telephone useful?
    Q: How was it invented?

Before the Telephone

    Q: How did people talk to each other before the telephone?

The Invention

    Q: Who invented the telephone?

    Q: When was it invented?

    Q: How was it invented?

After the Invention

    Q: What happened after the invention?

    Q: How did the telephone change people's lives?

The teacher asks the students to READ the selection, keeping the questions in mind. They are told to actively but silently RECITE the answers to questions as they occur. Answers can also be written down. When finished reading, students REVIEW answers with the teacher or individually by rereading parts of the passage that provide answers. A postdiscussion, referring to the text and to children's background knowledge, also takes place.

Although SQ3R has been shown to be an effective study strategy when used as described, it appears to be rarely spontaneously used by students (Cheek & Cheek, 1983) and needs to be taught and reinforced. Some (Vacca, 1981) feel that students need more structure than is provided by SQ3R. Pauk (1984) has added a record step after reading (thus

SQ4R: A more structured study tool than SQ3R, including surveying, questioning, reading, recording, reciting, and reflecting.

calling his technique **SQ4R**), and suggests a more structured method of presenting the technique, stressing the setting of purposes at each step. Pauk feels that after reading, a student should be recording succinct notes of ideas, facts, and details in the margins, thus establishing cues for immediate and future reviews. Above all, students need to be stingy, parsimonious, and selective in choosing what to note and what to underline.

The steps in SQ3R and SQ4R are ways to increase and focus students' attention on what they will be reading. The review and question steps are especially suited to expository selections because content-area texts are written around a superordinate and subordinate structure. Content texts have headings and other organizational features that make them suitable for fairly rapid previewing.

READING IN FOUR CONTENT AREAS

The preceding section has presented several techniques that can aid students' reading in expository material. Try to keep these techniques in mind when reading the following sections, for they can be used in any subject area. However, while there are general reading skills applicable to reading in all content areas, certain skills are required more often in some content areas than in others. The sections that follow present some of the specific demands that are faced by readers in the areas of social studies, science, mathematics, and language arts.

Reading in Social Studies

Often students who have difficulty reading mathematics and science texts appear to have less difficulty with reading material in their language arts and social studies classes (Muhtadi, 1977). This may be due to patterns of text organization. The majority of reading materials in language arts consist of narrative texts, organized along the time sequence discussed earlier. Science and mathematics texts are, most consistently, organized hierarchically. Social studies texts, however, may be organized either along a time sequence, or along the superordinate/subordinate pattern found in mathematics and science.

Think of the different social studies textbooks you have encountered. What component of social studies involves a time sequence? If you said *history,* you are correct. Since social studies often emphasizes history, and history is usually presented in a time-sequenced format, students would find some social studies texts similar to the narratives they are used to reading. What other kinds of organizational patterns are you familiar with in social studies?

BEFORE READING ON

Look at this list of titles and state how you feel the book probably would be organized. Use one of the following organization systems: time sequential or hierarchical.

Title   *Probable Organization*
1. Climates of the World   _____
2. Decline of the Dinosaurs   _____
3. Government in the U.S.A.   _____

Most people pick the first title as a heading for text organized along a hierarchical pattern, probably with a partial table of contents approximating

CLIMATES OF THE WORLD
Arid Climatic Regions
Arid Climate Defined
Arid Regions
African Continent
European Continent
American Continents

> Desert Climates
> > Desert Climate Defined
> > Desert Regions
> > > African Continent
> > > Asian Continent
> > > American Continents

The second title (Decline of the Dinosaurs) is usually picked as implying a time-sequenced organizational pattern, with the text moving from the evolution of dinosaurs through their most prolific period, to their decline and eventual extinction. The third title is hierarchical.

But there are several possibilities for organizing the texts that might follow each of the titles. To illustrate, although the third title is hierarchical, it can be organized sequentially (for example, the evolution of government to its present form). Organizational structures may also have a time sequence within a **hierarchical** organizational pattern. For example, even if the text were organized hierarchically, perhaps across federal and state governmental levels, it could approximate the following:

hierarchical organization: Where items are arranged so that each is subordinate to the one above it.

GOVERNMENT IN THE UNITED STATES

Government at the Federal Level
> Evolution of Federal Government
> > The Prerevolutionary Period
> > The Postrevolutionary Period

Government at the State Level
> Evolution of State Legislatures

In social studies material, therefore, students may be required to switch between different organizational structures within one reading selection. Students need to be aware that organizational patterns do not necessarily remain constant throughout a reading selection.

Readers in social studies are also confronted with graphic material that is not normally used in narrative texts. This material is usually in the form of maps, charts, or graphs. Although other content areas include such material (notably graphs in science and mathematics), the graphs and charts in social studies incorporate fairly unique symbolic material. Consider some of the graphic material predominantly found in social studies texts (see figure 8–5).

The examples shown in figure 8–5 demonstrate some figures and diagrams that students are confronted with in their social studies textbooks, in addition to more "normal" photographs, graphs and charts. Even good readers may have difficulty incorporating **graphic information.** They may be unsure how to move from the textual material to the graphic and back again. They may lose their place in moving back and forth, and may be unable to read or interpret the material presented in

graphic information: In this context, data presented in the form of charts, maps, graphs, or photographs.

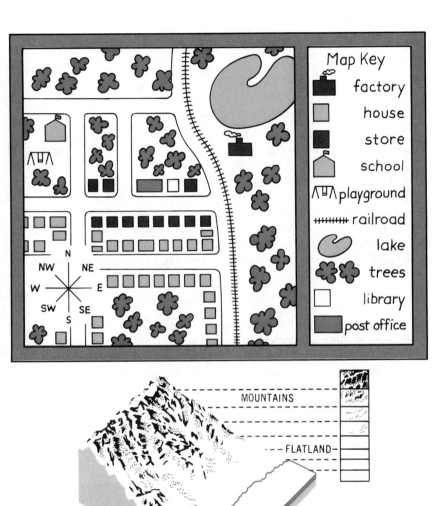

FIGURE 8–5

Sample graphic material from a third grade social studies text

graphic format. This is especially true since interpretation of maps and graphs is rarely taught as a specific skill, although the complexity of such reading has been noted (Summers, 1965; Vacca, 1981).

Fry (1981) presents a taxonomy of graphs. The main subdivisions of his taxonomy are:

1. *Lineal graphs*—sequential data. (For example, simple time lines, parallel time lines, and flow charts.)

2. *Quantitative graphs*—numerical data. (For example, growth curves, bar graphs, pie graphs, and multiple variable graphs.)
3. *Spatial graphs*—area and location. (For example, two-dimensional road maps and three-dimensional contour maps).
4. *Pictorial graphs*—visual concepts. (For example, realistic drawings, schematic drawings, and abstracted representations.)
5. *Hypothetical graphs*—interrelationship of ideas. (For example, conceptual, perhaps with a box labeled "short-term memory" leading to another labeled "long-term memory", verbal, and perhaps a sentence diagram or semantic map.)
6. *Intentional Omissions from the Taxonomy of Graphs: high verbal* (for example, posters and advertisements); *high numerical* (for example, statistical tables); *Symbols* (for example, word equivalents like the outline of a man on a restroom door); *Decorative design* (for example, designs whose main purpose is decorative rather than conceptual or informative).

Note: Nearly any kind of graph can be combined with any other.

map readers: Students who cannot interpret the information they successfully locate on a map.
map thinkers: Students who are able to locate information on a map and interpret it.

Summers (1965) has pointed out a discrepancy between what he calls **map readers** and **map thinkers** while discussing the various kinds of maps encountered by readers. He calls a map reader one who can locate information in a map but cannot interpret the presented information. This is similar to students who might be able to locate literal information in text, yet be unable to assimilate the information into existing knowledge structures or to interpret the information in the general context of the text as a whole. Obviously, a teacher's goal, especially in social studies, is to move students beyond being map readers, molding them into map thinkers.

Awareness of the following six points, according to Summers (1965) is required before a student has the potential to be a map thinker:

1. *Map title.* Similar to a book title, this provides the name of what the map depicts. Map titles should be read carefully for an introduction to the map and its features. Discussion of the title, and other activities similar to those performed with a book or story title, are appropriate for use with students.
2. *Legend.* This is often compared to the table of contents in a book since the legend indicates what map symbols stand for, as well as providing information such as the scale used on the map. The legend is usually separated in a box within the map or graph. It is suggested that students try to consciously focus on each item in the legend and visualize the things for which the symbols stand. For example, looking at the green of a map, one should try to "see" the rugged mountains which the legend says it represents.

3. *Direction.* The top of a map usually, but not always, indicates north. Students must be taught to realize that north is not just a direction, but is a concept with related understandings of true and magnetic north, intermediate distances, and polar regions.

4. *Distance scale.* Three types of scales are common: graphic; statement; and fractional scales. The scale must be kept in mind because it enables the reader to tell how far or how big something is. A small scale map depicts a large area made smaller while a large scale map depicts a small area made larger.

5. *Location.* This is usually depicted by a grid system which segment maps, usually by using horizontal and vertical lines. Township range lines and marginal letters and numbers are common grid systems, as are parallels and meridians (to locate places by latitude and longitude).

6. *Types of maps.* Major map types include land, elevation, climate, vegetation and water features, political, economic, and population. Combinations of these categories are often found on one map.

In addition to different kinds of graphic information that must be read, actively thought about, and incorporated into the text while reading, the following must also be attended to in social studies material.

■ Vocabulary terms may appear strange because they involve a larger than normal proportion of words with Latin and Greek roots, prefixes, or suffixes.

■ Vocabulary and concepts from a variety of disciplines make up the content of a social studies curriculum. These include anthropology, sociology, economics, political science, and other disciplines.

■ Many social studies textbooks are written in ways that focus on details to the extent that important major issues may be difficult to grasp. History segments in the social studies curriculum are often presented in ways that stress many details, often without drawing clear and obvious relationships to the "global picture."

■ In our world of rapid change, the material in social studies textbooks can become rapidly dated. Sometimes, information presented can be shown to be obsolete or even false. This can be confusing to children who have, perhaps, seen more recent or correct information in newspapers or news broadcasts.

■ Differentiating fact, opinion, and propaganda.

■ Since social studies often depends on time perspectives, some younger children may have difficulty grasping time-dependent concepts. We know that students at certain lower **cognitive levels** may have problems understanding concepts involving time, space and distance relationships—all things that are important to social studies; all appearing in various kinds of maps.

cognitive levels: Stages of intellectual development.

The teaching procedures noted in the first part of this chapter do, of course, apply to social studies material as well as to the other content areas. Building background, providing prereading activities and the other techniques discussed throughout this text are all important to the teacher concerned with students' abilities to read social studies material. Additionally, students will benefit from cloze and **maze procedures.** Both emphasize the use of context clues that serve to aid comprehension. Emphasis should also be placed on cause-and-effect activities. Crossword and word search puzzles can also be effectively used in social studies classrooms to build vocabulary background before reading is assigned. All of these techniques have been discussed in previous chapters.

maze procedure: A fill-in-the-blanks activity to measure comprehension.

SAMPLE ACTIVITIES

- Following discussion about information that can be found in various parts of a map, provide a list of questions that should be answered while referring to a specific map.

- Provide a summary of information in paragraph or list form. Have students use the information to draw a map or create a graph. Discuss how the information in graphic form has certain advantages over the listed form (for example, better overview, visual summary, easier to see relationships, and so on).

- Find factual and opinion statements in newspapers or create statements that would fit into these categories. Present the statements in pairs and have students decide and discuss which is a fact and which is an opinion, and why. For example:

Factual Statement	Opinion Statement
1. Trans World Airlines and Western Airlines both reported losses [in income] during the first quarter.	The airlines will close down if they lose money in the next quarter.
2. All land and buildings in Davidson County will be reassessed for their value before the next taxation year.	All taxes on real estate in Davidson County will go up next taxation year.

Using the same initial procedure, delete either a cause or an effect. Have students supply the deleted item. Follow up with students presenting and discussing their reasons for responses. For example:

Cause	Effect
1. Fewer people want to travel by airplane nowadays.	[The airlines are making less money.]

2. [All land and buildings in Davidson County will be reassessed for their value before the next taxation year.]

The county clerk needs to hire more staff to update Davidson County's tax records.

3. [There have been several airplane accidents recently.]

Fewer people want to travel by airplane nowadays.

Notice how the cause in number 1 is an effect in number 3. Such transpositions can serve as a basis for discussions centering around differences between causes and effects.

Reading in Mathematics

The examples in figure 8–6 are representative of the things children are commonly asked to read as part of mathematics instruction. Notice that there are a number of things in the mathematics passages that are not generally found in narrative texts. Perhaps the most obvious are the numeric symbols that must be "read." Just as a set of letters represent rather than are the concept (*c-h-a-i-r* represents rather than is a chair), so do numbers and other symbols represent meaning. For example, the number 50 represents or stands for a quantity of items totaling a certain amount. This amount could be stated as "two items more than the quantity of forty-eight items" or in innumerable other ways. Thus, just as a reader must learn the specific concepts that letter combinations represent, so must concepts be learned for other symbol sets. Look again at figure 8–6. Notice the categories of symbols that are generally not used in narrative texts, but that play a large part in the examples:

- numbers such as 1, 2, 3, or 57
- decimals such as 1.10 or 56.56
- fractions such as ½ or $^{15}/_{16}$
- mathematical symbols such as $\times$, /, %, +, [,], or =

In addition to different symbol sets, the following are also a part of reading in mathematics:

- Specialized vocabulary that is content specific; for example, set, square, division, quotient, digit, multiplication, product, numeral, and so on.
- A knowledge of specific shapes and diagrams; for example, triangle, parallelogram, and so on.
- A slower rate of reading than in narrative texts and also slower than in some expository texts such as history books. Word problems and theorems must be especially carefully read, and read more than once.

MULTIPLYING BY 2-DIGIT NUMBERS

When we use the long form to multiply, we write down each partial product. Then we add to find the product.

Step 1

```
 78   Multiply the ones.
×23   3 × 8 = 24.
 24   Write 24 ones.
```

Step 2

```
 78   Multiply 3 ones times 7 tens.
×23   3 × 70 = 210.
 24   Write 210.
210
```

Step 3

```
 78   Multiply 2 tens times 8 ones.
×23   20 × 8 = 160.
 24   Write 160.
210
160
```

Step 4

```
  78   Multiply 2 tens times 7 tens.
 ×23   20 × 70 = 1,400.
  24   Write 1,400.
 210
 160
1400
```

Step 5

```
  78   Add the partial products.
 ×23   Write the product.
  24
 210
 160
1 400
1,794
```

Shade the part of each region named by the fraction.

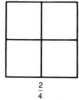
$\frac{2}{4}$

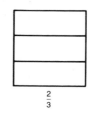
$\frac{5}{6}$

$\frac{2}{3}$

$\frac{3}{4}$

Complete these sentences.

1. $10 \div 2 =$ _5.0_   ½ of 10 is _5.0_

2. $12 \div 4 =$ _____   ¼ of 12 is _____

3. $5 \div 5 =$ _____   ⅕ of 5 is _____

Solve each of these word problems.

1. On Thursday Mr. Kincaid drove his car 7 kilometers, on Friday he drove 8 kilometers, and on Saturday he drove 13 kilometers. How far did he drive altogether?   _____ kilometers

FIGURE 8–6

Samples from elementary mathematics texts

- Eye movements that differ from the expected left-to-right sequence, as in

$$3 + 2 \times (6 + 1) = 17$$

Note that first, $6 + 1$ must be computed. Mathematical rules state that multiplication must be performed before addition, so the sum is next multiplied by 2, and then the product is added to 3. Eye movements also go up/down and down/up in addition and division problems, as well as diagonally in the multiplication of fractions.

- A different focus on comprehension. For example, word problems require one to attend to parts of the text not normally thought important.

The last point, that of a different focus, applies particularly to reading word problems. For example, consider the following problem.

> John was going to the store. First he stopped at Mary's house. Mary lived 2 blocks from John. John and Mary went to the store together. The store was 2 blocks past Mary's house. How far did John go to get to the store?

Normally, children would read to answer questions such as Who were the people in the story? Where were John and Mary going? or perhaps Why do you think John and Mary were going to the store? Yet in answering the problem, such things are unimportant. Students who are accustomed to focusing on the types of questions asked in narrative materials may attend to inappropriate items in a mathematics problem. In fact, reading ability may account for as much as thirty-five percent of student errors found on mathematics achievement tests (O'Mara, 1981). Clearly, teaching mathematics in a manner that ignores reading factors is inappropriate.

Fay (1965) suggests a strategy called **SQRQCQ** be used when reading to solve word problems. SQRQCQ stands for:

SQRQCQ: A study strategy for reading math word problems: survey, question, read, question, compute, and question.

Survey.	Read the problem rapidly, skimming to determine its nature.
Question.	Decide what is being asked; what the problem is.
Read.	Read for details and interrelationships.
Question.	Decide which processes and strategies should be used to address the problem.
Compute.	Carry out the necessary computations.
Question.	Ask if the answer seems correct. Check computations against the facts presented in the problem as well as against basic arithmetic facts.

**MODEL
LESSON**

SQRQCQ. Ms. Jackson knows that there are really only three reasons that a student is unable to correctly complete a word problem: reading the problem incorrectly, thus not finding the appropriate information; not performing the appropriate computation (perhaps subtracting when needing to add); or not performing the appropriate computation correctly (perhaps not knowing how to divide, or making a computational error). She has decided to address the first point—that which relates most directly to reading—by teaching her students to SQRQCQ.

Ms. Jackson tells her students that a technique called SQRQCQ will help them better understand their mathematics problems. She explains what the letters SQRQCQ stand for and demonstrates how she would read a mathematics problem (written on the blackboard) using the SQRQCQ technique. She asks several students what the letters stand for and what a reader would do at each stage of the procedure.

After Ms. Jackson is sure that her students know what SQRQCQ requires a reader to do, she tells her students that they will practice the technique together. She says that she will hand out a ditto sheet of simple word problems, but that they should not read them until she says to begin. After all the students have the ditto sheets, she tells her students that they will be working on the first problem. She asks several students to describe the first step in SQRQCQ, then reminds the class that they are to skim the problem rapidly, just to find out generally what it asks. She tells her students to turn their ditto papers over when they have finished skimming, and lets them begin.

After the students have finished, Ms. Jackson leads a discussion about what the problem is generally about. She then reminds the class about the next step in the procedure, tells them to use their pencils to make note of what is being asked if they wish, states that they should turn over their papers when finished, and allows them to start the question step.

Ms. Jackson continues the discussion of each step, both before and after it is attempted, for each part of the SQRQCQ procedure. This is practiced with several of the problems on the ditto sheet, and is reinforced several times throughout the next week and periodically thereafter.

---

modified cloze procedure: A comprehension assessment procedure which departs from the traditional procedure of deleting every fifth word.

Kane, Byrne, & Hater (1974) suggest a modification of the traditional cloze technique for mathematics. They refer to it as the **modified cloze procedure.** Their modification specifies areas of student difficulty in both textual aspects of mathematics material and in comprehension of mathematical concepts. As an instructional tool, this modification of the cloze procedure is completed as a joint activity between students, or teacher and students. Working through the exercise should proceed together with discussion that focuses students' attention on pertinent information that helps complete the deleted areas. An example of a mathematics cloze passage is shown in figure 8–7.

The final point in this section deals with teaching specialized vocabulary to students in mathematics. Since all content areas have unique vocabulary, it is necessary to teach content-specific terms in all reading materials. Yet the specialized symbolic vocabulary in mathe-

---

Following is a brief passage which could occur in a mathematics book written for upper elementary or junior high school students. To the right is a cloze test constructed for the passage. When actually constructing cloze tests, longer passages are used so that many more blanks are obtained.

Divide 20 by 5. Now, multiply 20 by $\frac{1}{5}$. Is dividing by 5 the same as multiplying by $\frac{1}{5}$? Are these sentences true?

Divide 20 by ___. Now multiply 20 ___$\frac{1}{5}$. Is ____by 5 the same ___ multiplying by $\underline{1/}$? Are these sentences true?

$36 \div 18 = 36 \times \frac{1}{18}$

$72 \div 8\ = 72 \times \frac{1}{8}$

___$6 \div 18$ ___$36 \times \frac{1}{18}$

72 ___$8 =\ \ \ 72$ ___$\frac{1}{8}$

Here are some observations you should note concerning the cloze test:

1. Word tokens and math tokens are counted in the deletion.
   Word tokens deleted: by, dividing, as
   Math tokens deleted: 5, 5, 3, $=$, $-$, $\div$, $\times$.
2. The percent of word tokens to total tokens in the passage is 32%.
   The percent of word tokens deleted to total tokens deleted is 30%.
   The percent is about the same for the passage and cloze test.
3. Every fifth token is deleted, starting with the fifth token.
4. Every token is capable of being deleted by simply selecting different starting points.
5. Deleted tokens are replaced by blanks of two sizes. The shorter blanks are used for math tokens where the context demands this.
6. Tokens are ordered according to the words used to read them. For example, $\frac{1}{5}$ can be read as "one-over-five." Therefore, these tokens are thought of as ordered 1, $-$, 5. A problem exists in ordering tokens since the verbalization of math tokens is not uniquely ordered. What is most important is that consistency of translation to words be maintained within a passage.

FIGURE 8–7

Adaptation of the cloze procedure for mathematics

matics is often forgotten. We do not mean simply the numeric symbols, but also the symbols that stand for addition, subtraction, multiplication, and so on. All of these have the same properties as regular vocabulary, and include synonyms. Consider, for example, the number of symbols there are for division or multiplication:

$$3 \times 2 \qquad 3 \cdot 2 \qquad 3(2)$$
$$3\overline{)2} \qquad 3 \div 2 \qquad 3/2$$

The various division and multiplication signs all mean the same thing and can be considered synonymous. They can be sources of confusion to students and might best be taught as synonyms. Since teaching vocabulary essentially means teaching concepts and their symbols, any symbols that stand for concepts can be considered vocabulary items. The vocabulary teaching techniques presented in chapter 5 apply to teaching in all symbol sets.

Reading in the Science Content Area

BEFORE READING ON

On these lines, state what you feel to be some of the specific demands of reading in science.

_____

_____

_____

As do texts in other content areas, science materials make their own unique demands of a reader. The following sample from an elementary science textbook illustrates some of the reading demands in science texts.

The chart below shows several common compounds. It also shows the chemical formula and the phase of the compound.

Compound	Formula	Phase of Matter
Carbon Dioxide	CO_2	gas
Water	H_2O	liquid
Ammonia	NH_3	gas
Salt	$NaCl$	solid

There are simple rules for writing chemical formulas. The formula for water is H_2O. The small number 2 means that a water molecule has two hydrogen atoms. The O has no number after it. No number means there is only one atom of oxygen. The number 1 is not written in chemical formulas. A molecule of water has 2 atoms of hydrogen and 1 atom of oxygen. CO_2 is the formula for carbon dioxide. What elements make up carbon dioxide? How many atoms of each element are in a molecule of carbon dioxide?

From Sund, R. B.; Adams, D. K.; & Hackett, J. K. *Accent on Science.* (Columbus, OH: C. E. Merrill, 1980), p. 90.

You may have noticed that the sample science text seemed much more technical than the examples used so far in this chapter. The explanation of the rules for writing formulas, for example, is specific and reflects technical writing. It must be carefully read and nothing must be missed, or the concept of formulas may not be grasped. There were also several terms that are specific to science.

| element | compound | dioxide |
| molecule | atom | formula |

You may also have noticed that, as in mathematics and social studies, science has several symbol sets. The symbols used in the formulas to represent the chemicals discussed in the example, along with the specific meaning of the subscripted numbers in the formulas, must all be mastered to read the science passage correctly.

As does social studies, science draws on several disciplines for its knowledge base. In fact, there is some overlap with social studies in science materials. Units on space exploration or weather and climate are examples. Thus, the previous discussion of maps and charts applies to the science area as well. Also consistent with social studies, science has a great many words with Latin and Greek **morphemes.**

morphemes: The smallest meaningful linguistic units.

One difference in the vocabulary found in science materials is the high number of words with a meaning specific only to science—words that are not found in everyday speech. Recall that there are several different kinds of vocabulary: vocabulary that is general; vocabulary that has general meaning as well as content-specific meaning; and vocabulary that has only content-specific meaning. While social studies and mathematics have many words in the second category, science has a large number of words in the third. This means that teachers may need to preteach specific science vocabulary concepts before students encounter them in text. Although context often helps readers learn new vocabulary, it is not good practice to assume that unknown words will become clear through reading alone.

Another key component in reading science material is reading to follow directions. This is particularly noticeable in laboratory exercises, where even the slightest digression from the directions can result in a failed experiment. Experiments that must be read (and written) also have a structure different from other text materials. Much scientific writing is presented in strict categories, with understood requirements for what is allowable in each. You may recall, from your own days in the science classroom, the emphasis on the following structure as related to reading and reporting science experiments even in elementary classes.

I.	Problem	IV.	Observation
II.	Hypothesis	V.	Collection of Data (Results)
III.	Procedure	VI.	Conclusion(s)

This is a structure with which students may be unfamiliar before encountering it in the science classroom, and it must be taught. As in any text, structure that is familiar is more easily comprehended. Looking at the organizational structure for scientific reporting, it is easy to see that reading in science requires organizing ideas so that relationships are clear and, further, so that inferences and conclusions can be made on the basis of the noted relationships.

An effective study technique specific to science has been suggested (Spache, 1963; Spache & Berg, 1966). Called **PQRST,** it recommends that students reading science materials:

PQRST: A science study technique stressing previewing, questioning, reading, summarizing, and testing.

Preview.   Rapidly skim the selection to be read. The reader should not move on until the passage's generalization or theory has been identified.

Question.   Raise questions for study purposes.

Read.   With questions in mind, read the selection. The questions should be answered. Sometimes experiments will need to be done before questions can be answered.

Summarize.   Organize and summarize the information gathered through reading. This is best done in writing. Group relevant facts and summarize answers to each question.

Test.   Go back to the reading selection and check the summary statement for accuracy. Can the generalization or theory identified in the first step be supported through the answers and summaries?

Although similar to SQ3R discussed earlier, Forgan & Mangrum (1985, p. 184) note that the difference between SQ3R and PQRST is "more than semantic" and agree with Fay (1965) that PQRST rather than SQ3R be used in science material.

MODEL LESSON

PQRST. Mr. Hernandez, a fourth-grade teacher, has decided to teach his science class the PQRST study technique. He carefully explains that science textbooks are structured so that a generalization or theory is stated near the beginning of a selection; that the generalization is expanded and supported through the rest of the selection; and that a summary statement of the generalization or theory, along with some supporting details, is usually presented at the end. He has his students look at a section in their science textbooks that demonstrates this structure.

Mr. Hernandez then explains that a technique called PQRST helps readers consciously identify the generalization or theory, as well as become more aware of the supporting details. He reminds his students that they should be active readers who anticipate what might come up in the reading, based on what has come before. He then presents each of the steps in PQRST, demonstrates what a reader might do at each step, and verbally tests a number of students to make sure that they know what should be done at each step.

After reminding his students that they should preview the selection, jotting a note about the generalization or theory, he asks his students to open their books to a specific selection that has not been read before. When done, students are asked what they thought the generalization was. Several students are then asked to refer to their books and supply the reasons for their decision. After this step, students are reminded about the procedure for the next (question) stage, are told to write down questions they might have about the generalizations or theory, as well as what questions might be answered as they read through the selection, and are asked to begin. They do not need to refer to their books at this stage. Questions should relate to the generalization or theory noted in step 1.

When step 2 has been completed, the students are told to keep their questions in mind and to read the selection. They are told to write brief notes as they read that might help answer their questions. Following this, Mr. Hernandez reminds his students about the "summarize" step, and students begin to summarize the information in the selection. They attempt to summarize by grouping relevant facts, and also attempt to specifically answer the questions they posed in step 1 by using, but moving beyond, the brief notes they made while reading.

Mr. Hernandez has chosen to do the final step (test) as a group activity. He leads a discussion about the summaries, allowing five or six students to read theirs while the other students silently compare theirs to those read. As a group, students are asked about the accuracy of the summary statement, as well as about the accuracy of answers to the questions identified in step 2. During this process, students are asked to use the selection as a reference to justify their decisions about accuracy.

Mr. Hernandez reinforces use of PQRST on a continuing basis. He also knows that for some classes, the initial lesson might need to be spread across two class sessions, usually between steps 2 (question) and 3 (read).

Reading in the Language Arts Content Area

In some ways, the reading task in the language arts or English classroom can be the most demanding of all. While the various subject areas do make specific demands on a reader, the language arts reading assignment has the potential of including any and all of the demands and text structures previously discussed. Although we have repeatedly noted that the general reading requirements in language arts revolve around narrative text structures, we have been careful to note that this is especially true in grades one through three. Once students are able to read on their own, they are frequently required to read everything from biographies to historical fiction.

The structure of a mathematics text may appear in the context of a biography of a mathematician, or the structure of a history text may appear in a historically based novel. In language arts reading materials, students must cope with different structures in different genre forms and with concepts such as mood, setting, imagery, characterization, plot, foreshadowing, and other literary techniques. Additionally, each literary selection may incorporate vocabulary ranging throughout other content areas as well as having its own, unique vocabulary demands (the terms listed in the previous sentence, for example, are specific to language arts). Thus a breadth of vocabulary concepts may be encountered in literature, including vocabulary and language structures which may be archaic or reflect unfamiliar dialects or language structures, as in the following passage.

Study strategies and study guides can help students more effectively read their content-area textbooks.

"Say, Tom, let *me* whitewash a little."

Tom considered, was about to consent; but he altered his mind:

"No—no—I reckon it wouldn't hardly do, Ben. You see, Aunt Polly's awful particular about this fence—right here on the street, you know— but if it was the back fence I wouldn't mind and *she* wouldn't. Yes, she's awful particular about this fence; it's got to be done very careful; I reckon there ain't one boy in a thousand, maybe two thousand, that can do it the way it's got to be done."

"No—is that so? Oh come, now—lemme just try. Only just a little— I'd let *you,* if you was me, Tom."

From Mark Twain, *The Adventures of Tom Sawyer.* (New York: Wanderer Books, 1982), p. 25.

The various demands in language arts reading material require that prereading preparation of concepts and a discussion of the textual organization take place before students begin reading. Give particular care to understanding of concepts of literary techniques, as well as to activities that target visual imagery. You may want to review the specific teaching suggestions presented in chapter 7 since they are appropriate to the various genres found in language arts reading requirements.

PERSONAL FRAMEWORKS AND TEACHING EXPOSITORY MATERIALS

Near the beginning of the chapter, you were asked to keep in mind the three explanations of how one reads that have been discussed through-out this book: text based, reader based, and interactive. Here is a list of the various methods discussed as appropriate for use in content-area reading instruction, with space for you to note the explanation which you feel each one exemplifies. Try to specify the explanation under which the respective methods fall.

Method	Explanation
SQ3R	_____
Directed Reading Approach	_____
Marginal Gloss Technique	_____
Advance Organizers	_____
Semantic Mapping	_____
Structured Concept Outlines	_____
SQRQCQ	_____
PQRST	_____

Would it surprise you to find that all of these strategies would form part of a comprehension framework with an interactive explanation for how one reads? An interactive explanation hypothesizes that the reader and text interact to find meaning. Meaning is not thought of as "residing" in either the text or the reader, but is seen as resulting from the interaction between text and reader. Viewed from this perspective, it is clear that each of the strategies requires that the reader bring his or her knowledge to bear on the text, while at the same time using information in the text to comprehend. Recall our statement that a common trait among several of these methods was the expectation that the reader identify main ideas and supporting details. To do this, the reader must have some knowledge about the text, and must also actively bring to bear existing world knowledge about the topic being read.

You should also note that many of the techniques used in content-area reading, as in other reading, require that the reader "monitor" comprehension while reading (Baker & Brown, 1983; Markam, 1981). Such **comprehension monitoring** means that the reader actively attends to the reading content, is aware of key ideas, can separate important information from unimportant, and knows when something has not been properly understood. In essence, all of the techniques discussed in this chapter are an attempt to foster a reader's internal comprehension-monitoring abilities.

comprehension monitoring: The ongoing process of checking one's understanding as one reads.

If you follow the teaching suggestions in this chapter, you will be using techniques based in interactive explanations for how one reads. This is not to say that teachers in content-area classrooms do not have comprehension frameworks involving text-based or reader-based explanations. We have often observed teachers who say that students need to read a content-area selection again and the meaning will become clear, thus implying that meaning resides only in the text. Conversely, we have observed teachers who might be said to "talk around" a subject, rarely referring to the textual material to be read. But it seems valid to say that effective and thus advocated techniques for content-area reading instruction are based on interactive explanations of how one reads.

THE MAJOR POINTS

1. Knowledge of book parts and general research skills helps children's comprehension, and should be a part of reading instruction.
2. Reading teachers and teachers who expect children to read texts within specific subject areas must provide students with reading instruction specifically related to that subject area.
3. The organization of narrative texts, generally used to teach reading, and expository texts that students are most often required to read after third grade, differ greatly. Text organization also differs throughout subject areas.
4. Flexibility in reading rate needs to be taught. Rate largely depends on one's purpose for reading.

5. Some general content-area reading and study skills are available to students, as are specific techniques that can be taught for use within subject areas.
6. Most effective reading and study skill strategies are founded on an interactive explanation for how one reads.

**QUESTIONS
AND
ACTIVITIES**

1. Examine a basal reader at second-, fourth-, and sixth-grade levels. How is the issue of content-area reading addressed in these grade levels? What is the approximate proportion of narrative or literary selections to expository or content-area selections?
2. Find a reading unit in any content-area subject. Construct a directed reading activity for the reading selection. Then, construct a three-level study guide and a set of marginal glosses for the same material.
3. Specify the general differences in organization patterns and reading requirements for social studies, mathematics, science, and language arts.
4. If possible, practice using the SQ3R technique with an elementary school student. If not, practice guiding a classmate through SQ3R or use it yourself in your own reading.
5. How does a map reader differ from a map thinker?
6. Describe the similarities and differences between semantic mapping and structured concept outline.
7. Why are the reading and study strategies described in this chapter said to stem mainly from interactive explanations for how reading takes place?

**FURTHER
READING**

Herber, H. (1978). *Teaching reading in content areas* (2nd Edition). Englewood Cliffs, NJ: Prentice-Hall.

Moore, D. W. & Readence, J. E. (1983). Approaches to content area reading instruction. *Journal of Reading, 26,* 397–402.
    Discusses four approaches, adaptable to primary or secondary grades, for teaching content-area reading.

Moore, D. W.; Readence, J. E.; & Rickelman, R. J. (1982). *Prereading activities for content area reading and learning.* Newark, DE: International Reading Association.
    Describes and provides activities useful for pre- and postcontent-area reading in all grade levels.

Ogle, D. M. (1986). K–W–L: A teaching model that develops active reading of expository text. *The Reading Teacher, 39,* 564–70.
    Presents a procedure that models for students the thought processes involved in reading informational material, and notes how teachers can become more aware of and responsive to students' knowledge and interests in such texts.

Vacca, R. & Vacca, J. (1986). *Content area reading* (2nd Edition). Boston: Little, Brown.
    Both this book and the book by Herber are well-known, readable texts in the area of teaching content reading. Although targeted at secondary grades, most activities can be adapted for elementary school use.

REFERENCES

Baker, L. & Brown, A. C. (1983). Metacognition and the reading process. In P. D. Pearson (ed.). *Handbook of reading research.* New York: Plenum Press.

Cheek, E. J., Jr. & Cheek, M. C. (1983). *Reading instruction through content teaching.* Columbus, OH: C. E. Merrill.

Daines, D. (1982). *Reading in the content areas: Strategies for teachers.* Glenview, IL: Scott, Foresman.

Davis, A. R. (1983). Study skills. In J. E. Alexander (ed.). *Teaching reading* (2nd Edition). Boston: Little, Brown.

Dupuis, M. M. (Ed.). (1984). *Reading in the content areas: Research for teachers.* Newark, DE: International Reading Association.

Farr, R. & Roser, N. (1979). *Teaching a child to read.* New York: Harcourt Brace Jovanovich.

Fay, L. (1965). Reading study skills: Math and Science. In J. A. Figurel (ed.), *Reading and inquiry* (pp. 93–94). Newark, DE: International Reading Association.

Forgan, H. W. & Mangrum II, C. T. (1985). *Teaching content area reading skills* (3rd Edition). Columbus, OH: C. E. Merrill.

Fry, E. (1981). Graphical literacy. *Journal of Reading, 24,* 383–89.

Hanf, M. B. (1971). Mapping: A technique for translating reading into thinking. *Journal of Reading, 13,* 225–30.

Kane, R. B., Byrne, M. A. & Hater, M. A. (1974). *Helping children read mathematics.* New York: American Book Co.

Markham, E. M. (1981). Comprehension monitoring. In *Children's oral communication skills.* New York: Academic Press.

Muhtadi, N. A. (1977). Personal Communication.

O'Mara, D. A. (1981). The process of reading mathematics. *Journal of Reading, 25,* 22–30.

Pauk, W. (1984). The new SQ4R. *Reading World, 23,* 274–75.

Pieroneck, F. T. (1979). Using basal reader guidebooks—the ideal integrated reading lesson plan. *Reading Teacher, 33,* 167–72.

Robinson, F. P. (1961). *Effective Study,* New York: Harper & Row.

Rubin, D. (1983). *Teaching reading and study skills in content areas.* New York: Holt, Rinehart & Winston.

Shepherd, D. L. (1982). *Comprehensive high school reading methods.* Columbus, OH: C. E. Merrill.

Singer, H. & Donlan, D. (1985). *Reading and learning from text.* Boston: Little, Brown.

Spache, G. D. (1963). *Toward better reading.* Champaign, IL: Garrard Press.

Spache, G. D. & Berg, P. C. (1966). *The art of efficient reading.* New York: MacMillan.

Summers, E. G. (1965). Utilizing visual aids in reading materials for effective reading. In H. L. Herber (ed.). *Developing study skills in secondary schools.* Newark, DE: International Reading Association.

Thomas, E. L. & Alexander, H. A. (1982). *Improving reading in every class* (Abridged 3rd Edition.) Boston: Allyn & Bacon.

Tierney, R. J., Readence, J. E.; & Dishner, E. K. (1985). *Reading strategies and practices: A guide for improving instruction* (2nd Edition). Boston: Allyn & Bacon.

Vacca, R. (1981). *Content area reading.* Boston: Little, Brown.

9 Materials

INSTRUCTIONAL MATERIALS ■ BASAL READING
SERIES ■ SUPPLEMENTAL MATERIALS FOR SPECIFIC SKILL
AREAS ■ MATERIALS WITH MODIFIED ORTHOGRAPHIES ■ TRADE
BOOKS AND INDIVIDUALIZED READING ■ SELECTING AND ADAPTING
MATERIALS

"I don't know, Mrs. Sanchez. First I have to read the story in my reading book. Then I have to do my workbook. Then I have to finish my Bonus Book. And then I have to finish those two ditto pages from yesterday. Who makes up all of these things anyway? They sure must never get to go out to recess."

(Overheard in a first grade classroom.)

By now you have developed an understanding of the knowledge sources required for effective reading comprehension and the methods used to develop each source. In addition, you are continuing to develop a clear sense of how one reads and how reading ability develops. This chapter will help you select and adapt a variety of materials to your framework of reading comprehension. You will see that decisions about materials are often influenced by the type of comprehension framework you have. Each set of instructional materials reflects a specific set of assumptions about how one reads and how reading ability develops. It is important that you be able to identify the assumptions inherent in any set of instructional materials. Knowing the assumptions behind a set of instructional materials will enable you to select materials that are more consistent with your framework or to modify materials to more closely fit your framework.

After reading this chapter you will be able to

1. explain what a basal reading program is and what the advantages and disadvantages are of using such a program;
2. discuss how different basal reading programs are alike and different;
3. identify several types of additional instructional materials and explain how each might be used to teach reading;
4. discuss how you might make modifications to a basal reading program that is inconsistent with your comprehension framework.

INSTRUCTIONAL MATERIALS

There are two major decisions you must make about the materials you will use to teach reading comprehension. First, you must decide which materials to use in your classroom. Second, you must decide how to use the materials which you have chosen. Each decision is influenced by the type of comprehension framework you have.

When you begin teaching, it is likely that the first decision will have already been made for you. Many school districts adopt a single reading program (or perhaps two or three reading programs), which all teachers are expected to use. This makes instruction more consistent as children move up through the grade levels. Often, however, groups of teachers are actively involved whenever a district adopts a new reading program, a decision that takes place about every five to seven years. Thus, if you remain in the same district for a period of time, you may participate in deciding which of several available reading programs your district will use.

Even if the first decision has been made for you when you first begin teaching, you must still decide how you will actually use the available instructional materials to teach reading comprehension. This decision (actually it is a number of separate decisions made each day) requires a clear understanding of your own particular comprehension framework, of the comprehension framework your materials reflect, and of the ways in which you can adapt a set of materials to be more consistent with your own framework. Since we assume that you have already identified your own framework of reading comprehension, your tasks in this chapter are to become familiar with the materials used to teach reading comprehension; to understand how each set of materials reflects the assumptions of a particular comprehension framework; and to understand how to modify instructional materials to be more consistent with your own framework of reading comprehension. There are several major categories of materials used to teach reading in the elementary grades: basal reading series; supplemental materials in specific skill areas; materials with modified orthographies; and trade books.

BASAL READING SERIES

Basal reading series (basal reading programs or basal readers) are published, comprehensive, graded sets of materials used to teach reading in grades kindergarten through six or eight. They are developed by one of several large publishing houses, usually under the direction of a senior author who is a respected figure in reading education. Basal reading series are typically referred to by the publisher's name: Scott, Foresman; Houghton Mifflin; Harcourt Brace Jovanovich; Ginn; Harper & Row; Economy; and so on. Typically, basal reading series update their publication dates every few years. A major revision in any series usually occurs every five to six years, coinciding with state adoptions in the two largest states that review basals for their schools: Texas and California. Basal reading programs often found in elementary schools are produced by the following publishers:

basal reading series: A published, comprehensive, graded set of materials used to teach reading comprehension in grades K–6 or K–8.

- Allyn & Bacon
- American Book Company
- Economy Book Company
- Ginn and Company
- Harcourt Brace Jovanovich
- Harper & Row–*Reading Basics Plus*
- Harper & Row–*Lippincott Basic Reading Series*
- D. C. Heath & Co.
- Holt, Rinehart and Winston
- Houghton Mifflin
- Macmillan
- Merrill Publishing Co.
- Open Court Publishing Co.
- Riverside Publishing Co.
- Scott, Foresman

Components

Often, it is mistakenly thought that a basal reading program contains all materials necessary to teach reading comprehension in the elementary grades. This assumption is not surprising when one considers the comprehensive array of materials available in most basal programs. Typically, the components of a basal program include the following:

- *Teacher's manual.* The teacher's manual contains an extensive and precise set of lesson plans for teachers. The manual almost always includes copies of the pages in the students' book along with discussion questions and correct answers to assist the teacher.
- *Student's book.* Students usually receive their own texts containing the stories, articles, and other selections used in the program. Several graded books are often used in each of the primary grades (one through three). A single book usually is used in each of the intermediate grades (four through six).
- *Student workbook.* Students also receive their own workbook containing practice activities for skills taught in the program.
- *Teacher's edition of the workbook.* This is usually an exact copy of the student workbook with additional directions and correct answers included.

Basal reading programs, including student books, teacher's manuals, and student workbooks are the most common instructional materials found in elementary classrooms.

- *Tests.* Several types of assessment instruments are often available including placement tests for making entry-level decisions at the beginning of the year; mastery tests for assessing each student's mastery of specific skills; section tests to assess each student's grasp of the major skills taught in a unit; and end-of-book tests to assess each student's grasp of the major skills taught in a book.
- *Duplicating and copying masters.* Additional skill practice is usually provided with duplicating and copying masters. Duplicating masters contain skill practice identical to that in students' workbooks but with different content.
- *Picture and word cards.* Picture and word cards are often used to teach decoding and vocabulary knowledge in the primary grades.
- *Pocket charts.* Pocket charts are often included to hold and display picture and word cards.
- *Additional supplementary materials.* Often programs make additional materials available such as read-along audio tapes, activity kits, language skills kits, reading filmstrips, and other ancillary materials.

Despite the comprehensive nature of materials available in any single basal reading series, there are several reasons one is likely to supplement a basal program: to be more consistent with one's framework; to meet the unique needs of students; to introduce variety into the program and raise students' interest levels; to bring real-world reading tasks into the classroom; and to include successful instructional activities that are not included in the basal series. Exactly how to adjust a basal program to classroom needs is covered in the final section of this chapter.

Organization

Levels. Basal reading series are organized according to graded levels of difficulty. It is assumed that instruction will take place at the level of difficulty most appropriate for any individual student. Traditionally, publishers have designated difficulty levels by grade. In kindergarten, children traditionally receive the readiness materials of a program. In first grade, students traditionally receive five levels of materials: three **preprimers** (PP); a **primer** (P); and a **first reader** (1). In both the second and third grades, students traditionally receive two levels of materials: a **first semester reader** (2–1 and 3–1) and a **second semester reader** (2–2 and 3–2). In grades four through eight, students traditionally receive a single level of materials: a fourth- (4), fifth- (5), sixth- (6), seventh- (7), or eighth- (8) grade reader. Recently, publishers have begun to replace grade-level designations with systems based on sequentially ordered numbers (1, 2, 3, 4, 5, 6, 7, 8) or sequentially ordered letters (A, B, C, D, E, F, G, H). Both the traditional and the more contemporary labeling systems for basal readers can be seen in figure 9–1. Most basal series

preprimers: Transition books between readiness materials and the first primer in a basal reading series.

primer: Usually the first hard-cover book with stories that students encounter in a basal program.

first reader: The book average students traditionally receive in a basal reading program during the second semester of the first grade.

first-semester reader: The book average students traditionally receive in a basal reading program during the first semester of either second (2–1) or third (3–1) grade.

second-semester reader: The book average students traditionally receive in a basal reading program during the second semester of either second (2–2) or third (3–2) grade.

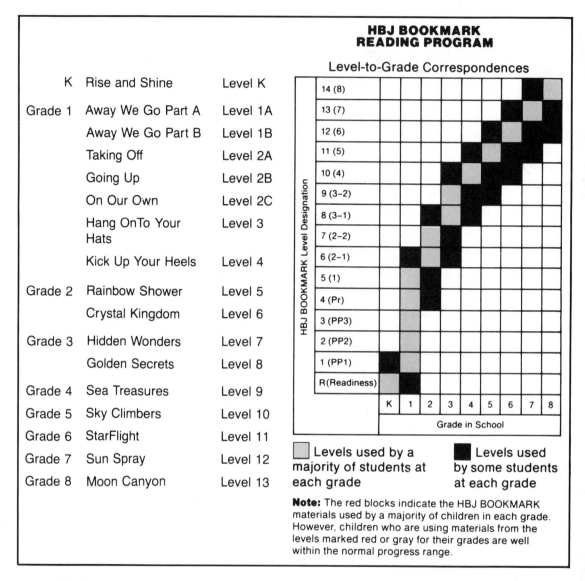

	K	Rise and Shine	Level K
Grade 1		Away We Go Part A	Level 1A
		Away We Go Part B	Level 1B
		Taking Off	Level 2A
		Going Up	Level 2B
		On Our Own	Level 2C
		Hang OnTo Your Hats	Level 3
		Kick Up Your Heels	Level 4
Grade 2		Rainbow Shower	Level 5
		Crystal Kingdom	Level 6
Grade 3		Hidden Wonders	Level 7
		Golden Secrets	Level 8
Grade 4		Sea Treasures	Level 9
Grade 5		Sky Climbers	Level 10
Grade 6		StarFlight	Level 11
Grade 7		Sun Spray	Level 12
Grade 8		Moon Canyon	Level 13

HBJ BOOKMARK READING PROGRAM

Level-to-Grade Correspondences

Levels used by a majority of students at each grade

Levels used by some students at each grade

Note: The red blocks indicate the HBJ BOOKMARK materials used by a majority of children in each grade. However, children who are using materials from the levels marked red or gray for their grades are well within the normal progress range.

FIGURE 9–1
Two examples of grade level equivalency tables

scope: The range of skills taught in any one basal reading series.
sequence: The order of introduction of reading skills in any basal reading series.

provide this information somewhere at the beginning of each teacher's manual.

Skills. All basal programs teach a fixed set of reading skills in a particular sequence. The range of skills taught in any one program is the **scope** of reading skill development. The order of introduction is the **sequence** of reading skill development. All basal programs share certain

similarities in their scopes and sequences of reading skills. All, for example, teach decoding skills early in the program and strictly order the
skills that are taught. Nevertheless, no two programs teach an identical
set of skills in the same order. An example of a portion of a scope and
sequence chart is shown in figure 9–2.

Analyze the scope and sequence charts of several basal reading series to observe the similarities or differences of their scopes and sequences of reading
skills. Scope and sequence charts are usually found at the beginning of the
teacher's manual for any level. Occasionally, they are found at the back of a
teacher's manual. Look first to see if the major skill categories are identical:
decoding (often called word identification or word recognition); vocabulary;
study skills; comprehension; literary understanding; and so on. Then compare
closely the specific skills listed within a common skill category such as decoding, study skills, or comprehension. Are the major skill categories identical? Are
the specific skills within a common skill category the same? Is the sequencing
of common skills the same? What skill consistencies do you find between the
two basal programs? What inconsistencies do you find?

**A POINT
TO PONDER**

The sequencing of a specific set of skills facilitates instruction but
it also has certain consequences for children learning to read. The most
important consequence for you to consider is the limited language that
exists at the beginning levels of any reading program. At beginning levels, the words in basal selections are often limited to previously introduced sight words or words following previously introduced phonic generalizations. The result is a series of reading selections that differ in
substantial ways from the language children are accustomed to hearing
in oral language contexts. Often this has an effect opposite from the one
intended by publishers: comprehension is actually more difficult for
young readers, rather than easier, *because* a sequenced set of skills was
incorporated into the reading program (Beck, Omanson & McKeown,
1982).

Consider, for example, the following sentences from a first-grade
reader:

> It is night. A man is very sick. The man comes here in a fast car (*Sun and
> Shadow,* Harcourt Brace Jovanovich, 1983, p. 28).

In this passage, the writers have chosen to use the word *here* for *hospital*
and the words *a fast car* for *ambulance.* These decisions were undoubtedly made because children had not yet been taught to recognize the
words *hospital* or *ambulance,* but had been taught the words *here* and *a
fast car.* As a result, children must infer the real meanings of these
seemingly easier words; a task that can make the comprehension of this
passage more difficult. The problems created by a fixed sequence of

Program Scope and Sequence

	K	1	2	3	4	5	6	7	8	9	10	11	12	13
Level	K	1	2	3	4	5	6	7	8	9	10	11	12	13
Grade	K	R	PP	P	1	2^1	2^2	3^1	3^2	4	5	6	7	8
READINESS SKILLS														
Discriminates auditorily (*See also* WORD IDENTIFICATION, Uses Phonics)	★	ᵀ△	□	□	□	□	□	□	□	□	□	□	□	□
Discriminates visually	★	ᵀ△	□	□	□	□	□	□	□	□	□	□	□	□
Increases concepts and vocabulary (*See* LANGUAGE SKILLS, Develops vocabulary)														
Uses language skills (*See* LANGUAGE SKILLS)														
Follows oral directions	★	△	△	□	□	□	□	□	□	□	□	□	□	□
Marks responses	★	△	□	□	□	□	□	□	□	□	□	□	□	□
Recognizes small and capital letters	★	ᵀ△	□	□	□	□	□	□	□	□	□	□	□	□
Uses left-to-right, top-to-bottom progression	★	△	□	□	□	□	□	□	□	□	□	□	□	□
Uses numbered items	★	△	□	□	□	□	□	□	□	□	□	□	□	□
WORD IDENTIFICATION														
Uses Context														
Pictures	○	★	△	△	△	□	□	□	□	□	□	□	□	□
Meaning and syntax	○	★	△	△	ᵀ△	ᵀ△	ᵀ△	ᵀ△	△	ᵀ△	ᵀ△	ᵀ△	ᵀ△	ᵀ△
Uses Phonics														
Consonants														
Initial	★	ᵀ△	ᵀ△	ᵀ△	ᵀ△	ᵀ△	ᵀ△	ᵀ△	△	ᵀ△	ᵀ△	ᵀ△	ᵀ△	ᵀ△
Auditory discrimination	★	△	□	□	□	□	□	□	□	□	□	□	□	□
Letter/sound relationships	○	ᵀ★	ᵀ△	ᵀ△	△	△	ᵀ△	△	△	□	□	□	□	□
b, c/k/,d,f,g,h,k,l,m,n,p,r,s,t		ᵀ★	ᵀ△	△	△	△	△	△	△	□	□	□	□	□
j,qu,v,w,y,z			ᵀ★	△	△	△	△	△	△	□	□	□	□	□
c/s/,g/j/			ᵀ★	ᵀ△	△	△	△	△	△	□	□	□	□	□
kn, wr								ᵀ★	△	△	□	□	□	□
Final		ᵀ★	ᵀ△	ᵀ△	ᵀ△	ᵀ△	ᵀ△	△	ᵀ△	ᵀ△	ᵀ△	ᵀ△	△	△
Auditory discrimination		★	□	□	□	□	□	□	□	□	□	□	□	□
Letter/sound relationships		ᵀ★	ᵀ△	ᵀ△	△	ᵀ△	△	△	□	□	□	□	□	□
b,g,k,l,n,p,s,t				★	△	△	△	△	△	□	□	□	□	□
d,m,r,x			ᵀ★	ᵀ△	△	△	△	△	△	□	□	□	□	□
ck			ᵀ★	ᵀ△	△	△	△	△	△	□	□	□	□	□

FIGURE 9-2

An example of a scope and sequence chart

reading skills, as well as the instructional advantages, must be considered while you teach reading and observe young children's behavior. In this case, you would want to check children's comprehension of the real meaning behind the words in this passage.

Teacher's Manuals. In addition to becoming familiar with the organization of skills, it is also important for you to become familiar with the organization of teacher's manuals used in basal reading programs. While the organization of teacher's manuals is not identical in all reading series, there are several structural characteristics that are commonly found. Knowing the structure of teacher's manuals will assist you as you read and interpret the manuals you encounter. Generally, there are three sections to the teacher's manual for any basal series: an introduction; teaching plans for each selection; and appendices.

The first section of most manuals provides the teacher with an introduction to the reading series. The authors and their consultants often are listed to provide you with a sense of the expertise which went into the program's development. A grade-level equivalency chart such as those depicted in figure 9–1 usually is provided to help you put each book into a developmental perspective. Frequently, the publisher includes a scope and sequence chart in the first section specifying the skills developed in the program and indicating when each skill is taught. Some programs only provide you with a list of the general categories of skills and do not indicate when each is taught. The complete range of materials used in each program also is listed in the introductory section: student books; student workbooks; teacher's manuals; duplicating and copying masters; test packets; and ancillary materials. Finally, the introductory section contains an overview which states the general goals of the program; the framework or philosophy behind the program; the structure of the teaching plans; and pacing suggestions for proceeding through the materials.

The second section of most teacher's manuals contains the lesson-by-lesson teaching plans that guide the instruction. Within each series, the teaching plans follow a consistent organizational pattern.

I. Overview
   A. New vocabulary
   B. Skill objectives
   C. Resource materials
   D. Summary of the selection

II. Preparation
   A. Vocabulary development
   B. Purpose setting
   C. Motivation

III. Guided reading
   A. Reading the selection (silently and then, sometimes, orally)
   B. Discussion
IV. Skill development and practice
V. Follow-up activities
   A. Review
   B. Enrichment

overview: The first section of most teaching plans in the teacher's manual of a basal reading series.

The first portion of most teaching plans contains an **overview** for the teacher, typically including a list of new vocabulary words; a list of skill objectives; a list of necessary resource materials; and a summary of the story. This information is helpful for planning decisions teachers must make as they prepare to teach the lesson. Figure 9–3 contains a sample lesson plan. Notice how the first two pages (pp. 432–33) contains the overview. Also notice that the story summary is not located on these first two pages. In this program the story summary is always located at the beginning of the next page (see p. 434).

preparation section: The second section of most teaching plans in the teacher's manual of a basal reading series. Designed to prepare students for reading the selection.

The second portion of most teaching plans often consists of activities designed to prepare students for reading the selection. During this **preparation section,** any new vocabulary words that need to be taught for either decoding or word-meaning purposes are specified. Suggestions for presenting the new words are usually given. Sometimes specific reading skills may also be taught or reviewed. These skills (using letter sounds and context, sequencing, cause-and-effect relationships, and so on) are usually directly related to some aspect of the reading selection. In addition, a motivating discussion will usually take place and the teacher will provide several purpose-setting questions or statements. Sometimes students simply are told what the next selection will be about. In figure 9–3, most of this information is contained on pages 434–35 in the section labeled Preparation. Note, however, that purpose setting takes place in the following section in conjunction with silent reading.

guided reading: The third section of most teaching plans in the teacher's manual of a basal reading series. Designed to assist the students in reading silently and then (sometimes) orally.

skill development and practice: The fourth section of most teaching plans in the teacher's manual of a basal reading series. Designed to teach and allow students to practice previously taught skills.

The third section of most teaching plans consists of suggestions for how to conduct a **guided reading** of the passage. Directions are provided for having students read the passage silently and then, sometimes, orally. In addition, discussion questions and possible answers are given. Seldom, however, are directions provided indicating what to do to help students who failed to comprehend portions of the selection (Durkin, 1981). The lesson in figure 9–3 models fairly closely the characteristics of most guided-reading sections on pages 436–41.

Following the guided reading, many basal lessons contain suggestions for developing and practicing specific reading skills. In the lesson example, a **skill development** section is missing since this is the last lesson at the first grade level. The **skill practice** section in most basal lessons includes workbook and other activities designed to practice

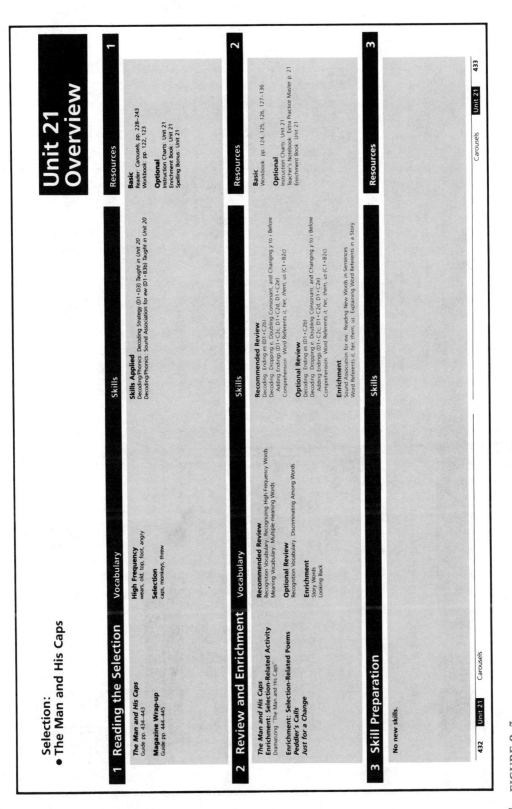

Selection:
• The Man and His Caps

Unit 21 Overview

1 Reading the Selection

Vocabulary

High Frequency
wears, old, top, foot, angry

Selection
caps, monkeys, threw

Skills

Skills Applied
Decoding/Phonics: Decoding Strategy (D1•D3) *Taught in Unit 20*
Decoding/Phonics: Sound Association for *ew* (D1•B3b) *Taught in Unit 20*

Resources **1**

Basic
Reader: Carousels, pp. 228–243
Workbook: pp. 122, 123

Optional
Instruction Charts: Unit 21
Enrichment Book: Unit 21
Spelling Bonus: Unit 21

The Man and His Caps
Guide pp. 434–443

Magazine Wrap-up
Guide pp. 444–445

2 Review and Enrichment

Vocabulary

Recommended Review
Recognition Vocabulary: Recognizing High-Frequency Words
Meaning Vocabulary: Multiple-meaning Words

Optional Review
Recognition Vocabulary: Discriminating Among Words

Enrichment
Story Words
Looking Back

Skills

Recommended Review
Decoding: Ending *es* (D1•C2b)
Decoding: Dropping *e*, Doubling Consonant, and Changing *y* to *i*; Before
  Adding Endings (D1•C2c, D1•C2d, D1•C2e)
Comprehension: Word Referents *it, her, them, us* (C1•B2c)

Optional Review
Decoding: Ending *es* (D1•C2b)
Decoding: Dropping *e*, Doubling Consonant, and Changing *y* to *i*; Before
  Adding Endings (D1•C2c, D1•C2d, D1•C2e)
Comprehension: Word Referents *it, her, them, us* (C1•B2c)

Enrichment
Sound Association for *ew*: Reading New Words in Sentences
Word Referents *it, her, them, us*: Explaining Word Referents in a Story

Resources **2**

Basic
Workbook: pp. 124, 125, 126, 127–136

Optional
Instruction Charts: Unit 21
Teacher's Notebook: Extra Practice Master p. 21
Enrichment Book: Unit 21

The Man and His Caps
Enrichment: Selection-Related Activity
Dramatizing "The Man and His Caps"
Enrichment: Selection-Related Poems
Peddler's Calls
Just for a Change

3 Skill Preparation

Vocabulary

Skills

Resources **3**

No new skills.

FIGURE 9–3
An example of a lesson plan from a basal reader

1 Reading the Selection

The Man and His Caps

pages 228–239

Summary

"The Man and His Caps" is the Medallion Selection in *Carousels*. Medallion Selections are those stories in Houghton Mifflin Reading which have been chosen for their popularity with children and teachers and for their literary merit.

This is the folktale of the peddler who carries a stack of many colored caps on his head. One day, when the man has had no luck selling the caps, he decides to nap beneath a tree. When the man wakes up, he discovers that all he has is his own cap! Bewildered at first, the man finally looks up into the tree. There in the tree are monkeys, and each one is wearing one of the missing caps. The man shouts and gestures at the monkeys but to no avail for the monkeys only mimic him. Finally the man throws down his cap in disgust, and that solves his dilemma. To his relief the monkeys mimic him once again and they all throw down his caps!

You may wish to include this selection in a unit on folktales.

Preparation

Vocabulary/Concept Development

Tell children that they are going to read a story about a man who sells caps. Explain that before they begin reading the story, they are going to read some words that may be new to them.

Skill Reminder

Decoding/Phonics: **Using Letter Sounds and Context** (D1 · D3)
Decoding/Phonics: **Sound Association for ew** (D1 · B3b)

Tell children that as they try to figure out the new words in the following sentences, they should re-

---

member what they know about reading new words. Review with children the steps for decoding new words:

1. Think about the sense of the words you can read.
2. Think about the sounds for the letters in the new word.
3. Think about what makes sense in the sentence.

Recall with children that recently they learned the sound for the letters *ew*. Remind them that they know that when the letters *ew* come together in a word, they usually stand for the sound they hear at the end of *grew*.

Note

All the words in this vocabulary section are Skill Applications of the skill Using Letter Sounds and Context. The word *threw* is also an application of the skill Sound Association for *ew*.

Display the following sentences, underlining the word *threw*.

Display *Jay wanted the ball.*
I threw it to him.

1. Tell children that the letters *thr* together stand for the sounds they hear at the beginning of the word *three*.
2. Have children read the sentences silently, using the sounds for letters and the sense of the other words to help them figure out the underlined word.
3. Have the sentences read aloud.
4. Use the word *throat* to check the use of context clues.
5. Use the word *tossed* to check the use of phonic clues.

Display *Mom has a special hat.*
She wears it at ball games.

Say waves *(wrong middle sounds)*
worse *(no sense)*

Display *Lee and Max were going out.*
They both put on coats and caps.

Say cups *(no sense)*
scarves *(wrong beginning and middle sounds)*

Display *Animals have many kinds of homes.*
Some monkeys live in trees.

Say chimps *(wrong beginning and middle sounds)*
Mondays *(no sense)*

Display *Don't walk on that grasshopper!*
Don't put your foot on it!

Say fit *(no sense)*
heel *(wrong sounds)*

Display *Dad is getting a new coat.*
This one is too old.

Say small *(wrong sounds)*
oil *(no sense)*

Display *Please put the book away.*
Put it in the top row of the bookcase.

Say tape *(no sense)*
bottom *(wrong sounds)*

Display *John broke his brother's new game.*
That made his brother very angry.

Say enjoy *(no sense)*
upset *(wrong sounds)*

Remind children that they are going to read about a man who sells caps. If necessary, explain to them that a cap is a kind of hat. Tell children that if they open their books to **Reader** page 229 they will see the man and the kinds of caps that he has for sale. Ask children if they think it's strange that the man carries all the caps on his head instead of in a bag or a basket. Tell children that sometimes people carry things on their heads. If anyone has ever seen people doing that either in person, on television, or in books or magazines, have them tell about what they saw. Then ask children to tell how many caps the man has and to tell what colors they are.

Have children read the title silently. Call on one child to read it aloud. Then point out that there is no author name. Instead there are the words "a folktale." Explain to children that a folktale is a story that people have been telling for many years. It is such an old story that no one knows who was the first person who ever told it. (Literary Skill Readiness)

Direct children's attention to page 228 and tell them that this page tells about the story. "The Man and His Caps." Point out the gold stamp and ask children what they think it is. Tell them that the gold stamp is a medallion and that a medallion is an award or prize. Explain that it is there to show them that "The Man and His Caps" is the Medallion Selection in *Carousels*. Point out the words "Medallion Selection." Explain that "The Man and His Caps" was chosen to be the Medallion Selection because it is an especially good story that people have enjoyed hearing and reading for a very long time.

FIGURE 9–3 *continued*

Page 231 / Page 230

Once there was a man who had many caps for sale.
He had the caps on his head.

First he had on his old brown cap.
On top of the brown cap, he had orange caps.
On top of the orange caps, he had blue caps.
On top of the blue caps, he had yellow caps.
And on the very top, he had red caps.

Every day the man would walk up one street and down another.
He would call, "Caps for sale! Caps for sale!"

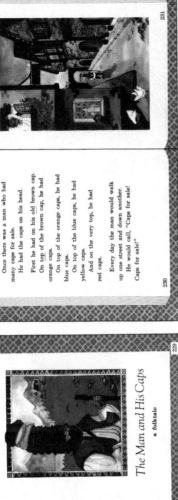

The Man and His Caps
a folktale

pictures by Jane Dyer

This is a story about a man who has caps for sale.
He has many caps, and he wears them all on his head.
One day all but one of the man's caps are missing.
Find out if he gets back his caps.

The Man and His Caps
a folktale

Reading

Pages 228–229: Purpose Setting for *The Man and His Caps*

Direct children to the material printed on the left-hand side of page 228. Have them notice that the title "The Man and His Caps" and the words "a folktale" appear again. In addition they can see the words "pictures by Jane Dyer." Explain that Jane Dyer is the person who drew all the pictures that they will see in the story.

Tell children that the rest of the sentences tell what "The Man and His Caps" is about. Ask them to read the sentences silently. When children have finished reading, ask a volunteer to read all the sentences aloud. Ask children what they think could have happened to all the caps. Encourage divergent thinking. Then tell children that as they read they'll find out if any of them were right and if the man will be able to get back his caps.

Pages 230–233 Purpose Setting/Silent Reading

Find the man with his caps on page 231. . . . What do you think he is doing? . . . (coming into town to sell his caps; accept any reasonable answer) What is the man doing on page 232? . . . (sitting by a tree) Has he sold all his caps? . . . Then why do you suppose he's sitting down instead of trying to sell the caps? . . . (Accept any reasonable answer.)

Does the man still have all his caps on page 233?

Read pages 230, 232, and 233 silently and find out what the man does when he discovers that his caps are missing. If you come to a word that you don't know, read to the end of the sentence and use the other words to help you think of a word that makes sense and has the right sounds.

Checking and Developing Comprehension

What did the man do when he woke up and found his caps were missing?

Page 230

In what order did the man wear the caps? . . . Who will read aloud all the sentences that tell that order?

Which cap do you think the man didn't want to sell? Why? . . . (probably the brown one because it was old and so was probably his own cap)

What did the man call as he walked up and down the streets trying to sell his caps?

FIGURE 9–3 continued

One day no one wanted a cap,
not even a red one.

"Well," thought the man,
"I may as well get some sleep."

So he walked off and found
a big tree to sleep under.

The man made sure all his caps
were in place, then he went to sleep.

232

When the man got up,
he put up his hand to see if his caps
were all in place.

All he had was his old brown cap!

He looked in front of him.
No caps.
He looked to the right of him.
No caps.
He looked to the left of him.
No caps.
He looked all around the tree.
No caps.

233

The man looked up in the tree.
There he saw monkeys, and
each monkey had a cap on its head!

234

"You monkeys, you!" the man
shouted, shaking his right hand.
"You give me back my caps."

The monkeys only shook
their hands back at him
and shouted, "Tsk! Tsk! Tsk!"

235

Page 232

Why did the man decide to sleep under the tree?

What did he do before he went to sleep?

Page 233

What did the man do as soon as he woke up from his nap?

Remember that before you started reading the story, you made some suggestions about what might have happened to the caps. Turn the page and see if you were right.

Pages 234–237
Purpose Setting/Silent Reading

Look at page 234. What happened to the caps?

Direct children's attention to the word tsk on page 235. Tell children that "Tsk!" is a way of using letters to stand for the sounds that monkeys make. Ask children how they think that sound should be said. If necessary, model the sound for them.

Now read silently pages 234, 235, 236, and 237 to see how the man tries to get his caps back from the monkeys.

Checking and Developing Comprehension

The man did four things to try to get back his caps. Let's see if you can tell what he did in the order in which he did them. Working with the entire group, establish that the man first shook his right hand at the monkeys, then his left hand. Next he stamped first his right foot, and then his left foot.

Each time he did these things he shouted at the monkeys, telling them to give him back his caps.

What did the monkeys do each time the man did one of these things? . . . (They just copied what he did.) Explain to children that some monkeys will copy what people do. Tell them that another word for copy is imitate.

Page 234

Where did the monkeys put the caps? . . . Why do you think they put them on their heads instead of just playing with them or doing something else with them? . . . (probably they saw the man wearing his cap and they were imitating him)

Page 235

Who will read aloud the sentence that tells what the monkeys did when the man shouted and shook his hand at them?

FIGURE 9–3 *continued*

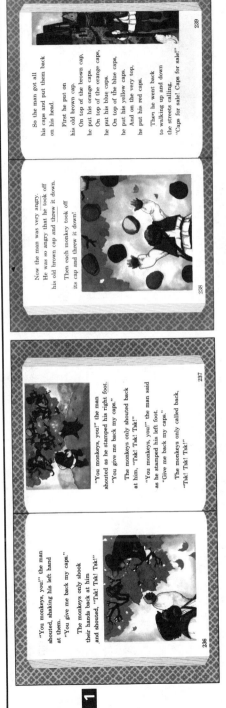

"You monkeys, you!" the man shouted, shaking his left hand at them.

"You give me back my caps."

The monkeys only shook their hands back at him and shouted, "Tsk! Tsk! Tsk!"

237

"You monkeys, you!" the man shouted as he stamped his right foot.

"You give me back my caps."

The monkeys only shouted back at him, "Tsk! Tsk!"

"You monkeys, you!" the man said as he stamped his left foot.

"Give me back my caps."

The monkeys only called back,

"Tsk! Tsk!"

238

Now the man was very angry.
He was so angry that he took off his old brown cap and threw it down.

Then each monkey took off its cap and threw it down!

239

So the man got all his caps and put them back on his head.

First he put on his old brown cap.
On top of the brown cap, he put his orange caps.
On top of the orange caps, he put his blue caps.
On top of the blue caps, he put his yellow caps.
And on the very top, he put his red caps.

Then he went back to walking up and down the streets calling.

"Caps for sale! Caps for sale!"

Page 236

On this page the monkeys shook their hands at the man again. How do you suppose the man was beginning to feel? . . . *(angry; accept any reasonable answer)*

Page 237

Why do you think the man stopped shaking his hands at the monkeys and stamped his feet instead? . . . *(shaking his hands hadn't helped him get his caps; he was getting angrier; accept any reasonable answer)*

Pages 238-239
Purpose Setting/Silent Reading

Finish the story now by reading silently pages 238 and 239. Find out whether or not the man can get back his caps.

Checking and Developing Comprehension

Did the man get back his caps? . . . How?

Page 238

Who will read aloud the sentences that tell why the man threw his brown cap on the ground?

How do you think the man felt when the monkeys imitated him and threw down all the caps? . . . *(surprised, happy, accept any reasonable answer)*

Page 239

What did the man do when he got back his caps? . . . Did he put them in any special order? . . . Who will read aloud the sentences that tell what that order was? . . . That's the same order that he had the caps on in the picture on the first page. Why do you suppose he always puts them that way? . . . *(Accept any reasonable answer.)*

FIGURE 9–3 *continued*

Left panel (page 240 / 442)

Thinking It Over

Comprehension Questions

1. How did the man get back his caps? Why do you think that the monkeys threw down the caps?
2. How do you think the man felt when he found that his caps were missing?
3. What do you think the man will do the next time he decides to sleep under a tree?

240

Oral Reading

Children may enjoy performing this story as a play. Assign children to the parts of the man and the monkeys. Because the story is largely narration, you may wish to choose several children to be the storyteller. Encourage those children playing the parts of the man and the monkeys to perform the actions stated in the story, and also encourage the person playing the man to read the words in a way that shows his growing anger and frustration.

Thinking It Over

Comprehension
Page 240

Comprehension Questions: Text

Ask children to read silently the three questions on page 240 in their reader. Then call on children in turn to read aloud and answer each question.

442　Unit 21　Carousels (228–243)

Middle panel (page 241)

Word Watch

These words name animals.

monkey　goat　goose
owl　mouse

Write some sentences about one of these animals.

Then draw a picture of the animal.

Take a Cap

The man had many, many caps. Make believe that you could wear one of them.

Draw a picture of yourself wearing the cap.

241

1. **Purpose How did the man get back his caps?** *(He threw his brown cap on the ground and that made the monkeys throw down their caps.)* **Why do you think the monkeys threw down the caps?** *(They were imitating the man.)* **Page 238**
   — Literal: noting important details
   — Interpretive: drawing conclusions

2. **How do you think the man felt when he found that his caps were missing?** *(surprised, confused; accept any reasonable answer)* **Page 234**
   — Interpretive: drawing conclusions

3. **What do you think the man will do the next time he decides to sleep under a tree?**
   — Evaluative: thinking creatively

Additional Questions

1. **Why do you suppose the man didn't go home to sleep instead of sleeping under the tree?**
   — Evaluative: thinking creatively

Right panel (top)

Have the remaining two sentences read silently, then aloud. Tell children that they may write some of the things that were already mentioned about each animal or they may write something new. Tell children that they should write their sentences first, then draw their animal. With some groups you may wish to have children write and draw about more than one animal. When children have finished, allow time for them to read aloud their sentences and share their drawings.

Take a Cap
Page 241

Have children read silently the title and the sentences below it. Then have a volunteer read everything aloud. When children have finished drawing, you may wish to allow time for them to show their pictures.

Workbook
page 122 Vocabulary Reinforcement
page 123 Story Comprehension

2. **In the story "Nate the Great and the Lost Stamp," Nate had to get a lost stamp back for Claude. Was the way the man got his caps back the same as or different from the way Nate got the stamp back?** *(different)* **Explain how each of them solved his problem.** *(Nate worked hard to figure out where the stamp was. The man got his caps back because he was lucky.)* **Pages 106–130; 228–241**
   — Interpretive: making comparisons

Word Watch (Vocabulary)
Page 241

Have children read silently the first sentence and the words below it. Then have one child read them aloud. Say each animal name again and call on individual children to tell one thing about the animal.

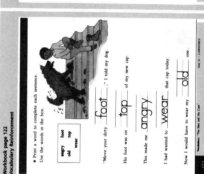

Workbook page 122
Vocabulary Reinforcement

• Print a word to complete each sentence. Use the words in the box.

[angry　foot　old　top　wear]

"Move your dirty **foot** ..." "I told my dog.

His foot was on **top** of my new cap.

This made me **angry**.

I had wanted to **wear** that cap today.

Now I would have to wear my **old** one.

122　Vocabulary: "The Man and His Cap"

Workbook page 123
Story Comprehension

• Think about "The Man and His Caps."
Read each question.
Print the answer.
The page number tells where to find it.

1. Who took all but one of the caps? (page 234)
some monkeys

2. What did the monkeys do when the man shouted at them? (page 235, 236 or 237)
they shouted back

3. What did the monkeys do when the man threw down his brown cap? (page 238)
They threw down their caps.

123　Comprehension: "The Man and His Caps"　Unit 21 · CAROUSELS

Carousels (228–243)　Unit 21　443

FIGURE 9–3 *continued*

Student page 242

Magazine Wrap-up

Looking Back

1. Mary Jo, Clyde, and Grady each had a family.
Tell about each family.

2. Mary Jo, Clyde, Grady, and the man who had caps all had problems.
Who worked out their problems without help from anyone?
Who got help from others?

Student page 243

Writing a Note

Write the name of the one you liked most in this part of the book
Write a note to that someone

Books to Enjoy

Follow Me by Mordicai Gerstein
See what happens when some ducks get lost on their way home

Curious George Flies a Kite
by Margaret Rey
Here's a funny story about a monkey who tries to fly a kite and to fish

Molly and the Slow Teeth by Pat Ross
Molly is waiting for her first tooth to come out
Find out what happens to her

243

Teacher page 444

Magazine Wrap-up
pages 242–243

Looking Back

Ask children to read silently the two questions on page 242 in their reader. Then call on children in turn to read aloud and answer each question.

1.   Mary Jo, Clyde, and Grady each had a family. Name the ones in each family. *(Mary Jo: father, mother, sister, brother; Clyde: mother, father, Grady: Grandpa, Mom, Dad)* **Pages 166–186; 188 –200; 208–223**

Literal: noting important details

2.   Mary Jo, Clyde, Grady, and the man who had caps each had problems. Who worked out their problems without anyone's help? *(Mary Jo and the man)* **Who got help from others?** *(Clyde and Grady)* **Pages 166–186; 188–200; 208–223**

Interpretive: drawing conclusions

Writing a Note

Have children read silently the title and the sentences below it. Then have one child read everything aloud. Before children begin writing, you may wish to review with them the format of a letter by going back to the note that Nate the Great wrote to his mother. This note appears on page 109 in the reader.

Teacher page 445

Books to Enjoy

Have children look at the bibliography, Books to Enjoy, on page 243 of *Carousels.* Tell them that these are the titles of three books that they might enjoy reading on their own. Tell children that they know most of the words in these books and that they can use what they know about the sounds letters stand for and the meaning of the sentences to figure out any words they don't know.

Children can probably read this page by themselves but you may prefer to read the page aloud while they follow along in their reader. Encourage discussion of those titles in which children show an interest. You may wish to obtain the books in advance in order to have them available in the classroom or you may prefer to suggest that children look for them in their school or local library.

Optional Resources

Instruction Charts:
Unit 21

Enrichment Book:
Unit 21

Spelling Bonus:
Unit 21

2 Review and Enrichment

Recommended Review

Vocabulary

Recognition Vocabulary:
Recognizing High-Frequency Words

See page 47 for model

Display: wear foot been part
angry never old ever
also off main top

Meaning Vocabulary:
Multiple-meaning Words

Display: The man stamped his foot.
The box is one foot long.

Remind children that they know that some words have more than one meaning. Tell them to read these sentences silently and think about what the word foot means in each one. After sufficient time, have volunteers read aloud each sentence and tell what the word foot means. (the part of the body that is used for standing and walking; a measurement that equals twelve inches)

Continue this activity with the words top, stick, and last, using the following sentences.

Display:
1. Let's play with your new top.
I put it on the top of the table.
(a toy that spins; the uppermost part)
2. The stamp will stick.
I have a wooden stick.
(stay attached to; a long thin piece of wood)
3. He was last in line.
The show won't last too long.
(coming after all the others; go on)

Skills

Decoding:
Ending es (D1·C2b)

Remind children that they know that the ending es can be added to some words to make new words. Point out that the words to which es is added usually end with s, x, ch, or sh.

Display: wish wishes

Have children identify the words. Ask what two letters come at the end of wish. Then ask what letters were added to wish to make wishes. Tell children to say the word wishes softly and listen for the sounds that the es ending stands for.

Tell children that they are going to read some sentences with new words in them. Explain that the new words are words that they already know with the es ending added to them.

Display:
1. She never finishes her supper.
2. Henry misses his friends.
3. Dad fixes breakfast every morning.
4. Mom made our lunches.
5. These sandwiches are great!

Have children read the sentences silently. Then call on individual children to read each sentence aloud and to identify the underlined word and its base word.

Workbook page 124

Decoding:
Dropping e, Doubling Consonant, and Changing y to i Before Adding Endings
(D1·C2d, D1·C2c, D1·C2e)

Remind children that they have learned that sometimes when endings are added to base words, the base words change. Remind them that they know that: when a word ends in final e, the e usually is dropped before an ending is added; when a word

ends with a consonant, that consonant is often doubled before an ending is added; when the final y in a base word comes right after a consonant, the y is usually changed to i before an ending beginning with the letter e is added.

Display: leave begin happy
leaving beginner happier

Point to leave and have children identify it. Ask them to tell what letter appears at the end of leave. Point to leaving and have children identify it. Ask them to tell how the base word leave was changed before the ing ending was added.

Continue in the same manner with the other words, having children notice that the final consonant was doubled before the er ending was added to the base word begin, and that the y was changed to i before the er ending was added to the base word happy.

Tell children to use what they know about how base words can change before endings are added to help them read some sentences with new words in them.

Display:
1. Dad is letting me go to the movies.
2. I never saw an uglier monster.
3. Why are you shaking like that?
4. Annie tried hard to win the race.
5. You are hitting the ball just right.
6. My best friend is moving away.

Have children read the sentences silently. Then call on individual children to read each sentence aloud, to identify the underlined word and its base word, and to tell how the base word was changed before the ending was added.

Comprehension:
Word Referents it, her, them, us
(C1·B2c)

Remind children that they have learned that the words it, her, them, and us are often used in place of other words.

Workbook page 124
Ending es

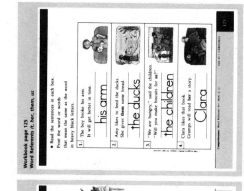

Workbook page 125
Word Referents it, her, them, us

FIGURE 9–3 continued

352

Display "You monkeys, you!" the man shouted, shaking his right hand at them. He was so angry that he took off his old brown cap and threw it down.

Tell children that here are two sentences that they read in the story "The Man and His Caps." Have children read the first sentence silently. Then have it read aloud. Ask what word *them* takes the place of.

Follow the same procedure with the second sentence, this time asking what word *it* takes the place of.

Remind children that when they are reading they will often come to a word that takes the place of another word or words. Point out that to understand what these words mean, they need to know what words they take the place of.

Tell children they are going to practice figuring out what words *it, her, them,* and *us* take the place of as they read a story.

2

Workbook page 126
Vocabulary Test

Display Ana and Bea were going to the movies. Pam asked if she could go with them. Ana and Bea thought that would be OK. "You can come with us," Ana said. Then Bea asked, "Do you have money? You'll need it to get in." Pam had some, but needed a little more. So Ana gave her some money.

Have children read the sentences silently.

Then call on individual children to read the first two sentences aloud. Point to *them* in the second sentence and ask what words it takes the place of. (Ana and Bea)

Remind children that when they are reading they will often come to a word that takes the place of another word or words. Point out that to understand what these words mean, they need to know what words they take the place of.

Have the third and fourth sentences read aloud. Point to *us* in the fourth sentence and ask what words it takes the place of. (Ana and Bea)

Have the fifth and sixth sentences read aloud. Point to *it* in the sixth sentence and ask what word *it* takes the place of. (money)

Have the last two sentences read aloud. Point to *her* in the last sentence and ask what word it takes the place of. (Pam)

Workbook page 125

Workbook page 126 Vocabulary Test

Optional Review

Vocabulary

Recognition Vocabulary: Discriminating Among Words

See page 34 for model.

Display
1. felt   foot   flat
2. took   top   told
3. angry   again   after
4. one   old   only
5. west   where   wear
6. paint   put   part

Words to be checked for instant recognition:
1. foot, 2. top, 3. angry, 4. old, 5. wear, 6. part.

Skills

Decoding: Ending *es* (D1 · C2b)

Remind children that they know that the ending *es* can be added to some words to make new words. The sounds for the *es* ending are the sounds they hear at the end of the word *wishes.*

Display
wish   box   glass   lunch
wishes   boxes   glasses   lunches

Point to *wish* and ask one child to say that word. Point to *wishes* and ask the child to tell what letters were added to *wish* to make *wishes*. Tell children to say the word *wishes* softly and listen for the sounds that the *es* ending stands for.

Repeat this procedure with the remaining pairs of words. Then point out to children that *wish* ends with the letters *sh*, *box* ends with *x*, *glass* ends with *s*, and *lunch* ends with *ch*. Remind children that the *es* ending is usually added to words ending with *sh, ch, x,* or *s.*

Display   teaches   messes   foxes

Point to *teaches*. Tell children that you are going to say a sentence and leave out this word. Explain that they should listen carefully and then be ready to tell you what the word is.

Read aloud the first sentence below, pausing briefly at the blank. Then point to *teaches* and have children identify it. Reread the sentence, pointing to *teaches* and having children say it with you at the point where it belongs in the sentence.

Follow the same procedure with *messes* and *foxes,* using the remaining sentences.

Say   Mr. Yee ___ me how to play the piano.
Everytime the dog goes into the garden, she ___ it up.
Karen saw a family of ___ at the zoo.

Decoding: Dropping *e*, Doubling Consonant, and Changing *y* to *i* Before Adding Endings (D1 · C2d, D1 · C2c, D1 · C2e)

Remind children that they have learned that sometimes when endings are added to base words, the base words change.

Remind children that they have learned that when a word ends with *e*, the *e* is usually dropped before an ending is added.

Display   love   loving

Point to *love* and have children identify it. Then point to *loving* and tell children they are going to figure out this word. Tell children that you will say a sentence and leave out this word. Say: **My new little rabbit is very ___.** Ask children what the word is. Ask them what ending was added to the base word *love* to make *loving.* Have a child tell how the word *love* changed before the *ing* ending was added.

Remind children that they know that when a word ends with a consonant, that consonant is usually doubled before an ending is added.

Display   sad   sadder

Point to *sad* and have children identify it. Then point to *sadder* and tell children they are going to figure out this word. Tell children that you will say a sentence and leave out this word. Say: **Jed is ___ than Amy about moving.** Ask children what the word is. Ask them what ending was added to the base word *sad* to make *sadder.* Have a child tell how the word *sad* changed before the *er* ending was added.

Remind children that they know that when a final *y* in a base word comes right after a consonant, the *y* is usually changed to an *i* before an ending beginning with the letter *e* is added.

Display   story   stories

Point to *story* and have children identify it. Then point to *stories* and tell children they are going to figure out this word. Tell children that you will say a sentence and leave out this word. Say: **Mother has read many ___ to us.** Ask children what the word

FIGURE 9–3 continued

353

is. Ask them what ending was added to the base word story to make stories. Have a child tell how the word story changed before the *es* ending was added.

Display: *hugged* *mixes* *saving*

Point to *hugged.* Tell children that you are going to say a sentence and leave out this word. Explain that they should listen carefully and then be ready to tell you what the word is.

Read aloud the first sentence below, pausing briefly at the blank. Then point to *hugged* and have children identify it. Reread the sentence, pointing to *hugged* and having children say it with you at the point where it belongs in the sentence.

Follow the same procedure with *mixes* and *saving,* using the remaining sentences.

Say: I ran up to Grandma and I ____ her.
Dad ____ the paints before he uses them.
Marshall is ____ his money to buy a bike.

2 Comprehension: Word Referents *it, her, them, us* (C1-B2c)

Remind children that they have learned that the words *it, her, them,* and *us* are often used in place of other words. Tell children that thinking about what words *it, her, them,* and *us* take the place of will help them understand what they read.

Have children listen to the following sentence and think about who the word *her* means. Then ask them if they could tell from the sentence who Pip walks to school with.

Say: Pip walks to school with her every day.

Then tell children they are going to read two sentences and see if they can tell now who *her* means.

Display: Mary is Pip's sister.
Pip walks to school with her every day.

Ask children to read both sentences silently, then have one child read them aloud. Point to the word *her* and ask what word in the first sentence *her* takes the place of. (*Mary*) Point out to children that

they needed to read the first sentence in order to understand who the word *her* meant in the second sentence.

Remind children that words such as *it, her, them,* and *us* don't mean much all by themselves. Explain that to understand what those words mean, you need to know what words they take the place of.

Tell children that they will practice figuring out what words *it, her, them,* and *us* stand for as they read some sentences.

Display:
1. *Lisa was going swimming.*
Jay asked if he could go with her.
"You can come, Jay," said Lisa.
2. *"Lee wants to swim with us, too."*
"This water isn't warm," said Lisa.
3. *"I don't think I can swim in it."*
4. *But Lee and Jay went swimming.*
The water felt good to them.

Have each pair of sentences read silently. Then call on individual children to read each pair aloud and to tell what word or words the underlined word takes the place of (1. her: *Lisa,* 2. us: *Jay and Lisa,* 3. it: *this water,* 4. them: *Lee and Jay*)

Teacher's Notebook
Extra Practice Master page 21

Enrichment

Vocabulary-Related Activities

Story Words
Print the following words on the board. Have children identify each one and tell which story the word reminds them of.

library ("Beatrice")
mile ("The Big Mile Race")
game ("Sports Day")
move ("We Are Best Friends")
flower ("Harriet")
dinosaur ("Nate the Great")
leaves ("The Little Pine Tree")
grasshopper ("What Mary Jo Shared")
monster ("Clyde Monster")
monkeys ("The Man and His Caps")

Looking Back
Now that children have reached the end of the book, it would be fun for them to see how far they have progressed as readers. Give them a copy of the first preprimer and ask them to read the first few stories. They will probably be surprised at how easy the reading is for them.

4. The necklace had many ____ in it. (*jewels*)
5. We ate beef ____ for dinner. (*stew*)

Word Referents *it, her, them, us*:
Explaining Word Referents in a Story
Read the following story to children, pausing at the places indicated to ask questions about the word referents.

Harriet wrote a funny story that Sally wanted to hear. So Harriet read the story to her. (Ask: Who do I mean by *her?*)
Harriet's mom and dad heard Sally laughing. "Read the story to us, Harriet," they said. (Ask: Who do I mean by *us?*)
"We heard Sally laughing when you read the story," said Mom. "We want to hear it, too." (Ask: What do I mean by *it?*)
So Harriet read the story again for Mom and Dad. The story made them laugh, too. (Ask: Who do I mean by *them?*)

2 Selection-Related Activity

Dramatizing "The Man and His Caps"
With children, make caps out of construction paper as shown below. Then choose one child to be the narrator and one child to be the man. The rest of the children can be the monkeys.

1. Cut strips of paper long enough to go around children's heads.

2. Cut visors for each band

3. Tape each visor to the backside of a band, making sure that the visor overlaps the band

4. Fit the bands to children, and staple or tape the edges together. Then fold up the visor.

Skill-Related Activities

Sound Association for *ew*:
Reading New Words in Sentences
For each sentence below, print on the board the word in parentheses. Then read the sentence aloud pausing briefly at the blank. Finally, point to the word on the board and have children say it aloud.

1. The ____ in the boat rowed hard. (*crew*)
2. Five big birds ____ over our house this morning. (*flew*)
3. I have only skated a ____ times. (*few*)

Extra Practice Master 21
or Teacher's Notebook Extra Practice page 21

EXTRA PRACTICE MASTER   Carousels • Unit 21

Read the sentences by each number.
Circle the base word for the underlined word.
Then print the base word on the lines.

1. Amy is *hungry.* She is *hungrier* than Ira.   hungry
2. I will *leave* tonight. I'm *leaving* with friends.   leave
3. I enjoy *playing* cards. *Playing* cards is fun!   save
4. We like to go *swimming.* Let's go *swimming.*   swim
5. That *story* is short. Other *stories* are long.   story
6. My rabbit can *hop.* It *hopped* to me.   hop

FIGURE 9–3 *continued*

skills related to the lesson. These can be found on pp. 442–45 of the lesson example.

Finally, **follow-up activities** are often listed, which include review activities for specific skills and possible enrichment activities. Review activities are used to provide additional skill practice for those who might need this work. Enrichment activities provide enjoyable learning activities for students who complete their work early or for students who can gain from motivating activities. Follow-up activities are located on pp. 446–51 in the lesson example.

follow-up activities: The fifth section of most teaching plans in the teacher's manual of a basal reading series. Usually contains review and enrichment activities.

Note the slight differences between the "ideal" outline of a teaching plan and the actual outline in the series illustrated in figure 9–3. Similar differences appear in all basal reading programs. While each program defines and organizes lesson structures slightly differently, almost all programs follow the general structural characteristics just listed.

You may recall seeing sections II throught V of the structural outline in chapter 8, where it illustrated one type of method framework: a **directed reading activity (DRA).** Directed reading activities are, in fact, the traditional way basal reading programs have organized instructional lessons. After using a basal series for several months, you will quickly acquire this method framework and incorporate it into your instructional repertoire.

directed reading activity (DRA): A method framework for teaching reading consisting of preparation, guided reading, skill development and practice, and enrichment activities.

One final note needs to be made, and made strongly, about the use of basal teaching plans. *Never attempt to accomplish everything in any single plan.* Basal teaching plans are intended to provide you with a range of suggestions about how you might teach a lesson. They are not to be followed exactly from beginning to end. At the very least, you need to be selective about activities designed to review skills and only use those you feel are necessary. As you will see, many teachers modify lessons more substantially. It is not uncommon for beginning teachers to ignore this point and begin the year by having children do every activity in every teaching plan. Quickly, however, they discover that it is impossible to complete all of the activities for a single grade in a single year. There simply is not enough time. Instead, you must quickly develop skills at selecting only those activities that are most appropriate for your students. You must also develop the ability to add new activities when appropriate. Flexibility is important in using basal teaching plans.

Types of Basal Programs

Basal reading programs vary in the emphasis they place on developing each of the knowledge sources discussed in previous chapters. To a large extent, differences between basal programs reflect differences between the comprehension frameworks of each author team. The greatest variation between programs exists in their assumptions about how one reads, not in how reading ability develops.

text-based assumptions: An explanation for how one reads. Readers are thought to translate print into sounds to uncover meaning in a text.

reader-based assumptions: An explanation for how one reads. The reader's prior knowledge is used to predict meaning. This prediction is then checked against the words in the text.

interactive assumptions: An explanation for how one reads. Reading is seen as an interaction between text and reader.

At different times, basal reading programs have been published that clearly reflected either **text-based assumptions** (Merrill Linguistic Reading Program [1980]), **reader-based assumptions** (Scott, Foresman: Reading Unlimited [1976]), or **interactive assumptions** (Allyn & Bacon: Pathfinder [1978]) for how one reads. Today, basal programs increasingly reflect interactive assumptions and, as a result, differences between programs are becoming less noticeable.

Differences between programs are especially visible at beginning levels. The most obvious differences appear in the relative emphasis assigned to decoding instruction and in the type of decoding knowledge developed. At upper levels, differences between programs are less noticeable.

Each basal reading program can be located somewhere on a continuum of basal programs that are more or less consistent with text-based, interactive, or reader-based explanations for how one reads. Figure 9–4 illustrates this relationship and specifies where several reading programs fall along this continuum. Note that no current basal series strongly reflects reader-based assumptions for how one reads.

While there is some variation among basal programs with respect to assumptions about how one reads, there is little or no difference between programs with respect to assumptions about how reading ability develops. All basal reading programs assume that reading comprehension is best developed by direct instruction. Thus, every basal program tends to reflect a mastery of specific skills explanation of reading development. Within basal programs, however, there are usually ways to be more or less consistent with a mastery of specific skills explanation. There are, for example, programmatic features more likely to be selected and emphasized by a teacher who has a mastery of specific skills explanation for development. There are also options that are more likely to be selected by a teacher who has a holistic language learning explanation but is, nevertheless, required by a district to teach reading com-

Greater Text-Based Assumptions	Interactive Assumptions	Greater Reader-Based Assumptions

1. Merrill, 1980
    2. Open Court, 1982
    3. Lippincott, 1985
	1. Scott, Foresman, 1985
	2. Harcourt, Brace, Jovanovich, 1985
	3. Macmillan, 1985
	4. Ginn, 1985
	5. Houghton Mifflin, 1984	

FIGURE 9–4

A continuum of basal reading programs based on different assumptions about how one reads

prehension from a basal reading program. These particular features are described in the final section of this chapter.

Basal Programs Reflecting More of a Text-Based Explanation for How One Reads

Basal programs that reflect more of a text-based explanation for how one reads share two distinguishing features: they emphasize the development of decoding knowledge over the development of other knowledge sources, particularly when children are beginning to read, and they less frequently provide instruction in using contextual knowledge.

Some basal reading programs devote substantial instructional time at an early level to the development of decoding skills. These same programs tend to postpone intensive development of higher-level knowledge sources until later. The early emphasis on decoding skills is consistent with a text-based explanation for how one reads. These programs tend to assume that meaning is in the text and that the reader's task is to determine the oral equivalent of the graphic information on the page.

Basal programs reflecting more of a text-based explanation for how one reads vary greatly in the way in which decoding skills are taught. Some adopt an analytic approach to phonics, some adopt a synthetic approach to phonics, some teach phonics inductively, and some teach phonics deductively. Almost all provide instruction in sight word knowledge, word structure knowledge, and (at later levels) dictionary knowledge, although substantial differences in both the content and method of instruction exist. What distinguishes these programs from other programs, in addition to the early emphasis on developing decoding knowledge, is that they tend not to spend much time developing context knowledge. Occasionally, new words may be presented in context but this almost always takes place after children are first shown the new word in isolation. Moreover, the contexts in which new words are presented usually provide little assistance for decoding; for example, Look at the bat on the *mat.* Deemphasizing the development of contextual knowledge is consistent with the text-based assumption that the direction of processing proceeds from lower- to higher-level knowledge sources. Thus, the lower-level decoding process is assumed to be relatively independent of contextual information available at vocabulary, syntactic, and discourse levels.

Consider, for example, the list of decoding and comprehension skills at level B (first grade, first semester) of the Open Court Headway Program. Table 9–1 indicates that decoding knowledge (particularly phonics knowledge and sight word knowledge) receives far greater emphasis than the development of higher-level knowledge sources (listed under "Comprehension Skills"). Note, too, that contextual analysis as a decoding strategy is not specifically identified as a decoding skill. Tasks that may promote context use do exist in this program, however, under

TABLE 9–1

Decoding and comprehension skills in Level B of the Open Court Headway Program (1982)

Decoding Skills	Comprehension Skills
1. 6 long-vowel sounds and 28 associated spellings.	1. Oral comprehension questions.
2. 19 consonant sounds and 20 associated spellings.	2. Preparation for the comprehension work sheets.
3. The *schwa* sound.	3. Picture exercises: words with long-vowel sounds.
4. The consonant-vowel combinations *er, ir,* and *ur.*	4. Picture exercises: words with long- and short-vowel sounds.
5. 5 short-vowel sounds and 6 associated spellings.	5. Comprehension work sheets.
6. 8 consonant sounds and 16 associated spellings.	
7. 11 new spellings for previously introduced consonant sounds.	
8. 4 other vowel sounds *(ow, aw, oi,* and *oo)* and 10 associated spellings.	
9. The consonant-vowel combination *ar.*	
10. The consonant-vowel combination *wor.*	
11. Sounding and blending sample words with long-vowel sounds.	
12. Sounding and blending sample words with long- and short-vowel sounds.	
13. Sounding and blending words in word lines, long-vowel sounds.	
14. Sounding and blending words in word lines, long- and short-vowel sounds.	
15. Reading irregular sight words.	
16. Reading words with long-vowel sounds.	
17. Reading words with long- and short-vowel sounds.	
18. In multiple choice exercises, long-vowel sounds and irregular words.	
19. In multiple choice exercises, long- and short-vowel sounds, irregular words.	
20. Isolated words with long-vowel sounds.	
21. Picture exercises. Words with long-vowel sounds.	
22. Picture exercises. Words with short-vowel sounds.	

skill labels such as "Sounding and blending sample words in word lines, long vowel sounds." Nevertheless, the relative frequency of these tasks as well as the emphasis on sounding and blending in the skill label suggests that phonics is valued more than the use of contextual information to form expectations for upcoming words.

Basal Programs Reflecting More of an Interactive Explanation for How One Reads

The majority of basal reading programs tend to fall somewhere between text-based and reader-based assumptions about how one reads. These eclectic programs tend to reflect interactive assumptions and share several distinguishing features. First, the development of both decoding skills and higher-level knowledge sources are stressed at early levels. When developing decoding knowledge, some programs devote greater attention to vowel generalizations than to consonant generalizations; some devote greater attention to consonant generalizations than to vowel generalizations. All, however, stress both the development of decoding knowledge and the development of higher-level aspects of comprehension. Second, decoding skills are often taught in relation to a reader's expectations. That is, new words and new letter-sound relationships are frequently taught in context. These instructional characteristics are consistent with the assumptions of an interactive explanation.

Consider, for example, the list of decoding and comprehension skills at level B (the first preprimer) of the Houghton-Mifflin Program (1984). Table 9–2 presents a very different picture of skill emphasis compared to table 9–1. Houghton-Mifflin devotes substantial attention to developing both decoding knowledge and higher-level knowledge sources (listed under *Comprehension Skills*). Less visible from table 9–2 is that Houghton-Mifflin emphasizes the development of contextual analysis; each lesson presents new words in context. As stated in one of the teacher's manuals for the Houghton-Mifflin program:

> If students are taught to expect what they read to make sense and if they use just the consonant correspondences at the outset, they will almost invariably be able to decode a word that is new in printed form if it is the only unknown word in a sentence or brief passage (Rockets, p. 1-18).

Both observations are consistent with basal programs that reflect more of an interactive explanation for how one reads.

Strengths and Weaknesses of Basal Programs

Basal reading programs are the most frequently used materials for teaching reading in the elementary school. They are used in approximately ninety percent of elementary classrooms (Zintz & Maggart,

A POINT
TO PONDER

Since basal reading programs sometimes change assumptions in new editions and since new basal programs may appear before you first begin teaching, it is important to be able to determine independently the assumptions of any individual program. The following are data from two separate reading series. See if you can determine which framework each program reflects. Check your answers with the information in figure 9–4.

The Merrill Linguistic Reading Program (1980)

1. From the Teacher's Manual (p. 5): ". . . pictures that illustrate the text have been omitted from the instructional sections of the readers to prevent the pupil from using picture cues to guess words and their meanings. A page that is free of illustrations also allows the reader to concentrate on the words without being distracted—a distinct advantage to beginning readers."
2. Initial reading instruction is built around the recognition of words. Decoding instruction initially consists of learning to recognize words with C-V-C spelling patterns (for example, *cat, bat,* and *cap*) and C-V-C-e spelling patterns (for example, *mate, mane,* and *made*). Vowels are taught in these environments because of the greater regularity in letter-sound relationships.
3. Contextual analysis is not taught for decoding purposes.
4. Vocabulary is carefully controlled to reflect only the spelling patterns and sight words that have been taught. From a page in the preprimer: "Nat! Nat! Look at the bat. Nat! Nat! Look at the bat on the mat. Cat! Cat! Pat the bat" (p. 19).

The Ginn Reading Program (1985)

1. Both decoding and higher-level knowledge sources receive considerable attention at beginning levels.
2. Vowel generalizations and consonant generalizations are introduced in the first preprimer. Contextual analysis also begins at this level.
3. Words are sometimes taught and practiced in isolation. Frequently words are taught in context.

1984). There are several reasons for the popularity of basal reading programs in contemporary reading instruction.

1. Basal reading programs save time. Having a complete set of stories, instructional activities, assessment instruments, and answer keys means that teachers do not have to spend large amounts of time developing or acquiring each of these components.
2. Basal reading programs include a comprehensive set of reading skills.
3. Basal reading programs organize skills hierarchically. Skills taught at earlier levels are sequenced so that they contribute to skill development at later levels.

TABLE 9–2

Decoding and comprehension skills at Level B of the Houghton-Mifflin Reading Program (1984)

Decoding Skills	Comprehension Skills
1. Using the meaning of spoken context as a clue to a missing word.	1. Interpreting pictures.
2. Associating a single consonant with the sound it stands for in initial position.	2. Using spoken context and letter-sound associations.
3. Associating a single consonant with the sound or sounds it can stand for in medial or final position.	3. Following directions.
	4. Noting important details.
	5. Noting correct sequence—order of events.
4. Associating a consonant digraph with the sounds that the consonants together stand for in initial, medial, or final position.	6. Recognizing pronoun referents.
	7. Recognizing adverb referents.
5. Associating a consonant cluster with the sounds that the consonants together stand for.	8. Recognizing and reading a simple sentence.
6. Associating a vowel combination with the sound or sounds it most commonly represents.	9. Drawing conclusions and inferences and making generalizations.
7. Recognizing common phonograms or rhyming elements.	10. Using direct and/or indirect experiences to get implied meanings.
8. Mastering grapheme-phoneme correspondences for affixes.	11. Classifying objects and concepts.
9. Associating common inflections with the sounds they stand for.	12. Appreciating poetry.
10. Recognizing the base word when one or more affixes have been added.	
11. Using consonant-sound associations together with context to decode words.	
12. Identifying contractions in context.	
13. Recognizing basal words instantaneously.	

4. Basal reading programs generally organize reading selections in terms of difficulty. Selections in earlier levels are usually easier to read than selections in later levels.
5. Basal reading programs provide for regular review of reading skills.
6. Basal reading programs provide opportunities for teachers to adapt the materials to the needs of individual students.
7. Basal reading programs provide explicit lesson plans for each day and, therefore, provide guidance to new teachers or teachers who begin teaching at a new grade level.

Basal reading materials are not without faults, however. They have been criticized for several reasons.

1. Basal reading selections often lack educational content. Stories and articles are often selected for teaching a particular skill and not for providing children with substantive knowledge about their environment (Schmidt, Caul, Byers & Buchmann, 1984).
2. Basal reading selections often are uninteresting to readers. Because stories are often written for particular instructional purposes and vocabulary and syntax are often controlled, basal selections tend not to interest young readers to the same extent as quality children's literature (Burns, Roe & Ross, 1984; Zintz & Maggart, 1984. See, however, Aukerman, 1981).
3. Basal reading materials often direct teachers to assess children's performance more than teach children how to read. Many of the tasks in basal materials call for answers that are either correct or incorrect. Less frequently, children are actually shown how to comprehend (Durkin, 1981).
4. Often, the use of basal readers is associated with spending substantial time managing peripheral aspects of instruction: giving assignments; clarifying directions; collecting work; correcting work; and returning work. As a result, less time is sometimes available for teaching or learning (Durkin, 1979).

SUPPLEMENTAL MATERIALS FOR SPECIFIC SKILL AREAS

Often teachers incorporate supplemental materials into the classroom reading program. Most frequently, supplemental materials are used to provide instruction and practice in a variety of specific skill areas.

Phonics

It is not uncommon in primary-grade classrooms to find teachers supplementing the decoding program of a basal series with separate phonics materials. This occurs whenever a teacher believes that the basal

Dolores Durkin (1979), in a study of concern to all teachers, found that less than two percent of class time was spent on comprehension instruction. She defined comprehension instruction as a teacher doing or saying something that helped students understand units of writing greater than a single word. Thus, helping students understand the meaning of new vocabulary words was not counted as comprehension instruction, but showing students how to determine an inferred cause-and-effect relationship was counted. Rather than helping students comprehend, much class time was spent on assessment tasks, defined as a teacher asking questions and telling students if their answers were correct or incorrect, but not telling them how to obtain correct answers. Similar results were obtained (Durkin, 1981) when several major basal reading series were evaluated. Do basal reading programs really test children instead of teach them? Analyze the lesson plan in figure 9–3 using Durkin's definitions and independently determine the answer to this question. What can you do to increase the amount of comprehension instruction you provide to your students? You may want to review the information in chapters 6 through 8 if you have difficulty answering this question. Keep Durkin's definition of comprehension in mind as you continue your professional development. Continually check to see if you are actually helping children comprehend or if you are only testing their abilities to comprehend.

series does not provide enough instruction or practice in phonic skills. It may also occur when a teacher wants to teach phonics in a manner (inductive, deductive, synthetic, or analytic) that is different from the way in which phonics is taught in the basal program. There are at least three different categories of supplemental phonics materials: phonics games and manipulative devices; phonics workbooks or ditto masters; and elaborated supplemental phonics programs.

Chapter 4 presented several ideas for creating your own phonics games and manipulative devices. In addition to the suggestions presented in chapter 4, there are a wide variety of commercially available games and manipulative devices incorporated into classroom reading instruction. Often these materials are available as **reading center** tasks or located in a classroom's **reading corner** as independent learning activities. Sometimes teachers will have one group of students working with these materials while they provide more direct instruction to a separate group. A small portion of the phonics games and manipulative devices commercially available include:

1. *Consonant Lotto.* Garrard Publishing Company, 1607 North Market Street, Champaign, IL 61820. A bingo-like game with letters and sounds rather than numbers.
2. *Consonant Flip Book.* DLM Teaching Resources, One DLM Park, Box 400, Allen, TX 75002. Children flip initial and final consonants on a page to form new words.

reading center: A learning center where children participate in a rotating series of independent, self-guided reading activities.

reading corner: A portion of a classroom devoted solely to reading. It might contain book shelves, a magazine rack, a newspaper rack, a carpet, comfortable chairs or pillows, and a display table.

3. *Crossword Puzzles for Phonics.* Continental Press, Incorporated, 520 East Bainbridge Street, Elizabethtown, PA 17022. A series of crossword puzzles designed to reinforce phonics skills.

4. *Go Fish.* Remedial Educational Press, Kingsbury Center, 2138 Bancroft Place NW, Washington, DC 20008. Based on the game "Go Fish", this card game contains decks for both consonants and vowels.

5. *Phonetic Word Analyzer.* Milton Bradley, 74 Park Street, Springfield, MA 01101. A set of interchangeable phonics wheels.

6. *Phonic Rummy Card Games.* Kenworthy Educational Service, Incorporated, Box 60, 138 Allen Street, Buffalo, NY 14205. Several decks of cards for working on phonic knowledge while playing rummy.

7. *Rainbow Word Builders.* Kenworthy Educational Service, Incorporated, Box 60, 138 Allen Street, Buffalo, NY 14205. Separate phonic strips with consonants, vowels, clusters, and digraphs are inserted into a viewing port. Children create different combinations of letters that form words.

8. *Vowel Digraph Word-Making Cards.* Educational Teaching Aids, 159 West Kinzie Street, Chicago, IL 60610. Puzzle-like strips that, when joined together correctly, show a picture and a word with a vowel digraph.

9. *Take.* Garrard Publishing Company, 1607 North Market Street, Champaign, IL 61820. Sounds at the beginning, middle, or end of words are matched in a card game.

10. *63 Webster Word Wheels.* Webster/McGraw-Hill, 1221 Avenue of the Americas, New York, NY 10020. A phonic wheel device.

Teachers in the primary grades may also choose to supplement their phonics program with phonics workbooks or ditto masters. These are sometimes used in place of basal workbook pages to develop phonic skills. More frequently, they are used to provide additional instructional and practice opportunities for students who require it. Whenever supplementary phonics workbooks or ditto masters are used, they must be for clearly defined instructional purposes. Do not use workbook and ditto page activities simply to keep children busy.

A partial list of the many phonics workbooks or ditto master packets that are commercially available include:

1. *Conquests in Reading.* Webster/McGraw-Hill, 1221 Avenue of the Americas, New York, NY 10020. Designed for the intermediate grade level. Presents phonics skills in meaningful contexts.

2. *Merrill Phonics Skilltext Series.* Merrill Publishing Company, 1300 Alum Creek Drive, Columbus, OH 43216. Five workbooks, one at each level for grades kindergarten through four.

3. *Macmillan Reading Spectrum.* Macmillan Publishing Company Incorporated, 886 Third Avenue, New York, NY 10022. A self-checking workbook series which may be used in the intermediate grades.

Supplemental materials, often incorporated into classroom reading instruction, typically serve to provide instruction and practice in specific skill areas.

4. *Discovering Phonics We Use.* The Riverside Publishing Company, 8420 Bryn Mawr Avenue, Chicago, IL 60631. Eight phonics workbooks that also combine meaning cues with phonic cues.
5. *Phonics is Fun.* Modern Curriculum Press. 13900 Prospect Road, Cleveland, OH 44136. A series of phonic workbooks. Short readers and flashcards also can be purchased separately.

Elaborated supplemental phonics programs contain more than a single game, device, or series of workbooks. They come with an elaborate set of integrated materials that teach phonic knowledge to young children. These materials often are used as a package to replace the phonics program in a basal series. Sometimes, too, they are used as the only materials for reading instruction during the end of kindergarten or the beginning of first grade. Several of the more popular elaborated supplemental phonics programs include:

elaborated supplemental phonics programs: Comprehensive instructional materials used to teach a complete and integrated set of phonic skills to young children.

1. *Alpha Time.* New Dimensions in Education, 83 Keeler Ave., P. O. Box 5080, Norwalk, CT 06856. A kit with puppets, pictures, filmstrips, wall charts, hand puppets, and songs used to teach letter names and letter sounds. Often used in kindergarten or the beginning of first grade.
2. *Alpha One: Breaking the Code.* New Dimensions in Education, 83 Keeler Ave., P.O. Box 5080, Norwalk, CT 06856. A continuation of *Alpha Time.* Includes a series of small books.

3. *Speech-to-Print Phonics.* Harcourt Brace Jovanovich, 757 Third Avenue, New York, NY 10017. First develops letter-name knowledge and then knowledge of letter-sound relationships. Sounds are always presented within words.

4. *SRA Kits.* Science Research Associates, Incorporated, North Wacker Drive, Chicago, IL 60606. Three kits which develop phonic knowledge of consonants, vowels, blends, and digraphs.

Context Use

Supplemental materials designed to promote context use often are used by teachers who want to make their instructional program reflect more interactive or reader-based assumptions about how one reads. These teachers want to provide more opportunities for students to learn to form appropriate expectations, at least more than their basal reading program may provide. Some of the many supplemental materials designed to promote context use as a decoding strategy include:

1. *Context Phonetic Clues.* Curriculum Associates, 5 Esquire Road, North Billerica, MA 01862. A specific skills program that develops knowledge of context use for grades three through six.

2. *Cloze Connections.* Barnell-Loft, Limited, 958 Church Street, Baldwin, NY 11510. Separate workbooks on nine levels (Grades one through nine) focusing on using vocabulary and syntactic knowledge during context use.

3. *Reading Power through Cloze.* Globe Book Company, 50 West Twenty-third Street, New York, NY 10010. Workbooks with stories followed by cloze sentences. Four books for grades four through seven.

4. *Building Language Power with Cloze.* Modern Curriculum Press, 13900 Prospect Road, Cleveland, OH 44136. Workbooks with cloze tasks at five grade levels (two through six).

Vocabulary Knowledge

Supplemental materials designed to promote the development of vocabulary knowledge will often be used by teachers who want to expand students' vocabulary instruction beyond the vocabulary program found in some basal readers. Often these are teachers with more of a reader-based or interactive explanation for how one reads who are required to use a program reflecting more text-based assumptions. At other times, teachers will want to provide supplemental vocabulary instruction for students who are weak in this area. A few of the commercially available materials to enhance the development of vocabulary knowledge include:

1. *Vocabulary Fluency.* Curriculum Associates, 5 Esquire Road, North Billerica, MA 01862. Two books (grades four through six and seven

through nine). Especially designed for remedial students and non-native speakers of English.
2. *Word Theatre.* Barnell-Loft, Limited, 958 Church Street, Baldwin, NY. 11510. Contains four books at each of four grade levels (three through six). Teaches word meanings in context.
3. *Talking Picture Dictionary.* Troll, 320 Route 17, Mahwah, NJ 07430. Contains audio cassettes and student picture dictionaries. For grades one through four.
4. *Wordly Wise.* Educators Publishing Service, Incorporated, 75 Moulton Street, Cambridge, MA 02238. Nine vocabulary workbooks using crossword puzzles, riddles, and games. For grades four through twelve.

Comprehension

Supplemental materials designed to promote general comprehension ability usually develop syntactic and discourse knowledge. They frequently include activities designed to provide additional practice on tasks described in chapters 6 through 8 as inferential reasoning, sequencing, predicting outcomes, drawing conclusions, identifying main ideas, determining cause-and-effect relationships, and developing familiarity with the structure of different discourse forms. Often these materials take two different forms: kits that promote a range of specific skills or supplemental workbooks and ditto master books. A few of the specific skills kits that are available include:

1. *Sports Reading Series.* Bowmar/Noble Publishers, Inc. 4563 Colorado Blvd., Los Angeles, CA 90036. Three separate skill kits developing a wide range of comprehension skills with stories about the Olympics, baseball, basketball, and football.
2. *Clues for Better Reading.* Curriculum Associates, 5 Esquire Road North Billerica, MA 01862. Three levels of skills kits for grades two through nine focusing on knowledge of discourse structure.
3. *Reading Skills Kits.* Zaner-Bloser, 612 North Park, Columbus, OH 43215. Presents specific comprehension skills in visual, auditory, and kinesthetic modes.
4. *A Need to Read.* Globe Book Company, 50 West Twenty-third Street, New York, NY 10010. Develops separate skills in main ideas, vocabulary, sequencing, drawing conclusions, and critical reading for grades three through six.
5. *SRA Reading Laboratories.* Science Research Associates, Incorporated, North Wacker Drive, Chicago, IL 60606. Ten different kits for primary grade levels through high school. Stories with self-checking questions.

Supplemental workbooks and ditto master books include:

1. *Comprehension We Use.* The Riverside Publishing Company, 8420 Bryn Mawr Avenue, Chicago, IL 60631. Six workbooks for grades one through six teaching specific reading-thinking strategies such as determining main ideas, sequencing, drawing conclusions, and so on.
2. *Reading Reinforcement Skilltext Series.* Merrill Publishing Company, 1300 Alum Creek Drive, Columbus, OH 43216. Ten workbooks for grades one through five.
3. *Reading Comprehension K-6.* Frank Schaffer Publications, Teachers Center, Department C, P.O. Box 727, 138 North Street, Middletown, NY 10940. Ditto master books developing a range of comprehension skills.
4. *Reading Comprehension Series.* Steck-Vaughn Company, 807 Brazos, P.O. Box 2028, Austin, TX 78768. Seven workbooks for grades one through six.
5. *Specific Skills Series.* Barnell-Loft, Limited, 958 Church Street, Baldwin, NY. 11510. Nonconsumable workbooks focusing on eight specific skills at fourteen different levels (grades one through twelve).

MATERIALS WITH MODIFIED ORTHOGRAPHIES

There are several reading programs that change their orthographic system, or alphabet, in an attempt to ease the learning tasks for beginning readers: UNIFON; Words in Color; i/t/a; and DISTAR. In these programs, beginning readers learn to read with an orthographic system that consistently represents symbol-sound relationships; each letter is intended to represent only one sound. Thus, children have two initial learning tasks: to recognize a limited set of regular letter-sound relationships and to learn to blend these sounds together. All the reading materials use the orthography. Teachers and students are sometimes expected to write in the modified orthography until students make the transition to the regular English alphabet.

Typically, programs that have modified orthographies are used as the sole materials of instruction only during the first year or two of school. Usually, children make the transition to regular texts before the third grade. Since these programs are not used frequently today (Harris & Sipay, 1985), we will only discuss one, *DISTAR®,* as an example of this type of instructional material.

The DISTAR (Direct Instruction Systems for Teaching Arithmetic and Reading) program was designed to teach initial reading skills to culturally different children in the beginning primary grades. It has been frequently used as a program to teach beginning reading skills to low-achieving readers before they begin a basal series.

At beginning levels, the DISTAR program modifies the normal orthography in four basic ways.

1. Long vowels are marked with a short line over the vowel.
2. Silent vowels and consonants are greatly reduced in size.
3. Some consonant digraphs have unique forms.
4. Capital letters are not used.

All of these changes were made to reduce the irregularities in the letter-sound relationships of the English orthography and, thus, ease the learning tasks of beginning readers. An example of the orthography used at the first level of the DISTAR program can be seen in figure 9–5.

did	thōse	are
clap	thēse	farm
do	there	yard
of	then	her
fōr	whȳ	hēre
dōn't	when	at
didn't	were	āte
very	where	hē
every	her	shē
ēven	hēre	thē

FIGURE 9–5
An example of DISTAR orthography

The DISTAR program is also known for several other distinguishing characteristics. Most prominent, perhaps, is the tightly structured nature of instructional lessons. Teachers are directed to read and reproduce exactly the dialogue written in their teacher's manuals. Student responses are cued with formulaic hand signals at appropriate points in the lesson. Teachers are admonished not to deviate from these scripts at all. A second characteristic of the program is the frequent use of **behavior modification** techniques. Children are rewarded for appropriate behavior at various points with take-home books, raisins, praise, or small pieces of candy.

DISTAR materials include short stories, workbooks, take-home blending sheets, sound-symbol sheets, writing sheets, and a teacher's manual. The program uses a highly structured synthetic blending approach for teaching phonics.

behavior modification: A technique where one identifies valued behaviors, defines conditions where valued behaviors will take place, and immediately reinforces positive behaviors with praise or tokens.

TRADE BOOKS AND INDIVIDUALIZED READING

A final source of reading materials outside of the basal program consists of children's literature selections, or trade books. Chapter 7 presented a general discussion of why and how these materials should be incorporated into the instructional program.

individualized read-ing: Relies on the use of self-selected trade books in the reading program.

In addition to the activities described in chapter 7, there is also a somewhat formalized instructional approach that uses trade books to teach reading comprehension: **individualized reading.** Although there are many individualizing techniques and many materials intended to provide individual instruction, *individualized reading* usually is a partic-ular instructional procedure relying solely on the use of trade books in the classroom reading program. Sometimes, individualized reading is the central core of an instructional program. More frequently it is used to supplement a basal reading program in the elementary grades. Indi-vidualized reading is described in a variety of ways, but a number of characteristics appear in most descriptions.

First, students always select their own reading materials. Instead of selections being determined by a publisher or teacher, students de-termine what they will read based on their interests and achievement levels. Teachers, however, do play a very important role in helping chil-dren to identify interest areas and in putting students in touch with a range of books in each area. Methods for accomplishing both of these tasks were presented in chapter 7.

Second, to implement an individualized reading program you need to have a wide range and substantial number of trade books available

Trade books in a class-room or school library may be used to de-velop an individualized reading program. This may either supplement or serve as core mate-rials for a classroom reading program.

in your classroom. As an alternative, you might consider the use of the school library, although there will be times when your library is not available for your students. Usually, it is suggested that you have four to five books for each student in your class to begin an individualized reading program. This number is sufficient to provide the number and variety of books you will need to begin the program.

Third, students usually read independently. Teachers provide instructional assistance when it is necessary, but this typically takes place individually. Children usually read by themselves at their desks, in a quiet and comfortable location in the classroom, and at home.

Fourth, when students complete a selection they are asked to have a conference with the teacher. Sometimes a teacher will have an appointment chart so students can sign up in advance. In other classes the teacher will arrange for conferences as students require them. During the conference, the teacher informally assesses how well the student comprehended the selection by asking discussion questions. The development of reading competence is observed and appropriate instruction is provided. Finally, the teacher and student will discuss books that might be read next. In some classes, the conference also includes a discussion about how the student plans to share the book with the class. This might be something as simple as a short oral report or as elaborate as constructing a diorama with a written synopsis of the book. Individual progress can be recorded on a form similar to the one in figure 9–6.

If you would like additional information on individualized reading, you may want to read the reference by Jeanette Veatch (1978) at the end of this chapter.

SELECTING AND ADAPTING MATERIALS

BEFORE READING ON

This chapter has described typical instructional materials used in elementary programs. It is important for you to recognize that no single set of materials is inherently superior to any other. During the late 1960s, a number of studies were conducted to investigate this very issue (Bond & Dykstra, 1967; Dykstra, 1968). The results indicated that teachers, not materials, make the difference in helping children develop proficiency in reading comprehension. Your role as a knowing and caring reading teacher is crucial to helping children learn to read. The more you understand about how materials are appropriately employed to assist children, the more you will be able to contribute to their development. Consider how your comprehension framework might influence decisions about materials in your classroom.

At the beginning of this chapter you learned there are two basic decisions that must be made about materials: Which materials should be used to teach reading comprehension? and How do I use the materials

Name: _____   Date: _____

Book: _____   Status: _____

Comprehension: _____

_____

_____

_____

_____

_____

Other Observations: _____

_____

_____

_____

_____

How the Book Will Be Shared: _____

_____

Ideas for Additional Assistance: _____

_____

_____

FIGURE 9–6

An example of a conference record for individualized reading

which have been chosen? The first question is basically a selection issue with long-term consequences; that is, Which materials should I select for my reading program this year? The second question is more of an adaptation issue with more immediate consequences; that is, On a day-to-day basis, how do I go about adapting the materials that have been chosen?

Both issues are important to consider, although it is far more common for teachers to confront decisions related to adaptation. Adaptation decisions occur every day as teachers regularly decide how to adapt their instructional programs to meet immediate learning needs. Selection decisions occur far less frequently and sometimes not at all, since these decisions are often made by administrators, local committees, or state adoption committees. Nevertheless, we will first consider how to use a framework of reading comprehension to select the appropriate materials for instruction, since teachers are sometimes involved in local selections.

To clearly specify how comprehension frameworks influence selection decisions, we will assume that you, as a classroom teacher, are able to select your own materials of instruction. Although this is seldom true, we take this approach since it can most clearly demonstrate relationships between types of comprehension frameworks and the materials you use for instruction. After considering the selection decision, we then consider how to adapt materials to be consistent with one's comprehension framework, particularly when one's framework is inconsistent with the materials that have been chosen.

Using a Comprehension Framework to Select Materials

So far, whenever we have considered comprehension frameworks, we have always first addressed the question of how one reads and only then considered how reading ability develops. If you are fortunate enough to be able to participate in selection of materials, however, first consider how reading ability develops and only then consider how one reads. The most important decision you must make about materials is whether your comprehension framework is consistent with the use of a basal program. This decision is severely constrained by your answer to the question of how reading ability develops.

If, for example, you have a mastery of specific skills explanation for how reading ability develops, your comprehension framework is consistent with the use of one of the several basal reading series described in this chapter. All basals are consistent with the assumptions of a mastery of specific skills explanation. Recall from chapter 2 that teachers with a mastery of specific skills explanation operate from a hierarchically organized list of specific skills that are all taught directly. This is precisely the set of instructional assumptions behind any basal reading program. If you have a mastery of specific skills explanation for how reading ability develops, this part of your comprehension framework will be consistent with the use of a basal reading program.

On the other hand, if you have a holistic language learning explanation for how reading ability develops, your framework will be most consistent with the use of trade books and other more naturally occurring reading materials. You will probably prefer to use individualized reading and language experience activities to develop children's reading competence, not basal reading programs. Both are more consistent with the assumptions of a holistic language learning framework.

Finally, if you have a differential acquisition explanation for how reading ability develops, your comprehension framework will be most consistent with using basal materials more frequently with less proficient readers. A differential acquisition explanation assumes that direct instruction is most appropriate for less proficient readers, while more inductive learning opportunities, such as those found in functional literacy tasks, are appropriate for more proficient readers. Thus, you would prefer to increasingly supplement and ultimately replace, a basal program with individualized reading activities as students developed in proficiency.

Having addressed the issue of how reading ability develops, we can now address the issue of how one reads. If the use of a basal program is consistent with your explanation for how reading ability develops, you would prefer to use a program that also shares your assumptions for how one reads. Thus, if you have more of a text-based explanation, you would prefer a program reflecting more text-based assumptions. If you have more of a interactive explanation, you would prefer a program reflecting more interactive assumptions.

If a school system requires you to use a basal series with assumptions about how one reads that are different from yours, you will find yourself in conflict with the instructional activities in that program. This may happen, for example, if you have more of a reader-based explanation for how one reads since few basal programs strongly reflect these assumptions. Still, as long as your explanation for how reading ability develops is consistent with the use of a basal series, it will not be too difficult for you to adapt the program to your comprehension framework.

In summary, the decision about which materials are consistent and inconsistent with your comprehension framework is most appropriately made by first identifying your answer to the question: How does reading ability develop? This will determine if the use of a basal reading series in your classroom is consistent with your comprehension framework or if you should consider individualized reading or language experience activities. If using a basal reading series is consistent with your comprehension framework, you must then identify your answer to the question: How does one read? This will help you determine the particular type of basal program that is most consistent with your particular framework.

Using a Comprehension Framework to Adapt Materials

Consider the ideal situation where teachers find their comprehension frameworks to be totally consistent with the materials of instruction. It may be that the teachers made the final selection decision themselves or, more likely, it may be that the district's decision is entirely consistent with their particular comprehension framework. In either case, it is important for you to recognize that these teachers must still continually adapt the instructional materials they have selected. A number of decisions must be made each day about how to best engage students in learning activities. Teachers who use a basal reading series, for example, must decide which of the many suggested instructional experiences they will provide their students. Teachers who use an individualized reading program must decide how to structure a student book conference. Each of these situations requires that a teacher decide exactly how to implement the materials that have been selected for instruction.

When materials are consistent with a teacher's comprehension framework, adaptation decisions are made largely on the basis of three considerations. First, materials may be adapted on the basis of one's perception of students' needs. If, for example, you are using a basal reading series you may need to repeat instruction in a particular skill area that students have not completely mastered. Often, basal series provide you with additional suggestions for instruction. You will need to select from the range of review activities at the end of a lesson to meet your students' unique needs. Or, you may choose to use instructional materials from outside the basal program. If, on the other hand, you are using trade books in an individualized reading program, you will need to carefully consider the recommendations you make for future reading selections based on your perception of students' needs. In either case, you must adapt materials to meet the individual needs of your students.

You must also adapt the materials of instruction to meet the time constraints of your instructional program. This is a particular concern with basal materials which assume that you will only select a portion of the suggested activities. It will not always be possible for you to teach every suggested skill, complete every suggested workbook page, or read every suggested story in a basal program. Time constraints will quickly force you to make decisions about what to include in and exclude from instruction. Given limited amounts of time, these adaptation decisions must be made on the basis of the priorities you establish for your students. Your evaluation of individual progress (see chapter 10) will help you in this process.

Finally, you will come to adapt the materials of instruction based on your evaluation of previous learning tasks. Over time, you will begin to identify learning tasks that seem to work better than others. You will recall an enjoyable and successful activity from the year before and repeat the activity with similarly situated students. The second year through any basal series, for example, you are likely to discard instructional tasks that seemed not to help children and repeat tasks that seemed to help students over a difficult skill area. Part of good teaching is simply to remember your effective instructional lessons and use them whenever the situation is again appropriate.

All of these examples, though, consider only the ideal situation where a teacher's comprehension framework is entirely consistent with the materials of instruction. More typically, perhaps, you will find yourself in a position where the materials of instruction are somewhat inconsistent with your comprehension framework. This often takes place when a district selects a basal reading series that is to be used by all teachers and all students.

There are two ways in which basal materials might be inconsistent with your framework. First, basal materials might be inconsistent with your explanation for how reading ability develops. You may, for example, believe that reading comprehension develops through either holistic language learning or differential acquisition but are, nevertheless, asked to teach from a basal program. If you are to be consistent with your framework in this situation you must adapt the basal materials in the direction of your explanation for the development of reading ability. How, though, does one accomplish this? One suggestion is to make certain that a portion of each reading period provides opportunities for children to engage in either language experience or individualized reading experiences. In fact, you will find many suggestions for activities of this type in the enrichment section of basal lesson plans. You, of course, will supplement these with your own ideas and materials. Another suggestion is to schedule periods regularly when you provide children with literature or language experience activities. For example, you may want to set aside a two-week period for children to complete an individualized reading project. Or, you may regularly schedule time for read-aloud sessions, Sustained Silent Reading, and other more holistic reading experiences, as described in chapter 7.

It is possible for basal materials to be inconsistent with your framework in a second way; the required basal program may be inconsistent with your explanation for how one reads. You may be asked to teach from a program reflecting mostly text-based assumptions when your explanation for how one reads reflects mostly reader-based or interactive assumptions. In this situation, you must consider ways in which different aspects of each lesson can be modified to be more consistent with your assumptions about how one reads. You might choose, for example, to reduce the extent of phonics instruction, concentrating on the consonant generalizations and limiting vowel generalizations to the short vowels and a few vowel digraphs. You might also choose to always present new words and phonic generalizations in context. Some of the supplemental phonics materials which have been listed in this chapter could be used for this purpose or you could make your own sentences to introduce new words. Also, you might revise the nature of the purpose-setting task for each story to generate expectations for what the story might be about. In addition, you would probably pay greater attention to developing inferential reasoning and less attention to literal recall of factual information since reader-based and interactive explanations assume that readers contribute substantial meaning to comprehension. Finally, you might choose to use a DRTA procedure for conducting the guided reading for each story. All would be consistent with the assumptions of a reader-based framework.

Should you find yourself in the opposite situation (having a text-based explanation for how one reads, but asked to teach with materials consistent with a mostly interactive explanation) you could adapt your instruction in several ways. You might first attempt to supplement your basal with any of the supplemental phonics materials described in this chapter. Second, you might consider presenting new words in isolation rather than in context. Third, you would probably pay greater attention to your students' oral reading. Fourth, you might be less likely to use any activities designed to promote the use of context. Finally, you would probably emphasize the recall of literal information since text-based explanations assume that meaning is in the text, not in what the reader brings to the text.

1. When using a comprehension framework, the selection and use of instructional materials requires a clear understanding of your own particular framework and the framework which your materials reflect. You also must know ways to adapt a set of materials to be more consistent with your own framework.

2. There are two major categories of materials used to teach reading in the elementary grades: basal and nonbasal.

3. Despite the comprehensive nature of basal reading programs, there are a number of reasons to modify or supplement them.

4. Lesson plans in the teacher's manuals of basal reading programs usually contain the following components: overview; preparation; guided reading; skill development and practice; and follow-up activities.

5. Today, basal reading programs tend to reflect either more text-based assumptions or more interactive assumptions about how reading takes place. All basal reading programs are consistent with a mastery of specific skills explanation for how reading ability develops.

6. When considering how the materials of instruction are consistent or inconsistent with your comprehension framework, compare your assumptions about how one reads and how reading ability develops to the implicit assumptions of the materials you use.

7. Adaptations can be made to the materials you use for instruction to make them more consistent with your comprehension framework.

THE MAJOR POINTS

QUESTIONS AND ACTIVITIES

1. Consider the situation where teachers in the same school have different frameworks of reading comprehension yet are asked to use the same basal reading series for instruction. Will students be put in jeopardy by receiving different instruction in successive years? Should this be taken into consideration in your decisions to adapt instructional materials? Explain why you believe this is or is not an important factor to consider. How might any problems you identify be overcome?

2. Review the characteristics of the DISTAR program. Which assumptions about the reading comprehension process and the nature of reading development are reflected in this program?

   After you have decided, consider the following situation. Your district requires that DISTAR be used to teach reading at your grade level. DISTAR requires that *no* changes be made in the way that instruction takes place. Teachers are expected to follow exactly the directions in each manual. If you had a framework based on holistic language learning assumptions of development and reader-based assumptions of the comprehension process, how would you help children learn to read? What could you do in this situation? What would you do?

3. It is not too early in your career to consider your first teaching position. Prospective teachers are usually interviewed by the school principal and sometimes by a committee of teachers as well. You will have an opportunity to ask questions as well as to answer them. What questions do you think will be asked about materials? What questions about materials should you ask?

4. Identify several conditions when supplemental phonics materials might be used to adapt a set of instructional materials. Identify several conditions when these same materials should not be used.

5. Assume that you have a framework based on mastery of specific skills and reader-based assumptions. You are asked, nevertheless, to teach the lesson illustrated in Figure 9–3. This comes from a program reflecting more interactive assumptions. How might you modify this lesson plan? Consider which activities you might select and which you might delete to be consistent with your comprehension framework.

6. Using the outline on pages 343–44, evaluate the structure of teaching plans in several basal reading series. How consistently do other basal programs follow this structure? Which sections seem to be most consistently found in basal reading programs? Which sections are least consistently found?

Baumann, J. F. (1984). How to expand a basal reader program. *The Reading Teacher, 37,* 604–607.

Shows how to supplement a basal program with language experience activities, individualized reading, and other language arts activities along with the use of parent aides and peer tutors.

Dasch, A. (1983). Aligning basal reader instruction with cognitive stage theory. *The Reading Teacher, 36,* 428–34.

Shows how basal reading lessons might be rearranged to be more consistent with Piagetian notions of cognitive stages. Provides specific examples from one reading series.

Durkin, D. (1984). Is there a match between what elementary teachers do and what basal reader manuals recommend? *The Reading Teacher, 37,* 734–44.

A study of fourteen teachers comparing what they did in the classroom to what basal manuals suggested. Results confirmed other findings that much time was spent on oral reading, assessment, and completing worksheets. Other results suggested that teachers often fail to introduce new vocabulary, ask prereading questions, and give instruction on essential topics.

Fry, E. & Sakiey, E. (1986). Common words not taught in basal reading series. *The Reading Teacher, 39,* 395–98.

Identifies 382 very common words not often taught in basal reading programs. Suggests that teachers may wish to supplement their basal program with these words.

Allen, R. V. & Allen, C. (1976). *Language experience activities.* Boston: Houghton Mifflin.

Aukerman, R. C. (1981). *The basal reader approach to reading.* New York: John Wiley and Sons.

Beck, I. L.; Omanson, R. C. & McKeown, M. G. (1982). An instructional redesign of reading lessons: Effects on comprehension. *Reading Research Quarterly, 17,* 462–81.

Bond, G. L. & Dykstra, R. (1967). The cooperative research program in first grade reading instruction. *Reading Research Quarterly, 2,* 5–142.

Burns, P. C.; Roe, B. D.; & Ross, E. P. (1984). *Teaching reading in today's elementary school.* Boston: Houghton Mifflin.

Dykstra, R. (1968). Summary of the second-grade phase of the cooperative research program in primary reading instruction. *Reading Research Quarterly, 4,* 49–70.

Durkin, D. (1979). What classroom observations reveal about reading comprehension instruction. *Reading Research Quarterly, 14,* 481–533.

Durkin, D. (1981). Reading comprehension instruction in five basal reader series. *Reading Research Quarterly, 16,* 515–44.

Harris, A. J. & Sipay, E. R. (1985). *How to increase reading ability,* 8th Edition. New York: Longman.

Schmidt, W. H.; Caul, J.; Byers, J. L.; & Buchman, M. (1984). Content of the basal text selections: Implications for comprehension instruction. In G. G. Duffy, L. R. Roehler, and J. Mason (eds.) *Comprehension instruction: Perspectives and suggestions.* New York: Longman.

Veatch, J. (1978). *Reading in the elementary school* (2nd Edition). New York: John Wiley and Sons, Inc.

Zintz, M. V. & Maggart, Z. R. (1984). *The reading process: The teacher and the learner* (4th Edition) Dubuque, IA: Wm. C. Brown.

SECTION THREE
DETERMINING INSTRUCTIONAL NEEDS

10 Assessment of Readers and Reading Materials

GENERAL ISSUES IN ASSESSMENT ■ THE MANY TYPES OF TESTS ■ EVALUATING READERS ■ TEACHER-MADE TESTS AND OTHER INFORMATION SOURCES ■ EVALUATING MATERIALS ■ ASSESSMENT AND YOUR READING FRAMEWORK

George looked at the test. It said:

Rabbits eat

☐ lettuce ☐ dog food

☐ sandwiches

"Rabbits have to eat carrots, or their teeth will get too long and stick into them," he said.

The teacher nodded and smiled, but she put her finger to her lips.

George carefully drew in a carrot so the test people would know.

(M. Cohen, *First Grade Takes a Test,* (New York: William Morrow & Co., Inc, 1980), p. 5–6.

Previous chapters have stated that a teacher can be considered a type of researcher in the classroom, using a variety of data to make instructional decisions. These data range from informal observations of students to formal, standardized tests. This chapter examines different strategies and techniques that may be used by teachers to evaluate (1) students; (2) reading materials; and (3) the interaction between students and materials.

After reading this chapter, you will be able to

1. use different formal and informal measurement tools for assessing readers and materials;
2. discuss what an assessment tool measures when assessing readers and reading materials;
3. state the differences between formal and informal evaluation instruments and how they differ in their usefulness;
4. state the different goals that assessment serves for a teacher, principal, district superintendent, and parents.

GENERAL ISSUES IN ASSESSMENT

Teachers may sometimes feel that a great deal of their time is spent testing. Often, much of the first week of a new school year is spent using various measurement instruments to determine students' instructional needs. Additionally, school districts regularly require yearly **standardized testing** to compare their students' progress to the progress of students in other districts or from previous years. Tests are a central part of many basal reader programs, requiring that students demonstrate competency on certain skills before attempting the next unit or lesson. Such testing is often paralleled by evaluation requirements at the school district level. School districts now commonly require detailed record keeping by their teachers in the form of a management system. Such a system delineates skills to be learned by students and requires an ongoing **assessment program** to document progress.

Clearly, testing can demand substantial amounts of a teacher's time. This is especially true when one considers not just test administration time, but also time for preparation before testing, for scoring and for interpretation after testing is completed. Obviously, it is important to use this time in the best possible way, choosing assessment instruments to match specific measurement objectives.

The test you choose will largely be determined by your reasons for testing. Although teachers may sometimes feel that testing might not be the best use of instructional time, one must realize that there are many reasons and purposes for administering tests in school (Ruddell & Kinzer, 1982). Some of these goals are:

standardized testing: Evaluation using published tests which include specific directions for administration and scoring.

assessment program: Systematic checking of students' academic progress by various testing methods.

1. to provide information on the strengths and weaknesses of specific students to aid teachers' specific instructional planning;
2. to discover strengths and weaknesses of students and curriculum to aid in decisions for general program improvement;
3. to provide the general public with evidence of student growth or success of instruction;
4. to provide data to contribute to the evaluation of special programs such as **Chapter I;**
5. to provide information for research into effective instructional programs;
6. to improve the educational system in relation to decisions regarding the allocation of tax dollars; to provide data for budgetary planning.

> **Chapter I:** A federally funded program that supplements instruction for disadvantaged students, especially in reading and mathematics.

Test results are used by many people in a school system, each having slightly different goals and purposes. These purposes range from decisions that must be made at the district level for curriculum planning to local school and classroom planning. Yet different tests and types of tests are more appropriate to some of these goals than to others. Some tests measure specific skills and are closely tied to individual students' instructional situations. Other tests provide only group or survey data which cannot be used for specific diagnostic purposes. Still other measures are appropriate for comparing different sets of materials—perhaps before purchasing decisions are made.

Tests range from highly sophisticated tests purchased from test publishers to simple tests constructed by the teacher. Yet there are certain aspects, common to all measurement instruments, which determine whether a test is good or bad, relative to its intended use. Your understanding of these factors will help you choose a test or type of test to best meet your measurement objective.

BEFORE READING ON

At some point in your teaching career, you will probably be asked to recommend a reading test for use in your classroom or you may be asked to serve on a committee that must choose a test for use in your school or school district. What would your criteria be? What should a good test do? What would you look for in a test?

Many people, when asked to define a good test, answer that

- It measures what it is supposed to measure—what it says it measures.
- It gives consistent results, not random or fluctuating results over time.
- It is manageable in terms of administration time.
- It is easy to score and interpret.

These factors are all important considerations when choosing a test. The following terms are generally used to describe the preceding factors.

Validity

validity: A test characteristic which refers to the test's ability to measure what it claims to measure.

Validity is whether a test measures what it is supposed to measure, or what it says it will measure. If a test measures what it is supposed to, then it is said to be valid. A test that attempts to measure oral reading ability would be valid if students were required to read orally while their reading was appropriately scored. A test stating that it measures oral reading and then does so through silent reading procedures would be invalid. Sometimes a test will state that it measures a particular skill or ability when an examination of the actual test items, procedures, or testing tasks shows that this may not be the case.

Consider, however, a test might be used in a manner not intended by its authors. It might be a survey test (thus providing information about general reading ability) that is being inappropriately used to infer areas of specific reading disability. It would be inappropriate to say that the test is invalid in such a situation. The fact that a test is misused does not make it a bad test. We must be careful not to dismiss an instrument because of factors beyond the intent of the instrument.

Your job in choosing between various tests is to be aware of the reading process and the relationship and interrelationship of reading subskills. You must examine carefully not only what a test claims to do, but also what it actually does. This can only be done by looking carefully at the test items. Only then will you be able to say with some certainty that a test is valid. This type of validity, which determines whether the test measures appropriate reading skills, is called **content** validity.

content validity: A test characteristic which looks at the appropriateness of items for measuring the skills to be tested.
curricular validity: A test characteristic which indicates if the test given to students measures what the students have been taught.

Another kind of validity, **curricular** validity, refers to whether the test measures what children are taught. Most respected tests acknowledge that curricular validity depends, in large part, on the given curriculum and students being tested. The classroom teacher is in the best position to determine if a test has curricular validity with regard to the curriculum used in the respective classroom.

Reliability

reliability: A test characteristic which looks at the test's ability to measure consistently.

Reliability tells whether a test is consistent in the information it provides. If a test were given to a student over and over again, and if the test yielded the same score each time, then it would be extremely reliable. In fact, if the scores were identical each time, the test would be 100 percent reliable. Of course, tests are not 100 percent reliable. Differences due to student learning between testing times, or because of affective, physical or environmental factors, all influence test/retest results.

Many assessment tools are available for evaluating readers. Whichever instrument is used, issues of validity and reliability need to be considered.

We need to be able to assume that a test provides consistent information. Then, if differences in pre- and posttest results are found, we can more confidently attribute the change to factors such as learning. This is also why it is very important to hold the testing situation as constant as possible. As much as possible, it is important to administer tests identically each time, or differences in results become difficult to attribute to specific learning factors.

Reliability estimates are generally listed in the teachers' or technical manuals provided with published tests. Always make a special effort to look through such manuals, requesting that they be provided for you if necessary. When examining test manuals, notice that there are several ways of determining reliability of an assessment instrument. Three common methods are **split-half, test/retest,** and **alternate-form** reliability estimates. Readers interested in the differences between the forms of reliability assessment are referred to any introductory book on measurement. For now, it is enough to note that all three methods provide reliability estimates that are in effect correlations showing the degree of relationship between factors. In this case, for example, the relationship might be between scores on different administrations of a test (test/retest reliability).

The degree of relationship between the two test administrations is indicated by a **reliability coefficient,** with 1.00 indicating a perfect relationship between the two sets of scores. A coefficient of 1.00 means

split-half reliability: A way of determining test reliability through dividing the test in half, usually by even and odd numbers.

test/retest reliability: A check to determine if two separate administrations of the same test produce similar scores.

alternate-form reliability: A check to see if different forms of the same test produce similar scores.

reliability coefficient: Indicates the degree of relationship between tests or several administrations of the same test.

that a test is 100 percent reliable; that a student taking the same test twice, with no increase in learning, will receive identical scores both times. In education, tests with reliability coefficients above 0.80 are considered reliable.

Standard Error of Measurement

standard error of measurement: How much a score can vary before the difference can be said to be the result of something more than chance.

Since we know that tests are not 100 percent reliable, it is necessary for teachers to know how widely students' scores will vary by chance. Thus, where reliability coefficients indicate whether a test is reliable, **standard error of measurement** specifies exactly how much a score can move before the difference is attributed to something other than chance. Such information can be viewed in plus-and-minus terms. If the standard error of measurement were 2 and a student scored 17 on a twenty-item test, then that student's actual score is really 17 plus or minus 2, or between 15 and 19.

If the student were to be tested again on the same test, receiving a score of 19, it would not be appropriate to assume that improvement had been shown. This is because the two scores are in the range of standard error of measurement; that is, they are within two points of each other and the difference could be due to chance. All high-quality tests provide information regarding standard error of measurement.

THE MANY TYPES OF TESTS

When asked what measurement is used for in their classrooms, teachers commonly answer

1. to find a student's general reading competency for placement purposes.
2. to see if one book is, in general, more difficult than another.
3. to find motivational material for a student or class.
4. to match a student with appropriate materials.
5. to find out whether a student has mastered a particular instructional lesson, unit or skill.

Think carefully about these statements. Notice that the purposes and the targets of assessment differ. For example, goals 1, 3, and 5 are student centered. The student is the target of measurement, with the assessment conducted directly on the student alone. Goal 3 differs slightly from 1 and 5 in that it measures an affective rather than a skills-based response, but still deals with reader rather than text factors. Such measures include attitude and interest surveys that might be administered to help select motivational reading materials for specific students. Goal 2 does not deal directly with measuring the student, but the material itself, and might be determined through an analysis examining factors such as print size and density of ideas. Goal 4 combines two categories; that is, 4 measures both the materials and student in combination, perhaps to match materials to a specific student or set of students. Thus, assessment can focus on the student, the materials, or the student together with the materials. The target and goals of assessment determine the type of measurement tool and technique used.

There are three types of measurement devices for classroom use: formal assessment instruments; informal assessment instruments; and teacher-made assessment instruments. All are equally valuable to the teacher, but it is important to know the strengths and weaknesses of each, and when each can be appropriately used. The three types of measures are defined as follows:

- **Formal Tests.** Tests which have strict guidelines for administration, scoring and interpretation. Such tests are purchased from test publishers and are often called standardized tests. They may be either norm or criterion referenced.

    formal tests: Have specific rules for administering, scoring, and interpreting.

- **Informal Tests.** Tests which allow for teacher judgment in administration, scoring, and interpretation. Such tests may be purchased as stand-alone items or may be included as part of a larger set of materials. Although tests in this category have a general procedure that must be followed, the teacher's judgment is critical within the procedure. For example, such a test might indicate that the testing session be discontinued when a student's frustration level is reached, but it is teacher judgment that plays a major part in this determination.

    informal tests: Allow for teacher decision making when administering, scoring, and interpreting.

- **Teacher-made Tests.** Tests devised or used by teachers to test students' knowledge of a particular instructional unit or lesson. Tests in this category differ from the above since there is no set procedure that must be followed in administration or scoring, beyond that determined by the teacher.

    teacher-made tests: Cover material currently under study and are designed, administered, and interpreted by the teacher.

These three types of measurement tools can be combined with the several targets of assessment. This provides a structure (presented in figure 10–1) for discussing the various aspects of reading assessment.

To determine where different tests fall in figure 10–1, one must be aware of the testing goal as well as the test's target. In fact, this is the key to the value of any testing program—having a goal, or valid reason for testing. Knowing the testing goal and the testing target is also basic to the process of choosing a test. Keep figure 10–1 in mind as you read the rest of this chapter. Try to decide how the different measurement tools discussed in the following sections fit into the grid.

Within the grid presented in figure 10–1, however, there are specific assessment considerations that range throughout formal, informal, and teacher-made test categories. These considerations relate to these four questions.

Test Types

Targets of Assessment	Formal Tests	Informal Tests	Teacher-Made Tests
Readers			
Materials			

FIGURE 10–1
An overview of test types and targets of assessment

group tests: Are given to more than one student at the same time.

1. *Is the test intended for group administration?* **Group tests** are administered to several students at the same time. Such tests result in overall time savings when a class or an entire school of students needs to be evaluated.

individual tests: Are designed for one-on-one administration.

2. *Is the test intended for individual administration?* **Individual tests** are administered in one-on-one situations. Such tests allow more controlled conditions than do group tests and can add specific information due to examiner observation of student behavior during test administration.

survey tests: Provide measures of only general ability in a certain area.

3. *Is the test intended to survey general reading ability?* **Survey tests** are measures that provide indications of general ability. Reading tests that indicate general reading level, but do not provide indications of specific strengths and weaknesses, fall into this category.

diagnostic tests: Measure very specific skills so that instructional decisions can be made.

4. *Is the test intended to diagnose a specific reading deficiency?* **Diagnostic tests** assess very specific skills and provide information leading to specific instructional practice. Such tests may be group tests (for example, *Stanford Diagnostic Reading Test*) or individual tests (for example, *Durrell Analysis of Reading Difficulty*), but not survey tests.

Implicit in this discussion is the assumption that tests not be used indiscriminately. Generally, teachers gather initial information about students from cumulative records. These are records that follow a student throughout school, providing a compilation of information about strengths, weaknesses, other teachers' observations and comments, and so on. Using the cumulative record as a guide, students can be observed in the classroom situation. Specific tests can be administered to discover areas of perceived weakness so that instructional decisions can be made more reliably.

EVALUATING READERS

Formal Norm-Referenced Tests

Norm-referenced tests compare an individual or a group to a "norm" group of similar individuals. A norm-referenced test usually contains several subtests within an overall area of emphasis. For example, a survey reading test might include subtests in vocabulary, reading rate, comprehension, and study skills. A diagnostic reading test might include subtests in knowledge of word parts, blending ability, inferential and literal comprehension, identifying relationships (for example, cause and effect), oral vocabulary, and so on.

norm-referenced tests: Compare an individual or a group to a group of other, similar individuals.

In norm-referenced assessment, test results are interpreted through a comparison with the **norm group,** providing information about how well a student or students have performed relative to similar students. When choosing a norm-referenced test, therefore, examine the test manual(s) to find out about the group to which your students will be compared. The manual provides information such as the distribution of males and females, the distribution of age ranges, the distribution of the norm population across geographical regions, the distribution of rural and urban students, the distribution of ethnic groups, and other facts which allow you to determine if the norm group is similar enough to your own students to ensure a valid comparison.

norm group: The group whose test performances were used to establish the levels of performances for a standardized test.

Further, it is important to know that since the norm group scores are presented as an average or norm, individual student comparisons are less reliable than comparisons of groups to the norm. For example, comparing a class average on a test would be more accurate than comparing an individual student to the norm.

Interpreting Results

Students' scores on reading tests are commonly reported in five ways:

- as **raw scores**
- as **percentage scores**
- as **percentile scores**
- as **stanine scores**
- as **grade equivalent scores**

Each of these reporting methods yields different information and can be misleading if not used properly.

raw scores: The number of correct responses.

Raw scores are determined simply by adding up the number of correct responses. If you were to give a ten-item test to a student who got eight items right, the raw score would be 8. When giving a single test to a student or group of students, such scores can be valuable since all students are taking the same test and there are no variations among students in the length of test or the skill(s) tested. Remember, however, that norm-referenced reading tests generally consist of a series of subtests. These subtests measure different reading skills and have different numbers of items per subtest. A comprehension subtest, for example, might include twenty-five items while a vocabulary subtest might include forty items. Stating that a student got a raw score of 20 on both subtests does not provide an overview of relative ability across subtests.

percentage scores: Calculated by comparing the number of correct responses to the total possible or total attempted and relating that number to a theoretical number out of 100.

Percentage scores are one way to remove some of the shortcomings of raw scores. Since percentages are calculated by comparing the number correct to the total possible, or total attempted, a percentage can provide a comparison of various subtests of different lengths. To continue this example, the student who had a raw score of 20 on both the twenty-five-item comprehension subtest and on the forty-item vocabulary subtest has percentage scores of 80 and 50, respectively. That is, the student would have received 80 and 50 out of 100. Percentage scores, therefore, allow clearer comparisons across subtests than do raw scores.

percentiles: Points on the raw score scale below which given percentages of the cases in the distribution fall.

Percentile scores indicate the percent of the norm population scoring below a student's score. Percentile scores allow a comparative mea-

Formal assessment tools can be survey or diagnostic; group- or individually-administered tests.

sure of **relative standing** between a student and his or her norm group. Thus, a percentile score of 80 indicates that 80 percent of the norm group scored below the student's raw score.

If a student receives a raw score of 20 (or 80 percent) on a twenty-five-item comprehension subtest, we may feel that the student has done fairly well. Yet a percentage or raw score does not indicate how the student compares with the peer group. If students similar in ability scored fifteen correct (75 percent), then the student scoring 80 percent appears above average. Conversely, if the student's peer group also scored 20 (80 percent) or scored 24 (95 percent), the student's scores would be at or perhaps below those students of similar ability. Percentile scores provide such relative-standing information.

Stanine scores also allow a comparison of relative standing. Stanine scores are reported in numbers between 1 and 9, inclusively. Stanines indicate where in the overall distribution of scores the score in question lies. This reporting technique assumes that the total distribution of scores falls into a **normal curve.** The curve is then divided into nine bands, corresponding to predetermined percentages of scores falling into each band. The illustration in the margin shows the nine stanine bands and the respective percentage of scores falling into each stanine.

Notice that a student whose score is the fifth stanine falls in the range of scores in the middle of the curve. The fifth stanine, as shown in margin note, encompasses twenty percent of the total test scores; ten percent on each side of the mean, or average. Where would a student whose score was the second or ninth stanine fall? If you said in the lower eleven percent and in the upper four percent of test scores, respectively, you would be correct. Thus, while percentile scores allow a comparison of relative standing, stanine scores additionally provide an indication of where a student lies in the overall distribution of scores.

Grade equivalent scores are also commonly used to provide information about relative standing. If a student received a grade equivalent score of 7.0, then that student's raw score was equivalent to the average score of beginning seventh graders in the norm population. Grade equivalent scores can be deceptive and can inadvertently label students. For these reasons, the International Reading Association has released a policy statement opposed to reporting grade equivalent scores, and test publishers have moved away from providing grade equivalent scores for interpreting results.

relative standing: How one student's score compares to scores made by other students in the same group.

stanine scores: Reported in numbers between 1 and 9. Allow a comparison of relative standing.

normal curve: A symmetrical, bell-shaped curve.

grade equivalent scores: Provide relative standing by comparing a student's raw score to the average score across grade levels.

MODEL LESSON

Formal Norm-Referenced Tests. Ms. Henshaw had just come out of a faculty meeting where an announcement had confirmed the memo she received last week: all students in third grade would be tested, using a norm-referenced test, in two weeks. Some teachers had questioned the validity and reliability of the test, and the principal, who had the manual with her, explained that the test was both reliable and valid. The norm group was also discussed, and it was thought that the school's third-grade population adequately reflected this group for comparative purposes. Teachers would be given the test manuals in three days. There was another faculty meeting called to discuss test administration shortly after that time.

During the meeting about test administration, the principal and third-grade teachers discussed the test's instructions for administration. It was made clear that these instructions needed to be followed to the letter. Instructions that were to be read to students were to be read as stated in the test manual, a stopwatch was to be used to make sure that timed sections were accurate, subtests were to be done in order, and so on. Test booklets and answer sheets were to be collected and would be scored electronically, with the results returned to the teachers.

On receiving the results, Ms. Henshaw noticed that there were several parts to the results: a section listing overall scores for her class; a section comparing her class to a norm group; a section that noted how many students had missed particular items; and a section that listed her students' names along with the items each student missed. This information was clustered within question types that appeared on the test, for example, questions dealing with syllabication, vocabulary, literal comprehension, inferencing, and so on.

Since the test had been given late in the school year (the goal of the assessment was to compare students' achievement over several years, as well as to see how the third graders in her school district performed relative to other third graders across the nation), the results could not be incorporated into her instruction. She did record individual students' deficiencies on her class record sheet, as well as on the students' official cumulative record cards. Ms. Henshaw knew that her students' next teacher would be looking at these records and would thus have a better idea of general areas needing particular focus. Further, she would use the information as a discussion point at the faculty meeting at the beginning of next year, when teachers told each other about their observations and comments about the class they had taught the previous year.

Formal Criterion-Referenced Tests

criterion-referenced tests: Compare a student's performance to a predetermined level of success.

A **criterion-referenced test** (CRT) does not compare a student to a norm group. The intent of a CRT is to provide a picture of student performance without comparing that performance to others'. To this end, performance is compared with an established criterion rather than to other students' performance (Popham, 1978). In norm-referenced assessment, a student's score (and thereby the student's performance) is compared to a norm group of peers. In criterion-referenced assessment, the student is compared to a predetermined criterion of success. As Mehrens & Lehman (1984) have stated, "To polarize the distinction, we could say that the focus of a normative score is on how many of Johnny's peers do not perform (score) as well as he does; the focus of a criterion-referenced score is on what it is that Johnny can do" (p. 18).

In part, the popularity of criterion-referenced assessment lies in its use to determine whether a student has mastered a specific set of skills and may be moved on to the next level of instruction. This has been criticized, however, because it implies that a strict sequence of instruction is known to be best for all students and that all necessary reading subskills have been correctly sequenced and identified. Unfortunately, this is not the case. Although much is known about reading, there is still much to learn. Also, even though certain skills are generally thought to be necessary in reading, these skills are interrelated and are difficult to separate. A difficult issue to resolve in criterion-referenced measurement is that deleting any one skill in the large number usually present in a criterion reading test does not usually result in inability to read. This is true of almost all subskills included on most criterion referenced tests and thus, one-by-one, tested skills on a CRT can be questioned.

Criterion-referenced measures are included in almost every basal reading series used in today's schools. Their advantage over norm-referenced assessment is that they can be closely tied to instruction. This makes criterion-referenced assessment an ideal tool on which to base **management systems.** A management system provides a detailed record of each student's progress through an instructional program and records when mastery of specific skills occurs. Such systems are extremely attractive to school systems that are being increasingly faced with accountability issues.

> **management system:** A detailed, systematic record of a student's progress through an instructional program.

Criterion-referenced assessment easily can be used to monitor each student's progress through instructional materials at a pace dictated by how well the current lesson has been mastered. Suppose, for example, that a reader is learning the two-letter blend *st*. If the instructional program introduces the *str* blend at a more difficult level and feels that *str* should not be attempted until *st* has been mastered, then a criterion-referenced test is often used to make a determination of mastery. Perhaps five items testing mastery of *st* are administered, with the criterion set at 3. If the student answers three of the five items correctly, then instruction moves on to the *str* blend. If not, more instruction is provided for *st* and the test (usually in a different form) is again administered. This close tie to instruction is a major reason for criterion-referenced assessment's popularity. Figure 10–2 provides an illustration of a criterion-referenced measure.

One misconception about the differences between norm- and criterion-referenced scores needs to addressed before concluding this section. We often hear the statement that norm-referenced assessment results in relatively arbitrary comparisons of individual students to a norm group, while criterion assessment is somehow fairer because it only examines students' performances against their own strengths. One needs to remember that criterion-referenced tests also compare students' performances against an externally imposed criterion. In fact, one could argue that the criterion is more arbitrary than are norms, since norm-referenced tests provide a comprehensive and valuable discussion of the norm group and norming procedure, while the rationale for a given criterion level is rarely addressed in teacher's manuals, leaving unan-

---

The learner will read a story and sequence sentences. Given a story and 5 sentences, the learner will number each sentence in the correct sequence.

NOTE: *Teacher may give unknown words. However, if the child requests more than 3 words per page, the instructional level may be too difficult. Teacher may identify the first sentence in the correct sequence.*

POST TEST 4.3.1

1. Read the story and the sentences.

2. Number the sentences in the order in which they happened in the story.

NAME: _____
DATE: _____
MINIMUM: 5
SCORE: _____

Carlos and Rosa

Carlos saw Rosa come down the street.

"Come in, Rosa," he said. "I have something you want."

"What is it?" said Rosa. "What do you have for me?"

"Look at my toys," said Carlos. "You will soon see."

Rosa and Carlos ran to look at the toys. Rosa saw big airplanes and trains. She saw little things, too.

Soon Rosa saw a little kitten.

"My kitten!" she said. "My kitten is not a toy! Thank you,

Carlos. I do want my little kitten."

_3_ Rosa and Carlos ran to look at the toys.

_4_ Rosa saw her kitten.

_1_ Rosa came in.

_5_ "Thank you, Carlos," said Rosa.

_2_ Carlos had something for Rosa.

FIGURE 10–2

An example of a criterion-referenced test

swered questions such as How is a criterion determined? or Where does it come from?

Usually, a criterion is set at the level where average students, in relation to students being tested, perform. Thus the difference between a norm and a criterion that is based on average students' performances does not appear substantially different. The major difference between criterion- and norm-referenced assessment lies in philosophy and in the way scores are used, rather than in any substantive difference in how appropriate performance is determined. This is reflected in the frequency of administration of the two types of assessment. Criterion-referenced tests are used often and are usually specifically keyed to the instructional situation, while formal norm-referenced tests are generally used only once per year.

MODEL LESSON

Formal Criterion-Referenced Tests. Mr. Washington had just completed a lesson on cause-and-effect relationships. The lesson format and suggestions came from a basal reader that includes criterion-referenced tests as part of the program. On completing the unit on cause and effect, the teacher's manual suggests that the criterion-referenced test be given to see whether students have mastered the concept of cause and effect and its application.

The test provided in the basal program contained ten items, with 8 as the criterion. The teacher's guide suggested reteaching if the criterion was not met, and new lessons were provided for the reteaching, if needed. An additional criterion assessment, with new items, was provided for use after reteaching.

All but five of Mr. Washington's students met the criterion. His teacher's aide worked with this group of five students, using the reteaching lesson and, on retesting, all five met the criterion. Instruction was thus begun on the next skill, as suggested in the guide provided with his basal reader program.

Informal Tests: The Informal Reading Inventory

Informal reading inventories (IRIs) allow a teacher to match students and materials. They provide information that helps a teacher place students at appropriate instructional levels within a set of graded materials. This is done by having students read passages at varying levels of difficulty until a passage is encountered that is too difficult. This indicates the level of materials that are too difficult, as well as those that could be used appropriately with a particular student. IRIs are included as part of most basal reading programs, can be purchased separately, or can be teacher developed.

informal reading inventory (IRI): Individualized tests consisting of graded word lists and passages used to determine a student's reading ability, and to provide diagnostic information.

In addition to sets of graded word lists and passages, some published IRIs also include tests of spelling and listening comprehension. Although an informal reading inventory is administered individually and requires some expertise to score and interpret (thus requiring somewhat more time that other measures), it provides information that can be of great value in instructional decision making. Teachers typically use IRIs near the beginning of a school year as one information source to help determine instructional groupings and appropriate level of materials for students. They also often are used when a teacher desires more information about some observed reading behavior.

Teachers find IRIs useful partly because they provide an indication of a student's independent, instructional, and frustration reading level. These are important concepts, for they are used to indicate the functioning level of a reader. As a reading educator, you will encounter these terms often. The three reading levels are defined as follows:

■ Independent Reading Level. The level at which students can read on their own without teacher assistance. Reading is fluent and free of undue hesitations. Intonation is appropriate for the punctuation and phrasing of the material.
■ Instructional Reading Level. The level at which one can read if support and instruction are provided. Material at this level is challenging, but not frustrating to read.
■ Frustration Reading Level. The level at which one has great difficulty even with teacher guidance and instruction. In effect, one is unable to read the selection even with support.

Typically, an IRI provides three grade equivalent scores, each corresponding to one of these three general levels of reading. For example, an IRI might determine that a particular student's independent reading level is at approximately the third-grade level, while the instructional and frustration levels may be placed at about the fourth and fifth grades, respectively. This provides some indication of the difficulty of materials appropriate for instruction, practice, free-reading, and supplementary materials and additionally indicates which materials might be too difficult for a particular student.

miscue: An oral reading response different from the text being read.

Published informal reading inventories usually include two copies of each reading selection. The teacher notes any **miscues** and other comments on one copy while the student reads from another. Typically, the teacher's copy is double spaced to allow written comments, and includes suggested comprehension questions with spaces to record students' responses.

Administering an Informal Reading Inventory. Since an informal reading inventory includes passages with varying difficulty levels, a decision must be made when testing a student about which passage should begin the test. There is no need for a student to read passages that might be either too easy or too hard. Passages that are so difficult that they frustrate the student or so easy that time is used unnecessarily need not be administered.

Published IRIs attempt to provide an entry level to the oral reading passages through a set of graded word lists. These lists are read by the student, beginning with the list suggested by the IRI being used, until a certain number of errors occur within a given list. Most IRIs then suggest that the student begin oral reading with the passage corresponding to the level of the word list that was read perfectly, or with a passage one level below this list. The word lists are in two forms: one for the teacher; the other, for the student. The teacher's copy provides space for noting student answers. Specific student responses must be noted, since miscues (or word recognition mistakes) on the word list can provide valuable supplementary information when looking for miscue patterns throughout the oral reading passages. The marking system in table 10–1 should be used to indicate reading behaviors on the word list as well as on subsequently administered passages.

We have attempted to be consistent with recommended marking systems. Different tests, however, use different symbols or methods to mark reading miscues and behaviors. Since the miscue types are well accepted, it is not important for you to accept one marking system over another. We do recommend that you choose one system and use it consistently. Now let us look at an example of an IRI given to Debby, an average second-grade student (figures 10–3 and 10–4).

Debby made no errors on the first ten words on the initial list so she was moved to the next level. On the second-grade list she stumbled on *beautiful,* but did read the word correctly. *I'm* was read as *am* but was self corrected. Thus the only miscue is the last word on the list. The next (third-grade) word list resulted in three miscues and one self correction, and Debby was asked to read the words on the fourth-grade list.

Note that the teacher allowed Debby to finish the fourth-grade list even after five miscues. This was thought appropriate for two reasons. First, Debby immediately went on after her fifth miscue and second, she did not exhibit signs of frustration. The teacher felt that it would be more detrimental to discontinue after *is-land,* thus sending the message that too many mistakes had taken place, than allowing Debby to continue to the end of the list. Remember, this is an informal reading inventory, where the teacher's judgment largely determines administration and interpretation. The key to decisions made during an IRI center around the child. If signs of frustration are evident, then discontinue. If not, additional information can appropriately be gathered.

Following the fourth-grade list, Debby was told she would be reading several short passages out loud. The flexibility of the informal reading inventory is again evident at this point. Debby told the teacher that she was insecure reading out loud, and the teacher decided to begin at

TABLE 10–1

Informal reading inventory marking system and examples

Miscue/Behavior and Definition	Marking	Example
Omissions, insertions, substitutions, and no-response behaviors are always considered as word recognition miscues.		
Omission Not reading something in the text, e.g., part or whole word, phrase, punctuation.	Circle the omission.	He likes the big, (yellow) car.
Insertion Adding something not originally present in the text.	Use caret (^), add insertion.	(and blue) He likes the big, yellow ^ car.
Substitution Replacing something in the text with something else, e.g., *this* for *the.*	Cross out original, add substitution.	(takes) He likes the big, yellow car.
No Response (Teacher Pronounced) Substantial pause indicating inability to read the word, resulting in the teacher's pronouncing the word.	Write *P* over pronounced items.	(P) He likes the big, yellow car.
Although always marked, some IRIs do not count the following as word recognition miscues, or do not count them as a full, one-point miscue.		
Repetition Repeated reading of a word or group of words.	Put dome over repeated items.	He likes the big, yellow car.
Hesitation Pause, interrupting the flow or pattern of reading.	Put checkmark at point of hesitation.	✓ He likes the big, yellow car.
Transposition Reversing order of letters in words or words in sentences.	Put reverse *S* around transposed items.	He likes the big, yellow car.
Mispronunciation Pronunciation clearly different from normal, e.g., *k* in *knife* or *w* in *sword.*	Write phonetic pronunciation or use diacritical marks.	(līkĕs) He likes the big, yellow car.
Self-Correction Corrected by the student without teacher help.	Write *C* above the miscue.	C large He likes the big, yellow car.

Name *Debby*

Form A Part 1/Graded Word Lists

PP		P		1		2	
1 for	+	1 was	+	1 many	+	1 stood	+
2 blue	+	2 day	+	2 painted	+	2 climb	+
3 car	+	3 three	+	3 feet	+	3 isn't	+
4 to	+	4 farming	+	4 them	+	4 beautiful *bōw-beautiful*	
5 and	+	5 bus	+	5 food	+	5 waiting	+
6 it	+	6 now	+	6 tell	+	6 head	+
7 helps	+	7 read	+	7 her	+	7 cowboy	+
8 stop	+	8 children	+	8 please	+	8 high	+
9 funny	+	9 went	+	9 peanut	+	9 people	+
10 can	+	10 then	+	10 cannot	+	10 mice	+
11 big		11 black		11 eight		11 corn	+
12 said		12 barn		12 trucks		12 everyone	+
13 green		13 trees		13 garden		13 strong	+
14 look		14 brown		14 drop		14 I'm	*am*ᶜ
15 play		15 good		15 stopping		15 room	+
16 see		16 into		16 frog		16 blows	+
17 there		17 she		17 street		17 gray	+
18 little		18 something		18 fireman		18 that's	+
19 is		19 what		19 birthday		19 throw	+
20 work		20 saw		20 let's		20 own	*on*

Teacher note: If the child missed five words in any column—stop Part I. Begin oral paragraphs, Part II, (Form A), at highest level in which child recognized all 20 words. To save time, if the first ten words were correct, go on to the next list. If one of the first ten words were missed, continue the entire list.

FIGURE 10–3
Debby's informal reading inventory (word lists)—Grades one and two

Form A Part 1

3		4		5		6	
1 hour	*hoar*	1 spoon	*+*	1 whether	_____	1 sentinel	_____
2 senseless	*sendless*	2 dozen	*+*	2 hymn	_____	2 nostrils	_____
3 turkeys	*+*	3 trail	*+*	3 sharpness	_____	3 marsh	_____
4 anything	*+*	4 machine	*matching*	4 amount	_____	4 sensitive	_____
5 chief	*+*	5 bound	*brown* ᶜ	5 shrill	_____	5 calmly	_____
6 foolish	*+*	6 exercise	*ex* ––– ᴾ	6 freedom	_____	6 tangle	_____
7 enough	*+*	7 disturbed	*dis-disturb*	7 loudly	_____	7 wreath	_____
8 either	*other*	8 force	*+*	8 scientists	_____	8 teamwork	_____
9 chased	*+*	9 weather	*+*	9 musical	_____	9 billows	_____
10 robe	*+*	10 rooster	*+*	10 considerable	_____	10 knights	_____
11 crowd	*+*	11 mountain(s)	_____	11 examined	_____	11 instinct	_____
12 crawl	*+*	12 island	*is-land*	12 scarf	_____	12 liberty	_____
13 unhappy	*+*	13 hook	*+*	13 muffled	_____	13 pounce	_____
14 clothes	*+*	14 guides	*+*	14 pacing	_____	14 rumored	_____
15 hose	*house* ᶜ	15 moan	*+*	15 oars	_____	15 strutted	_____
16 pencil	*+*	16 settlers	*sletters*	16 delicious	_____	16 dragon	_____
17 meat	*+*	17 pitching	*+*	17 octave	_____	17 hearth	_____
18 discover	*+*	18 prepared	*period*	18 terrific	_____	18 shifted	_____
19 picture	*+*	19 west	*+*	19 salmon	_____	19 customers	_____
20 nail	*+*	20 (k)nowledge	*nowledge*	20 briskly	_____	20 blond	_____

FIGURE 10–4
Debby's informal reading inventory (word lists)—Grades three through six

a level slightly lower than indicated by the word lists. Figure 10–5 shows the two passages that Debby read. These correspond to grade levels one and two. Notice that Debby appears to be reading for meaning in passage 1. She self-corrects several places where her initial effort did not make sense, and her reading of the last sentence is syntactically correct, preserving the text's intended meaning. She does appear to have some difficulty with the latter half of the passage. In one instance she omits punctuation; in another, she makes a question out of a statement. Word recognition miscues were scored as above 4, or frustration level. Yet Debby's comprehension of the passage is at independent level even though she missed one factual question.

Teacher judgment again determines whether to continue with the next passage. When asked whether she wanted to read another passage, Debby answered yes. This, coupled with the fact that comprehension was still at the independent level, prompted the teacher to continue to the next passage. Remember, also, that Debby's admitted nervousness at reading aloud may have contributed to the number of miscues in her reading.

The second passage also indicates that Debby is actively processing the text and that she is trying to derive meaning from what she reads. The comments that she makes during the reading (for example, "ride *at* midnight—or is that the horse's name?") show that she is interacting with what she reads and that she is trying to relate the text to her existing knowledge base. Unfortunately, her answer to the third comprehension question indicates that she never did understand that *midnight* was the horse's name and not a time of day. However, the fact that she is attempting to process what she reads rather than simply reading words without thinking about meaning is important.

Following this passage, the teacher decided to discontinue the test. During the comprehension questioning, Debby began exhibiting signs of frustration. She fidgeted in her chair and often looked around the room. She began drumming her fingers and showed signs of stress between questions. Since the scoring of Debby's miscues and comprehension questions indicated that both aspects bordered on the frustration level, the test was discontinued. At this point the teacher began reading the next passage to Debby, asking questions as before. This procedure, discontinued when frustration level on the comprehension questions is reached, evaluates one's listening comprehension.

After completing an informal reading inventory, a summary sheet is compiled. Published IRIs usually include summary pages as part of the inventory. An example of a summary sheet is shown in figure 10–6 including the information on Debby's reading.

The summary includes information about the word lists as well as Debby's miscues on the IRI passages. The summary is divided into word recognition (WR) miscues and comprehension (COMP) errors. Addition-

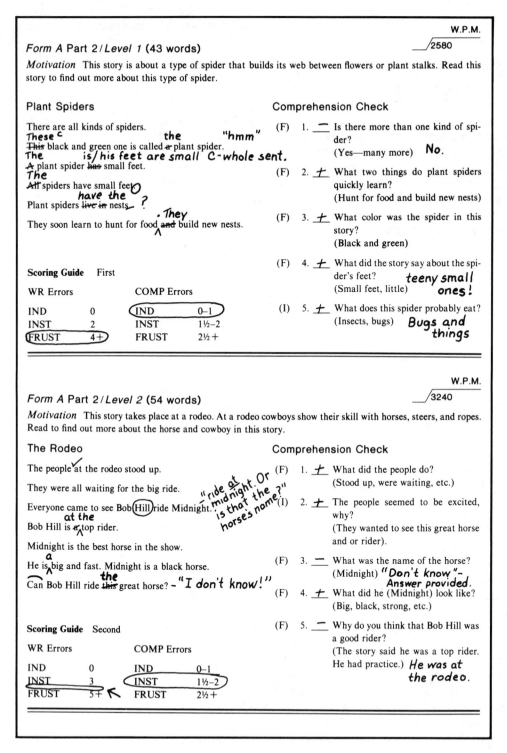

Form A Part 2/*Level 1* (43 words)

W.P.M.

___/2580

Motivation This story is about a type of spider that builds its web between flowers or plant stalks. Read this story to find out more about this type of spider.

Plant Spiders

There are all kinds of spiders.
These ᶜ the "hmm"
~~This~~ black and green one is called ~~a~~ plant spider.
The   is/his feet are small C-whole sent.
~~A~~ plant spider ~~has~~ small feet.
The
~~All~~ spiders have small feet⟲
have the ⟲ ?
Plant spiders ~~live in~~ nests⌐
. They
They soon learn to hunt for food ~~and~~ build new nests.
                    ∧

Comprehension Check

(F) 1. ⎺ Is there more than one kind of spider?
(Yes—many more) **No.**

(F) 2. ✚ What two things do plant spiders quickly learn?
(Hunt for food and build new nests)

(F) 3. ✚ What color was the spider in this story?
(Black and green)

(F) 4. ✚ What did the story say about the spider's feet? **teeny small**
(Small feet, little) **ones!**

(I) 5. ✚ What does this spider probably eat?
(Insects, bugs) **Bugs and things**

Scoring Guide First

WR Errors		COMP Errors	
IND	0	(IND	0–1)
INST	2	INST	1½–2
(FRUST	4+)	FRUST	2½+

W.P.M.

___/3240

Form A Part 2/*Level 2* (54 words)

Motivation This story takes place at a rodeo. At a rodeo cowboys show their skill with horses, steers, and ropes. Read to find out more about the horse and cowboy in this story.

The Rodeo

The people✓at the rodeo stood up.

They were all waiting for the big ride.

Everyone came to see Bob (Hill) ride Midnight. *"ride at midnight. Or is that the horse's name?"*
at the
Bob Hill is ~~a~~ top rider.
        ∧
Midnight is the best horse in the show.
    a
He is⌐big and fast. Midnight is a black horse.
⌐   the
Can Bob Hill ride ~~this~~ great horse? – *"I don't know!"*

Comprehension Check

(F) 1. ✚ What did the people do?
(Stood up, were waiting, etc.)

(I) 2. ✚ The people seemed to be excited, why?
(They wanted to see this great horse and or rider).

(F) 3. ⎺ What was the name of the horse?
(Midnight) *"Don't know"–*
Answer provided.

(F) 4. ✚ What did he (Midnight) look like?
(Big, black, strong, etc.)

(F) 5. ⎺ Why do you think that Bob Hill was a good rider?
(The story said he was a top rider. He had practice.) *He was at the rodeo.*

Scoring Guide Second

WR Errors		COMP Errors	
IND	0	IND	0–1
INST	3	(INST	1½–2)
FRUST	5+ ↖	FRUST	2½+

FIGURE 10–5
Debby's informal reading inventory (passages)—Grades one and two

Form A Inventory Record

Summary Sheet

Student's Name __Debby__ Grade __2__ Age (Chronological) __7-2__
yrs. mos.

Date __9/8__ School _____ Administered by _____

Part 1 Word Lists			Part 2 Oral Paragraphs			
Grade Level	Percent of Words Correct	Word Recognition Errors		WR	Comp	H.C.

PP	___	*Consonants* ___ Consonants	PP			
1 P	___	___ blends	P			
1	_100_	✓ digraphs	1	*FRUST*	*IND*	
		___ endings	2	*INST/FRUST*	*INST*	
		___ compounds	3			90
		___ contractions	4			90
		Vowels	5			75
		✓ long	6			
		___ short	7			
2	_95_	___ long/short oo	8			
		___ vowel + r				
		___ diphthong		Estimated Levels		
		✓ vowel comb.				Grade
		___ a + 1 or w		Independent		_1_
		Syllable		Instructional		_2_ (range)
3	_85_	___ visual patterns		Frustration		_3_
4	_65_	✓ prefix		Listening Capacity		_5_
		___ suffix				
5	___	Word Recognition reinforcement and				
6	___	Vocabulary development				

Comp Errors

_3_ Factual (F)
_0_ Inference (I)
_0_ Vocabulary (V)
_N/A_ "Word Caller" (A student who reads without associating meaning)
_N/A_ Poor Memory

Summary of Specific needs:

Note: Minimal information on which to base word recognition error patterns. Suggest diagnostic test if classroom observations confirm the patterns noted here.

Permission is granted by the publisher to reproduce pp. 49 through 60.

FIGURE 10–6
Debby's informal reading inventory (summary sheet)

hearing capacity (HC) level: The highest level of material that a student can understand when listening.

ally, a **hearing capacity (HC) level** has been determined. This was done by asking comprehension questions after reading passages to the student. The hearing capacity is valuable because it indicates students' comprehension levels removed from any decoding factors. Theoretically, the difference between one's hearing capacity (or listening comprehension) and one's reading comprehension indicates whether a student is at level or slightly below level (Harris & Sipay, 1985). Passages to determine hearing capacity are read to the student beginning with the passage immediately beyond the passage at which the oral reading test was discontinued, concluding when frustration level in comprehension is reached. The second part of the summary sheet includes information arrived at through an evaluation of trends noticed in Debby's reading.

A Checklist for IRI Administration

1. Have all materials ready. This includes typing word lists on separate sheets of paper or cards, as needed. Avoid having to shuffle papers during the session with the student. Be familiar with the marking system and passages.
2. Have a tape recorder ready. It is sometimes very difficult to keep up with the student, and most students don't mind if a tape recorder is used unobtrusively. Don't turn the tape on and off throughout the session, because this draws undue attention to the machine.
3. Begin with a word list one or two grade levels below the student's actual grade. This may vary, depending on your knowledge of that student.
4. Continue with word lists until the criterion level for miscues has been reached, recording any discrepancies between the student's reading and the words on the list.
5. Begin the IRI passages at a level one or two grades below that of the word list where the criterion error level was reached. Use your knowledge about the student and your observation of the student during administration of the word lists to modify the entry level for the passage as necessary.
6. Make sure to read the motivating focusing statement to the student before allowing the student to begin reading the passage.
7. Mark any miscues during oral reading of the passages and record any discrepancies between the student's reading and the original text.
8. Ask the student the comprehension questions for each passage, noting errors and recording the student's responses. Do not allow the student to refer to the passage. It is appropriate to give partial credit for answers.
9. Discontinue the student's oral reading of the IRI passages when frustration level has been reached. Again, you will need to use your judgment. Some students will reach frustration level on word recognition

errors before reaching frustration level on the comprehension questions. Other students will show the reverse pattern. Still others will reach frustration level, as indicated by the test, simultaneously in both aspects. A rule of thumb is to discontinue if both word recognition and comprehension aspects test at frustration level. If only one aspect is at this level, then you may continue the test. In any case, let your observations of the student in the testing situation be your guide regarding a decision about when to stop the test.

10. To find a listening comprehension level (or hearing capacity), begin reading the next passage to the student, asking comprehension questions as before. Hearing capacity indicates the level at which students can comprehend information presented orally, rather than in written form. Discontinue testing hearing capacity after the frustration level has been reached, as indicated by the score on the comprehension questions.

Scoring and Interpretation. As the student reads IRI passages to the teacher, any inconsistencies between the student's oral reading and the text being read are recorded. Independent, instructional, and frustration levels are then determined by the number of miscues the student makes. Although published IRIs indicate specific numbers of miscues that correspond to each of the reading levels for a given passage, the numbers are arrived at through determining the percentage of miscues to total words read (for word recognition) or to the number of comprehension questions (for comprehension). This is called the scoring criteria.

There has been some disagreement regarding scoring criteria for IRIs (Aulls, 1982; Betts, 1946; Cooper, 1952; Powell, 1973). To resolve these differences, Burns, Roe & Ross (1984, p. 396) have combined the criteria proposed by Johnson & Kress (1965) with those of Powell (1970). The result shown here is suggested for use when determining reading levels on an IRI. The percentages that correspond to the three reading levels are important guidelines to use should you decide to construct your own IRI. Remember, however, that they are only approximate guidelines.

Reading Level	Word Recognition Accuracy		Comprehension Accuracy
Independent	99% or higher	and	90% or higher
Instructional	85% or higher (grades 1–2) and 95% or higher (grades 3 and above)	and	75% or higher
Frustration	below 90%	or	below 50%
Hearing Capacity	—		75% or higher

BEFORE READING ON

There are differences in the type of miscues that are demonstrated in the following examples. Can you describe them?
Text to be read:

> The boy likes the kitten. Ask him where it is.

Student 1 reads: The boy likes the cat. Ask him where it is.
Student 2 reads: The boy likes the kitchen. Ask him where it is.
Student 3 reads: The boy like da kitt'n. Ax him where it is.
                   (black dialect speaker)
Student 4 reads: The boy likes the kitten let's ask where she is.
Student 5 reads: The boy likes the kitten. Ask him to go where it is.

In these examples, you may have noticed that some of the miscue(s) preserved the essential meaning of the text while others changed the meaning. Disregarding student 3 for the moment, student 1 provides an example of this, as does student 4. The substitution of *cat* for *kitten* and combining the two sentences did not substantially alter the original meaning of the text, although neither student read exactly what was presented. This raises an important and interesting question with regard to scoring of miscues.

Do you think it appropriate to term the inconsistencies noticed in student 1's and student 4's reading as mistakes, or do you feel it appropriate to "let it go," calling the reading correct? If such reading occurred in your classroom, would you immediately stop and correct the reader or would you allow the reader to go on? Your answer will depend largely on whether you view reading as essentially a text-based or as a reader-based process. Clearly, the reading of students 1 and 4 indicates that the text has been comprehended. Although the students did not read exactly what was written, the author's message has been grasped. Note such occurrences on the answer sheet for later analysis, but realize that the miscue was semantically correct. Some systems encourage you to count these; others do not.

What does reader 2's miscue tell us? Does the substitution of *kitchen* for *kitten* indicate anything more than the fact that comprehension has not taken place? If the question What did the boy like? were asked of the student, there is a high probability that the boy would answer with *kitchen*, demonstrating that the meaning of the sentence has not been grasped. Yet there is much that student 2's miscue allows us to infer about the student's reading process. Notice that the substitution makes sense in the sentence, even though the sentence now means something different than the original. The student has used syntactic cues effectively, correctly placing a noun where it belongs in the sentence. The student knows, for example, that articles must be followed by nouns in English.

Notice also that the student used many of the letters in the original work (kitten) in the substitution. Indeed, the only difference between the two words is the replacement of the second *t* in *kitten* with a *ch*. This indicates that the student is not making wild guesses about what is to be read. Active and logical processing is taking place. This may also be said of student 5. Although the meaning of the original sentences has been altered, the miscue is not arbitrary. Obviously, such inferences should not be based on only one such instance in a student's reading. When interpreting an IRI, it is the **pattern of miscues** that is used to draw generalizations about the reader.

Let's now examine student 3's reading. How did you categorize this student's miscues? Did you feel that this student read incorrectly or that the reading reflected the student's normal dialect pattern, thus allowing the inconsistencies between the reading and the text to be disregarded? Once again, your answer will depend on your framework of reading and on the importance you place on exact pronunciation and apprehending meaning. Most people feel that there may be instances when dialect differences may be focused on to make a student aware of some more-accepted standard but that dialect variations should not be counted as miscues (Goodman & Buck, 1973; Harris & Sipay, 1985).

pattern of miscues: A group of similar miscues from which a teacher can begin to draw generalizations about a reader.

MODEL LESSON

Informal Reading Inventory. School had been in session for just over one month when Joann and her parents moved to a new neighborhood. On Joann's first day, Ms. Chen welcomed Joann to her new third-grade class. Ms. Chen wanted Joann to have a good experience in her new school and, after introducing her to her classmates, decided to administer an informal reading inventory to help place Joann with materials appropriate to her level. This was especially valuable since, on talking to Joann, Ms. Chen discovered that the basal reader used in Joann's other school was different from the one used by Ms. Chen. The testing took place while the other students were involved in art activities, under the supervision of Ms. Chen's parent volunteer aide.

Ms. Chen used the IRI provided with her basal reader program. After administering the appropriate word lists and passages, Ms. Chen decided that Joann was able to read material just a little more difficult than what was being read by the average readers in her class. Since Ms. Chen wanted to confirm this finding through some regular classroom work, and since she wanted Joann to experience success in her new situation, Ms. Chen placed her with the group of average readers. She made a note in her class record sheet, however, to review Joann's work after a short period of time in case she should be moved to other, more difficult material.

Creating Your Own Informal Reading Inventory. Although there are a number of published IRIs readily available (for example, almost all basal readers now contain IRIs appropriate for use with the given basal program), you may at times want to construct your own. For example, you might want your IRI to reflect a set of materials that does not include its own IRI, since this would have more curricular validity than a generic IRI or one constructed for another set of materials.

Informal Tests: The Cloze Procedure

cloze procedure: A fill-in-the-blanks activity used to estimate the level at which a child can read with assistance.

The preceding section has pointed out that informal reading inventories are one way to match students with materials. Another useful technique for doing this, however, is sometimes preferred because it can be administered to a group and it involves the student directly with the text, without the intervening step of teacher questions. This technique is called the **cloze procedure.** Cloze gained widespread use after its modification by Taylor (1953). Having its roots in gestalt psychology, cloze uses the human drive to provide closure to incomplete items. In the reading cloze procedure, this has been translated to the reader's use of context to complete passages from which words have been systematically deleted, and is essentially a fill-in-the-blanks task (see Warwick, 1978; Rankin, 1974, 1978).

In the cloze procedure, students are given a passage that has blanks in place of some of the words. Students attempt to fill in the blanks with the word that was deleted from the original passage. Using the scoring procedure described later in this section, the teacher has an indication about whether the passage is at independent, instructional, or frustration level for the student and, by extension, whether the material from which the passage came is appropriate. When attempting to match students and materials, construct cloze passages from selections taken from the material that will be read. Since both cloze and the IRI attempt to match students and materials, table 10–2 provides an outline of the major differences between the two measures.

Constructing a Cloze Test. Constructing a cloze test is a simple task. One needs only to choose a passage representative of the material from which it came and systematically delete words. The passage chosen should not be broken up by illustrations or other potentially distractive features. Blanks are substituted for the deleted words. The following list describes the construction of a cloze test in detail and table 10–3 provides an illustration of a cloze test ready for use.

1. Choose representative passages from the beginning, middle, and end of the material (usually a book) you wish to use with your student(s). To ensure high reliability, each passage should contain approximately 250 words. Obviously, this may not be possible in primary grade materials. It is strongly recommended that a number of rep-

TABLE 10–2

General differences between cloze and IRI

	Cloze	IRI
Administration	Group or individual	Individual
	Written (or oral)	Oral
	Passages	Word lists, passages, oral questions
Uses	Match students and materials	Match students and materials
	Find a student's general reading level	Find a student's general reading level
	General readability measure	General readability measure
		Inferences about student's reading process
Type of Information	Ability to use context	Word recognition score
	Comprehension score	Comprehension score
		Hearing capacity score
	Independent, instructional, frustration reading level	Independent, instructional, frustration reading level

resentative passages be used, since averaging the results from a number of passages serves to increase the validity and reliability of the assessment procedure.

2. Leave the first sentence of the passage intact. This provides a contextual base.
3. Beginning with the second sentence, replace every fifth word with a blank. Be sure that your blanks are the same size. The blanks should not provide the reader with a clue as to the length of word deleted.

   Continue, if possible, until fifty words have been deleted. The following, however, are usually not deleted: proper names, dates, abbreviations, or acronyms (for example, IBM). When these are encountered, the next word is deleted and the every-fifth-word rule proceeds from that point.
4. After the final deletion, leave the rest of the sentence intact. The cloze passage is then concluded with an additional complete, intact sentence.

TABLE 10–3

Sample cloze passage

That evening they all had dinner together in the enchanter's cozy kitchen. Then Albion took Petronella _____ to a stone building _____ unbolted its door. Inside _____ seven huge black dogs.

"_____ must watch my hounds _____ night," said he.

Petronella _____ in, and Albion closed _____ locked the door.

At _____ the hounds began to _____ and bark. They showed _____ teeth at her. But Petronella _____ a real princess. She _____ up her courage. Instead _____ backing away, she went _____ the dogs. She began _____ speak to them in _____ quiet voice. They stopped _____ and sniffed at her. _____ patted their heads.

"I _____ what it is," she _____. "You are lonely here. _____ will keep you company." _____ so all night long, _____ sat on the floor _____ talked to the hounds _____ stroked them. They lay _____ to her.

In the _____, Albion came and let _____ out. "Ah," said he, "_____ see that you are _____. If you had run _____ the dogs, they would _____ torn you to pieces. _____ you may ask for _____ you want."

"I want _____ comb for my hair," _____ Petronella.

The enchanter gave _____ a comb carved from _____ piece of black wood.

Prince Ferdinand _____ sunning himself and working _____ a crossword puzzle. Petronella _____ to him in a _____ voice, "I am doing _____ for you."

"That's nice," _____ the prince. "What's 'selfish' _____ nine letters?"

"You are," _____ Petronella. She went to _____ enchanter. "I will work _____ you once more," she _____. That night Albion led _____ to a stable. Inside were seven huge horses.

Scoring and Interpreting Your Cloze Test. A cloze test is similar to an informal reading inventory in that it too provides an indication of a reader's independent, instructional, and frustration reading levels. Cloze tests determine the reading level by calculating the percentage of exact replacements of deleted words. Synonyms are not counted as correct in scoring a cloze test. Using the cloze test shown in table 10–3, the following replacements were provided by Lee, a third-grade student.

	Original Deletion	Lee's Replacement		Original Deletion	Lee's Replacement
1.	out	away	26.	close	beside
2.	and	and	27.	morning	morning
3.	were	sat	28.	her	her
4.	you	we	29.	I	I
5.	all	all	30.	brave	alive
6.	went	went	31.	from	NO RESPONSE
7.	and	and	32.	have	have
8.	once	NO RESPONSE	33.	now	so
9.	snarl	growl	34.	what	anything
10.	their	their	35.	a	a
11.	was	NO RESPONSE	36.	said	said
12.	plucked	NO RESPONSE	37.	her	her
13.	of	of	38.	a	a
14.	toward	toward	39.	was	lay
15.	to	to	40.	at	NO RESPONSE
16.	a	her	41.	said	said
17.	snarling	NO RESPONSE	42.	low	nice
18.	she	she	43.	this	this
19.	see	know	44.	said	said
20.	said	said	45.	in	about
21.	I	NO RESPONSE	46.	snapped	said
22.	and	then	47.	the	the
23.	she	she	48.	for	with
24.	and	and	49.	said	cried
25.	and	then	50.	her	Petronella

12 replacements out of 25   12 replacements out of 25

SCORE: 24/50 * 100 = 48%

Several researchers have attempted to specify the scoring criterion for interpreting cloze results (Bormuth, 1968; Rankin & Culhane, 1969; Rankin, 1971). Although complete agreement does not exist, we suggest the percentage bands noted by Rankin & Culhane, as does Aulls (1982, p. 552).

Reading Level	Percentage of Exact Replacements (Rankin & Culhane)	Percentage of Exact Replacement (Bormuth)
Independent Reading Level	above 60%	above 57%
Instructional Reading Level	40%–59%	44%–57%
Frustration Reading Level	below 40%	below 44%

Lee's percentage of replacements was forty-eight. Using this scale, Lee's reading of the passage is at the instructional level.

Common Questions about Cloze

Question: Why are only exact replacements counted? Isn't it unfair to reject synonyms like *home* for *house* as in "that is a nice _____"?

Answer: The cloze procedure has been extensively used and tested. The **exact replacement criterion** has been shown to be accurate and does not penalize students because the percentage bands for the various reading levels are so wide (a range of twenty percent for instructional level). The exact replacements allow more accurate scoring and resolve potential problems of different semantic interpretations by different people. Some might argue, for example, that *home* and *house* are not the same—that a house is only a building, while home implies much more. Because of the exact replacement criterion, the percentages corresponding to the various reading levels are quite low. A student can replace as few as four out of ten deletions (forty percent), yet still be placed at the instructional reading level. Some people do score synonyms as correct, but higher scoring percentages must then be used and the test becomes more difficult to score, thus taking more teacher time.

Question: How accurate is the cloze procedure?

Answer: The cloze procedure has been studied and shown to be quick, easy-to-use, and able to provide approximate measurements consistently. Teacher judgment must play a significant part in cloze interpretation. Give students the benefit of doubt if their percentage score borders the bands separating the different reading levels. Remember that the test is most accurate when at least three cloze passages are used from throughout the material under consideration.

Question: Should there be a time limit when administering a cloze test?

exact replacement criterion: A scoring procedure that accepts as correct only those replacements which were the actual words deleted from the text.

Answer: No. Generally, students are given as much time as they wish to complete the cloze passage. They are certainly allowed to go through the passage more than once.

Question: Does spelling count when marking the student's replacements?

Answer: No.

Other Uses of the Cloze Procedure. Although the cloze test has traditionally been used to examine the potential match between readers and specific reading material, there are other ways in which the cloze procedure benefits the reading teacher. First, the cloze test can be used with a graded set of materials to determine a student's general reading level. This allows the teacher to generalize the student's score beyond the material from which the cloze test was constructed. If this modification is made, then a set of graded passages is used to construct a series of cloze tests. A student is then asked to work through the passages, attempting to replace deletions. Scoring the series of cloze tests provides a rough guide to the grade level (corresponding to the grade level of the passage) at which frustration reading level is reached. Readability formulas (discussed later in this chapter) can be used, instead of a leveled set of passages taken from a basal reader, to determine the reading grade level of the passages chosen for use with this procedure.

The other common use for the cloze is as a teaching technique. There have been several variations of the cloze proposed for use in instruction instead of assessment. For example, deleting specific parts of speech (nouns, adjectives, or verbs) has been used in instructional situations, as has providing choices above the blanks. When used as an instructional aid, however, it is important to provide time for meaningful discussion of the replacements. It is not enough to simply grade the student's effort. You will have to lead students into an awareness of why given replacements are appropriate, what other options might fit, and why some replacements are not very good choices.

Informal Tests: Additional Measures

In addition to informal reading inventories and cloze tests, there are other informal assessment tools that teachers commonly use as part of their reading instructional program. Two are described in the following sections.

Retelling Scores. **Retelling scores** are derived when students are asked to read a passage and then retell what was read in their own words. Retellings are useful measures of comprehension. They have been used in informal reading inventories to supplement or, at times, replace the comprehension questions generally asked after an IRI passage has been

retelling scores: A measure of comprehension obtained by having the children tell in their own words what they have just read.

passage independent:
Describes questions
which can be answered
from general knowledge
rather than from having to
read the text from which
the questions were drawn.
idea units: Complete,
related thoughts.

read. Some feel that retellings are more accurate than answers to questions, because questions can sometimes be answered from general knowledge even without reading a passage. In fact, Allington, Choolos, Domarack & Truex (1977) have shown that approximately thirty percent of the questions asked in informal reading inventories are **passage independent;** that is, they may be answered without first reading the passage to which they refer.

When using retelling scores, one first divides the original passage into units, often called **idea units** or thought units. These units should represent a complete, related thought. For example

The boy ran.

would be considered as one idea unit, while

The boy ran although his leg was hurt.

consists of two idea units. If possible, two people should work together to segment the passage. This increases the reliability of this procedure.

The student's retelling of the passage is then compared to and matched with the original, now segmented passage. Instructional reading level is determined by the degree of consistency between the retelling and the segmented passage. Generally, a sixty to seventy percent match is used as the criterion for the instructional reading level. Teacher judgment, of course, plays a part in this informal test situation. Teachers use information such as the amount and specificity of the ideas recalled and the order and fluency of the retelling when considering whether a student may be placed at the instructional level for a given passage.

Assessment of Attitudes and Interests. One of the most powerful pieces of information available to a teacher concerned with motivating students is an awareness of each student's attitudes and interests. Informal measures can be used to discover motivational topics that can enhance instruction.

Attitude and interest measures have been placed in the informal assessment category because basal readers provide suggested assessment inventories and because there are a number of published inventories available. Clearly, however, these can also be teacher made.

Naturally teachers want to show that reading is interesting and common sense dictates using materials with a topic the child thinks is worth reading. Unfortunately, it is easy to get so involved in ensuring that a student learns to read that reading ability becomes an end in itself. No wonder some graduates can read but dislike reading intensely and simply *don't* or don't want to read. When students develop a love of reading, it becomes lifelong activity; thus the best educators go beyond simply providing students with the capability to read.

Figures 10–7 and 10–8 show items from the *Wisconsin Reading Attitude and Interest Scales* (Dulin & Chester, 1984). The test items re-

I. The first part of the inventory consists of a series of choices to be made between different leisure-time activities, some dealing with reading and others not. You're to indicate your choices by marking a series of scales, and it works like this.

At each of the two ends of each scale there'll be an activity, something you could do in your spare time if you wanted to. If you'd much rather do one of the activities than the other, mark the box nearest to that activity, like this:

read a book	X					watch TV

II. Now, to take the next part of the inventory, you're to grade twenty statements in terms of how you feel about them. If you STRONGLY AGREE with a statement, give it an A; if you TEND TO AGREE with it, give it a B; if you feel FAIRLY NEUTRAL about it, give it a C; if you TEND TO DISAGREE with it, give it a D; and if you STRONGLY DISAGREE with it, give it an E. Be sure to read each statement carefully before you circle a grade for it, and be sure to grade every statement.

1. Reading is for learning but not for enjoyment.   A   B   C   D   E

III. This third part of the inventory calls for a bit of math ability. Your job this time is to divide up 100 points among the following ten things in terms of how desirable you feel they are as leisure activities. Remember, the total should come out to 100.

Activities	Points
Reading books	
Reading magazines and newspapers	
Watching television	

IV. And finally, to tell us a few things about you personally, please respond to the following scales by circling the answer to each which best describes you.

1. Compared to other people your own age, about how well do you think that you read?

1	2	3	4	5
a good deal better than most	somewhat better than most	about as well as most	somewhat less well than most	a good deal less well than most

2. Compared to other people your own age, about how much do you feel you like to read?

1	2	3	4	5
a good deal more than most	somewhat more than most	about as much as most	somewhat less than most	a good deal less than most

FIGURE 10–7
Excerpts from Dulin & Chester's Reading Interest Questionnaire

I. Here are possible rewards people get for reading. For each reward, circle the grade you're giving it.

1. getting a grade for how much reading you do   A   B   C   D   E

2. getting extra credit for how much reading you do   A   B   C   D   E

3. getting your name on a bulletin board for how much reading you do   A   B   C   D   E

II. Sometimes things teachers do encourage us to read. Please grade the following ten things to show how much you think they'd encourage you to read. Here's what the grades mean this time. Again, circle the grade you're giving the activity.

1. having the teacher read a book to the class at a chapter a day   A   B   C   D   E

2. having the teacher read to the class the first few pages of books that you can then check out if you want to   A   B   C   D   E

III. Now, here are some things you might do after reading a book or story in class. Grade them by these grades.

3. take an oral test on a story or book you've read   A   B   C   D   E

4. use some of the new words in a story or book you've read for word-study   A   B   C   D   E

IV. And finally, here are some extra things you could do after reading a story or book. Grade them with these grades.

A = I'd really like to do this.
B = I'd sort of like to do this.
C = I might or might not like to do this.
D = I'm fairly sure I wouldn't like to do this.
E = I'm quite sure I wouldn't like to do this.

1. make a play out of a story or book you've read   A   B   C   D   E
2. make a picture to go with a story or book you've read   A   B   C   D   E
3. have a discussion in class about a story or book you've read   A   B   C   D   E

V. And finally, for the last part of the questionnaire, divide up 100 points to show how much you like different types of reading material. Any one type can get from 0 to 100 points, but you should try to give at least some points to each.

TYPES OF READING MATERIAL	POINTS
magazines	
newspapers	
comic-books	
hard-bound books	
paper-back books	
TOTAL	100

FIGURE 10–8
Excerpts from Dulin & Chester's Reading Attitude Scale

produced in figures 10–7 and 10–8 demonstrate that attitude/interest measures can examine various important aspects related to reading instruction such as how students feel about reading, how they feel about various instructional methods and reward systems, or how they feel about different types of materials. Notice also the different response methods that can be used by students to indicate their attitudes and interests.

The affective information gathered through interest/attitude inventories should be added to the informal classroom records previously discussed. Remember also that children's interests and attitudes change fairly quickly. Attempt an attitude/interest measure several times during a year, in addition to keeping anecdotal records of current trends, fads, and interests as they crop up.

TEACHER-MADE TESTS AND OTHER INFORMATION SOURCES

Perhaps the most common assessment instruments used in reading classrooms are teacher made. Obviously, such measures have the advantage of being closely tied to the curriculum and program being taught. Teacher-made tests can be written to apply specifically to one or more students in a class. Length and number of items, testing duration, and format all vary in teacher-made tests.

Observing student performance during normal classroom activities provides valuable information on which teachers can base instructional decisions.

Teachers use a wide variety of data sources to make their daily instructional decisions. Various assignments, worksheets, graded tests, interviews with parents and students, and other methods are used to reach decisions about students' needs and capabilities on an ongoing basis. We feel that to be informed and effective instructors in their classrooms, teachers need to be aware of the wealth of information available to them and use it in an informed manner. Thus, assignments and worksheets that are part of purchased materials become more than simple practice pieces for students; they become parts of an overall process of gathering data on which to base instructional decisions. Teacher-made tests, in this context, go beyond quizzes or other graded requirements to include all things which a teacher might ask a student to do as part of the learning process. This includes items that are required in class as well as homework or other such outside activities.

Using all aspects of a student's performance requires that a clear and comprehensive up-to-date record-keeping system be kept. Maintaining a record of students' strengths and weaknesses as demonstrated in aspects such as class discussions and written assignments will allow you to be much more focused in your instruction, targeting specific students' individual needs. An informal record-keeping system might look like the one in figure 10–9.

To use incidental and teacher-initiated information in your classroom you will need to become both a keen observer of student behavior and a conscious implementer of your knowledge of the reading process. For example, when creating an assignment or worksheet in the comprehension area, ensure that all levels of comprehension are included in your assignment. Then, when responding to a student's work, you will be able to note areas of difficulty and initiate instructional efforts aimed at these difficulties.

EVALUATING MATERIALS

The preceding sections have presented and discussed formal and informal assessment of students, including both skills and affective measurement. This section presents methods for evaluating reading materials. Both evaluation of readers and materials is important, since teachers are necessarily involved in matching students and materials. This section, however, presents the evaluation of materials independently.

The Readability Formula

A **readability formula** provides a rough guideline for determining the difficulty level of reading material in terms of a grade-level score. Although useful, the results of a readability formula must be interpreted carefully. In fact, the International Reading Association and the National Council of Teachers of English (1984/85) have recently noted that read-

readability formulas: Determine the difficulty of written text. A combination of word length and sentence length is commonly used.

This was compiled by a teacher while grading students' vocabulary exercises. They were to use words from the vocabulary lesson in sentences, then in a story. As the teacher graded the assignment, a list of student names was kept handy. Comments about students' errors were written on this sheet. The sheet was then used to target specific students for additional instruction. It was also added to individual students' files, where such records were kept.

ASSIGNMENT: *Vocabulary — write words in sentence, then use all words in story or paragraph. Words: Observe, suspect, strut, elegant, modest.*

NAME	COMMENTS	DATE: *10/12/86*
Allison	*Used words correctly. Misspelled elegant both times used "elegent"*	
Bobby	*Left out strut, modest.*	
Julio	*No problems.*	
Kathleen	*Words used correctly. Neatness and hand-writing still a problem.*	
Latisha	*modest, elegant used incorrectly*	
Wanda	*modest used incorrectly.*	

GENERAL COMMENTS: *Reteach modest. Have Kathleen recopy - grade only on neatness. See Bobby individually about this assignment. Add elegant, modest to spelling list*

FIGURE 10–9
Sample informal class record sheet

ability formulas, on their own, are insufficient for matching books with students. They suggest that teachers

1. evaluate proposed texts, based on knowledge of their students' prior information, experiences, reading abilities, and interests;
2. observe students using proposed texts in instructional settings to evaluate the effectiveness of the material;
3. use checklists for evaluating the readability of the proposed materials, involving attention to variables such as student interests, text graphics, number of ideas and concepts in the material, length of lines in the text, and other factors which contribute to relative difficulty of text material.

Although several readability formulas are available, all are essentially similar in their manner of analyzing text difficulty. Two factors are usually considered by a readability formula in order to determine difficulty level: one deals with word difficulty; the other, with sentence difficulty.

In attempting to determine word difficulty, many readability formulas use the premise that longer words are more difficult, implying that difficult words contain more syllables than easier words. Many formulas thus require that the number of syllables in a given sample of text be counted. Some formulas, however, use word lists that are compared to the words in the material being examined. These word lists serve as guides for estimating word difficulty in the material.

In attempting to determine sentence difficulty, readability formulas use similar logic, reasoning that more difficult sentences are longer. Many readability formulas thus require that the number of sentences in a given sample of material be counted. Few sentences are taken as an indication that the sentences are long, and thus more difficult. The relationship between the number of syllables and the number of sentences in a passage is then used to determine the approximate reading grade level (RGL) for the text being evaluated.

A Common Readability Measure. Readability formulas, because of their method of approximating reading grade level, are necessarily more accurate at higher (above second) grade levels. This is because most materials written for lower elementary grade children use controlled vocabulary, many words of one syllable, and relatively short sentences. Additionally, reading selections for young students are usually quite short. For a readability measure to be valid, however, a continuous passage of approximately 100 words (depending on the formula used), should be used, and it is strongly suggested that at least three representative passages from several sections of the material be averaged to estimate the overall reading grade level. Thus, some formulas specifically state that they are not intended for use below given grade levels. Other formulas, however, may be used throughout a broad range of grades. A popular readability measure, the Fry Readability Scale, is shown in figure 10–10.

The popularity of the Fry formula results from its ease of use and its wide range of grade levels. Directions for using the formula are also presented in figure 10–10.

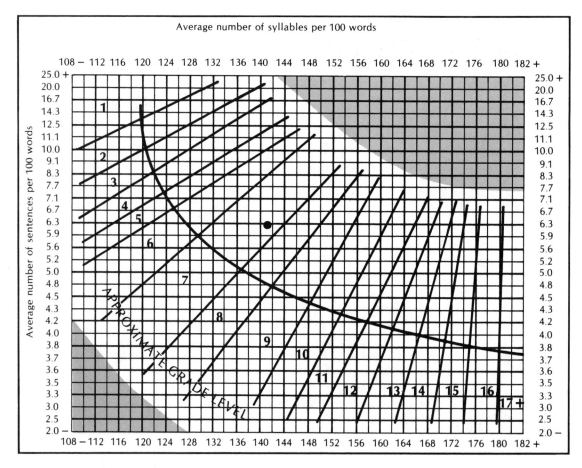

FIGURE 10–10
The Fry Readability Scale

BEFORE READING ON

Try using the Fry Readability Scale to estimate the reading grade level of the following passage. One hundred words end at the double slash mark (//).

That evening they all had dinner together in the enchanter's cozy kitchen. Then Albion took Petronella out to a stone building and unbolted its door. Inside were seven huge black dogs.

"You must watch my hounds all night," said he.

Petronella went in, and Albion closed and locked the door.

At once the hounds began to snarl and bark. They showed their teeth at her. But Petronella was a real princess. She plucked up her courage. Instead of backing away, she went toward the dogs. She began to speak to them in a quiet voice. They stopped snarling and sniffed // at her.

There are, of course, other highly regarded readability formulas. Formulas devised by Spache (1953, 1976), appropriate for grades one through three; Dale & Chall (1948), for grades four through six; and Flesch (1948), for grades five and above, are extensively used to estimate readability of textual material. Many publishers and other private businesses offer computerized services to determine readability estimates based on a variety of formulas. Readability analyses can also be performed using microcomputers since there are several commercially available programs, as well as programs in the public domain (and thus available at no or minimal cost) that will apply one or more formulas to a passage.

The Limitations of Readability Formulas

BEFORE READING ON

Decide which sentence in each of the following pairs would be easiest for a second grader to understand.

1. **(a)** The boy ran down the street.
    (b) The boy ran down the street.
2. **(a)** The boy ran down the street.

    (b) The boy ran down the street.
3. **(a)** The boy ran down the street.
    (b) Down the street ran the boy.
4. **(a)** The boy ran down the long, busy street.
    (b) The boy ran down the street. The street was busy. The street was long.

These examples illustrate some factors that make texts more or less difficult to read. In each of the sentence pairs, sentence *(a)* is generally considered to be easier than sentence *(b)*. This is because things such as print size, supportive illustrations, and word order can affect reading difficulty. Additionally, short sentences do not always yield better comprehension. Example 4*(a)* is easier for a second grader to read than 4*(b)* (Pearson, 1974–75). Since readability formulas only consider word and sentence difficulty based on features such as length, factors just noted do not affect determination of difficulty level when a formula is used.

Another aspect of reading difficulty that formulas do not address is concept difficulty. Since readability formulas generally assume that more syllables in a word imply more difficulty, misleading results can sometimes occur. For example, a formula would estimate *television* as more difficult than *vector,* yet second graders would have much less trouble reading and conceptualizing *television.* This demonstrates a major issue regarding the use of readability formulas: they do not take a reader's background knowledge into account.

Still, a readability formula is an easy-to-use method for estimating the relative difficulty level of reading materials. If carefully and thoughtfully interpreted, they can provide an indication of the RGL of a specific piece of text. Remember, however, that formulas can be "fooled" and that reading selections, especially at lower grade levels, often become more difficult as one moves through the book. In this case, a readability measurement using a passage at the beginning of the material would yield different results than a measurement using a passage from the end.

Evaluating Materials—Additional Considerations

Because readability formulas do not consider several important factors when estimating text difficulty, teachers often find it necessary to supplement readability formulas with other information when asked to choose between two different sets of materials. A form that considers readability, as well as other data, is presented in figure 10–11.

The example in figure 10–11 is intended for analysis of content-area material or textbooks. A form for evaluating general reading material would not include questions such as those regarding the accuracy of content or the appropriateness of deductive and inductive presentation methods. The form should be used as appropriate, with the realization that not all questions apply to every type of reading material.

Notice that the form compiles a summary of factors such as student interests and attitudes, datedness of the material, balance of narrative to non-narrative selections (poems, dramatic scripts, informational material, and so on), quality and appropriateness of illustrations, stereotyping, students' background knowledge, and other factors that teachers might consider important for their students and instructional situation. Examined with the information provided by readability formulas, such evaluation forms serve a valuable function in clarifying differences between reading materials and help in budgetary decision making.

1. Readability
   Formula used: _____   Reading grade level: _____
   Reading grade level is: a) one grade off _____
                            b) appropriate _____
                            c) more than one grade off _____

   Literary style (rate using 5-excellent to 1-unsatisfactory)
   use of lead sentences _____   sentence complexity _____
   use of technical terms _____   appropriate summaries _____

2. Content (rate using 5-excellent to 1-unsatisfactory)
   suitability for chosen objective _____
   up-to-date (current accuracy) _____
   appropriate to student readiness _____
   probable interest to students _____
   organization: use of underlying theme _____
                  units and subunits logically placed _____
                  logical chapter sequence _____
   treatment of controversial subjects _____

3. Presentation of materials
   authoritarian _____   prescriptive _____   deductive _____   inductive _____

4. Background demands
   Note background requirements (mathematical concepts, prior knowledge, prerequisite coursework, etc.) _____

5. Appearance (rate using 5-excellent to 1-unsatisfactory)
   total book size _____   print size and quality _____
   eye appeal _____   durability _____

6. Quality of illustrations (rate using 5-excellent to 1-unsatisfactory)
   modern, high quality _____   useful learning devices _____
   appropriate supplements to the written text _____

7. Learning aids (rate using 5-excellent to 1-unsatisfactory)
   appendices _____   table of contents _____   glossary _____
   activities (pertinent) _____   activities (variable difficulty) _____   references _____
   teacher's manual (appropriate and easy to use) _____

8. Other comments and Overall rating

FIGURE 10–11
Material analysis form

ASSESSMENT AND YOUR READING FRAMEWORK

In all measurement, your comprehension framework will play a significant, though secondary role in determining your selection or construction of a test. Consider a teacher whose comprehension framework includes mastery of specific skills explanations for how reading ability develops. This teacher is happier with a test that attempts to separate the reading process into a set of various specific subskills. Often, such tests will include items that make little use of context, perhaps testing letters, blends, or vocabulary knowledge in isolation. Teacher-made tests would closely reflect the specific skills taught.

Teachers with comprehension frameworks that include a holistic language explanation for how reading ability develops tend to choose tests that present test items in context and that do not attempt to split reading into closely defined subskills. Informal and teacher-made tests would generally not be used to test isolated skills. Test formats would tend to test student's knowledge in real-language situations, providing opportunity to apply skills and knowledge in context. Such tests might, for example, present readers with picture clues or include prediscussion of the test's reading selection(s). Teachers with comprehension frameworks that include holistic explanations for how reading ability develops may also look for a test that allows students to refer back to a reading selection to find answers—thus more closely approximating the real reading situation.

Teachers with differential skills explanations for how reading ability develops look for a test that examines specific skills for less mature readers, changing to less formal and global assessment methods as readers become more proficient. Teachers with such comprehension frameworks expect a test to change as it moves from measuring students at lower to higher grade levels.

Although instructional frameworks play a part in test selection, their major role is in interpretation of test results. This was hinted at in the discussion of informal reading inventories, where it was noted that some teachers would count as miscues anything that differed from the material to be read. These teachers would count a reading of *cat* or *kitty* for *kitten* as a miscue. Other teachers would not count such a deviation as a miscue. What explanation for the reading process do you think the teachers in these examples have? One reflects a text-based; the other, a reader-based explanation for how one reads.

Teachers with text-based explanations for how one reads count as inappropriate any response that deviates from the text. In tests using oral responses, this may not extend to dialect variation, but would apply to the *cat-kitty-kitten* example. In written tests, synonyms or explanations that may make sense but are not those required by the test's scoring key would be scored as incorrect. A reader-based explanation allows much more flexibility in scoring, focusing more on whether the reader had understood the intent of the passage. Cloze tests, for example, might be scored with synonyms counted as correct. Teachers with an interactive explanation for how one reads attempt to examine both the text and the background knowledge of the reader, basing interpretations of mismatches between responses and test requirements on how the material, in combination with reader factors, may have led to the response.

Finally, realize that a test in itself is relatively meaningless. It is the goal of testing, in conjunction with the use to which results are finally put, that determine a test's value to the instructional situation. This is true for formal, informal, and teacher-made tests. Having a clear understanding of why a test is given and ensuring that results are used consistently with the specified goal help make testing a valuable addition to your instructional program.

THE MAJOR POINTS

1. Assessment instruments are used to evaluate readers, reading materials, and the interaction between readers and materials.
2. Measurement instruments can be categorized as formal, informal, or teacher made. They are also categorized as either norm- or criterion-referenced.
3. When choosing or making a test, strive for validity (both content and curricular) and reliability.
4. The informal reading inventory provides valuable information regarding students' reading processes and instructional needs. Depending on whether it has been created based on classroom materials, it can evaluate readers or the interaction of readers with specific instructional material. This is also true of cloze tests.
5. Evaluation of materials cannot be done using a readability formula alone. Factors such as density of ideas, appropriate visual aids, print size, and students' background are only some of the factors that additionally must be considered.

QUESTIONS AND ACTIVITIES

1. Your curriculum library should have a file of commonly used reading tests. Choose three or four tests recommended for use with students at the same grade level and compare their testing of reading. How do they test word attack? Vocabulary? Comprehension?
2. Write a brief definition of the following terms:

standardized test	norm referenced
criterion referenced	standard error of measurement
cloze procedure	informal reading inventory
retelling score	percentile
raw score	stanine
readability formula	miscue

3. Interview both a primary and an intermediate grade teacher. Ask about the different kinds of measurement that are used in their classrooms. What are the purposes of the testing? How are tests used to help in instruction?

4. Interview a teacher, a parent, and a school principal. Ask about their philosophy of testing and how they use test results. Do the goals and purposes for testing differ across the people you interviewed? What implications does this have for a teacher?

5. Construct and administer a cloze test. This may be done with elementary students or with some of your college-age friends. Choose appropriate materials for your practice group.

6. Choose two passages from two different basal readers and perform a readability analysis using the Fry formula. Compare your results with readability information provided in the teacher's manual of the basal readers you chose.

7. Using the IRI marking system and examining Debby's efforts on the fourth-grade word list (see figure 10–4) answer the following questions: Which two words were self-corrected? Which word was pronounced by the teacher? Which word had its plural ending omitted? How many total miscues would you count for this level?

8. Answer the following questions about Debby's reading of the second-grade IRI passage (see figure 10–5). At what two points did Debby hesitate before reading on? What word did Debby repeat? What word did Debby omit? What word did Debby insert?

9. Borrow a copy of a published IRI from your library. Using the checklist for IRI administration, practice giving an informal reading inventory to a second-grade student and a fourth-grade student. How did you have to change your administrative technique to account for the differences in the students' level? Practice until you feel comfortable with the scoring system.

FURTHER READING

Jongsma, E. (1980). *Cloze instruction research: A second look.* Newark, DE: International Reading Assoc.

Discusses the history and uses of the cloze procedure, including its weaknesses and its use as a teaching tool.

Pikulski, J. J. & Shanahan, T. (eds.). (1982). *Approaches to the informal evaluation of reading.* Newark, DE: International Reading Assoc.

Describes informal assessment techniques that are useful with a range of reading materials and in instructional planning.

Pumfry, P. (1985). Tests and assessment techniques (2nd Edition) Newark, Delaware: International Reading Association.

Describes the justification, use, and interpretation of reading tests. Includes an extensive list of tests for specified purposes and age ranges.

Schell, L. M. & Hanna, G. S. (1981). Can informal reading inventories reveal strengths and weaknesses in comprehension subskills? *Reading Teacher, 35,* 263–68.

Points out potential problems of informal reading inventories when used to test comprehension subskills.

Aulls, M. W. (1982). *Developing readers in today's elementary schools.* Boston: Allyn & Bacon.

Betts, E. A. (1946). *Foundations of reading instruction.* New York: American Book Co.

Bormuth, J. R. (1968). The cloze readability procedure. In J. R. Bormuth (ed.), *Readability in 1968* (pp. 40–47). Champaign, IL: NCTE.

Burns, P. C.; Roe, B. D.; & Ross, E. P. (1984). *Teaching reading in today's elementary schools.* (3rd Edition). Boston: Houghton Mifflin.

Cooper, J. L. (1952). *The effect of adjustment of basal reading materials on reading achievement.* Unpublished doctoral dissertation, Boston University.

Dale, E. & Chall, J. S. (1948). A formula for predicting readability. *Educational Research Bulletin, Ohio State University, 27,* 11–20; *28,* 37–54.

Englert, C. S. & Semmel, M. I. (1981). The relationship of oral reading substitution miscues to comprehension. *Reading Teacher, 35,* 273–80.

Dulin, K. L. (1984). Assessing reading interests of elementary and middle school students. In A. J. Harris & E. R. Sipay (eds.). *Readings on reading instruction* (pp. 346–57). New York: Longman.

Flesch, R. F. (1948). A new readability yardstick. *Journal of Applied Psychology, 32,* 221–23.

Flesch, R. F. (1949). *The art of readable writing.* New York: Harper.

Goodman, K. S. & Buck, C. (1973). Dialect barriers to reading comprehension revisited. *Reading Teacher, 27,* 6–12.

Harris, A. J. & Sipay, E. R. (1985). *How to increase reading ability* (8th Edition). New York: Longman.

IRA, NCTE take stand on readability formulae. (December 1984–January 1985). *Reading Today, 2,* 1.

Johns, J. L. & Kuhn, M. K. (1983). The informal reading inventory: 1910–1980. *Reading World, 23,* 8–19.

Johnson, M. S. & Kress, R. A. (1965). *Informal reading inventories.* Newark, DE: International Reading Assoc.

Mehrens, W. A. & Lehman, I. J. (1984). *Measurement and evaluation in education and psychology* (3rd edition). New York: Holt, Rinehart & Winston.

Nitko, A. J. (1980). Distinguishing the many varieties of criterion-referenced tests. *Review of Educational Research, 50,* 461–85.

Pearson, D. (1974–75). The effects of grammatical complexity on children's comprehension, recall and conception of certain semantic relations. *Reading Research Quarterly, 10,* 155–92.

Popham, W. J. (1978). *Criterion referenced measurement.* Englewood Cliffs, NJ: Prentice-Hall.

Powell, W. R. (1970). Reappraising the criteria for interpreting informal reading inventories. In J. DeBoer (ed.), *Reading diagnosis and evaluation.* Newark, DE: International Reading Assoc.

Rankin, E. F. (1971). Grade level interpretations of cloze readability scores. In F. Greene (ed.), *The right to participate.* Milwaukee, WI: National Reading Conference.

Rankin, E. F. & Culhane, J. W. (1969). Comparable cloze and multiple choice comprehension test scores. *Journal of Reading, 13,* 193–98.

Ruddell, R. B. & Kinzer, C. K. (1982). Test preferences and competencies of field educators. In J. Niles & L. Harris (eds.), *New inquiries in reading research and instruction.* New York: National Reading Conference.

Spache, G. S. (1953). A new readability formula for primary grade reading material. *Elementary English, 53,* 410–13.

Spache, G. S. (1976). The new Spache readability formula. In *Good reading for poor readers* (pp. 195–207). Champaign, IL: Garrard Publishing.

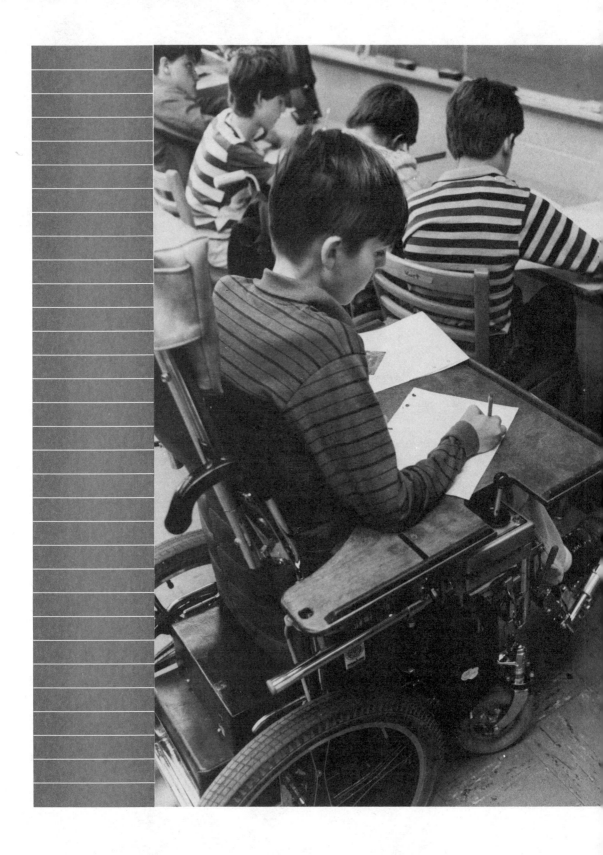

11 Teaching Reading to Children with Special Needs

CONSIDERING CHILDREN WITH SPECIAL NEEDS ■ EXCEPTIONAL
CHILDREN, SPECIAL EDUCATION, AND MAINSTREAMING ■ CHILDREN
WITH UNIQUE LINGUISTIC AND CULTURAL BACKGROUNDS

"They were all—all laughing—whenever I made a mistake—and I kept making
mistakes. I couldn't help it . . . Because I can't," Maybeth wailed, "I can't—
read, and I—can't learn."

"Who says?" James's cool voice cut across her tears . . . "I say—you *can* learn.
I say, I can teach you . . . ."

A little smile lifted the corners of Maybeth's mouth, like a wave licking at the
shore.

"Have you ever known me to be wrong?" James asked. He sounded so
confident . . . .

"All right," Maybeth said, in a little voice.

Cynthia Voigt, *Dicey's Song,* (New York: Atheneum, 1982) pp. 89–90

everal recent trends have made the role of today's teacher of reading more important than ever before: federal and state legislation requiring schools to provide a free and appropriate public education for all handicapped students, increasing local sensitivity to the unique needs of individual students, and increasing respect for the multicultural and multilingual nature of our society. It is now imperative that teachers understand federally defined categories of special-education students and become familiar with instructional strategies that can assist these students in reading comprehension. It is also imperative that teachers understand the reading needs of students who are gifted or have unique cultural and linguistic backgrounds. This chapter will help you develop a better understanding of all these students and provide instructional suggestions to help you better meet their special needs.

After reading this chapter you will be able to

1. explain how each of your students is actually a student with special needs;
2. identify the different categories of exceptional children and describe appropriate instructional considerations for each;
3. explain how recent federal legislation regarding exceptional children will affect you as a classroom teacher of reading;
4. identify two different populations of students with unique linguistic and cultural backgrounds and describe appropriate instructional considerations for each.

CONSIDERING CHILDREN WITH SPECIAL NEEDS

We wish to make two points that should guide all of your considerations about students with special needs. The most important is that each of your students is, in fact, a student with special needs. Each and every student you encounter will have unique needs that must be acknowledged as you make instructional decisions in reading. You must continuously consider each student's set of background experiences and abilities as you plan to teach each lesson and as you interpret children's responses to your instruction. Nothing is more important.

The second point is related to the first: do not allow the categorical designations used for pedagogical, legal, or administrative purposes (for example, mentally retarded, learning disabled, emotionally disabled, average learner, or gifted) limit your instructional decisions about individual children or your expectations for achievement. We have used categorical designations for different populations in this chapter for three reasons: because they have been used in legal definitions for categorical aid programs; because they are sometimes used for administrative purposes; and because they facilitate your learning as a new teacher. Recognize that the definition we use for any single category is not consistently held by all educators. You must also recognize the inherent variation within any category. All children who have been labeled as either learning disabled, mentally retarded, bilingual, or any other designation are not alike. As a result, instructional decisions must always take into account the unique needs, aspirations, and experiences of each and every individual in your room. While the use of labels has brought considerable benefits to students whose needs have been ignored, we must ensure that labels do not blind us to the individuality that each of us expresses in our daily life.

EXCEPTIONAL CHILDREN, SPECIAL EDUCATION, AND MAINSTREAMING

Exceptional children are unable to reach their full potential without services, instructional materials, and/or facilities that go beyond the requirements of the average child. Typically, exceptional children include those who are mentally retarded, learning disabled, emotionally disturbed, hearing impaired, visually impaired, speech or language disordered, and gifted. According to federal estimates of the number of exceptional children (Hallahan & Kauffman, 1982; Lerner, 1985; United States Department of Education, 1984), approximately thirteen to sixteen percent of school-age children fall into one or several of these categories.

exceptional children: Children unable to reach their full potential without services, materials and/or facilities which go beyond the requirements of the average child.

Special education encompasses the educational services, materials, and/or facilities provided to help exceptional children reach their full potential. Special educational services, for example, may include a special educator in an elementary school who teaches basic skills such as reading to exceptional children, a school psychologist who performs psychological assessment, or special **home-bound teachers** who teach children unable to come to school. In an increasing number of situations, classroom teachers provide at least a portion of the special education services for exceptional children.

special education: Services, materials, and/or facilities provided to exceptional children.

home-bound teachers: Teachers who teach children unable to come to school.

The nature of the special educational assistance varies on a continuum that ranges from less restrictive environments to more restrictive environments as shown in figure 11–1. Generally, children with less severe handicaps are placed in less restrictive environments; children with more severe handicaps are placed in more restrictive environments. You can see from figure 11–1 that self-contained classroom teachers may have opportunities to work with exceptional students in several different contexts. There is also an effort being made to get those with more severe handicapping conditions into less restrictive environments (like classrooms) for part of the day—primarily for socialization and language stimulation.

<table>
<tr><td rowspan="8" style="writing-mode: vertical-lr">← LEAST RESTRICTIVE — MORE RESTRICTIVE →</td></tr>
</table>

1. Classroom instruction by a regular classroom teacher, who is provided with special materials or who adapts existing materials to meet individual needs.

2. Classroom instruction by the regular classroom teacher in consultation with a specialist in special education.

3. Itinerant services provided by a special educator who regularly visits and teaches the exceptional child within the regular classroom. Itinerant teachers will also make suggestions for instruction to the regular classroom teacher.

4. Resource services provided by a special educator outside of the classroom. Exceptional children receive instruction in a resource center for a portion of the day. The resource teacher will also consult with the classroom teacher regarding instruction within the classroom.

5. Self-contained special education classrooms within the regular school for homogeneous classes of exceptional children.

6. Special day schools for homogeneous groups of exceptional children.

7. Hospital or home-bound instruction by itinerant special education teachers.

8. Residential school in a segregated institution.

After D. P. Hallahan & J. M. Kauffman, *Exceptional Children*, 2nd Edition. (Englewood Cliffs, NJ: Prentice-Hall, 1982), pp. 6–7.

FIGURE 11–1

A continuum of special educational environments and services

PL 94–142: The Education for All Handicapped Children Act

PL 94–142, The Education for All Handicapped Children Act: Federal legislation mandating a free public education for all children regardless of handicap.

The most powerful recent influence on the education of exceptional children has been the federal law which was passed in 1975: **The Education for All Handicapped Children Act, or Public Law (PL) 94–142.** The most important provision of PL 94–142 states that:

> . . . in order to receive funds under the Act every school system in the nation must make provision for a free, appropriate public education for every child . . . regardless of how, or how seriously, he may be handicapped.

Besides requiring schools to provide a free public education for all handicapped children, two other provisions of this legislation affect classroom teachers of reading: individualized educational programs (IEPs) and the concept of a least restrictive environment.

Individualized Educational Programs (IEPs). PL 94–142 requires that a multidisciplinary team consisting of trained educational specialists

An individualized education program (IEP) will be developed at a case conference meeting for each exceptional child.

evaluate each exceptional student and potential exceptional student. This team then submits a report to a case conference meeting where a school representative, the teacher, the parents, and other appropriate individuals are responsible for developing an **IEP** for each exceptional child. An IEP, according to federal guidelines, must contain the following:

> (A) a statement of the present levels of educational performance . . . ,
> (B) a statement of annual goals, including short-term instructional objectives, (C) a statement of the specific educational services to be provided
> . . . , and the extent to which [each] child will be able to participate in
> regular educational programs, (D) the projected date for initiation and
> anticipated duration of such services, and appropriate objective criteria
> and evaluation procedures and schedules for determining, on at least an
> annual basis, whether instructional objectives are being achieved (Education for All Handicapped Children Act of 1975, p. 3).

The IEP is used to guide instruction and monitor student progress.

individualized educational programs (IEPs): Specialized instructional outlines for each exceptional child, used to guide and evaluate instruction.

The Least Restrictive Environment. One of the most important decisions made at the case conference, aside from the initial decision to include a child in a special education program, concerns the recommended instructional environment. Participants in the case conference meeting must state in the IEP the extent to which a handicapped child

mainstreaming: Placing exceptional students into learning environments with nonexceptional students.

least restrictive environment (LRE): A learning situation where maximum opportunity is provided for exceptional students.

will be **mainstreamed** into the regular instructional environment. PL 94–142 requires that handicapped children be placed in the **least restrictive environment (LRE)** possible. A least restrictive environment is one where maximum opportunity is provided for students to engage in the full measure of school life, consistent with their educational needs. Thus, children should not be educated in a separate special education classroom if their needs can be adequately met in a regular classroom with outside instruction by a resource teacher. Or, children should not leave the regular classroom for resource assistance if their needs can be adequately met by the regular classroom teacher. Exceptional children are to be included as much as possible into the mainstream of educational environments.

The principle of LRE and the concomitant increase in mainstreaming has increased the role regular classroom teachers play in the education of handicapped children. How will this affect you as a classroom teacher of reading? Should you have an opportunity to have an exceptional student in your classroom, you may be affected in several ways. First, you will be required to attend the case conference meeting where you will assist in planning the student's IEP. If the decision of the multidisciplinary team is to mainstream your student for reading instruction you will also be affected in a second way: you will be responsible for implementing the IEP in your classroom. Your role may include being totally responsible for reading instruction or providing reading instruction but consulting with a special education teacher regarding materials and methods. Should the multidisciplinary team decide not to mainstream your student for reading instruction, you will be responsible for coordinating the classroom visits of a reading teacher or your student's trips for outside assistance. Finally, as a member of the case conference meeting, you will be responsible for evaluating the degree to which your student has met the specified instructional objectives.

General Guidelines for Exceptional Children

Besides accommodating a child's particular handicap, reading instruction for special education students does not differ substantially from the activities, strategies, and materials described in previous chapters. This does not mean that identical instruction is given to both handicapped and nonhandicapped students. Instead, reading instruction for the handicapped child requires judicious selection from the range of instructional suggestions presented in this text. You may want to keep in mind the following general guidelines as you work with exceptional children in the classroom.

1. *Prepare your other students for exceptional children.* Include literature selections that deal with exceptional children in your classroom library and in your read-aloud sessions. A list of appropriate

selections can be found at the end of this chapter. Discussing the concerns and feelings of exceptional children will help your students respect the unique qualities of each and every child in your classroom.

2. *Capitalize on individual strengths.* Where it is required, work around a handicap by taking advantage of a particular strength. A hearing impaired child, for example, may require a more visual approach than the hearing child during instruction. Pictures may be needed to complement a verbal definition of a new vocabulary word. Or, affective considerations such as interest and motivation can often be used to increase successful learning experiences. Carefully consider a student's interests when selecting reading materials.

3. *Ensure successful learning experiences.* Try to build success into your instruction by carefully considering what each child can be expected to do. Positive experiences lead to continued success with increasingly difficult tasks.

4. *Record and chart individual growth to demonstrate gains to students and parents.* Listing individual achievements in a progress chart, keeping selected work examples in a personal folder, or recording accomplishments in a diary makes individual growth more visible. Recording growth makes success concrete and tangible. In addition, a cumulative set of observational notes can lead to important insights about children as you see patterns of success in certain tasks and under certain conditions.

5. *Establish an accepting and positive environment.* Praise success with compliments. Accept failure with tolerance. Develop the attitude in your students that mistakes are an important part of learning. Try to compliment each child in your class each day. Encourage all of your students to do the same with their peers.

6. *Regularly discuss your students' progress and your instructional program with parents, special educators, and other teachers with exceptional children in their classrooms.* Keep a list of ideas that others have found successful.

7. *Use background knowledge to provide entry into difficult learning tasks.* When a student is experiencing difficulty with a particular learning task, try to redefine the content of the task to match the child's background knowledge. This will make the task easier and lead to initial success. Once the child has met with success and understands the nature of the task, increasingly remove the familiar content.

8. *Do not continuously repeat unsuccessful learning experiences.* Be willing to change materials, strategies, and activities when a student has not met with success. Find successful approaches and maintain them.

9. *Be certain that you do not search for a single solution to reading failure.* Reading is a complicated developmental process. No single set of materials or activities will ever solve a reading problem.
10. *Be certain to provide real reading opportunities.* Do not forget to make time for all children to experience real reading experiences such as reading a book for pleasure or personal information.

Reading and the Mentally Retarded. The American Association on Mental Deficiency (AAMD) has defined **mental retardation** as follows.

mental retardation: Describes individuals with inadequate adaptive behavior and intellectual functioning significantly below average.

> Mental retardation refers to significantly subaverage general intellectual functioning existing concurrently with deficits in adaptive behavior and manifested during the developmental period (Grossman, 1973, p. 11).

Thus, two factors must be present for a child to be categorized as mentally retarded: intellectual functioning that is significantly below average and inadequate adaptive behavior. What, however, is "significantly subaverage general intellectual functioning"? According to the AAMD, this requires an IQ score on the most commonly used test (WISC–R) of 69 or below. Children with IQ scores between 70 and 85 may learn more slowly than their peers and may sometimes be called slow learners. Typically, they are not formally labeled as mentally retarded. Figure 11–2 illustrates the various categories of mental retardation used by the AAMD and a separate system used by American educators that you may also encounter.

In evaluating adaptive behavior, the AAMD suggests that one consider the age of the child. In early childhood, sensorimotor, communication, self-help, and socialization skills are evaluated. In middle childhood and early adolescence, learning processes and interpersonal social skills are evaluated.

IQ	100	95	90	85	80	75	70	65	60	55	50	45	40	35	30	25	20	15	10
American Association on Mental Deficiency								Mild		Moderate			Severe			Profound			
American Educators							Educable				Trainable								

After D. P. Hallahan & J. M. Kauffman, *Exceptional Children,* 2nd Edition. (Englewood Cliffs, NJ: Prentice-Hall, 1982), pp. 42–43.

FIGURE 11–2

Categories of mental retardation used by the AAMD and by American educators

According to federal estimates, approximately 1.9% of school-age children are mentally retarded (United States Department of Education, 1984).

Learning Characteristics. Mentally retarded students tend to progress through the same developmental stages as normal students, but their rate of progress is much slower. This is especially true with respect to academic learning tasks such as reading. Other important characteristics that might need to be accommodated during instruction include:

1. *Short attention spans.*   Students might be easily distracted, especially in environments with many visual and auditory signals.
2. *Poor short-term memory.*   The ability to remember words, numbers, and ideas for short periods of time is limited. Long-term memory is less of a problem.
3. *Delayed language development.*   Language development is often slower than normal but progresses in a sequence that is similar to most children. However, a higher frequency of language and speech problems can be anticipated.
4. *Difficulty in grasping abstract ideas.*   Children tend to have more difficulty with abstract concepts and do better with concrete concepts.

Keep in mind that each of these characteristics varies with each child and with the severity of mental retardation. Thus, each characteristic will be more likely to appear and be more pronounced as the extent of mental retardation increases.

Instruction. The most important instructional consideration for retarded children and slow learners is to remember that their development will lag behind that of other children in your classroom. Thus, while second graders may be putting the final touches on decoding skills and learning new vocabulary meanings, new syntactic patterns, and new discourse forms, retarded children of the same age may still be consolidating important readiness skills. Readiness activities are often a major aspect of reading programs for the mildly retarded in the early elementary years (Hallahan & Kauffman, 1982). Developing oral language skills, teaching letter names, listening to stories, doing simple language experience activities, and learning to write and read one's name might all be appropriate components in an instructional program. All have been described in previous chapters.

In working with mentally retarded children, consider the extent to which reading instruction will focus on academic aspects of reading development as in the regular developmental reading program or focus on more functional aspects of reading development such as reading signs, following simple written directions, using the yellow pages, reading and ordering from catalogs, reading labels, locating bus routes on a map, or

functional reading skills: Abilities required to successfully interact with basic aspects of written language during daily life.

reading recipes. Generally, the lower the level of intellectual functioning, the more you will need to teach **functional reading skills** with activities similar to the following sample activities. Consider having other students in your class help your mentally retarded students with these games and learning activities.

SAMPLE ACTIVITIES

Learning Environmental Print. Teach the common environmental print that children experience as sight words. Street signs, traffic signals, labels, children's names, and bus or transit markers might all be considered. Also, consider imperative words such as *Danger, Poison,* or *Keep Out.* All these words could be put on flash cards or used in a card game (see chapter 4).

Catalog Reading. Show children how to read a catalog including the name and price for each object. Help them make out a holiday order of gifts for others.

Reading Students' Names. Give students frequent opportunities to read class names by passing back papers that have been corrected or by checking off names of students who have turned work in.

Reading a Shopping List. For a language experience activity, have children dictate shopping lists for a trip to buy their favorite foods. Have them read back their lists and tell at which meal they will eat each food. Children may then draw a picture labeling each of their favorite foods.

Reading and Writing Personal Information. Teach children how to read and write their names, addresses, and phone numbers. Practice by filling out employment forms for favorite jobs in the class.

Reading TV Guides. Bring in TV program listings and show children how to read them. Have children plan TV viewing schedules, assuming that they may only watch one or two hours of television each day.

Reading and the Learning Disabled

learning disability: Describes individuals with substantial gaps between expected and actual achievement levels in at least one academic area, not attributed to mental retardation or emotional disturbance.

Learning disability was first used in 1963 by Samuel Kirk to refer to children who, despite normal intelligence, had great difficulty learning in school. Since then, a variety of definitions have evolved. The most common characteristics include:

1. A substantial gap between expected achievement levels (based on intelligence scores) and actual performance in at least one academic area (math, reading, writing, and so on).

2. An uneven profile in achievement. Achievement in some areas will be very high. In others, achievement will be very low.
3. Low achievement levels not due to environmental factors.
4. Low achievement levels not due to mental retardation or emotional disturbance.

The federal definition of specific learning disability, the most widely used definition, states that:

> "specific learning disability" means a disorder in one or more of the basic psychological processes involved in understanding or in using language, spoken or written, which may manifest itself in an imperfect ability to listen, think, speak, read, write, spell, or do mathematical calculations. The term includes such conditions as perceptual handicaps, brain injury, minimal brain dysfunction, dyslexia, and developmental aphasia. The term does not include children who have learning problems which are primarily the result of visual, hearing, or motor handicaps, of mental retardation, of emotional disturbance, or of environmental, cultural, or economic disadvantage.

> From Federal Register 42, no. 250, December 29, 1977, p. 65083.

Approximately five percent of school age children are considered learning disabled (United States Department of Education, 1984).

Consider a student who is achieving substantially lower in reading and social studies than in mathematics. This student is also new to our country and has not yet developed proficiency in English. Should you recommend this student to a specialist for screening into the learning disabilities program at school? Why or why not?

A POINT TO PONDER

Learning Characteristics. It is difficult to identify a common set of learning characteristics that all learning disabled students manifest. This is due to the nature of the disability; different children have different impaired psychological processes. The most common characteristic found in learning disabled students is some disruption in language processing. Because reading is a language-based process, learning disabled children often have extreme difficulty in learning how to read. They may be more than two years behind grade level in reading achievement. Often, they have difficulty with automatic decoding and need more direct instruction to develop this skill (Chall, 1983). Other characteristics that are likely to appear and will need to be accommodated during instruction include:

1. *Perceptual-motor problems.* Lack of both fine and gross motor coordination. Students may appear clumsy. Writing is often labored,

hard to read, with many reversals in letter formation (for example, *d* for *b* or *z* for *s*) and letter order (for example, *tac* for *cat*) that persist beyond the age of seven or eight.

2. *Attention problems.* Students may have very short attention spans, be easily distracted, and have difficulty completing regular class assignments on time.

3. *Lacks effective learning and problem-solving strategies.* The child does not appear to use effective strategies for learning and problem solving.

Instruction. Learning disabled students who have difficulty learning to read often receive additional reading instruction from a resource teacher, a learning disability specialist, or a reading specialist. The emphasis is on maintaining the child, to the extent possible, in some modified regular class reading program (Lerner, 1985). It is most important for you and the specialist to communicate regularly and extensively regarding the instructional approaches and materials that are being used to teach reading. Also, it is essential to share teaching strategies that seem to be especially productive. You may want to schedule regular lunch periods together, communicate via a memo each day that indicates the materials, approaches, and results from that day, or share tape-recorded observations. The latter can be quickly recorded at the end of each day, indicating the activities and progress of the students with whom you are jointly working.

At least three general categories of instructional approaches have been used to teach reading to learning disabled children: visual, auditory, kinesthetic, and tactile (VAKT) approaches; behavior modification approaches; and cognitive behavior modification approaches.

VAKT approaches: Teaching reading to children through visual, auditory, kinesthetic, and tactile modalities.

When **VAKT approaches** are used, children are taught by simultaneously receiving information through visual, auditory, kinesthetic (movement), and tactile (touch) modalities. It is thought that receiving information through multiple channels of sensory input makes learning more likely. The most common VAKT method is one originally developed by Fernald (Fernald, 1943; Gearhart, 1985; Tierney, Readence, & Dishner, 1985). Words are initially taught by having children see (visual), hear (auditory), and trace (kinesthetic and tactile) words with their fingers. Sometimes sandpaper letters are used to enhance tactile input. Children learn to read what they write themselves, similar to language experience methods.

behavior modification: Instruction where one identifies valued behaviors, defines conditions where valued behaviors will take place, and immediately reinforces positive behaviors with praise or tokens.

Behavior modification approaches attempt to overcome the attention problems that some learning disabled readers exhibit. Behavior modification involves identifying valued behaviors, defining conditions where valued behaviors take place, and then immediately reinforcing positive behaviors with praise or tokens (Savage & Mooney, 1979). Gradually, a set of discrete behaviors contributing to successful learning experiences is built up. Usually behavior modification approaches are used with the regular school reading program. The materials and instructional strategies remain the same while attempts are made to modify a student's inappropriate behaviors which interfere with learning. For example, the use of sight word envelopes (described in chapter 4) might be combined with a daily recording of student gains in sight word knowledge on a chart, as in figure 11–3. This helps reinforce and make visible daily gains in word recognition.

Recently, **cognitive behavior modification (CBM)** approaches have been developed to overcome the frequent lack of effective problem solving and learning strategies among the learning disabled (Lloyd, 1980; Wong, 1980). These approaches attempt to modify cognitive behaviors and help students use explicit learning strategies. Modeling of a specific strategy by the teacher is often used. It appears that the four-step method framework developed by Meichenbaum (1977) may be useful in teaching specific learning from text strategies such as SQ3R discussed in chapter 8.

cognitive behavior modification (CBM): Approaches that attempt to modify the cognitive behaviors of students and help them use specific learning strategies.

1. The teacher performs a task such as reading comprehension while explaining his mental processes out loud. ("First I want to survey the material and see what it is about. Now I need to ask some questions. . . .")

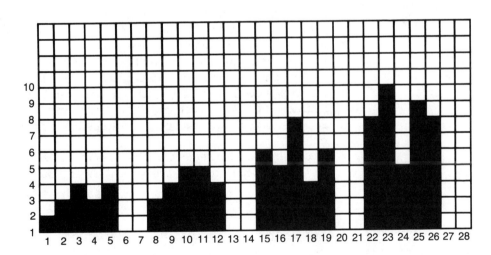

FIGURE 11–3

Charting student gains as a behavior modification technique

2. The student repeats a similar task attempting to overtly repeat the procedures of the modeled behavior.
3. The student repeats similar tasks while whispering the instructions to himself.
4. The student repeats similar tasks and independently guides his mental behavior with silent "inner speech."

There is no consistent evidence to suggest that any one of these approaches is superior to the others or to individualized instruction that is carefully paced, clearly presented, and uses regular classroom materials. Rather than a single type of approach, you should keep several general principles in mind as you work with learning disabled children on reading tasks.

1. *Structure the learning environment.* Regularize the rules and conventions followed during reading instruction. Provide clear and unambiguous directions and explanations. Note that structuring a learning environment does not necessarily mean that a mastery of specific skills type of framework must be implemented (Ringler & Weber, 1984).
2. *Provide a warm and supportive atmosphere for learning.* Praise successful achievements even if they are small ones. Do not ignore failures but acknowledge them as necessary for learning to take place. Let students know that mistakes are acceptable as long as they use them to learn.
3. *Individualize instruction.* As much as possible, provide individual instruction to learning disabled children. Do not assume that all learning disabled readers have the same type of weaknesses. Each is likely to be unique and respond best to a unique form of instruction.
4. *Continually evaluate instructional effectiveness.* Is the student meeting with success in the approach you are using? Continually modify instruction based on each child's successful experiences. Keep what appears to work and disregard unsuccessful approaches and materials.
5. *Be certain that each student is working at a level consistent with actual performance, not expected achievement levels.* Build from successful experiences.

Reading and the Emotionally Disturbed

emotionally disturbed: Describes individuals with normal intelligence who achieve substantially below expected levels because of chronic and extreme withdrawal, anxiety, and/or aggressive behavior.

No single definition of children who are **emotionally disturbed** is widely accepted. There are, however, three features that are often found in any definition of emotional disturbance:

1. behavior that goes to an extreme—behavior that is not just slightly different from the usual;

2. a problem that is chronic—one that does not disappear;

3. behavior that is unacceptable because of social or cultural expectations.

Note that emotional disturbance is often defined in terms of physical behavior. Thus it is not surprising that emotionally disturbed children are often called emotionally and behaviorally disturbed.

According to federal estimates (United States Department of Education, 1984), approximately one percent of the school-aged population is emotionally disturbed. Kauffman (1981), however, has put the actual estimate at six to ten percent. Thus, you are likely to encounter children who experience serious and persistent emotional and behavioral problems who have not been formally identified as exceptional students.

Learning Characteristics. Emotionally disturbed children have at least normal intellectual ability but achieve substantially below expected levels because of withdrawal, anxiety, and/or aggressive behavior (Savage & Mooney, 1979; Zinz & Maggart, 1984). Each reflects a different set of learning characteristics that need to be accommodated during instruction. Often these characteristics appear in combination.

Withdrawal

1. The child may be without friends and have difficulty working cooperatively in groups.

2. The child often daydreams more than normal for an age group.

3. Often the child appears secretive.

Anxiety

1. The child may cry much more frequently than normal.

2. Often the child appears tense and nervous. The child may be easily embarrassed and overly sensitive to criticism.

3. The child may appear depressed, sad, or troubled.

4. Frequently the child is reluctant to attempt new tasks independently.

5. The child may be afraid of making mistakes.

Aggression

1. The child may deliberately disrupt the classroom environment.

2. The child may be frequently involved in physical aggression. The child may fight and bully others.

3. The child may intentionally destroy the property of others.

Instruction. Several instructional approaches are often used with children experiencing emotional turmoil: contract reading; bibliotherapy; and cross-age tutoring. These approaches usually supplement or modify slightly the normal developmental reading program in your classroom. Except in extreme cases, they do not replace your normal reading program. Contract reading, bibliotherapy, and cross-age tutoring are also approaches which are not necessarily limited to emotionally disturbed students. They are often found incorporated into reading instruction for other students as well.

contract reading: When student and teacher formally agree upon the learning tasks to be completed, when they will be completed, and how they will be completed.

Contract reading requires that you and a student mutually agree that a specific set of reading activities be completed within a fixed time period. Usually, a reading contract is written by the teacher and then signed by the student. Upon completion, it is evaluated by the teacher or by both the teacher and student. Sometimes parents also evaluate the contract. Reading contracts can cover a period as short as a single reading period or extend over a number of periods. Contract reading may be particularly useful in helping aggressive students control disruptive behavior and complete work on time or in helping anxious students meet with structured, repeated successes. It can also assist a withdrawn child to begin greater interaction with others in the midst of academic tasks. An example of a contract covering one day's reading activities is shown in figure 11–4.

bibliotherapy: Using literature to promote mental and emotional health.

Bibliotherapy, according to Harris & Sipay (1985), ". . . is the attempt to promote mental and emotional health by using reading materials to fulfill needs, relieve pressure, or help an individual in his development as a person" (p. 542). By interacting with a piece of literature, often thematically related to the particular emotional difficulty experienced by the reader, one may find solace and solutions to life's problems. Seeing that others may experience the same problems and seeing how others solve their particular difficulties provides an important therapeutic experience.

Implementing a program of bibliotherapy requires a number of literature selections related to the emotional difficulties experienced by a child. Your librarian may be able to suggest several selections or you may want to consult annotated bibliographies by Baskin & Harris (1977); Coody (1983), Lass & Bromfield (1981); Hormann (1977); or Horner (1978). It also requires putting children in touch with the appropriate materials in a gentle and caring way. This may happen through self-selection; you may wish to introduce a number of related books to the entire class and hope that the child you are concerned about selects one. Or you may need to put the appropriate books directly in the hands of the appropriate child. A program of bibliotherapy requires follow-up activities through discussions of the book and its characters, through retellings or role playing, through art projects related to the book, or in other ways that allow children to respond to a work they have read. Throughout this process, maintain close contact with your school psychologist, informing this specialist of your plans and seeking guidance as you work with your student.

<u>READING CONTRACT</u>

This reading contract is an agreement between <u>Tommy P.</u> and <u>Mrs. Satherswaite</u>

Date: <u>November 20, 1986</u>

<u>TIME</u>	<u>ACTIVITY</u>	<u>COMMENTS</u>
8:30–8:45	Learn about main ideas. Learn new words for "Actions speak louder than words."	
8:45–9:00	Read "Actions speak louder than words." Find the main idea of this article. Share your answer with Bill. Do you agree? Be ready to discuss the article tomorrow.	
9:00–9:10	Work with Sam and complete workbook pages 11 & 12 together.	
9:10–9:30	Read quietly in the reading corner on your independent book project. Write down any new words you find. (OR) Work on a reading center activity with a friend.	

Signed: _____   _____
　　　　　　　　Tommy P.　　　　　　　　　　Mrs. Satherswaite

Self-evaluation:

Teacher Evaluation:

Parent Comments and Signature:

_____

FIGURE 11–4

An example of a daily reading contract covering regular classroom activities

DETERMINING INSTRUCTIONAL NEEDS

cross-age tutoring:
Where older or more proficient students assist younger or less proficient students.

Cross-age tutoring may also be used with children who are experiencing emotional difficulties. Cross-age tutoring requires that older children assist younger children with reading activities. The reading activities may include reading stories aloud regularly to a group of younger children; helping younger children with independent seat work activities; listening to younger children read aloud and correcting their oral reading when necessary; working with younger children on simple word recognition activities such as sight words; or working with children on an independent reading activity in a reading center. Children experiencing emotional problems may benefit by either tutoring younger children or receiving instruction from an older tutor, depending upon the child, the situation, and your best judgment. In either case, children often feel a bit special with the new role and the relationships they develop. You will want to carefully choose, train, and supervise any students who work as tutors for younger children. Provide them with clear and unambiguous directions regarding their specific responsibilities. This increases the likelihood of successful experiences.

In addition to contract reading, bibliotherapy, and cross-age tutoring, there are several general suggestions (Hallahan & Kauffman, 1982; Savage & Mooney, 1979) to keep in mind during reading instruction with children who are emotionally disturbed.

1. Motivation and interest are critically important for these children. Begin first with materials and reading selections that are interesting and engaging to the children. Be certain that you complete an interest inventory before beginning reading instruction.
2. If a student is receiving special education services, be certain to communicate regularly with the specialist who provides the service. Try to provide your student with consistent management and instructional approaches inside and outside the classroom. Share observations on a regular basis with specialists.
3. Communicate regularly with parents or other adults who may be responsible for your students. If particular problems occur at home, ask that you be kept informed.
4. Be certain to explain your classroom rules and expectations. Be very clear about rules you may take for granted. Children need to understand exactly what your expectations are.
5. Be certain that reading instruction is within the instructional level of the child. Try to begin with successful experiences and gradually raise the difficulty level of discussion questions, assignments, and other reading tasks.
6. If reprimands are necessary, try to make them as private as possible. Praise children in public; reprimand in private.
7. Maintain a happy, calm, orderly, and protective environment for the children in your classroom. Model your concern for others and expect your children to treat others with the same respect.

Reading and the Hearing Impaired

Hearing impaired children have permanently reduced sensitivities to sounds in their environment because of genetic factors, illness, or trauma. Usually, hearing impaired children are not sensitive to sounds softer than about 26 decibels (dB, a unit for measuring the relative loudness of sounds). One categorization system used by the Conference of Executives of American Schools for the Deaf defines degrees of hearing impairment as follows:

hearing impaired: Describes individuals with permanently reduced sensitivity to sounds (<26dB) in their environment because of genetic factors, illness, or trauma.

Category of Hearing Impairment	Amount of Hearing Loss
mild	26–54 dB
moderate	55–69 dB
severe	70–89 dB
profound	>90 dB

From a strictly physiological definition, individuals with hearing losses greater than 90 dB are usually considered deaf and those with less are considered hard of hearing.

Besides knowing the extent of hearing loss, it is also important for you to know when the hearing loss took place. The earlier that a hearing loss takes place, the more likely that a child will have inadequately developed language skills. Since reading comprehension depends so strongly on language knowledge, a child with a hearing loss that took place at an early age may have great difficulty acquiring high levels of reading comprehension. This is especially true for hearing losses which go undetected for some time. Approximately two-tenths of one percent of school-age children are considered to be deaf and hard of hearing (United States Department of Education, 1984).

Learning Characteristics. Depending upon the degree of hearing loss, hearing impaired children can compensate by using amplifying devices, speechreading (lipreading), and sign language or finger spelling. Some students may be receiving a strictly oral communication program dependent upon amplification and speechreading. Some may be receiving a strictly manual communication program dependent upon sign language and/or finger spelling. Recently, an increasing number of students have been receiving a total communication program which incorporates both oral and manual aspects. Regardless of the communication program that hearing impaired children receive, the most important learning characteristic for you to consider is that children will be very dependent upon the visual information in your classroom for acquiring information. This includes your facial expression, lip movements, and written information around the classroom.

During instruction, keep in mind the following considerations.

1. The language development of hearing impaired children is likely to be less completely developed than the language of hearing children.
2. Hearing impaired children must concentrate very carefully on orally presented learning tasks. Fatigue can quickly develop which may lead to inattentive behavior.
3. Hearing impaired children with amplifying devices tend to be distracted by extraneous noises in the environment. These devices amplify both target and background sounds.
4. Sometimes, hearing impaired children are initially reluctant to actively participate with hearing children because they fear being rejected (Savage & Mooney, 1979). This usually disappears when a class is tolerant of individual differences.

Despite the fact that many schools now screen children for hearing impairments, some children with mild or moderate hearing losses still go undetected. Thus, it is important for you to be aware of classroom behaviors that often are associated with hearing loss. Using your own judgment, you may want to request a hearing evaluation for a child with some of the following symptoms:

1. Complains of frequent ear aches, head colds, or sinus difficulties
2. Has difficulty following directions and frequently asks to have explanations repeated
3. Is easily fatigued during listening tasks
4. Suspected of being learning disabled, mentally retarded, or emotionally disturbed
5. Is easily distracted by external noises
6. Mispronounces words
7. Uses immature language

BEFORE READING ON

Knowing the learning characteristics of the hearing impaired will help you anticipate a number of instructional considerations teachers need to keep in mind as they teach reading to hearing impaired students. See if you can state at least three of these instructional considerations before reading the next section.

Instruction. Increasingly, children with hearing impairments are being mainstreamed and educated in regular classrooms. Of those who are mainstreamed, the majority have mild or moderate hearing losses; thirty-eight percent have severe or profound losses (Karchmer & Trybus, 1977). Most children who are mainstreamed with profound or severe hearing loss have sign language interpreters who accompany them in the classroom (Hallahan & Kauffman, 1982). If you work with children who have hearing losses, consider the following instructional suggestions.

1. Phonics instruction to develop decoding knowledge presents particular problems to hearing impaired children. You will need to depend more upon sight word instruction in conjunction with contextual analysis to promote decoding skills. Present all new words in context, especially when you are teaching word meanings.
2. Have hearing impaired children sit close to you where they can always see your face and lips.
3. Lipreading will be facilitated if you speak normally. Do not exaggerate lip movements, do not speak either too quickly or too slowly, and maintain eye contact with the student. Stand still when speaking. Movement makes lipreading more difficult.
4. Because an amplifying device amplifies all ambient sound, attempt to limit extraneous sound, especially during verbal instruction.
5. Limit periods of oral instruction. Several short sessions, broken with independent work, are better than a single long session.
6. Use visual aids as much as possible to communicate concepts or explain directions.
7. Use an overhead projector in place of a blackboard when you can. This enables a hearing impaired student to maintain visual contact with your lips.
8. If a child does not understand your directions, rephrase them. Some words are difficult to speechread. Encourage children to ask you to repeat explanations when something is not clear.

Reading and the Visually Impaired

The **visually impaired** include the legally blind and the partially sighted. Individuals who are legally blind have visual acuity which is less than 20/200. With their best eye, the legally blind can see at twenty feet (or less) what a normally sighted individual can see at two hundred feet, even with correction. The partially sighted have visual acuity which falls between 20/70 and 20/200, even with correction, in their best eye.

visually impaired:
Describes individuals who are legally blind (<20/200) or partially sighted (20/70 to 20/200), even with correction

Contrary to popular opinion, legally blind individuals are not necessarily totally blind. Eighty-two percent of the legally blind have some vision, often enough to be able to read print with the assistance of large print books or magnifying devices (Willis, 1976). Only twenty-one percent of the legally blind depend solely upon Braille for reading. Over half (fifty-two percent) use large- or regular-print books for most or all of their reading. One-tenth of one percent of school-age children in the United States are thought to be visually impaired (United States Department of Education, 1984).

Learning Characteristics. Visual impairment does not substantially alter one's language development like hearing impairment does. In addition, IQ scores of the visually impaired are not significantly different from those of their normally sighted peers (Hallahan & Kauffman, 1982). Visual impairment, thus, has little direct effect on either linguistic or cognitive functioning.

There are several ways through which the visually impaired compensate for their handicap: tactile sensation; listening skills; and greater attention. The visually impaired may require, however, some formal training to take maximum advantage of each compensatory strategy.

It is important, too, for teachers to be able to recognize behaviors that may indicate some type of visual difficulty in children. Vision testing is commonly found in elementary schools, but occasionally undetected vision problems occur. You may wish to inquire about visual screening for children who

1. squint;
2. hold reading materials very close or very far away from the eyes;
3. have red or watery eyes;
4. rub their eyes frequently;
5. cover one eye when reading;
6. have crusty material around their eyes and lashes.

Instruction. The visually impaired increasingly are mainstreamed into elementary schools. Should you have the opportunity to have a visually impaired child in your classroom, you will need to consult closely with the resource teacher or other specialist to learn the extent of your student's impairment; which methods and strategies are being used to teach reading; which mechanical and optical devices your student needs to use when reading in other content areas; and particular strategies you might take.

In addition, try to maintain a relatively constant physical environment in your classroom. This will help a visually impaired child move around the room. When you introduce new materials or equipment into your classroom or alter the seating arrangement, introduce the changes to a visually impaired child. Help the new child get acquainted with the physical arrangement of the school. Classmates can help you with this.

When introducing new vocabulary or conceptual knowledge in content-area subjects, take advantage of tactile and auditory strengths. New concepts need to be more extensively described than for the normally sighted student. Although visually impaired students may have had identical background experiences, their interpretation of those experiences is determined by nonvisual senses. You may find that science programs based on self-exploration, experimentation, and reasoning such as the Science Curriculum Improvement Study (SCIS) and Elementary Science Study (ESS) are more appropriate than science programs depending entirely upon reading.

One important way to develop conceptual knowledge is to provide a rich listening environment. Tape recordings of favorite literature selections are particularly useful and enjoyable for younger children. You may want to develop a listening center with a central tape or record player and separate headphones for individuals. Most major publishers of trade books make audio cassettes or records of popular children's literature. You also can get books on tape for the blind through your local public library or by contacting Recordings for the Blind, 214 East Fifty-Eighth Street, New York, NY 10022.

Reading and Children with Speech or Language Disorders

Children with **speech disorders** produce oral language abnormal in how it is said, not in what is said. Several categories of speech disorders exist: phonological disorders (for example, substituting *w* for *r* or omitting all *l* sounds); voice disorders (for example, unusual pitch, loudness, or quality of voice); disorders associated with abnormalities in the mouth and nose (for example, an orofacial cleft); disorders of speech flow (for example, stuttering); or disorders associated with the muscles associated with speech production. It is important to recognize that children who speak nonstandard dialects of English or who are acquiring English as a second (or third) language do not typically have speech disorders. These children's speech needs to be compared to the speech of their peers in their community to determine if speech disorders exist. The speech pathologist in your school will help you make this distinction.

> **speech disorders:** Describes abnormal oral language behavior due to phonological, voice, or other disorders.

Children who have **language disorders** have difficulty expressing their ideas in oral language clearly or have difficulty understanding the ideas expressed by others. Children with language disorders may not have developed verbal language; may use words in abnormal ways such as echoing words spoken to them; may have delayed language development; or may have interrupted language development (Naremore, 1980). As with speech disorders, language disorders do not include children who speak nonstandard dialects or are acquiring English as an additional language.

> **language disorder:** Describes difficulty with expressing ideas in oral language or difficulty understanding the ideas expressed by others.

According to federal estimates, about three percent of the school-age population have speech disorders and approximately one-half of one percent have language disorders (United States Office of Education, 1975; United States Department of Education, 1984).

Learning Characteristics. Some generalizations appropriately can be made about the learning characteristics of speech and language disordered children. Children with language disorders may have a particularly difficult time developing proficiency in reading comprehension since reading is so dependent on adequate language proficiency. On the other hand, some children with oral language disorders actually do quite well in reading.

As a classroom teacher, there may be times when you want to refer a student for formal speech and language assessment by a speech pathologist. It helps the speech pathologist if you provide specific information about a child's speech or language and not simply statements like "Karen's speech seems to be different." In addition, consider the following before making a referral.

1. Is the child's language substantially less mature than that of peers? How does vocabulary and syntax differ from peers? Can the student tell a complete story with all appropriate elements?
2. What regular substitutions or omissions of sounds does the student make? Some of the more common include /w/ for /r/ or /l/ (*wead* for *read* or *lead*); /b/ for /v/ (*berry* for *very*); /t/ for /k/ (*tat* for *cat*); /f/ for voiceless /th/ (*wif* for *with*); voiceless /th/ for /s/ (*thith* for *sis*); /d/ for voiced /th/ (*dis* for *this*); and voiced /th/ for /z/ (*thew* for *zoo*). Are these unusual for the students in your class?
3. Do the students in your class often have trouble understanding what this child is saying? Why is the child hard to understand?
4. Does the child speak much more rapidly than others in your class, to the point where intelligibility suffers?
5. Does the child use normal intonation patterns? Is the pitch, loudness, or quality noticeably different from peers?
6. Does the child have particular difficulty following directions?

Instruction. Classrooms can be excellent places for speech and language disordered youngsters to make progress with their communications skills if the use of oral language is encouraged, valued, and well-integrated into the day's schedule. Regular sharing times, formal oral presentations, informal conversation and discussion as children complete their independent work, and class projects that require cooperation between students can all be used to foster development of effective communication skills.

For younger children with speech disorders, consider independent reading opportunities with books that have rhyming or rhythmic patterns. Opportunities to independently practice appropriate speech behaviors while reading may benefit the child. Books by Dr. Suess and Bill Martin are particularly enjoyable for young children.

For the child who stutters, you and all your students need to keep four things in mind: attend carefully to what the child has to say; let the child finish talking before you respond or interrupt; do not become tense or frustrated at waiting for the entire message; and do not tease or ridicule the condition or the child. It is perfectly acceptable to talk about the disorder with the child; do not ignore it. It will help considerably, though, if you discuss the condition matter-of-factly. Anxiety, for the stutterer, is likely to exaggerate the difficulty.

Reading and the Gifted

A universally accepted working definition of **giftedness** has yet to emerge. Depending upon the defining characteristics of giftedness, different children will be identified. Creativity, intelligence (as measured by an intelligence test or by "street smarts"), motivation, artistic talent, verbal ability, scientific curiosity, and the ability to see unique and novel relationships might all be used to define giftedness. Each, however, would end up identifying a different population of students. We tend to agree with Renzulli's (1978) definition of giftedness which incorporates three characteristics:

giftedness: Describes individuals with high cognitive ability, creativity, and motivation.

1. High cognitive ability
2. Creativity
3. Motivation

Alone or in combination, these factors distinguish gifted children sufficiently from peers to make it possible that they are likely to contribute something of exceptional value to society. Hallahan & Kauffman (1982) estimate that approximately two to five percent of school-age students might be labeled as gifted according to this definition.

However, the federal definition is somewhat different:

"gifted and talented children" means children and, whenever applicable, youth, who are identified at the preschool, elementary, or secondary level as possessing demonstrated or potential abilities that give evidence of high performance capabilities in areas such as intellectual, creative, specific academic, or leadership ability, or in the performing and visual arts, and who by reason thereof, require services or activities not ordinarily provided by the school.

From the Gifted and Talented Children's Act of 1978, PL 95–561, section 902.

Learning Characteristics. Gifted children tend to demonstrate exceptional performance on most cognitive and linguistic tasks. Indeed, often a teacher's first observation about a gifted child is precocious language development. Gifted children often talk about topics which are advanced for their ages. In addition, the way in which they talk is often noticeably more mature. Some individuals believe early reading to be a mark of giftedness, thus reflecting the high social value we place on literacy skills. While it is true that early reading as well as exceptional performance on most cognitive and linguistic tasks is often found among the gifted, not all children who have unique creative, intellectual, or motivational ability read at an early age.

Gifted children tend to demonstrate a high level of curiosity about their environment and have accumulated a substantial amount of background knowledge in a short amount of time. Extensive background knowledge may be reflected by a vocabulary that is noticeably different from their classmates'. Sometimes, however, their background knowledge and superior vocabulary is concentrated in a fairly limited area. Gifted children tend to achieve to a higher degree in reading than in areas which require fine motor skills such as beginning writing. Socially, they tend to be liked by their classmates. The gifted may be concerned at an earlier age with notions of right and wrong and moral and immoral behavior.

While research has established that gifted children often have these characteristics, every gifted child will not have all, or even most, of these attributes (Callahan, 1981; Clark, 1979; Fisch, Bilek, Horrobin & Chang, 1976). Teachers should be concerned with helping the gifted (and indeed all children) develop their abilities in all areas, not merely the areas in which they excel.

Instruction. Three types of instructional accommodations are often provided for gifted children: enrichment programs; ability grouping; and acceleration. **Enrichment programs** provide opportunities outside and inside of the regular classroom for gifted children to pursue special interests. **Ability grouping** involves placing the gifted permanently together in homogeneous classrooms or schools such as New York's School of the Arts. **Acceleration programs** advance gifted children into classrooms with older students. Since both ability grouping and acceleration procedures are discussed in chapter 12, we will only discuss enrichment programs here.

Renzulli (1977) and Renzulli and Smith (1980) have defined a popular enrichment program for the gifted which consists of three types of activities used with a "revolving-door" plan. Type I activities are designed to help children learn about their environment and develop particular interests. Type II activities are developed around group process tasks such as gaming and simulations that enhance problem solving skills, critical thinking, and creative thinking. Type III activities allow individual or group study of actual problems such as determining community feelings about a new shopping center, preserving traditional folk knowledge, or studying the effects of changes in the local environment. Reading activities can be built into each of these types of tasks for children as they explore the environment around them and learn how to acquire the knowledge which is necessary for completing their projects. Research skills need to be developed during Type II tasks and then applied to real-life problems with Type III tasks.

The unique aspect of this program, however, concerns the notion of having a revolving door for students. Renzulli argues that children are

enrichment programs: Learning activities often provided to gifted students outside of the regular classroom.

ability grouping: When children of similar abilities are placed in the same class.

acceleration programs: When children who achieve at high levels in one grade are advanced in order to learn with children of similar achievement levels.

gifted for particular tasks and at particular times. He advocates selecting children for inclusion in the gifted program when they show an interest and talent for the particular topic which will be covered. If they are successful and make a substantial contribution to the project, they may remain. If they lose interest or do not succeed in making a substantive contribution, other children are allowed to participate in the next project in their place. This approach opens enrichment programs to a wider population.

Cassidy (1981) has described another approach for the gifted which is more directly tied to the needs of the classroom teacher of reading: **inquiry reading.** Inquiry reading follows a weekly sequence of procedures, allowing students to define, research and report on a project of interest. It allows gifted students to read and explore topics of individual interest in grades three through six.

inquiry reading:
Permits students to define projects, read and do research, and then present the projects to the class.

Week 1	Children learn the procedures, purpose, and goals of inquiry reading. Students then identify a topic, locate the necessary resources, specify a tangible project which can be completed, and, finally, develop a contract. The contract indicates the nature of the project and due dates. It is signed by both the student and the teacher.
Weeks 2–3	Children spend this time researching their topics independently or in small groups. Often this will require independent library work or interviews in the community as students read, listen, take notes, and develop the necessary resources for completing their project. The teacher may want to confer with the child during this time to provide suggestions and to review the nature of the final project.
Week 4	The fourth week is spent completing the project and preparing it to be presented. Students may present the results of their work in a variety of ways: oral reports with visual aids, a play, a story, written reports, art, dioramas, models, or a slide presentation are just a few of the ways in which projects can be shared with the class.

SAMPLE ACTIVITIES

Establishing Mentor Relationships. Attempt to locate local experts in areas in which your gifted students are interested. See if they would be willing to contribute an hour or so a week to work on an independent project with your students. Design a contract around this project. Display the results in your classroom and your school.

Publishing a Classroom Magazine. Have a rotating group of students be responsible for gathering, editing, and printing articles, essays, stories, poetry, crossword puzzles, and other features from students in the classroom. Make arrangements to use the school's duplicating machine for printing the results.

Tutoring. Involve your gifted students in tutoring situations with students in younger classes as well as students in your own classroom. Help them to carefully plan and evaluate their tutoring activities.

Independent Library Research. Encourage small groups to gather information in the library relevant to particular class needs. Have them present this information to the class when they are done. Focus these projects on real, not make-work, tasks. For example, one group may investigate how to set up and maintain an aquarium and then take responsibility for setting up an unused classroom aquarium.

CHILDREN WITH UNIQUE LINGUISTIC AND CULTURAL BACKGROUNDS

Reading and Speakers of Nonstandard Dialects

dialect: An alternative language form commonly used by a regional, social, or cultural group.

Nearly every major language evolves a number of different **dialects.** Dialects are alternative language forms commonly used by regional, social, or cultural groups. Dialects are mutually understandable by speak-

Independent library research can be effectively integrated into classroom reading instruction and provide challenging opportunities for students.

ers of the same language group but differ in several important ways: sounds (*this* or *dis*); vocabulary (*soda* or *pop*); and syntax (*He is tired* or *He tired*).

All dialects are equally logical, precise, and rule governed; no dialect is inherently superior to another. Usually, however, one dialect becomes the standard language form in a society because it is used by the socially, economically, and politically advantaged members of that society. In our country, the standard language form is called **Standard American English** (SAE). Although it is difficult to define precisely, Standard American English is commonly identified as the form of English spoken by newscasters in most parts of the United States. It is thought to be most similar to the main dialect found in the midwestern states. Today, however, many newscasters reflect slight regional variations of SAE. A common nonstandard dialect in our country is **Black English.** Others, however, also exist including a dialect common to the Appalachian region and one common to New England.

Speakers of each of these dialects share certain language conventions, but there is some degree of variation within a dialect. Thus, when we speak of a Black English dialect, recognize that speakers of Black English in one region may differ slightly from speakers of Black English in another region. We will use Black English as an example of a nonstandard dialect in the following discussion. What is said about this dialect, however, also applies to other nonstandard dialects.

Characteristics. When students who speak a nonstandard dialect read aloud, they often alter the sounds, words, and syntax of the text to be consistent with their particular dialect. A speaker of Black English, for example, may read the sentence *He is playing* as *He playing*. While it may appear to you that the child has not read the sentence correctly, there is no evidence to indicate that this behavior interferes with comprehension (Simons, 1979). Indeed, this type of oral reading behavior reflects an attempt to get to the underlying meaning of a message in the dialect of the reader. Thus, when oral reading reflects the correct translation of a text into a particular dialect, we do not want to stop to have students correct their reading behavior. Indeed, to do so would impede comprehension, not promote it, since it would force students to attend to the surface conventions in the print at the expense of maintaining attention on the meaning of the message. We do, however, wish to have a student correct reading behavior that interferes with comprehension and is unrelated to a dialect; for example, *He painting* for *He is playing*. Teachers, therefore, need to be aware of the dialects of their students; they need to be able to discriminate between oral reading errors reflecting dialect differences and oral reading errors reflecting actual comprehension difficulties.

Table 11–1 summarizes some of the more common differences between Standard American English and Black English. While it is important for you to learn to recognize these features when they appear dur-

Standard American English (SAE): The language form spoken by newscasters in most parts of the United States.

Black English: A dialect spoken by many blacks and some whites in the United States.

TABLE 11–1

A partial summary of common differences between Standard American English and Black English

Language Trait	Standard American English	Black English
	Phonological Differences	
<u>Initial</u>		
th—d	this	dis
th—t	thin	tin
str—skr	stream	scream
thr—tr	three	tree
<u>Final</u>		
sks—ses	tasks	tasses
sk—ks	ask	aks
th—f	teeth	teef
l—no sound	tool	too
r—no sound	four	foe
<u>General</u>		
Simplify final	best	bess
consonant clusters	walked	walk
	books	book
	talks	talk
i—e before nasals	pin	pen
	Syntactic Differences	
Dropping *to be* verbs	He is playing.	He playing.
Using *be* for extended time	He is always here.	He be here.
Subject-predicate agreement		
To be verbs	I am going.	I is going.
	There were two girls.	There was two girls.
Third-person singular verbs	Tom plays ball.	Tom play ball.
Irregular Verbs	She rode her bike.	She rided her bike.
Omission of indefinite article	Give him a book.	Give him book.
Use of more for comparatives	He is bigger than you.	He is more bigger than you.
Double negatives	I don't want any.	I don't want none.

ing children's reading, it is equally important for you to recognize that every dialect will contain similar, regular, and predictable differences from the standard dialect. By listening to your students speak, try to discover these regularities and use them to guide your behavior during oral reading.

A speaker of Black English read the sentence in the following example. Which deviations from the text are probably due to the child's dialect, do not impede comprehension, and should not be corrected by a teacher who wants the child to focus on the meaning of the message? Which deviations from the text impede comprehension and need to be corrected?

A POINT TO PONDER

Child:	Day won ax for duh two book.	Day (pause) after?
Text:	They won't ask for the two books.	They are afraid.

Instruction. Because reading is a language-based process and because speakers of nonstandard dialects as a whole have achieved at lower levels in reading, it is, perhaps, natural to assume that nonstandard dialects interfere with reading comprehension. This was, in fact, a common assumption before the 1970s. Several instructional practices were recommended in an attempt to correct this situation.

1. Teach the students with reading materials that matched their dialect.
2. Teach the students with dialect-neutral stories; reading materials that avoid conflicts with the nonstandard dialect.
3. Teach the students to speak Standard American English before teaching them to read.

None of these approaches, however, were particularly effective at increasing students' abilities to comprehend (Simons, 1979). In addition, each proposal assumed that speakers of nonstandard dialects had deficits that needed to be "fixed." Children were implicitly being told that their language was inferior.

Research and debate during the 1970s have largely settled this issue in favor of a **difference explanation,** not a **deficit explanation.** That is, nonstandard dialects are now recognized by researchers as different but equally logical, precise, and rule governed. Moreover, it is acknowledged that speakers of nonstandard dialects can understand Standard American English very well even when they can not speak or write in this dialect. Dialect differences, by themselves, are not the cause for reading failure.

Today, three instructional practices are usually encouraged in classrooms with nonstandard dialect speakers.

1. Language experience approaches are used at the very beginning stages of reading so that children see the close connection between their language and the meaning of printed words.

difference explanation: An interpretation of nonstandard dialects as being different but equally logical, precise, and rule-governed as the standard dialect.

deficit explanation: An interpretation of nonstandard dialects not simply as different, but as illogical, imprecise, and not as rule-governed as the standard dialect.

2. Culturally relevant materials written in Standard American English are used whenever possible to ensure that students' background knowledge is consistent with the background knowledge required to comprehend the text as well as to increase interest and motivation. Many reading programs have now incorporated stories about different cultural groups.

3. Teachers ignore oral reading errors when they reflect the correct translation of a text into a particular dialect and when they do not alter the underlying meaning of material written in Standard American English.

The preceding discussion is not meant to suggest that it may be socially, economically, and politically unimportant for a speaker of nonstandard English to acquire the standard dialect. Teachers want to provide learning experiences that promote competency in a standard dialect and an awareness of when one can effectively use both the standard dialect and a student's regular dialect. On the other hand, it is important to recognize that this need not be done when students are demonstrating competence at comprehending written material.

SAMPLE ACTIVITIES

Dictated Sentences. Using sentence dictation tasks during spelling and language arts activities is often a useful way to direct students' attention to the conventions of Standard American English.

Read-Aloud Sessions. Incorporate culturally appropriate materials into read-aloud sessions for students. Use these to generate discussions of dialect differences. You may want to write examples of the ways that two dialects can be used to communicate the same message.

Two-sided Stories. Have students write stories in their dialects, putting a few sentences and an illustration on one side of each page. Then help them to rewrite the story in Standard American English on the other side of each page. This may initially be done as a language experience activity where you write down the sentences dictated by students.

Defining Dialects. Attempt to listen carefully and identify the regular, rule-governed differences in the dialects of your students. To help you become proficient at deciding when you should correct oral reading and when you should not, you may want to ask students questions about what they have read. Gradually you will develop skill at determining when an error interferes with comprehension.

Reading and Limited English Speaking Students

It has been estimated that at least seven and one-half million school-aged children in the United States are non-native speakers of English (Gonzales, 1981). A substantial portion are **limited English-speaking students**—students who have not yet developed fluency with the English language. Limited English speakers may come from a variety of linguistic backgrounds: Spanish; Cajun; one of several Native American languages; Vietnamese; Cambodian; Haitian; Korean; Cantonese; or Mandarin. At least one public school district on the west coast has students who speak more than eighty different primary languages (McNeil, Donant & Alkin, 1980). Although more of these students are being provided with special educational services, many limited English-speaking students still receive most of their instruction from the regular elementary classroom teacher (Feeley, 1983; Gonzales, 1981). Thus, it is important for you to develop an awareness of the needs of these students and an understanding of the accommodations that are necessary during reading instruction.

limited English-speaking students: Students who have not yet developed fluency with the English language.

Characteristics. One major difference exists between students who speak nonstandard dialects and limited English-speaking students. Speakers of nonstandard dialects can understand spoken English and

Students of different language and cultural backgrounds can add much to other students' understanding of the world. Use their special knowledge to help comprehension of stories set in areas where they have unique backgrounds and ask them to share their knowledge.

need only develop proficiency at reading. Limited English speakers lack the knowledge of spoken English that will permit them to comprehend what they read. Acquiring oral language competence in English is, therefore, fundamental to developing proficiency in reading comprehension for the limited English-speaking student.

A second difference also exists: while nonstandard dialects do not appear to impede reading comprehension in Standard American English, the same is not necessarily true among students who are learning to speak English. Differences between Standard American English and another language often impede comprehension. This makes it important to become familiar with the differences between English and a child's native language. The major differences between English and Spanish, one of the more common languages of limited English-speaking students, are listed in table 11–2.

TABLE 11–2

A partial summary of differences between Standard American English and Spanish

Language Trait	Standard American English	Spanish
	Phonological Differences	
i—e	bit	beet
a—e	pat	pet
a—e	late	let
b—p	bar	par
z—s	buzz	bus
j—ch or *y*	Jane	chain or yane
th—s	thank	sank
th—d	this	dis
	Syntactic Differences	
Negatives	Bill is not here.	Bill is no here.
	They do not go to school.	They no go school.
	Don't go.	No go.
Use of *be*	I am eight.	I have eight years.
	I am hungry.	I have hunger.
Tense	I will see you later.	I see you later.
	I needed help yesterday.	I need help yesterday.
Omission of determiner	He is a teacher.	He is teacher.
Omission of pronoun		
in questions	Is it time to go?	Is time to go?
in statements	It is time.	Is time.

It is important that you become sensitive to differences between Standard American English and any language that your limited English-speaking students bring to the classroom, not just Spanish. To acquire this understanding, you may seek advice from another speaker of this language who also speaks English, your local or state coordinator of bilingual educational services, or write to one of these organizations.

Center for Applied Linguistics
1611 North Kent Street
Arlington, VA 22209

Dissemination Center for Bilingual Bicultural Education
6504 Tracor Lane
Austin, TX 78721

Instruction. Research in teaching reading to limited English-speaking students is still in its infancy. Consistent findings regarding effective instructional approaches have yet to be generated. Several instructional approaches, however, are often found in schools: immersion approaches; English-as-a-second-language (ESL) approaches; and bilingual approaches. **Immersion approaches** make no special provisions for the limited English-speaking student. As teachers instruct all students in oral and written language skills, limited English-speaking students are expected to pick up as much as they can, as fast as they can, from immersion in their new language. This has been the traditional form of instruction to limited English-speaking students in our country, although not necessarily the most effective. **ESL approaches** teach limited English-speaking students oral English skills first, before any reading instruction begins. Usually, ESL approaches require that students leave the classroom for this instruction. Special ESL teachers work with students, usually in structured oral drills, to develop fluency in oral English. After students have begun to establish fluency in oral English, reading instruction is started. **Bilingual approaches** promote the development of reading and writing skills in students' native language concurrently with either formal or informal instruction in oral English. After students have learned to read and write in their own language and acquired proficiency in oral English, reading instruction in English begins. Bilingual approaches require special teachers who are fluent in the native language of the children they work with.

immersion approaches: When students are expected to pick up English as rapidly as they can without any special instructional intervention.

ESL approaches: When limited English-speaking students learn oral English in structured lessons before learning how to read in English.

bilingual approaches: When limited English-speaking students learn reading and writing skills in their native language concurrently with formal or informal instruction in oral English.

Regardless of approach that your students receive, it is important for you to keep a number of instructional recommendations in mind as you work with students who are just learning to speak English.

1. Encourage talking among all your students, but especially between other students and your limited English-speaking students.
2. Be patient with your limited English-speaking students. Often students first go through a "silent period" before they begin to experiment with their new language (Krashen, 1978).

3. Pay less attention at the beginning to pronunciation and accent. Concentrate on meaning and communication.

4. Try to understand the difficulty of the task your student faces and help your other students to also appreciate the challenge. Encourage them to help your new student whenever they can.

5. Select books for read-aloud sessions that are culturally appropriate for your limited English-speaking students. Encourage them to discuss the book with you and the class.

6. Respect your students' cultural and linguistic heritages. Attempt to work them into classroom activities whenever possible.

7. Use language experience activities frequently to teach beginning reading skills.

SAMPLE ACTIVITIES

Picture Dictionaries. Have your limited English-speaking students begin a picture dictionary using common school objects, activities, or locations (desk, book, library, office, recess, music, and gym). Have other students help them in this task.

Teaching Cultural Units. Develop a unit on the country or culture that your student comes from. Use this unit to teach new vocabulary words in English. Have your limited English-speaking student share the native words for these items.

Peer Tutoring. Have one student in your class work with a limited English-speaking student regularly, completing tasks such as reading a storybook together and talking about the pictures; writing and illustrating a story together; practicing spelling words from the student's picture dictionary; writing sentences together about a topic of interest; or playing "Simon Says."

Readers Theatre. (See chapter 7.) Readers Theatre experiences are often useful as students begin to develop some confidence in their abilities. This activity gives them an opportunity to practice reading their part a number of times before they have to read it in public.

A FINAL NOTE

This chapter has attempted to expose you to the variety of special needs children that you will be likely to encounter among your students. It has provided you with instructional suggestions for helping each of your students reach their potential in reading proficiency. While this information will undoubtedly broaden your perspective on reading instruction, we feel that your developing perspective will almost certainly require additional study on the needs of special children in our schools. We encourage you to consider taking at least one course on the needs of exceptional children and, if possible, one course on the needs of limited English-speaking children and children who speak nonstandard dialects.

THE MAJOR POINTS

1. Each of your students is, in fact, a student with special needs. Each student you encounter will have unique needs that must be acknowledged as you make instructional decisions in reading. You must consider each student's set of background experiences and abilities as you plan to teach each lesson and as you interpret children's responses to your instruction.
2. Exceptional children include those who are mentally retarded, learning disabled, emotionally disturbed, hearing impaired, visually impaired, those who have speech or language disorders, and the gifted. Federal legislation has mandated that a free and appropriate education be provided to meet the unique needs of these students.
3. Increasingly, exceptional students are being mainstreamed into classrooms. This has resulted in additional opportunities, challenges, and responsibilities for elementary classroom teachers.
4. Besides accommodating a child's particular handicap, reading instruction for exceptional children does not differ substantially from the activities, strategies, and materials that have been described in previous chapters. Reading instruction for the exceptional child does, however, require some instructional accommodations and judicious selection from a range of instructional activities.
5. Children with unique linguistic and cultural backgrounds include those who speak nonstandard dialects and those who are limited English speakers. Both populations require considerable sensitivity, additional knowledge, and particular instructional adaptations by the teacher.

QUESTIONS AND ACTIVITIES

1. Federal, state, and local requirements based on the categorical designations defined in this chapter have brought considerable benefit to populations previously excluded from the mainstream of education. Categories and labels have clearly benefitted these children. Is it possible for categories and labels to jeopardize the educational opportunities afforded these children? How? What must you do to prevent this?
2. Identify at least three ways in which recent federal legislation affects you as a classroom teacher of reading. What must you do to prepare for these responsibilities?
3. It is the beginning of the school year. Your school psychologist informs you that you will have a student in your room that was tested

for but not admitted into the district's special education program for mentally retarded youngsters. This child, the school psychologist tells you, has ". . . below average intellectual functioning but not low enough to qualify for special assistance." Identify several learning characteristics you might look for during the first few weeks of school. Also, specify the major instructional consideration you may need to consider when planning reading instruction for this student. Finally, and most importantly, consider how you will provide appropriate instruction without having expectations that are too low for this student and prevent the student from being sufficiently challenged.

4. Students with learning disabilities sometimes receive instruction from a classroom teacher with one type of comprehension framework and instruction from a learning disability specialist or a reading specialist with another type of comprehension framework. What might you and the specialist do to avoid this problem?

5. Discuss the similarities and the differences in the learning characteristics and instruction for the hearing impaired and the visually impaired.

6. Interview specialists who work with exceptional children in an elementary school. Discuss their role, the learning characteristics of the children they see, and how they work with their students on reading or how they assist classroom teachers to provide appropriate instruction in reading. Prepare a list of interview questions in advance and use these to guide your discussions. Write up the results of your interviews, summarizing the major points.

7. One student who was a speaker of Black English read the following sentences. Identify the deviations from the text that are probably due to the child's dialect, probably do not impede comprehension, and probably should not be corrected by a teacher who wants the child to focus on the meaning of the message? Which deviations from the text impede comprehension and probably should be corrected?

   a. Child: One day five childrens went out to play.
       Text: One day five children went out to play.

   b. Child: The children laugh.
       Text: The children laughed.

   c. Child: The childrens were watching for the parade.
       Text: The children were waiting for the parade.

   d. Child: She want to play. One morning a boy made a bus.
       Text: She wants to play. One morning a boy made a boat.

FURTHER READING

Carlsen, J. M. (1985). Between the deaf child and reading: The language connection. *The Reading Teacher, 38,* 424–26.

Describes differences in the ways that deaf and hearing children learn to read. Presents a list of useful instructional suggestions when teaching reading to the deaf and hard of hearing.

Feeley, J. T. (1983). Help for the reading teacher: Dealing with the Limited English Proficient (LEP) child in the elementary classroom. *The Reading Teacher, 36,* 650–55.

Outlines a number of instructional suggestions for classroom teachers of reading who have students with limited English proficiency and no outside assistance.

Lukasevich, A. (1983). Three dozen useful information sources on reading for the gifted. *The Reading Teacher, 36,* 542–48.

An annotated bibliography of ideas and activities for classroom teachers who teach reading to gifted students.

Sinatra, R. C.; Stahl-Gemake, J. & Berg, D. N. (1984). Improving reading comprehension of disabled readers through semantic mapping. *The Reading Teacher, 38,* 22–29.

Describes how the use of story-mapping activities (see chapter 7) enhanced reading comprehension among a group of disabled readers in grades two through eight. Describes a number of different types of story maps that can be used for instructional purposes.

Wagoner, S. A. (1984). The portrayal of the cognitively disabled in children's literature. *The Reading Teacher, 37,* 502–508.

Reviews the negative attitudes that sometimes enter portrayals of the cognitively disabled (mentally retarded) in children's literature. Includes an annotated bibliography of children's literature that deals with the cognitively disabled.

REFERENCES

Baskin, B. H. & Harris, K. H. (1977). *Notes from a different drummer: a guide to juvenile fiction portraying the handicapped.* New York: R. R. Bowker.

Callahan, C. M. (1981). Superior abilities. In J. M. Kauffman & D. P. Hallahan (eds.). *Handbook of special education.* Englewood Cliffs, NJ: Prentice-Hall.

Chall, J. (1983). *Stages of reading development.* New York: McGraw-Hill.

Clark, B. (1979). *Growing up gifted.* Columbus, OH: Charles E. Merrill.

Cody, B. (1983). *Using literature with young children* (3rd Edition). Dubuque, IA: William C. Brown.

Feeley, J. T. (1983). Help for the reading teacher: Dealing with the Limited English Proficient (LEP) child in the elementary classroom. *The Reading Teacher, 36,* 650–55.

Fernald, G. (1943). *Remedial techniques in basic school subjects.* New York: McGraw-Hill.

Fisch, R. O.; Bilek, M. K.; Horrobin, J. M.; & Chang, P. (1976). Children with superior intelligence at 7 years of age. *American Journal of Diseases of Children 130,* 481–87.

Gearhart, B. R. (1985). *Learning disabilities: Educational strategies* (4th Edition). St. Louis: C. V. Mosby.

Gonzales, P. C. (1981). Beginning English reading for ESL students. *Reading Teacher, 35,* 154–62.

Grossman, H. J. (ed.). (1973) *Manual on terminology and classification in mental retardation, 1973 revision.* Washington, D.C.: American Association on Mental Deficiency.

Hallahan, D. P. & Kauffman, J. M. (1982). *Exceptional children.* (2nd Edition). New York: Prentice-Hall.

Harris, A. J. & Sipay, E. R. (1985). *How to increase reading ability* (8th Edition). New York: Longman.

Hormann, E. (1977). Children's crisis literature. *Language Arts, 54,* 559–66.

Horner, C. (1978). *The single-parent family in children's books: An analysis and annotated bibliography with an appendix on audiovisual material.* Metuchen, NJ: Scarecrow.

Karchmer, M. A. & Trybus, R. J. (1977). *Who are the deaf children in the mainstream programs?* Washington, DC: Office of Democratic Studies, Gallaudet College.

Kauffman, J. M. (1981). Characteristics of children's behavior disorders, (2nd Edition). Columbus: Charles E. Merrill.

Krashen, S. (1978). The mother-model for second language acquisition. In R. C. Gingras (ed.) *Second language acquisition and foreign language teaching.* Arlington, VA: Center for Applied Linguistics.

Lass, B. & Bromfield, M. (1981). Books about children with special needs: An annotated bibliography. *The Reading Teacher, 10*(1), 12–13.

Lerner, J. (1985). *Learning Disabilities: Theories, diagnosis, and teaching strategies* (4th Edition). Boston: Houghton Mifflin.

Lloyd, J. (1980). Academic instruction and cognitive behavior modification: The need for attack strategy training. *Exceptional Education Quarterly, 1*, 53–63.

McNeil, J. D.; Donant, L.; & Alkin, M. C. (1980). *How to teach reading successfully.* Boston: Little, Brown.

Meichenbaum, D. (1977). *Cognitive-behavior modification: An integrative approach.* New York: Plenum Press.

Naremore, R. C. (1980). Language disorders in children. In T. J. Hixon; L. D. Shriberg; & J. H. Saxman (eds.) *Introduction to communication disorders.* Englewood Cliffs, NJ: Prentice-Hall.

Renzulli, J. S. (1978) What makes giftedness? Re-examining a definition. *Phi Delta Kappan, 60*(3), 180–84, 261.

Ringler, L. H. & Weber, C. K. (1984). *A language-thinking approach to reading.* New York: Harcourt Brace Jovanovich.

Savage, J. & Mooney, J. F. (1979). *Teaching reading to children with special needs.* Boston: Allyn and Bacon.

Simons, H. D. (1979). Black dialect, reading interference and classroom interaction. In L. B. Resnick & P. A. Weaver (eds.) *Theory and practice of early reading,* Volume 3. Hillsdale, NJ: Erlbaum.

Tierney, R. J.; Readence, J. E.; & Dishner, E. K. (1985). *Reading strategies and practices: Guide for improving instruction* (2nd Edition). Boston: Allyn and Bacon, Inc.

United States Department of Education. (1984). *To assure the free, appropriate public education of all handicapped children.* Sixth Annual Report to Congress on the Implementation of PL 94–172. Washington, DC: United States Department of Education.

United States Office of Education. (1975). Estimated number of handicapped children in the United States, 1974–75. Washington, DC: Bureau of Education for the Handicapped.

Van Riper, C. (1978). *Speech correction: Principles and methods* (6th Edition). Englewood Cliffs, NJ: Prentice-Hall.

Willis, D. H. (1976). *A study of the relationship between visual acuity, reading mode, and school systems for blind students–1976.* Louisville, KY: American Printing House for the Blind.

Wong, B. Y. L. (1980). Increasing retention of main ideas through questioning strategies. *Learning Disability Quarterly, 2*, 42–47.

CHILDREN'S LITERATURE AND SPECIAL EDUCATION: A SELECTED BIBLIOGRAPHY

General Information

Adams, B. (1979). *Like it is: Facts and feelings about handicaps from kids who know.* New York: Walker and Co.

Biklen, D. & Barnes, E. (1977). *You don't have to hear to cook pancakes: A workbook on understanding people.* Syracuse, NY: Human Policy Press.

Biklen, D. & Sokoloff, M. (1977). *What do you do when your wheelchair gets a flat tire? Questions and answers about disabilities.* Syracuse, NY: Human Policy Press.

Kamien, J. (1979). *What if you couldn't . . . ? A book about special needs.* New York: Scribner's.

Mental Retardation

Baldwin, A. (1978). *A little time.* New York: Viking Press.

Brightman, A. (1976). *Like me.* New York: Little, Brown.

Byars, B. (1970). *Summer of the swans.* New York: Viking Press.
Carpelan, B. (1971). *Bow island.* New York: Delacorte.
Christopher, M. (1966). *Long shot for Paul.* Boston: Little, Brown.
Cleaver, B. & Cleaver, V. (1973). *Me too.* New York: Lippincott.
Little, J. (1968). *Take wing.* Boston: Little, Brown.
Sobol, H. (1977). *My brother Stephen is retarded.* New York: Macmillan.

Learning Disabilities

Albert, L. (1977). *But I'm ready to go.* Scarsdale, NY: Bradbury Press.
Gilson, J. (1980). *Do bananas chew gum?* New York: Lathrop.
Hunter, E. (1969). *Sue Ellen.* New York: Houghton Mifflin.
Lasker, J. (1974). *He's my brother.* Chicago: Albert Whitman.
Smith, D. B. (1975). *Kelly's creek.* New York: Crowell.

Hearing Impairment

Charlip, R. & Charlip, M. B. (1980). *Hand talk: An abc of finger spelling and sign language.*
New York: Four Winds Press.
Corcoran, B. (1974). *Dance to still music.* New York: Atheneum.
Levine, E. S. (1974). *Lisa and her soundless world.* New York: Human Sciences.
Litchfield, A. (1976). *A button in her ear.* New York: Whitman.
Peter, D. (1976). *Claire and Emma.* New York: John Day.
Peterson, J. W. *I have a sister. My sister is deaf.* New York: Harper & Row.
Riskind, M. (1981). *Apple is my sign.* Boston: Houghton Mifflin.
Wolf, B. (1977). *Anna's silent world.* New York: Lippincott.

Visual Impairment

Butler, B. (1962). *Light a single candle.* New York: Dodd, Mead, and Co.
Butler, B. (1972). *Gift of gold.* New York: Dodd, Mead, and Co.
Cohen, M. (1983). *See you tomorrow, Charles.* New York: Greenwillow Books.
Jensen, V. A. & Dorcas, W. (1977). *What's that?* New York: Philomel.
Keats, E. J. (1971). *Apartment 3.* New York: Macmillan.
Little, J. (1977). *Listen for the singing.* E. P. Dutton.
Peterson, P. (1977). *Sally can't see.* New York: John Day.
Wolf, B. (1976). *Connie's new eyes.* New York: Lippincott.
Yalen, J. (1977). *The seeing stick.* New York: Thomas Y. Crowell Co.

Speech and Language Disorders

Christopher, M. (1975). *Glue fingers.* Toronto: Little, Brown.
Fleischman, P. (1980). *The half-a-moon-inn.* New York: Harper & Row.
Gupo, F. (1967). *Atu, the silent one.* New York: Holiday Press.
Lee, M. (1969). *The skating rink.* New York: Seabury.
White, E. B. (1970). *The trumpet of the swan.* New York: Harper & Row.

SECTION FOUR
INSTRUCTIONAL PATTERNS IN THE READING CLASSROOM

12 Classroom Organization

"And Abe put on his buckskin breeches, washed his face and hands in the brook, and went off to school with his sister, Sally . . . . There they sat together, big and small, reading and writing and reckoning aloud, all at one time together. There was such a chatter that it could be heard a long way off. But when Abe was six years old he had learned both to read and write."

Ingri & Edgar Parin d'Aulaire, *Abraham Lincoln.* (New York: Doubleday, 1939), p. 5–6.

How can you best organize your classroom for reading instruction? Should you provide instruction to the whole class as one group, divide the class into achievement groups for instruction, have each student work on individualized reading projects, or provide some combination of these organizational patterns? In Abraham Lincoln's day, decisions related to classroom organization were simple; it was common for all students in a one-room school to learn ". . . all at one time together." In this chapter, you will learn how organizational decisions have become much more complex as we have begun to value and accommodate individual differences in reading achievement levels, reading interests, specific skill competencies, and background knowledge. The natural variation between individuals demands your attention. It requires that you make informed decisions related to classroom organization.

After reading this chapter, you will be able to

1. identify the types of individual differences you need to accommodate in your classroom organization and explain why these differences are important;
2. identify the two major categories of organizational accommodations used during reading instruction to meet the unique needs of individuals;
3. describe several different types of organizational accommodations that can be made between and within classes;
4. describe two different methods that can be used to individualize instruction within a classroom;
5. explain how your developing framework of reading comprehension is related to the organizational decisions you must make.

THE CHALLENGE: INDIVIDUAL DIFFERENCES

individual differences: Specific ways in which students vary such as reading achievement level, reading interests, specific skill competencies, or background knowledge.

As a developing professional, you are undoubtedly familiar with the concept of **individual differences** in educational settings. You know that your classroom will contain a unique collection of individual children, no two of whom will be the same. You also know that instruction must attempt to meet the unique needs of each student in your classroom. The diversity that exists within classrooms presents a unique opportunity for teachers concerned with providing appropriate instruction for every student. You can take advantage of this opportunity and meet the individual needs of your students by making appropriate decisions about how to organize your classroom.

Individual students differ along many dimensions. Within the realm of reading instruction, however, we need to accommodate differences between students in four major areas:

1. reading achievement levels
2. reading interests
3. specific skill competencies
4. background knowledge

Consider, for example, individual differences in reading achievement levels that might be expected in an average fourth-grade classroom. Which do you think might best describe the likely variation in reading achievement levels between the highest and lowest achieving readers: one year; two years; three years; four or more years? A very conservative rule of thumb is that the variation in reading achievement levels will at least equal the grade level of a class. According to Harris & Sipay (1985), for example, you can expect a minimum of four years difference in achievement levels between the highest achieving and lowest achieving readers.

BEFORE READING ON

Burmeister (1983) suggests that reading achievement levels within individual classrooms are likely to vary according to the following parameters:

Grade Level	Lowest Reader	Highest Reader	Achievement Range (In Years)
1st	preschool	3.0	4.0
2nd	preschool	4.3	5.3
3rd	kindergarten	5.7	5.7
4th	1.0	7.0	6.0
5th	1.7	8.3	6.6
6th	2.3	9.7	7.4
7th	3.0	11.0	8.0

Notice that the achievement range between lowest and highest achieving readers increases as grade level increases; the gap between lowest and highest achieving readers is greater in seventh grade than it is in first grade. Does the increasing difference between lowest and highest achieving readers result from the more rapid growth of high-achieving readers, the slower growth of low-achieving readers, or both factors? Should we take comfort in this information or be distressed? Before reading on, consider how these individual differences might be accommodated in your instructional program.

Because reading achievement levels vary so substantially within classrooms, one cannot expect to accommodate individual differences in reading achievement levels by teaching all students using a basal reader at a single level. Some students will not be challenged sufficiently and thus lose interest in learning. Others will be unable to benefit from instruction because the learning tasks are extraordinarily difficult. Only a few students will find the reading tasks appropriate for their level of competence. You will need to accommodate the range of differences in achievement levels by effectively organizing for reading instruction.

Differences in reading achievement levels are the most apparent type of difference between individuals. Differences in reading interests are equally important to consider when planning how to best meet individual needs in reading. Each student in your classroom is likely to have unique reading interests; some will prefer to read narratives, others will prefer exposition; some will prefer stories about animals and others will prefer stories about dirt bikes. As a teacher of reading, you need to anticipate that instructional activities for students who are interested in the topic will probably be more meaningful than for students who are not interested in the topic.

Specific skill competencies is a third dimension on which individuals in your classroom will differ. Each student will bring a unique combination of reading skills to your instructional lessons. Some may have comprehensive decoding knowledge but poorly developed vocabulary knowledge. Others may have comprehensive vocabulary knowledge but poorly developed decoding knowledge. Other combinations of strong and weak knowledge sources (decoding, vocabulary, syntactic, and discourse) are also possible. It is not unusual to find two students who are both reading at the same achievement level and are both equally interested in the selection used for instruction, but exhibit a different pattern of skill needs that must be met during the same lesson. If you multiply this situation by the number of students in your class, you can appreciate the importance of accommodating each child's instructional needs in specific skill areas. Accommodating differences in specific skill competencies is especially important to teachers who adopt more of a mastery of specific skills explanation for the development of reading comprehension.

A fourth dimension on which individuals in your classroom will differ is the background knowledge that each brings to any reading task. Each child's previous experiences are unique. As a result, each has a different type of background knowledge to assist in the comprehension process. Two students may both be reading at the same level of achievement, be equally interested in a story about backpacking which is used for instruction, and have a similar set of skill competencies. Differences in background knowledge may, however, lead one child to make the required inferences while another child struggles to understand even the most basic information in the story. Somehow, each child's unique background knowledge needs to be accommodated in your classroom reading program as you attempt to provide appropriate instruction for all of your students.

Each child in your classroom is unique along a number of dimensions: reading achievement level, specific skill competencies, reading interests, and background knowledge. Classroom organization attempts to use these differences to provide more appropriate, individualized instruction.

Thus, your students are unique in the reading achievement level, reading interests, skill competencies, and background knowledge that each brings to the reading task. An important challenge for any teacher of reading consists of how to most effectively exploit this inherent diversity and further the development of reading comprehension for each individual in a classroom. Schools and teachers attempt to meet this challenge through organizational decisions. By accommodating differences in reading achievement levels, reading interests, skill competencies, and background knowledge, schools and teachers attempt to provide more appropriate reading instruction for individuals. There are two general categories of organizational accommodations used during reading instruction to meet the unique needs of individuals: interclass accommodations and intraclass accommodations.

INTERCLASS ACCOMMODATIONS

Interclass accommodations alter the manner in which reading instruction is organized between classes. Generally, interclass accommodations only accommodate differences in reading achievement levels. They do

interclass accommodations: Account for individual differences by altering the manner in which reading instruction is organized *between* classes.

not usually accommodate differences between students in reading interests, skill competencies, or background knowledge. Interclass accommodations include homogeneous grouping (tracking); departmentalized reading instruction; team teaching; cross-grade and cross-class grouping; split-half classes; retention and acceleration; and assistance by reading specialists or special educators.

Homogeneous Grouping (Tracking)

homogeneously grouped classrooms: Classes where students are grouped on at least one dimension, usually reading achievement levels.

tracking: An interclass organization structure using classes that are homogeneously grouped according to achievement levels.

Most elementary classrooms are heterogeneous; they contain children from a wide range of reading achievement levels (Hiebert, 1983). To reduce the range of reading achievement levels within any single classroom, schools sometimes attempt to form **homogeneously grouped classrooms.** If there are three fourth-grade classes, for example, one will contain the high-achieving readers; one, the average-achieving readers; and one, the low-achieving readers. This solution is sometimes called **tracking,** since children are placed in different educational tracks (high, average, low) depending on achievement level. Homogeneous grouping is more frequently found in the upper elementary grades (fourth through sixth) rather than in the primary grades (Kindergarten through third). There is no evidence to suggest that low-achieving readers do better in a homogeneous instructional environment (Harris & Sipay, 1985). Limited evidence suggests that high-achieving readers benefit from a homogeneous instructional environment (Guthrie, 1979).

BEFORE READING ON

Is it possible to ever form a truly homogeneous class for reading instruction? Why or why not? Be certain to consider all types of individual differences important to reading instruction.

Departmentalized Reading Instruction

departmentalized reading instruction: Where one or several teachers is solely responsible for reading instruction while other teachers are responsible for instruction in other subject areas.

Occasionally, an elementary school will use **departmentalized reading instruction;** that is, one or several teachers will be solely responsible for reading instruction while other teachers are responsible for instruction in another subject area. Students move from one subject-area classroom to another as the day progresses, receiving instruction from the teacher responsible for reading, the teacher responsible for mathematics, the teacher responsible for science, and so forth. The traditional organizational plan for high schools is, in effect, implemented at the elementary school. This interclass accommodation is almost always limited to the intermediate grade levels. It is seldom, if ever, found in the primary grades.

By itself, departmentalized reading instruction does not solve the challenge created by individual differences. Often, however, departmentalized reading instruction is combined with some form of homogeneous grouping. The teacher responsible for reading at the fourth-grade level, for example, will teach reading to classes which have been homogeneously grouped on the basis of reading achievement.

Team Teaching

There are probably as many different definitions of **team teaching** as there are groups of teachers who decide to cooperate for instructional purposes, sharing instructional ideas and students. Often, team teaching in reading involves several teachers who pool their students for instruction, each assuming responsibility for teaching a specific subject area. This form of team teaching usually, but not always, takes place between two or more teachers at the same grade level. Two sixth-grade teachers, for example, may decide to team teach the subject areas of reading and mathematics, each teacher being responsible for instruction in one of these areas for all of the students in both classes. Both teachers would also be responsible for teaching their own class in the remaining subject areas. In this situation, reading and mathematics are taught at the same time; half of the students would receive instruction in reading from one teacher and the other half would receive instruction in mathematics, from the other teacher. After one period of either reading or mathematics, the students would switch classrooms and receive instruction in the other subject.

> **team teaching:** Where two or more teachers decide to cooperate for instructional purposes, sharing instructional ideas and students.

As with departmentalization, team teaching by itself does not solve the challenge created by individual differences. Again, however, team teaching usually takes place in conjunction with some form of homogeneous grouping based on achievement levels. In the previous example, the sixth graders might be grouped on the basis of their combined achievement levels in reading and mathematics with high achievers receiving reading instruction while low achievers received mathematics instruction. Then each group would change subjects and teachers for a second period of instruction before returning to their home classroom.

Cross-Grade and Cross-Class Grouping

Cross-grade and cross-class grouping for reading instruction involves homogeneously regrouping students in several grades and classes based on reading achievement levels. Only reading instruction is affected. Students receive instruction in all other areas in their regular classroom.

> **cross-grade and cross-class grouping (Joplin Plan):** Where students are homogeneously regrouped over several grades or classes based on reading achievement levels.

Under this scheme, children in all classes leave their regular classroom at the same time each day and go to their assigned reading classes. In each class, reading is taught to a group of children who are reading at about the same grade level. All children from a school who read at about the second-grade level, for example, receive reading instruction from the same teacher, even if their nominal grade level was anywhere between kindergarten to sixth grade. Sometimes cross-grade and cross-class grouping is called the Joplin Plan, after the Missouri town where it first received notice.

There are several potential problems with cross-grade and cross-class grouping plans. It is sometimes difficult for teachers to get to know their reading students when they only see them for one period a day. Also, it is not easy to integrate reading with content-area instruction since content-area instruction takes place with different teachers in different classrooms.

Split-Half Classes

split-half classes: Where each heterogeneously grouped classroom is divided into two halves based on reading achievement levels.

Schools that use **split-half classes** divide each heterogeneously grouped classroom into two halves based on reading achievement levels. Within each class, half the students (usually the low-achieving readers) come to school an hour before the other students. During this hour, the classroom teacher teaches reading to half of the class. After this reading period, the remaining students arrive and the school day proceeds normally. One hour before the end of school, however, the early students return home, leaving the teacher alone for reading instruction with the other half of the class. In effect, half of the students in each classroom learn to read during the first hour, before the other students arrive. The other half of the students learn to read during the final hour of school when the early students have left for home.

Split-half classes sometimes create difficulties for families when several children are in school and both parents are working. It requires additional juggling of an often busy schedule since children will be leaving and returning home from school at different times. Also, split-half classes end up sacrificing one additional period each day from the regular schedule to reading instruction.

Retention and Acceleration

retention: Repeating a grade level.
acceleration: Skipping a grade level.

Retaining slower students for another year at the same grade level and accelerating faster students to a higher grade level was one of the earliest interclass accommodations to the challenge of individual differences (Harris & Sipay, 1985). In most cases of **retention** and **acceleration,** the notions of *slower* and *faster* were usually closely associated with achievement in reading comprehension. Recently, retention is finding increasing favor, despite evidence that neither retention nor social promotion have been consistently successful solutions to the challenge of individual differences (Jackson, 1975). Whenever children are being considered for retention or promotion, it is important for the teacher, the principal, the parents, and possibly the school psychologist to carefully review the particular child's situation.

Assistance by Special Educators or Reading Specialists

In many classrooms, children who achieve at low levels in reading are often provided with additional assistance by the school system. This is a final form of interclass accommodation. Children who have been formally identified as special education students because of a particular physical, mental, or emotional disability sometimes receive reading instruction by a special educator. Others who have not been formally identified as special education students may still require remedial assistance. These students often receive reading instruction from a **reading specialist,** a teacher specially trained to diagnose and teach children with reading difficulties. Students who receive remedial assistance may receive all of their reading instruction from a reading specialist or only receive assistance which supplements the regular classroom reading program.

reading specialist: A teacher specially trained to diagnose and provide remedial assistance to children with reading difficulties.

A Summary of Interclass Accommodations

Although many schools use interclass accommodations to adjust for individual differences between students' achievement levels they have two basic weaknesses. First, interclass accommodations tend to give the false impression that students have been homogeneously grouped on the basis of achievement levels when, in fact, significant achievement differences remain. Teachers tend to believe that since all students are high-, low-, or average-ability students they should all receive identical instruction. This is almost never appropriate. Every classroom, despite the best attempts at grouping children on the basis of reading achievement levels, will almost always contain close to two years' difference in reading achievement (Harris & Sipay, 1985). Thus, most interclass accommodations do not completely account for the range of reading achievement levels found in classrooms.

Assume that you are teaching in a school with departmentalized reading for grades four and five. You teach reading to all three classes of fourth graders and all three classes of fifth graders. Both fourth- and fifth-grade classes have been homogeneously grouped on the basis of reading achievement levels. Thus, you have one high-, one average-, and one low-achieving class of readers in both the fourth and fifth grades. Using the data from Burmeister on page 479, calculate the likely range of reading achievement levels in each of your six reading classes. Has a departmentalized reading program solved the challenge presented by individual differences? Why or why not?

A POINT TO PONDER

A second problem associated with interclass accommodations is that each usually accommodates only one type of individual difference—differences in reading achievement levels. None of the interclass accommodations address the variation in reading interests, specific skill competencies, or background knowledge that will always exist in a classroom and are important to accommodate in reading instruction. Students in a class of high-achieving readers, for example, do not all share identical skill needs. Some require work in vocabulary knowledge. Others require work in content-area reading skills. Still others have difficulty with narrative discourse forms. Additional organizational accommodations must be made to account for other types of individual differences.

INTRACLASS ACCOMMODATIONS

intraclass accommodations: Accommodates individual differences by altering the way in which reading instruction is organized *within* classes.

Because interclass accommodations never accommodate all of the individual differences important to reading instruction, it is also necessary to consider **intraclass accommodations.** Intraclass accommodations alter the manner in which reading instruction is organized *within* classes.

Reading Groups

reading groups: Small groups of students who share similar reading achievement levels, interests, or skill needs.

The most common intraclass accommodation consists of small group instruction in **reading groups** (Hiebert, 1983; Pikulski & Kirsch, 1979). A teacher works with one or several of the reading groups each day while others are working on independent activities. Working with a group smaller than the entire class reduces the range of individual differences that a teacher must accommodate during any single instructional lesson. It seldom, however, completely eliminates individual differences between students.

Typically, reading groups are formed to accommodate individual differences in reading achievement levels. High-, average-, and low-achieving reading groups are often used with a basal reading program to provide the bulk of developmental reading instruction. Less frequently, reading groups are formed to accommodate individual differences in skill needs or interests. We will discuss the use of reading groups based on achievement levels first. Then we will consider ways in which groups based on specific reading skill needs and reading interests might be used to accommodate other individual differences.

Forming Reading Groups Based on Achievement Levels. Three questions need to be considered when first attempting to form reading groups based on achievement levels.

1. What information can I use to determine achievement levels?
2. How many groups should I have in my classroom?
3. How many students should be in each of my groups?

Reading groups are often formed in classrooms to accommodate individual differences in reading achievement levels, specific skill competencies, or interests.

The answers to these questions are discussed in the following paragraphs.

What information can I use to determine achievement levels? Achievement data on your students can be obtained from a number of sources at the beginning of the year. Two sources in particular are often used: achievement data from a student's cumulative file and informal assessment of reading achievement during the first few weeks of school.

Each student in your class will have a **cumulative file** containing achievement, physical, and health records. Cumulative files are typically located in your school's office. You, as a classroom teacher, have access to this information and may review all your students' files before the beginning of the school year. In particular, look for two types of information in students' cumulative files: placement recommendations from last year's teacher and standardized, norm-referenced test scores in reading.

In June, each teacher is usually expected to make recommendations to next year's teacher about where, in a basal reading program, each student should begin. Usually, this will be a record of the materials that a student completed in the basal program during the previous year and some indication of general skill strengths and weaknesses. Often this information will be combined from the several teachers who are sending their students on to you, and is placed on a single form. In table 12–1 you will find the placement recommendations for a new fourth-

cumulative files:
Contain students' achievement, physical, and health records.

TABLE 12–1

Classroom assessment data collected by one teacher at the beginning of the year

Name	Materials Completed	Stanine Decod/Voc/Comp	IRI Instructional Level	Informal Observation	Interests
FROM MR. NELSON:					
Tommy	Sea Treasures (4th)	8/9/8	Sky Climbers (5th)	Fluent. Read The Hobbit.	Myths & legends
Anne	Sea Treasures (4th)	9/9/9	Sky Climbers (5th)/ Star Flight (6th)	Spends lunch in library.	Olympics, ballet
Tama	Golden Secrets (3–2) Weak decoding skills	3/9/6	Sea Treasures (4th)/ Sky Climbers (5th)	Excellent comprehension.	Poetry
Sharon	Golden Secrets (3–2) Weak vocabulary	8/4/7	Sky Climbers (5th)	Summer library reader	Basketball, sports
Brian	Golden Secrets (3–2) Good comprehension	8/6/8	Sea Treasures (4th)	Summer library reader	Mysteries
Jo	Golden Secrets (3–2)	5/5/5	Sea Treasures (4th)	Exposition a problem	Sports
Katie	Golden Secrets (3–2) Weak vocabulary	6/4/5	Sea Treasures (4th)/ Golden Secrets (3–2)	Good reader	Horses, skiing
Sarah	Golden Secrets (3–2)	7/5/5	Sea Treasures (4th)	Fluent reader	Science, computers
FROM MRS. BLASIUS:					
Kathy	Golden Secrets (3–2)	6/7/7	Sky Climbers (5th)	Excellent inferences Good vocabulary	Mysteries
Nelima	Golden Secrets (3–2)	7/5/7	Sky Climbers (5th)	Summer library reader	Computers
Billy	Golden Secrets (3–2)	6/4/5	Sky Climbers (5th)/ Star Flight (6th)	Excellent vocabulary	Ballet, sports

Name	Reading Level	Scores	Assignment	Notes	Interests
Jesus	Golden Secrets (3–2)	6/8/7	Sky Climbers (5th)	Excellent vocabulary	Basketball, poetry
Tim	Golden Secrets (3–2)	5/8/7	Sky Climbers (5th)	Fluent. Excellent vocabulary	Computers, sports.
Roberto	Golden Secrets (3–2)	5/4/5	Sea Treasures (4th)	Weak vocabulary Exposition a problem	Mysteries, Olympics
Jessica	Golden Secrets (3–2)	4/6/5	Sea Treasures (4th)/ Golden Secrets (3–2)	Good inferences Weak vocabulary	Reading, sports
Vanessa	Golden Secrets (3–2) Weak in exposition	5/3/3	Hidden Wonders (5–1)	Weak vocabulary knowledge	Pets, baseball
Jeff	Golden Secrets (3–2)	5/3/3	Hidden Wonders (3–1)	Exposition a problem	Bowling, pets
Kurt	Crystal Kingdom (2–2) Weak vocabulary	4/3/4	Hidden Wonders (3–1)	Poor vocabulary Weak in exposition	Olympics
Warren	Crystal Kingdom (2–2) Weak in exposition	3/2/3	Crystal Kingdom (2–2)	Poor decoding skills Halting reader	Basketball, dirt bikes
Becky	Crystal Kingdom (2–2)	2/3/4	Hidden Wonders (5–1)	Weak decoding skills	Magic, travel

NEW STUDENTS:

Name			Assignment	Notes	Interests
Erica	_____		Sky Climbers (5th)	Writes own stories at home	Adventure stories
John	_____		Sea Treasures (4th)	Weak vocabulary	Science fiction
Vanita	_____		Sky Climbers (5th)/ Star Flight (6th)	Excellent vocabulary	Ballet, sports
Gene	_____		Sea Treasures (4th)	Lacks prefix/suffix knowledge	Dirt bikes
Daniel	_____		Kick Up Your Heels (1–2)	Poor decoding skills Little comprehension	Hamsters, baseball

grade class listed under *Materials Completed.* Two separate third-grade teachers (Mrs. Blasius and Mr. Nelson) have listed their students' names along with an indication of the last materials completed in the Scott, Foresman program. Notice, too, that five students are without placement recommendations. These are new students who have transferred into the school at the beginning of the year.

Table 12–1 also presents standardized, norm-referenced test scores from a test of reading achievement administered at the end of the third grade. Notice that separate **stanine scores** are reported for the subtests of decoding knowledge, vocabulary knowledge, and passage comprehension. Sometimes you will be able to obtain separate subtest scores. At other times you will only have a single score reflecting total reading achievement. Usually, test results are in students' cumulative files. It is often useful to combine them with other assessment information in a single chart for your class as in table 12–1.

stanine scores: Scores, ranging from 1 to 9, that represent a range of scores on a norm-referenced test.

A POINT TO PONDER

Using the information in cumulative files at the beginning of the year is somewhat controversial. Some professionals argue that the use of this information often biases a teacher's perception of a child and results in a self-fulfilling prophecy (Rosenthal & Jacobson, 1968) that is most damaging to the least able. They suggest that achievement information in cumulative files should not be used. Others argue that, used correctly, achievement information in cumulative files is but one source of information that a teacher should consider. These professionals point out that it is inappropriate to ignore any information when making a decision as important as reading group placement. Consider this issue for a moment. If you decide to use the achievement information in cumulative files at the beginning of the year, what might you do to reduce the possibility of creating inappropriate self-fulfilling prophecies for your students? Would waiting until after you have had an opportunity to independently evaluate the achievement levels of your students solve this problem?

In addition to the information in students' cumulative files, consider obtaining achievement information informally by observing children's performance within the context of your classroom. This is especially important at the beginning of the year when some children will have read widely during the summer and others will not have read anything at all. Some students make gains in reading achievement over a summer vacation; others lose ground. In either case, last year's assessment information may be inaccurate. You may wish to administer an informal reading inventory (IRI) at the beginning of the year to obtain informal data on achievement levels. Useful information can also be obtained by simply watching and listening to children read individually during the first few weeks of school.

Table 12–1 includes the instructional level for each student that resulted from the administration of an informal reading inventory during the first two weeks of school. The IRI was created by this teacher using passages from each level in the Scott, Foresman reading series. Table 12–1 also includes the results of informal classroom observations made during this time. Notice that some students' instructional level on the IRI fell between two books in the series (for example, Anne, Tama, and Katie). Notice, too, that information from informal reading inventories and informal observations is particularly important for your new students whose cumulative files are not likely to have arrived at the beginning of the school year.

Seldom are multiple sources of assessment information completely consistent. One source may indicate that a child is a stronger reader than another source. Interpreting assessment information requires a certain "feel" for the types of information that are collected as well as the ability to make reasoned guesses. To provide you with a sense of the ambiguity that may sometimes appear, consider the cases of Tama and Sharon from Table 12–1.

A POINT TO PONDER

Tama completed the 3–2 reader in the Scott Foresman series last year and the teacher felt she was weak in decoding skills. One would think that Tama might benefit from instruction at the beginning of the fourth-grade reader with an emphasis on decoding skills. This year, however, IRI performance indicates an instructional level at the end of the fourth-grade level or at the beginning of the fifth-grade level. In addition, the teacher was impressed with Tama's comprehension during several informal observations. Tama appears to be able to function at a level somewhat higher than would be expected from the assessment information collected last year. What might explain the discrepancy? Where should Tama begin receiving instruction in the new series?

Sharon, like Tama, completed the 3–2 reader in the Scott Foresman series last year. The teacher felt that Sharon needed some help with vocabulary development. One would also think that Sharon's instructional level would be at the beginning of the fourth-grade reader. On the IRI, however, Sharon's instructional level was at the fifth grade. How do you explain this discrepancy? Where would you probably have Sharon begin in the new series?

How many groups should I have in my classroom? When forming reading groups based on achievement levels, one must decide how many groups to have in a single classroom. The most common number of reading achievement groups that you will observe in classrooms is three (high, average, and low). You may, however, see as few as one and as many as six. As a new teacher, you will need to consider three factors in deciding how many achievement groups are best for you. First, consider the extent of your students' previous experience with small-group instruction. Children who have no experience working in reading groups need more initial supervision; you may need to consider having fewer initial groups than you might like. Some teachers begin the year with a single reading group and then gradually increase the number of groups as children are able to work more independently.

Children who are familiar with working in small groups need less initial supervision. With these students you may be able to establish more groups at an earlier point in the school year.

Second, consider your own experience with reading groups. If you have never had to monitor the independent activities of one or more groups while teaching an instructional lesson to another group, you may want to begin slowly. Perhaps you might begin with only one or two groups and gradually increase the number of groups to a level where you feel comfortable and where the children continue to benefit from the increasingly individualized nature of your classroom organization. If you have experienced the demands of simultaneously monitoring and teaching separate groups you will know how many groups you can effectively manage.

Finally, consider the amount and quality of supplemental material available to you in reading. If you have no reading materials other than those provided in the basal reading series (student books, workbooks, and perhaps a set of spirit masters) it will be more difficult to organize independent activities for your students. You may want to consider having fewer groups. If, on the other hand, you have acquired a number of reading-center activities, a classroom library collection, and other independent reading activities you will be more able to form and effectively manage several reading groups.

How many students should be in each of my groups? When forming reading groups based on achievement levels, one must also consider the number of students to place in each group. Determining the appropriate number of students for each of the reading groups in your particular situation depends on the distribution of achievement levels in your classroom and the ability of your students to work independently.

When you look at achievement data, you may find that a logical division exists between several groups of students. If possible, you want to accommodate any clear distinctions in the achievement levels of your students when you make reading groups. At other times, logical divisions will not exist; students' achievement levels will be continuous. Such is the case for the information collected by one teacher in figure 12–1. Here, a teacher has combined stanine scores on a standardized, norm-referenced achievement test with IRI data on instructional levels. When achievement scores appear continuous (as in figure 12–1), you may want to initially look for divisions between the top three stanines (stanines 9–7), the middle three stanines (stanines 6–4), and the bottom three stanines (3–1). Then see if this distribution is consistent with IRI instructional levels and make any minor adjustments that may be necessary. You can see how one third-grade teacher has done this in figure 12–1.

When making decisions about the number of students in each reading group, also take into consideration your students' ability to work independently. It is often best to reduce the number of students in a

Name	Total Reading Stanine Score	IRI Instructional Level
1. Bill	9	4th
2. Maria	9	3–2
3. Pete	8	3–2
4. Alvin	8	3–2
5. Jodi	8	3–2
6. Marti	8	4th
7. Diane	8	3–2
8. Cindy	7	4th
9. Jinny	7	3–2
10. Daniel	7	3–2
11. Fran	6	3–1
12. Tina	5	3–1
13. Joanne	5	3–1
14. Lee	5	3–2
15. Joey	4	3–1
16. Denny	4	3–1
17. Cora	4	2–2/3–1
18. Roger	4	2–2/3–1
19. Patty	4	3–1
20. Rosa	3	2–2
21. Marsha	3	2–2
22. Pat	3	2–1
23. Jinny	3	2–2
24. Paul	3	2–1
25. Mark	2	2–1
26. Jim	2	2–1
27. Ed	2	2–1

FIGURE 12–1
Achievement data from a third-grade classroom

group that requires more individual attention. The lowest achieving group in any classroom is frequently the smallest since these children often require more direction and instructional time from a teacher.

When forming instructional groups based on reading achievement keep in mind that any decisions you make should be considered tentative especially during the first few weeks after you form groups and begin instruction. Use this time as a trial period to see how well individual students seem to fit into the organizational scheme that you have established. It is often useful when making initial grouping decisions to be conservative with students who fall on the borderline between groups. Placing these students in the lower group gives you an opportunity to evaluate their performance for a short period of time and move them to a higher group if observation reveals that such a move is warranted. As the year progresses, continuously reevaluate your grouping decisions. Be prepared to accommodate individual students who show they might benefit from a change in group assignment. Flexibility is important when considering the organization of your classroom.

A POINT TO PONDER	It is important now for you to apply your knowledge about achievement groups. Attempting to make grouping decisions will make much of the previous discussion more meaningful. It will also help you see how grouping decisions are actually more complicated and subjective than has been described. Assume that you are a fourth-grade teacher with some experience in working with achievement groups during reading. Your students come from classes with three achievement groups and can work independently. Table 12–1 contains the data you have collected on your students during the first week of classes. You must now begin to form reading groups and begin formal instruction with the school's new reading series. Place these students into two or three instructional groups based on reading achievement. Which factors did you consider while making your decisions? Which specific instructional needs will require your attention? Which students will you want to observe carefully for possible regrouping?

Individualizing within Achievement-Level Groups

The use of achievement groups suffers from the same two problems associated with the various interclass accommodations for individual differences. The use of achievement groups tends to give the false impression that students have been homogeneously grouped on the basis of achievement levels when, in fact, significant achievement differences remain within each group. Also, the use of achievement groups fails to account for individual differences in other areas important to reading instruction: reading interests; specific skill competencies; and background knowledge. Thus, it is important to consider ways in which you might further individualize instruction within the constraints imposed by achievement grouping. The following suggestions are intended to help you begin to further individualize instruction within achievement groups.

SAMPLE ACTIVITIES	**During Oral Reading.** Whenever you have students orally read portions of a story, assign paragraphs on the basis of difficulty and students' achievement levels. Long paragraphs with a number of difficult vocabulary words might be given to a better reader within a group. Shorter paragraphs with less difficult vocabulary might be given to a weaker reader.

Rechecking at the End of Instruction. When you know that one or several of your students have particular difficulty with the skill being taught, be certain that those students have grasped the skill before providing independent skill practice.

Students Helping Students. Encourage your students to help each other if they are stumped while they are doing independent skill practice at their seats. To avoid students simply copying answers with no understanding of why an answer is correct, establish the rule that only the way to find an answer is to be given, not the answer itself.

Review Lessons. When a few of your students fail to grasp the instructional objective for any lesson, provide a short review lesson specifically designed for these students. Other students in the group can use this time to work on one of the independent reading tasks you have set up in the room.

Special Oral Reports to a Group. When you know that one of your students is especially interested in the topic of a reading selection or has considerable background knowledge about the topic, ask that student to prepare a short oral report for the group. Give clear directions about what the report should touch upon. Have the student focus on background knowledge that other students might not have and will be important for comprehending the story. Just before reading the selection, have the student present the report.

Regrouping Students on Interests and Skills. Periodically regroup all of the students in your classroom into interest or specific skill groups for several weeks.

Providing Independent Reading Activities. Be certain that you have a sufficient number of independent reading activities for children to choose from when they complete regular seatwork assignments.

These suggestions are not intended to accommodate all of the individual differences you will encounter within achievement groups. Indeed, accommodating all of the individual differences in any single classroom will be difficult if reading groups based on achievement are the only form of grouping that you use. Any effective classroom program of reading instruction will also incorporate reading groups based on specific skills, reading groups based on interests, and individualized reading activities.

Reading Groups Based on Specific Skills. Teachers often find it useful to use reading groups based on specific skill needs. When this happens, the students in a classroom are grouped according to the types of specific skills with which each needs additional instruction: main ideas; inferencing; decoding; vocabulary; study skills; knowledge of narrative discourse structure; or other aspects of reading comprehension.

Grouping students on the basis of specific skill needs will occur for several reasons. Sometimes a teacher finds that specific skill needs appear to cut across the established achievement groups. Several students in each of the achievement groups may have similar skill weaknesses although their achievement levels differ. The teacher in this situation may find it useful to regroup the students on the basis of skill needs for a short period of time, independent of achievement levels.

Sometimes the school district (or any other governing body) mandates a specific skill list that must be mastered by each student in a particular grade level. In conjunction with the list of specific skills, an elaborate sequence of pretests, instructional activities, and posttests can be used to assess and teach each skill to some specified criterion level. In this situation, the teacher will find it appropriate to periodically group and regroup students based on specific skill needs. A basal reading program can be used with achievement groups, but set aside a short time during each term for instruction in the mandated set of specific skills.

In either case, the set of questions that were considered when forming achievement groups also applies to grouping decisions based on specific skills: What information can I use to determine specific skill needs? How many groups should I have in my classroom? and How many students should be in each of my groups?

What information can I use to determine specific skill needs? There are three major sources of information on individual skill needs that may be available to you as a teacher: data from criterion-referenced tests; informal information from last year's teachers about specific students' needs; and your own informal observations.

Criterion-referenced test information may come from several sources. First, it may come from a specific skills testing program incorporated into your basal reading series. Nearly all basal series include criterion-referenced tests. Usually, these tests are administered at the end of a unit or book to determine which of your students have mastered the reading skills taught in that section. In June, your school may have teachers record the skill tests that students have passed (and not passed) in students' cumulative files for next year's teacher.

Criterion-referenced test information also can come from a criterion-referenced testing program purchased separately from your basal reading series. Often, these programs are used to ensure some consistency in skill development between teachers in districts where several different basals are used. Teachers are expected to teach and assess students' performance on these skills and record this information for each new teacher that a student has. Again this information usually is found in students' cumulative files. One example of a record-keeping form which you might encounter is illustrated in figure 12–2.

3.0

3.1.1   The learner will read words from a basic primer sight vocabulary list. Given 50 words, the learner will read each word orally.
MINIMUM: 45 correct   DATE OF COMPLETION: _____

3.2.1   The learner will identify rhyming words and pictures. Given 14 rows of 3 pictures each, the learner will circle the picture in each row having a name that rhymes with the printed word in each row.
MINIMUM: 13 correct rows DATE OF COMPLETION: _____

3.2.2   The learner will identify the initial sounds and letters *b, c, d, f, g, h, j, k, l, m, n, p, r, s, t, v, w, y*, and *z*. Given 19 pictures with 3 letters beneath each, the learner will circle the letter with which the name of each picture begins.
MINIMUM: 18 correct   DATE OF COMPLETION: _____

3.3.1   The learner will read a story and sequence sentences. Given a story and 4 sentences, the learner will number each sentence in the correct sequence.
MINIMUM: 4 correct   DATE OF COMPLETION: _____

3.3.2   The learner will read a story and recall details. Given a story and 5 questions with 3 choices each, the learner will select the correct answer for each question.
MINIMUM: 4 correct   DATE OF COMPLETION: _____

3.3.3   The learner will read stories and select main ideas. Given 3 stories with 4 titles each, the learner will select the best title for each story.
MINIMUM: 3 correct   DATE OF COMPLETION: _____

3.4.1   The learner will demonstrate oral reading skill by reading orally a story written at the primer level.
MINIMUM: approval   DATE OF COMPLETION: _____

4.0

4.1.1   The learner will read words from a first reader vocabulary list. Given 70 words, the learner will read each word orally.
MINIMUM: 63 correct   DATE OF COMPLETION: _____

4.2.1   The learner will identify final sounds and letters *d, g, k, l, m, n, p, r, s*, and *t*. Given 10 pictures with 4 letters beneath each picture, the learner will circle the letter that represents the final sound of each picture name.
MINIMUM: 9 correct   DATE OF COMPLETION: _____

FIGURE 12–2
An example of a record-keeping form for a criterion-referenced testing program

In addition to these formal sources of information on specific skill needs, you can use informal observational information from last year's teachers and from your own impressions of students' reading skill needs. Information from last year's teachers about specific students' needs is sometimes included with end-of-year information on materials completed (see table 12–1). You may also talk to last year's teachers during the first few weeks of school, which often provides useful information about students. Also value your own observations. You may want to maintain an observational log for your students or you may prefer to mentally record your observations. An observational log can be something as simple as a single notebook for your entire class with separate pages for notes on the specific skill behavior of each student. An example is illustrated in figure 12–3.

Decisions about how many groups and how many students to have per group closely parallel the situation one finds when working with reading groups based on achievement levels. The number of specific skill groups that you will have depends on your students' previous ex-

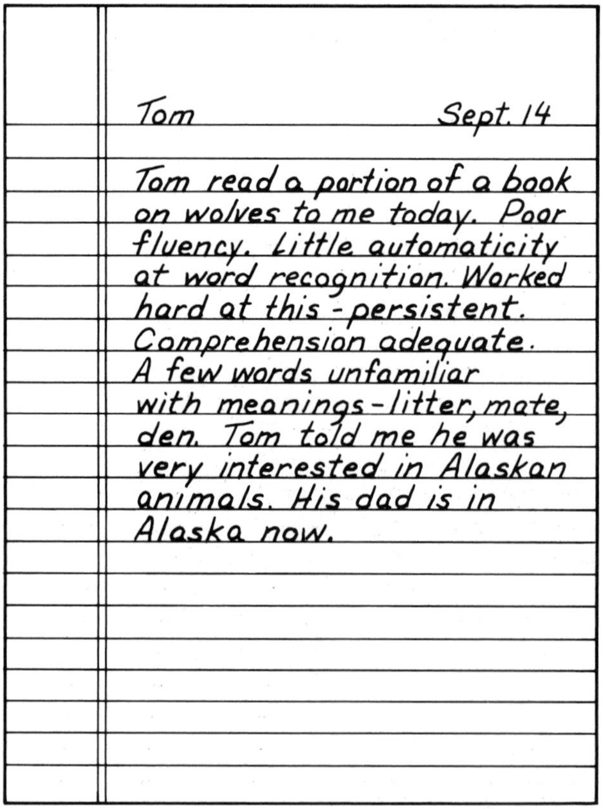

Tom   Sept. 14

Tom read a portion of a book on wolves to me today. Poor fluency. Little automaticity at word recognition. Worked hard at this - persistent. Comprehension adequate. A few words unfamiliar with meanings - litter, mate, den. Tom told me he was very interested in Alaskan animals. His dad is in Alaska now.

FIGURE 12–3
An example of an observational log

perience in group work, your own experience, and the amount and quality of supplemental instructional material that you have available. The number of children in each group will be determined by the distribution of students with similar skill needs and the ability of your students to work independently.

There are, however, two important differences when working with specific skill groups that you must be aware of. First, specific skill groups typically last for only a few reading periods before children are regrouped for instruction on new skills. Second, all of your students will not necessarily require instruction in the specific skill areas used to group students. As a consequence, you may frequently have one additional group of students who do not require instruction in one of the specific skill areas you use to group students. In this situation, you may want to have your additional group of students work on an independent reading contract or complete one of the reading center activities that you have set up around the room.

Reading Groups Based on Students' Interests. Often, it may be appropriate to group students by their particular interests and let them explore, in groups, topics that are personally very important. After reading about the exploration of the western United States in social studies, a sixth-grade class may decide to work in separate groups for a week during their regular reading period reading, collecting information and reporting on the discovery and early history of their favorite state. A third-grade class, after reading about different types of mammals in science, may decide to work in different animal groups and collect information to be presented in bulletin board displays. Other groups may last longer, but meet less frequently. Once a month, different interest groups can get together to share books and information about their favorite topics: sports, pets, science fiction, music, or computers. In each case, grouping decisions are based on students' interests independent of achievement levels or performance on specific skills.

Interest groups can be used for several reasons in a classroom reading program. A teacher may consider it essential to regularly incorporate functional reading activities into the classroom program. Giving students opportunities to actually practice what they have been learning is an important consideration in any program. A teacher may also want to heighten interest and motivation in reading by blocking in time for interest group activities. Making certain that you have students who not only can read, but also want to read, is an important consideration in a classroom reading program. Or, a teacher may be concerned about the negative effects on self-concept that may result from permanent achievement grouping. This teacher would periodically use interest groups as a way of improving self-concept, since even the weakest reader would have an opportunity to display his or her abilities on a topic that was personally interesting.

To determine students' interests, teachers often will administer an interest inventory to children at the beginning of the school year (see chapter 3). In addition to using interest inventories to collect this information, you may informally accumulate information about each of your students as you begin to work with them and discover what motivates your students. Finally, you can simply ask students what they would be interested in learning more about as you complete a discussion on a topic. Keep in mind that with young children interests are often short-lived. Do not assume that an interest expressed at the beginning of the year will last throughout the year.

When grouping children by interests, the number of groups in the class and students in each group becomes less important than for grouping children by achievement levels or specific skill needs. Although all of the considerations listed earlier should be taken into account, the most important consideration is the pattern of interest areas expressed by students. As much as possible, encourage children to make the final decisions about grouping assignments.

It is likely that you will have more interest groups than achievement or specific skills groups. This is possible since the teacher's role is somewhat different when working with interest groups. Instead of providing direct instruction, a teacher's role is more of a guide and resource person. You will not teach each group at a fixed time each day as much as you will circulate around the room, listening to ideas, contributing your own, and helping children to implement their plans by directing them to the appropriate resources.

INDIVIDUALIZED ACTIVITIES

individualized reading activities: Attempts to provide learning experiences that meet the unique needs of individual students during reading instruction.

Another way to accommodate individual differences within a classroom is to provide **individualized reading activities.** Individualized reading activities attempt to provide learning experiences that meet the unique needs of individual students in your classroom. While individualized activities accommodate all types of individual differences important to reading instruction, they are especially useful for accommodating individual differences in background knowledge. You have already read about many different types of individualized activities in previous chapters: cross-age tutoring; board games; card games; independently selected reading corner activities; individualized instruction within small groups; individual instructional assistance provided by special educators or reading specialists; word banks; sight word envelopes; independent book projects; reading center activities; and contract reading activities. But consider in greater detail two formats for individualizing instruction that are often incorporated into the organization of classrooms: reading centers and contract reading projects. Each format has enormous potential for helping you individualize instruction to meet the unique combination of achievement levels, reading interests, specific skill competencies, or background knowledge that will always exist in a classroom. Both may be used with classroom reading groups, or independently from classroom reading groups.

Reading Centers

A **reading center** is a location in a classroom where children participate in a rotating series of independent, self-guided reading activities. Reading centers may take many forms but they usually share several characteristics.

reading center: A location in a classroom where students participate in a rotating series of independent, self-guided reading activities.

First, reading centers usually contain all of the materials that students will require to complete the learning tasks. The following materials, for example, came from one reading center activity which was used at the third-grade level to provide experience with locating factual information in expository discourse.

1. Ten different articles about exotic animals from the nature magazine *Ranger Rick.* Each had been separated from the magazine and separately bound by stapling construction paper covers around the article.
2. A box containing ditto copies of a fact sheet. This was a partial outline with major headings such as: name of animal; size and description; where it lives; what it eats; family life; and unusual facts. Children had previously learned how to use this form for collecting information about animals in a science project.
3. Writing paper and felt-tip pens.
4. A box to collect students' finished work.

Second, reading centers usually have clear directions to students about the procedures for completing a particular learning activity. Display directions prominently on a bulletin board or wall. Often these take the form of a set of procedures to follow to complete the learning task. Figure 12–4 shows the directions for a reading center.

Third, reading center activities usually contain some form of record-keeping system where individual student's progress can be noted. Usually, this is simply a chart listing the names of the students in your class and the numbers of the different reading center activities. Often teachers duplicate many copies of these forms and place one next to each reading center in the classroom. Because the activities at any single reading center are changed regularly by a teacher, students need to record each activity that they have an opportunity to complete.

Finally, reading centers often have a place to turn in or display completed work. This may consist of a box as in the example. Frequently, completed work is displayed at a bulletin board near the center to provide children who are beginning a reading center task with examples of what might be done.

UNUSUAL ANIMAL STORIES

1. Look through the <u>Ranger Rick</u> articles about unusual animals from different countries. Choose one animal that you want to learn more about.

2. Read the article about the animal you have selected.

3. Look back through the article and locate the information requested by your "Fact Sheet". Write this down.

4. Use the information in your "Fact Sheet" to write an interesting story about your animal. Share your story with a friend. Revise your story based on your friend's suggestions. Illustrate your story.

6. When finished, turn in your story to the "Work Completed Box".

7. Check off activity #5 next to your name.

FIGURE 12–4
An example of the directions found at a reading center activity

Sometimes a teacher has a single reading center located in the classroom. Different reading center activities are displayed regularly and children are expected to accomplish as many activities as they can whenever their regularly assigned seatwork is completed.

Another approach may also be used, however, that attempts to use reading center activities more individually. This requires developing several different reading centers at various locations around the classroom. One reading center contains activities for promoting each of the major aspects of the reading comprehension process described in chapter 2: decoding knowledge; vocabulary knowledge; syntactic knowledge; discourse knowledge; and affective considerations. Activities within each center are regularly changed by the teacher during the year. A teacher determines, in conjunction with each student, a specified number of activities that should be completed during each month or quarter. A student who is having particular problems with decoding skills, for example, might be expected to complete eight different activities at the center devoted to decoding knowledge and only one or two at the center devoted to developing discourse-level knowledge. A student who is mak-

Reading center activities can also be effectively used to accommodate individual differences within a classroom.

ing average progress in reading might be expected to complete two or three activities at each of the five reading centers. What is important to notice with this approach to reading centers is that a different combination of learning experiences will be established for each student in your room, depending upon their particular instructional needs. Participation in reading center activities is defined, at least partially, by each student's needs.

Holiday Crossword Puzzles. For every holiday during the school year, make a reading center with a holiday crossword puzzle. You can make these yourself and duplicate enough copies for your students. You also can purchase commercial versions (often in a complete set of ditto masters for all of the year's holidays). Try to find puzzles where the clues are given in cloze sentences, which provides practice in context use. Post an answer key (perhaps covered by a sheet of paper) to make this activity self-checking.

Color Lacing. For very young children, display a heavy-duty sheet of paper with color patches in a column on the left and color words in a column on the right. Punch out holes next to each color and each word. Attach laces through the color words on the right. Have students attempt to match color words and color patches by putting the laces through the correct holes. Post an answer key and make this activity self-checking.

FIGURE 12–5
An example of a reading center activity—Color lacing

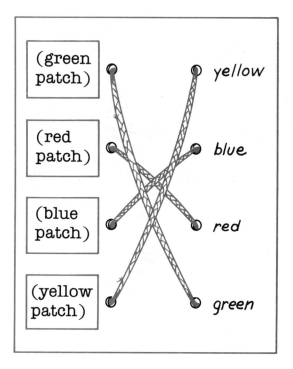

Similar cards can be made for shape words, size words, or other logical sets of words (see figure 12–5).

Sequencing Silly Stories. Cut out four or five cartoon strips from the Sunday paper. Cut each cartoon strip into individual frames. Then post the frames out of order on a bulletin board. Repeat for each of the cartoon strips. To identify each frame and the correct sequence of frames for each cartoon strip, write a letter under each frame. Ask students to write the correct sequence of letters for each strip. This activity can be made self-checking by making the correct letter sequence for each cartoon strip spell a word. You also could have all of the answers for the separate cartoons make a sentence.

A Pair Tree. To develop familiarity with homonyms, cut out an outline of a tree without any leaves from brown construction paper and post it on a bulletin board. Cut out leaves from construction paper with fall colors. Write sets of homonyms (*pair, pear; too, to;* or *mane-main*) on these leaves, one word on each leaf. Mix up the leaves and place them in a small container. Also put out a set of paper clips. Have students attempt to find all of the homonym pairs and put each pair on the tree with paper clips. You may make copies of an answer key and have students check off their answers when they are completed. Encourage children to bring in other homonym pairs and add them to your set.

Contract Reading Projects

In contract reading, the student and teacher formally agree on the learning tasks to be completed, when they will be completed, and how they will be completed. Daily contracts were described in chapter 11 as a method that might help exceptional children deal with emotional and behavioral difficulties. Contracts also can be used over a longer period of time with all of your students to formalize the nature of reading center activities and **independent book projects.**

With reading center activities, contracts can formally specify the number of activities at each separate reading center that the student will complete in a fixed time. You may want to establish reading center contracts for each of your students at the beginning of each grading period in the school year and then evaluate students' independent reading progress at the end of each period.

With independent book projects, contracts can be used to formally identify (1) the book each child selects to read; (2) when the book will be completed; and (3) how the book project will be presented to the class in a culminating project. An example of a contract used with an independent book project is illustrated in figure 12–6. Independent book projects are more fully described in chapter 7 along with a number of activities that might be considered for culminating projects.

independent book projects: Provide independent reading opportunities. Students select a minimum number of books to read during a fixed time.

WHOLE-CLASS ACTIVITIES

There are some situations during reading instruction where whole-class experiences can be valuable. Even though you should be concerned about accommodating the individual differences within your classroom, do not overlook the use of the entire class for some reading activities. The following activities often can best be done with the entire class:

1. Any reading activity where an audience is required. This might include oral book reports, Readers Theatre presentations, and read-aloud sessions.
2. Short sessions where you introduce the students to new materials in the room. Examples include book talks that introduce a set of new books in the reading corner, author of the week introductions where you or a student introduce a favorite author, or reading center introductions where you explain a new reading center activity in the room.
3. Teaching a new reading skill that has not yet appeared in the regular instructional program but that you want to introduce. These might

---

CONTRACT

I _Megan Fredricks_ plan to read the following book and complete my independent book project by _May 15_ .

Book: _The Little Prince_

My independent book project will include:

making a paper-mâché model of the asteroid and giving an oral report on my book.

Signed _Megan Fredricks_ _Ms. Keenery_
(Student) (Teacher)

Date _____

FIGURE 12–6

An example of contract reading used with an independent book project

include reference skills in the library, map-reading skills, the use of a thesaurus, learning a new poetry form, or a new phonic generalization.

4. Reading about current events. Often teachers subscribe to a weekly school newspaper and have the class read and discuss the articles together.

5. Sustained silent reading (SSR). SSR is often incorporated into the daily reading schedule outside of the period devoted to reading instruction.
6. Choral reading to develop an appreciation for rhythm, poetry, and stylistic conventions of unique discourse forms.

INTEGRATING DIFFERENT ORGANIZATIONAL SOLUTIONS

One of the more difficult challenges you face as a classroom teacher of reading is to develop an organizational scheme that accommodates the individual differences in your classroom and, at the same time, is not so overwhelming that your instruction becomes lost in the process. Over time, you will develop an organizational structure in your classroom that feels comfortable and permits you to provide individual assistance to each student. It is likely that you will take advantage of multiple forms of intraclass organization in an attempt to efficiently meet the individual needs within your classroom. Many teachers find this to be the solution that fits their situation. To help you see how different organizational solutions are possible within a single classroom, consider the organizational decisions in reading that one teacher made during the course of a year.

Mr. Graham's Class

Bill Graham is one of three third-grade teachers in a school with heterogeneously grouped classes. The twenty-seven students in his classroom range in reading achievement from early first grade to the beginning of fifth grade. He has one learning disabled student who receives reading instruction each day outside of the classroom with a learning disabilities specialist. Mr. Graham uses the single basal reading series that has been adopted by his school for the core of his instructional program. He is also required to see that his students make continuous progress on a district-wide set of reading skills that are assessed in a criterion-referenced testing program. Mr. Graham has established a **reading corner** with a wide selection of children's literature, magazines, newspapers, and books written by students. He has managed over the years to establish five different reading centers around the room. One reading center contains activities designed for promoting each of the following aspects of reading comprehension: decoding knowledge; vocabulary knowledge; syntactic knowledge; and discourse knowledge. He has approximately thirty different reading center activities filed away for each reading center. The school schedule is organized into four nine-week quarters.

reading corner: A portion of a classroom devoted solely to reading.

yearly plan: An outline of organizational patterns that will be used in a classroom.

Mr. Graham's Yearly Plan for Reading. Each year Mr. Graham begins with a **yearly plan** for reading which he outlines on a weekly basis. In his yearly plan, he specifies when children will be grouped by achievement groups, interest groups, and skills groups. He also indicates how much time will be devoted to read-aloud sessions and sustained silent reading (SSR). Finally, he specifies when reading contracts (for both independent book projects and reading center activities) are introduced and when each of eight different independent book projects are due. Mr. Graham's yearly plan is outlined in table 12–2.

Mr. Graham spends the first two weeks of each year getting acquainted with his students' abilities and getting them acquainted with the organization of his classroom. He introduces students to reading contracts for their first independent book project. Mr. Graham uses this time to evaluate students individually. He administers an IRI and an interest inventory, and informally observes his students as they read various materials in the classroom. Afterwards, he checks his students' cumulative files for reading achievement information. All this information is used to make tentative grouping decisions at the end of the second week. During the first few weeks of school, Mr. Graham also introduces and begins his read-aloud sessions to his class. These are fifteen-minute periods once a day (usually after lunch) when Mr. Graham reads quality children's literature to his students. Read-aloud sessions continue throughout the school year.

In week three, Mr. Graham begins instruction with the basal series using his previously determined achievement groups. This year he has decided to work with three different achievement groups in his class. He observes his students carefully during weeks three through five and makes any necessary changes in achievement groups. Also during week three, Mr. Graham introduces his five different reading centers (a new one each day of the third week) and explains the center contracts he has developed. He sits down with each student to consider how many activities from each center they will complete during the first quarter of the school year. New contracts are drawn up at the beginning of each quarter.

Mr. Graham uses achievement groups as the primary grouping pattern during the first quarter. He wants the children to get settled into the routine of his classroom during this time while he observes each student's performance. Beginning with the second quarter, Mr. Graham spends the first week of each quarter in skills groups. During this time he works with the district's criterion-referenced skills program testing, teaching, and retesting the students for specific skill mastery. The next three weeks of quarters two through four are then spent in achievement groups before switching for two weeks into interest groups. The final three weeks are then spent back in achievement groups. Though flexible throughout, during the final week of each quarter, Mr. Graham reviews

TABLE 12–2

Mr. Graham's yearly plan for reading instruction

Weeks 1–2	Introduce and begin reading contracts for independent book project #1.
	Administer IRI and interest inventory.
	Informal assessment.
	Check cumulative files for assessment information.
	Make tentative grouping decisions.
	Introduce and begin read aloud sessions.

Week	Grouping Pattern	Read Aloud Sessions	SSR	Independent Book Projects	Reading Center Activities
3	Achievement (tentative)	15 min.		Contract #1	Intro. Centers
4	Achievement (tentative)	15 min.	Intro.	Contract #1	Cont. Centers
5	Achievement (regroup?)	15 min.	5 min.	Contract #1	Cont. Centers
6	Achievement	15 min.	10 min.	Contract #1	Cont. Centers
7	Achievement	15 min.	15 min.	#1 due	Cont. Centers
8	Achievement	15 min.	15 min.	Begin #2	Cont. Centers
9	Achievement	15 min.	15 min.	Contract #2	Cont. Centers
10	Skills: test, teach, test	15 min.	20 min.	Contract #2	New Contract
11	Achievement	15 min.	20 min.	Contract #2	Cont. Centers
12	Achievement	15 min.	20 min.	Contract #2	Cont. Centers
13	Achievement	15 min.	20 min.	# 2 due	Cont. Centers
14	Interest	15 min.	20 min.	Begin #3	No Centers
15	Interest	15 min.	20 min.	Contract #3	No Centers
16	Achievement	15 min.	20 min.	Contract #3	Cont. Centers
17	Achievement	15 min.	20 min.	Contract #3	Cont. Centers
18	Achievement (regroup, if necessary)	15 min.	20 min.	#3 due.	Cont. Centers
19	Skills: test, teach, test	15 min.	25 min.	Begin #4.	New Contract
20	Achievement	15 min.	25 min.	Contract #4	Cont. Centers
21	Achievement	15 min.	25 min.	Contract #4	Cont. Centers
22	Achievement	15 min.	25 min.	#4 due.	Cont. Centers
23	Interest	15 min.	25 min.	Begin #5.	No Centers
24	Interest	15 min.	25 min.	Contract #5	No Centers
25	Achievement	15 min.	25 min.	Contract #5	Cont. Centers
26	Achievement	15 min.	25 min.	#5 due.	Cont. Centers
27	Achievement (regroup, if necessary)	15 min.	25 min.	Begin #6.	Cont. Centers
28	Skills: test, teach, test	15 min.	30 min.	Contract #6.	New Contract
29	Achievement	15 min.	30 min.	#6 due.	Cont. Centers
30	Achievement	15 min.	30 min.	Begin #7.	Cont. Centers
31	Achievement	15 min.	30 min.	Contract #7	Cont. Centers
32	Interest	15 min.	30 min.	#7 due.	No Centers
33	Interest	15 min.	30 min.	Begin #8.	No Centers
34	Achievement	15 min.	30 min.	Contract #8	Cont. Centers
35	Achievement	15 min.	30 min.	#8 due.	Cont. Centers
36	Achievement	15 min.	30 min.		

each student's performance and considers any possible changes in group assignment.

Sustained silent reading (SSR) is an important part of Mr. Graham's program. He is careful to introduce this activity slowly to his students. He finds it useful to spend a few minutes each day during week four to describe the activity to students and explain his procedures. Beginning with week five, Mr. Graham and his students begin to participate in SSR for five minutes each day. Throughout the year, Mr. Graham gradually increases the amount of time set aside for SSR to thirty minutes each day. SSR takes place immediately after the read-aloud session in the early afternoon.

Mr. Graham expects each student to complete eight independent book projects during the year. Students have seven weeks to complete their first contract, because Mr. Graham wants each student to have plenty of time to successfully complete this first task. Beginning with the second contract, the time period is shortened to six weeks, then five weeks, four weeks, and finally three weeks are given for each of the last three contracts. Students are free to work on their independent book projects during sustained silent reading (SSR) or whenever they have completed their regularly assigned work in reading or any of the other subjects. He finds that children enjoy their independent book projects more than any other classroom activity.

Individual reading center contracts are also a popular part of Mr. Graham's classroom. Each week, Mr. Graham changes the five reading center activities with the exception of weeks when children are working in their interest groups. During this time, Mr. Graham has found that the students are so involved in their two-week projects that they have little time for reading center work. As with individual contracts for independent book projects, children may work on their reading center contracts when their regularly assigned work is completed during the day.

One Weekly Plan for Reading: Week Twelve. Mr. Graham's schedule for reading instruction during week twelve is listed in table 12–3. By week twelve, Mr. Graham's class has adapted to his organizational structure quite nicely. Students know how independent contracts for both book projects and reading centers operate. Also, students have a clear sense of Mr. Graham's expectations. The time that Mr. Graham spent carefully introducing each new aspect of the reading program has had its intended effect; students are able to work cooperatively and independently. Students can now work on their own while Mr. Graham works with others at the reading table, a semicircular table located in one corner of his classroom used for direct instruction with different achievement groups.

Mr. Graham has set up three different achievement groups (green = low, blue = average, red = high) and uses the school's basal reading series for the core of his developmental reading program. The lowest

TABLE 12–3

Mr. Graham's weekly plan for reading: Week 12

Time	Group	Monday	Tuesday	Wednesday	Thursday	Friday
8:30–9:20	Green	Table: Map Reading "The Way to Go" Intro: "Eddie . . ."	Table: Discuss Eddie Ck in WB 70 Dictionary	Table: Ck in WB p. 91 Master p. 91 Intro "A Quiet Place"	Table: Discuss "A Quiet Place" Read "At the Library"	Newspaper reading (current events.) Oral Book Reports. Readers Theatre.
		Seats: Read "Eddie . . ." WB 70 Contracts	Seats: WB 91 Master 91 Contracts or choose.	Seats: Read "A Quiet Place" Choose	Seats: Describe your own quiet place (Writing). Contracts	
	Blue	Seats: Vocabulary review. WB 9 & 10 Master 9. Contracts	Seats: Read "Anya's Adventures". WB 12. Master 12 Contracts or choose.	Seats: Answer quest. on p. 48. Choose.	Seats: Read p. 51 WB 17. Master 17. Contracts or Write: "If I were as small as Anya"	
		Table: Intro Table of Contents. Intro "Anya's Adventures".		Table: Discuss "Anya's Adventure". Ck in WB 12. Ck in Master 12. Intro Context Use.		
	Red	Seats: p. 31B WB 135 Contracts or Write: What happened after Jenny & Peter went to the park?	Seats: Master 135 Contracts	Seats: Read "The Day . . ." WB 138. Choose	Seats: Master 138. p. 32B. Contracts.	
			Table: Ck in 31B Ck in WB 135 Intro Drawing Conclusions. Intro "The day . . ."		Table: Discuss "The Day . . ." Ck in WB 138. Intro Analogies.	
9:20–9:30		Intro 6 new biographies	Intro "Author of the Week" (Sam)	Readers Theatre	Oral Book Reports	

group has six students working out of the 2–2 reader. They are currently learning about map reading, dictionary use, and reference skills. The average group has eight students working out of the beginning of the 3–2 reader. These students are learning about different types of tables of contents and developing strategies to use initial consonant letters with context to recognize words. The high group also has eight students. They are working at the end of the fourth-grade reader on several types of inference tasks including drawing conclusions.

From Monday through Thursday of each week, Mr. Graham works with two of the reading groups for about twenty-five minutes each, providing direct instruction in the major components of the basal reading series. When students are not working with Mr. Graham at the reading table, they can work at one of several activities: completing assigned seatwork related to their most recent instructional session with Mr. Graham; working on their contracts for independent book projects or reading center activities; or choosing one of the many magazines, books, or reading games from the reading corner in the classroom. The final ten minutes of each period of reading are always reserved for introducing new books in the classroom library, introducing the Author-of-the-Week bulletin board, presenting short selections in Readers Theatre, or giving oral book reports. On Friday of each week, the reading period is devoted to current events. The class reads and discusses a weekly newspaper which the parent's organization has purchased for each student in each classroom.

Notice three particular aspects of Mr. Graham's organizational structure. First, Mr. Graham begins instruction each day with the achievement group that is having the most difficulty with reading (green). He wants to adequately prepare these students for the independent activities which will follow. He has found that the other two groups (blue and red) do much better than the green group when they begin the independent work period.

Second, notice that devoting half of each period to the low-achieving readers leaves the second half of the class for instruction with either the blue group or the red group. Mr. Graham sees the students in the two higher-achieving groups only once every other day for direct instruction. On the other day, these students spend the entire day working independently.

Third, notice that at the end of every schedule for independent seatwork activities is listed either contracts or choose. When students complete their regularly assigned work in reading they must work on literature contracts, reading center contracts, or choose a book, magazine, or activity from the reading corner. Wednesdays are usually set aside for children to explore the materials in the reading corner. On other days students usually are expected to work on their contracts or one of several different writing projects.

FRAMEWORKS AND CLASSROOM ORGANIZATION

Generally, only one of the two questions associated with your evolving comprehension framework affects organizational decisions. Your answer to the question How does reading ability develop? strongly influences the type of classroom organization you will find most appropriate. Your answer to the question How does one read? does not profoundly influence organizational decisions.

The reason for this is fairly straightforward. You have seen how explanations for how one reads influence what you teach and how often you teach it, not how to teach any particular skill. For example, you have learned that text-based explanations for how one reads are consistent with teaching many decoding skills and few higher-level skills. Reader-based explanations for how one reads are consistent with teaching more higher-level skills and few decoding skills. Interactive explanations for how one reads are consistent with teaching relatively equal amounts of decoding skills and higher-level skills. Explanations for how one reads do not influence how you teach any of the skills associated with reading comprehension.

Instead, decisions related to how to teach reading are usually constrained by your answer to the question How does reading ability develop? Since classroom organization is one of several issues involved in how one teaches reading instruction, it is an area constrained by your explanation for how reading ability develops.

Consider the situation of a teacher with a holistic language learning explanation for the development of reading comprehension. This teacher believes that reading comprehension develops similarly to oral language; the important generalizations associated with reading comprehension are induced by children as they naturally interact with print for real, not artificial, purposes. The important generalizations for reading are learned by the child, not directly taught by the teacher. A teacher with this type of perspective is likely to provide little direct instruction of specific reading skills in isolation. Instead, children would be expected to read real literature selections not the artificial text of workbook pages which work on a single isolated skill. Children spend much of their time engaged in individual activities such as contracts for reading centers, contracts for literature, Readers Theatre, drama, reading in content areas, or similar activities. Reading center tasks would always consist of engaging activities with real, complete texts, not isolated and specific skills. Interest groups would probably be used extensively since these would provide real purposes for reading and learning about reading.

Teachers with a mastery of specific skills explanation for the development of reading comprehension organize their classrooms differently. These teachers believe that reading comprehension develops as a result of specific skill instruction; the important generalizations associated with reading comprehension are learned by children as a result of direct instruction. Specific reading skills are taught and then tested to ensure mastery. If students fail to master a particular skill, they receive additional instruction until they master the skill. Teachers with this type of perspective undoubtedly spend substantial time teaching specific skills in instructional groups formed around specific skills or achievement levels. Reading center activities are limited to instruction or practice on very specific and isolated reading skills. Contracts for independent book projects might be used but be viewed as important for affective factors and for practicing the skills taught in reading groups. Interest groups only are used for affective reasons. They are not seen as crucial for the development of new insights about reading.

A teacher with a differential acquisition explanation for the development of reading ability provides for a wide range of organizational patterns, but distinguishes between proficient and less proficient readers. Proficient readers are likely to spend more time in realistic reading experiences with interest groups or contracts for independent book projects. Less proficient readers are likely to spend more time in skills or achievement groups. Often, this occurs when teachers decide (like Mr. Graham) to provide more direct instructional time to low reading groups, and allow higher reading groups to do more independent work.

THE MAJOR POINTS

1. To help students understand what they read, reading instruction must accommodate individual differences in four areas: reading achievement levels; reading interests; specific skill competencies; and background knowledge. Organizational decisions usually are used to accommodate individual differences in these four areas.

2. There are two general categories of organizational accommodations used during reading instruction to meet the unique needs of individuals: interclass and intraclass. Generally, interclass accommodations only deal with differences in reading achievement levels. They include a variety of means by which students are more homogeneously grouped on the basis of reading achievement levels. They do not usually accommodate differences between students in reading interests, skill competencies, or background knowledge.

3. Intraclass accommodations can: (1) partially account for differences in reading achievement levels through the use of achievement groups; (2) account for differences in reading interests through the use of interest groups; (3) account for differences in specific skill competencies through the use of skill groups; and (4) account for differences in background knowledge through the use of individualized activities.

4. When considering intraclass grouping decisions, consider the answers to three questions: What information can I use to determine grouping patterns? How many groups should I have in my classroom? and How many students should be in each of my groups?
5. The use of reading center activities and contract reading projects are useful formats for individualizing learning experiences in reading.
6. Weekly and yearly plans are often helpful in planning the organizational patterns you want to introduce into your classroom.
7. Organizational decisions are most strongly affected by only one of the two questions associated with your evolving comprehension framework: How does reading ability develop? Teachers with either a mastery of specific skill explanation, a holistic language learning explanation, or a differential acquisition explanation value different patterns of classroom organization.

QUESTIONS AND ACTIVITIES

1. Define the classroom organizational scheme that you intend to employ in your first classroom teaching assignment. Explain your decisions. What materials do you need to acquire or develop to implement your organizational scheme? Explain how your classroom organization is consistent with your evolving comprehension framework.
2. Use the data in table 12–1 to form several different interest groups. Identify several different reading projects or activities that each group might be expected to complete.
3. Define one reading center activity that you might develop for each of the following aspects of reading comprehension.

   a. decoding knowledge
   b. vocabulary knowledge
   c. syntactic knowledge
   d. discourse knowledge
   e. affective considerations

   Identify all the materials you will need for each center activity.
4. Describe the type of comprehension framework that Mr. Graham is likely to have. Identify the assumptions he is likely to make about how one reads and how reading ability develops. Explain your answers. Also identify any additional information that would help you to develop a more precise picture of his framework.
5. Which type of grouping pattern would be likely to result in a greater number of reading groups within a single classroom: achievement groups; interest groups; or skill groups? Explain.
6. Develop a yearly plan for your first classroom teaching assignment. Specify, in your yearly plan, all of the accommodations you will

make to provide for individual differences, when you will begin each accommodation, and how much time will be spent on each during each day.

FURTHER READING

Anderson, L. (1984). The environment of instruction: The function of seatwork in a commercially developed curriculum. In G. G. Duffy, L. R. Roehler, & J. Mason (eds.), *Comprehension instruction: Perspectives and suggestions.* New York: Longman.

Describes the results of a study investigating responses of students to independent seatwork tasks in a basal reading series. Suggests that students may define success on seatwork tasks in terms of completion, not understanding.

Ehly, S. & Larsen, S. C. (1984). Peer tutoring in the regular classroom. In A. J. Harris and E. R. Sipay (eds.), *Readings on reading instruction,* 3rd Edition. New York: Longman.

Explains how to establish a program of peer tutoring in reading within an elementary classroom. Describes how to select pairs, train tutors, schedule tutoring sessions, and supervise students' progress. Shows how peer tutoring may supplement more traditional forms of classroom organization.

McKenzie, G. R. (1984). Personalize your group teaching. In A. J. Harris and E. R. Sipay (eds.) *Readings on reading instruction,* 3rd Edition. New York: Longman.

Describes several ways to individualize instruction within the context of reading achievement groups by individualizing your communication with students.

Unsworth, L. (1985). Meeting individual needs through flexible within-class grouping of pupils. *The Reading Teacher, 38*(3), 298–303.

Describes a method for using flexible reading groups with students of varying reading achievement levels. Outlines a six-day sequence of activities with rotating membership in each group. Argues that this type of approach provides a viable alternative to more traditional and static forms of group organization within a classroom.

REFERENCES

Burmeister, L. (1983). *Foundations and strategies for teaching children to read.* Reading, MA: Addison-Wesley.

Guthrie, J. T. (1979). Grouping for reading. *The Reading Teacher 32,* 500–501.

Harris, A. J. & Sipay, E. R. (1985). *How to increase reading ability* (7th Edition). New York: Longman.

Hiebert, E. H. (1983). An examination of ability grouping for reading instruction. *Reading Research Quarterly, 18*(2), 231–55.

Jackson, G. B. (1975). The research evidence on the effects of grade retention. *Review of Educational Research, 45,* 613–35.

Pikulski, J. J. & Kirsch, I. S. (1979). Organization for instruction. In R. C. Calfee & P. A. Drum (eds.), *Contemporary reading survey.* Newark, DE: IRA.

Rosenthal, R. & Jacobson, J. (1968). *Pygmalion in the classroom.* New York: Holt, Rinehart and Winston.

13 Effective Teaching of Reading

TEACHER EFFECTIVENESS: AN OVERVIEW ■ GENERALIZATIONS ABOUT EFFECTIVE TEACHERS ■ TWO SAMPLE CLASSROOMS ■ ORGANIZATIONAL FACTORS ■ USING INSTRUCTIONAL TIME ■ PEER INTERACTIONS IN THE CLASSROOM ■ THE IMPORTANCE OF EXPECTATIONS ■ THE DIRECT INSTRUCTION MODEL ■ EFFECTIVE READING PROGRAMS ■ A CONCLUDING STATEMENT

The teacher's role in orchestrating and managing the many messages, contexts, and levels of interaction in the classroom requires considerable skill. In any one lesson, teachers must effectively communicate (through verbal and nonverbal cues) the academic task and the participation rules, distribute turns at talk, manage the discipline of the group, monitor and interpret student messages in several channels, and repair any frame clashes. Of course, teachers do much more than teach one lesson to one group at a time. They also (1) construct methods for moving students from lesson to lesson or place to place, (2) arrange and monitor groups, (3) monitor and respond to messages from several groups simultaneously engaged in other tasks, and (4) manage the discipline of the whole class without disturbing the flow of the immediate lesson in which they are involved. . . . From this perspective, the task of instruction involves much more than planning the sequence of presentation of academic content.

Adapted from J. L. Green & D. Smith, Teaching and learning: a linguistic perspective. *Elementary School Journal, 83,* 1983, pp. 361–62.

This chapter presents major findings regarding the effective teaching of reading, not from a specific teaching or methodological viewpoint, but based on general research on effective teaching practices. It is an outgrowth of a belief that there are two vital participants in the classroom—the teacher and the student—and that certain interactions between these participants have greater instructional benefits than do others. This chapter is also an outgrowth of our experiences in teaching future teachers of reading, who consistently state that they feel they know the methodology of reading instruction, but feel that they do not know how to act in the classroom.

After reading this chapter, you will be able to

1. discuss effective teaching of reading and probable classroom behaviors of effective reading teachers;
2. state how effective teaching practices might differ throughout the elementary grades;
3. discuss the measurement of effective teaching of reading.

TEACHER EFFECTIVENESS: AN OVERVIEW

Teacher effectiveness is an issue of growing importance in education and in the mind of the general public. In Washington, DC, the National Institute of Education (NIE) has made research into teacher effectiveness a major goal and parents often say that they want their children placed with the best (that is, the most effective) teachers in a particular school. In fact, some states have enacted legislation resulting in a **career ladder,** paying substantial salary incentives for teachers deemed master teachers.

career ladder: A system where teachers are ranked and rewarded for effectiveness, experience, or a combination of both.

Definitions and measurement of effective teaching have resulted from a tradition of curiosity about what happens in classrooms. At first, researchers attempted to document what happens in classrooms. They simply went into classrooms and carefully documented what teachers did during a given period of instructional time. Such research was conducted until the early 1960s and resulted in a wealth of descriptive data about teacher behavior (see Wallen & Travers, 1963).

This period was followed by an interest in correlating the documented, descriptive teacher behaviors with student achievement scores, usually in mathematics or reading. It was thought that finding a relationship between student test scores and possible consistent teacher behaviors would indicate effective teaching practices. Of course, such studies only point to *relationships* and did not actually test the effectiveness of specific practices. It remained questionable whether the behaviors that correlated with high student achievement scores actually were responsible for the scores. Also, defining appropriate teacher behaviors in terms of student achievement scores was and is still debated. Yet interest in matching teacher behaviors with test scores remained high for some years (the peak of such research activity was from the mid-1960s to the mid-1970s), and is still of current interest (Brophy & Good, 1986; Evertson, Anderson, Anderson & Brophy, 1980; Fisher, Berliner, Filby, Marliave, Cahen & Dishaw, 1980).

Beginning in the mid-1970s, the question of whether student test scores were caused by, rather than being simply related to certain teacher behaviors began to be studied directly. Researchers still used student achievement test data and relied heavily on the descriptive research documenting teacher behaviors. But researchers began using the behaviors that correlated positively with achievement scores to develop modules to train teachers in those behaviors. The general reasoning used by these researchers (Anderson, Evertson & Brophy, 1979; Good & Grouws, 1979; Gage & Giaconia, 1981; Stallings, Needels & Stayrook, 1979) was that assigning a random group of teachers into groups and training one group in behaviors that correlated highly with student achievement scores while leaving the other group to teach as they normally did, allowed closer examination of the effectiveness of specific teaching behaviors throughout the groups. This would then provide an indication of the value of the hypothesized, effective teaching behaviors.

Although a relatively large number of studies appear to show that certain behaviors seem to result in increased student achievement test scores, such research is really still in its infancy and has some conceptual and methodological problems. Yet the results of such studies are consistent enough to have already made an impact on educational practices, and future teachers need to be aware of this research and its implications. Partly due to the debate that surrounds some of the research methods and results in this area, we present and discuss only findings that are most consistent.

GENERALIZATIONS ABOUT EFFECTIVE TEACHERS

Although it is always difficult to generalize about human behavior, the body of research on effective teaching does yield some consistent results that correlate teacher behaviors with high student achievement scores. Using such test scores as the basis on which to judge effectiveness is still, in our opinion, a debatable question. However, since effective teaching research has used such measures, we also will, but with the caution that there is more to schooling than standardized achievement test scores. Other, perhaps more balanced measures must be explored to measure learning outcomes and effective instruction.

Rosenshine (1983, pp. 336–37) presents an overview of the research on successful teaching practices. He finds that when students are younger, slower, or have little prior background, teachers are most effective when they:

- structure the learning;
- proceed in small steps but at a brisk pace;
- give detailed and redundant instructions and explanations;
- provide many examples;
- ask many questions and provide overt, active practice;
- provide feedback and corrections, particularly in the initial stages of learning new material;
- have a student success rate of eighty percent or higher in initial learning;
- divide seatwork into smaller assignments;
- provide for continued student practice so that students have a success rate of ninety to one-hundred percent and become rapid, confident, and firm.

Although there are questions that can be raised (for example, it seems obvious that if student success rate is initially over eighty percent, the teacher is doing something right. The question might then be how to get the initial eighty-percent.), these points are important in effective instruction for students of all abilities, not only those who are younger, slower, or have little background. Rosenshine (1983, p. 337) goes on to outline a six-item list of teaching functions that are synthesized from the studies on effective teaching that he reviewed. The six points are noted in table 13–1, and form an outline for stages in teaching a skills lesson.

Rosenshine expands each of the six points noted in table 13–1. Here we discuss his comments relating to point 4 and readers interested in his more extensive discussion can refer to the original source.

- present material in small steps;
- focus on one thought (point, direction) at a time;
- avoid digressions;
- organize and present material so that one point is mastered before the next point is given;
- model the skill (when appropriate);
- have many, varied, and specific examples;
- give detailed and redundant explanations for difficult points;
- check for student understanding on one point before proceeding to the next point;
- ask questions to monitor student progress;
- stay with the topic, repeating material until students understand (pp. 338–39).

Related to this synthesis of successful presentation methods is his compilation of suggestions for checking for students' understanding.

TABLE 13-1
Teaching functions in instructional programs

1. Daily review, checking previous day's work, and reteaching (if necessary): Checking homework Reteaching areas where there were student errors
2. Presenting new content/skills: Provide overview Proceed in small steps (if necessary), but at a rapid pace If necessary, give detailed or redundant instructions and explanations New skills are phased in while old skills are being mastered
3. Initial student practice: High frequency of questions and overt student practice (from teacher and materials) Prompts are provided during initial learning (when appropriate) All students have a chance to respond and receive feedback Teacher *checks for understanding* by evaluating student responses Continue practice until students are firm Success rate of 80% or higher during initial learning
4. Feedback and correctives (and recycling of instruction, if necessary): Feedback to students, particularly when they are correct but hesitant Student errors provide feedback to the teacher that corrections and/or reteaching is necessary Corrections by simplifying question, giving clues, explaining or reviewing steps, or reteaching last steps When necessary, reteach using smaller steps
5. Independent practice so that students are firm and automatic: Seatwork Unitization and automaticity (practice to overlearning) Need for procedure to ensure student engagement during seatwork (i.e., teacher or aide monitoring) 95% correct or higher
6. Weekly and monthly reviews: reteaching, if necessary

Note—With older, more mature learners *(a)* the size of steps in the presentation is larger, *(b)* student practice is more covert, and *(c)* the practice involves covert rehearsal, restating, and reviewing (i.e., deep processing or "whirling").

This is a vital area in effective teaching, for if students have not understood a particular point or concept, then there is little use in attempting to build on that concept. When checking for understanding, it has been suggested that a teacher

- prepare a large number of oral questions beforehand;
- ask many brief questions on main points, on supplementary points, and on the process being taught;

- call on students whose hands are not raised;
- have all students write answers (on paper or a chalkboard) while the teacher circulates;
- have all students write the answer and check their answers with a neighbor (usually done with older students);
- at the end of a lecture/discussion (usually with older students) write the main points on the board and have the class meet in groups and summarize the main points to each other.

TWO SAMPLE CLASSROOMS

To this point you have examined aspects of effective instruction that have been consistently found in research on teacher effectiveness. Additionally, it is important to know how the effective teaching practices might be applied. This section illustrates the application of effective teaching practices by comparing teachers across classrooms. In addition to illustrating the concepts presented to this point, the examples should make you think about which effective teaching behaviors are missing and how they might be included.

Classroom 1: A Scenario

Mr. Alexis' focus for the past and current lesson is cause-and-effect relationships. Yesterday, Mr. Alexis began by reading the following passage to his students and allowed discussion of what might have caused the tire to go flat.

> The pavement in front of Andy's house was very bumpy. Some new homes were being built at the end of the street, and trucks went back and forth along the street all day long. There were large lumber trucks, heavy concrete trucks, and small delivery trucks. One day a pane of glass fell from one of the trucks that was delivering building materials. When the glass hit the pavement, it broke into hundreds of pieces. When Andy's father drove home that evening, he tried very hard not to drive over any of the glass. But the next morning when Andy's father went out to go to work, he found that his car had a flat tire.
>
> From Teacher's Guide to *Towers*, Houghton Mifflin Reading Program, 1983, pp. 146–47.

Mr. Alexis had previously prepared the following questions.

- What was happening in Andy's neighborhood?
- What was the street like in front of Andy's house?
- Why were there so many different kinds of trucks going back and forth along Andy's street all day?

- What fell from one of the trucks that was delivering building materials?
- What happened to the pane of glass?
- Did Andy's father care whether or not he drove over the glass?
- What was wrong with Andy's father's car the next morning?

This was the end of the class, which was cut short due to a fire drill. Mr Alexis continued the cause-and-effect lesson the next day. Mr. Alexis began the class by asking several students what was covered during the previous lesson. He asked several others to provide a restatement of as much of the paragraph about Andy's father's car as they remembered. He asked additional students specifically, by name, whether they could add anything to the restatements they had just heard. Students who did not volunteer to answer were also often questioned. Shouted-out answers were not encouraged.

Mr. Alexis then went on to restate the purpose of the lesson: learning about cause-and-effect relationships. He had students reread the paragraph about Andy's father and had students quickly turn to the student beside them and tell each other the answers to the questions from the previous day. (These had been written on the chalkboard.) He then went on to define and discuss cause and effect and let students discover cause-and-effect relationships in the paragraph, using prepared questions such as these.

- What does *cause* mean?
- If something happens because of something else, can we say that one thing *caused* another to happen?
- If something called *querb* (a nonsense word) makes *benerf* (another nonsense word) happen, which one would you call the cause?

The discussion proceeded with Mr. Alexis pointing out that the cause and what was caused (for example, *querb* and *benerf*) are related because one does not happen without the other also happening. He went on to define and then ask questions about effect(s) and further discussed the relationship between a cause and an effect.

Following the definition and discussion, Mr. Alexis provided students with the opportunity to work quickly (five to ten minutes) in pairs. He had written several sets of items on the blackboard. The students in the pairs were to alternate telling each other which are cause-and-effect relationships and which are not. Disagreements were to be noted. After a brief discussion of the students' agreements and disagreements, Mr. Alexis had the class copy a definition of cause-and-effect relationship into their notebooks. He then went back to the passage about Andy's father's flat tire. Students were to write answers to the following questions in their notebooks. The questions and passage were handed out on a teacher-prepared worksheet (shown here).

---

1. The paragraph says that Andy's father tried not to drive over the glass. Do you think he was able to miss all of the glass on the road? Explain your answer.
2. Find as many cause-and-effect relationships in the paragraph as you can. You should be able to find at least three.
3. What do you think caused the tire to go flat?
4. What was the effect of the bumpy road?
5. What was the effect of driving over the glass?
6. Explain the cause-and-effect relationship between the glass and the flat tire.
7. Explain one other cause-and-effect relationship in the paragraph.
8. In your own words, define a cause-and-effect relationship.

Note that, for number 2 there are at least four answers: construction related to movement of trucks; bumpy road related to glass falling; glass hitting pavement related to glass shattering; glass on road related to flat tire. One could even draw further relationships, such as the flat tire causing the father to be late for work.

While students were working, Mr. Alexis walked around the classroom, stopping to talk to various students, making sure that they were working properly on the assignment.

Mr. Alexis then had students trade papers and check answers. For open-ended, inferential questions, students used the following as guidelines: Does the answer make sense? Can it be logically supported by other aspects or events in the story (be specific)? All answers were discussed. He then collected the papers to tabulate answers into his informal record-keeping system, thus allowing him to provide special help during the next class period for students who may not yet have grasped the concept. He also asked questions and discussed why cause-and-effect relationships help readers understand a passage. He explained that many cause-and-effect relationships must be inferred rather than specifically found in a passage. For example, the tire may have gone flat because it already had a slow leak, or the glass fell off the truck because it was improperly secured.

Students were encouraged to think of other causes and effects for the cause-and-effect relationships found in the paragraph, and then discussed the fact that readers must choose the most logical reason using information provided in the text, together with one's knowledge. Mr. Alexis concluded the class period by asking various students to restate what had been learned that day. These main points were written on the board by the teacher and copied into students' notebooks. Mr. Alexis

Effective teachers are aware of students' needs and provide individual help when necessary.

then described what would follow from the current lesson. A brief, pertinent homework assignment, due the following day, was given. Students were told that the homework would be discussed first thing during the next class. He also planned follow-up activities to test and reinforce the cause-and-effect lesson for the following week and at several longer intervals throughout the school term.

Classroom 2: A Scenario

Ms. Pleasant also is providing instruction on cause-and-effect relationships to a group of students who are very similar to Mr. Alexis' students. Ms. Pleasant begins her class by talking about causes of things. She provides several examples of causes (for example, turning on a light switch) and asks students to provide some possible effects. She listens to the answers and tries to write as many as possible on the blackboard beside the appropriate cause. She then provides examples of effects and follows the same procedure with potential causes that students present.

Ms. Pleasant uses the causes and effects written on the blackboard to provoke a discussion of the relationship between what makes things happen and what happens. She asks students to define *cause* and *effect*.

She asks the class in general if they know what a cause-and-effect relationship is, and asks them to raise their hands if they would like to provide an example of a cause-and-effect relationship. Several students do so, and she asks for their examples, writing them on the chalkboard. Ms. Pleasant then hands out copies of the passage about Andy's father and asks her students to read it to themselves and to turn the page over so that she knows when they finish.

When most of the students finish, Ms. Pleasant asks several questions based on the paragraph:

- How many people have been in a car with a flat tire? (Ms. Pleasant elicits the circumstances and causes from those students who indicate they have had such an experience.)
- What kinds of things can cause a flat tire?
- How does a tire become flat? (Here, she searches for an answer approximating "the air gets let out of the tire.")
- Is there anything in the story that can cut a tire? What?
- Do you think that Andy's father drove over the glass?
- What do you think caused the tire to go flat in the paragraph you just read?
- Why do you think it took overnight for the tire to go flat? Why didn't it happen right away?
- If Andy's father drove over the glass, what do you think the effect was?
- What would you do if you were in Andy's father's situation?
- Do we know for certain that the glass caused the flat tire?
- Write another paragraph to continue what you just read. Be sure to include at least one cause-and-effect relationship in the paragraph you write.

Ms. Pleasant concludes the class by thanking students for their attention, stating that much was learned today, and that she looks forward to completing the lesson tomorrow.

The Scenarios Discussed

BEFORE READING ON

Look back at the two scenarios, and at table 13–1. State which teacher you think exhibited most of the listed behaviors. Using table 13–2, place a mark in each category if the teacher exhibited the effective teaching practice. You will need to refer to the scenarios as you complete the checklist.

You may have been surprised at the number of behaviors that Ms. Pleasant did not exhibit even though, on the face of it, her lesson probably sounded fine. You may have noticed that the most serious deficit in Ms.

TABLE 13–2

Checklist related to the two classroom scenarios

Effective Teaching Practice	Mr. Alexis	Ms. Pleasant
Review/restatement of previous day's work, reteaching if necessary.	_____	_____
Presenting new content and/or skills.	_____	_____
Provision for initial student practice and checking for understanding.	_____	_____
Feedback and reteaching if necessary.	_____	_____
Provision for student independent practice.	_____	_____
Provision for weekly and monthly reviews.	_____	_____
Presentation of material in small, manageable steps.	_____	_____
Avoidance of digressions.	_____	_____
Provision of many, varied examples.	_____	_____
Preparation of questions ahead of time.	_____	_____
Call on students who do not volunteer.	_____	_____
Have all students write answers.	_____	_____
Teacher circulates while students practice to provide needed help.	_____	_____
Summarize main points at end of lesson.	_____	_____
Provide homework and/or other independent practice.	_____	_____

Pleasant's lesson was a lack of focus. Often, her questions did not reflect the goal of the lesson: to teach cause-and-effect relationships. Her questions also did not appear to range across students. She did not ask questions of specific students, thereby checking for understanding, but relied mainly on asking a general question that students could or could not respond to. Although this has its place in a lesson, it should be used cautiously. Students do not benefit as much from hearing another student provide a correct answer as giving a response themselves. This is especially true when answers are spoken out loud, because such answers are often hard to understand since there are several students speaking at once.

Other instances can support an argument that Mr. Alexis' lesson was more effective. For example, he began with a recap of the previous lesson, thus setting the stage for his students, reminding them of what was learned and what to anticipate in the coming lesson. Similarly, he ended his lesson by recapping what was learned that day and discussing its importance. These two steps should not be left out. They are important aspects in learning because they provide the feeling that an overall plan to learning and a **continuum of instruction** exist.

continuum of instruction: Instruction that is clearly connected, with lessons building on each other.

Students should not be made to feel that instruction is a set of haphazard or disjointed steps. In fact, students who have difficulty seeing how their lessons fit together into a cohesive learning experience may think that their teacher is disorganized, basing their opinion on the overall class rather than on specific lessons. Even though individual lessons may be well planned, a thread woven throughout the school year should be present. This is accomplished in part by the summarizing strategy at the end of a lesson, the recapping strategy at a lesson's beginning, and the weekly and monthly discussion and review of prior work.

ORGANIZATIONAL FACTORS

Organized teachers are regarded more highly by their students and also appear to impart more information than disorganized instructors (Nash, 1976; Brophy, 1979; Good, 1979). A key factor in organization is being prepared. This means organizing lessons; preparing questions; prereading material; working through exercises and preparing answer sheets; arriving at school early enough to write exercises, notes, or other items on the blackboard; preparing bulletin boards, posters, learning centers, and practice exercises; ensuring there are enough materials for all students; and numerous other items that are part of an effective teacher's daily routine. Time will also be spent providing continuous and (as much as possible) immediate feedback to students. This means promptly correcting homework, worksheets, students' writing, and other assignments. The organized teacher also uses parents as partners in the educational process, and keeps records allowing feedback to parents in the form of letters or notes, parent-teacher conferences, or similar forms of contact.

Most generally, organizing instruction means being fully prepared. For example, prepare questions ahead of time because it is not easy to ask good, wide-ranging comprehension questions "off the top of your head." With experience, fewer questions will have to be prepared, but an outline of questions to be asked will always be a valuable aid.

Being an organized, effective teacher also means having a detailed lesson plan ready before class. Often, experienced teachers may not consistently refer to the plan that was made, but the step of sitting down and thinking about the lesson in advance allows them to be secure in the knowledge that they are prepared and helps ensure that an important point is not neglected. As teachers become more experienced, the necessity of extremely detailed plans becomes less important. But effective teachers do take the time to make a comprehensive outline of their lesson ahead of time. This is done in a **teacher's day book.** To ensure that your instruction builds systematically, you should also have some idea of a long range plan. Often, teachers make outlines for a month or more at one time, filling in details of lessons as they become more immediate. Such a strategy helps ensure that there is cohesion in your instruction beyond your daily classes.

teacher's day book: A log book where teachers write their lesson plans, ideas, and comments.

USING INSTRUCTIONAL TIME

One of the most consistent research findings in effective teaching comes under the label **time on task studies** (Rosenshine & Berliner, 1977). These studies consistently find that teachers are more effective when they structure their lessons in ways that provide students with more time that is directly related to the objective being taught. That is, students who spend more time on the content of a lesson learn more than students who spend less time on the content to be learned.

time on task studies: Research that examines the amount of time actually spent on the objectives of a lesson.

It seems almost self-evident that students who spend more class time directly related to the objective(s) to be mastered learn more than students who spend relatively less time. In fact, this relates directly to the previous discussion on organization. An organized teacher, due to preparation of questions and of the overall structure of a lesson, spends less time digressing.

Although you might feel that there is little down time (time not being used directly for instruction) in the classroom, much research indicates otherwise. This can be due to interruptions in the instructional routine (a student asking to go to the restroom or a public-address announcement from the main office), teachers' spending time handing out books or other materials, or students' daydreaming or otherwise not engaged in the learning task. Time actively spent by students on the learning task is often called **engaged time** by researchers who study whether students are "on" or "off" task (Brookover, Schweitzer, Scheider, Beady, Flood & Wisenbarker, 1978).

engaged time: Spent by students while actively attending to objectives the teacher sets.

BEFORE READING ON

How much on task or engaged time do you think that fifth-grade students spend in a reading class? What percentage of time per class is engaged time and what percentage of instructional time during reading period is off task? Note your opinion: _____. If an average school year consists of 150 days, how many hours do you think that average fifth-grade students are actively engaged in learning to read throughout the school year? Note your answer: _____.

It may surprise you that research indicates that students are engaged in learning to read between 120 and 298 hours per 150-hour school year (Berliner, 1981). Thus, students are not active learners, for one reason or another, between eighteen and twenty-five percent of the time. This finding is based on a study of four fifth-grade classrooms, where some classes spent substantially less time than others in on-task behaviors. The importance of this finding is not in the actual number of hours spent on or off task but, as Berliner (1981) points out, in the wide variability of engaged time across classes and teachers. There appears to be a wide range in the amount of engaged time that teachers foster. Relating student achievement to engaged time provides the finding that classrooms with high student-engaged rates have students with higher achievement scores than students in classrooms with lower engaged rates.

You may feel that the engaged rates shown here are quite low. In fact, Berliner points out that the numbers are probably artificially high

> [since the numbers] are an artifact of the observational system that was in use . . . transition time and certain other classroom phenomena [were] coded as separate events . . . . [Thus] engagement rates are for the time spent in reading, after a class has settled down and before the class starts to put their work away. If engagement were coded for the entire block denoted by teachers as reading time, the engaged time rates would be considerably lower because during transitions or when waiting for help students are usually not engaged. . . . in *many* fifth grade classes cumulative engaged time in reading is well under 100 hours for the entire school year . . . (pp. 207–209).

Since the relationship between time on task and achievement scores is positive and high, and since a prepared teacher is less likely to use instructional time for tasks not directly related to instruction, we stress again the need for careful preparation. Time that is used for transitions, as Berliner calls it in this passage, is necessary, but can often take much more time than is really needed. Passing out paper or worksheets, putting away books or other supplies and materials, or finding the right page in the reading text should all be done systematically and as quickly as possible. Careful preparation, including **preplanning question outlines,** will do much to ensure student interest and an instructional pace that will enhance student-engaged time.

Thus, keeping students engaged in the instructional task at hand is an important function for a teacher, although one must keep in mind the importance of providing instruction at a level which is manageable for students. Material presented in chunks that are too large or too difficult for the students will decrease effective learning, result in lower success rates, and ultimately yield negative student attitudes. Remember also that these considerations apply to all instructional frameworks. One of the best statements of how one's personal teaching philosophy and style should not be downgraded, but rather complement the structure of a lesson, is reprinted here (italics have been added for emphasis).

> Teaching *functions,* rather than teaching *methods* or skills are important. 'No one technique of instruction is clearly associated with disastrous outcomes or successful ones' (Cooley & Leinhart, 1978, p. 40). McDonald and Elias (1976), in related research, found that there were patterns of instruction that were effective, but these differed from teacher to teacher, from grade to grade, and from context to context. Certain teaching functions, however, always need to be met for successful classroom experiences to occur. Academic monitoring must be accomplished in some form, though many different teaching behaviors can fulfill the function. Diagnostic and prescriptive functions must be carried out, though these can be accomplished in many different ways and can be done well or poorly, in individualized or nonindividualized settings. Nonetheless, some diagnosis and prescription must take place. Feedback must be given to learners. Dozens of ways to provide such feedback are known. What is important is that feedback in some form takes place. We have . . . lost sight of the fact that certain teaching functions must be met regardless of the method used. *There is probably no one best way to teach anything to all students, but there are probably similarities in the teaching functions met in all successful ways of teaching* (Berliner, 1981, p. 223).

PEER INTERACTIONS IN THE CLASSROOM

The instructional situation in classrooms may be thought of as a set of interactions between (1) teacher and students and (2) student and peers. This classification, of course, includes other types of interaction patterns, such as teacher with single student, but in general the two broad categories are valid. Often, teachers teach with the whole class or a group of students as the target. The structure of such lessons has been discussed in the earlier sections of this chapter, from the perspective of what we know about effective teaching based on observational and correlational research in the classroom. It has also been noted that such research sometimes makes no value judgment about the content taught and does not examine the appropriateness of skill sequence or content-specific factors. That is, if a student is told by the teacher to look at the floor, then students who look at the chalkboard would be identified as being off task, even though the task may be inappropriate to the goal of the lesson.

This section considers interactions between students in the classroom. It is an accepted practice for teachers to place students into reading groups for instructional purposes. Chapter 12 discussed how such groups might be formed, their potential value (and pitfalls), and the special danger of not being flexible in grouping arrangements. Yet certain conditions arise within any grouping arrangement and must be considered if teachers want to provide equal opportunity for all students to present their ideas and opinions. Many potential problems can result from unconsidered interactions that occur within a group. These usually stem from **perceived** and actual **status** of members in the student group.

perceived status: One's idea of one's own or another's status, regardless of actual status.

Rosenholtz (1982) provides research indicating that students are very aware of their peers' reading abilities and, further, that their perceptions of reading ability translate into judgments of the "worth" of other students in relation to themselves. In short, reading ability has been found to be a **status characteristic** that students focus on to make decisions about how bright other students are in relation to themselves, and also about the relative value of their own ideas and opinions. Rosenholtz has conducted further research showing that the amount of interaction in a group of students—the amount of participation of each group member—depends to a large degree on the perception of status in the group (Rosenholtz, 1982; 1984; Rosenholtz & Cohen, 1983).

status characteristics: Concepts that influence perception of status.

BEFORE READING ON

Of the following two groups of students, who do you think will participate more, in terms of voicing opinions and suggesting strategies and ideas? The assignment is to discuss a story line and to write a short play extending a selection that has been read and discussed by the class as a whole. Assume that Josh and Dina are the same students and could be placed in either group.

GROUP 1	GROUP 2
Bob (high-ability reader)	Josh (average-ability reader
Pat (high-ability reader)	Dina (average-ability reader)
Josh (average-ability reader)	Sam (low-ability reader)
Dina (average-ability reader)	Eileen (low-ability reader)

Researchers have found that students who perceive other group members as being better readers do not take as active a part in group work (Cohen, 1982). Such students appear to be content to allow their perceived higher-ability peers to dominate discussion and to provide strategies to complete the learning task. This seems true even when they have alternate solutions or suggestions that are equally valid. Interestingly, students who are not active participants in one group become active in another group, provided group membership changes so that they are (or perceive that they are) of higher reading ability than their group peers. Thus, average students in a group of high-ability students often show the same behaviors as do low-ability students placed with average students.

In this example, you would have been correct had you stated that Bob and Pat in Group 1, and Josh and Dina in Group 2, would have dominated discussion and generally shown leadership within the groups. This is true even though Josh and Dina would have shown low participatory behavior in Group 1. The reason for this seeming "flip-flop" is that the perception within the group about each member's reading ability, and thus about status, shifted from one group to the other. This is an important statement, for it indicates that students can be encouraged to participate depending on the situation or group of students with whom they are placed. Further, it is important to stress that it is the *students'* perception of *each other's* reading abilities that results in their behaviors.

This may not be a surprise, since reading is so strongly stressed in the elementary school curriculum. Since oral reading and verbal questioning based on silent reading plays a significant part in primary school instruction, students can quickly and easily determine who are the good and the poor readers. Often, teachers' praise and other rewards (allowing those who finish reading first to help with classroom tasks, carrying messages, and so on) are visible and are consistently given to the good readers.

Such interactions quickly result in perceptions and evaluations of others in relation to self. This is a strong basis for both positive and negative feelings of self-worth in relation to others, and directly results from a perception of what is valued (ability to read well) by the authority figure in the classroom. Of course, there are other factors that influence perceptions of status in students; sex and race are two obvious examples. Yet perceptions of reading ability are consistently found to be strong influences on student behavior and student interactions in group learning situations, regardless of other factors.

Since perceptions of peers, related to self, appear to modify behavior to such a large extent, you may be wondering how to increase participatory behavior by all students in group learning (including paired) situations. Rosenholtz has extended her research into studying whether teachers can change interaction patterns between students. She has found that in classrooms where teachers interact with students in ways that apply equal praise for reading-related behaviors as well as for other

Teachers must carefully consider group dynamics when providing opportunities for group work.

tasks, relatively equal participation and willingness to take risks (in answering questions, for example) is noted in all students. Such classrooms also appear to contribute to higher feelings of self-worth in low-achieving students.

Rosenholtz calls such classrooms **multidimensional,** contrasting them to **unidimensional classrooms** (Rosenholtz, 1984). Her suggested curriculum is based on the philosophy that all students have areas of strength, but that the educational system often does not adequately reward strengths other than reading ability in elementary grades. She suggests activities such as illustrating stories, using movement or drama, and other less directly print-based activities to teach concepts and reading skills. Although such activities are present in reading instruction, often they are performed as supplementary activities, overshadowed by oral and silent reading, and not singled out for special praise. Providing praise through overt actions by the teacher can

multidimensional classrooms: Where successes in print-based activities and other activities are generally equally rewarded.

unidimensional classrooms: Where successes in print-based activities are rewarded more than successes in other activities.

- raise self-esteem in all students, but especially in those often called below-average readers
- increase student perceptions of other individuals' worth
- result in learning that all individuals have specific strengths and weaknesses
- encourage participation in group situations requiring interactions across students of all levels of reading ability.

The following activities represent some ways to implement these suggestions. We stress, however, that these activities are currently part of most teachers' reading lessons. The key is that teachers, through actions and modeling, make students aware that all students have strengths and weaknesses and that each can be a valuable contributor in group activities. The goal, of course, is that students not perceive reading ability as the indicator of intelligence and relative worth, but rather as one area in which particular individuals might do well.

- Tell or read a brief story to children. Discuss the story's events in sequence. Have students draw to illustrate the sequence of events or draw one event and state where in the sequence it took place. Grade the work as any other assignment and post the students' work on bulletin boards or in conspicuous places around the classroom.

- After such an activity, have students discuss what they like best about the drawings. A subset of drawings can be used, spread across several sessions. Focus on what is good about each work and discuss how it fits into the story that was the basis for the assignment. Poorer readers will thus find their work, or at least certain segments of it, being praised by their peers.

- Give poorer readers responsibilities of their own and on which other students must focus. For example, a small group of poorer readers might work with the teacher to develop the story line for a play that is based on a reading assignment, perhaps continuing a story beyond its ending. The whole class then is asked to write the play along the suggested story line. The group who created the story line is given responsibility to "approve" the direction of the other students' efforts. This activity must be done under careful teacher supervision.

- Occasionally allow students to respond to reading assignments in ways that are not print based. For example, if a reading selection on pioneering includes a clear description of a fort, students might use clay or flour and water paste to build the fort. Discussion about the fort, its importance, hardships endured by its residents, and importance in the reading selection should form part of the activity. Grade, praise, and display the students' work.

- Average and slightly below-average readers can be asked to read to lower-grade students. For example, fourth-grade students could read to first-grade students. This would provide a feeling of worth in a print-based activity. Teachers must choose the fourth-grade students carefully and allow them to practice the reading selection.

- Allow poorer achieving readers to practice a reading selection (or a short play) and read to the rest of the class. This can effectively be done as a choral reading activity, where the poorer readers can read as a group.

THE IMPORTANCE OF EXPECTATIONS

A teacher's actions can indicate clearly to students both what is expected from them and the value that is placed on answers and contributions. Students quickly learn that teachers place more worth on some students' answers than on others'. This results from calling on specific students more than on other students or calling on given individuals in specific situations. Students perceived as below-average readers are asked more lower-level questions than are those designated by teachers as above-average readers. Such students are asked more detail and fact questions than are other students. Usually, the incidence of students who are called on to answer **high-order comprehension questions** is significantly greater for students perceived as being average or above-average readers.

Differences in teacher-student interactions have also been noted during the **interruption and correction behaviors** that teachers exhibit during students' oral reading. When a student reads aloud and miscues, teachers have the choice of interrupting the student or ignoring the miscue. Students who are thought to be below-average readers are interrupted and corrected during oral reading even when their miscues do not change the intended meaning of the text. That is, if two readers, one the teacher perceives as good and the other as poor, read "The *kitty* was in the hall" instead of "The *kitten* was in the hall," the poor reader is much more likely to be interrupted and corrected than is the student perceived as being a good reader (Allington, 1980). Such correction patterns are readily observed by students and can quickly influence a student's self-esteem.

In the instructional situation a teacher is involved in an on-the-spot, sometimes stressful, and always demanding situation. When questions are asked of students, it is not surprising that teachers are more prone to call on those students who consistently raise their hands or otherwise indicate their eagerness to provide a response. Since it is more likely that students who feel that they know the answer will raise their hands and since correct answers result in positive reinforcement and feedback, students can quickly fall into two groups—those who consistently attempt to respond and those who do not. It is often the case that most answers to teacher questions are provided by a small percentage of the students in a class. This is one reason for the written practice suggested by Rosenshine, discussed earlier. Remember, students may learn relatively little from simply hearing another providing the answer. In fact, it is not easy to even hear an answer if you happen to sit behind the responding student.

Another reason that teachers often rely on a fairly consistent core of students to provide responses to questions is a simple, human factor. Teachers, as well as students, require positive reinforcement for their efforts. When correct answers are provided to teachers' questions and

high-order comprehension questions: Questions beyond the literal level.

interruption and correction behavior: The different way(s) to correct students during a reading assignment.

Teachers interact with students in many different ways, from whole-class to individual situations and, in these diverse situations, provide instruction and expect specific responses.

assignments, there is an indication that learning has taken place. In effect, a correct answer tells teachers that their teaching has been effective, while an incorrect answer implies that the teaching is not being understood and may thus be ineffective. Thus, perhaps due to a subconscious urge for positive feedback, teachers may more often call on students who regularly provide correct responses.

Calling on some students on a regular basis is also an effect of many teachers' seeming fear of "dead air." A common pattern seen in questioning is the lack of waiting time for student response(s). For example, Rowe (1974) found that on the average, teachers waited only one second before repeating a question and moving to another student for an answer. Other studies (Swift & Gooding, 1983; Tobin & Capie, 1982) have found that lengthening the time that a teacher waits for a response, even only for a few seconds, provides benefits such as improved student-engaged rates and longer verbal responses.

Taken together, such research suggests that teachers need to provide more time for students to think about an answer to a question rather than expecting an almost instant response. Too often, it almost appears as if there might be a fear that silence indicates that nothing is happening. This is far from the truth. If a question is important enough to be asked, there should be an answer given before moving to another question. Also, help and a reasonable amount of time should be provided to one student before another is asked to attempt to answer the question.

In your other classes you may have heard of what is commonly called the **self-fulfilling prophecy** in education. This can be thought of in the following way:

self-fulfilling prophecy: The phenomenon that students who are expected to achieve highly do so; those expected to do poorly do so.

Students who are expected to do well generally do well.
Students who are not expected to do well generally do not do well.

Teachers use a number of ways to form perceptions about their students' abilities. For example, all of the following can affect perceptions of students' abilities and thus influence a teacher's expectations relative to a student or a group of students:

- oral language (including dialect)
- general behavior
- attitude
- cleanliness
- test scores
- comments on permanent record card (by previous teachers)
- informal comments by other teachers

Additionally, factors such as stereotyping due to racial factors and applying one sibling's achievement to expectations for another member of the same family can influence a teacher's judgment. It is not too unusual to hear comments like "I remember Sam's brother. He was in my class three years ago. He was nice enough, but sure didn't do very well!" or "Sue's sister was sure a good student. Her parents come to all the parent/teacher's days, too. They sure are interested in what we do here!" Such comments, although casual and not ill intended, can influence Sam's or Sue's teachers who might have overheard the comment. Teachers' judgments and expectations can, in subtle ways, be inadvertently transferred into student's achievement. Knowing this, and knowing the major factors influencing teacher expectations, will help you recognize and guard against problems that can result from factors other than instructional considerations.

THE DIRECT INSTRUCTION MODEL

direct instruction model: Teaching model where general subject content is broken into small components or skills that become specific instructional objectives.

One model of teaching behavior that attempts to incorporate research findings on effective teaching practices is the **direct instruction model.** This model gained popularity after a study called Project Follow Through, which compared nine different models or approaches for students' learning of academic skills. Each of the nine approaches was tested on students in areas of academic skills, cognitive-conceptual skills, and through instruments evaluating students' self-images. In his review of this research, Samuels (1981, p. 261) correctly points out that the project did not, in the strictest sense, use an experimental design, although each model was compared to its own control group. The approaches examined ranged from whole person, **open classroom models** to **skills-emphasis approaches.**

The study concluded that the direct instruction model resulted in more effective teaching and learning of reading compared to the other eight approaches examined. This model focuses on mastery of component skills in reading, breaking down the reading task into subskill components, and using principles of educational psychology to teach these subskills. Such principles include immediate feedback, consistent reinforcement, appropriate practice, and overlearning.

One of the reasons for the popularity gained by the direct instruction model is that students instructed using this approach ranked highest in both subject-matter learning and in attitudinal measures of self-esteem. This is a fairly striking finding, for **mastery-learning approaches** are generally criticized as being regimented, thus perhaps stifling creativity and resulting in negative attitudes. Yet students in the direct instruction approach group were found to have the highest score on measures of self-worth, even when compared to teaching approaches or programs that stated the fostering of self-esteem was an important objective. The assumptions and characteristics of the direct instruction model are shown in figure 13–1.

Although the direct instruction model is well known and enjoys current popularity, it is only one of several advocated teaching models and you should not view it as the only teaching method. There are several other promising approaches that are currently being researched. Often, these attempt to incorporate the suggestions of the direct instruction model into research findings that examine the classroom from a sociological perspective. One reason for this direction is the possibility those that were based on the direct instruction model are not easily transferred to other situations. That is, performance of students in new sites is sometimes below that of students in the original research site, and even successful programs have difficulty in maintaining performance levels over several years.

In the future, models of effective teaching are expected to incorporate more holistic approaches, while not discarding the findings of the direct instruction model. The impetus for such a direction comes from researchers who view the classroom as a combination of social context and communicative environment. That is, students and teachers interact with each other socially (this is partially discussed in the preceding section on peer interactions) and through language. Readers interested in such research are referred to Baghban, 1984; DeStefano & Pepinsky, 1981; Green & Harker, 1982; Green & Wallat, 1981; Harste, Woodward & Burke, 1984; Hymes, 1981.

open classroom model: Student-centered teaching method involving large, open areas for learning centers.
skills-emphasis approach: Where specific subskills related to reading are identified and taught as units.

mastery-learning approach: Where students are expected to show competence in what is taught before moving to another unit.

The Direct Instruction Model has the following characteristics:

Assumptions

1. All children, regardless of socio-economic status, are capable of mastering basic academic skills.
2. Teaching failure is not excused.
3. Children from disadvantaged homes have less well developed prerequisite skills necessary for academic achievement.
4. Students from disadvantaged homes must be taught more in less time in order to catch up with other students.

The Rationale for Six Essential Teaching Components in the Direct Instruction Model

1. Teach the general case. By teaching a subset, the whole set is learned. For example, by teaching 40 sounds and skills for blending them together and saying them fast, generalized decoding skill, relevant to one-half of the common English words, is learned.
2. Use teacher aides in direct instruction. This increases the number of instructors in a classroom.
3. Daily program is carefully structured. Routines are established so that time is used efficiently.
4. Maintain student attention. This is done through rapid paced, teacher-directed, small group instruction.
5. Provide training and supervision. Teachers are carefully trained and supervised to ensure

that appropriate skills are taught and utilized in the classroom.

6. Maintain quality control. Student progress is monitored with bi-weekly, criterion-referenced tests which help to detect problems while there is time to correct them.

The Rationale for Distinctive Features of the Direct Instruction Model

1. Scripted presentation of the lessons. The purpose is to provide quality control in the instructional delivery system.
2. Small group instruction. It is more efficient than one-to-one instruction and allows for better supervision than large group instruction.
3. Reinforcement. Although most people would agree that learning should be its own reward, there are many students who need extensive rewards to encourage learning. Hence, token economies may be used for students who do not respond to games, praise, or attention.
4. Training and supervision. Teachers are trained to use this approach to reading and are supervised to ensure implementation of instructional methods.
5. Program design. Utilizes task analysis, specifying objectives, analysis of objectives into component subskills, identifying prerequisite skills, selecting examples and sequencing the skills.

FIGURE 13–1

Assumptions and characteristics of the direct instruction model

EFFECTIVE READING PROGRAMS

So far we have discussed effective teaching from the perspective of the interactions that take place between students and teachers as well as between students and their peers. This section presents a brief discussion of the general factors that have been found to correlate with effective reading **instructional programs.** As usual, the effective programs are defined in terms of high student achievement scores. In discussing these factors, *program* is defined as everything that is included in and contributes to reading instruction. An instructional method, therefore, is only one part of an instructional program. Samuels (1981, p. 256) summarizes this point:

instructional program: The entire set of factors involved in reading instruction.

> in addition to the reading method, other components which can affect program outcome include staff, administration, parents, and students. Thus, a program can be thought of as a set of interrelated components consisting of human, material, and procedural factors which influence the extent to which institutional objectives are realized.

Samuels presents an excellent overview of research that has examined factors common to successful instructional programs in reading. He reviewed the findings of six major research projects that focused on the issue of program effectiveness and presented their common findings. These are summarized here.

1. Staff in effective reading programs hold the belief that the school can make a difference, and that responsibility for student achievement (including failure) rests with the teacher and the school. Teachers take primary responsibility for their students' progress. They also assume that most students are capable of learning basic academic skills.
2. All personnel throughout the school were committed to a successful program. Administrative leadership and support were found to be important, as was the inclusion of well-trained teacher aides in the instructional program. Reading specialists were involved in training teachers and aides, rather than in remedial work with students.
3. Everyone realized that change comes slowly and that implementation of a new program requires at least two years of unhurried planning time and better implementation of effective teaching practices.
4. The curriculum was composed of clear, specific objectives, with material to be taught divided into manageable components that are sequentially taught. Ample time for practice was provided.
5. Available instructional time was used efficiently. Successful programs used the majority of available time on structured learning activities rather than transitional aspects such as collecting papers or handing out books.

6. Teachers were structured and were good classroom managers. Established routines were often used to facilitate movement of students and materials.
7. Student progress was frequently monitored. Evaluation took place after subskills were taught, as well as at consistent, longer intervals. This allowed diagnosis and remediation.

You may want to compare these findings to the six points advocated by Rosenshine presented earlier in this chapter. Although Samuels focuses on effective programs and Rosenshine examines effective practices, you should see much similarity.

A CONCLUDING STATEMENT

This chapter discussed findings of several research projects aimed at discovering effective teaching practices in reading instruction. In doing so, we attempted to translate the findings into suggestions for ways that teachers might best interact with students to enhance instruction. Findings have been presented that argue that teachers need to be well organized in the classroom and well prepared before the class begins. This helps ensure that time is used to meet specific instructional goals.

We also attempted to provide knowledge about peer interactions in group situations and ways that teachers might deal with unwanted dominance by certain members of a group. Similarly, we tried to provide cautions about teacher questioning techniques that might lower certain students' self-images and that might inadvertently, and inappropriately, differentiate between the types of questions asked of students whose abilities vary. This was related to teachers' perceptions of students' abilities in a discussion of the self-fulfilling prophecy and how teacher perceptions might influence student achievement.

Throughout this chapter, we stressed that the findings presented here are those that have been found by several researchers in a number of research studies. What we presented, therefore, are consistent findings. Several of the questions and activities at the end of the chapter are designed to make you think about ways to incorporate what was presented into your personal framework of reading. We strongly suggest that you take the time to work through the questions.

We have also noted that the effective teaching practices discussed in this chapter can, in some sense, be applied within all frameworks of reading. Yet teachers who have mastery of specific skills explanations for how reading ability develops are more comfortable with the direct instruction model than are teachers with holistic explanations for how reading ability develops. This is because the direct instruction model, as noted earlier, is most effective with specific skills that are directly taught and measured for mastery.

The direct instruction model is a teacher-centered approach. Teachers who have a holistic explanation for how reading ability develops may want less structure than is usually seen in the direct instruction model. While the direct instruction model works best when there is a prescribed curriculum based on mastery of specific skills, teachers with alternative explanations often teach based on students' language and experiential base. This does not always allow a narrow constraint on what is to be taught, since curriculum may be determined based on readers' needs at given points in time rather than potentially on mastery of predetermined skills.

Teachers with comprehension frameworks that include differential acquisition explanations for how reading ability develops may teach specific skills at lower grade levels or to less proficient readers. They may use the direct instruction model more comfortably at lower rather than higher grade levels, moving to more holistic approaches as readers become more proficient.

Finally, you may feel that the research on effective teaching practices (that is, effective teacher-student interactions) are really based on common sense. In fact, research in this area has been criticized precisely for its strong **intuitive base.** You are urged to carefully consider Smith's (1983, p. 489) response to one who makes such a criticism.

intuitive base: The use of instructional practices or the acceptance of findings or claims due to common sense or general feelings regarding accuracy.

> . . . we have had some effective teachers for a long time, but we did not know precisely what they did or how and when they did it. What you point to now as facts we have always known you have acquired from recent literature. It strikes you as so plausible that you think you have always known them. To know that clarity is essential to good teaching is not the same as knowing what clear discourse is or how teachers who are clear in their teaching actually perform. Yes, we have always known that children are not likely to learn unless they are aware of their mistakes and how to correct them. But it took the work of Thorndike to show us that we do not learn unless we are aware of the outcome of our effort and that such awareness is a necessary, though not sufficient, condition for learning. We now call this "feedback," and it has taken many hours of research to discover for us the characteristics of effective feedback, characteristics of which we had no previous knowledge. Yes, we have a long way to go before we have a highly developed scientific pedagogy, but we have come a long way.

1. There are consistent research results indicating that certain teaching behaviors are related to student achievement. These behaviors include clear lesson structure, appropriate questioning, provision of different kinds of practice, pacing instruction, and classroom management.

THE MAJOR POINTS

2. Organized teachers take time to prepare beforehand and use little instructional time for management activities. This relates to more student time on task, which has been found to correlate highly with achievement.

3. The structure of small groups and the perceptions of each others' abilities by the students within the group influences participatory behavior.

4. Teacher expectations, the type of questions they ask, and their behavior toward students influence a student's perception of self and influence achievement.

QUESTIONS AND ACTIVITIES

1. How do the factors that are associated with effective reading instruction fit into your framework of reading? (Look back at the six aspects as summarized in table 13–1.)

2. Look back at classroom scenario 2. Rewrite the scenario so that it more closely uses the knowledge we have about effective reading instruction.

3. Pretend you are being interviewed for a teaching job by an elementary school principal. The principal has just stated that a commitment has recently been made to make the school a model of effective reading instruction. You are then asked to discuss your views on effective instructional reading programs and to provide some suggestions as to what the school will need to do to reach the stated goal. What would you say?

4. How are effective use of instructional time and teachers' organizational and managerial skills related?

5. Discuss the concept of time on task and explain how teachers can use this concept in reading instruction.

6. Pretend you will be teaching a unit on main idea to a group of second-grade students. Write a detailed lesson plan that clearly incorporates what you know about effective instructional practices. Do the same for a lesson on short vowels intended for first graders.

7. Find one basal reader teacher's manual for any grade level. Does the manual present a discussion of effective teaching practices? (This might be in a section discussing the general format or structure of the lessons in the manual, or in a separate section.) How does it deal with the issue of effective teaching?

8. Using the same basal reader teacher's manual, examine several suggested lessons or lesson plans. How is what you know about effective teaching practices incorporated into the lesson? If necessary, how would you have to modify the plan to incorporate your knowledge?

Berliner, D. C. (1981). Academic learning time and reading achievement. In Guthrie, J. T. (ed.). *Comprehension and teaching: research reviews,* Newark, DE: IRA.

A basic discussion of how time on task relates to organization and to students' reading achievement.

Durkin, D. (1984). Is there a match between what elementary teachers do and what basal reader manuals recommend? *The Reading Teacher, 37,* 734–44.

A discussion of the relationship between basal reader instructional guides and teaching behaviors.

Guzzetti, B. J. & Marzano, R. J. (1984). Correlates of effective reading instruction. *The Reading Teacher, 37,* 754–58.

A basic introduction to reading teachers' behaviors as they relate to effective instruction.

Hoffman, J. (ed.). (1986). Effective teaching of reading: Research and practice. Newark, DE: International Reading Association.

A readable volume by a number of authors. Papers range from a history of research, to correlates, to future directions in effective teaching from both a research and implementation perspective.

FURTHER READING

Allington, R. L. (1980). Teacher interruption behaviors during primary grade oral reading. *Journal of Educational Psychology, 72,* 371–77.

Anderson, L. M.; Evertson, C. M. & Brophy, J. E. (1979). An experimental study of effective teaching in first-grade reading groups. *Elementary School Journal, 79,* 193–222.

Baghban, M. (1984). *Our daughter learns to read and write: A case study from birth to three.* Newark, DE: International Reading Association.

Berliner, D. C. (1981). Academic learning time and reading achievement. In J. T. Guthrie (ed.). *Comprehension and teaching: research reviews,* Newark, DE: IRA.

Brookower, V.; Schweitzer, J.; Scheider, J.; Beady, C.; Flood, P.; & Weisenbarker, J. (1978). Elementary school social climate and school achievement. *American Educational Research Journal, 15,* 301–18.

Brophy, J. (1979). Teacher behavior and its effects. *Journal of Educational Psychology, 71,* 733–50.

Cohen, E. G. (1982). Expectation states and interracial interaction in school settings. In R. H. Turner & J. F. Short (eds.). *Annual Review of Sociology, 8,* 209–35.

DeStefano, J. & Pepinsky, H. (1981). *The learning of discourse rules of culturally different children in first-grade literacy instruction.* (Final Report, NIE G-79-0032). Washington, DC: NIE.

Durkin, D. (1984). Is there a match between what elementary teachers do and what basal reader manuals recommend? *The Reading Teacher, 37,* 734–44.

Evertson, C.; Anderson, C.; Anderson, L.; & Brophy, J. (1980). Relationship between classroom behaviors and student outcomes in junior high mathematics and English classes. *American Education Research Journal, 17,* 43–60.

Fisher, C. W.; Berliner, D. C.; Filby, N. N.; Marliave, R.; Cahen, L. S.; & Dishaw, N. M. (1980). Teaching behaviors, academic learning time, and student achievement: An overview. In C. Denham & A. Lieberman (eds.), *Time to learn.* Washington, DC: United States Department of Education.

Gage, N. & Giaconia, R. (1981). Teaching practices and student achievement: Causal connections. *New York University Education Quarterly 13,* 2–9.

Good, T. (1979). Teacher effectiveness in elementary school: What we know about it now. *Journal of Teacher Education, 30,* 52–64.

Good, T. L. & Grouws, D. A. (1979). The Missouri mathematics effectiveness project. *Journal of Educational Psychology 71,* 355–62.

REFERENCES

Green, J. & Harker, J. (1982). Gaining access to learning: Conversational, social, and cognitive demands of group participation. In L. C. Wilkinson (ed.), *Communicating in the classroom.* New York: Academic Press.

Green, J. & Wallat, C. (eds.). (1981). *Ethnography and language in educational settings.* Norwood, NJ: Ablex.

Green, J. L. & Smith, D. (1983). Teaching and learning: A linguistic perspective. *Elementary School Journal, 83,* pp. 353–91.

Guzzetti, B. J. & Marzano, R. J. (1984). Correlates of effective reading instruction. *The Reading Teacher 37,* 754–58.

Harste, J.; Woodward, V.; Burke, C. (1984). *Language stories and literacy lessons.* Portsmouth, NH: Heineman Books.

Hymes, D. (1981). *Ethnographic monitoring project.* (Final Report, NIE–G–78–0038). Washington, DC: NIE.

Nash, R. (1976). Pupils' expectations of their teachers. In M. Stubbs & S. Delamont (eds.), *Explorations in classroom observation.* New York: Wiley.

Rosenholtz, S. J. (1984). Modifying a status-organizing process of the traditional classroom. In J. Berger & M. Zelditch Jr. (ed.) *Pure and applied studies in expectation states theory,* San Francisco: Jossey-Bass.

Rosenholtz, S. J. & Cohen, E. G. (1983). Back to basics and the desegregated school. *Elementary School Journal 83,* 515–27.

Rosenshine, B. (1983). Teaching functions in instructional programs. *Elementary School Journal 83,* 335–51.

Rosenshine, B. & Berliner, D. (1978). Academic engaged time. *British Journal of Teacher Education 4,* 3–16.

Rowe, M. B. (1974). Wait-time and rewards as instructional variables: Their influence on language, logic and fate control. Part I. Wait time. *Journal of Research in Science Teaching 11,* 81–94.

Samuels, S. J. (1981). Characteristics of exemplary reading programs. In J. T. Guthrie (ed.). *Comprehension and teaching: research reviews.* Newark, DE: IRA.

Smith, B. O. (1983). Some comments on educational research in the twentieth century. *Elementary School Journal 83,* 487–492.

Stallings, J.; Needles, M; & Stayrook, N. (1979). *How to change the process of teaching basic reading skills in secondary schools.* Menlo Park, CA: SRI International.

Swift, J. N. & Gooding, C. T. (1983). Interaction of wait time feedback and questioning instruction in middle school science teaching. *Journal of Research on Science Teaching 20,* 721–730.

Tobin, K. G. & Capie, W. (1982). Relationships between classroom process variables and middle school science achievement. *Journal of Educational Psychology 74,* 441–54.

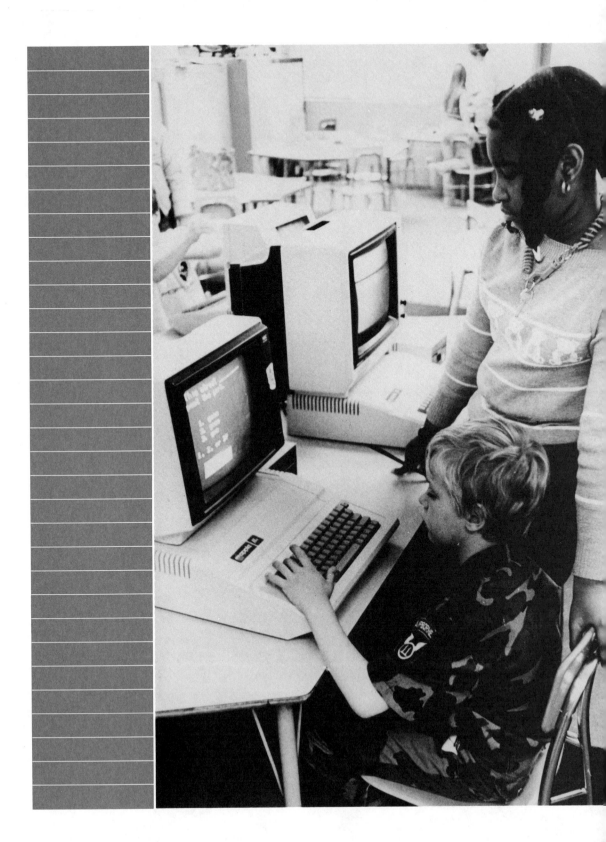

14 Microcomputers in the Reading Classroom

A MODEL OF MICROCOMPUTER USE FOR THE READING
CLASSROOM ■ BASIC COMPUTER LITERACY CONCEPTS FOR THE
READING TEACHER ■ SPECIFIC USES OF MICROCOMPUTERS IN
READING INSTRUCTION ■ FINDING, CHOOSING, AND EVALUATING
SOFTWARE ■ INSTRUCTIONAL FRAMEWORKS AND MICROCOMPUTER
TECHNOLOGY

"Wait a minute! This is exactly like something I saw on television." . . .
"See," Linda went on, pausing to get a tray, "this boy and girl started
communicating by computer, and they met at McDonald's and fell in love."
. . .
"Linda, this is nothing like that program. I don't know who sent this message.
It could have been a girl or a boy or a ninety-year-old man. You don't
understand—."
"Of course I don't understand. How could I? I have never in my life touched a
computer that it didn't go, 'ILLEGAL COMMAND.' . . ."

From Betsy Byars, *The Computer Nut.* (New York: Viking Press, 1984), pp. 15–16.

I n chapter 1 we asked you to keep in mind that first-grade students will graduate from college (should they choose to attend) sixteen years after they begin formal instruction in reading. We also noted that the technology of instruction will increasingly reflect changes and trends in the general use of technology in society. The increasing availability and use of **microcomputers** in society is paralleled in schools. This chapter discusses various uses of microcomputers, based on a five-stage model. Its goal is to provide you with a working knowledge of microcomputer use in reading instruction, as well as to enable you to intelligently evaluate and choose both presently available software and the more sophisticated programs still to be developed.

After reading this chapter, you will be able to

1. discuss how the increased availability of microcomputers in schools will affect reading instruction;
2. use a working knowledge of what can and should be done to integrate microcomputers into a reading instructional program;
3. use microcomputers for different applications in reading instruction;
4. discuss how microcomputers fit into your framework of reading.

A MODEL OF MICROCOMPUTER USE FOR THE READING CLASSROOM

By now you will have realized that the reading teacher's job is a demanding one, requiring skills of management and decision making while designing curriculum and imparting knowledge, information, and skills. There are those who view microcomputers in education as a force that will radically change instructional practice, almost replacing the teacher. Others, however, believe that the microcomputer is an expensive fad—which will ultimately die as school systems realize that instruction requires a human quality that can never be supplanted by electronics.

We feel that neither view adequately reflects the potential educational enhancements that can be provided by thoughtful implementation of microcomputers into the reading curriculum. We view the microcomputer as an educational tool that reflects society's technological advancements. Although the microcomputer can be a good tool for reading instruction, it also can be misused and lead to detriments in learning. This is true of all technology and teaching materials. For example, basal readers or ditto machines provide no more guarantee of benefitting instruction than do microcomputers. The key element is the teacher, who must make appropriate decisions regarding the use of the basal reader or what to ditto, or what software to assign to a student.

microcomputer: A self-contained computer system generally used in homes, schools, or small businesses.

BEFORE READING ON

Think of different ways in which microcomputers might be useful to both reading teachers and their students. Try to address possible uses beyond student drill and practice.

Taylor (1980) has suggested that the computer has three potential functions, tutor, tool, and tutee. By tutor, he meant that the computer can be a patient instructor, providing practice exercises or information. Used as a tool, the computer can be an aid to the teacher, perhaps providing record-keeping or other functions. Finally, as a tutee, the computer has the capability to be programmed or "educated," in contrast to the tutor function where the computer is seen as doing the educating.

Taylor's classification system was modified by Luehrmann (1982), who renamed the functions as learning about computers, learning from computers, and learning with computers. More recently, Goldberg and Sherwood (1982) have expanded Luehrmann's categories to include managing learning with computers and learning about thinking with computers. We present this classification system as a five-part model that includes present and potential uses in the reading classroom. Throughout this chapter, we will refer to the five categories to present a scheme for implementing and using microcomputers in reading instruc-

A microcomputer system will sometimes be placed in a central location for teachers' use.

hardware: The parts of a computer and its peripheral equipment that are fixed; for example, the video screen.

program: In this sense, a set of instructions that tells the computer what to do.

BASIC: A programming language commonly distributed with most microcomputers used in education.

Pascal: A more structured computer language than BASIC.

Logo: A popular computer language that uses simple commands and is easy to program for graphics.

applications software: Programs that are useful in everyday life, for example, word-processing software.

spreadsheet: A computer applications program that allows entry of data in rows and columns for later manipulation.

tion, as well as to discuss useful software. Table 14–1 presents an overview and examples of the five categories of computer use.

Learning about Computers in the Reading Classroom

As table 14–1 notes, this category deals mainly with computer literacy. When students learn about the computer, they learn about its components, or **hardware,** as well as its common peripheral equipment such as printers. This category also includes learning to **program** computers in any one of many computer languages; in education, usually **BASIC, Pascal,** or **Logo.**

Also often included in the learning about computers category is an introduction to the most useful generic or **applications software:** word processing; filing; and **spreadsheet** programs. In this category, such software is generally taught to demonstrate the potential usefulness of computers in everyday life. Some of this depends, of course, on the age of the students being instructed, but there are programs available in each of these applications areas that can be used with children in primary grades.

Since your concern will be reading instruction, learning about computers will not be a primary focus in your classroom. Yet you will need to ensure that students know enough about the equipment to use it intelligently. For example, to effectively perform specific activities related to your reading instructional program, your students will need to know how your particular microcomputer turns on and off, how to load

TABLE 14–1

A classification system of computer use

Classification	Examples
Learning about Computers	Computer literacy. This includes learning about the equipment as well as learning programming languages.
Learning from Computers	Drill and practice. This includes most games and tutorial software.
Learning with Computers	Simulations. This includes software modeling a real-world situation and attempting to enhance problem-solving abilities.
Learning about Thinking with Computers	Problem solving. This includes the influence that working with computers and some types of software potentially has on students' thinking skills.
Managing Learning with Computers	Classroom management. This includes record-keeping, filing, and other such functions.

and run specific software, how to use the printer, and so on. This chapter has a section dealing with basic issues in computer literacy. It is not intended to replace a course in computers for educators, but if you know little about such technology, it will provide a basis for future, more detailed understanding.

Learning from Computers

In this category, the computer acts as a drill-and-practice instructor, with communication being a relatively one-way affair: from microcomputer to student. Most of the applications in learning from computers are in the area of drill-and-practice software, but tutorial and gaming software also falls into this category.

Drill-and-Practice Software. Although software in the learning from computer category is often criticized, **drill-and-practice software** is the most commonly available software specifically marketed for reading instruction. In this kind of software, the student is presented with a series of questions to which responses are expected. A correct response results in some form of feedback and a new question. An incorrect response results in feedback and the opportunity for another try at the correct answer. If the answer is still incorrect, most drill-and-practice software programs give the answer and move to a new question. Such software usually keeps records of students' responses and provides either the student, teacher, or both with the students' overall score. Such software is available in all skill areas of reading, from initial sounds to finding main ideas. The following is an example of a typical session that a student might have with a drill-and-practice program.

drill-and-practice software: Nonteaching programs that do not go beyond activities intended to reinforce knowledge.

Software for Drill and Practice on Prefixes

This is a lesson on PREFIXES.
Please tell me your name: <student enters *Tony*>

Hello, Tony. I will show you a sentence with a word underlined. That word will have a PREFIX. You will have to tell me the prefix and choose what it means from a list of choices. Here is your first question:

> That water is <u>impure</u>.

> The prefix in <u>impure</u> is: <student enters response>

> (If incorrect, student is told the answer is not right and is asked to try again. If correct, the program continues. . . .)

> Good for you! You're right! The prefix in <u>impure</u> is <u>im</u>.

**MODEL
LESSON**

```
In impure, the prefix im means
     a.  with
     b.  in
     c.  not
Choose one of the meanings: <student responds>
```

(If incorrect, the student is told the answer is not right and is asked to try again. If correct, the student receives feedback and the program continues with the drill and practice exercise. At the conclusion of the program, the student is presented with the number correct and number attempted.)

Drill-and-practice software is common because it is easy to program. Yet many drill-and-practice programs are little more than computerized worksheets. If this is true, then one should seriously consider whether the microcomputer provides an advantage over the worksheet. In fact, availability of a program such as that described in the model lesson may not be sufficient reason to justify purchase of a microcomputer for your class.

BEFORE READING ON

What is the role and value of drill and practice in a reading lesson? What would your purpose(s) be in assigning students to worksheets or computer software for drill and practice?

Yet drill and practice, if used appropriately, has a place in a lesson. It is appropriately used after teaching and initial learning has taken place. It does not teach; it only reinforces what has already been taught. This is as true for paper-and-pencil worksheets as it is for microcomputer software. Reinforcement, however, is an important part of learning.

Even in the drill-and-practice area, however, microcomputers may have several advantages over worksheets. Microcomputers appear to stimulate and motivate students to a greater extent than do workbooks. Students spend more time, even when tasks are similar, on computer drill and practice than on worksheets. Yet the recent decline in popularity of video games may be an indication that this is due to a novel experience rather than due to some inherently motivational aspect of the microcomputer.

Further, the capacity for drill-and-practice software to tabulate student scores so that teachers can be relieved of the burden of manually checking student answers is not trivial. Teachers can quickly see who has understood a concept or who needs additional instruction, and are thus given needed information which forms part of the decision-making process.

Also, the microcomputer, together with well-written drill-and-practice software, can present items more closely matched to student ability level than can a workbook. For example, if a student answers three consecutive problems incorrectly, the software can **branch** to items of less difficulty. The reverse, of course, can take place if a student responds correctly a predetermined number of times. Not all drill-and-practice software includes branching capabilities, however.

branch: The selection of one of several possible responses by a computer program based on its user's input.

Tutorial Software. Tutorial software also is part of the learning-from-computer category. While drill-and-practice software does not teach a new concept, tutorial software is designed so that a student can learn as well as practice. The following illustration, also on prefixes, provides an example (modified from Hasselbring & Cavanaugh, 1986).

tutorial software: Programs that attempt to teach as well as reinforce concepts.

Software for Tutorial on Prefixes

MODEL LESSON

```
This is a lesson on PREFIXES.
Please tell me your name: <student enters Tony>

Hello, Tony. Let me tell you about prefixes.

A prefix is found at the beginning of a word.
It almost always changes the meaning of the word.

re is a prefix
re means back or again.

Replace means to place back.
Replay means to play again.


Tony, read this sentence:
Sue repaid the money she owed Mary.

This means:
Sue paid back the money she owed Mary.

Re can mean back.
Repaid means paid back.

Read this sentence:
The corn must be replanted.

This means:
The corn must be planted again.

Re means again.
Replanted means planted again.
```

Try these activities, Tony.
Draw a line under all letters in the
prefix by pressing the → key.

Underline the Prefix

repaint

(if the student correctly underlines *re,* the computer responds with:)

THAT'S RIGHT, Tony.

repaint means to paint again

(if the student incorrectly underlines the prefix, the program responds with:)

TRY AGAIN, Tony.

(if the response is still incorrect, the program responds with:)

No, the answer is re.
Repaint means to paint again.

(The program continues until there are no more items in the lesson or, in some programs, until the student elects to stop. Most tutorial programs provide the student and/or the teacher with an indication of number correct, number attempted, and overall progress.)

Note that tutorial software goes beyond a simple presentation of items to which a student responds. Tutorial programs are written so that someone is taught a concept that is later drilled. Further, tutorial software almost always includes branches that attempt to move the student into further presentation and practice, as appropriate. The inclusion of explanation, beyond simple feedback, and a request to try again if a response is incorrect, completes the basic differences between drill-and-practice and tutorial software.

Although tutorial software is preferred by teachers over simple drill-and-practice offerings, it too can be misused. You will need to remember that, while the computer can patiently present a tutorial, it cannot decide whether the tutorial includes content that is important in a student's reading development, or whether the content, format, sequencing of concepts, pacing, and other factors are appropriate to your instructional program, the reading process, or reading instruction in general.

gaming software:
Computer programs that use games or gamelike formats to teach and reinforce concepts.

Gaming Software. The motivational potential of microcomputers is most obvious in software that presents material, whether drill and practice or tutorial, in a game format. **Gaming software** uses the color, sound, and animation capabilities of microcomputers to catch and hold student attention. These are used to present instruction in a format allowing a student to play against others or the computer while learning.

As microcomputers that feature advanced **graphics** and sound become less expensive and more available in schools, software that teaches in a game format will become more and more prevalent. Although teachers need to be careful that the concepts being presented are not overshadowed by the peripheral aspects of the presentation, well-constructed gaming software that is pedagogically sound has great potential for instruction.

Awareness of several problems with gaming software will help ensure that software is chosen for its educational rather than gaming value. First, gaming software often has violent overtones. One must carefully evaluate these programs and consider their consequences. Second, problems with reinforcement can occur if getting a wrong answer is more interesting than getting an answer correct. For example, seeing something explode, in full color and with sound, may tend to motivate errors if a correct response only has a written "good for you" statement. Third, the instructional value of gaming software must be closely examined. Students must be learning while using the program, not simply playing a game. This relates to potential dangers in that gaming software is sometimes used far beyond its value. That is, students like to play the game and may continue to use the software with the teacher's blessing long after the concept the software teaches has been mastered. In this case, instructional time is being used inappropriately, since students should have moved on to learning new items.

To illustrate how gaming software might appear to a student, imagine that a student is learning prefixes in a format modeled after the *Space Invaders* video game. At the top of the screen, several prefixes appear, enclosed in various shapes and in different colors, and begin to move down the screen. At the bottom of the screen a definition is presented inside a cannon. The student must fire the definition at the appropriate prefix. The object, of course, is to "shoot" all the prefixes with their definitions before they reach the bottom of the screen. Such a format is also used to teach typing, where different letters float to the bottom of the screen. If a student successfully presses the proper keys in the correct order, the letters disappear and the student wins the game. Consider, however, the comments in the previous paragraph about such software, and be aware that these types of gaming programs involve things such as eye-hand coordination and reflexes—which may cause incorrect responses due to factors unrelated to learning to read.

Learning with Computers

Software in this category also attempts to teach rather than only to provide practice, but it provides a much richer context for the student. Mi-

graphics: Items that are drawings rather than text or numerical displays.

learning with computers: Simulations that actively involve students.

simulations:
Presentations of events similar to those found in the real world.

crocomputers in the science and social studies content areas have been used for some time to present **simulations.** Although this type of software is less prevalent in reading education than in other subject areas, it holds tremendous potential for teachers of reading. Microcomputers have the ability to present simulations (models of real-world events or situations) and thus allow students to "experience" things that are impossible to experience in the classroom. Some of these experiences might be too dangerous, too time consuming, or simply unavailable to students. For example, simulations dealing with mixing dangerous chemical compounds or studying the ecology of a lake as an active participant are commonly used in science.

Simulation software presents situations and expects the student to become a participant in solving problems as they are presented in the context of the situations. In social studies, for example, a program called *Oregon Trail* presents a simulation where the student is an explorer moving through the wilderness, attempting to reach a fort. As the journey proceeds, the student must make decisions about how and where to travel, how much money to spend on things such as supplies and ammunition, when to stop and where to camp, and generally is faced with problems along the way.

Another popular simulation, *Odell Lake,* is used in science ecology lessons. This software teaches the food chain by having students pretend they are a fish in a pond. The student is confronted with other fish and situations where they must make decisions about running from predators, chasing fish that are food sources, or ignoring things that are nonthreatening. As a result, the student learns about this particular food chain.

In reading education, some simulation software allows a student to learn that plot development depends on a series of decisions. That is, students learn that later developments in a story are constrained by what happens earlier. Simulations allow students to become a character in a story and make decisions about that character's actions. As the plot changes based on what the student's character does, plot development is learned.

Similarly, other software simulates writing a newspaper article, making the student a reporter who is sent out to get a story. The student must search out pertinent facts and write the story, submitting it to the "editor" (the computer) who checks key words in the story to determine whether the facts have been correctly interpreted and presented. The editor then provides the student feedback about the logic of the facts chosen, as well as providing hints for rewriting the story. A specific objective of such software is to teach who, why, what, when, where, and how questions.

Simulation software generally use all of the color, sound, and graphics capabilities available to the microcomputer, as well as providing record-keeping functions for the teacher. The same cautions presented for tutorial software apply here. You will have to decide whether the skill being presented is appropriate to your instructional program and framework.

Learning about Thinking with Computers

Recently, there have been claims that working with computers and with certain programming languages generalizes certain problem-solving strategies to areas beyond the computer (Papert, 1980). These claims are closely related to the tutee category originally used by Taylor (1980). In general, the proponents of this view argue that the computer can be used in one of two ways: either the computer dominates the situation, in effect controlling the student; or the student dominates the situation, controlling the computer.

In the former, the computer might be viewed as teaching the student, presenting content, questions, and feedback, as well as branching to appropriate difficulty levels. In the latter view, the student teaches the computer—usually through programming. Teachers often say that to really learn something, one should attempt to teach it to others. This is the rationale for a student's using the computer as a tutee.

Among the main advocates of the potential of microcomputers to influence thinking and problem-solving abilities through programming is Seymore Papert and his colleagues, developers of the Logo computer language. In fact, most of the advocates of using Logo in schools believe that working with Logo will have positive effects across the school curriculum, although such claims are more often heard for mathematics than for other areas. Similar claims, however, have been made for teaching students to program and work with microcomputers using **structured BASIC,** another common computer language. In fact, Luehrmann (1983; 1984a, b, c) advocates using structured BASIC programming precisely because he feels that teaching BASIC in this way influences the development of logical thinking skills. Such claims, however, must be carefully considered. There are, as yet, few consistent research findings, and some conflicting evidence, regarding these viewpoints.

An illustration of how programming might be related to reading skills follows. Consider this example program:

```
10   PRINT "HOW OLD ARE YOU?"
20   INPUT A
30   IF A > 10 THEN PRINT "THAT'S NICE!"
40   IF A < 11 THEN PRINT "GREAT!"
RUN
```

This program asks the user's age, waits for a response and, depending on whether the age given is more than 10 or less than 11, prints

learning about thinking with computers: Refers to the claims that using certain kinds of programs or performing certain kinds of activities using a computer will enhance general problem-solving and thinking skills.

structured BASIC: A way of teaching BASIC that uses logical modules.

either "That's nice!" or "Great!". Note that the way in which the computer responds depends on the student's answer. IF-THEN statements in the computer program allow different responses to the user.

IF-THEN statements might be considered somewhat similar to cause-and-effect relationships in reading. Although one must be cautious before advocating such uses as a major part of a reading instructional program, teachers may find that relating such simple programs to other cause-and-effect examples may help clarify this concept for some students. Although research in the area of learning about thinking with computers is relatively new, it is possible that it will yield benefits to certain areas of reading instruction in the future.

Another example of possible similarity between programming and reading is that in both one needs to be aware of possible outcomes. When programming, students need to keep in mind the expected outcome(s) for their program, as well as being aware of the fact that what they will be able to do later in the program results from their earlier decisions. This may parallel what the reader must do in anticipating and hypothesizing possible outcomes during reading.

Finally, although simulations were discussed under the learning-with-computers category, they really bridge into the learning-about-thinking category as well. Simulations have traditionally been developed mainly to teach specific content. In this light, they may be placed in the former category. Yet simulation software requires students to make decisions and anticipate the consequences of their actions. It may be that general thinking skills are also being developed and that simulation software goes beyond simply imparting information. If this is true (as yet there is no research specifically addressing this issue), then simulations may also be placed in the learning-about-thinking category. If simulation software does in fact both teach specific content and expand general thinking skills, then the category in which you place this software will depend on your instructional goal for the simulation you are using with your students.

managing learning with computers: The use of computers to perform everyday, work-related functions.

Managing Learning with Computers

BEFORE READING ON

What are some of the management functions faced by the reading teacher? How could a microcomputer be used to aid the teacher in these tasks?

Reading teachers who have the use of one or more microcomputers in their classrooms often use them only with their students, forgetting that the machine can be used to make their jobs easier. There is an increasing amount of software available that can be used for keeping student

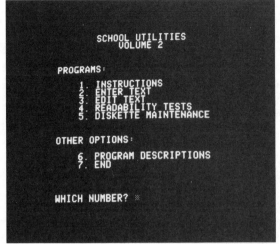

Screen one

```
         SCHOOL UTILITIES
             VOLUME 2

PROGRAMS:
     1. INSTRUCTIONS
     2. ENTER TEXT
     3. EDIT TEXT
     4. READABILITY TESTS
     5. DISKETTE MAINTENANCE

OTHER OPTIONS:
     6. PROGRAM DESCRIPTIONS
     7. END


WHICH NUMBER? ▓
```

Screen two

```
        - READABILITY TESTS -

WHERE DO YOU WANT THE TEXT DISPLAYED?
     ✱ S - ON THE SCREEN
       P - ON A PRINTER
       N - NOT DISPLAYED

WHERE DO YOU WANT THE WORD LIST?
     ✱ S - ON THE SCREEN
       P - ON A PRINTER
       N - NOT DISPLAYED

WHERE DO YOU WANT THE ANALYSIS?
     ✱ S - ON THE SCREEN
       P - ON A PRINTER
```

Screen three

```
          - READABILITY TESTS -
               PASSAGE 1

   NUMBER OF SENTENCES:            8

   NUMBER OF WORDS:              184

   NUMBER OF SYLLABLES:         269

   WORDS OF 6 OR MORE LETTERS:   58

   3 OR MORE SYLLABLE WORDS:     19

   % OF 3 OR MORE SYLLABLE WORDS: 10.3

   AVERAGE SENTENCE LENGTH:      23

   AVERAGE LETTERS PER WORD:     4.5

   AVERAGE SYLLABLES PER WORD:   1.5


       PRESS ▌SPACE BAR▐ TO CONTINUE
```

Software such as pictured here allows teachers to quickly perform a readability analysis using any or all of several formulas.

records, indicating student progress, tracking lunch money, writing form letters to parents, and other time-consuming functions.

Almost all publishers of basal reading series now also have microcomputer management systems available. These computerized systems are generally tied into the basal reader's criterion-referenced testing plan. The computerized system indicates to the teacher which students have mastered specific concepts and which might need additional help.

Additionally, the system indicates which lessons in the basal reader may be used to teach needed skills for specific students. With a printer attached, the basal management system often has the capability to write personalized notes to students or parents, thus providing encouragement and an indication of progress.

The microcomputer, together with filing system software, can be used to keep track of anything that normally requires time-consuming entries on file cards. For example, a classroom library can easily and quickly be entered into a computerized filing system, by author, title, reading difficulty level, topic area(s), genre, or any other descriptive area. Similarly, a file can be made of students' attitudes and interests as collected on attitude/interest inventories (see table 14–2).

Such a file system allows the teacher to quickly and easily choose or recommend reading material for a student based on, for example, the student's interest area. Or, conversely, the computer could search for any student(s) who might be interested in pet stories and for any books in the class library that are about pets. The teacher can then personalize motivational, supplementary reading for any student or group of students in the class.

We provide one more example of the use of microcomputers as helpful tools that can be used by teachers to lighten their loads. Think back to the discussion of cloze tests and reading formulas in chapter 10. There are several software programs that allow the teacher to create cloze tests, either on the screen or on paper. The teacher simply types in a passage and the computer deletes the appropriate words and replaces them with blanks. Most such software allow the teacher to specify

TABLE 14–2

Example of filing system software

```
AUTHOR      Silverstein, Shel
TITLE       Where the Sidewalk Ends
GENRE       Poetry
RDGLEVEL    All
DESCRIPTOR  Appropriate for all students.
COMMENT     No reading level or descriptors because the
            book has a variety of poems. In previous
            use, has been of high interest across all
            students/grades

STUDENT     Alex Smith
AGE         8
INTERESTS   Pets, Science Fiction, Poems, Cars, TV
RDGLEVEL    3.0
COMMENTS    Likes to read aloud to her friends—espe-
            cially poems.
```

which words (for example, every fifth or seventh) or types of words (for example, all nouns or adjectives) to delete. The test is then printed for student use or appears on the screen. If the cloze test appears on the screen for students' use, then the program scores the test (the microcomputer "remembers" the deletions for later comparison) and provides the teacher with a printout of each student's rating.

Readability analyses are also possible through microcomputer use. The teacher need only type in a passage and the computer will provide an analysis, often based on a choice of more than one readability formula. A listing of number of syllables, sentences, and other data on the passage is also often presented. Both cloze and readability software are available from commercial vendors, but can also be found in the **public domain.**

public domain:
Available for general use with no copyright restrictions.

BASIC COMPUTER LITERACY CONCEPTS FOR THE READING TEACHER

It is not the goal of this chapter to replace a course in computer literacy. Yet we feel that it is important for future teachers of reading to know about the technology which is finding its way into reading classrooms. Thus, the sections that follow provide a brief discussion of microcomputer systems that may be found in reading classes.

All microcomputers can be thought of as having three general parts. These parts can be different in different models or brands of machines, but all have these three components: a way of providing input to the computer (an input component); a memory/storage component; and an output component (see figure 14–1).

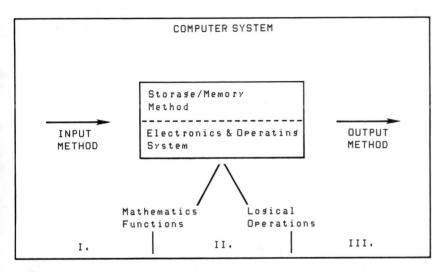

FIGURE 14–1

Schematic of a simple computer system

The components of a microcomputer system may be thought of in much the same way as a textbook. Textbooks differ in their number of chapters or the detail in the index, yet almost all have the same parts: table of contents; chapters; index; and so on. So, too, do different microcomputers have certain differences within their three basic components, but all have the same components. The following sections briefly discuss each of these three components. The discussions are not exhaustive, and limit themselves to input, memory/storage, and output devices that are commonly found in normal classroom settings.

Computer Input Devices

computer input device: Equipment that allows one to communicate with a computer, such as a keyboard.

central processing unit: The part of a computer that contains the circuitry and other necessities to execute commands and perform mathematical functions.

Before the computer can respond to a question, analyze data, or process words, the question, data, or words must be somehow communicated to the **central processing unit** (CPU)—what might be called the "brains" of the microcomputer. There are several ways that information can reach the processor. Five input devices are commonly used in education: keyboards; voice-activated input devices; joystick-type devices; and touch- and light-sensitive devices.

Keyboards are the most common input device used with microcomputers. They are very similar to typewriter keyboards and are used in the same manner. Yet there are several keys on a computer keyboard that do not appear on a normal typewriter. For example, most microcomputer keyboards have keys labeled DELETE (or DEL) and CONTROL (or CTRL). These keys allow specific commands to be entered into the microcomputer. Up-, down-, right-, and left-arrow keys are also common on computer keyboards. These allow the user to move to specific areas on the screen before touching a key that will input data. For example, if one typed "The big house" while word processing, and really wanted to type "The very big house", then the left arrow key would move you back in front of the word *big*.

The four other kinds of input devices found in school settings (voice-activated, joystick-type, and light- and touch-sensitive devices) are much less common than keyboards, but have great potential in education. Because their cost is already reasonable and continues to decrease, we believe they will become more common in the future. Their main advantage is for use with students who cannot, for one reason or another, type accurately on a keyboard. This includes young students who may lack the coordination necessary for accurate typing or handicapped students who may be **mainstreamed** into your classroom.

mainstreamed: Placing exceptional students into learning environments with non-exceptional students.

Computer Storage Devices

Once you have entered information into the microcomputer, you will want to save it for future use. For example, if you are writing letters to your students' parents, you may not finish the task in one sitting. You will want to store what you have written so that you can later continue from your point of departure.

Microcomputer systems store information in several ways. These storage systems may be compared to human memory. Theorists have described human memory as being composed of short-term and long-term memory. This is analogous to storage of data on microcomputers, which have two internal, built-in memory systems: **random-access memory (RAM)** and **read-only memory (ROM).** The former may be thought of as short-term memory; the latter, as long-term memory. Also, just as we might write something down and file it to access it and be able to remember it clearly at a later date, the microcomputer can write information on magnetic media (such as recording tape or diskettes) for later retrieval.

random-access memory (RAM): Computer memory installed at the factory. RAM can usually be easily expanded.
read-only memory (ROM): Computer memory installed at the factory. ROM is relatively difficult to change.

Read-only memory, or ROM, may be viewed as built-in long-term memory. Installed at the factory, ROM resides on a computer chip that has permanently encoded information on it. This information is generally what tells the computer what to do when the computer is turned on. It tells the computer to look for information from a long-term storage device or to print "Please insert a diskette into drive A" on the screen when the computer is first turned on. Different computers have different amounts of ROM. Information in ROM is not lost when the microcomputer is turned off.

Random-access memory (RAM) is memory that is also built into the microcomputer at the factory. This memory is electronic, with information stored on silicon computer chips. Since the factory determines how many chips are provided with the microcomputer, the amount of information that can be stored in RAM (that is, the amount of RAM) varies. When you see computers advertised as being 128K or 256K machines, the number refers to the amount of RAM that has been made available. Most microcomputers allow easy and relatively inexpensive ways to add more chips, thus expanding random-access memory. The amount of RAM is an important consideration when buying most software. If, for example, a program requires 128K or more memory, a microcomputer with only 64K of RAM will not be able to run the program.

When you enter information into a microcomputer and see it immediately echoed back to you on the computer screen, the information resides in RAM. If you were to turn off your microcomputer before giving a command to store the information on tape or diskette, it would be lost. Since turning off the microcomputer turns off the electric circuits on the chips where the information was stored, the information is irretrievable. For this reason RAM is often thought of as short-term memory. To keep information from being erased when the machine is turned off, data must be written to a long-term storage system.

The most common storage device in school settings is the floppy disk system, consisting of a disk drive and diskettes. Although cassette tape and recorders are still in use as storage devices, they are much slower and less accurate than diskette storage systems. There is, of course, a limited amount of information that can be stored on a storage device. The amount that can be stored on a diskette varies according to two factors: how densely the information is packed onto the diskette surface and whether both sides of a diskette can be used. The type of diskette format that a microcomputer uses for storage is determined by the microcomputer and disk drive used. Hard disks, consisting of metal plates with a recording surface, are more accurate, faster, and store more information than a floppy diskette. Since hard disks are becoming increasingly cheaper, they may become more prevalent in classrooms in the future.

Computer Output Devices

computer output device: Equipment that allows a computer to communicate with its user.

Output devices are used to communicate information in usable form from the microcomputer to the user. This information might be an echo of one's input on a screen or paper; a teacher's request for a student's score on a drill-and-practice exercise; a finished letter or document that has been prepared using the microcomputer as a word processor; the results of some numerical calculations that have been asked for through a statistics or other program; or the result of a request by a teacher using a cross-reference filing system to find book titles for students who are interested in baseball. In any case, some way for information to flow from the computer to the user must be present. The two most common output devices found in reading classrooms are video devices and printers.

Video devices, or monitors, are much like televisions and can be either monochrome (single color, usually white, green, or amber on black) or color units. Software that is written to include color graphics often will not work acceptably on video monitors that do not have color capabilities.

dot-matrix printer: A computer output device that prints by firing a series of small pins.

The other output device commonly used in classrooms is a printer. Printers are desirable for making copies for long-term use. They are of two general types: dot matrix and letter quality. **Dot-matrix printers** are fast (printing at about 120 characters per second) and inexpensive, but their print quality may not be acceptable for final copies of important documents, although they are completely adequate for classroom uses. Letter-quality printers are relatively slow and are substantially more expensive than dot-matrix printers, but produce print identical to high-quality, business typewriters.

The Compatibility Problem

One of the common questions teachers ask is whether programs written for one microcomputer will work on another and, if not, why not. In general, the answer is that most software is written for one microcomputer and that it will not run on other microcomputers. This is because each microcomputer has an **operating system** that controls what the machine will do. One part of the operating system allows blank diskettes to be **formatted** into a form readable by a particular machine.

Operating systems are generally machine specific. The operating system that controls an Apple IIc will not control an IBM-PC. In fact, some operating systems written for identical machines are not compatible. Thus, it is the operating system that causes much of the compatibility problem. Most software, however, is available in a number of formats for use in the microcomputers most commonly found in schools. When ordering software, be sure to specify the make, as well as the model, the operating system, and amount of RAM available in the microcomputer, on which the software will be used.

operating system: Software that forms the command structure and characteristics that make one computer incompatible with another.
format: In this sense, the structure of a diskette that allows it to be read by a particular computer.

Computer Languages and Reading Teachers

Reading educators may have the initial reaction that there is little or no need for them to have a sophisticated knowledge of computer programming, and we agree. Yet rudimentary knowledge may facilitate appropriate use of a microcomputer, in all its aspects, in reading instruction. Teachers need not be programmers to use a microcomputer just as teachers have no need to be textbook authors in order to use a textbook. But an understanding of the parts of a textbook help in its use, and a general knowledge of programming languages and how they function will alleviate some fears you may have about computers and will also clarify some potential uses.

Future teachers may wish to develop an introductory knowledge of BASIC and Logo—the most common languages currently used in education. Reading teachers should make an effort to become aware of how these languages might be used as potential examples to illustrate aspects of reading. Although teaching such languages is beyond the scope of this book, courses in computer literacy for educators now attempt to closely relate knowledge of microcomputers to teaching and learning in specific subjects. Such courses do not teach programming, but attempt to link knowledge of computer languages to educators' specific needs.

It is not the purpose of this text to teach programming. A brief discussion of artificial intelligence and authoring systems languages, however, follows, since these languages might be used by teachers to build specific instructional segments.

You may have heard of artificial-intelligence languages, called so because they give the computer the opportunity to "learn" from input. The following example illustrates how this might occur.

Screen Display   `Think of an animal. I will try to guess what it is. Type GO when you are ready.`
Response: `GO`
Screen Display: `Is it a dog?`

Response:	NO
Screen Display:	What were you thinking of?
Response:	CAT
Screen Display:	How is a CAT different from a DOG?
Response:	IT MEOWS.
Screen Display:	Let me try again. Think of an animal. I will try to guess what it is. Type GO when you are ready.
Response:	GO
Screen Display:	Is it a dog?
Response:	NO
Screen Display:	Is it a cat?
Response:	NO
Screen Display:	What were you thinking of?
Response:	BIRD
Screen Display:	How is a BIRD different from a DOG and a CAT?
Response:	IT FLIES.
Screen Display:	Let me try again. Think of an animal. I will try to guess what it is. Type GO when you are ready.

The more input that is provided the "smarter" the program becomes. Theoretically, the point will be reached when the program will have "learned" enough to consistently guess the animal. Artificial intelligence-languages hold great promise for education because they will more easily and appropriately react to students' responses. Also, they are better able to search and handle textual rather than numerical information.

Other languages, called authoring systems, also hold promise for the future. These languages allow teachers to create customized programs without being programmers. Authoring systems provide a series of prompts to which the user responds. For example, if a teacher wanted to create a multiple-choice test, the language might ask how many items and how many choices per item are desired. The teacher might then be asked to type the first item, followed by the choices. Next, the correct choice would be requested, along with any feedback that is desired for both correct and incorrect answers. This proceeds until the entire test has been entered. When finished, the language does the programming functions, compiling the program so that correct screen displays and tabulations of responses are presented to students on demand. Using authoring systems in such ways, teachers will be able to design software and use their classroom microcomputers for specialized applications, without being sophisticated programmers.

Authoring languages are now available that allow relatively unsophisticated computer users to write programs controlling videotape and/or videodisc players. For example, a videotape segment may play for several minutes, then stop while a text display asks the students for responses to questions that are paired with reading selections (also displayed on the computer) that relate to the videotape. This method allows background knowledge to be enhanced, and preliminary research suggests that gains are made in vocabulary knowledge and comprehension of what was read (Bransford, Sherwood, Kinzer & Hasselbring, 1985). The potential of authoring languages that control video players is still relatively unexplored, but seems to be great. Such systems may provide instruction in reading that accesses the learner's auditory and visual channels in ways that are specific to the needs of a given student or group of students.

SPECIFIC USES OF MICROCOMPUTERS IN READING INSTRUCTION

This chapter has stayed away from discussing specific software. This is because software is frequently updated and improved, and sometimes becomes unavailable after a period of time. Thus, we have tried to provide a discussion, in the sections presenting the five-part model of microcomputer use, of types of uses and software rather than discussing software per se. Where software has been mentioned by name, it is not being recommended over other offerings, but is used as one example within a category. Your local computer store, educational computer publications, and school district resource and curriculum center will recommend specific software titles for the uses mentioned. Software exists for use at all elementary grade levels and for all major skill areas.

Although there is much software available for use in reading instruction, students can also use software that is intended for other content areas or applications. For example, word processing software can be used in language experience applications. As the student or students dictate a story to the teacher, it can be typed directly into the microcomputer. The students' story can then be quickly printed for each student. This is highly motivational, since students receive physical copies of their story. Later, also using the word processor, teachers can more easily build individual lessons for students that are based on the words used in their language experience stories. For example, if the teacher will be teaching a lesson on -ing words, the word processor can search for all words ending in -ing in a student's story. These words can then be used to make the lesson more personal and relevant.

Students can also use the microcomputer with word processing software to type their own stories or to access and read stories written by other class members. Messages to other students also can be left on the microcomputer, used in this case as a form of bulletin board. These messages can be reactions to others' stories or simply be conversational messages. As students read and respond to these messages, they develop audience awareness in their writing and have a strong motivation to read meaningful communication written specifically for them.

Software that checks students' spelling can also be used to form the basis of lessons. Most spelling-checker programs create a file of words that were not recognized as correct. Teachers can access these files, print them, and use their contents as a basis for periodic spelling lessons on the most frequently misspelled words used by their students.

Other software that has been written for business use, such as spreadsheets, may also be successfully used in reading instruction. Spreadsheets present the user with a series of rows and columns on the monitor screen (see table 14–3). Information is entered in the rows or columns and, if it is numerical data, it can be manipulated in a number of ways, either with or without the use of mathematical formulas. In the reading instructional situation, the mathematics functions are less important than are the possibilities available as a result of the row-and-column format.

Since one of the important elements in reading instruction is the ability to classify (that is, to see the relationships and nonrelationships

TABLE 14–3
Spreadsheet with entries

	a	b	c	d	e	f	g	h
2					NOT			
3			ACTION		ACTION			
4			WORDS		WORDS			
5			————		————			
6								
7			RUN		THE			
8			JUMP		SHE			
9			SIT		FLOOR			
10								
11								
12		Taken from the following exercise:						
13								
14		Which of the following underlined words are action words?						
15		Which are not?						
16								
17		1. He will _run_ to _the_ store.						
18								
19		2. _She_ will _jump_ down from the chair.						
20								
21		3. _Sit_ down on the _floor_.						
22								
23								

between items) the rows and columns on a spreadsheet allow the students an opportunity to classify in easily visible categories and to change errors easily. If, for example, you were teaching a lesson on action words, you might write a series of words on the chalkboard, or simply on a piece of paper beside the microcomputer. If provision is made so that students, at some time during the day, all have an opportunity to use the microcomputer, they could use the spreadsheet to type their own, additional words into appropriate columns headed *Action Words* and *Not Action Words.* Saving the students' categorizations would allow you to access individual students' responses quickly and teach accordingly. Of course, this example describes a practice or testing activity and not a teaching function.

Simulations intended for science or social studies classrooms, such as *Odell Lake* and *Oregon Trail,* mentioned earlier, can provide opportunities to build needed background knowledge prior to reading stories about a fish surviving in a lake or settlers in the west. Allowing students to work through relevant computer simulations results in increased background knowledge and more interest in reading specific stories. Of course, appropriate prediscussion and a clear goal for using the simulation are required. Further, in this use the simulation should be com-

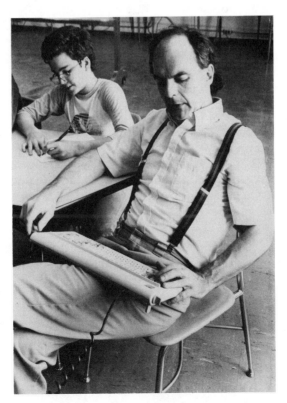

Teachers can use the microcomputer, with appropriate software, to enhance group instruction.

pleted as a small or large group activity. This facilitates discussion and uses class time more effectively while meeting the goal of a prereading activity.

One common question teachers ask is what can be done with only one or two microcomputers in a class of twenty-five or more students. In fact, many people advocate that students work in groups of two or three per microcomputer (Berger, 1984; Bransford, 1984). If only one or two microcomputers are available in the classroom, teachers can allow students to work on the machine in much the same way that learning centers are used. Students can work in pairs or groups of three on one microcomputer. The resulting discussion, as problems are encountered and solved, is valuable and can enhance learning in this situation.

Teachers must also guard against allowing some students freer access to the class microcomputer than is available to others. It is especially inadvisable to use time on the microcomputer as a reward for finishing assigned reading or other work. Since more advanced students often complete assignments faster than average or below-average students, there is a danger in further differentiation between high and low achievers. Such differentiation is also possible between males and females, as well as between high and low socioeconomic-level students. Care must be taken to ensure that those who have a microcomputer at home do not, simply due to background knowledge, monopolize microcomputer time in the classroom. Similarly, stereotypes can arise from a mistaken view that males are more mechanically or mathematically inclined than females. Such stereotypes can lead to sex differences in computer use in the classroom.

Finally, reading teachers must be aware that microcomputers are appropriate for use in any grade level—they are not only the domain of students in intermediate grades and above. Although younger students will have difficulty using keyboards to input information, most software intended for their use asks only for yes/no responses, or for touching a letter indicating their choice. In fact, keyboarding skills should not be a concern when deciding whether to use a microcomputer with students. A more relevant issue is whether the material presented by the software requires reading skills beyond those in the range of the intended audience.

In summary, teachers can use microcomputers in a variety of ways in reading instruction. Available uses include drill-and-practice, tutorials, and problem-solving activities. Also, software intended for other subjects or uses can be adapted for reading-instruction applications.

FINDING, CHOOSING, AND EVALUATING SOFTWARE

There are literally thousands of software programs marketed for the reading classroom. Yet teachers often ask where they can find reading-instruction software and how to tell whether it is appropriate for their instructional program.

A good place to start is a software catalog. These are published monthly or yearly by general publishers and by computer software reviewers. Most publishers of educational materials, including basal readers, now publish software and include their offerings in their general catalogs. These catalogs compile, list, and briefly describe available educational software, though they often do not provide an evaluation of what is listed. Catalogs are available from publishers on request and are automatically sent to school and university libraries and curriculum centers. Finally, computer journals, both those intended specifically for educators as well as for the general public, include listings and evaluations of educational software. Check the following journals and review publications under "new product announcements" or "software evaluation" departments:

BYTE—The Small Systems Journal
Classroom Computer News
Computers in Reading and Language Arts
Digest of Software Reviews: Education
Educational Technology
Microcomputers in Education
T.H.E. Journal (Technological Horizons in Education)
The Computing Teacher

Perhaps one of the largest distributors of educational software is the Minnesota Educational Computing Consortium (MECC). MECC's extensive software catalog is available from 3490 Lexington Avenue North, Saint Paul, Minnesota 55112. MECC offers a subscription service to school systems and other educational users that automatically provides every piece of software it distributes as well as updates of new offerings as they appear. Many school districts subscribe to MECC, keeping a software depository in their district resource center from which individual schools and teachers can borrow software for use in their classrooms.

Once you find software that interests you, you will have to decide whether it is appropriate for your students and instructional program. Some software publishers will send their programs (or a demonstration copy) on approval so that you can try them and evaluate them yourself. Others do not allow the return of software for refund after the package has been opened. In this case, you are well advised to find one or more independent reviews of the software before you order it. Reviews and articles are available in the previously mentioned journals and from agencies that evaluate educational software. Additionally, most state departments of education and many school districts have compilations of software evaluations that are available to teachers on request. Of course, the most relevant evaluation will be the one that you conduct yourself. You will have the best knowledge about your students' needs, your instructional program, and how the software will fit into your framework of reading.

There are two things to consider when evaluating software. First, one must ask if the software is appropriate to the hardware, the microcomputer equipment available in one's classroom. Second, one must consider aspects of the software itself, together with one's instructional program. Use the following hardware-specific evaluation checklist before you order any software. Since it is not dependent on having the software in hand (the questions can usually be answered from information provided in catalogs or advertising brochures), use of this checklist will help identify inappropriate software before further time, effort, and money are expended (Kinzer, 1986).

Hardware-Specific Software Checklist

1. Will the software work on your particular input/storage system? For example, if your storage device is a cassette-tape system, is the software available in that medium or is it, perhaps, only available on diskettes?

2. Is the software compatible with your operating system? Remember that, even if the software is available for your particular microcomputer, it must still be compatible with the operating system you are using with that microcomputer.

3. Does the software require a certain amount of RAM? Some software must be loaded into RAM and does not later access information on the diskette. If this is true, a certain amount of memory is required for the software program to run.

4. Does the software require any programmable, function, or special keys to run? Is a full-ASCII keyboard necessary?

5. Does the software require any specific output device? Some software sends output directly to a printer and, if a printer is unavailable, the program simply stops or "hangs up."

6. Does the software require any specific output capabilities? For example, the software might require output devices with graphics capabilities or 80-column (or more) displays.

7. Does the software require any other software to be useful? For example, some software requires word processing software to be used to input information. Thus, the software might be useless without first acquiring a word processing package.

The following two questions assume that you are using a diskette storage system.

8. Is the software available in your diskette format? For example, if the software is available only on double-density, double-sided diskettes,

and your system uses single-sided, double-density diskettes, then the software cannot be read into your microcomputer system.

9. Does the software require one or two disk drives? Sometimes, software programs require that the applications program be placed in one drive, and the data files be stored and accessed from another.

Once you have determined that the software you want to order is suitable for your classroom microcomputer system, consider the questions in the following list. (Kinzer, Hynds & Loofbourrow, 1986). These questions require that you have the software in hand. If your school district or school library catalogs such evaluations, forward yours for inclusion. Additionally, some software is developed and distributed without appropriate **field testing.** If you have suggestions for improvements or complaints regarding the software, send these to the publisher so that modifications can be made.

field testing: Presale experimentation by people who would normally be using a product.

Teachers need to carefully examine software before using it in their classrooms. Ideally, hands-on evaluation should take place. Some software may be inappropriate for intended students with regard to their reading level or typing skills. Also, the reinforcement provided for correct and incorrect answers should be critically viewed. Some software uses the microcomputer's graphics and sound capabilities to draw a great deal of attention to wrong answers. This might lead to students' making incorrect responses on purpose, simply to see their answer explode (with appropriate sound effects) on the screen. Guard against such reinforcement.

Questions for Evaluating Reading and Writing Instructional Software

Title and Version:
Publisher and Address:
Cost:

1. What are the skills targeted, according to the publisher? Do you agree?
2. Are the skills targeted by the software appropriate to your students and to your curriculum? (In what way(s); for how many of your students would the software be useful?)
3. What is the intended age/grade level(s), according to the publisher? Do you agree?
4. How do you intend to use the software? What will its purpose be in your overall program?
5. How many of your students are at a level where the software would be useful?
6. In what area does the software fall: (a) learning *from* computers; (b) learning *with* computers; (c) *managing* learning with computers; (d) other: _____.

7. Do you have the proper equipment to run the software (see the hardware-specific checklist)?

8. Does the software do more than a workbook could in the same skill area? In what way?

9. Is the software, in terms of screen display, appropriate for your students' reading level?

10. Will the software be easy to use and understand for your students? Are commands, required typing skills, or complexity of screen displays beyond your students' abilities?

11. Does the software make appropriate use of graphics, color, and sound to enhance motivation and learning? Are these necessary, given your intended use of the software (relate this to question 4)?

12. Does the software make use of branching to provide instruction when errors are made? Is this necessary, given your intended use (relate this to question 4)?

13. How long will it take one of your students to go through the program? Is this an appropriate amount of time, given your goals and instructional situation?

14. Will your students have to go through the entire program, perhaps in some predetermined sequence, or will they be able to stop and start at various points? (Perhaps where they stopped the previous day, or at a higher difficulty level.)

15. Does the software provide a pretest so that students may begin at an appropriate level of difficulty, and/or a posttest to measure learning? Are these important, given your intended use (relate this to question 4)?

16. Can your students load and use the software by themselves? How much teacher support in a stand-by capacity will be needed? Is this appropriate to your instructional situation?

17. Does the software score students' work and store the result under individual students' names so that it can later be accessed by the teacher?

18. Can the software be used by more than one student at a time? Would this detract from your intended use?

19. Is there overt sex, racial, or socioeconomic-status bias in the software?

20. What suggestions for improvement(s) should the publisher be made aware of?

INSTRUCTIONAL FRAMEWORKS AND MICROCOMPUTER TECHNOLOGY

Your framework will determine how you use microcomputers and their attendant software in your reading instructional program. It will also result in an emphasis on one part of the five-part model discussed at the beginning of this chapter—perhaps on learning from computers as opposed to learning with or learning about thinking with computers.

Teachers with mastery of specific skills explanations for how reading ability develops tend to choose drill-and-practice or tutorial software that relate to specifically defined skills that parallel those taught outside the computer environment. Teachers with reader-based or holistic explanations for how reading ability develops may find simulations useful, or use word processors to enhance language experience activities. Comprehension frameworks based on interactive explanations for how one reads or differential explanations for how reading ability develops will have no difficulty incorporating a range of software as appropriate for specific learners. They may use drill-and-practice programs for specific, low-level skills development with less proficient readers and software that allows selection of story endings (thus using high-level discourse knowledge), or that targets other high-level knowledge sources with more proficient readers.

Remember, however, that computers are simply tools for teachers to use in reading instruction. They are affected by similar considerations, regarding one's framework, that apply to printed supplemental materials as discussed in chapter 9.

You are on the forefront of educational opportunities resulting from a combination of new and traditional technologies. The concepts, theories, and teaching methods suggested throughout this book, together with the conscious use of your personal framework of reading, ensure that you will be a professional and effective teacher of reading even as technology continues to impact our society.

THE MAJOR POINTS

1. The use of microcomputers in reading instruction falls into five general categories: learning about computers; learning from computers; learning with computers; learning about thinking with computers; and managing learning with computers.
2. All types of software, including drill-and-practice software, tutorial software, gaming software, simulation software, and programming software can have a place in reading instruction if appropriately used.
3. Microcomputers can help the teacher with record-keeping functions and with things such as performing readability analyses and cloze testing.
4. If thoughtfully applied, software intended for use in other subject areas can be used in reading instruction.
5. Teachers should carefully evaluate software before it is adopted for use in reading instruction.

QUESTIONS AND ACTIVITIES

1. Interview several teachers who use microcomputers in their reading-instruction programs. Ask how they use their microcomputer system in their reading lessons and how they perceive the microcomputer as moving beyond more traditional instructional practices (for example, workbooks).

2. Interview several students who have been allowed to use microcomputers as part of their reading instruction. Ask how they feel about the microcomputer and how it helps them learn.

3. Your curriculum library or microcomputer laboratory will probably have software that is marketed as being appropriate for reading instruction. Evaluate several software packages using the checklist shown on page 576 of this chapter. Are there any common problems that you perceive? How might the software be used in a reading instructional program? If such software is unavailable in the library or laboratory, go to a microcomputer store and ask to see and use such software.

4. Specify three uses of microcomputers in reading instruction from each of these categories: learning from computers; learning with computers; managing learning with computers.

5. How would microcomputers fit into your framework of reading?

FURTHER READING

Balajthy, E. (1986). *Microcomputers in reading and language arts.* Englewood Cliffs, NJ: Prentice Hall.

Includes chapters on evaluating software as well as applications in readiness, word recognition, vocabulary, comprehension, and study skills, as well as discussions of other general issues of microcomputer uses in reading instruction.

Geoffrion, L. D. & Geoffrion, O. P. (1983). *Computers and reading instruction.* Menlo Park, CA: Addison-Wesley.

A readable paperback that presents basic computer terminology for the novice. The book discusses ways of using microcomputers in reading instruction. Specific chapters focus on reading readiness, word identification, comprehension, and other reading skills.

Mason, G. E.; Blanchard, J. S.; & Daniel, D. B. (1983). *Computer applications in reading* (2nd Edition). Newark, DE: International Reading Assoc.

A popular publication by the International Reading Association, this brief volume is a good introduction and resource for teachers wishing to implement microcomputers in the reading program.

Toong, H. D. & Gupta, A. (1982). Personal Computers. *Scientific American,* 87–88, 92, 94, 96, 99–100, 102–107.

An article that provides a good introduction and overview relating to microcomputers, their components, and their potential.

REFERENCES

Awad, E. M. (1983). *Introduction to computers* (2nd Edition). Englewood Cliffs, NJ: Prentice-Hall.

Berger, C. (April, 1984). Assessing cognitive consequences of computer environments for learning science: research findings and policy implications. Paper presented at National Association for Research in Science Teaching.

Bransford, J. (April, 1984). Personal communication.

Bransford, J.; Sherwood, R.; Kinzer, C.; & Hasselbring, T. (1985). *Frameworks for learning: Toward a framework for developing effective uses of technology.* Technical Report No. 85.1.1, Nashville, TN: Learning Technology Center, Peabody College, Vanderbilt University.

Goldberg, K. & Sherwood, R. D. (1983). *Microcomputers: A parent's guide.* New York: Wiley.

Hasselbring, T. & Cavanaugh, K. (1986). Computer applications for the mildly handicapped. In C. Kinzer, R. Sherwood, & J. Bransford (eds.), *Computer strategies for education: Foundations and content-area applications,* Columbus, OH: C. E. Merrill.

Kinzer, C. K. (1986). Universals of computer systems. In C. K. Kinzer, R. Sherwood, & J. D. Bransford (eds.), *Computer strategies for education: Foundations and content-area applications,* Columbus, OH: C. E. Merrill.

Kinzer, C. K.; Hynds, S.; & Loufbourrow, M. (1986). Applications of microcomputers in reading and writing. In C. Kinzer, R. Sherwood, & J. D. Bransford (eds.), *Computer strategies for education: Foundations and content-area applications,* Columbus, OH: C. E. Merrill.

Luehrmann, A. (1983). *Computer literacy: A hands-on approach.* New York: McGraw-Hill.

Luehrmann, A. (1984a). Structured programming in BASIC, Part I: Top-down BASIC. *Creative Computing,* 152–56.

Luehrmann, A. (1984b). Structured programming in BASIC, Part II: Control blocks. *Creative Computing,* 152–63.

Luehrmann, A. (1984c). Structured programming in BASIC part III: an application. *Creative Computing,* 125–36.

Papert, S. (1980). *Mindstorms: Children, computers, and powerful ideas.* New York: Basic Books.

Taylor, R. P. (ed.). (1980). *The computer in the school: Tutor, tool, tutee.* New York: Teachers College Press.

Toong, H. D. & Gupta, A. (1982). Personal Computers. *Scientific American.* 87–88, 92, 94, 96, 99–100, 102–107.

Name Index

Subject Index